Teach®
Yourself

Essential Gaelic Dictionary

Boyd Robertson and
Ian MacDonald

For UK order enquiries: please contact Bookpoint Ltd.,
130 Milton Park, Abingdon, Oxon OX14 4SB.
Telephone: +44 (0) 1235 827720. *Fax:* +44 (0) 1235 400454.
Lines are open 09.00–18.00, Monday to Saturday, with a 24-hour
message answering service. Details about our titles and how to
order are available at www.teachyourself.com

For USA order enquiries: please contact McGraw-Hill
Customer Services, PO Box 545, Blacklick, OH 43004-0545, USA.
Telephone: 1-800-722-4726. *Fax:* 1-614-755-5645.

For Canada order enquiries: please contact McGraw-Hill
Ryerson Ltd., 300 Water St, Whitby, Ontario L1N 9B6, Canada.
Telephone: 905 430 5000. *Fax:* 905 430 5020.

Long renowned as the authoritative source for self-guided
learning – with more than 30 million copies sold worldwide –
the *Teach Yourself* series includes over 500 titles in the fields of
languages, crafts, hobbies, business, computing and education.

British Library Cataloguing in Publication Data: a catalogue record
for this title is available from The British Library.

Library of Congress Catalog Card Number: on file.

First published in UK 2004 by Hodder Education, 338 Euston Road,
London NW1 3BH, as *Teach Yourself Gaelic Dictionary.*

**First published in US 2004 by Contemporary Books,
a Division of the McGraw-Hill Companies,** 1 Prudential Plaza,
130 East Randolph Street, Chicago, IL 60601, USA.

This edition published 2010.

The *Teach Yourself* name is a registered trade mark of
Hachette UK.

Typeset by MPS Limited, a Macmillan Company.

Printed in Great Britain for Hodder Education, a division of
Hachette UK, 338 Euston Road, London NW1 3BH, by
CPI Group (UK) Ltd., Croydon, CR0 4YY.

The publisher has used its best endeavours to ensure that the
URLs for external websites referred to in this book are correct and
active at the time of going to press. However, the publisher has no
responsibility for the websites and can give no guarantee that a site
will remain live or that the content is or will remain appropriate.

Hachette UK's policy is to use papers that are natural, renewable
and recyclable products and made from wood grown in sustainable
forests. The logging and manufacturing processes are expected to
conform to the environmental regulations of the country of origin.

Impression number   10 9 8 7
Year   2013

Contents

Credits

Front cover: Oxford Illustrators Ltd

Back cover: © Jakub Semeniuk/iStockphoto.com, © Royalty-Free/Corbis, © agencyby/iStockphoto.com, © Andy Cook/iStockphoto.com, © Christopher Ewing/iStockphoto.com, © zebicho – Fotolia.com, © Geoffrey Holman/iStockphoto.com, © Photodisc/Getty Images, © James C. Pruitt/iStockphoto.com, © Mohamed Saber – Fotolia.com

Only got a minute?

Gaelic is Scotland's oldest living language and part of Scotland's heritage, life and culture. It is a Celtic language related to Irish and to Welsh and Breton. Gaelic was, in the tenth and eleventh centuries, the language of the Crown and Government of Scotland and was spoken in most parts of the country.

The language declined over the centuries because of political attempts to suppress Gaelic culture. Fewer than 60,000 Scots were recorded as Gaelic speakers in the 2001 Census. Most reside in the Hebrides and on the western seaboard of the Highlands but concentrations of speakers are also found in conurbations such as Glasgow and Edinburgh.

Gaelic is not confined to Scotland. There are emigrant communities around the world in which Gaelic is spoken, for example in parts of Nova Scotia, Canada. Some of these communities date back to the Highland Clearances in the eighteenth and nineteenth centuries.

Vigorous attempts are being made to halt the decline in the number of Gaelic speakers. The Scottish Government passed a Gaelic Language Act in 2005 giving the language a measure of official status and introducing a coherent system of language planning.

The footprint of the language can be seen in place names, topographical features and in personal names. Surnames with Mac or Mc abound, deriving from the Gaelic word *mac* meaning 'son'. MacDonald is 'son of Donald'. Place names also reveal how widely Gaelic has been spoken. Prefixes Ach/Auch (field), Bal (town), Dun/Dum (fort), Inver (river mouth), Kil (church), Kin/Ken (head or end) and Strath (valley) come from Gaelic, and are found in places like Auchinleck, Balmoral, Dundee, Inverness, Kilmarnock, Kingussie, and Strathclyde, all around Scotland.

Tartan, bagpipes and whisky derive from Gaelic culture, and Gaelic song and music are celebrated and transmitted in *fèisean* (festivals) and *cèilidhean* (ceilidhs).

5 Only got five minutes?

Gaelic is the longest established of Scotland's languages and is an intrinsic part of the country's heritage and culture. It is a Celtic language that belongs to the same Goidelic group as Irish Gaelic. The influence of the Gael is evident in the very name of the country. The Gaelic-speaking people who arrived in modern day Argyll and Galloway in the fourth and fifth centuries AD were known to the Romans as *Scotti* and the country in which they settled came to be known as Scotland. Gaelic was, for a period in the tenth and eleventh centuries, the language of the Crown and Government and was spoken in most parts of the country.

The area known as the Lordship of the Isles, which covered the western seaboard and the Inner and Outer Hebrides, was a powerful principality within the kingdom of Scotland in the fourteenth and fifteenth centuries and came to be regarded by the monarchs as a threat to the stability of the country. That led to several attempts by the State to emasculate its power base and its Gaelic culture. The fortunes of the language declined over the centuries in the face of initially overt and, later, more subtle and sustained policies aimed at homogenization.

The 58,000 Scots recorded by the 2001 Census as speakers of the language are found mainly in the Highlands and Islands. The strongest Gaelic-speaking communities are in the Outer Hebrides, but concentrations of speakers are also found in urban centres like Glasgow and Edinburgh. A further 30,000 Scots claim to have a passive knowledge of the language.

But Gaelic is not confined to Scotland. There are emigrant communities around the world in which Gaelic may still be heard, for example in Nova Scotia, Canada. Some of these communities date back to the Highland Clearances in the eighteenth and nineteenth centuries, when tenants were forcibly evicted from their land to make way for more sheep farms.

Gaelic elements are found widely in place names across Scotland, providing evidence of the historical reach of the language. The Gaelic element often occurs as the first part of a name, as in the forms Ach/Auch (a field), Bal (town, township), Dun/Dum (fort), Inver (river mouth), Kil (church or cell), Kin/Ken (head of, end of) and Strath (wide valley). The names Auchinleck, Balmoral, Dundee, Inverness, Kilmarnock, Kingussie and Strathclyde contain these elements. Adjectives such as *mòr* (big), *beag* (small), *bàn* (fair) and *dubh* (black) are common as second or third elements in names and often appear in anglicized form as *-more*, *-beg*, *-bane* and *-du/-dhu*. Bens, glens, cairns, craigs, lochs and skerries, signifying various topographical features, abound on maps of Scotland and all derive from Gaelic.

A quick scan of a telephone directory in any area of the country reveals the extent to which surnames beginning with Mac or Mc predominate. These names derive from the Gaelic word *mac*, meaning 'son'. So *MacDhùghaill* or MacDougall is Son of Dougal, while *Mac an t-Sagairt* or MacTaggart is Son of the Priest. Surnames beginning in Gil or Gill are derived from the word for a lad or servant, *gille*. Examples are Gillies, Gilchrist and Gillespie, where the second element refers to Jesus, Christ and bishop respectively. The word 'clan' itself comes from the Gaelic word for children, *clann*. There are many Scottish first names which also come from Gaelic. Alasdair, Calum, Catriona, Eilidh, Fiona, Hamish, Iain, Kirsty and Mairi are just some of the best known.

Many of the badges of Scottish identity including tartan, bagpipes and whisky are derived from Gaelic culture, and Gaelic song and music are celebrated and transmitted in *fèisean* (festivals) and *cèilidhean* (ceilidhs). Music, song and poetry were integral to Clan society and culture and continue to play a prominent part in community life. The great Highland bagpipe and the *clàrsach*, or harp, were the traditional instruments of Gaelic society. One form of bagpipe music, *ceòl-mòr* (great music), is considered by some experts to be Scotland's most significant contribution to world music.

Gaelic features in the curriculum of a small minority of Scottish schools as a subject of study for learners, as a subject for fluent speakers and as a medium of education. Most schools with Gaelic are in the Highlands and Islands. Provision of Gaelic-medium education was first made in 1985 in two urban primary schools. Today, over 3,000 pupils are educated through the medium of Gaelic in 137 nursery, primary and secondary centres across Scotland. The Gaelic College, Sabhal Mòr Ostaig, on the Isle of Skye, offers further and higher education courses through the medium of Gaelic and the Universities of Aberdeen, Edinburgh and Glasgow have long-established Celtic Departments.

The BBC is the main producer of Gaelic radio and television programmes. Residents in most parts of Scotland can tune in to a good variety of Gaelic radio programmes 15 hours each weekday. Gaelic television expanded greatly in 2008 with the setting-up of a Gaelic channel, BBC Alba, which broadcasts for over six hours per day. Gaelic language broadcasts and online resources can be accessed at any time on the BBC Scotland Gaelic website.

Provision for learning Gaelic ranges from weekly evening classes to full-time immersion courses. Many local authorities and some universities and colleges offer evening classes, while Sabhal Mòr Ostaig and a few FE colleges provide immersion courses. The Gaelic College also runs a series of short courses in the language and in aspects of the culture.

For learners working independently, there are distance learning or online options. Sabhal Mòr Ostaig has a Gaelic access course which takes beginners to a level at which they can undertake studies in Gaelic and which attracts students from all over the world. Gaelic is also taught in other countries, including Canada and the USA.

Meet the authors

Professor Boyd Robertson

Boyd Robertson is Principal of Sabhal Mòr Ostaig, Scotland's Gaelic College, on the Isle of Skye. He has extensive experience of teaching and lecturing in Gaelic and of devising language acquisition materials. He is co-author of the *Complete Gaelic* course and the *Speak Gaelic with Confidence* audio course in the Teach Yourself series and was Language Adviser for the Scottish Television series, *Speaking our Language*. A native Gaelic speaker, he was brought up on the island of North Uist in the Outer Hebrides. After graduating in Celtic Studies from Aberdeen University, he taught Gaelic at Oban High School before becoming a lecturer at Jordanhill College of Education in Glasgow and then Reader in Gaelic at the University of Strathclyde. He was Convener of the Steering Committee of *Faclair na Gàidhlig*, the inter-university Historical Dictionary of Scottish Gaelic project.

Ian MacDonald

Ian MacDonald is from the island of Grimsay in North Uist, and worked there and in Birmingham, Glasgow and London, where he had a spell in the Civil Service, before joining Comhairle nan Leabhraichean (the Gaelic Books Council, of which he later became Director). Comhairle nan Leabhraichean is based in Glasgow and is a support agency for Gaelic writers and publishers. A native Gaelic speaker, Ian attended schools in Uist and Inverness and Glasgow University. He has edited many books, Gaelic and English, and translated several others, including *Am Mabinogi*, the first Gaelic version of the classic Welsh tales. He is on the Executive Council of the Scottish Gaelic Texts Society, and has been Treasurer of the Gaelic Society of Glasgow for some years.

Introduction to the first edition

This *faclair* or dictionary was compiled in response to an invitation from the publishers to produce a publication that would complement the course book *Gaelic* in the Teach Yourself series and be useful to learners and to Gaelic speakers generally. The publishers were aware that there was a need and demand for a compact two-way dictionary of this kind.

One of the problems with a concise dictionary is that difficult decisions have to be taken as to what should be included and what left out. On occasion, therefore, there will be a noun here, but not the related adjective – and so on. This can be frustrating for the user, but within the constraints of the prescribed format we have tried to make the selection the most practically useful we could.

Anyone compiling a dictionary, whatever its length, must have recourse to the work of others, and we were grateful to have ready access to several existing dictionaries. The older Gaelic–English works by MacBain and Dwelly were consulted extensively, as were Derick Thomson's more recent *The New English–Gaelic Dictionary*, the all-Gaelic *Brìgh nam Facal* by Richard Cox and Clò Ostaig's *An Stòr-Dàta Briathrachais Gàidhlig*. We also drew on *Faclair na Pàrlamaid: Dictionary of Terms*, produced by the European Language Initiative and published by the Scottish Parliament, the Secondary Review Group's word list for schools, *Faclan Ùra Gàidhlig*, and two Irish dictionaries, Tomás de Bhaldraithe's *English–Irish Dictionary* and Séamus Mac Mathúna and Ailbhe Ó Corráin's *Pocket Irish Dictionary*.

Ian Quick read the dictionary in draft and contributed many useful suggestions. We are much obliged to him for his painstaking and perceptive commentary. Any shortcomings that remain are our responsibility. Katie Kennedy had the major task of keying in the text and formatting it onto disk. She has played a vital role in the production process, and we greatly appreciate her input and sustained commitment. We would also wish to acknowledge the support and encouragement given to us by Sheila Robertson and other members of our families, by John De Cecco of the University of Strathclyde and by Sue Hart and Ginny Catmur of the publishers, Hodder and Stoughton.

Detailed guidance on how to use the book is given in **The layout of the dictionary**. We hope it will prove a user-friendly work.

Tha sinn an dòchas gum bi am faclair feumail do luchd-labhairt na Gàidhlig, co-dhiù a tha iad fileanta no aig toiseach tòiseachaidh.

Boyd Robertson and Ian MacDonald

The layout of the dictionary

Selection and format of entries

For reasons of space, it has been possible to include only a small number of the many variants (including plurals) to be found in the language. These are indicated in the form used in 'Also **gàireachdaich**' under the main entry, **gàireachdainn**. Elsewhere, we have used oblique strokes, as in **neach-iùil/treòrachaidh**. In the case of hyphenated words like these, the oblique stroke indicates that the first element and the hyphen should also be added to the second word – ie, that the alternatives are **neach-iùil** and **neach-treòrachaidh**. Similarly, the oblique stroke in **gun toinisg/chiall** shows that the alternatives are **gun toinisg** and **gun chiall**.

We have also, to save space, usually given only the forms that are appropriate for the third person singular, masculine and feminine, in many phrases – eg, the translation of awake is given as **na d(h)ùisg**, etc, where the full paradigm would be **nam dhùisg**, **nad dhùisg**, **na dhùisg**, **na dùisg**, **nar dùisg**, **nur dùisg**, **nan dùisg**. Users should change the third person to another as required.

The language has more than one form of the prepositional pronouns that express 'to the, for the' etc and 'of the'/'off the', **don**, **dhan** and **dan** all being used for the first meaning and **den**, **dhen** and **dhan** for the second, but we have confined ourselves here to using only **dhan** for the first of these meanings and only **dhen** for the second.

We have used contractions throughout, as given in the **Abbreviations** section, and contracted forms of the headword are often used in entries. But the full headword is given where its form has changed – for example, where a consonant has been lenited (followed by h), and also if the word has fewer than four letters or if there may be ambiguity.

We have occasionally provided grammatical information – for instance, where a word or phrase should be followed by the genitive case – and short sections after the two main sections of the dictionary provide tabular information on the definite article, verbs and prepositional pronouns. These are intended to enable the user to have convenient access to basic forms, but it is not possible in any dictionary to provide the detailed guidance to be found in a grammar book. Similarly, the lists of personal and place names at the end are intended to be handy and useful, but they are necessarily selective.

A grammar book is also the best place in which to learn in detail where Gaelic greatly differs from English in the way certain meanings are expressed – for example, the fact that 'never' is not rendered by a separate word but is expressed by a negative form of a verb with one of the words used to render 'ever'. In such situations we have tried to give guidance as clear as space permitted, but we could not go into detail.

Nouns are nearly always listed before a related adjective, and an adjective before a related verb, but in cases in which, for example, an adjective is commoner than the noun, the adjective has been given first.

Headwords are in bold, translations are in roman and explanatory notes such as '+ *gen*' are in italics.

Current orthographic conventions are adopted throughout but earlier forms of spelling which users will encounter are provided as appropriate, and introduced by the term *Formerly*.

English words with one spelling but different meanings are included within one entry, but Gaelic ones are listed separately.

Layout of Gaelic–English section

All Gaelic text is in bold type.

Where a number of alternative translations of a Gaelic word are given, the order in which they appear aims to reflect currency and frequency of use.

When a Gaelic word has entirely distinct meanings, these are separated by semi-colons.

Some translations are glossed in brackets to clarify the context.

Alternative spellings of words are given either within the entry or as a separate entry:
>   eg **naoi** *n, a* nine *Also* **naodh**
>   **maith** *v See* **math**

Secondary forms of entries show the element to be added to the basic form:
>   eg **màileid** *n* -e, -ean *f* bag, suitcase

In many cases, the secondary form involves an internal adaptation of the primary form. The secondary form begins with the last unchanged letter of the original or, sometimes, the last unchanged letter before h:
>   eg **mòinteach** *n* -tich, -tichean *f* moor, moorland
>   **easbhaidheach** *a* -dhiche deficient, defective

The full secondary form is given in words where the primary form changes radically:
>   eg **sgian** *n* **sgeine, sgeinean** *f* knife

Where a secondary form of the word appears in the example, it is given in full.

NOUNS

The gender of nouns is given after the last secondary form, usually the nominative plural. Some nouns can be feminine (*f*) in certain areas and masculine (*m*) in others.

Nouns are normally entered in their nominative singular form. The genitive singular and nominative plural forms are also indicated:
  eg **faoileag** *n* **-eig, -an** *f* seagull

Where the genitive singular has the same form as the nominative singular, only the nominative plural form appears:
  eg **slabhraidh** *n* **-ean** *f* chain

Where there are alternative forms of the genitive singular or nominative plural, these are given with an oblique:
  eg **rathad** *n* **-aid/rothaid, -aidean/ròidean** *m* road, route, way

When nouns are normally accompanied by the definite article (*the* in English), the entry gives the full form:
  eg **griùthrach** *n* **-aich** *f* a' ghriùthrach measles

In compound nouns, only the element that shows change from the basic form is shown in the genitive singular and nominative plural:
  eg **ball-coise** *n* **buill-, buill-** *m* football

Where a noun and adjective have the same form, they are listed together under the same headword:
  eg **ceithir** *n*, *a* four
  Diùrach *n* **-aich, -aich** *m* someone from Jura *a* from, or pertaining to, Jura

ADJECTIVES

The comparative/superlative form of the adjective is indicated along with the primary form except where the two are identical or in cases where they have little practical application.

VERBS

Verbs are entered in their root form, the second singular imperative or command form. The verbal noun (equivalent to the -ing ending in verbs in English) is also given where it differs from the root, but not otherwise:

eg **coisich** *v* **-seachd** walk

Where a verb is normally followed by a preposition, that is indicated thus:

eg **èist** *v* **-eachd** (+ **ri**) listen (to)

Common forms of irregular verbs are entered separately and most forms are listed in the **Grammar**.

PREPOSITIONS

Prepositions are usually followed by the dative case form of the noun. When the preposition is followed by the genitive case of the noun, this is indicated thus: (+ *gen*).

PREPOSITIONAL PRONOUNS

Each form of prepositional pronoun is included as a separate entry.

Layout of English–Gaelic section

The English headwords are in bold type.

Where a number of Gaelic words are given for an English headword, the order in which they appear reflects currency and frequency of use.

When an English word has entirely distinct meanings, these are separated by semi-colons and their sphere of application is specified in brackets.

Where a verb is intransitive, this is indicated thus: (*intrans*).

Abbreviations

a	adjective	*dem pron*	demonstrative pronoun
abb	abbreviation		
acad	academic	*descr*	description
ad	advertisement	*dom*	domestic
adj phr	adjectival phrase		
adv	adverb	*eccl*	ecclesiastical
adv phr	adverbial phrase	*educ*	education(al)
adv pref	adverbial prefix	*emph (pron)*	emphatic (pronoun)
abstr	abstract	*exam*	examination
agric	agriculture	*exclam*	exclamation
anat	anatomical		
atmos	atmosphere	*f*	feminine
aug conj	augmented conjunction	*fig*	figurative
		fin	financial
aug prep	augmented preposition		
		gen	genitive case
Bibl	Biblical	*geneal*	genealogical
biol	biological	*gen pl*	genitive plural
bot	botanical	*geog*	geography, geographical
caps	capital letters	*geol*	geology, geological
coll	collective	*gram*	grammar
colloq	colloquial		
comp	comparative	*impl*	implement
comp a	comparative adjective	*ind*	industry, industrial
con	concrete	*infin part*	infinitive particle
conj	conjunction	*instit*	institution
corresp	correspondence	*intens*	intensive
contr	contraction	*interj*	interjection
cult	cultural	*interr*	interrogative
		int part	interrogative particle
dat	dative case	*int pron*	interrogative pronoun
def art	definite article	*intrans*	intransitive
def v	defective verb	*irreg v*	irregular verb
dem a	demonstrative adjective		
		jud	judicial

lang	language	*pl*	plural
leg	legal, legislation	*pol*	polite
len	lenition	*polit*	politics, political
ling	linguistics, linguistically	*pop*	population
		poss pron	possessive pronoun
lit	literal(ly)	*pref*	prefix
liter	literature, literary	*prep*	preposition
		prep phr	prepositional phrase
m	masculine	*prep pron*	prepositional pronoun
math	mathematics		
mech	mechanical	*pron*	pronoun
med	medical	*punct*	punctuation
met	metaphorical		
metr	metrical	*rel*	relative
mil	military	*rel part*	relative particle
mus	music(al)	*rel pron*	relative pronoun
		relig	religion, religious
n	noun		
naut	nautical	*sg*	singular
neg	negative	*stat*	statistics
neg conj	negative conjunction	*suff*	suffix
neg part	negative particle	*sup a*	superlative adjective
neg pref	negative prefix		
nf	noun feminine	*temp*	temperature
nm	noun masculine	*topog*	topographical
nom	nominative case	*trad*	traditional(ly)
num a	numerical adjective	*trans*	transitive
num part	numerical particle	*typ*	typographical
org	organization	*v*	verb
		veg	vegetable
past part	past participle	*voc*	vocative case
pej	pejorative	*voc part*	vocative particle
pers pron	personal pronoun	*vn*	verbal noun
phil	philosophical	*v part*	verbal particle
phot	photographic	*vulg*	vulgar
phr	phrase	+	followed by
phys	physical		

A

a *num part* used before the numbers 1–19 in counting or when they are not followed by a noun **a h-aon, a dhà, a trì, a h-ochd, a h-aon-deug, a dhà-dheug, trithead 's a naoi, seachdad 's a ceithir**

a *voc part* when addressing someone **A Mhairead!** Margaret! **A Dhonnchaidh!** Duncan! **A Charaid/Bhanacharaid** Dear Sir/Madam (*at start of letter*)

a *prep* (*contr of* **do**) to (+ *len*) **a' dol a Pheairt** going to Perth

a *prep* (*contr of* **de**) of (+ *len*) **uair a thìde** an hour (*of time*)

a *rel part* who, whom, which, that **an tè a thachair rium** the one whom I met **an t-aodach a cheannaich sinn** the clothes that we bought

a *infin part* (*contr of* **do**) to (+ *len*) **a bheil sibh a' dol a thadhal?** are you going to call? (*becomes* **a dh'** *before vowels*) **a' dol a dh'èirigh** going to get up

a *poss pron* her (*without len*); his (+ *len*) **a màthair 's a h-athair** her mother and father **a phiuthar is a bhràthair** his sister and brother

a' *def art* the (*See Forms of the article in Grammar*)

a' *v part* (*used before verbal nouns not beginning in vowels*) **a' ceannach** buying **a' suidhe** sitting

à *prep* from, out of

aba *n* -chan *m* abbot

abachadh *n* -aidh *m* ripening **gealach an abachaidh** the harvest moon *f*

abaich *v* abachadh ripen, mature

abaich *a* -e ripe, mature

abaid *n* -e *f* abbey

abair *irr v* ràdh say (*See irr v* **abair** *in Grammar*); used to give emphasis **a. sealladh!** what a sight!/some sight! **a. e!** indeed!/you can say that again!

abairt *n* -e, -ean *f* saying, expression, phrase

àbhachd *n* *f* fun, joking, mirth

àbhachdach *a* -aiche funny, given to joking

àbhachdas *n* -ais *m* fun, joking, mirth

abhag *n* -aig, -an *f* small dog, tyke, terrier

abhainn *n* aibhne/-e, aibhneachan/aibhnichean *f* river

àbhaist *n* *f* norm, custom, habit **'s à. dhomh ...** I usually ... **mar as à.** as usual

àbhaisteach *a* -tiche usual, normal

a-bhàn *adv* down, downward(s)

a bharrachd *adv phr* in addition, extra; either **fhuair mi £5 a bh.** I got £5 extra **chan eil sin fìor a bh.** that isn't true either *prep phr* (+ **air**) in addition to

abharsair *n* -ean *m* adversary **an t-A.** the Devil

a bhith *v* to be (*See verb* **to be** *in Grammar*)

a' bhòn-dè *adv phr* the day before yesterday

a' bhòn-raoir *adv phr* the night before last

a' bhòn-uiridh *adv phr* the year before last *Also* **a' bhèan-uiridh**

a-bhos *adv* (being) over here/on this side

abhsadh *n* -aidh *m* slackening **gun a.** non-stop, without halting

ablach *n* -aich, -aich/-aichean *m* carcase; person affected by illness or something suffering from wear and tear **tha e na a.** he is in poor shape **seann a. de chàr** an old wreck of a car

abstol *n* -oil, -oil/-an *m* apostle

aca(san) *prep pron* their; they **bha aca ri falbh** they had to go

acadamh *n* -aimh, -an *f* academy

acaid *n* -e, -ean *f* stabbing pain, stitch

acair(e) *n* (-e), acraichean *f m* anchor

acair(e) *n* (-e), acraichean *f m* acre

acarsaid *n* -(e), -ean *f* anchorage, harbour

acfhainn *n* -(e), -ean *f* equipment, instruments, tools **a. eich** horse harness

acfhainneach *a* -niche equipped; expert

ach *conj* but; (*after neg*) only, except **cha robh ann ach fathann** it was only a rumour

ach am/an *conj See* **feuch**

achadh *n* **-aidh/acha, -aidhean/ achannan** *m* field

a-chaoidh *adv* forever, always; (*after neg v*) never **cha tig iad a-ch.** they'll never come

achd *n* **-a, -an** *f* Act (*of Parliament*)

achdarra *a* skilful, expert, methodical

a-cheana *adv* already, previously

a-chianaibh *adv* recently, a short time ago

a chionn ('s) *adv phr* because, since **a ch. gu bheil mi sgìth** because I'm tired

achlais *n* **-(e), -ean** *f* armpit, oxter

achmhasan *n* **-ain, -ain** *m* rebuke, reprimand, reproach *v* **thoir a. do** rebuke, reprimand

a chum *prep phr* (+ *gen*) to **a chum an taighe** to the house *Also* **chum**

a chum is gu *conj* in order that **a chum is gum faic thu iad** in order that/so that you will see them

acrach *a* **-aiche** hungry

acraich *v* **-achadh** anchor

acras *n* **-ais** *m* hunger **a bheil an t-a. ort?** are you hungry?

actair *n* **-ean** *m* actor

ad(a) *n* **aide, -(a)n/-(a)ichean** *f* hat

adag *n* **-aig, -an** *f* haddock; stook (*eg of corn*)

a dh'aindeoin *prep phr* (+ *gen*) despite *adv phr* despite, even although, nevertheless **thig e a dh'. sin** he'll come despite that **a dheòin no (a) dh'.** willy-nilly/like it or not

adha *n* **àinean** *m* liver

adhairc *n See* **adharc**

adhaltranach *a* **-aiche** adulterous

adhaltranas *n* **-ais** *m* adultery

adhar *n* **-air** sky *m*

adharc *n* **-airc(e), -an/-aircean** *f* horn

adhartach *a* **-aiche** progressive

adhartas *n* **-ais** *m* progress

adhbhar *n* **-air, -air/-an** *m* cause, reason **air an a. sin** for that reason, that being so, hence

adhbh(a)raich *v* **adhbh(a)rachadh** cause

a dh'ionnsaigh *prep phr* (+ *gen*) to, towards

adhbrann *n* **-ainn, -ainn/-an** *f m* ankle

a dhìth *adv phr* needed; lost (forever) **tha sin a dh. orm** I need that **chaidh an sreapadair a dh.** the climber perished

adhlacadh *n* **-aidh, -aidh/-aidhean** *m* funeral, burial, interment

adhlaic *v* **-acadh** bury, inter

adhradh *n* **-aidh, -aidhean** *m* worship, act of worship **a. teaghlaich** family worship **dèan a.** *v* worship

Afraganach *n* **-aich, -aich** *m* African *a* African

ag *v part* (*used before verbal nouns beginning in vowels*) **ag ithe 's ag òl** eating and drinking

agad(sa) *prep pron* your (*sg*) **a bheil càr agad?** do you have a car?

agaibh(se) *prep pron* your (*pl & pol*) **cò agaibh a bh' ann?** which of you were there?

againn(e) *prep pron* our **tha iad a' fuireach againne** they're staying with us

agair *v* **-t** petition, demand **ag agairt a chòraichean** demanding his rights

agallaich *v* **-adh/-achadh** interview; give abuse, quarrel with

agallaiche *n* **-an** *m* interviewer

agallamh *n* **-aimh, -an** *m* interview **dèan a.** *v* interview

agam(sa) *prep pron* my **cò th' agam an seo?** who's this?

agh *n* **aighe, aighean** *f m* heifer; hind

àgh *n* **àigh** *m* joy, bliss; good fortune **An ainm an Àigh!** For goodness's sake! **Gun sealladh an t-Àgh orm!** Goodness gracious me!

aghaidh *n* **-(e), -ean** *f* face (*human or geog*), facade **a. ri a.** face to face **nach ann ort a tha 'n a.!** what a cheek you've got! **bhithinn an a. sin** I'd be against that **air a.** forward **thug e an a. orm** *v* he (*verbally*) attacked/rebuked me

aghaidh-choimheach *n* **-coimhich, aghaidhean-coimheach** *f* mask, false-face

àghmhor *a* **-oire** happy; fortunate

a-ghnàth *adv* always (*past, present, future*), ever

agus *conj* and (*also contracted to* **is, 's**)

a h-uile *a* (*precedes n*) every, each, all **a h-uile h-oidhche** every night

àibheis *n* **(-e), -ean** *f* abyss, the deep; (*colloq*) large structure; ruin

àibheiseach *a* **-siche** large, huge; remarkable

aibidil *n* **-ean** *f* alphabet **òrdugh na h-a.** *m* alphabetical order

aice(se) *prep pron* her **an tèid aice air tighinn?** can she come?

àicheadh *n* **-eidh, -eidhean** *m* denial **rach às à.** *v* deny

àicheidh *v* **-eadh** deny

àicheil *a* negative

aideachadh *n* **-aidh, -aidhean** *m* admission, confession

aidh *excl* aye, yes

àidhear *n See* **èadhar**

aidich *v* **aideachadh** admit, confess

aidmheil *n* **(-e), -ean** *f* creed, faith

aifreann *n* **-rinn(e), -rinnean** *f m* Mass (*relig*)

aig *prep* at; (*also used to denote possession*) **tha càr aig Sìm** Simon has a car

aige(san) *prep pron* his **bidh fios aigesan** he'll know

àigeach *n* **-gich, -gich** *m* stallion

aigeann *n* **-ginn** *m* sea-bed *Also* **aigeal**

aigeannach *a* **-aiche** spirited, lively

aighear *n* **-eir** *m* joy, high spirits, merriment

aighearach *a* **-aiche** joyful, in high spirits, merry

aigne *n f* mind, consciousness, spirits

ailbhean *n* **-ein, -an** *m* elephant

àile *n m* air, atmosphere

àileadh *n m See* **fàileadh**

aileag *n* **-eig** *f* hiccups **bha an a. orm** I had the hiccups

àilgheas *n* **-eis** *f* will, inclination, desire

àilgheasach *a* **-aiche** choosy, fussy, fastidious, hard to please

ailisich *v* **-seachadh** criticize strongly

àill *n f* wish, desire **dè b' àill leibh?** what is your wish? **b' àill leibh?/bàillibh?** pardon?

àilleachd *n f* beauty, loveliness

àilleag *n* **-eig, -an** *f* jewel

àilleagan *n* **-ain, -ain** *m* little jewel, treasure

àillidh *a* **-e** beautiful, lovely

aillse *n f* cancer **tha a. air** he has cancer **a. sgamhain** lung cancer

ailm *n* **-e, -ean** *f* elm tree

ailtire *n* **-an** *m* architect

ailtireachd *n f* architecture

aimhleas *n* **-eis** *m* harm, hurt; misfortune

aimhleasach *a* **-aiche** harmful, hurtful; unfortunate

aimhreit *n* **(-e), -ean** *f* argument, dispute

aimhreiteach *a* **-tiche** argumentative, disputatious

aimlisg *n* **-e, -ean** *f* confusion, disorder; mischief **'s e a. a th' ann** he's a mischief

aimlisgeach *a* **-giche** mischievous

aimsir *n* **(-e), -ean** *f* time, era; weather **san t-seann a.** in days gone by

aimsireil *a* **-e** temporal, of this world; climatic

ain-deòin *n f* unwillingness, reluctance

ain-deònach *a* **-aiche** unwilling, reluctant

aineol *n* **-oil** *m* stranger, foreigner; lack of acquaintance **bha mi air m' a. sa bhaile** I was a stranger in the town

aineolach *a* **-aiche** ignorant, unaware, ill-informed

aineolas *n* **-ais** *m* ignorance

aingeal *n* **-gil, ainglean** *m* angel

aingidh *a* **-e** wicked, heinous

aingidheachd *n f* wickedness, iniquity

ainm *n* **(-e), -ean/-eannan** *m* name **a. sgrìobhte** signature **dè an t-a. a th' ort?** what's your name?

ainmeachadh *n* **-aidh** *m* nomination; mention

ainmear *n* **-eir, -an** *m* noun **a. gnìomhaireach** verbal noun

ainmeil *a* **-e** famous

ainmhidh *n* **-ean** *m* animal

ainmich *v* **ainmeachadh** name, mention; announce

ainmichte *a* designated, nominated

ainmig *adv* seldom, rarely

ainmneach *a* nominative **an tuiseal a.** the nominative case

ainneamh *a* **-eimhe** rare, infrequent **gu h-a.** rarely, infrequently

ainneart *n* **-eirt** *m* oppression, violence

ainneartach *a* **-aiche** oppressive, violent

ainnir *n* (**-e**), **-ean** *f* maiden

ainnis *n* **-e** *f* need, poverty

ainniseach *a* **-siche** needy, indigent, destitute

aintighearn(a) *n* (**-a**), **-an** *m* tyrant, oppressor, abuser of power

aintighearnas *n* **-ais** *m* tyranny, oppression, abuse of power

air *adv* on **tha an solas air** the light is on

air *prep* on; by; about; at; however, no matter; (*used to describe feelings and states*) **tha an t-acras/an t-eagal orm** I'm hungry/I'm afraid (*sometimes with len*) **air chuairt** on a trip **rug mi air chois air** I caught him by the foot **a' bruidhinn air na rudan sin** speaking about these things **bha sinn a' bruidhinn ort** we were speaking about you **air banais** at a wedding **math air ...** good at ... **air cho anmoch 's gum bi sinn** however late we are/will be

air *adv* after (*used before vn*) **tha iad air tilleadh** they've returned (*lit* they're after returning) **tha iad air an doras fhosgladh** they've opened the door

air(san) *prep pron* on him/it

air adhart *adv phr* ahead, forward(s), onwards **dol-air-adhart** *f* carry-on, undesirable behaviour

air aghaidh *adv phr* ahead, forward(s), onwards

air ais *adv phr* back, backwards **air ais 's air adhart** backwards and forwards

air ball *adv phr* at once, immediately

air beulaibh *prep phr* (+ *gen*) in front of **a. b. an taighe** in front of the house **air mo bheulaibh** in front of me

air bhog *adv phr* afloat **cuir a. b.** *v* launch

air bhonn *adv phr* in operation, up and running **cuir a. b.** *v* establish, set up

airc *n* **-e** *f* distress, want

àirc(e) *n* (**-e**), **-ean** *f* ark **À. Nòah** Noah's Ark

air chall *adv phr* lost

air chois *adv phr* in operation **cuir a. ch.** *v* establish, set up, institute

air choreigin *adv phr* or other **fear/tè a. ch.** someone or other

air chùl *adv phr* behind, rejected, lost

air cùl *prep phr* (+ *gen*) behind

air cùlaibh *comp prep* (+ *gen*) behind, at the back of **tha e air do chùlaibh** he/it is behind you

àird(e) *n* **-e**, **-ean** *f* height, high place, point, headland **sia troighean a dh'àirde** six feet tall

àird *n* **-e**, **-ean** *f* point of the compass, airt **an àird an iar** the west

air dheireadh *adv phr* behind, last; late **bha am bàta a. dh.** the boat was late

aire *n* heed, attention *f* **thoir an a.** notice; watch! look out! **thoir an a. ort fhèin** take care (of yourself)

air eagal ('s) gu *conj* lest, in case **a. e ('s). gun tuit thu** in case you fall

àireamh *n f* **-eimh, -an** number **à. fòn** phone number

àireamhair *n* **-ean** *m* calculator

air fad *adv* altogether, in total

air falbh *adv* away, in a different place

air feadh *prep phr* (+ *gen*) throughout, all around

airgead *n* **-gid** *m* money, currency; silver **a.-pòcaid** pocket money **a. ullamh** cash

airidh *a* **-e** worthy, deserving **a. air duais** deserving a prize **'s math an a.** it's richly deserved (*whether good or bad*)

airidheachd *n f* merit

àirigh *n* **-ean** *f* sheiling, hill pasture; bothy

àirleas *n* **-eis, -an** *m* token **a.-leabhair** book token *Also* **eàrlas**

air leth *adv* separate; exceptional, outstanding **cùm an dà rud sin a. l. o chèile** keep these two things separate from each other **duine a. l.** an exceptional man **a. l. math** exceptionally good

air-loidhne *a* online

air muin *prep phr* (+ *gen*) on top of, astride **a. m. eich** on horseback

àirne *n* **-an** *f* kidney
àirneis *n f* furniture **ball a.** an item
of furniture
air neo *conj* or, or else
air sàillibh *prep phr* (+ *gen*) because
of *Also* **air tàillibh**
air sgàth *prep phr* for the sake of, in the
interests of **air mo sgàth-sa** for my sake
a. s. na sìthe in the interests of peace
airson *prep* (+ *gen*) for, for the sake of;
(*before a vn*) desirous of, wanting to
tha iad a. falbh they want to go
airson gu *conj* because, since
air thoiseach *adv* ahead, in front;
(*of a clock*) fast
air thoiseach air *prep phr* ahead of
air thuaiream *adv* at random
airtneal *n* **-eil** *m* weariness, sorrow,
dejection *Also* **airsneal**
airtnealach *a* **-aiche** weary, sorrowful,
dejected *Also* **airsnealach**
aiseag *n* **-eig/-sig, -an** *m* ferry
aiseal *n* **-eil, -an** *m* axle
aisean *n* **-ein, aisnean** *f* rib *Also* **asna**
f pl **asnaichean**
aiseirigh *n f* resurrection, resurgence
Àisianach *n* **-aich, -aich** *m* Asian
a Asian
aisig *v* **aiseag** ferry; restore
aisling *n* **-e, -ean** *f* dream
aiste *prep pron* from/out of her/it
ait *a* **-e** glad, joyful; funny
àite *n* **-an/-achan/-tichean** *m* place
à.-fuirich dwelling-place, accommodation,
habitation **à.-obrach** workplace **à.-suidhe**
seat **à. bàn** vacancy **an à.** (+ *gen*) in place
of, instead of
àiteigin *n m* somewhere
àiteach *n* **-tich** *m* cultivation, farming
talamh-àitich *m* arable land

àiteachas *n* **-ais** *m* agriculture
aiteal *n* **-eil, -an** *m* glimpse, ray; breeze;
small quantity **a. grèine** a glimpse of
sunshine
aiteamh *n* **-eimh** *m* thaw **tha beagan
aiteimh ann** it's thawing a little *Also vn*
ag aiteamh
aiteann *n* **-tinn** *m* juniper
aitheamh *n* **-eimh, -an** *m* fathom
aithghearr *a* **-a** fast, swift, sudden; short,
brief *f* **a dh'a.** *adv phr* soon, shortly
fhuair i bàs a. she died suddenly
aithghearrachd *n f* shortness, brevity;
shortcut **ann an a.** soon, swiftly; in brief
aithisg *n* **(-e), -ean** *f* report
a. bhliadhnail annual report
àithn *v* **-e** command, ordain
aithne *n f* knowledge; acquaintance
an a. dhut e? do you know him? **cuir a.
air** *v* get to know **cuir an a. (a chèile)**
v introduce (to each other)
àithne *n* **-ntean** *f* order, commandment
na Deich Àithntean the Ten
Commandments
àithneach *a* imperative (*gram*)
aithnich *v* **-neachadh** know, recognize,
acknowledge **a bheil thu ga
h-aithneachadh?** do you recognize her?
aithreachas *n* **-ais** *m* regret, repentance
ghabh iad (an t-)a. they regretted it
aithris *n* **-ean** *f* account, report
aithris *v* relate, report, recite
àitich *v* **àiteach/àiteachadh** cultivate;
inhabit
aitreabh *n* **-eibh, -an** *m* building,
dwelling
àl *n* **àil, àil** *m* brood, young, litter
àlainn *a* **-e/àille** lovely, beautiful, fine
Albàinianach *n* **-aich, -aich** *m* Albanian
a Albanian

Insight: Alba

The Gaelic name for Scotland. In the genitive case it can take the
definite article – *muinntir na h-Alba*, the people of Scotland – but it
doesn't always: *muinntir Alba* is OK. One of these words with a vowel
sound not written, it's pronounced '*Al*-ab-uh'. *Albannach* (noun) –
'*Al*-ab-un-uch' – is a Scot, while *Albannach* (adjective) is Scottish.

Albais *n f* the Scots language, Scots

Albannach *n* **-aich, -aich** *m* Scot *a* Scottish

alcol *n* **-oil** *m* alcohol

allaban *n* **-ain** *m* wandering **air an a.** wandering; homeless

allail *a* **-e** noble, illustrious

allmharach *n* **-aich, -aich** *m* foreigner, alien

allaidh *a* **-e** wild, fierce

allt *n* **uillt, uillt** *m* stream, burn

alltan *n* **-ain, -ain** *m* little stream, brook

alt *n* **uilt, -an/uilt** *m* joint (*of the body*); aptitude, knack; article (*liter, gram*) **tha alt aice air ceòl** she has an aptitude for music

altachadh *n* **-aidh, -aidhean** *m* grace (*before meals*) **dèan/gabh a.** *v* say grace

altaich *v* **altachadh** relax the joints; salute, thank **tha mi airson mo chasan altachadh** I want to stretch my legs

altair *n* **altarach, -ean/altraichean** *f* altar

altraim *v* **-am/-amas** nurse, dandle, foster, nurture

altram *n* **-aim** *m* fosterage, fostering, nursing

am *def art* the (*used before b, f, m, p*) (*See Forms of the article in Grammar*)

am *poss pron* their (*used before b, f, m, p*)

am *int part* **am pòs thu mi?** will you marry me?

am *prep* equivalent to **an** in (*used before b, f, m, p*) **am Peairt** in Perth

àm *n* **ama, amannan** *m* time, period of time **àm nam Fuadaichean** the time of the Clearances **tha an t-àm agad falbh** it's time you went **tha an t-àm agad!** it's high time! (you did) **anns an eadar-àm** in the meantime, at present **san àm ri teachd** in future

a-mach *adv* out, outwards (*implying motion*)

amadan *n* **-ain, -ain** *m* fool

amaideach *a* **-diche** foolish, silly, ridiculous

amaideas *n* **-eis** *m* foolishness, folly, silliness

a-màireach *adv* tomorrow

amais *v* **amas (+ air)** aim at; chance on, chance to be **ag amas air an targaid** aiming at the target **dh'amais dhomh a bhith ann** I happened/chanced to be there

amar *n* **-air, -an** *m* container for liquid, trough, bath **a.-snà(i)mh** swimming pool

amas *n* **-ais, -an** *m* aim, objective; chance **cha robh ann ach a. gun d' fhuair mi e** it was only by chance that I found it

ambaileans *n* **-ean** *f* ambulance

am bàrr *prep phr* (*+ gen*), *adv* on top of, on the surface of **chì sinn dè thig am b.** we'll see what comes to the surface/ to light

ambasaid *n* **-ean** *f* embassy

am-bliadhna *adv* this year

am broinn *prep phr* (*+ gen*) inside, within

Ameireaganach *n* **-aich, -aich** *m* American *a* American

amen *exclam* amen, so let it be

am-feast *adv phr* forever; (*after neg*) never **cha ruig iad a.-f.** they'll never get there

amh *a* **aimhe** raw; (*of a person*) uncouth

amhach *n* **-aich, -aichean** *f* neck *Also* **amhaich**

a-mhàin *adv* only, alone

àmhainn *n* **-ean** *f* oven

amhairc *v* **amharc (+ air)** see, look at, view

amharas *n* **-ais** *m* suspicion **fo a.** under suspicion, suspect **tha a. agam gu bheil** I suspect so

amharasach *a* **-aiche** suspicious, distrustful

amharc *n* **-airc** *m* seeing, looking, view **dè th' agad san a. a-nis?** what have you in view/in mind now?

àmhghar *n* **-air, -an** *f m* affliction, adversity, anguish, severe trouble

àmhghair *n See* **àmhghar**

amhlaidh *adv* as, in the way that

amhran *n* **-ain, -ain** *m* song

am measg *prep phr* (*+ gen*) among

a-muigh *adv* out, outside (*not implying motion*)

an *def art* the (*See Forms of the article in Grammar*)

an *poss pron* their

an *int part* **an tàinig iad?** have they arrived?

an *prep* in **an Èirinn** in Ireland

an-abaich *a* **-e** unripe

anabarr *n* **-a** *m* excess, too much

anabarrach *a* **-aiche** greatly, extremely, remarkably, excessively **a. mòr** extraordinarily large

ana-cainnt *n* **-e** *f* abusive language, verbal abuse

ana-caith *v* **-eamh** waste, misuse

ana-caitheanaich *n f* waste, misuse **a. air biadh math** a waste of good food

ana-ceartas *n* **-ais** *m* injustice

anacladh *n* **-aidh** *m* handling; protecting

anacothrom *n* **-uim** *m* injustice, hardship, handicap

ana-creideas *n* **-eis** *m* disbelief, scepticism

an aghaidh *prep phr* (+ *gen*) against

anail *n* **-e/analach, -ean** *f* breath; rest **a. na beatha** the breath of life **a. a' Ghàidheil am mullach** the Gael's rest is (*when he/she reaches*) the summit **leig d' a.** get your breath back/have a rest

an-àird(e) *adv* up, upwards

analachadh *n* **-aidh** *m* aspiration (*gram*)

a-nall *adv* over (*from the other side*), to this side

anam *n* **-a, anman/anmannan** *m* soul

anann *n* **-ainn** *m* pineapple

anarag *n* **-aig, -an** *f* anorak

anart *n* **anairt** *m* linen **anartan** clothes on a line **a.-leapa** bed linen **a.-bùird** table linen

an-asgaidh *adv* free (of charge), for nothing **saor is an-a.** free, gratis

an-ath- *pref* (*usually lenites*) next **an-ath-d(h)oras** *adv* next door **an-ath-bhliadhna** *adv* next year **an-ath-oidhch'** *adv* tomorrow night **an-ath-sheachdain** *adv* next week

an ath *pref* (*usually lenites*) the following **an ath bhliadhna** *adv* the following year, **an ath sheachdain** *adv* the following week

an ceann *prep phr* (+ *gen*) after, at the end of

an-ceartuair *adv* at present, just now; shortly **thig iad an-c.** they'll come shortly/presently

an cois *prep phr* (+ *gen*) beside; (*met*) in the course of, as part of

an comhair *prep phr* (+ *gen*) in the direction of **an c. a etc chùil** backwards **an c. a etc chinn** forwards, head first

an-còmhnaidh *adv* always, constantly

an-dè *adv* yesterday

an deaghaidh *prep phr* See **an dèidh**

an dèidh *prep phr* (+ *gen*) after; despite **cairteal an d. uair** quarter past one **is toigh leam e an d. sin** I like him nevertheless/despite that **an d. sin 's na dhèidh** for all that, after all **an d. làimhe** afterwards, subsequently

an-diugh *adv* today **feasgar a.** this afternoon **san latha a.** these days

an-dràsta *adv* just now, now, at present **a. 's a-rithist** now and again

an ear *adv* east, eastern, eastwards **an àird an ear** the east

an-earar *adv* the day after next/tomorrow

an ear-dheas *adv* south-east, south-eastwards **gaoth an e.** a south-east wind

an ear-thuath *adv* north-east, north eastwards **a' dol dhan ear-thuath** going north-eastwards

anfhann *a* **-ainne** weak, feeble, infirm

an-fhoiseil *a* **-e** restless, uneasy, ill-at-ease, troubled

an iar *adv* west, western, westwards **na h-Eileanan an Iar** the Western Isles

an iar-dheas *adv* south-west, south-westwards **oiteag on i.** a breeze from the south-west

an iar-thuath *adv* north-west, north-westwards

an impis *adv* about to, on the point of

an-iochdmhor *a* **-oire** unmerciful, unpitying, unfeeling

an làthair *adv* present *prep phr* (+ *gen*) in the presence of

an lùib *prep phr* (+ *gen*) among, involved in, in the course of, attached to

a-nìos *adv* up (*from below*)

a-nis *adv* now *Also* **a-nise, a-nist**

anmoch *a* **-oiche** late

ann(san) *rel pron* in him/it; he, it **'s e oileanach a th' ann** he's a student

ann *adv* in existence, there; in it **'s e latha math a th' ann** it's a fine day

ann *prep* in a (*followed by* **an**, *by* **am** *before b, f, m, p, by* **a** *before h*) **ann an taigh** in a house **ann am bùth** in a shop **ann a Hiort** in St Kilda

annad(sa) *prep pron* in you (*sg*); you

annaibh(se) *prep pron* in you (*pl & pol*); you

annainn(e) *prep pron* in us; we

annam(sa) *prep pron* in me; I

annas *n* **-ais, -an** *m* rarity, novelty; unusual object/event **thug iad an t-a. às** the novelty wore off for them

annasach *a* **-aiche** unusual, novel; strange, odd

annlan *n* **-ain** *m* condiment, accompaniment to main food being eaten

anns *prep* (+ *art*) in (the) *Also used before* **gach a. gach taigh** in every house

annsa *a* better/best liked, preferred **an tè a b' a. leam** the woman I liked best

annsachd *n f* love, affection or object of these **m' a.** my beloved

ann(san) *prep pron* in him/it; he/it

annta(san) *prep pron* in them; they

a-nochd *adv* tonight

ànradh *n* **-aidh** *m* misfortune, distress

an seo *adv* here

anshocair *n* **-ean/-ocran** *f* unease; discomfort; illness

anshocrach *a* **-aiche** uneasy; discomforted, distressed, distressing; suffering from illness *Also* **anshocair**

an sin *adv* there

an siud *adv* over there

antaidh *n* **-ean** *f* aunt(ie)

an toiseach *adv* first, to begin with

an uair a *conj* when (*equivalent to* **nuair)**

an uair sin *adv phr* then, after that

a-nuas *adv* down (*from above*) *See also* **a-nìos**

an-uiridh *adv* last year

a-null *adv* over (*to the other side*) **a-null 's a-nall** hither and thither

a-nunn *adv See* **a-null**

aobhar *n See* **adhbhar**

aobrann *n See* **adhbrann**

aocoltach *a* **-aiche** unlike, unalike, dissimilar **glè a. ri chèile** very unlike one another

aodach *n* **-aich/-aichean** *m* clothes, cloth, material *pl* cloths of different kinds, clothes on a line **a.-leapa** bedclothes **a.-oidhche** night-clothes

aodann *n* **-ainn** *m* face (*human or geog*)

aodannan *n* **-ain, -ain** *m* false-face, mask

aodomhainn *a* **-e** shallow

aog *n* **aoig** *m* **an t-aog** death

aogas *n* **-ais** *m* face, appearance, countenance

aoibhinn *a* **-e** joyful, glad; pleasant

aoibhneach *a* **-niche** joyful, happy, glad; delightful, pleasant

aoibhneas *n* **-eis** *m* joy, gladness; delight

aoidion *n* **-a, -an** *m* leak

aoidionach *a* **-aiche** leaky, leaking

aoigh *n* **-ean** *m* guest

aoigheachd *n f* hospitality **bha iad air a. againn** we had them as guests/they were our guests

aoigheil *a* **-e** hospitable; genial

aoir *n* **-e, -ean** *f* satire

aois *n* **-e, -ean** *f* age **dè an a. a tha i?** how old is she? **A. an Iarainn** the Iron Age

aol *n* **aoil** *m* lime

aom *v* **-adh** incline, bend **sna lathaichean a dh'aom** in days gone by

aomadh *n* **-aidh** *m* act of inclining or bending; inclination, tendency

aon *n* **aoin** *m* one (*of anything*) *normally written* **a h-aon**; each *not* **an t-aon** £1 each

aon *num a* one; only; same **sin an (t-) aon dath** that's the same colour *Also* **aona**

aonach *n* **-aich, -aich** *m* high or steep place, ridge **A. Eagach** the Serrated Ridge (in Glencoe)

aonach *n* **-aich** *f m* panting, state of being out of breath **bha a. orm** I was out of breath

aonachd *n f* unity

aonad *n* **-aid, -an** *m* unit

aonadh *n* **-aidh, -aidhean** *m* union, unity, merger **a. ciùird** (trade) union **an t-A. Eòrpach** the European Union

aonaich *v* **-achadh** unite, integrate, combine

aonaichte *a* united, integrated

aonan *n* **-ain** *m* one (*of anything*)

aonar *n* **-air** *m* one person; state of being alone **bha i na h-a.** she was alone *Also* **ònar**

aonaran *n* **-ain, -ain** *m* hermit, loner, recluse *Also* **ònaran**

aonar(an)ach *a* **-aiche** lonely, solitary

aonaranachd *n f* isolation, loneliness, solitude *Also* **aonranas**, **ònrachd**

aon-deug *n, a* eleven **aon duine deug** eleven men/persons

aon-ghuthach *a* **-aiche** unanimous

aonta *n* **-n** *m* agreement, assent, consent **cuir a. ri** *v* agree to, approve

aontachadh *n* **-aidh** *m* agreement, act of agreeing

aontaich *v* **-achadh** agree, consent

aontaichte *a* agreed

aoradh *n* See **adhradh**

aosta *a* old, elderly, aged *Formerly* **aosda**

aotraman *n* **-ain, -ain** *m* bladder

aotrom *a* **-ruime** light; light-hearted

aotromaich *v* **-achadh** lighten; alleviate

apa *n* **-ichean** *m* ape

aparan *n* **-ain, -ain** *m* apron

ar *poss pron* our **Ar n-Athair a tha air Nèamh** Our Father which art in Heaven

ar *def v* seems *in phr* **ar leam** it seems to me, I think

àr *n* **àir** *m* battle, battlefield, slaughter

ar-a-mach *n* rebellion, rising **A. nan Seumasach** the Jacobite Rebellion/Rising

àra *n* **àrann, àirnean** *f* kidney

Arabach *n* **-aich, -aich** *m* Arab *a* Arabian, Arabic

àrachas *n* **-ais** *m* insurance

àrach *n* **-aich** *m* raising, upbringing, rearing

àradh *n* **-aidh, -aidhean** *m* ladder

àraich *v* **àrach** raise, bring up, rear

àraid(h) *a* **-e** certain, particular; odd, peculiar

Arainneach *n* **-nich, -nich** *m* someone from Arran *a* from, or pertaining to, Arran

àrainneachd *n f* environment

aran *n* **arain** *m* bread **a.-coirce** oat bread, oatcake **a.-cridhe** gingerbread

a-raoir *adv* last night

araon *adv* together, both **a. mise is tusa** both you and I

arbhar *n* **-air** *m* corn

àrc *n* **-a/àirce, -an** *f* cork, cork cap (*in bottle*)

Arcach *n* **-aich, -aich** *m* Orcadian *a* Orcadian

arc-eòlaiche *n* **-an** *m* archaeologist

arc-eòlas *n* **-ais** *m* archaeology

àrd *a* **àirde** high, tall; loud (*of sound*) *pref* principal, high, chief

àrd *n* See **àird(e)**

àrdachadh *n* **-aidh** *m* raising, increasing, elevation; promotion **fhuair sinn à. pàighidh** we got a pay rise

àrdaich *v* **-achadh** raise, increase, elevate; promote

àrdaichear *n* **-eir, -an** *m* lift, elevator

àrdan *n* **-ain** *m* pride, arrogance, haughtiness

àrdanach *a* **-aiche** proud, arrogant, haughty

àrd-chùirt *n* **-e, -ean** *f* high court

àrd-doras *n* **-ais** *m* lintel

àrd-easbaig *n* **(-e), -ean** *m* archbishop

àrd-ghuthach *a* **-aiche** loud-voiced

àrd-ìre *n* **-an** *f* higher, higher grade/level **deuchainnean na h-Àrd Ìre** Higher exams **foghlam a.** *m* higher education

àrd-oifigear *n* **-eir, -an** *m* chief executive, senior officer

àrd-sgoil *n* **-e, -tean** *f* secondary school, high school

àrd-sheanadh *n* **-aidh, -aidhean** *m* general assembly (*eg of a Church*)

àrd-urram *n* **-aim, -an** *m* high honour, distinction; renown

àrd-ùrlar *n* **-air, -air** *m* stage, platform

a rèir *prep phr* (+ *gen*) according to **a. r. c(h)oltais** apparently

a-rèist(e) *adv* then, therefore, in that case

argamaid *n* **-e, -ean** *f* argument, dispute

argamaidich *v* **argamaid** argue

(a-)riamh *adv* ever, always

a-rithist *adv* again **an-dràsta 's a.** now and again, occasionally *Also* **a-rìs**

arm *n* **airm, airm** *m* army *Also* **armailt**

armachd *n f* arms, armour, weaponry

armaich *v* **-achadh** arm, equip with weapons

armaichte *a* armed

àrmann *n* **-ainn, -ainn** *m* hero, warrior

armlann *n* **-ainn, -an** *f* armoury, arsenal

àros *n* **àrois, -an** *m* dwelling place, mansion

ars *def v* said (**arsa** *before consonants*)

àrsaidh *a* **-e** ancient, antiquated

àrsair *n* **-ean** *m* antiquarian

àrsaidheachd *n f* quality of being ancient; antiquarianism; archaeology

artaigil *n* **-ean** *m* article

as *v rel form* of **is** (who/that) is **am fear as motha** the one that is biggest, the biggest one

as *prep* in *contr* of **anns** *used in phrases* **as t-earrach, as t-samhradh, as t-fhoghar** in spring, in summer, in autumn

às *adv* out **chaidh an teine às** the fire went out **leig às e** let it go **rinn e às** he made off/ran for it/escaped **thàrr e às** he escaped

às *prep* out of

às(-san) *prep pron* from/out of him/it

asad(sa) *prep pron* out of you (*sg*)

asaibh(se) *prep pron* out of you (*pl & pol*)

asainn(e) *prep pron* out of us

asal *n* **-ail, -ail** *f m* ass, donkey **a.-stiallach** zebra *Also* **aiseal**

asam(sa) *prep pron* out of me

às aonais *prep phr* (+ *gen*) without, in the absence of

asbhuain *n f* stubble (*in field*)

às dèidh *prep phr* (+ *gen*) after, following *Also* **às deaghaidh**

às eugmhais *prep phr* (+ *gen*) without, lacking

asgaidh *n* **-ean** *f* gift *normally only used in phr* **an-a.** free (*of charge*), for nothing

asgair *n* **-ean** *m* apostrophe

aslaich *v* **-achadh** supplicate, beseech

às leth *prep phr* (+ *gen*) on behalf of **rinn e sin às mo leth-sa** he did that on my behalf

asta(san) *prep pron* from/out of them

a-staigh *adv* in, inside; at home

astar *n* **-air, -air/-an** *m* distance; speed; journey **a. dheich mìle** a distance of ten miles **aig a.** at speed

a-steach *adv* in, into (*implying motion*) **thig a.** come in **chaidh iad a. dhan bhaile** they went into (the) town **cha tàinig e riamh a. orm** it never crossed my mind

Astràilianach *n* **-aich, -aich** *m* Australian *a* Australian

at *n* **-an** *m* swelling **an t-at-busach** mumps

at *v* **at/-adh** swell, puff up

ath *a* (+ *len*) (*preceded by def art*) next **an ath uair** the next time **an ath choinneamh** the next meeting

àth *n* **-an** *m* ford

àth *n* **-a, -an** *f* kiln; old barn/outhouse

ath- *pref* (+ *len*) re- **ath-aithris** *v* repeat, reiterate **ath-chruthaich** *v* recreate

athair *n* **athar, athraichean** *m* father **a.-cèile** father-in-law **athraichean** forefathers

athaiseach *a* **-siche** dilatory, tardy

a thaobh *prep phr* (+ *gen*) concerning, regarding, on that account **na biodh dragh ort a th. sin** don't worry on that account

atharrachadh *n* **-aidh, -aidhean/ atharraichean** *m* change, alteration **a. nan gràs** religious conversion **thàinig a. air** he changed

atharraich *v* **-achadh** change, alter **tha an t-àite air atharrachadh** the place has changed

atharrais *n f* imitation, mimicry **dèan a. air** *v* imitate

atharrais (+ **air**) *v* mimic, imitate **bha e ag a. orm** he was mimicking me
ath-bheothachadh *n* -**aidh** *m* revival, rejuvenation **Linn an Ath-Bheothachaidh** the Renaissance Period
ath-bheothaich *v* -**achadh** revive, rejuvenate, revitalize
ath-chruthaich *v* -**achadh** re-create
athchuinge *n* -**an** *f* entreaty, petition
ath-dhìol *v* -**adh** repay
ath-leasachadh *n* -**aidh** *m* reform, redevelopment, amendment **an t-A.** the Reformation

ath-leasaich *v* -**achadh** reform, redevelop, amend
ath-nuadhachadh *n* -**aidh** *m* renewal, renovation
ath-nuadhaich *v* -**achadh** renew, renovate, reinvigorate, (*intrans*) be reinvigorated
àth-sgrìobh *v* -**adh** rewrite; transcribe
ath-sgrùdadh *n* -**aidh**, -**aidhean** *m* revision, review
a thuilleadh *prep phr* (+ **air**) in addition to, as well as
atmhorachd *n f* inflation **ire na h-a.** the inflation rate

B

b' *v part* shortened version of **bu**, was (*used before vowels*)
bà-bà *n* soothing sound made to child indicating sleep
bac *n* **baic/baca**, -**an** *m* impediment, hindrance, obstruction, restraint; rowlock; bank
bac *v* -**adh** impede, hinder, obstruct, restrain, prevent
bacach *n* -**aich**, -**aich** *m* lame person, cripple
bacach *a* -**aiche** lame, crippled
bacadh *n* -**aidh**, -**aidhean** *m* impediment, hindrance, obstruction, restraint, delay, handicap **cuir b. air** *v* obstruct, hinder
bacan *n* -**ain**, -**ain** *m* stake, tether-stake; crook, crooked staff; hindrance **b.-dorais** hinge of a door
bachall *n* -**aill**, -**aill/-an** *m* staff, crozier
bachlach *a* -**aiche** curly, curled
bachlag *n* -**aig**, -**an** *f* curl, ringlet; shoot (*of plant*)
bachlagach *a* -**aiche** curly, curled
bad *n* **baid**, -**an** *m* spot, place, part, area; tuft, bunch, cluster; clump, thicket **anns a' bhad** at once, immediately
badan *n* -**ain**, -**anan/-ain** *m* a small cluster or tuft, thicket; nappy
badeigin *adv* somewhere
badhbh *n* **baidhbh**, -**an** *f* witch, old hag

Badhlach *n* -**aich**, -**aich** *m* someone from Benbecula *a* from, or pertaining to, Benbecula
badhg *n* -**an** *m* fancy, notion **dè am b. a bhuail e?** what fancy took him?
baga *n* -**ichean/-nnan** *m* bag, case
bagaid *n* -**e**, -**ean** *f* cluster, bunch
bagair *v* -**t/bagradh** threaten, menace
bagairt *n* -**e**, -**ean** *f* threat, threatening
bagarrach *a* -**aiche** threatening, ominous, menacing
bàgh *n* **bàigh, bàigh/ (ann)an** *m* bay
bagradh *n* -**aidh**, -**aidhean** *m* threat, threatening, menacing
bàibheil *a* -**e** marvellous, tremendous, terrific
baic *n* -**ichean** *m* bike, motorbike
bàidh *n* -**e** *f* kindness, affection, tenderness
bàidheil *a* -**e** kind, affectionate, friendly **b. ri** affectionate to, well-disposed to
baidhsagal *n* -**ail**, -**an** *m* bicycle
baile *n* **bailtean** *m* town, village, township **b. beag** village **b.-mòr** city **aig b.** at home
bailiùn *n* -**aichean** *m* balloon
bàillidh *n* -**ean** *m* factor; baillie, magistrate
bainne *n m* milk **b. goirt** sour milk
baintighearna *n* -**n** *f* lady
bàirligeadh *n* -**gidh**, -**gidhean** *m* summons of removal, eviction order

bàirlinn f See **bàirligeadh**

bàirneach n **-nich, -nich** f barnacle, limpet

baist v **-eadh** baptize

Baisteach n **-tich, -tich** m Baptist a Baptist **an Eaglais Bhaisteach** the Baptist Church

baisteadh n **-tidh, -tidhean** m baptism, christening

bàl n **bàil, bàil/bàiltean** m ball, dance

balach n **-aich, -aich** m boy, lad **bu tu am b.!** well done, lad!

balachan n **-ain, -ain** m young boy, young lad

balaist(e) n f m ballast

balbh a **-a/bailbhe** dumb, mute, silent, quiet (of weather)

balbhachd n f dumbness, muteness

balbhan n **-ain, -ain** m dumb person, mute

balg n **builg, builg** m blister; abdomen; leather bag **b.-sèididh** bellows **b.-shaighead** quiver

balgair n **-e, -ean** m rogue, rotter, scoundrel

balgam n **-aim, -(ann)an** m mouthful (of drink), sip **b. tì** a drop of tea

balgan-buachair n **balgain-b., balgain-b.** m mushroom

ball n **buill, buill** m member, limb **Ball Pàrlamaid, Buill Phàrlamaid** m Member of Parliament **B. P. na h-Alba** Member of the Scottish Parliament

ball n **buill, buill** m ball Also **bàl(l)a**

balla n **-chan/-ichean** m wall, rampart

ballach a **-aiche** spotted, speckled

ball-basgaid n **buill-, buill-** m basketball

ball-coise n **buill-, buill-** m football

ball-dòbhrain n **buill-** m mole (on skin)

ball-lìn n **buill-, buill-** m netball

ball-maise n **buill-, buill-** m accessory, ornament

ballrachd n f membership

ball-seirce n **buill-, buill-** m beauty spot

ball-stèidhe n **buill-, buill-** m baseball

bàn a **bàine** fair, fair-haired; white, pale; vacant, fallow, blank **talamh bàn** m fallow ground **duilleag bhàn** f blank sheet **eaglais bhàn** f vacant charge (relig)

bàn- pref light, pale **bàn-dhearg** light red

ban(a) pref used to give female version of one's identity or occupation, female, woman **ban-Albannach** f Scotswoman

bana-chlèireach f clerkess

bana-bhuidseach n **-sich, -sichean** f witch

banacharaid n **-ean** f female friend, girlfriend

banachdach n **-aich** f a' **bhanachdach** vaccination

bana-chliamhainn n **-chleamhna, -chleamhnan** f daughter-in-law

banachrach n **-aich** f a' **bhanachrach** smallpox

bànag n **-aig, -an** f grilse, sea trout

bana-ghaisgeach n **-gich, -gich** f heroine, female warrior

bana-ghoistidh n **-ean** f godmother

banail a **-e/-ala** feminine, womanly, modest

banais n **bainnse, bainnsean** f wedding **bean na bainnse** f the bride **fear na bainnse** m the bridegroom

banaltram n **-aim, -an** f nurse

bana-mhaighstir-sgoile n **-mhaighstirean-** f headmistress

bana-mhaighstir n **-ean** f mistress (figure of authority)

banana n **-than** m banana

bana-phrionnsa n **-n** f princess

banas-taighe n f housekeeping; home economics

banca n **-ichean** m bank (fin) **B. na h-Alba** Bank of Scotland **B. Rìoghail na h-Alba** Royal Bank of Scotland **B. Dhail Chluaidh** Clydesdale Bank

bancair n **-ean** m banker

bancaireachd n f banking

ban-diùc n **-an** f duchess

bangaid n **-ean** f banquet, feast

ban-iarla n **-n** f countess

bann n **-a, -an/-tan** m band, belt, bandage; tie, hinge

bannal n **-ail, -an** m band, troupe, group, panel (of people)

bannas n **-ais** m gum

banntrach n **-aich, -aichean** f widow, m widower

ban-ogha n -**oghaichean/-oghachan**
f grand-daughter
banrigh n -**rean** f queen Also
ban-righinn
baobh n See **badhbh**
baoghalta a foolish, silly, idiotic
baoit n f bait
baoth a **baoithe** foolish, simple
(of mind), vacuous
bàr n **bàir, -aichean** m bar (pub)
bara n -**chan/-ichean** m barrow,
wheelbarrow
barail n -**e, -ean** f opinion **dè do
bharail?** what do you think?
baraille n -**ean** m barrel
barantaich v -**achadh** accredit
barantas n -**ais, -ais/-an** m guarantee,
authority, surety, commission
bàrd n **bàird, bàird** m poet, bard
bàrdachd n f poetry
bargan n -**ain, -ain/-an** f m bargain
barganaich v -**achadh** bargain,
make a deal
bàrr n **barra, barran** m top, surface,
crest; cream **a bhàrr air** besides **thig
am b.** v surface
Barrach n -**aich, -aich** m someone from
Barra a from, or pertaining to, Barra
barrachd n f more **b. air** more than
barraichte a super, supreme, superlative,
excellent
barraid n -**e, -ean** f terrace
barrall n -**aill, -aill** m shoelace
bas n **boise, -an** f palm (of hand)
bàs n **bàis, bàis** m death **a' dol bàs**
dying out
bàsaich v -**achadh** die
basgaid n -**e, -ean** f basket **b.-sgudail**
waste-basket
bàsmhor a -**a** mortal
bàsmhorachd n f mortality
bata n -**ichean** m stick, staff
bàta n -**ichean** m boat **bàt'-aiseig** ferry
b.-cargu cargo boat **bàt'-iasgaich**
fishing boat **b.- sàbhalaidh** lifeboat
b.-siùil sailing boat **b.-smùid** steamer,
steamboat **b.-teasairginn** lifeboat
b.-tumaidh submarine

batail n -**ean** m battle
batal n -**ail** m battle
bataraidh n -**ean** f m battery
bàth v -**adh** drown, extinguish, muffle
(sound)
bàthach n **bàthcha/-aich,
bàthchannan/-aichean** f byre, cowshed
Also **bàthaich**
bàthadh n -**aidh, -aidhean** m
drowning
bathais n -**ean** f forehead, brow
bathar n -**air** m goods, wares,
merchandise **b. bog** software
bàthte a drowned
beach n -**a, -an** m bee; wasp
beachd n -**a, -an** m opinion, view,
viewpoint; idea **dè do bheachd?**
what do you think? **bha i a' dol às a
b.** she was going crazy **gabh b. air** v
consider
beachdaich v -**achadh** consider, think
about, speculate, reflect on
beachdail a -**e** reflective, meditative,
observant
beachd-smaoinich/smuainich v
-**neachadh** meditate, contemplate
beachd-smaoin/smuain n -**tean** f idea,
theory
beachlann n -**ainn, -annan** f beehive
beadaidh a -**e** disrespectful, impudent,
forward
beadradh n -**aidh** m flirting, fondling,
caressing
beag a **bige/lugha** small, little, wee
b. air bheag little by little **is b. orm ...**
I dislike ...
beagaich v -**achadh** diminish, lessen
b. air cut down on, reduce
beagan adv a little, a trifle, somewhat
b. tràth a little early
beagan n -**ain** m a little, a few
beag-chuid n -**chodach, -chodaichean**
f minority
beairt n -**e, -ean** f machine, equipment,
engine **b.-fhighe** loom **b.-iasgaich**
fishing tackle Also **beart**
beairteach a -**tiche** rich, wealthy
Also **beartach**

beairteas n -eis m riches, wealth
Also **beartas**
bealach n -aich, -aichean m mountain
pass, way, gap
bealaidh n -ean m broom (plant)
Bealltainn n -e f May Day, first day of
May, Beltane
bean n mnà/mnatha, mnathan f wife,
woman dat mnaoi gen pl bhan
a mhnathan- 's a dhaoin'-uaisle!
ladies and gentlemen!
bean v -tainn (+ ri/do) touch, handle,
meddle with
bean-bainnse n f bride **bean na
bainnse** the bride
bean-ghlùine n mnà-glùine,
mnathan-glùine f midwife
beannachadh n -aidh, -aidhean
m blessing, benediction
beannachd n -an f blessing **b. leat**
goodbye **mo bheannachd ort!** well
done!
beannag n -aige, -an f shawl
beannaich v -achadh bless
beannaichte a blessed, religious
bean-phòsta n mnà-pòsta,
mnathan-pòsta f wife **a' Bhean-
Phòsta (A' Bh) NicLeòid** Mrs MacLeod
Formerly **bean-phòsda**
bean-sìthe n mnà-, mnathan- f fairy
Also **bean-shìth**
bean-taighe n mnà-, mnathan- f
housewife **b. an taighe** the lady of the
house
bean-teagaisg n mnà-, mnathan-
f teacher
bean-uasal n mnà-uaisle, mnathan-
uaisle f lady
beàrn n beàirn, -an f m gap, space,
hiatus, breach, cleft
beàrnan-bride n beàrnain-, beàrnain-
m dandelion
Beàrnarach n -aich m someone from
Bernera(y) a from, or pertaining to,
Bernera(y)
beàrr v bearradh cut (hair), shave, clip,
shear, prune
bearradair n -ean m barber, cutter

bearradaireachd n f sharp wit
bearradh n -aidh, -aidhean m precipice,
steep rockface; shearing, shaving,
cutting hair
beatha n -nnan f life **'s e do bheatha**
you're welcome
beathach n -aich, -aichean m beast,
animal **b.-mara** sea mammal
beathachadh n -aidh, -aidhean m
living, sustenance, nourishment
beathadach n -aich m beaver
beathaich v -achadh feed, nourish, sustain
beath-eachdraiche n -an m biographer
beath-eachdraidh n (-e), -ean f
biography
bèibidh n -ean m baby
beic n -ean/-eannan f curtsy **dèan b.** v
curtsey
bèicear n -eir, -an m baker
bèicearachd n f baking
Beilgeach n -gich, -gich m Belgian
a Belgian
being n -e, -ean f bench
beinn n -e, beanntan f mountain, ben
beinn-theine n -teine, beanntan-teine
f volcano
beir irr v breith/beireachdainn bear,
catch, take (See irr v **beir** in Grammar)
b. air catch hold of, catch up with
b. leanabh give birth to a child **b. ugh**
lay an egg
beirm n -e, -ean f yeast
beirmear n -an m enzyme
beithe n -an f birch, birch wood **craobh
b.** f birch tree
beithir n beathrach, beathraichean
f m thunderbolt
beò a beotha alive **cha robh duine
b. ann** there wasn't a soul there
beò n m lifetime **rim bheò** during my life
beò-ghainmheach n -ghainmhich f
quicksand
beò-ghlacadh n -aidhean m obsession
beòshlaint n -ean f livelihood, living
beothachadh n -aidh m animation,
enlivening, kindling
beothaich v -achadh enliven, animate,
quicken, kindle, stir Also intrans

beothail a -e/-ala lively, vital, vivacious, animated
beothalachd n f liveliness, vitality, animation
beothaman n -ain m vitamin
beuc n -an m roar, bellow
beuc v -adh/-ail roar, bellow
beud n -an m pity, shame; harm, loss, damage **is mòr am b.!** what a pity!
beugaileid n -ean f bayonet Also **bèigneid**
beul n beòil, beòil m mouth, opening **dùin do bheul!** be quiet! **b. an latha** daybreak, dawn **b. na h-oidhche** twilight, dusk **droch bheul** verbal abuse **air a b(h)eul fodha** face down
beulach a -aiche talkative, plausible
beulaibh n m front (part) **air b.** (+ gen) in front of
beul-aithris n beòil-, -aithrisean f oral tradition, folklore
beum n -a, -an/-annan m blow, stroke; reproach
beurla n f speech, language **Beurla** English **B. Ghallta** Scots (lang) **B. Shasannach** English
beus n -a, -an f virtue, conduct
beus n -a, -an f bass, bass (instrument)
beus a -a/bèise bass (mus)
beusach a -aiche virtuous, moral
beusail a -e/-ala ethical
beusalachd n f moral behaviour, ethics
bha irr v was, were (See verb **to be** in Grammar)
bhan n -aichean f van
bhàn adv See **a-bhàn**
bhàrnais n f varnish
bhàrr prep (+ gen) from, from off, down from
bhàs(a) n -ichean f vase
bhathar/bhathas irr v was, were (passive form) (See verb **to be** in Grammar)
bheat n -a, -aichean m veterinary surgeon
bheil irr v am? is? are? (See verb **to be** in Grammar)
bheir irr v will give, will bring, will take (See irr v **thoir** in Grammar)

bhidio n -than f m video
bhiodh irr v would be (See verb **to be** in Grammar)
bhìoras n -ais, -an m virus
bhìosa n -than f visa
bhith irr v See **a bhith**
bhitheadh irr v would be (See verb **to be** in Grammar)
bho conj since
bho prep from
bho chionn prep phr since, ago (equivalent to **o chionn**) **b. c. mìos** a month ago **b. c. ghoirid** recently, a short time ago
bhod aug prep from your (sg)
b(h)olcàno n -than m volcano
bhom aug prep from my; from their
bhon aug prep from the; from their
bhon (a) conj since
bhor aug prep from our; from your
bhos adv See **a-bhos**
bhòt n -a, -aichean f vote
bhòt v -adh vote
bhòtadh n -aidh m voting, poll
bhuaibh(se) prep pron from you (pl & pol)
bhuainn(e) prep pron from us
bhuaipe(se) prep pron from her; from it
bhuaithe(san) prep pron from him, from it adv **chaidh e bhuaithe** he/it deteriorated
bhuam(sa) prep pron from me
bhuapa(san) prep pron from them
bhuat(sa) prep pron from you (sg)
bhur poss pron your (pl & pol)
bi irr v be (See verb **to be** in Grammar)
biadh n bìdh, -an m food, meal
biadhlann n -ainne, -an f canteen, refectory, dining-hall
bian n bèin, bèin m hide, skin (of animals), pelt; fur
biast n bèiste, -an f beast; wretch
biastag n -aig, -an f beastie; insect
biast-dhubh n bèiste-duibhe, biastan-dubha f otter Also **biast-dubh**
biath v -adh feed
biathadh n -aidh m feeding; bait
bìd n -e, -ean m bite; cheep

bìd v **-eadh** bite
bìdeadh n **-didh** m biting, bite
bìdeag n **-eig, -an** f a little bit, morsel
bidean n **-ein, -an** m pinnacle
bidh irr v will be (See verb **to be** in Grammar)
bidse n **-achan** f bitch (person)
bigein n **-ean** m rock-pipit, any little bird; (colloq) willie (penis)
bile n **-an** f lip, rim, blade (of grass etc)
bile n **-an** m bill (parliamentary)
bileag n **-eig(e), -an** f little blade (of grass etc); label; leaflet
bile-bhuidhe n **-buidhe, bilean-buidhe** f marigold
binid n **-e** f rennet
binn n **-e** f judgement, sentence (of court), verdict
binn a **-e** melodious, harmonious, musical, sweet
binndich v **-deachadh** curdle, coagulate
binnean n **-ein, -an** m pinnacle, highest point, apex, high conical hill
binneas n **-eis** m melody, sweetness
Bìoball n **-aill, -aill** m Bible Also **Bìobla**
bìodach a **-aiche** minute, tiny
biodag n **-aig(e), -an** f dagger, dirk
biodh irr v (would) be (See verb **to be** in Grammar) **B. e a' dol!** To pot with it!
bìog n **-a, -an** f chirp, squeak, cheep
bìog v **-ail** chirp, squeak
bìogail n f chirping, squeaking
biolair n **-ean** f cress, water-cress
biona n **-ichean** f m bin
biona-sgudail n f m rubbish bin
bior n **-a, -an** m prickle; knitting needle
biorach n **-aich, -aich** f dogfish
biorach a **-aiche** sharp, prickly
bioraich v **-achadh** sharpen, make pointed
bioran n **-ain, -ain/-an** m stick, kindler
biorgadh n **-aidh, -aidhean** m twitch, tingle, sensation of pain
biotais n m beet, beetroot
birlinn n **-e, -ean** f galley (ship)
bith n **-e, -ean** f life, being, existence **nì air b.** anything **às b.** whoever, whatever, wherever **sam b.** any **a' dol à b.** going out of existence

bìth n **-e** f gum, resin; bitumen, pitch
bith-beò n f m livelihood
bith-bhuan a **-bhuaine** eternal, everlasting Also **biothbhuan**
bith-bhuantachd n f eternity Also **biothbhuantachd**
bith-cheimigeachd n f biochemistry
bith-cheimigear n **-eir, -an** m biochemist
bitheadh irr v (would) be (See verb **to be** in Grammar)
bitheag n **-eige, -an** f microbe, germ
bitheanta a often, common, frequent **gu b.** often, regularly
bitheantas n **-ais** m frequency, generality, normality **am b.** generally, normally
bithear irr v am, is, are, will be (passive form) (See verb **to be** in Grammar)
bith-eòlas n **-ais** m biology
bith-eòlasach a biological
bithibh irr v be (pl & pol command) **b. sàmhach!** be quiet! (See verb **to be** in Grammar)
biùg n m sound; faint light
biùgan n **-ain, -ain/-anan** m torch, faint light
biùro n **-than** m bureau
biurocrasaidh n **-ean** m bureaucracy
blaigeard n **-eird, -an** m brat, blackguard, scoundrel Also **bleigeard**
blais v blasad(h) taste
blàr n **blàir, -an** m battle; plain, sward **cuir b.** v fight a battle
blas n **blais** m taste, flavour; accent
blasad n **-aid** m taste, tasting, bite **b. bìdh** a taste/bite of food
blasaich v **-achadh** add flavour to
blasta a tasty, savoury, delicious Formerly **blasda**
blàth a **blàithe** warm
blàth n **blàith, -an** m blossom, bloom **fo bhlàth** in bloom
blàthach n **-aich** f buttermilk
blàthaich v **-achadh** warm
blàths n **blàiths** m warmth
bleideag n **-eig(e), -an** f flake **bleideagan sneachda** snowflakes **bleideagan coirce** cornflakes

bleith v grind
bleoghain v -an milk
bliadhna n -chan/-ichean f year am-b. this year a' **Bhliadhn'** Ùr New Year **B. Mhath Ùr!** Happy New Year!
bliadhnail a annual, yearly **coinneamh bhliadhnail** f annual meeting
blian a -a insipid
blian v -adh sunbathe, bask in sun
blobhs(a) n -ichean f m blouse
bloc n -a, -aichean m block
bloigh n -e, -ean f fragment, scrap (of); incomplete state **dh'fhàg sibh e na bhloigh** you left it half-finished **rinn mi b. èisteachd ris** I half-listened to it
bloinigean-gàrraidh n **bloinigein-** m spinach
blonag n -aig, -an f lard Also **blonaig**
bò n **bà, bà** f cow dat **boin** gen pl **bò b. bhainne** milking cow, milch-cow
boban n -ain, -ain/-an m bobbin
bobhla n -ichean m bowl
bobhstair n -ean m bolster, mattress Also **babhstair**
boc n **buic, buic** m buck **boc-earba** roebuck
boc v -adh/-ail leap, skip
bòc v -adh swell, bloat, inflate
bocadaich n c f leaping, skipping
bòcadh n -aidh, -aidhean m swelling, eruption
bòcan n -ain, -ain m hobgoblin, spectre, apparition, ghost
bochd n -a m poor person **na bochdan** the poor a -a poor, wretched, ill
bochdainn n -e f poverty; ill-health
bod n **boid/buid, boid/buid** m penis
bodach n -aich, -aich m old man **b.-ròcais** scarecrow **b.-ruadh** cod **b.-sneachda** snowman **B. na Nollaig** Santa Claus
bodha n -chan/-ichean m submerged rock, reef
bodhaig n -e, -ean f body
bodhair v **bòdhradh** deafen
bodhar n -air, -air m deaf person
bodhar a **buidhre** deaf
bòdhradh n -aidh m deafening; boring

bòdhran n -ain, -ain/-an m bodhran (drum)
bodraig v -eadh bother **na b.** don't bother
bog v -adh dip, immerse, soak, steep
bog a **buige** soft, boggy, moist, damp (of weather) **b. fliuch** sodden, soaking wet
bogadaich n bobbing
bogadh n -aidh m dipping, immersing, steeping; bobbing
bogaich v -achadh soften, moisten; mellow
bog-chridheach a soft-hearted
bogha n -chan m bow; bulge
bogha-frois n -froise, **boghachan-** m rainbow
bog(l)ach n -aich, -aichean f bog, swamp, quagmire, marsh
bogsa n -ichean m box; accordion **b.-ciùil** accordion **b.-fòn** phone box **b.-litrichean** letter-box **b.-mhaidseachan** matchbox Formerly **bocsa**
bogsadh n -aidh m boxing Formerly **bocsadh**
bogsaig v -eadh box (fight) Formerly **bocsaig**
bogsaigeadh n -gidh m boxing Formerly **bocsaigeadh**
bogsair n -ean m boxer Formerly **bocsair**
bòid n -e, -ean f vow, oath
Bòideach n -dich, -dich m someone from Bute a from, or pertaining to, Bute
bòidhchead n -chid f beauty, comeliness
bòidheach a **bòidhche** beautiful, pretty, bonny
bòidich v -deachadh vow, swear
boil(e) n -e f frenzy, rage, madness **air bhoil(e)** in a frenzy
bòilich n f bawling, idle talk
boillsg n -e, -ean m gleam, shine, flash
boillsg v -eadh gleam, shine, flash
boillsgeach a -giche gleaming, shining
boillsgeadh n -gidh, -gidhean m gleam, shine, flashing
boineid n See **bonaid**
boinne n -an/-achan f drop (of liquid)
boinneag n -eige, -an f little drop (of liquid)
boireann a female, feminine (gram)
boireannach n -aich, -aich m woman

boireannta *a* effeminate; feminine (*gram*)
bois *n* -e, -ean *f* palm (*of hand*)
boiseag *n* -eige, -an *f* palmful, handful; slap **cuir b. air d' aodann** *v* wash your face quickly
boiteag *n* -eig, -an *f* worm *Also* **baoiteag**
boladh *n* -aidh, -aidhean *m* scent, smell
bolt *n* -a, -aichean *m* bolt, roll of wallpaper
boltaig *v* -eadh wallpaper
boltaigeadh *n* -gidh *m* wallpapering
boltrach *n* -aich, -aich *m* scent, fragrance
boma *n* -ichean *m* bomb
bonaid *n* -e, -ean *f m* bonnet
bonn *n* buinn, buinn *m* base, bottom, foundation; sole (*of foot*); coin, medal **b. airgid** silver coin, silver medal **b.-cuimhne** medal, medallion **b.-dubh** heel **b. òir** gold medal
bonnach *n* -aich, -aich *m* bannock, small cake
borb *a* buirbe fierce, barbaric, savage
borbair *n* -ean *m* barber, gents' hairdresser
bòrd *n* bùird, bùird *m* table, board **air b.** aboard **b. bàta** boat deck **b.-dubh** blackboard **b.-geal** whiteboard **b.-iarnaigidh** ironing table **b. locha** bank of loch **b.-sgeadachaidh** dressing table **b.-sgrìobhaidh** writing table, bureau **b.-stiùiridh** board of directors
bòst *n* -a, -an *m* boast *Formerly* **bòsd**
bòst *v* -adh boast *Formerly* **bòsd**
bòstail *a* -e boastful *Formerly* **bòsdail**
bòstair *n* -ean *m* boaster *Formerly* **bòsdair**
botal *n* -ail, -ail *m* bottle **b.-teth** hot-water bottle
bòtann *n* -ainn, -an *f m* boots, wellington boots
bothag *n* -aig, -an *f* bothy, small hut; hovel
brà *n* -than *f* quern
bracaist *n* -e, -ean *f* breakfast **leabaidh is b.** bed and breakfast
brach *v* -adh ferment, malt
brachadh *n* -aidh *m* fermenting, malting

bradan *n* -ain, -ain *m* salmon
brag *n* braig, -an *m* crack (*sound*), bang; report (*of gun*)
bragadaich *n m* crackling (*sound*), banging; gunfire
bragail *n f* crackling (*sound*), banging
bragail *a* -e cocky, self-confident
braich *n* -e *f* malt, fermented grain
braidhm *n* brama, bramannan *m* fart **leig b.** *v* break wind
braidseal *n* -eil, -an *m* roaring fire
bràigh *n* -e/bràghad, -eachan *m* brae, upper part; chest (*person*)
bràigh *n* -e, -dean *f m* hostage, captive
braighdeanas *n* -ais *m* captivity, bondage, confinement
bràiste *n* -an *f m* brooch
bràmair *n* -ar, -ean *m* lover, boyfriend, girlfriend
branndaidh *n f* brandy
braoisg *n* -e, -ean *f* grin
braoisgeil *n f* grinning; giggling
braon *n* braoin, braoin *m* drop (*of liquid*)
bras *a* braise rash, impetuous, hasty
bras-shruth *n* -an *m* torrent
brat *n* -a, -an *m* cover, sheet, mantle **b.-làir/b.-ùrlair** carpet, rug, mat **b.-grèise** tapestry **b.-gnùise** veil
bratach *n* -aich, -aichean *f* flag, banner
bratag *n* -aig, -an *f* caterpillar
brath *n* -a, -an *m* information, notice, message **b. naidheachd** press statement/release **cò aige tha b.?** who knows?
brath *v* -adh betray, inform on
brathadair *n* -ean *m* betrayer, informer
brathadh *n* -aidh *m* betraying, betrayal, treason
bràthair *n* -ar, bràithrean *m* brother **b.-athar** uncle (*father's brother*) **b.-cèile** brother-in-law **b.-màthar** uncle (*mother's brother*)
breab *n* -a, -an *f m* kick
breab *v* -adh kick, stamp
breabadair *n* -ean *m* weaver; daddy-longlegs

Insight: breac

The adjective *breac* has the general sense of speckled or spotted: *bò bhreac* – a brindled cow. The masculine noun *breac* means that speckled fish, a trout, while the feminine *a' bhreac* (always with the definite article) refers to smallpox. Hence the pockmarked Alan Breck Stewart in *Kidnapped*. And *breacadh-seunain*? Freckles!

breac *n* brice *f* a' bhreac pox, smallpox
breac *n* bric, bric *m* trout; salmon (*in some areas*)
breac *a* brice speckled, spotted, brindled
breacadh-seunain *n* breacaidh- *m* freckles *Also* **breac-sheunain** *f*
breacag *n* -aig, -an *f* scone, bannock, pancake
breacan *n* -ain, -ain/an *m* plaid, tartan
breacan-beithe *n* breacain-, breacain- *m* linnet, chaffinch
breac an t-sìl *n* bric-, bric- *m* wagtail
breac-bhallach *a* -bhallaiche freckled
breac-òtraich *n* bric- *f* a' bhreac- òtraich chickenpox
brèagha *a* beautiful, fine, lovely
Breatannach *n* -aich, -aich *m* Briton *a* British
brèid *n* -e, -ean *m* patch, kerchief
brèig *n* -e, -ean *f* brake (*as in car*)
breige *n* -gichean/-geachan *f m* brick
brèige *a* false, deceiving, artificial
breisleach *n* -lich *f m* confusion, delirium **ann am breislich** in a state, delirious
breisleachail *a* confused, delirious
breislich *v* -leachadh rave, confuse
breith *n* *f* birth **co-là-b.** birthday
breith *v* bear, catch (*See irr v* **beir** *in Grammar*) **b. air** catch hold of, catch up with
breith *n* *f* judgement, sentence, verdict **thoir b.** *v* pass judgement, give a verdict
breitheamh *n* *See* **britheamh**
breitheanas *n* -ais, -an *m* judgement **thig b. ort** *v* you'll suffer for it
breithneachadh *n* -aidh *m* judging, consideration
breithnich *v* -neachadh judge, consider
breòite *a* infirm, frail, sickly
breòiteachd *n* *f* infirmity, frailty

breoth *v* -adh rot, putrefy
breug *n* brèige, -an *f* lie, untruth
breug *v* -adh entice, coax, cajole
breugach *a* -aiche lying, dishonest, deceitful, false
breugaire *n* -an *m* liar
breugnaich *v* -achadh falsify; refute, rebut
breun *a* brèine putrid, stinking, nasty
briathar *n* -air, -thran *m* word, saying, term
briathrach *a* -aiche wordy, talkative, loquacious, verbose
briathrachas *n* -ais *m* terminology
brìb *n* -e, -ean/-eachan *f* bribe
brìb *v* -eadh bribe
brìbearachd *n* *f* bribery
brìgh *n* -ean *f* meaning; substance, essence; pith, juice **do bhrìgh** *conj* because (*of*)
briod *n* -a, -an/-aichean *m* breed, type
briod *v* -achadh/-adh breed
brìodal *n* -ail *m* expressions of endearment; flattery, lover's talk
briogais *n* -ean *f* trousers, breeches
brìoghmhor *a* -a meaningful; energetic, substantial, substantive; sappy, pithy
briosgaid *n* -e, -ean *f* biscuit
bris(t) *v* -(t)eadh break, smash
bris(t)eadh *n* -(t)idh *m* breaking, smashing, break, breach **b. an latha** daybreak **b.-cridhe** heartbreak **b.-dùil** disappointment
brisg *a* -e brittle, crisp
brisgean *n* -ein, -an *m* crisp; silverweed; gristle **brisgein** crisps
briste *past part* broken
britheamh *n* -eimh, -an *m* judge, adjudicator, umpire
broc *n* bruic, bruic *m* badger

brochan n **-ain** m gruel, porridge; hotch-potch **dèan b. de** v make a mess of

brod n **bruid, -an** m goad, prickle; the best of anything **brod na sìde** excellent weather

brod v **-adh** goad, poke; stimulate, spur

brodaich v **-achadh** stimulate, kindle

bròg n **bròige, -an** f shoe, boot **brògan-cleasachd** sports shoes, trainers **b. na cuthaig** pansy **brògan-spèilidh** skates

broidse n **-sichean** m brooch

broilleach n **-lich, -lichean** m breast, bosom, chest

bròinean n **-ein** m poor soul (male)

broinn n **-e** f belly **am b.** inside, within

bròn n **bròin** m sorrow, grief, sadness **fo bhròn** sad, sorrowful

brònach a **-aiche** sad, sorrowful, mournful

brònag n **-aig** f poor soul (female)

brosgal n **-ail** m flattery

brosnachadh n **-aidh** m encouragement, inspiration

brosnachail a **-e** encouraging, inspiring

brosnaich v **-achadh** encourage, inspire, spur, provoke

brot n **-a, -an** m broth, soup

broth n **-a, -an** m rash

brù n **broinne/bronn, brùthan** (dat **broinn**) f belly, womb

bruach n **-aich(e), -aichean/-an** f m bank (of river), edge

bruadair v **-ar** dream

bruadar n **-air, -an** m dream

bruaillean n **-ein** m trouble, confusion

brùchd v **-adh** belch **b. a-mach** break out

brùchd n **-a, -an** m belch

brù-dhearg n **brùthan-dearga** m robin (redbreast)

bruich v boil, cook

bruich a **-e** boiled, cooked

bruid n **-e, -ean** f captivity

brùid n **-e, -ean** f m brute, beast

brùidealachd n f brutality

brùideil a **-e** brutal; (intens) terribly

bruidhinn n **bruidhne** f talk, conversation

bruidhinn v talk, speak, say **b. ri** talk/speak to

bruis n **-e, -ean/-eachan** f brush **b.-chinn/fuilt** hairbrush **b.-fhiaclan** toothbrush **b.-pheant** paintbrush

bruis(ig) v **-eadh** brush

brùite a bruised, oppressed

brùth v **bruthadh** bruise; press, push

bruthach n **-aich, -aichean** f m hillside, slope, brae **le b.** downhill **ri b.** uphill

bruthainn n **-e** f sultriness, sultry heat

bruthainneach a sultry

bu v was, were (See verb **to be** in Grammar)

buabhall n **-aill** m buffalo, unicorn

buachaille n **-an** m herdsman, cowherd, shepherd

buachailleachd n f herding

buachaillich v **-leachd** herd, tend cattle

buachar n **-air** m dung

buadh n **buaidh, -an/annan** f quality, property, attribute, virtue, talent

buadhach a **-aiche** victorious; talented; influential

buadhaich v **-achadh** win, triumph

buadhair n **-ean** m adjective

buadhmhor a **-oire** victorious; talented; influential

buaic n **-e, -ean** f wick

buaidh n **-e, -ean** f success, victory, sway, influence, effect, impact **fo bhuaidh** under the influence of **thoir b. air** v affect; defeat

buail v **bualadh** hit, strike, beat, thresh, crash into

buaile n **-ltean** f fold (for animals); circle, ring

buailteach a **-tiche** liable (to), apt (to), inclined (to), susceptible (to)

buain n **buana** f harvest, reaping, cutting **b. mhòna** peat cutting

buain v reap, cut (eg hay), harvest

buair v **-eadh** tempt, lure, worry, trouble

buaireadh n **-ridh, -ridhean** m temptation, trouble

buaireas n **-eis, -an** m turbulence, trouble

buaireasach a **-aiche** turbulent, stormy, troublesome

bualadh n **-aidh** m hitting, striking, beating, threshing **b. bhasan** clapping, applause

buamastair n **-ean** m boor, blockhead, oaf

buan a **buaine** lasting, enduring

buannachd n **-an** f profit, gain, advantage

buannachdail a **-e** profitable, advantageous

buannaich v **-achadh** win, gain

buar n **-buair** m herd of cattle

buarach n **-aich, -aichean** f cow-fetter

bucaid n **-e, -ean** f bucket

bucall n **-aill** m buckle

bucas n **-ais, -ais** m box

bugair n **-ean** m bugger

buideal n **-eil** m bottle, flask, cask

buidhe a yellow **nach b. dhut!** aren't you lucky!

buidhe pref yellow-tinted **b.-ruadh** auburn

buidheach a **-iche** satisfied, grateful, thankful

buidheach n **-dhich** f **a' bhuidheach** jaundice

buidheachas n **-ais** m gratitude, thanks, thanksgiving

buidheag n **-eig, -an** f goldfinch

buidheagan n **-ain, -ain** m egg-yolk

buidheann n **buidhne/-dhinn, buidhnean** f m group, band, organization, agency **b.-ciùil** band **b.-obrach** working party

buidhinn v win, gain

buidhre n f deafness

buidseach n **-sich, -sichean/-seachan** f m wizard **bana-bhuidseach** f witch

buidseachd n f witchcraft

bùidsear n **-eir, -an** m butcher

buidseat n **-eit, -an** m budget

buidsidh n **-ean** m budgie

buil n **-e, -ean** f effect, consequence, outcome, impact **thoir gu b.** v bring into effect, carry out, complete **bidh a' bhuil ann!** you'll see what will happen!

buileach a complete, absolutely, fully **nas miosa b.** worse still **gu b.** completely, entirely **chan eil e b. deiseil** it is not quite ready

buileann n **-linn, -an** f loaf

builgean n **-ein, -an** m bubble, blister

builgeanach a bubbly, blistered

builich v **-leachadh** bestow, grant

buille n **-an** f blow, hit, strike; emphasis, stress; beat (mus) **b.-cinn** header (in football)

buin v **buntainn/buntail** belong to **b. do** belong to; concern **b. ri** apply (to)

buinneach n **-eich** f **a' bhuinneach** diarrhoea

buinneag Bhruisealach n **buinneig Bruisealaich, buinneagan Bruisealach** f Brussels sprout

buinnig v **-eadh** win

buinteanas n **-ais** m relationship, connection

bùirean n **-ein, -ein/-an** m roar, bellow

bùirich n **-e, -ean** f roaring, bellowing Also **bùireanaich**

Bulgàirianach n **-aich** m Bulgarian a Bulgarian

bumailear n **-eir, -an** m boor, oaf, bungler

bumpair n **-ean** m bumper

bun n **-a/buin, -an/buin** m base, bottom, stump; root; mouth (of river) **b.-craoibhe** stump of tree

bunait n **-e, -ean** f m foundation, base, basis

bunaiteach a **-tiche** fundamental, basic

bunasach a **-aiche** original, fundamental

bun-bheachd n **-a, -an** m concept, notion

bun-os-cionn adv upside-down, topsy-turvy **cuir b.** v turn upside-down

bun-reachd n **-a, -an** m constitution (of org)

bun-sgoil n **-e, -tean** f primary school

bun-stèidh n **buin-, buin-** m basis, constitution (of org)

buntainneach a **-niche** relevant

buntanas n See **buinteanas**

buntàta n m potato, potatoes (sg & pl)

bùrach n **-aich** m mess, guddle, shambles **abair b.!** what a shambles!

bùrn n **bùirn** m water

burraidh n **-ean** m boor, oaf; bully

burraidheachd n f bullying

burras n **-ais, -ais** m caterpillar

bùrt *v* mock, scoff, ridicule **bha e gam bhùrt às** he was ridiculing me
bus *n* **-aichean** *m* bus
bus *n* **buis, -an/buis** *m* mouth, lip, snout, cheek **bha b. air** he was sullen
busach *a* **-aiche** sullen, glum

C

cab *n* **caib, -an** *m* mouth (*colloq*) **dùin do chab!** shut your trap!
cabach *a* **-aiche** talkative (*often of a small child*), garrulous; gap-toothed
cabadaich *n f* blethering, chattering
càball *n* **-aill, -aill** *m* cable

butarrais *n f* hotch-potch **dèan b. de** *v* make a mess of
bùth *n* **-a, -an/bùith(t)ean** *f* shop, booth **b.-èisg** fish shop **b.-leabhraichean** bookshop
buthaid *n* **-e, -ean** *f* puffin

cagailt(e) *n* **(-e), -(e)an** *f* hearth
cagainn *v* **cagnadh** chew, gnaw
cagair *v* **-arsaich** whisper
cagar *n* **-air, -airean** *m* whisper; secret **a chagair** my darling **cuir c. na chluais** whisper in his ear

---

Insight: cabar

Cabar gives us the English caber which is tossed at Highland Games, but in Gaelic it refers to any long piece of wood – or to a roof-tree. *Fo mo chabair* is under my roof. It can also mean a deer's antler, *Cabar Fèidh* being the motto of the MacKenzies.

---

cabar *n* **-air, -air/-an** *m* rafter; any large piece of wood, eg caber (*for tossing*); deer's antler **fo mo chabair-sa** under my roof
cabhag *n* **-aig** *f* hurry, haste **a bheil c. ort?** are you in a hurry? **dèan c.!** *v* hurry! *Also* **cabhaig**
cabhagach *a* **-aiche** hurried, hasty; impatient
cabhlach *n* **-aich, -aich/-aichean** *m* fleet **an C. Rìoghail** the Royal Navy
cabhsair *n* **-ean** *m* pavement, sidewalk; causeway
cac *n* **cac(a)** *m* excrement, (*vulg*) crap, shit
cac *v* **cac/-adh** excrete, defecate
caca *a* rotten, nasty
càch *pron* **chàich** (*of people*) the rest, the others
cachaileith *n* **-ean** *f* gate, entrance
cadal *n* **-ail, -ail/an** *m* sleep **tha an c. orm** I'm sleepy **a bheil iad nan c.?** are they asleep? **c.-deilgneach** pins and needles
cadalach *a* **-aiche** sleepy
cafaidh *n* **-ean** *f m* cafe

caibeal *n* **-eil, -eil/-an** *m* chapel; family burial area
caibideil *n* **-ean** *f m* chapter
caidil *v* **cadal** sleep
caidreabh *n* **-eibh, -an** *m* fellowship, partnership, association
caidreachas *n* **-ais, -an** *m* alliance, federation; companionship
càil *n* **-e, -ean** *f* appetite, disposition, desire; appearance; anything **chan eil e a' tighinn rim chàil** it doesn't appeal to me **c. an latha** the first appearance of day **chan eil c. ann** there's nothing there **bheil c. às ùr?** is there anything new/any news?
cailc *n* **-e, -ean** *f* chalk, piece of chalk
caileag *n* **-eig, -an** *f* girl, lass, young woman
càilear *a* **-eire** attractive, pleasing
cailin *n* **-ean** *f* maiden, young woman
caill *v* **call** lose
cailleach *n* **-lich(e), -an** *f* old woman **c.-dhubh** nun **c.-oidhche** owl
càin *n* **-e, -tean** *f* fine **chaidh c. air** he was fined

càin v **-eadh** scold, criticize, denounce
cainb n **-e** f hemp, cannabis (*plant*)
càineadh n **-nidh** m criticism, scolding
caineal n **-eil** m cinnamon
cainnt n **-e, -ean** f speech, conversation,
language **droch c(h)ainnt** bad
language, swearing
caiptean n **-ein, -an** m captain, skipper,
ship's master
cairbh n **-e, -ean** f carcase, corpse
càirdeach a **-diche** related (to)
tha i c. dhomh she is related to me
càirdeas n **-eis** m kinship, relationship;
friendship **tha c. fad' às eadarainn**
we are distantly related **cha do mhair
an c.** the friendship did not last
càirdeil a **-e** friendly
càirean n **-ein, -an** m palate, gum
càirich v **càradh** repair, mend, arrange;
place, lay **a' càradh na leapa** making
the bed **c. an sin e** put it down there
cairt n **-e, -ean** f card; chart **c.-creideis**
credit card **c.-iùil** chart **c. Nollaig**
Christmas card **c.-p(h)uist** postcard
cairt n **-e/cartach, -ean** f cart
cairteal n **-eil, -an/-eil** m quarter
c. na h-uarach quarter of an hour
cuisbheart n **-eirt** f footwear
càis(e) n **-an** f m cheese
Càisg n **-e** f a' **Chàisg** Easter
caisg v **casg/casgadh** check, stop, proscribe
caismeachd n **-an** f march (*mus*),
martial song; alarm
caisteal n **-eil, -an/-eil** m castle
càit(e) int pron, adv where **c. a bheil
thu?** where are you? **chan eil fhios
aca c. a bheil i** they don't know where
she is
caith v **-eamh/caith** spend, use up; wear;
throw
caitheamh n **-eimh** f m spending, using up
a' chaitheamh consumption, tuberculosis
c.-beatha way of life, behaviour
caithris v watch at night, keep a vigil
caithriseach a watchful, vigilant;
sleepless
Caitligeach n **-gich, -gich** m Catholic,
Roman Catholic a Roman Catholic

càl n **càil** m cabbage, kail
caladh n **-aidh, -aidhean** m harbour,
port; (*met*) place of rest *Also* **cala**
calanas n **-ais** m spinning, working
of wool
càl-colaig n **càil-colaig** m cauliflower
calg-dhìreach adv direct, directly
c. an aghaidh completely against,
diametrically opposed to
call n **call(a)** m loss; defeat **air chall**
lost **'s e c. a bh' ann** it was a pity
callaid n **-e, -ean** f fence, hedge, partition
Callainn n **-e** f a' **Challainn** New Year's
Day **Oidhche Challainn** Hogmanay
calltainn n **-ean** m hazel
calma a brave, strong, hardy
calman n **-ain, -ain** m dove, pigeon
calpa n **-nnan** m calf of leg; (*fin*) capital
calpachas n **-ais** m capitalism
cam a **caime** crooked, bent; one-eyed
cama-chasach bow-legged
camag n **-aig(e), -an** f curl, ringlet of
hair; (*in writing*) bracket
caman n **-ain, -ain** m stick for shinty,
hockey etc.
camanachd nf shinty *Also* vn a' **c.**
playing shinty
camara n **-than** m camera
camas n **-ais, -ais/-an** m wide bay
càmhal n **-ail, -ail** m camel
camhana(i)ch n **-aich, -aich** f dawn
campa n **-ichean** m camp
campaich v **-achadh** camp, encamp
can v **-tainn/-tail/-ail** say
cana n **-ichean** m can, tin
canabhas n **-ais** m canvas
canach n **-aich** m bog-cotton, cotton-
grass
cànain n *See* **cànan**
canàl n **-àil, -aichean** m canal
cànan n **-ain, -an** f m language, tongue,
speech **mion-chànan** minority language
canastair n **-ean** m canister, can, tin
Canèidianach n **-aich, -aich** m
Canadian a Canadian
cangarù n **-than** m kangaroo
cànran n **-ain** m whingeing, grumbling,
girning

cànranach *a* **-aiche** whingeing, grumbling, girning; fretful (*of small child*)

caoch *See* **cuthach**

caochail *v* **caochladh** change, alter; die, pass away

caochladh *n* **-aidh** *m* change, variation, different state; death **tha fhios agamsa air a chaochladh** I know different(ly)

caochlaideach *a* **-diche** changeable, variable, fickle

caog *v* **-adh** wink, close one eye (so as) to take aim

caogad *n* **-aid, -an** *m* fifty

caoidh *v* mourn, grieve, lament

caoin *a* **-e** kind, gentle, mild

caoin *v* **-eadh** weep, weep for, cry

caol *n* **caoil, caoil/caoiltean** *m* channel, narrows, kyle; narrow part of anything **Caol Loch Aillse** Kyle of Lochalsh **c.- shràid** lane, alley **c. an dùirn** the wrist

caol *a* **caoile** slender, thin, narrow

caolan *n* **-ain, -ain/-an** *m* gut, intestine

caolas *n* **-ais, -ais** *m* channel, narrows, kyle

caomh *a* **caoimhe** tender, kind, gentle; beloved, dear **is c. leam** I like

caomhain *v* **caomhnadh** save, economize on; spare **ma bhios sinn air ar caomhnadh** if we are spared

caomhnadh *n* **-aidh** *m* saving, economizing

caora *n* **-ch, -ich** *f* sheep

caoran *n* **-ain, -ain** *m* small lump of peat; deeper part of a peat-bank

caorann *n* **-ainn, -ainn/-ainnean** *m* rowan, mountain ash

capall *n* **-aill, -aill** *m* mare; (*less commonly*) horse **c.-coille** capercaillie

car *n* **cuir, -an** *m* turn, twist, bend **cuir car dheth** capsize it/overturn it **a' cur charan** rolling/going round **car a' mhuiltein** somersault **thug e mo char asam** he got round me/tricked me **a' chiad char sa mhadainn** first thing in the morning

car *prep* during, for **car ùine** for some time *adv* about, somewhat **car daor** somewhat dear

càr *n* **càr/càir, -aichean** *m* car

carabhaidh *n* **-ean** *f m* boyfriend

carabhan *n* **-aichean** *f m* caravan

carach *a* **-aiche** cunning, wily, sly, crafty, underhand

carachd *n* *f* wrestling

caractar *n* **-air, -an** *m* character

càradh *n* **-aidh** *m* mending, act of mending, repairing; condition, state

caraich *v* **-achadh** move, stir **cha do charaich e** he didn't budge

càraich *v See* **càirich**

caraid *n* **(-e), -(e)an/càirdean** *m* friend; relative (*especially in plural* **càirdean**) (*in corresp*) **A charaid/bhanacharaid** Dear ...

càraid *n* **-e, -ean** *f* couple, pair, married couple

caran *adv* somewhat, a little **c. anmoch** a bit late

carbad *n* **-aid, -an** *m* vehicle, car, conveyance, chariot, coach **c.-eiridinn** ambulance

Carghas *n* **-ais** *m* **an Carghas** Lent, any period of suffering

càrn *n* **càirn/cùirn, càirn/cùirn** *m* cairn, heap of stones (*often found in hill/ mountain names*)

càrn *v* **-adh** heap, pile up; (*met*) accumulate **a' càrnadh airgid** accumulating/piling up money

càrnabhail *n* **-ean** *m* carnival

càrnan *n* **-ain, -ain** *m* small cairn; hill (*often found in place-names*)

càrn-slaoid *n* **cairn-s.** *m* sledge

carragh *n* **-aigh, -aighean** *m* pillar, erect stone **c.-cuimhne** memorial, monument

carraig *n* **(-e), -ean** *f* rock, pinnacle **C. nan Àl** the Rock of Ages

carraigean *n* **-ein** *m* carrageen (*seaweed used to make milk pudding*)

carson *int pron, adv* why

cartadh *n* **-aidh** *m* mucking out, clearing; clearance; tanning

carthannas *n* **-ais** *m* charity, compassion, tenderness **buidheann carthannais** *f m* a charity

cartùn *n* **-ùin, -aichean** *m* cartoon

cas n **coise, casan** f foot, leg; handle, shaft (broom, spade, hammer etc) **a bheil i air a cois?** is she up and about? **chaidh mi ann dhe mo chois** I went there on foot/I walked there **an cois** (+ gen) beside, as a result of, with **an cois na mara** close by the sea **an cois na litreach** enclosed with the letter **cuir air chois** v set up **thoir do chasan leat!** be off!/get off!

cas a **caise** steep, sudden, headlong; quick-tempered

càs n **càis, -an** m difficulty, emergency, predicament

casad n **-aid, -an** m cough **dèan c.** v cough

casadaich n f coughing Also vn **a' c.**

casa-gòbhlach, casa-gòbhlagain adv astride

casaid n **-e, -ean** f complaint, accusation, charge; prosecution **bha droch chasaid na aghaidh** he faced a serious accusation

cas-cheum n **-chèim/-a, -an** m path, footpath, track

cas-chrom n **coise-cruime, casan-croma** f foot-plough

casg/casgadh n **casg/casgaian** m checking, stopping, preventing **casg/casgadh-gineamhainn** contraception **casg/casgadh-breith** abortion **cuir c. air** v stop, restrain, check

casgairt n f slaughter Also **casgradh**

casruisgte a barefoot

casta a complex

cat n **cait, cait** m cat

catalog n **-oig, -an** f m catalogue

cath n **(-a), -an/-annan** m battle

cathadh n **-aidh, -aidhean** m snowstorm, snowdrift **c.-mara** sea-spray, spindrift Also **cabhadh**

cathag n **-aig, -an** f jackdaw

cathair n **cathrach, cathraichean** f chair; city **c.-bhaile** city **c.-chuibhle** wheelchair **c.-eaglais** cathedral

catharra a civil, civic

cathraiche n **-an** m chair (person)

ceacharra a awkward, perverse, cussed

cead n **-a, -an** m permission, permit **c.-siubhail** travel permit, passport **tha a chead aige** it serves him right, he well deserves it (whether good or bad) **c.-dealbha(cha)idh** planning permission

ceadaich v **-achadh** permit, allow

ceadaichte a permitted, allowed, permissible **chan eil e c. smocadh** smoking is not permitted

ceàird n **-e, -ean** f craft, trade, profession **fear-ceàirde** tradesman, craftsman

ceala-deug n f fortnight

cealg n **ceilge** f deceit, wiles, treachery

cealgach a **-aiche** deceitful, wily, treacherous, underhand

cealgair(e) n **-e, -ean** m deceiver, cheat

cealla n **cille, -n/cilltean** f cell (biol); cell, church, churchyard **Calum Cille** Columba

ceanalta a gentle, mild; comely, handsome

ceangail v **-al** tie, bind, connect, unite

ceangailte a tied up, connected, united

ceangal n **-ail, -glaichean** m tie, bond, connection, link

ceann n **cinn, cinn** m head; end; top **tha mo cheann goirt** I have a headache **cuir air c. dhiun bhotul** put the top back on the bottle **c. an rathaid** the end of the road **o cheann gu c.** from end to end **air a' cheann thall** eventually **an c. mìos** in/after a month **ag obair air a c(h)eann fhèin** self-employed

ceannach n **-aich** m buy, purchase, buying, purchasing

ceannaich v **-ach** buy, purchase

ceannaiche n **-an** m merchant, dealer, buyer

ceannairc n **-e** f terrorism, rebellion

ceannairceach n **-cich** m terrorist, rebel

ceannard n **-aird, -an** m head, chief, leader, commander

ceann-bhaile n **cinn-bhaile, -bhailtean** m capital city

ceann-bliadhna n **cinn-, cinn-** m birthday, anniversary

ceann-cinnidh n **cinn-, cinn-chinnidh** m clan chief

ceann-feadhna *n* **cinn-, cinn-** *m* clan chief

ceann-latha *n* **cinn-, cinn-** *m* deadline, day something is due, date

ceann-phollan *n* **cinn-phollain, -phollain** *m* tadpole

ceannruisgte *a* bare-headed

ceannsaich *v* **-achadh** subdue, conquer, master, control

ceann-suidhe *n* **cinn-, cinn-** *m* president **C. nan Stàitean Aonaichte** the President of the United States

ceann-uidhe *n* **cinn-, cinn-** *m* destination

ceap *n* **cip, -an/cip** *m* sod, piece of turf; block **c.-bròige** shoemaker's last

ceap *n* **-(a), -an** *m* cap

ceapaire *n* **-an** *m* sandwich

cearbach *a* **-aiche** awkward, inept, unfortunate, misguided

cearban *n* **-ain, -ain** *m* shark

cearc *n* **circe, -an** *f* hen **c.-fhraoich** grouse

cearcall *n* **-aill, -aill** *m* circle, hoop, ring **c. mun ghealaich** a ring round the moon

ceàrd *n* **ceàird, -an/-annan** *m* tinker

ceàrdach *n* **-aich, -aichean** *f* smithy, forge

ceàrn *n* **-a, -an/-aidhean** *f* quarter, particular area, zone, district

ceàrnach *a* square

ceàrnag *n* **-aig, -an** square *f* **C. Sheòrais** George Square

ceàrnaidh *n* **-ean** *f* quarter, area

ceàrr *a* **-a** wrong, incorrect; left **an làmh cheàrr** the left hand

ceart *a* **-a** right, correct, just; (*before noun + len*) same **an uair cheart** the correct time **an làmh cheart** the right hand **cuir c.** *v* correct **an c. dhuine** the very same man **aig a' cheart àm** at the same time **a cheart cho ... ri ...** just as ... as ...

ceartachadh *n* **-aidh, -aidhean** *m* correction, marking, the act of correction

ceartaich *v* **-achadh** correct, put right, rectify

ceartas *n* **-ais** *m* justice **le c. ...** strictly speaking ...

ceart-cheàrnach *a* right-angled

ceartuair *adv* preceded by **an-** at present, these days; shortly

ceas *n* **-a, -aichean** *m* suitcase

ceasnachadh *n* **-aidh, -aidhean** *m* questioning, interrogation; examination (*educ*)

ceasnaich *v* **-achadh** question, interrogate

ceatharnach *n* **-aich, -aich** *m* strongly built man, warrior

ceathrad *n* **-aid, -an** *m* forty

ceathramh *n* **-aimh, -an** *m* quarter; quatrain

ceathramh *a* fourth **an c. fear** the fourth one

ceathramh deug *a* fourteenth (*preceded by art* **an**) **an c. fear deug** the fourteenth one

ceathrar *n* *f m* four (people)

cèic *n* **-e, -ichean** *f m* cake

cèidse *n* **-achan/-sichean** *f* cage

ceigeach *a* **-giche** matted (*of hair*)

ceigean *n* **-ein, -an** *m* small quantity, puckle; (*person*) little upstart

ceil *v* **ceil/-tinn/cleith** conceal, hold back information

cèile *n* *f m* spouse; fellow, match, another **athair-c.** father-in-law **màthair-chèile** mother-in-law **bu toigh leotha a chèile** they liked one another/each other **thuit e às a chèile** it fell apart

ceileir *v* **-earadh** chirp, warble (*usually of birds*)

cèilidh *n* **-idhean** *f m* ceilidh, concert; visit **chaidh mi air chèilidh orra** I paid them a visit

ceilp *n* **-e** *f* kelp

Ceilteach *n* **-tich, -tich** *m* Celt *a* **-tiche** Celtic

ceimig *n* **-ean** *f* (a) chemical

ceimigeach *a* **-giche** chemical

ceimigeachd *n* *f* chemistry

ceimigear *n* **-eir, -an** *m* chemist

cèin *a* **-e** distant, foreign

cèir *n* **-e** *f* wax

ceirsle *n* **-an** *f* clew, ball (*of wool*) Also **ceirtle**

cèis *n* **-e, -ean** *f* receptacle, case **c.-litreach** envelope

cèiseag *n* **-eig, -an** *f* cassette
ceist *n* **-e, -ean** *f* question, query; issue, problem; sum in arithmetic **cuir c.** *v* ask a question
ceisteachan *n* **-ain, -ain** *m* questionnaire
ceistear *n* **-eir, -an** *m* questioner, quizmaster; catechist
Cèitean *n* **-ein** *m* **an C.** the month of May
ceithir *n, a* four **c.-chasach** four-legged
ceithir-deug *n, a* fourteen **ceithir taighean deug** fourteen houses
ceò *n* **ceò/ceotha, -than/ceothannan** *f m* mist, fog; smoke **Eilean a' Cheò** the Misty Isle (the Isle of Skye)
ceòl *n* **ciùil** *m* music **c.-mòr** pibroch **c.-beag** light music for the pipes **c.-gàire** mirth **luchd-ciùil** musicians
ceòlmhor *a* **-oire** musical, tuneful, melodious
ceòthach *a* **-aiche** misty, foggy
ceud *n* **-an** *m* a hundred *a* a hundred **bha c. cabhag orra** they were in a great hurry ... **sa cheud** ... per cent **c. taing** thanks a lot
ceudameatair *n* **-ean** *m* centimetre
ceudamh *a* (*preceded by art* **an**) hundredth
ceud-chasach *n* **-chasaich, -chasaich** *m* centipede
ceudna *a* (*preceded by art* **an**) same **air an dòigh cheudna** in the same way **mar an c.** also, likewise
ceum *n* **cèim/-a, -an/-annan** *m* step; footpath; (*university*) degree **c. air cheum** step by step
ceumnaich *v* **-achadh** graduate; take a step
ceus *v* **-adh** crucify **chaidh Crìosd a cheusadh** Christ was crucified
ceusadh *n* **-aidh** *m* affliction, trial: (*of person*) torment
cha *neg part* not (*often lenites*) **cha bheag sin** that is not small, that's quite a lot
chaidh *irr v* went (*See irr v* **rach** *in Grammar*)
chan *neg part* (*used before vowels and fh*) **chan aithne dhomh i** I don't know her **chan fhuirich mi** I won't stay
chaoidh *See* **a-chaoidh**

cheana *See* **a-cheana**
chì *irr v* will see, can see (*See irr v* **faic** *in Grammar*)
cho *adv* as, so **cho dearg ris an fhuil** as red as blood
chon *prep See* **chun**
chuala *irr v* heard (*See irr v* **cluinn** *in Grammar*)
chum *See* **a chum**
chun *prep* (+ *gen*) to, towards, as far as
chunnaic *irr v* saw (*See irr v* **faic** *in Grammar*)
cia *int pron* who, which, what; how *See* **cò**
ciad *a* first **an c. latha** the first day (*often takes feminine form*) **a' chiad latha**
ciadfath *n* **-a, -an** *f* sense, faculty
ciad-fhuasgladh *n* **-fhuasglaidh** *m* first aid
ciall *n* **cèille** *f* sense, reason, understanding **dìth na cèille** lack of sense **a' dol às a chiall** going mad, losing his reason **a chiall!** goodness!
ciallach *a* **-aiche** sensible, reasonable
ciallaich *v* **-achadh** mean, intend
ciamar *int pron, adv* how **c. a tha thu?** how are you?
cia mheud *int pron, adv* how many **cia mh. iasg a fhuair thu?** how many fish did you get? **cia mh. aca a bh' ann?** how many of them were there? *Also* **cò mheud**
cian *a* **cèine** distant, remote
cianail *a* **-e** mournful, melancholy; terrible **c. fuar** terribly cold
cianalas *n* **-ais** *m* nostalgia, homesickness, melancholy **bha an c. orm** I felt homesick/nostalgic
ciar *v* **-adh** darken, grow dark
ciar *a* **-a/cèire** dusky, darkening; swarthy
ciatach *a* **-aiche** *m* pleasant, elegant, graceful, becoming, agreeable **bidh sin c.** that will be fine
cidhe *n* **-achan** *m* quay, pier
cidsin *n* **-ean** *m* kitchen
cileagram *n* **-aim, -an** *m* kilogram
cilemeatair *n* **-ean** *m* kilometre
cill *n* **-e, -tean** *f* church, churchyard (*common in place names*) **Cill Rìmhinn** St Andrews

cinn v **-tinn** grow, increase

cinneach n **-nich** m nation; gentile; a character **'s e c. a th' ann!** he's a hard case!

cinneadh n **-nidh, -nidhean** m clan, tribe, race; surname

cinnt n **-e** f sureness, certainty **le c.** definitely, certainly

cinnteach a **-tiche** sure, certain, reliable

cìobair n **-ean** m shepherd

cìoch n **cìche, -an** f female breast

cion n m lack, want, shortage **c. cosnaidh** unemployment

cionnas int pron, adv how **c. a fhuair e sin?** how did he get that?

ciont(a) n **-(a), -(an)** m guilt

ciontach a **-aiche** guilty

ciopair n **-ean** m kipper

ciorram n **-aim** m disability

ciorramach n **-aich, -aich** m disabled person

ciorramach a **-aiche** disabled, handicapped

ciotach a **-aiche** left-handed

cìr n **-e, -ean** f comb; cud **cìr-mheala** honeycomb

cìr v **-eadh** comb

cìrean n **-ein** m comb or crest of a bird

cìs n **-e, -ean** f tax **Cìs Comhairle** Council Tax **cìs cosnaidh** income tax

ciste n **-achan** f chest **c.-dhràthraichean** chest of drawers **c.-laighe** coffin

ciùb n **-an** m cube

ciudha n **-ichean** f m queue

ciùin a **-e** calm, mild, meek **duine c.** an even-tempered man

ciùinich v **-neachadh** calm, pacify, appease

ciùrr v **-adh** hurt very painfully

ciutha n **-chan** m cue (hair)

ciùthran n **-ain, -ain** m drizzle

clach n **cloiche, -an** f stone **c.-ghràin** granite **c.-iùil** magnet **c.-mhuilinn** millstone **c.-sùla** eyeball

clach v **-adh** stone

clachair n **-ean** m stonemason

clachan n **-ain, -ain** m village, hamlet; stepping-stones

clach-mheallain n **cloiche-meallain, clachan-meallain** f hailstone

cladach n **-aich, -aichean** m shore, coast

cladh n **-a/claidh, -an/-annan** m cemetery

cladhaich v **-ach** dig

cladhan n **-ain, -ain** m channel

clag n **cluig, cluig/-an** m bell

claidheamh n **-eimh, -an/ claidhmhnean** m sword **c.-mòr** claymore

claigeann n **-ginn, -ginn** m skull **ag èigheach àird a claiginn** shouting at the top of her voice

clais n **-e, -ean** f furrow, ditch, trench

claisneachd n f hearing **cùm cluas ri c.** keep an ear to the ground

clamhan n **-ain, -ain** m buzzard; kite

clann n **cloinne** f (sg n) children (often lenited in gen) **triùir chloinne** three children Used in clan names, eg **Clann Dòmhnaill** Clan Donald

clann-nighean n **-nighinn** f (sg n) girls, young women

claoidh v **-eadh** weary, oppress, vex, harass

claoidhte a exhausted, worn out

claon a **-oine** slanting, inclining, squint; (met) partial **c.-bharail** prejudice **c.-bhreith** prejudice, unjust verdict

claon v **-adh** slope, veer; (met) incline

clapranaich v **claparan** pet, clap

clàr n **-àir, -àir** m board, table, level surface; table (of figures), programme (of events), form (for filling); record **c.-ama** timetable **c.-amais** index **c.-aodainn** brow, forehead **c.-bìdh** menu **c.-dùthcha** map **c.-gnothaich** agenda **c.-iarrtais** application form **c.-innse** contents list **c.-oideachais** curriculum

clàrachadh n **-aidh** m recording, registration

clàraich v **-achadh** record, register, tabulate, arrange into tables

clàrsach n **-aich, -aichean** f harp

clàrsair n **-ean** m harper, harpist

clas n **-aichean** m class (in schools etc)

clasaigeach a **-giche** classical

cleachd v **-adh** use, employ, deploy; practise, be accustomed (to), be used (to) **chleachd mi a bhith a' snàmh** I used to swim

cleachdadh n **-aidh, -aidhean** m use; custom, habit, practice, convention

cleachdte (ri) past part accustomed to, used to

cleamhnas n **-ais** m relationship by marriage

cleas n **-an** m play, trick, clever feat; way **rinn esan c. chàich** he did what the others did

cleasachd n f play, playing

cleasaich v **-achd** play, perform feats

cleasaiche n **-an** m actor, performer, conjurer

clèir n **-e, -ean** f **a' chlèir** the clergy; presbytery

clèireach n **-rich, -rich** m cleric; clerk a presbyterian

cleith See **ceil**

cleòc(a) n **-a, -aichean** m cloak

clì n **-the** f strength, vigour

clì a left; wrong **an làmh chlì** the left hand

cliabh n **clèibh, clèibh** m creel, basket, hamper; person's chest

cliamhainn n **cleamhna, cleamhnan** m son-in-law **bana-chliamhainn** f daughter-in-law

cliath n **clèithe, -an** f grid; harrow **c.-chruidh** cattle grid

cliath v **-adh** harrow

cliatha(i)ch n **-aich, -ean** f side (of person or thing)

cliobach a **-aiche** clumsy, awkward

clis a **-e** quick, nimble, agile

clisg v **-eadh** move suddenly, start (through fear or alarm); **bi air do chlisgeadh** be very afraid of something **bha mi air mo chlisgeadh roimhe** I was terrified of it

clisgear n **-eir, -an** m exclamation (gram)

clisg-phuing n **-phuing(e), -phuingean** f exclamation mark

cliù n m fame, reputation; praise **c.-mhilleadh** m libel, slander

cliùiteach a **-tiche** famous, celebrated

clò n **clò/-tha, clòith(n)tean** m cloth (especially tweed woven on looms), a piece of tweed **an Clò Mòr/Hearach** Harris Tweed

clò n m print; press **cuir an c.** v print

clobha n **-chan** m pair of tongs

clòbhar n **-air** m clover

clobhd(a) n **-(a), -a(n)** m cloth (for wiping), clout **c.-sgùraidh** scouring cloth

clobhsa n **-n/-ichean** close m (in tenement)

clò-bhuail v **bhualadh** print (a book) **-bhuailte** (past part) printed

clò-bhualadair n **-ean** m printer, printing firm; publisher

clò-bhualadh n **-aidh** m printing, the work of printing

cloc n **-aichean** m clock

clogad n **-aid, -an** f m helmet, headpiece Also **clogaid**

clòimh n **-e, -ean** f wool

closach n **-aich, -aichean** f carcase

clòsaid n **(-e), -ean** f closet, small back room

clostar n **-air, -air** m loud thump or noise of falling (person or thing); large specimen of something

cluain n **-e, -tean** f green plain, meadow, pasture

cluaineas n **-eis** m retirement **chaidh e air chluaineas** he retired (from work)

cluaran n **-ain, -ain** m thistle

cluas n **cluaise, -an** f ear Also **cluais**

cluasag n **-aig, -an** f pillow

club n **-aichean** m club (organization) **c. òigridh** youth club

cluich n **cluich(e), -an** f m play, game **c.-bùird** board game

cluich v **cluich/-e/-eadh** play (sport or musical instrument)

cluicheadair n **-ean** m player, actor **c.-chlàr** record-player

cluinn irr v hear, listen (See **irr** v **cluinn** in Grammar)

cnag n **cnaig(e), -an** f pin, peg, knob, piece of wood **c.-aodaich** clothes peg **c.-dealain** electric plug **sin c. na cùise** that's the nub of the matter

cnàimh n -e/cnàmha, -ean/cnàmhan m bone **c. an droma** the backbone

cnàimhneach n -nich, -nichean m skeleton

cnàimhseag n -eig, -an f pimple on face, acne

cnàmh v chew, digest; wear away, decay **tha a' bhò a' c. a cìre(adh)** the cow is chewing the cud

cnap n cnaip, -an m knob; lump, small hill

cnapach n -aich, -aich m young boy (not a small child)

cnapach a -aiche lumpy

cnap-starra n cnaip-, cnapan- m obstacle, obstruction (Also met)

cnatan n -ain, -ain m common cold **bha an c. orm** I had the cold

cnead n -a, -an m groan **cha robh c. air** there was nothing wrong with him

cneasta a humane, moderate, decent, modest Formerly **cneasda**

cnò n cnò/cnotha, cnothan/cnòithtean f nut **c.-challtainn** hazelnut **c.-còco** coconut **gall-chnò** walnut

cnoc n cnuic, cnuic/-an m hill

cnocach a -aiche hilly

cnocan n -ain, -ain m hillock, small hill

cnot n -an m knot that is tied; door-bar

cnòthach a -aiche nutty

cnuasaich v -achadh reflect, ponder, ruminate; collect, accumulate

cnuimh n -e, -ean f worm, maggot **c.-thalmhainn** earthworm Also **cruimh**

cò int pron, adv who? which? **cò sibh?** who are you? **cò agaibh a dhèanadh sin?** which of you would do that? **tha fhios aicese cò iad** she knows who they are **cò às a tha thu?** where are you from?

co-aimsireil a -e contemporary

co-aois n See **comhaois**

cobhair n còbhrach f help, aid, succour, relief **rinn iad c. oirnn** they came to our rescue

co-bhann n -bhuinn, -an f bond, league, confederacy **an co-bhoinn/co-bhuinn ri** in co-operation/league with

co-bhanntachd n -an f coalition

cobhar n -air m foam, froth

coc n -a, -an(nan) f (hay)stack

còc n -an m coke (drink & fuel)

còcaire n -an m cook, chef

còcaireachd n f cooking, cookery

cochall n -aill, -aill m husk, shell; hood **theab i a dhol à c. a cridhe** she nearly died of fright

co-cheangail v -al connect, bind together, involve with each other

co-cheangal n -ail, -ail/-glan m connection **an c. ri** in connection with

co-cheangailte a (+ ri) connected (to), in connection with, related (to)

co-chomann n -ainn, -ainn m society, association, co-operative **C. Nis** Ness Community Co-operative

co-chomhairle n -an f consultation

co-chòrdadh n -aidh, -aidhean m agreement, accord, alliance

co-chruinneachadh n -aidh, -aidhean m assembly, gathering, convention; compilation, collection

còco n m cocoa

còd n -aichean m code **còd puist** postcode

co-dheth adv See **co-dhiù**

co-dhiù adv anyway, in any case **c. no co-dheth** anyway

co-dhùin v -dhùnadh conclude, decide

co-dhùnadh n -aidh, -aidhean m conclusion, decision

co-èignich v -èigneachadh urge, persuade strongly, force, compel

cofaidh n f m coffee

co-fhaireachdainn n f sympathy

co-fharpais n (-e), -ean f competition, contest

co-fhlaitheas n -eis m confederation **An C.** The Commonwealth

co-fhreagair v -t match, correspond

cofhurtachd n f comfort

cofhurtaich v -achadh comfort, console

cofhurtail a -e comfortable

cogadh n -aidh, -aidhean m war **an Dàrna C.** the Second World War

cogais n (-e), -ean f conscience

cogaiseach a -siche conscientious, honest

co-ghin v **-eadh/-tinn** have sexual intercourse, copulate
co-ghnìomhair n **-ean** m adverb
coibhneas n **-eis, -an** m kindness, generosity
coibhneil a **-e** kind, kindly, generous
coidse n **-achan** f coach
còig n, a five
còig-cheàrnach n **-aich, -aichean** m pentagon
còig-deug n, a fifteen **còig mìosan deug** fifteen months
còigeamh n **-eimh** m a fifth a fifth **an c. fear** the fifth one
còignear n f m five (people)
coigreach n **-rich, -rich** m stranger, foreigner
coileach n **-lich, -lich** m cockerel **c.-gaoithe** weathercock
coilean v **-adh** fulfil, accomplish, complete *Formerly* **coimhlion**
coileanta a perfect, accomplished, complete **an tràth c.** the perfect tense
coilear n -eir, **-an** m collar
coilion v *See* **coilean**
coille n **-ltean** f wood, forest
coilleag n **-eig, -an** f cockle; sand-dune
coimeas n **-eis** f comparison, likeness **an c. ri** compared to, in comparison to **chan eil a c. ann** there's no-one like her **dèan c. eatarra** v compare them
coimeas v compare
coimeasgaich v **-achadh** mix together, mingle
coimheach a **-mhiche** foreign, alien; shy, 'strange' (*of a small child*), unfriendly
coimhead v look, look at; keep watch over
coimhearsnach n **-aich, -aich** m neighbour
coimhearsnachd n f neighbourhood, vicinity, community
coimisean n **-ein, -an** m commission **an C. Eòrpach** the European Commission
coimiseanair n **-ean** m commissioner
coimpiutair n **-ean** m computer
coimpiutaireachd n f computing
coineanach n **-aich, -aich** m rabbit
còinneach n **-nich** f moss

coinneachadh n **-aidh** m meeting, the act of meeting
coinneal n **coinnle, coinnlean** f candle
coinneamh n **-eimh, -an** f meeting, appointment; religious service **c. naidheachd** press conference
coinnich v **-neachadh** meet **c. ri** meet with
coinnlear n **-eir, -an** m candlestick *Also* **coinnleir**
co-ionann a equal, equivalent to
co-ionannachd n f state of being equal, equality **c. chothroman** equal opportunities (*policy*)
còir n **-e/còrach, -ean/còraichean** f what is right; obligation; right, privilege, claim **tha c. agad sin a dhèanamh** you ought to do that **bu chòir dhut fheuchainn** you should try it **ag agairt do chòraichean** claiming your rights
còir a **-e** worthy, decent; just, honest; kind, generous; gentle, docile **cho c. ris an fhaoileig** as kind as kind can be **cù c.** m a well-behaved dog
coirbte a corrupt
coirce n m oats **aran-c.** m oatmeal bread
coire n **-achan** m kettle, cauldron; corrie **C. a' Cheathaich** the Misty Corrie
coire n **-achan** f fault, wrongdoing; blame **na bi a' cur na c. ormsa** don't lay the blame on me
coireach a **-riche** at fault, blameworthy **'s tu fhèin as c.** you're the one who's to blame
coirich v **-reachadh** blame
coiridh n **-ean** m curry (*the food*)
coiseachd n f walking
coisich v **-seachd** walk
coisiche n **-an** m walker, pedestrian
coisinn v **cosnadh** earn, win, gain; deserve
còisir n **-e/còisre, -ean** f choir *Also* **c.-chiùil**
coisrig v **-eadh** consecrate, dedicate; sanctify
coisrigte a consecrated, sanctified **uisge c.** m holy water
coitcheann a **-chinne** common, public, general, standard

coitcheannas *n* **-ais** *m* generality
coitheanal *n* **-ail, -an** *m* congregation
coitich *v* **-teachadh** press, persuade; campaign, lobby
co-labhairt *n* **-ean** *f* conference, seminar
co-là-breith *n* **-làithean-/-lathaichean-** *m* birthday
cola-deug *n* *f* fortnight
colag *n* **-aig, -an** *f* cauliflower
colaiste *n* **-an** *f m* college *Formerly* **colaisde**
colann *n* **-ainn, -an/-ainnean** *f* body
colbh *n* **cuilbh, cuilbh/-an** *m* pillar, column; column (*in newspaper*)
Colach *n* **-aich, -aich** *m* someone from Coll *a* from, or pertaining to, Coll
coltach *a* **-aiche** like, apparent, likely; healthy/robust-looking (*pronounced in some areas with the t silent*) **tha i c. riut** she's like you **tha e c. gu bheil i tinn** it seems she's ill **chan eil sin glè choltach** that's not very likely **duine mòr c.** a big robust-looking man
coltaich *v* **-achadh** (+ **ri**) liken (to)
coltas *n* **-ais** *m* appearance, likeness; expression (*on face*) **a rèir c(h)oltais** apparently, seemingly, by the looks of it **bha c. an acrais orra** they looked hungry
com *n* **cuim** *m* chest, upper part of the body, trunk
coma *a* indifferent, unconcerned, uncaring **tha mi c. cò a thig** I don't care who comes **c. leat** never mind **tha mi c. dheth** I don't like it **c. co-dhiù/ co-aca** couldn't care less, past caring, totally indifferent
comaig *n* **-ean** *f m* comic (*children's paper*)
comaig *a* **-e** comical, funny
comain *n* **-ean** *f* obligation for something done for one **tha mi fada nad chomain** I'm much obliged to you
comain *n* **-ean** *m* communion **a ciad chomain** her first communion
comanachadh *n* **-aidh** *m* communion; season of communion services

comanaich *v* **-achadh** take communion, be a communicant in church
comann *n* **-ainn, -ainn** *m* society, association; company, fellowship
comas *n* **-ais, -an** *m* ability **tha e gun chomas labhairt** he is without the power of speech
comasach *a* **-aiche** able, capable, talented **dèan c.** *v* enable, facilitate
comataidh *n* **-ean** *f* committee
combaist *n* **-e, -ean** *f* compass (*for direction*)
comhair *n* *f* direction **thuit mi an c. mo chùil** I fell backwards **an c. gach ama** now and then, from time to time **bha e fa chomhair na cùirt** he was before/in front of the court
comhairle *n* **-an** *f* advice, counsel; council **thug i deagh chomhairle orm** she gave me good advice **C. na Gàidhealtachd** the Highland Council
comhairleach *n* **-lich, -lich** *m* adviser, counsellor
comhairlich *v* **-leachadh** advise, guide
comhairliche *n* **-an** *m* councillor, adviser
comhaois(e) *n* (**-e**), (**e**)**an** *m* person the same age, peer, contemporary **tha iad nan comhaoisean** they are the same age
comharra(dh) *n* **comharra/-aidh, comharran/-aidhean** *m* mark, sign **c.-ceiste** question mark **c.-stiùiridh** landmark
comharrachadh *n* **-aidh** *m* marking
comharraich *v* **-achadh** mark, indicate, earmark, identify
comharraichte *a* noteworthy, special, exceptional
comhart *n* **-airt, -an** *m* dog's bark
comhartaich *n* *f* (*continuous*) barking
còmhdach *n* **-aich** *m* covering, cover
còmhdaich *v* **-achadh** cover, clothe
còmhdaichte *a* covered, clothed
còmhdhail *n* **-dhala(ch), -ean** *f* congress, convention; meeting, tryst; transport
cò mheud *See* **cia mheud**

còmhla n **-chan/-idhean** f door, door-leaf, door of cupboard

còmhla adv together **ràinig iad c.** they arrived together **c. ri** prep phr along/together with

còmhlan n **-ain, -ain** m group, band (usually small) **c.-ciùil** music group, band

còmhnaidh n **-ean** f residence, dwelling, house

còmhnaich v **-aidh** reside, live, stay

còmhnard a **-airde** level, flat, even, smooth

còmhradh n **-aidh, -aidhean** m conversation, dialogue **dèan c.** v converse, chat

còmhrag n **-aig, -an** f fight, struggle, conflict, combat **c.-dithis** duel

còmhraideach a **-diche** talkative, chatty, fond of conversation

còmhstri n **-thean** f strife, struggle, conflict; rivalry, disagreement

com-pàirt n **(-e)** f partnership, share, participation

com-pàirteachas n **-ais** m partnership

com-pàirtich v **-teachadh** share, divide, take part, participate; communicate

companach n **-aich, -aich** m companion, partner; spouse

companaidh n **-ean** f m company (org), firm

companas n **-ais** m company (personal), companionship

comraich n **-ean** f sanctuary, protection **Comraich Ma-Ruibhe/a' Chomraich** Applecross **c. phoilitigeach** political asylum

còn n **-aichean** m cone

conair(e) n **(-e), -(e)an** f rosary; path, way

conaltradh n **-aidh** m conversation, communication; company (social)

conas n **-ais** m contention, quarrel; teasing **chuir e c. orm** it annoyed me Also vn **a' c. bha iad a' c. rithe** they were teasing her

conasg n **-aisg** m whin, gorse

connadh n **-aidh, -aidhean** m fuel **c. làmhaich** ammunition, munitions

connlach n **-aich** f straw

connrag n **-aig, -an** f consonant

connsachadh n **-aidh** m quarrel, argument, dispute, feud

connsaich v **-achadh** quarrel, argue, dispute, feud, wrangle

connspaid n **(-e), -ean** f quarrel, dispute, strife, contention

connspaideach a **-diche** disputatious, quarrelsome, contentious, confrontational

conntraigh n **-ean** f neap tide

consairt n **-ean** f m concert (music)

consal n **-ail, -an** m consul

co-obraich v **-obrachadh** work with, co-operate with, collaborate

co-obrachadh n **-aidh** m co-operation, collaboration

co-ogha n **-ichean** m cousin

co-òrdanaich v **-achadh** co-ordinate

co-òrdanaiche n **-an** m co-ordinator

cop n **coip** m foam, froth

còp v **-adh** tip up (a load); capsize

copag n **-aig, -an** f dock, docken

copan n **-ain, -an** m cup

copar n **-air** m copper (metal)

cor n **coir/cuir** m state, condition **cor an t-saoghail** the state the world is in **dè do chor?** how are you?/how are you doing? **air chor sam bith** under any circumstances

còrd v **-adh** agree, come to an agreement; (+ **ri**) give enjoyment/pleasure to **chòrd e rium** I enjoyed it

còrdadh n **-aidh, -aidhean** m agreement, pact

còrn n **cùirn, cùirn** m horn (mus), drinking horn; corn (on foot)

Còrnach n **-aich, -aich** m someone from Cornwall a Cornish

còrnair n **-ean** m corner

corp n **cuirp, cuirp** m body; corpse **c.-eòlas** anatomy

corporra a corporal, bodily; corporate

còrr n f m an excess; remainder, (fin) balance; more **na ith an c./a' chòrr** don't eat any more **còrr is mìle duine** over a thousand men

corra a odd, occasional, irregular **bidh c. dhuine a' dol ann** the odd person goes there **c. uair** occasionally, now and then

corra-biod(a) n m state of alertness/readiness; (preceded by **air**) on tiptoe **bha e air a chorra-biod(a)** he was on tiptoe

corrach a -aiche steep; rough; unsteady, unstable (eg boat)

corrag n -aig, -an f finger

corra-ghritheach n -g(h)rithich, **corrachan-gritheach** f heron

corran n -ain, -ain m sickle; point of land running into the sea; crescent

corraich n f anger

corrghail n f cooing (of infant)

còrr-mhial n -a, -an f gnat, hornet

còs n còis, -an m cave, hollow, recess; any sheltered place

còsach a -aiche cavernous; porous, hollow; sheltered, snug, cosy

cosamhlachd n -an f parable

cosg v cosg(adh) cost; spend; run out, be used up **dè a chosg sin?** how much did that cost? **dè a chosg thu air?** what did you spend on it? **tha an t-airgead air c.** the money has run out

cosgail a -e costly, expensive

cosgais n -e, -ean f cost, expense

co-sheirm n -e, -ean f harmony (mus)

co-shìnte a parallel

cosmhail a -e like, resembling

cosnadh n -aidh, -aidhean m earnings, way of earning, work, employment **gun chosnadh** unemployed **ionad-cosnaidh** m job centre

cost(a) n -taichean m coast, shore

còta n -ichean m coat **c.-bàn** petticoat

cotan n -ain m cotton, cotton-wool

cothaich (ri) v -achadh contend with, grapple with; (met) cope

cothlamadh n -aidh m mixture, merger, merging

cothrom a -ruime even

cothrom n cothruim, -an m chance, opportunity; equilibrium, balance; fair play **C. na Fèinne** fair play, a fair opportunity, a sporting chance **chan eil c. air** it can't be helped **a bheil thu air chothrom?** are you fit/able?

cothromach a -aiche just, equitable, reasonable, fair, balanced

cothromaich v -achadh weigh; make equal, balance; consider

co-thuiteamas n -ais, -an m coincidence

cràbhach a -aiche devout, religious, pious

cràbhadh n -aidh m piety, devoutness

crac n craic f chat, crack

cràdh n cràidh m pain, suffering **bha c. air** he was in pain

craiceann n -cinn, -an/-cinn m skin

cràidh v cràdh(adh) pain, torment

cràiteach a -tiche painful

crann n cruinn/croinn, cruinn/croinn/ crainn m mast or other long rod; plough (also **crann-treabhaidh**); bolt, bar, beam; lot; cran (measure for herring); tree **a' cur chrann** casting lots **an C.-ceusaidh** the Cross (of Christ) **c.-fìona** vine **c.-ola** oilrig **c.-sneachd(a)** snowplough

crannchur n -uir, -an m casting of lots, lottery **an C. Nàiseanta** the National Lottery **c.-gill** raffle

craobh n -oibhe, -an f tree **c.-challtainn** hazel tree **c.-dharaich** oak tree **c.-ghiuthais** pine tree

craobhag n -aig, -an f plant; bush; small tree

craobh-sgaoil v -eadh broadcast, transmit; promulgate, propagate

craol v -adh broadcast, transmit; promulgate, propagate

craoladair n -ean m broadcaster

craoladh n -aidh m broadcasting, broadcast, transmission

craos n -ois, -an m large mouth, maw; (met) gluttony

craosach a -aiche wide-/large-mouthed; gluttonous

crath v -adh shake, wave; sprinkle

crathadh-làimhe *n* **crathaidhean-** *m* handshake

creach *n* **creiche, -an** *f* plunder, booty; ruin, destruction **Mo chreach!** Alas! **Mo chreach-sa thàinig!** Goodness gracious me!

creach *v* **-adh** plunder, rob, ruin

creachan(n) *n* **-ain(n), -ain(n)** *m* scallop

crèadh *n* **crèadha/creadha** *f* clay

crèadhadair *n* **-ean** *m* potter

crèadhadaireachd *n* *f* pottery

creag *n* **creige, -an** *f* rock; crag, cliff, precipice

creagach *a* **-aiche** rocky

creamh *n* **-a** *m* garlic **c.-gàrraidh** leek, leeks

crèapailt(e) *n* **-(e)an** *m* garter *Also* **crèibilt(e)**

creathail *n* **(-e), -ean** *f* cradle *Also* **creathall**

creid *v* **-sinn** believe **chan eil mi ga chreidsinn** I don't believe it **cha chreid mi nach coisich mi** I think I shall walk

creideamh *n* **-eimh, -an** *m* faith; religion, religious belief

creideas *n* **-eis** *m* credit (*moral, fin*), credibility; faith, trust **chan eil cus creideis ugam ann** I don't have much faith in him

creidhean *n* **-ein, -an** *m* crayon

creim *See* **criom**

creithleag *n* **-eig, -an** *f* cleg

creuchd *n* **-a, -an** *f* wound

creud *n* **(-a), -an** *f* creed; belief

creutair *n* **-ean** *m* creature, animal; (*Lewis*) female **an c.!** the poor thing!

criathar *n* **-air, -an** *m* sieve, riddle

criathraich *v* **-rachadh/-radh** sieve; (*met*) weigh up, assess

cridhe *n* **-achan** *m* heart **na biodh a chridh' agad,...!** don't dare ...!

cridhealas *n* **-ais** *m* heartiness, merriment, conviviality

cridheil *a* **-e** hearty, cheerful

crìoch *n* **crìche, -an** *f* end, conclusion; limit, boundary, border **na Crìochan** the Borders **cuir c. air** *v* finish it **thoir gu crìch** *v* bring to a close/an end **c.-ghrèine** tropic

crìochnaich *v* **-achadh** finish, complete, bring to an end

crìochnaichte *a* finished, completed, concluded

criogaid *n* *f, m* cricket (*sport*)

criom *v* **-adh** gnaw, nibble, chew; erode

criomag *n* **-aig, -an** *f* small bit, fragment, morsel

crìon *a* **crìne, -a** small, mean, trifling; withered, shrunken, dried up

crìon *v* **-adh** wither, fade, decay

crìonadh *n* **-aidh** *m* withering, decay, decline

crioplach *n* **-aich, -aich** *m* cripple

crios *n* **(-a), -an/-achan** *m* belt, strap **c.-sàbhalaidh** lifebelt

Crìosdachd *n* *f* **a' Chrìosdachd** Christianity; Christendom

Crìosdaidh *n* **-ean** *m* Christian *a* **-e** Christian

Crìosdail *a* **-e** Christian **an creideamh C.** the Christian religion

Crìosdalachd *n* *f* Christianity; Christian disposition

criostal *n* **-ail, -an** *m* crystal *a* crystal

cripleach *See* **crioplach**

crith *n* **(-e), -ean** *f* trembling, shaking, shivering **air chrith leis an eagal** trembling with fear

critheanach *a* **-aiche** shaky, unsteady; causing shaking

critheann *n* **-thinn, -an** *m* aspen tree

crith-thalmhainn *n* **crithe-talmhainn/ -thalmhainn, crithean-talmhainn** *f* earthquake

crò *n* **-tha, -than** *m* pen for animals, fold; eye of a needle

croch *v* **-adh** hang (*person or thing*) **chaidh a chrochadh** he was hanged

crochadair *n* **-ean** *m* hangman; hanger

crochadh *n* **-aidh** *m* hanging (*of things or people*) **an c. air** dependent (on) **an c. air an t-sìde** depending on the weather

crochte *a* hung, hanging

crodh *n* **cruidh** *m* (*sg n*) cattle, kine **c.-bainne** dairy cows

crò-dhearg *a* crimson

cròg *n* **cròige, -an** *f* large hand; palm of the hand **làn cròige** a handful, fistful

crogall *n* **-aill, -aill** *m* crocodile

crogan *n* **-ain, -ain** *m* jar, pitcher, tin **c.-silidh** jam-jar

cròic *n* **-e, -ean** *f* antlers; foam on liquids or on the sea

croich *n* **-e, -ean** *f* gallows

cròileagan *n* **-ain, -ain** *m* playgroup

crois *n* **-e, -ean** *f* cross; difficulty, mishap **c.-rathaid** crossroads **bha e ann an c.** he was in a fix **bha e ri c.** he was up to no good

croiseil *a* **-e** awkward, problematic

croit *n* **-e, -ean** *f* croft *Also* **crait, cruit**

croit *n* **-e** *f* hump, hunch

croitear *n* **-eir, -an** *m* crofter

croitse *n* **-achan** *f* crutch

crom *a* **cruime** bent, crooked, curved **ceann c.** *m* a bowed head

crom *v* **-adh** bend, stoop; descend

crom-lus *n* **-lusa/-luis, -lusan** *m* poppy

cromag *n* **-aig, -an** *f* hook; shepherd's crook; apostrophe

cron *n* **croin, -an** *m* harm, damage, fault, crime **cha dèan e c. ort** it'll not harm you

cronaich *v* **-achadh** rebuke, reprimand, censure

cronail *a* **-e** harmful, damaging, pernicious

crònan *n* **-ain, -ain** *m* croon, low singing, humming, purring, any low murmuring sound **c. nan allt** the murmuring of the streams

crosgag *n* **-aig, -an** *f* starfish

crosta *a* cross, angry, irascible, irritable *Formerly* **crosda**

crotach *a* **-aiche** stooped, humpbacked

crotair(e) *n* **-an** *m* hunchback

crotal *n* **-ail** *m* lichen

cruach *n* **cruaiche, -an** *f* pile, heap, stack **c.-arbhair/fheòir/mhòna(ch)** corn-/hay-/peat-stack *Also found in hill/mountain names*

cruach *v* **-adh** pile or heap up; make into a stack

cruachann *n* **-ainn, -ainn/ cruaichnean/-an** *f m* hip, haunch *Also* **cruachan**

cruadal *n* **-ail, -an** *m* hardship, adversity, difficulty

cruadhaich *v* **-achadh** harden, solidify

cruaidh *n* **-adhach, -ean** *f* steel; stone (*used as anchor*)

cruaidh *a* **-e** hard; difficult; mean; hardy **c.-chàs** *m* danger, extremity, adversity **c.-cheasnaich** cross-examine **c.-chridheach** hard-hearted

cruas *n* **-ais** *m* hardness, hardihood; meanness

crùb *v* **-adh** crouch, squat

crùbach *a* **-aiche** lame or otherwise crippled

crùbag *n* **-aig, -an** *f* crab

crùban *n* **-ain** *m* crouch, squat **dèan c.** *v* crouch, squat **na c(h)rùban** crouching, squatting

crudha *n* **cruidhe, crùidhean** *m* horseshoe

cruinn *a* **-e** round, circular; gathered together; compact, neat **c.-leum** *m* standing jump

cruinne *n* *m* the world (*f in gen* **na cruinne**); roundness

cruinneachadh *n* **-aidh, -aidhean** *m* gathering; function; collection

cruinne-cè *n* *m* **an C.** the world, the universe

cruinn-eòlas *n* **c.-eòlais** *m* geography (*subject*)

cruinnich *v* **-neachadh** collect, assemble, gather together; come together

crùisgean *n* **-ein, -an** *m* cruisie, oil-lamp

Cruithneach *n* **-nich, -nich** *m* Pict *a* Pictish

cruithneachd *n* *f m* wheat

crùn *n* **crùin, crùintean** *m* crown

crùn *v* **-adh** crown

crùnadh *n* **-aidh** *m* crowning, coronation

cruth *n* **(-a), -an** *m* form, shape, appearance **c.-atharrachadh** *m* transformation

cruthachail *a* **-e** creative

cruthaich *v* **-achadh** create, make

cruthaidheachd n f a'
  Chruthaidheachd Creation, the world
  A Chruthaidheachd! My goodness!
cruthaidhear n -eir m **an C.** God, the
  Creator Also **cruthadair, cruithear**
cù n **coin, coin** m dog **cù-chaorach**
  sheepdog
cuach n **cuaiche, -an** f drinking cup,
  quaich; fold, curl of hair
cuagach a **-aiche** lame, limping
cuaille n **-an** m cudgel, club
cuairt n **-e, -ean** f circuit, round trip, trip
  (generally), excursion; round (sport);
  individual planks in a clinker-built boat
  chaidh sinn c. dhan Fhraing we
  took a trip to France **c. dheireannach**
  final round **c.-ghaoth** eddying wind,
  whirlwind **c.-litir** circular, newsletter
cuairtich v **-teachadh** circulate
cuan n **cuain, cuain/-tan** m ocean,
  sea **an C. Siar** the Atlantic Ocean
  an C. Sèimh the Pacific Ocean
cuaraidh n **-ean** f m quarry
cuaran n **-ain, -an** m light shoe,
  sandal
cuartaich v **-achadh** surround, enclose;
  perform, conduct **a' cuartachadh an
  adhraidh** conducting worship
cùbaid n **(-e), -ean** f pulpit Also **cùbainn**
cubhaidh a **-e** fit, becoming, seemly,
  appropriate, fitting
cùbhraidh a **-e** fragrant
cucair n **-ean** m cooker
cudromach a **-aiche** important,
  weighty; heavy
cudthrom See **cuideam**
cudthromach See **cudromach**
cugallach a **-aiche** unstable (also met),
  wobbly, shoogly, unsteady; precarious
cuibheall n **cuibhle, cuibhleachan,
  cuibhlichean** f wheel **c.-stiùiridh**
  steering-wheel **c.-shnìomh**
  spinning-wheel
cuibheasach a **-aiche** sufficient;
  tolerable, middling
cuibhil v **cuibhleadh** wheel, roll along
cuibhle n **-an/-lichean** f wheel
  See **cuibheall**

cuibhlich v **-leachadh** See **cuibhil**
cuibhreann n **-rinn, -an** f m portion,
  part, instalment, allowance; (met)
  portion in life, fate
cuibhrig(e) n **-e, -e(an)** f m cover,
  coverlet, bed-cover
cuid n **cuid/codach, -ean/codaichean**
  f share, part; belongings, property,
  resources; often used to indicate
  possession; some (people) **c. na
  h-oidhche** board and lodgings, bed
  and breakfast **mo chuid fhìn** my
  own/my own property/resources **mo
  chuid airgid/aodaich/chloinne** my
  money/clothes/children **canaidh c.
  nach eil sin ceart** some people say
  that's not right **chan eil e an dara c.
  fuar no teth** it is neither hot nor cold
  a' mhòr-chuid the majority
cuideachadh n **-aidh** m help,
  assistance, aid
cuideachail a **-e** helpful
cuideachd n f company, group of people
  bha e math a bhith nur c. it was good
  to be in your company
cuideachd adv also, as well;
  together
cuideachdail a **-e** sociable;
  companionable
cuideam n **-eim, -an** m weight
cuideigin pron someone, somebody
cuide ri prep with, along with, in the
  company of
cuidhteag n **-eig, -an** f whiting
cuidhteas n receipt; riddance **fhuair
  mi c. an cnatan mu dheireadh thall**
  I finally got rid of the cold
cuidich v **-deachadh** help, assist, aid
cùil n **(-e), -tean** f corner, nook,
  recess, any secluded or private place
  c.-chumhang a tight spot, a fix
cuilbheart n **-eirt, -an** f wile,
  stratagem
cuilc n **-e, -ean** f reed
cuileag n **-eig, -an** f fly **a bheil a'
  chuileag ann?** are the midges out?
cuilean n **-ein, -an** m puppy
cuileann n **-linn, -an** m holly

cuimhne *n f* memory, remembrance
tha c. mhath aige he has a good
memory **an robh cuimhn' aice ort?**
did she remember you? **mas math mo
chuimhne** if my memory serves me
right **chaidh e glan às mo chuimhne**
I completely forgot (about it) **cuir nan
c.** *v* remind them
cuimhneachan *n* **-ain, -ain** *m* memorial,
remembrance, commemoration,
keepsake **mar chuimhneachan ormsa**
in remembrance of me
cuimhnich *v* **-neachadh** remember,
recall, bear in mind, commemorate
cuimir *a* **-e** brief, concise; (*of person*)
shapely, well-proportioned, handsome
Cuimreach *n* **-rich, -rich** *m* someone
from Wales *a* Welsh
cuimse *n* **-an** *f* aim, mark; moderation
cuimseach *a* **-siche** moderate,
reasonable; (*of person*) sure of aim
c. math reasonably good
cuimsich *v* **-seachadh** aim; hit a mark
or target, target
cuin(e) *int pron, adv* when **c. a thig iad?**
when will they come? **chan eil fhios
agamsa c. a thig iad** I don't know
when they will come
cuing *n* **-e, -ean** *f* yoke, bond, restraint
c./a' chuing (*pronounced* **a' chaoidh**
but nasally) asthma
cuingealaich *v* **-achadh** restrict, limit
cuinneag *n* **-eig, -an** *f* pail, bucket
cuinnean *n* **-ein, -an** *m* nostril
cuinnseas *n* **-eis** *f* conscience
cuip *n* **-e, -ean/-eachan** *f* whip
cuip *v* **-eadh** whip
cuir *v* **cur** put, place, lay; send; set; sow,
plant; cast **c. buntàta** plant potatoes
c. clèibh/lìn set creels/nets **c. fios/litir**
send word/a letter **c. fios air** … send
for … **c. gaoisid** shed coat **c. sneachda**
snow *Also featured in many idioms eg*
c. air bhonn set up **c. air chois** set up,
establish **c. a-mach** issue; vomit, be
sick **c. an aghaidh** oppose **c. an cèill**
express, declare **c. an ìre** pretend **c. às
do** abolish **c. às leth** accuse **c. dheth**

postpone **c. fàilte air** welcome **c. geall**
bet, lay wager **c. ìmpidh air** urge **c. ri**
add to **c. romhad** decide (to) **dè tha cur
riut?** what's troubling you? **c. troimh-a-
chèile** upset, confuse
cuireadh *n* **-ridh, -idhean** *m* invitation
cuirm *n* **-e, -ean** *f* feast, banquet **c.-chiùil**
concert **c.-chnuic** picnic
cùirt *n* **-e/cùrtach, -ean** *f* court **c.-lagha**
court of law
cùirtear *n* **-eir, -an** *m* curtain
Also **cùirtean**
cùis *n* **-e, -ean** *f* matter, affair; cause;
object, butt **sin mar a tha a' chùis**
that's how things are/stand **c.-bhùirt/
bhùrta** a laughing-stock **c.-eagail**
something to be feared **c.-lagha** a court
case **c.-mhaslaidh** a disgrace **an dèan
thu a' chùis air?** will you manage it?
rinn iad a' chùis oirnn they defeated us
nì sin a' chùis that'll do/that'll suffice
cuisean *n* **-ein, -an** *f m* cushion
cuisle *n* **-an** *f* vein, blood-vessel, artery
c.-chiùil pipe (*mus*)
cuislean *n* **-ein, -an** *m* flute
cuithe *n* **-achan** *f* pit, trench; fold for
animals **c. sneachda** snowdrift
cùl *n* **cùil, cùil/cùiltean** *m* back; (*in
poetry*) hair **c. an taighe** the back of
the house **cuir c. ris** *v* abandon it/leave
it/stop it **c.-chàin** *v* backbite, slander
c.-chàineadh *n m* backbiting, slander
c.-taic *n f* support **'s e Gàidheal gu
chùl a th' ann** he's a Gael through
and through
cùlaibh *n m* back, back part of anything
air do chùlaibh behind you
culaidh *n* **-e, -ean** *f* garment, apparel;
object, butt **c.-choimheach** fancy dress
c.-mhagaidh object of scorn/mockery
cùlaist *n* **-e, -ean** *f* utility room, scullery
cularan *n* **-ain, -ain** *m* cucumber
cullach *n* **-aich, -aich** *m* male cat,
tomcat; boar
cùl-mhùtaireachd *n* **cùil-** *f* smuggling;
mutinying, plotting
cultar *n* **-air, -an** *m* culture
cultarach *a* **-aiche** cultural

cum v **-adh** shape, form, compose, fashion
cùm v **cumail** keep, retain; support; hold
  a bheil thu a' cumail gu math? are
  you keeping well? **dè na chumas e?** how
  much will it hold? **c. sin dhomh** hold
  that for me **c. a-mach** claim, make out
  c. coinneamh hold a meeting **c. grèim**
  air keep hold of **c. ort** keep going, carry
  on, keep at it **c. suas** keep up, maintain
cumadh n **-aidh, -aidhean** m shape,
  form; the act of shaping or forming
cumanta a common, ordinary
cumha n **-chan** m mourning,
  lamentation; elegy; condition, stipulation
cumhach a conditional (*gram*) **an**
  tràth c. the conditional tense
cumhachd n **-an** f m power, strength;
  authority
cumhachdach a **-aiche** powerful, mighty
cumhain v See **caomhain**
cumhang a **-ainge/cuinge** narrow,
  tight; narrow-minded
cùmhnant n **-aint, -an** m contract,
  agreement, covenant; condition
  c.-obrach contract of employment
cunbhalach a **-aiche** regular, constant,
  steady, consistent
cungaidh n **-ean** f ingredients,
  implement **c.-leighis** medicine, cure
cunnart n **-airt, -an** m danger, risk
cunnartach a **-aiche** dangerous, risky
cunnradh n **-aidh, -ean** m bargain,
  contract, deal; treaty
cunnt v **-adh/-as/-ais** count
cunntais n f m counting
cunntas n **-ais, -an** f m (*fin, general*)
  account; arithmetic **c.-beatha** CV
  c.-bheachd opinion poll **c.-sluaigh**
  census

cunntasachd n f accountancy,
  accounting
cunntasair n **-ean** m accountant
cuntair n **-ean** m counter (*in shop etc*)
  Also **cunntair**
cupa n **-nnan** m cup *Also* **cupan**
curaidh n **-ean** m hero, champion,
  warrior
cùram n **-aim, -an** m care, responsibility,
  charge, trust; anxiety, worry; religious
  conversion **ghabh mi c. a' ghille**
  I took care of/took responsibility for the
  boy **fo chùram** anxious/concerned **na**
  biodh c. ort don't be anxious/concerned
  tha an c. oirre she's been converted
  (*relig*)
cùramach a **-aiche** careful, responsible;
  anxious
cur na mara n m seasickness
currac n **-aic, -aicean** m cap, bonnet
curracag n **-aig, -an** f peewit, lapwing;
  haycock
curran n **-ain, -ain** m carrot
cùrsa n **-ichean** f m course
cur-seachad n **-an** m pastime,
  hobby
cus n m excess, too much, too many; (*less*
  usual) many **tha cus airgid aige** he has
  too much money **tha iad a' cur cus**
  bheannachdan thugad they send you
  lots of good wishes
cusbann n **-ainn** f customs, excise
cuspair n **-ean** m subject, topic
cut v **-adh** gut (*fish*)
cuthach n **-aich** m rage, fury; madness
  duine-cuthaich madman, wild man
  bha an c. dearg oirre she was mad
  with rage
cuthag n **-aig, -an** f cuckoo

D

dà a two (+ *dat sg & len*) **dà chaileig**
  two girls
da *aug prep* to his, for his
dachaigh n **(-e), -ean** f home
  gun d. homeless
dà-chànanach a bilingual

dà-chànanas n **-ais** m bilingualism
dà-chasach a **-aiche** two-footed
dad n f anything **dad ort!** hang on! wait
  a minute!
dadaidh n **-ean** m dad, daddy
dadam n **-aim, -an** m atom

dadamach a atomic
dà-dheug n, a twelve (*nouns in their singular form are inserted between* **dà** and **dheug** and are lenited) **dà dhuine dheug** twelve men/persons
dà-dhualach a two-ply
dà fhichead n, a forty (*lit* two score)
dà-fhillte a two-fold, double, compound
daga n **-ichean** m pistol
dàibhear n **-eir, -an** m diver
dàibh(ig) v **-eadh** dive
dail n **dalach, -ean** f dale, meadow
dàil n **dàlach, dàlaichean** f delay, procrastination; credit **cuir d. ann** v delay **air dhàil** on credit
dàimh n **-e** f m relationship, affinity, friendship
dàimheach a **-mhiche** related; relative (*gram*)
dàimhealachd n f friendliness
dàimheil a **-e** friendly
daingeann a **daingne** firm, steadfast, determined, committed
daingneach n **-nich, -nichean** f stronghold, fortification, fort
daingnich v **-neachadh** confirm, ratify; strengthen, consolidate
dàir n **dàra/dàrach** f breeding, heat, breeding together (*of cattle*) **tha an d. air a' bhoin** the cow is in heat/season
dall n **doill, doill** m blind person
dall a **doille** blind
dall v **-adh** blind
dallag an fheòir n **dallagan an fh.** f dormouse
dallag an fhraoich n **dallagan an fh.** f shrew
dalma a presumptuous; blatant
dalta n **-n** m foster-child
daltachd n f fosterage
daltag n **-aig, -an** f bat
dam n **-a, -aichean** m dam
dàmais n f draughts
damaiste n f damage; difficulty
damh n **daimh, daimh** m bullock, ox; stag
Dàmhair n f **an D.** October

damhan-allaidh n **damhain-, damhain-** m spider
dàn n **dàin** m fate, destiny **bha sin an dàn dhi** that was her destiny
dàn n **dàin, dàin** m poem
dàna a bold, intrepid, daring, presumptuous
dànachd n f boldness, daring
dànadas n **-ais** m boldness, daring
Danmhairgeach n **-gich, -gich** m Dane a Danish
danns v **-a(dh)** dance
danns(a) n **-(a)ichean** m dance
dannsa(dh) n **(-aidh)** m dancing
dannsair n **-ean** m dancer
daoimean n **-ein, -an** m diamond
daoine n m See **duine**
daolag n **-aig(e), -an** f beetle **d.-bhreac-dhearg** ladybird
daonna a human *Also* **daonda**
daonnachd n f humanity *Also* **daondachd**
daonnan adv always
daor a **daoire** dear, expensive, costly
daorach n f **-aich** intoxication, drunkenness **bha an d. air** he was drunk **air an daoraich** on a binge
daorsa n f bondage, captivity
dar aug prep to our, for our conj when
darach n **-aich** m oak (*tree*)
da-rìribh adv indeed, very, in earnest
dàrna a second *Also* **dara**
dà-sheaghach a **-aiche** ambiguous
dath n **-a, -an** m colour
dath v **-adh** colour; dye
dathadh n **-aidh** m colouring
dathte a coloured
dè int pron what? **dè an uair a tha e?** what's the time? **dè an t-ainm a th' ort?** what's your name? **dè cho fad' 's a tha e?** how far is it?
de prep of (+ dat & len)
deachd v **-adh** dictate
deachdadh n **-aidh, -aidhean** m dictation **inneal-deachdaidh** m dictaphone
deadhan n **-ain, -ain** m dean

deagh a (*precedes & lenites n*) good, fine, excellent **d. bhanais** a good wedding

deagh-bheus n -a, -an f virtue

deagh-ghean n -a m goodwill, benevolence

dealachadh n -aidh m parting, separation

dealaich v -achadh part, separate, differentiate **tha iad air dealachadh** they've separated (*of a couple*)

dealaichte a separate, separated

dealain a electric **teine d.** m electric fire **post-d.** m e-mail

dealan n -ain m electricity

dealanach n -aich, -aich m lightning

dealanaich v -achadh electrify

dealanair n -ean m electrician

dealan-dè n dealain-, dealain- m butterfly

dealas n -ais m zeal, eagerness, commitment

dealasach a -aiche zealous, eager, committed

dealbh n -a/deilbhe, -an/deilbh f m picture, illustration, photograph, form, figure, outline **tog d.** v take a picture **d.-chlulch(e)** play (*acted*) **d.-èibhinn** cartoon

dealbh v -adh design, plan

dealbhadair n -ean m photographer; designer

dealbhaiche n -an m draughtsman

dealg n deilg, -an f pin, prickle, skewer

dealgan n -ain, -an m spindle

deàlrach a -aiche shiny, shining

deàlradh n -aidh, -aidhean m shining, flashing

deàlraich v -adh shine, flash

dealt n -a f m dew

deamhais n -ean f m shears

deamhan n -ain, -ain m demon, devil **'s e d. a th' annad!** you're a devil!

deamhnaidh a -e devilish **tha fhios agad d. math** you know damned well

deamocrasaidh n -ean m democracy

deamocratach n -aich, -aich m democrat

deamocratach a -aiche democratic

dèan irr v -amh do, make **d. cabhag!** hurry! **d. gàire** laugh **d. air do shocair!** slow down! **d. an gnothach/a' chùis** suffice, manage (+ **air**) beat, overcome

dèanadach a -aiche industrious, hardworking

deann n -a, -an f force, haste

deannan n -ain, -an m a number, a good few **d. bhliadhnaichean** a good few years

deann-ruith n -e f movement at speed, travel at pace, headlong rush

deanntag n -aige, -an f nettle

dèanta a done, complete; stocky (*in build*)

dearbh v -adh prove, affirm

dearbh a (*precedes & lenites n*) certain, sure, identical **gu d. fhèin** indeed **an d. fhear/thè** the very one

dearbhadh n -aidh m proof, identification, trial

dearbhta a certain, sure, proven *Also* **dearbhte**

dearc n -an f berry

dearcag n -aig, -an f little berry, currant

dearg a deirge red, crimson (*also used as an intensive*) **d. amadan/òinseach** an utter fool **d. chuthach** mad rage **d. mhèirleach** a downright thief **d. rùisgte** stark naked

dearg- pref reddish **d.-dhonn** reddish brown

deargann n -ainn, -an f flea

dearmad n -aid, -an m omission, oversight (*error*), neglect **dèan d. air** v neglect, omit, overlook

dearmadach a -aiche negligent, forgetful

dearmaid v -ad neglect

deàrrs v -adh shine

deàrrsach a -aiche shining, gleaming, glistening **d. uisge** f downpour

deàrrsadh n -aidh, -aidhean m shining

deas n, a deise f south; right; ready (to) **Uibhist a D.** South Uist **an taobh a d.** the south side **an làmh dheas** the right hand **air an làimh dheis** on the right

deasachadh n -aidh m preparation, editing **neach-deasachaidh** m editor
deasaich v -achadh prepare, edit
deasaichte a prepared, edited
deasbad n -aid, -an f m debate **dèan d.** v debate
deas-bhriathrach a -aiche eloquent
deas-chainnt n -e f eloquence
deasg n -a, -an m desk
deas-ghnàth n -ghnàith, -ghnàthan m ceremony, ceremonial
deatach n -aiche, -aichean f smoke, fumes, vapour
deatamach a -aiche necessary, crucial, essential
ded aug prep of your
deic n -e, -ichean f m deck (of boat)
deich n, a ten
deichead n -eid, -an m decade
deicheamh n -eimh m decimal num a tenth
deichnear n f m ten (people) **d. fhear** ten men
dèideadh n -didh m toothache **a bheil an d. ort?** do you have toothache?
dèideag n -eig, -an f toy; pebble
dèidh n -e, -ean f desire; fondness; aspiration
dèidheil a -e fond **d. air ...** fond of ...
deidhseag n -eig, -an f smack
deifir n See diofar
deifrichte See diofraichte
deigh n -e f ice
dèile n -an/-achan f wooden board, plank **d.-bhogadain** see-saw
dèilig v -eadh (followed by ri) deal (with), treat
deimhinn(t)e a certain, categorical, conclusive
dèine n f keenness, commitment; impetus
dèirc n -e, -ean f alms, charity
dèirceach n -cich, -cich m beggar
deireadh n -ridh, -ridhean m end, rear, stern; (abstr) finish, conclusion **air d(h).** late ... **mu dheireadh** last **mu dheireadh thall** at (long) last, eventually

deireannach a -aiche last, latter, final, ultimate; backward
deis a **deise** ready, eager, willing
deisciobal n -ail, -ail m disciple
deise n -achan f suit, uniform **d. an Airm** Army uniform **d.-sgoile** school uniform **d.-snàimh** swimsuit
deiseil a -e/eala ready; finished (with); handy; clockwise
deit n -e, -ichean f date (fruit)
dem aug prep of my
den aug prep of the; of their
deò n f breath **thug e suas an d.** he breathed his last **d. gaoithe** a breath of wind
deoc v -adh suck
deoch n dighe/dibhe, -an/-annan f drink **d. an dorais** stirrup cup **d.-làidir** alcohol **d.-slàinte** toast (with drink)
deòin n -e f will, purpose
deònach a -aiche willing
deònaich v -achadh grant, vouchsafe, be willing to do
deothail v -al suck Formerly **deoghail**
der aug prep of/off our/your
deuchainn n -e, -ean f examination, test, trial; agony
deuchainneach a -niche trying, agonizing
deucon n -oin, -oin/-an m deacon
deud n -an m denture, tooth
deudach a -aiche toothy, dental
deug suff teen (in numbers) **sia-deug** sixteen
deugachadh n m a span of 13 to 19 years **d. bhliadhnaichean** a period of between 13 and 19 years
deugaich v -achadh enter teenage years
deugaire n -an m teenager
deur n **deòir, deòir** m tear (drop)
dha prep See do
dha aug prep to/for his
dha/dhàsan prep pron to/for him
dhà n two **a dhà** two **na dhà** the two
dhachaigh adv home (ie homewards)
dhad aug prep to/for your
dhà-dheug n twelve **a d.** twelve

dhaibh(san) *prep pron* to/for them
dham *aug prep* to/for my; to/for their
dhan *aug prep* to/for the/their
dha-rìribh *adv* indeed, very, in earnest
  math d. excellent, very good
dhe *aug prep* of/off him
dhed *aug prep* of/off your (*sg*)
dhem *aug prep* of/off my
dhen *aug prep* of/off the/their
dher *aug prep* of/off our/your
dheth *adv* off
dheth(san) *prep pron* of/off him
dhi/dhì(se) *prep pron* to/for her
dhibh(se) *prep pron* of/off you
dhinn(e) *prep pron* of/off us
dhìom(sa) *prep pron* of/off me
dhìot(sa) *prep pron* of/off you (*sg*)
dhith(se) *prep pron* of/off her
dhiubh(san) *prep pron* of/off them
dhòmh(sa) *prep pron* to/for me
dhuibh(se) *prep pron* to/for you

dibhearsain *n m* fun, entertainment, diversion; teasing
dìblidh *a* **-e** abject, wretched; in difficulty
dìcheall *n* **dìchill** *f m* diligence, utmost
  rinn iad an d. they did their best/utmost
dìcheallach *a* **-aiche** diligent, conscientious
dì-chuimhnich *v See* **dìochuimhnich**
Diciadain *n m* Wednesday
Didòmhnaich *n m* Sunday
dìg *n* **-e, -ean** *f* ditch
digear *n* **-eir, -an** *m* digger
Dihaoine *n m* Friday
dìle *n* **-ann, -an** *f* deluge, flood
  d. bhàthte torrential rain
dìleab *n* **-eib(e), -an** *f* legacy, bequest
dìleas *a* **dìlse** faithful, loyal
dilleachdan *n* **-ain, -an** *m* orphan
dìlseachd *n f* faithfulness, loyalty
Diluain *n m* Monday

Insight: Diluain

Monday in Gaelic. Names of days have the element *Di-* followed by suffixes of varying origin: *Diciadain* (the day of the first fast, Wednesday), *Disathairne* (the day of Saturn, Saturday), *Didòmhnaich* (the day of the Lord, Sunday). But for Sunday you can also say *Latha na Sàbaid*, the Sabbath Day.

dhuinn(e) *prep pron* to/for us
dhuit *See* **dhut**
dhur *aug prep* to/for your
dhut(sa) *prep pron* to/for you (*sg*)
di/dì(se) *prep pron* to/for her
dia *n* **dè, -than** *m* god **Dia** God
diabhal *n* **-ail, -ail/-bhlan** *m* devil
  an D. the Devil
diabhlaidh *a* devilish, diabolical
diadhachd *n f* divinity, godhead; theology, study of divinity; godliness
diadhaidh *a* **-e** godly, devout; divine
diadhaire *n* **-an** *m* theologian, divine
diallaid *n See* **dìollaid**
dian *a* **dèine** keen, vehement, impetuous; intensive, intense
Diardaoin *n m* Thursday
dias *n* **dèise, -an** *f* ear of corn
diathad *n* **-aid, -an** *f* dinner, lunch

Dimàirt *n m* Tuesday
dìmeas *n* **-a** *m* disregard, disrespect
  dèan d. air *v* disregard, look down on
dìneasair *n* **-ean** *m* dinosaur
dinn *v* **-eadh** stuff, cram, squeeze in
dinnear *n* **-eir/-ach, -an** *f* dinner
dinnsear *n* **-eir** *m* ginger
dìobair *v* **-bradh** desert, abandon; fail, come to nothing
dìobhair *v* **-t** vomit
dìochuimhne *n f* forgetfulness
dìochuimhneach *a* **-niche** forgetful
dìochuimhnich *v* **-neachadh** forget
diofar *n* **-air** *m* difference; variety
  chan eil e gu d. it doesn't matter
diofraichte *a* different
diog *n* **-an** *m* second (*unit of time*)
diogail *v* **-gladh** tickle
diogalach *a* **-aiche** tickly, ticklish

dìoghail v **-ghladh** avenge; pay back, compensate *Also* **dìol**

dìoghaltas n **-ais** m revenge, vengeance

dìoghras n **-ais** m enthusiasm

dìoghrasach a **-aiche** enthusiastic

dìogladh n **-aidh** m tickling

dìol n m abuse **dèan droch dhìol air** v badly abuse

dìolain a illegitimate (*as of child*)

dìol-dèirce n **diolacha-/diolan-** m beggar, wretch, poor soul

dìollaid n **-e, -ean** f saddle

diomb n f m displeasure, indignation, resentment

diombach a **-aiche** displeased, indignant, resentful

diombuan a **-uaine** transient, fleeting

dìomhain a **-e** vain; idle

dìomhair a **-e** mysterious; secret, confidential

dìomhaireachd n f mystery; secrecy, confidentiality

dìomhanas n **-ais** vanity; idleness

dìon n **-a** m protection, defence, security

dìon v protect, defend, guard

dìonach a **-aiche** watertight

dìongmhalta a determined, steadfast

dìosgan n **-ain, -ain** m creak

dìosganaich n **-e** f creaking

dìreach a **dìriche** straight, direct; upright

dìreach adv just **tha e d. air falbh** he has just gone **seadh, d.** just so

dìreadh n **-ridh, -ridhean** m climb, ascent

dìrich v **dìreadh/dìreachadh** climb, ascend; straighten, make straight

dis a prone to feeling cold, cauldrife; wimpish

Disathairne n m Saturday

dìsinn/dìsne n **dìsne, dìsnean** m dice, die

dìt v **-eadh** condemn, sentence

dìth n **-e** f m want, lack, deficiency **dè tha dhìth ort?** what do you want? **bha feadhainn a dhìth** there were some missing **a' dol a dhìth** perishing, dying

dìthean n **-ein, -ein/-an** m flower

dithis n f two (*people*); both; pair, couple **an d. aca** the two of them

diù n m worth, heed, attention **cha do chuir e d. ann** he paid no attention to it

diùc n **-an** m duke **ban-d.** f duchess

diùid a **-e** shy, bashful, reticent

diùlt v **-adh** refuse, reject

diùltadh n **-aidh, -aidhean** m refusal, rejection

Diùrach n **-aich, -aich** m someone from Jura a from, or pertaining to, Jura

dleastanas n **-ais, -an** m duty, obligation **mar dhleastanas** obligatory *Formerly* **dleasdanas**

dligheach a **-ghiche** due, legitimate

dlùth n **-a, dlùithe** m warp (*weaving*)

dlùth a **dlùithe** close (to), near

dlùthaich v **-achadh** approach, near; warp (*weaving*)

do poss pron your **d'** before vowels **d' athair** your father

do prep to, for (+ dat)

do v part (indicates past tense) **an do dh'èirich iad?** did they get up?

do neg pref in-, im-, un-

do-àireamh a innumerable, countless

dòbhran n **-ain, -ain** m otter

doca n **-n/-ichean** m dock; hollow, hole

docair n **-ean** m docker

dòcha a likely, probable **'s e sin as d.** that's most likely **'s d.** perhaps, maybe **is d. gun tig iad** perhaps they will come

dochainn v **-ann** beat up, hurt, injure

dochann n **-ainn** m hurt, injury

dòchas n **-ais, -an** m hope **tha mi an d. gum faic mi iad** I hope I'll see them

dòchasach a **-aiche** hopeful

dod aug prep to your (sg)

do-dhèanta a impossible, impractical, impracticable

do-fhaicsinneach a **-niche** invisible

doicheallach a **-aiche** churlish

dòigh n **-e, -ean** f way, method, manner **d.-beatha** way of life, lifestyle **cuir air d.** v repair; arrange, organize **tha i air a d.** she is happy

dòigheil a **-e** well-arranged, contented, sensible, reasonable **tha e gu d.** he is well

doile n **-lichean** f doll

doileag n **-eig, -an** f (small) doll

doilgheas n **-eis** m affliction, vexation, sorrow

doille n f blindness

doilleir a **-e** dark, gloomy

doimhearra a swarthy

doimhne n f depth **an d.** the sea

doimhneachd n f depth

doineann n **-ninn, -an** f tempest

doirbh a **-e/dorra** difficult

doire n **-an/-achan** f m grove, thicket

dòirt v **dòrtadh** pour; spill

dol n m going (See irr v **rach** in Grammar)

dol-a-mach n m exit; behaviour **anns a' chiad d.** initially **dè an d. a th' ort?** what are you up to?

dol-a-steach n m entrance

dolaidh n f harm, detriment **chaidh e a dholaidh** it perished/rotted

dolair n **-ean** m dollar

dol-air-adhart n m carry-on

dol-às n m escape **cha robh d. againn** we had no way out, we found it unavoidable

dòlas n **-ais, -an** m woe, grief, desolation

dom aug prep to/for my/their

domhainn a **doimhne/-e** deep; profound

domhan n **-ain** m universe

don prep pron to/for the/their

dona a **miosa** bad

donas n **-ais** m devil **an D.** the Devil **an D. ort!** Drat you!

donn a **duinne** brown, brown-haired

donnalaich n f howling

dor aug prep to/for you (pl & pol)

dòrainn n **-e, -ean** f anguish, agony

dòrainneach a **-niche** anguished, excruciating

doras n **-ais, dorsan** m door **d.-aghaidh** front door **d.-cùil** back door **d.-èiginn** emergency exit

dorch(a) a **duirch(e)** dark, dark-haired, dusky

dorchadas n **-ais** m darkness

dòrlach n **-aich, -aich** m handful

dòrn n **dùirn, dùirn** m fist

dorsair n **-ean** m doorman, janitor

dòrtadh n **-aidh, -aidhean** m pouring **bha d. uisge ann** it was pouring (with) rain

dos n **dois/duis, duis, -an** m bush, tuft; drone (of bagpipe)

dòs v **-adh** dose

do-sheachanta a unavoidable, inevitable

dotair n **-ean** m doctor

dòtaman n **-ain, -ain/-an** m spinning top

drabasta a lewd, obscene

dràbhadh n **-aidh** m falling away, dropping off, reduction

dragh n **-a, -annan** m bother, trouble; worry **bha d. oirre** she was worried **na gabh d.** v don't worry/go to any trouble

dragh v **-adh** tug

draghadh n **-aidh, -aidhean** m a tug **thug i d. air** v she gave it a tug

draghail a **-e/-ala** worried, worrying, troublesome

dràibhear n **-eir, -an** m driver

dràibh(ig) v **-eadh** drive

drama n **-ichean** f m dram (of whisky)

dràma n f drama

dranndan n **-ain** m murmur, drone; growl, snarl

draoidh n **-ean** m wizard, sorcerer, druid

draoidheachd n f wizardry, sorcery; magic; druidism

drathair n **dràthraichean** m drawer (in furniture)

drathais n **-e, -ean** f drawers, pants, knickers Also **drathars**

dreach n **-a, -an** m appearance

dreachd n **-an** f draft

dreag n **dreige, -an** f meteor

dreagaire n **-an** m satellite

dreallag n **-aige, -an** f swing (for play)

dream n **-a, -annan** m people, tribe

drèana n **-ichean** f drain, ditch

dreasa n **-ichean** f m dress

dreasair n **-ean** m dresser (furniture)

dreathan-donn n **dreathain-duinn, dreathain-donna** m wren

drèin n -e, -ean f scowl **chuir i d. oirre** v she pulled a face

dreuchd n -an f profession, occupation, office (*position*) **leig i dhith a d.** v she retired

driamlach n -aich, -aich/-aichean f m fishing line

drile n -lichean f drill (*mech*)

drilig v -eadh drill (*mech*)

drioftair n -ean m drifter (*fishing boat*)

drip n -e f bustle

dripeil a -e very busy, bustling

dris n -e, -ean f bramble

drithlinn n m malfunction **chaidh e d.** it malfunctioned

dr(i)ùchd n -an m dew

dròbh n dròibh/-a, -an f m drove

dròbhair n -ean m drover

droch a bad (*precedes & lenites* n) **d. shìde** bad weather

drochaid n -e, -ean f bridge

droch-bheus n -a, -an f bad behaviour, immorality

droch-nàdarrach a -aiche bad-natured, ill-tempered

droga n -ichean f drug

droigheann n -ghinn m thorn

droman n -ain m elder tree

drudhag n -aig, -an f drop (*of liquid*); sip *Also* **drùdhag**

druid n -e, -ean f starling

druid v -eadh shut

drùidh v drùdhadh soak, penetrate; impress, influence **dhrùidh e orm** it impressed me

drùidhteach a -tiche penetrating; impressive

druim n droma, dromannan m back; ridge (*topog*)

druma n -chan/-ichean f m drum

duainidh a -e drab, dowdy

duais n -e, -ean f prize, reward; wages

dual n duail, -an m lock (*of hair*), plait; strand

dual n duail m hereditary right, inherited character or quality **mar bu d. dha** as was his custom

dualach a -aiche curled, plaited

dualag n -aig, -an f curl (*of hair*), ringlet

dualchainnt n -e, -ean f speech of a particular area, dialect

dualchas n -ais m heritage, tradition

dualchasach a -aiche traditional

dual(t)ach a -aiche liable (to), inclined (to)

duan n duain, duain m poem

duanag n -aig, -an f ditty

duanaire n -an m anthology

dùbailte a double

dubh n duibh m black (*colour*); ink; pupil (*of eye*)

dubh a duibhe black **d. dorcha** pitch-dark/-black

dubh v -adh blacken **d. às** erase, excise

dubh- pref dark **d.-ghorm** dark blue

dubhach a -aiche sad, melancholy

dubhadh n -aidh m blackening, darkening, eclipse **d. na grèine/ gealaich** eclipse of the sun/moon

dubhag n -aig, -an f kidney

dubhan n -ain, -ain m hook

dubhar n -air m shade

dubh-cheist n -cheistean f puzzle

dubh-fhacal n -ail, -ail/-fhaclan m riddle, enigma

Dùbhlachd n f **an D.** December

dùbhlan n -ain, -ain m challenge, defiance **thug i d. dha** she defied/challenged him

dùblaich v -achadh double, duplicate

dùdach n -àich(e), -aichean f m horn (*in car*), hooter

dùil n -e, -ean f expectation, intention **tha d. aice ri leanabh** she's expecting (a baby) **ma-thà, tha mi 'n d.** I should think so (too)

dùil n -e, -ean f element

duileasg n -lisg m dulse

duilgheadas n -ais, -an m difficulty, problem

duilich a duilghe sad, regrettable; difficult **tha mi d.** I'm sorry

duilleach n -lich m foliage

duilleachan n -ain, -ain m leaflet

duilleag n -eige, -an f leaf; sheet (*of paper*); page **taobh-duilleig(e) 6** page 6

duilleagach a -aiche leafy

dùin v **dùnadh** close, shut
duine n **daoine** m man, person, anyone;
husband **a bheil d. a-staigh?** is there
anyone in? **a h-uile d.** everyone,
everybody **d.-uasal** gentleman,
nobleman **d. sam bith** anyone
duinealas n **-ais** m manliness
duineil a **-e** manly
dùinte a closed, shut; reserved, withdrawn
duiseal n **-eil, -an** f flute
dùisg v **dùsgadh** wake, awaken, rouse
Dùitseach n **-sich** m Dutch person a Dutch
dùmhail a **-e** dense; crowded, congested
dùn n **dùin, dùin** m fort; heap
dùnadh n **-aidh, -aidhean** m closure,
closing, ending
dùnan n **-ain, -ain** m small fort; small
heap; dunghill
dùr a **dùire** dour; stubborn
dur aug prep to your (pl & pol)
dùrachd n **-an** f sincerity, earnestness,
wish **le deagh dhùrachd** with best
wishes/yours sincerely

dùrachdach a **-aiche** sincere, fervent,
impassioned
dùraig v **-eadh** dare, venture; desire
dhùraiginn falbh I'd like to go
durcan n **-ain, -ain** m cone (on tree)
dùrdail n **-e** f crooning, cooing
durrag n **-aig, -an** f worm
dusan n **-ain** m dozen (+ sg) **d. ugh**
a dozen eggs **leth-d.** half a dozen
dùsgadh n **-aidh, -aidhean** m waking,
awakening, rousing **d. spioradail**
religious revival
duslach n **-aich** m dust; mortal remains
dust n m dust
dust/dustaig v **-adh/-eadh** dust
dustair n **-ean** m duster
dùthaich n **dùthcha, dùthchannan**
f country **air an d.** in the countryside
dùthchail a **-e** rural
dùthchas n **-ais** m place of origin,
homeland; heredity, heritage
dùthchasach a **-aiche** native,
indigenous, hereditary

E

e pron he, him, it
eabar n air m mud, mire
Eabhra n f Hebrew (lang)
Eabhra(idhea)ch n **-aich, -aich**
m Hebrew a Hebrew
eacarsaich n **-e, -ean** f exercise; capering
about
each n **eich, eich** m horse **e.-aibhne**
hippopotamus **e.-uisge** water-horse, kelpie
eachdraiche n **-an** m historian
eachdraidh n **-e, -ean** f history, chronicle
eachdraidheil a **-e** historic, historical
eaconamach a economic, economical

eaconamachd n f economics
eaconamaidh n **-ean** f m
economy
eaconamair n **-ean** m economist
eaconamas n **-ais** m economics
e. dachaigh home economics
Eadailteach n **-tich, -tich** m Italian
a Italian
Eadailtis n f Italian (lang)
eadar prep (+ len) between **e. ... agus ...**
both ... and ... **e. bheag is mhòr** both
large and small **e. dhà bharail** in two
minds Does not always lenite

Insight: eadar

A highly productive preposition, *eadar*, between, appears in
many phrases (*eadar samhradh is foghar*, between summer and
winter) but also very often as a prefix translated by inter: *eadar-
nàiseanta* (international), *an t-Eadar-lìon* (the Internet). There is
also a full set of inflected prepositional pronouns: *eadarainn fhìn* –
between ourselves.

eadaraibh(se) *prep pron* between you (*pl & pol*)

eadarainn(e) *prep pron* between us

eadar-àm *n* **-ama** *m* **-amannan** *m* interim period, interval **anns an e.** in the interim, meantime

eadar-bhreith *n* **-e, -ean** *f* arbitration

eadar-bhreithnich *v* **-neachadh** arbitrate

eadar-dhà-lionn *adv (met)* floundering; hesitating, undecided

eadar-dhà-shian *n f* a break in a spell of adverse weather

eadar-dhealachadh *n* **-aidh, -aidhean** *m* difference, distinction, differentiation

eadar-dhealaich *v* **-achadh** differentiate, distinguish, discriminate

eadar-dhealaichte *a* different, distinctive **e. bho** distinct from

eadar-ghuidhe *n* **-achan** *m* intercession, mediation

eadar-lìon *n* **-lìn** *m* **an t-Eadar-lìon** the Internet

eadar-mheadhanach *a* intermediate

eadar-mheadhanair *n* **-ean** *m* intermediary; Redeemer (*relig*)

eadar-nàiseanta *a* international

eadar-roinneil *a* inter-departmental, inter-regional

eadar-sholas *n* **-ais** *m* twilight

eadar-theangachadh *n* **-aidh, -aidhean** *m* translation (*of languages*) **e. mar-aon** simultaneous translation

eadar-theangaich *v* **-achadh** translate

eadar-theangaiche *n* **-an** *m* translator

eadar-ùine *n f* interval, intermission

eadhon *adv* even

eadradh *n* **-aidh, -aidhean** *m* milking time

eadraiginn *n* **-e, -ean** *f* intervention, mediation **rach san e.** *v* intervene, mediate

eag *n* **eige, -an** *f* nick, notch, jag

eagach *a* **-aiche** jagged, serrated, notched

eagal *n* **-ail** *m* fear, fright **an robh an t-eagal ort?** were you afraid? **bha e. mo bheatha orm** I was scared stiff **air e. 's gum faic iad sinn** in case/lest they see us

eagalach *a* **-aiche** fearful, afraid; frightful, dreadful **e. fuar** fearfully cold

eag-eòlas *n* **-ais** *m* ecology

eaglais *n* **-e, -ean** *f* church **E. na h-Alba** the Church of Scotland **an E. Bhaisteach** the Baptist Church **an E. Chaitligeach** the Catholic Church **an E. Easbaigeach** the Episcopal Church **an E. Shaor** the Free Church **an E. Shaor Chlèireach** the Free Presbyterian Church **an E. Stèidhichte** the Established Church

eagnaidh *a* **-e** exact, precise

eagranaich *v* **-achadh** arrange, organize, place in order

eala *n* **-chan** *f* swan

èalaidh *v* **-adh** creep, move stealthily, steal away

ealain *n* **-e, -ean** *f* art **Comhairle nan E.** the Arts Council

ealamh *a* **-aimhe** quick, swift, ready

ealanta *a* skilful, skilled, ingenious, expert, artistic

ealantas *n* **-ais** *m* skill, ingenuity

ealla *n f* watching **gabh e. ris** take stock of it, watch him

eallach *n* **-aich, -aich** *m* burden, load

ealt *n* **-a, -an** *f* flock of birds, bird life

ealtainn *n* **-e, -ean** *f* razor; flock of birds

eanchainn *n* **-e, -ean** *f* brain **tha deagh e. aice** she has a good brain

eangarra *a* irritable, cross

eanraich *n* **-e** *f* soup

ear *n f* east **an ear** the east **Cille Bhrìghde an Ear** East Kilbride **chaidh iad an ear 's an iar** they scattered **an ear-dheas** the south-east **an ear-thuath** the north-east **an Ear Mheadhanach** the Middle East

earail *n* **-alach, -alaichean** *f* exhortation; warning

earalaich *v* **-achadh** exhort, caution; warn

earalas *n* **-ais** *m* foresight, precaution

earb *n* **-a, -aichean** *f* roe-deer

earb *v* **earbsa** trust, rely, confide

earball *n* **-aill, -aill** *m* tail

earbsa n f reliance, confidence, trust **cha chuirinn e. ann** I wouldn't trust him/it
earbsach a **-aiche** reliable, trustworthy
eàrlas n **-ais, -ais** m pledge, (gift) token **e. leabhair** book token
eàrr n **-a, -an** f m tail, end, conclusion **e.-ràdh** m tailpiece, appendix
earrach n **-aich, -aich** m spring **as t-e.** in spring
earrann n **-ainn, -an** f section, portion, sector; (fin) share; (liter) passage, verse Also **earrainn**
earranta a limited (as of company)
eas n **-a, -an** m waterfall, cascade, cataract
easag n **-aig, -an** f pheasant
eas-aonta n **-n** f disagreement, dissent, discord, disunity
eas-aontach a **-aiche** dissenting, dissident, discordant
eas-aontachd n **-an** f disagreement, dissent, discord, disunity
eas-aontaich v **-achadh** disagree, dissent
easaontas n **-ais** m disobedience, transgression
easbaig n **-e, -ean** m bishop **àrd-e.** archbishop
Easbaigeach n **-gich, -gich** m Episcopalian a Episcopalian, episcopal
easbhaidh n **-e, -ean** f want, lack, defect **chan eil càil a dh'e. oirnn** we lack for nothing
easbhaidheach a **-dhiche** deficient, defective
eascaraid n **-cairdean** m enemy, foe
èasgaidh a **-e** willing, ready (to), keen, obliging; active
easgann n **-ainn, -an** f eel
eas-onair n **-e** f dishonour
eas-onarach a **-aiche** dishonest, dishonourable
eas-umhail a **-e** disobedient, insubordinate
eas-ùmhlachd n f disobedience, insubordination
eas-urram n **-aim** m dishonour, disrespect

eas-urramach a **-aiche** dishonourable, disrespectful
eathar n **-air, eathraichean** f m boat
eatarra(san) prep pron between them
èibh n **-e, -ean** f shout, call, cry
èibh v **-each** shout, call, cry
èibhinn a **-e** funny, amusing, humorous
èibhleag n **-eige, -an** f live coal, cinder
èideadh n **-didh, -didhean** m dress, clothing, garb, uniform
eidheann n **eidhne** f ivy
èifeachd n f effectiveness, efficacy
èifeachdach a **-aiche** effective, effectual, efficient
èifeachdail a **-e** effectual, effective
Eigeach n **Eigich, Eigich** m someone from Eigg a from, or pertaining to, Eigg
eigh n **-e** f ice
èigh n **-e, -ean** f shout, call, cry
èigh v **-each** shout, call, cry
eighe n **-achan** f file (impl)
èigheach n **-ghich** f shouting, calling, proclamation Also **èigheachd**
eighre n f ice
-eigin suff some **cuideigin** someone **rudeigin** something
èiginn n f necessity, emergency, straits **air e.** only just, with difficulty **ann an e.** as a last resort
èiginneach a **-niche** desperate, essential Also **èigeannach**
èignich v **èigneachadh** compel, force; rape
eil irr v was, were (never used on its own) (See verb **to be** in Grammar)
Eilbheiseach n **-sich, -sich** m someone from Switzerland a Swiss
èildear n **-eir, -an** m (church) elder
eile a other, another, else **fear e.** another one (m) **tè e.** another one (f) **cò e.?** who else?
èileadh n See **fèileadh**
eileamaid n **-e, -ean** f element
eilean n **-ein, -an** m island, isle
eileanach n **-aich, -aich** m islander
eileatrom n **-oim, -an** m hearse, bier
eilid n **èilde, èildean** f hind
eilthireach n **-rich, -rich** m exile, alien

eilthireachd *n f* exile
einnsean *n* **-ein, -an** *m* engine
  e.-smàlaidh fire engine
einnseanair *n* **-ean** *m* engineer
Èipheiteach *n* **-tich, -tich** *m* Egyptian
  a Egyptian
eireachdail *a* **-e** handsome, comely
eireag *n* **-eige, -an** *f* pullet, young hen
Èireannach *n* **-aich, -aich** *m* Irish person
  a Irish
èirich *v* **èirigh** rise, arise, get up; happen
  to, befall **dè dh'èirich dhaibh?** what
  happened to them? **chan eil càil ag**
  èirigh dhaibh they are all right, they
  are coming to no harm
èirig *n* **-e, -ean** *f* ransom, forfeit,
  reparation
èirigh *n f* rising, arising, getting up,
  uprising
Èirisgeach *n* **-gich, -gich** *m* someone
  from Eriskay *a* from, or pertaining to,
  Eriskay
eirmseach *a* **-siche** witty, sharp-witted
èis *n* **-e, -ean** *f* need, want; delay,
  impediment **Clann ann an Èis** Children
  in Need
èiseil *a* **-e** needy, urgently required
eisimeil *n* **-e** *f* dependence **an e. air**
  dependent on **an e. Dhòmhnaill**
  dependent on Donald
eisimeileach *a* **-liche** dependent
eisimpleir *n* **-ean** *f m* example
  mar e. for example
eisir *n* **-ean** *m* oyster
eisirean *n* **-ein, -an** *m* scallop, clam
èislean *n* **-ein** *m* grief, sorrow
  fo è. sorrowing, dejected
èist *v* **-eachd** (+ **ri**) listen (to)
  Formerly **èisd**
èisteachd *n f* listening, audition;
  confession (*relig*) **luchd-e.** *m* audience
  Formerly **èisdeachd**
eitean *n* **-ein** *m* core
eòlach *a* **-aiche** knowledgeable,
  acquainted (with) **a bheil thu e. air?**
  do you know him/it?
eòlaiche *n* **-an** *m* expert **e.-inntinn**
  psychologist

eòlas *n* **-ais, -an** *m* knowledge,
  acquaintance **e.-bodhaig** anatomy
  e.-inntinn psychology **cuir e. air** *v*
  get to know
eòrna *n m* barley **Tìr an E.** *lit* the Land
  of the Barley (*a poetic name for the*
  island of Tiree)
Eòrpach *n* **-aich, -aich** *m* European
  a **-aiche** European
esan *emph pron* he, him, it
eu- *neg pref* dis-, in-, mis-, un- *etc*
euchd *n* **-an** *m* feat, exploit, achievement
eucoir *n* **eucorach, -ean** *f* crime,
  misdemeanour, misdeed
eu-còir *a* **-e** unkind, stingy
eu-coltach *a* **-aiche** unlike, dissimilar,
  unlikely
eu-coltas *n* **-ais** *m* unlikelihood,
  dissimilarity
eu-comas *n* **-ais, -an** *m* inability
eu-comasach *a* **-aiche** (+ **do**)
  unable (to)
eucorach *n* **-aich, -aich** *m* criminal,
  miscreant, rascal **'s e e. a th' ann**
  he's a rascal
eud *n m* zeal, jealousy
eudach *n* **-aich** *m* jealousy **bha e ag**
  e. rithe he was jealous of her *a* **-aiche**
  jealous
eudail *n* **-ean** *f* dear, darling, treasure
  m' eudail my dear
eudar *n See* **feudar**
eudmhor *a* **-oire** zealous; jealous
eu-dòchas *n* **-ais** *m* hopelessness, despair
eu-dòchasach *a* **-aiche** hopeless,
  despairing
eu-domhainn *a* **-e** shallow
eug *n* **èig** *m* death
eug *def v* die, decease **dh'eug e** he died
eugsamhail *a* **-e/-mhla** various,
  manifold, miscellaneous, incomparable
eun *n* **eòin, eòin** *m* bird, fowl **e. dubh**
  an sgadain guillemot **e.-eòlas**
  m ornithology **e.-Frangach** turkey
  e.-fraoich grouse, moorhen **e.-mara**
  seabird **e.-tràghad** wader **e.-tumaidh**
  diver
eunlann *n* **-ainn, -an** *f m* cage, aviary

eunach n -aich m fowling
eunadair n -ean m fowler
eunlaith n -e f birds, fowls, bird life
euslaint n -e, -ean f ill-health, sickness

F

fàbhar n -air, -an m favour
fàbharach a -aiche favourable;
providential
fabhra n -n m eyelid
facal n -ail, -ail/faclan m word f. air an
fhacal word for word
fa chomhair prep phr (+ gen) opposite
faclair n -ean m dictionary
facs n -aichean m fax
factaraidh n -ean f m factory
fad n faid m length, distance air f. all,
altogether air fhad lengthways f. an
latha all day f. an t-siubhail all the
time fhad 's while
fàd n fàid/fòid, -an m a peat
fada a faide long dè cho f.? how long?
fad' às distant, remote f. nas fheàrr
much better f. gun èirigh late getting
up fad-ùine long term 's fhada bhon
uair sin long time no see
fadachd n f longing, yearning
bha f. oirnn ... we were longing for ...
a' gabhail f. longing, wearying
fadalach a -aiche late, slow
fadhail n -ail/fadhlach, fadhlaichean
f ford
fad-fhulangach a -fhulangaiche
long-suffering
fa-dheòidh adv at last
fàg v -ail leave; depart, go f. air ...
accuse ..., allege
fagas a faisge near am f. near
faghaid n -e, -ean f hunt
faic v -inn see (See irr v faic in Grammar)
faiceall n -cill f care, caution Also faicill
faiceallach a -aiche careful, cautious,
wary bi f.! be careful! Also faicilleach
faiche n -an f lawn, plain, meadow
faicsinneach a -niche visible,
conspicuous
fàidh n -e, -ean m prophet

euslainteach n -tich, -tich m invalid,
patient
euslainteach a -tiche ill, sickly,
unhealthy

faidhbhile n -an f m beech
fàidheadaireachd n -an f prophecy
faidhle n -achan m file (stationery)
faigh v -inn get, obtain, acquire, receive
f. a-mach find out, ascertain
faighean n -ein, -an m vagina
faighnich v -neachd question, ask,
enquire f. dhith ask her
failbheachan n -ain m earring
failc n -e, -ean f guillemot
fàileadh n -(e)idh, -(e)idhean m smell
faileas n -eis, -an m shadow
faileasach a -aiche shadowy
fàil(l)idh a -e stealthy gu f. quietly
faillich v -leachadh (+ air) defeat
dh'fhaillich e orm I failed to do it/I
couldn't manage it/he got the better
of me Also fairtlich
fàillig v -eadh fail
fàilligeadh n -gidh, -gidhean m failure;
flaw, defect
failmean n -ein, -an m kneecap
fail-mhuc n failean- f pigsty
fàilneachadh n -aidh, -aidhean m
failing
fàilt(e) n -(e)an f welcome cuir f. air ...
v welcome ... ceud mìle f. a hundred
thousand welcomes, the warmest of
welcomes
fàilteachadh n -aidh m welcoming,
reception
fàiltich v -teachadh welcome, greet
fàiltiche n -an m receptionist
faing n -e, -ean f fank, sheep-pen
fàinne n -achan f m ring f.-cluaise
earring f.-gealladh-pòsaidh
engagement ring f.-pòsaidh wedding
ring
faire n -an f watch, watching, guard
neach-f. guard
fàire n -an f horizon air f. on the horizon

faireachadh n -aidh m feeling,
sensation, sense
faireachdainn n -ean f feeling,
sensation, sense
fàireag n -eig, -an f gland
fairge n -achan/-annan f sea, ocean
fairich v -reachdainn/-reachadh
feel, sense
fairtleachadh n -aidh m failing
faisg a -e near **nas fhaisge** nearer
f. air near/close (to)
fàisg v **fàsgadh** squeeze, press
fàisneachd n -an f prophecy
fàisnich v -neachadh prophesy
fàitheam n -eim, -an m hem
fàl n **fàil, fàil** m hedge, dyke
fàl an rathaid (of road) verge
falach n -aich m hiding-place,
concealment **cuir am f. e** v hide it
chaidh iad am f. they hid **f.-fead**
hide and seek
falaich v -ach, hide, conceal
falaichte a hidden, concealed, secret
falamh a -aimhe empty, void
falamhachd n f emptiness, vacuum
falbh v go **air f.** gone away
falbhanach a -aiche wandering,
unsettled
fallain a -e healthy, wholesome, sound
slàn f. safe and sound
fallaineachd n f health
fallas n -ais m sweat, perspiration
bha (am) f. orm I was sweating
fallasach a -aiche sweaty
falmadair n -ean m helm
falmhaich v -achadh empty
falt n **fuilt, fuilt** m hair
famh n **faimh, faimh/-an** f m
mole (animal)
famhair n -ean m giant
fan v -tainn wait, stay, remain
fanaid n -e f mockery, mocking, derision
a' dèanamh f. air v mocking him,
deriding it
fànas n -ais m outer space **f.-long**
f spaceship
fa-near adv under consideration **thoir f.**
notice, observe, be aware of

fang n **faing, faing/-an** m fank,
sheep-pen
fann a -a/**fainne** faint, feeble, weak
fannaich v -achadh grow faint, faint,
weaken
fanntaig v -eadh faint
faobhar n -air, -an m edge (as of knife)
cuir f. air v sharpen it
faobharaich v -achadh sharpen
faochag n -aig, -an f whelk, winkle
faod def v may, can **am f. mi smocadh?**
may I smoke? **faodaidh tu fuireach**
you may/can wait/stay
faoileag n -eig, -an f seagull
faoilidh a -e generous, liberal, hospitable
Faoilleach/Faoilteach n -lich/-tich
m **am F.** January
faoin a -e vain, silly, pointless, futile
faoineas n -eis m vanity, futility **'s e f.
a th' ann** it's pointless
faoinsgeul n -eil/-a, -an m idle talk,
fiction, myth
faoisid n -e, -ean f confession (relig)
faoisidich v -deachadh confess (relig)
fao(tha)chadh n -aidh m relief, respite
far prep See **bhàrr**
far conj where **sin far a bheil iad** that's
where they are
faradh n -aidh, -aidhean m fare (price)
fàradh n -aidh, -aidhean m ladder
far-ainm n -e, -ean m nickname
faram n -aim m loud noise; percussion
faramach a -aiche noisy, resounding
farasta See **furasta**
farchluais n -e f eavesdropping
Also vn **a' f.**
fàrdach n -aich, -aichean f house,
dwelling, lodging
farmad n -aid m envy
farmadach a -aiche envious
farpais n -e, -ean f competition
farpaiseach n -sich, -sich m competitor
farsaing a -e wide, wide-ranging,
extensive **fad' is f.** far and wide
farsaingeachd n f width, extent, area
san fharsaingeachd in general, on the
whole
farsainn a -e See **farsaing**

farspag n **-aig, -an** f great black-backed gull

fàs n **fàis** m growth

fàs a **-a** empty, waste, desolate, fallow

fàs v grow, become **a' fàs sean** getting/growing old

fàsach n **-aich, -an** f m wilderness, desert

fàsachadh n **-aidh, -aidhean** m depopulation

fàsaich v **-achadh** depopulate, clear (of people), lay waste

fàsail a **-e/-ala** desolate (of places)

fasan n **-ain, -ain/-an** m fashion

fasanta a fashionable

fasgach a **-aiche** sheltered

fasgadh n **-aidh, -aidhean** m shelter

fa sgaoil adv loose

fasgnadh n **-aidh** m winnowing

fastadh n **-aidh, -aidhean** m hiring, employing, employment Formerly **fasdadh**

fastaidh v **-adh** hire, employ Formerly **fasdaidh**

fastaidhear n **-an** m employer Formerly **fasdaidhear**

fàth n m reason, cause, opportunity

fathann n **-ainn, -an** m rumour, hearsay

feabhas n **-ais** m improvement **a' dol am f.** getting better, improving, healing

feachd n **-an** f m army, host **F. an Adhair** the (Royal) Air Force

fead n **-an** f whistle (by person) **dèan/ geàrr f.** v whistle

fead v **-ail/-alaich/-arsaich/-aireachd** whistle

feadag n **-aige, -an** f whistle, flute; plover

feadaireachd n f whistling

feadan n **-ain, -ain** m chanter (of bagpipes); water pipe, water duct

feadh n m length **air f.** throughout, during (+ gen) **am f.** while, whilst

feadhainn n **feadhna/feadhnach** f people, some **f. aca** some of them **an fheadhainn sin** those **an fheadhainn dhearg** the red ones

feagal n See **eagal**

feàirrde a better **'s fheàirrd' thu sin** you are the better of that **b' fheàirrde mi norrag** I'd be the better of a nap

fealla-dhà n f fun, jest **ri f.** in fun/jest

feall-fhalach n **-aich, -aichean** m ambush

feallsanach n **-aich, -aich** m philosopher

feallsanachd n **-an** f philosophy

feamainn n **-ann/-mnach/feamad** f seaweed

feann v **-adh** skin, flay

feannag n **-aige, -an** f crow; lazybed (for planting), rig

feanntag n **-aige, -an** f nettle

feansa n **-ichean** f m fence

fear n **fir, fir** m man, male, one (referring to masculine subject) **am f. sin** that one **f. sam bith** anyone **f. an taighe** chairman (of concert)

fearail a **-e/-ala** manly, manful, brave

fearalachd n f manliness, manfulness

fearann n **-ainn** m land, ground **am mòr-fhearann** the common grazing

fearas-chuideachd n **fearais-** f diversion, pastime

fearas-feise n **fearais-** f homosexuality

fear-bainnse n **fir-, fir-** m bridegroom Also **fear na bainnse**

fear-breige n **fir-bhrèige, fir-** m puppet **na Fir Bhrèige** the Callanish Stones

fear-bùtha n **fir-, fir-** m shopkeeper Also **fear na bùtha**

fear-cathrach n **fir-, fir-** m chairman Also **fear na cathrach**

fear-ceàird n **fir-, fir-** m tradesman

fear-ciùil n **fir-, fir-** m musician

fear-deasachaidh n **fir-, fir-** m editor

fear-ealain n **fir-, fir-** m artist

feareigin pron someone (male)

fearg n **feirge** f anger, ire, wrath **cuir f. air** v anger, annoy **bha an fhearg air** he was angry/annoyed

feargach a **-aiche** angry

fear-gnothaich n **fir-, fir-** m businessman

fear-labhairt n **fir-, fir-** m spokesman

fear-lagha n **fir-, fir-** m lawyer (male)

feàrna n f alder

fear-pòsta n **fir-phòsta, fir-phòsta** m married man

feàrr a better **nas fheàrr** better **is fheàrr leis …** he prefers … **is fheàrr dhi …** she had better …

fearsaid n -e, -ean f spindle

fear-smàlaidh n **fir-, fir-** m fireman

fear-stiùiridh n **fir-, fir-** m director (male)

feart n **feirt, -an** f notice, attention **na toir f. air** pay no heed to him/it

feart n -a, -an m quality, virtue, characteristic

fear-teagaisg n **fir-, fir-** m teacher (male)

fear-togail n **fir-, fir-** m builder

feasgar n -air, -air/-an m afternoon, evening adv in the afternoon/evening **F. math** Good afternoon/evening **f. Diluain** Monday afternoon/evening

fèath n -a, -an f m calm (weather) **bha f. ann** it was calm

fèathach a calm (weather)

fèileadh n -lidh, -lidhean m kilt

fèill n -e, -(t)ean f festival; fair, market, sale **bha f. mhòr air** it/he was in great demand

fèin pron self, selves

fèin-àicheadh n -eidh m self-denial

fèin-dhìon n -a m self-defence

fèin-eachdraidh n -e, -ean f autobiography

fèineil a -e, -eala selfish

fèin-ìobairt n -e, -ean f self-sacrifice

fèin-mheas n m self-respect

fèin-mhurt n -mhuirt m suicide

fèin-riaghladh n -aidh m self-government

fèin-spèis n -e f self-regard, conceit, egotism

fèis n -e, -ean f festival **f. ciùil** music festival **Fèisean nan Gàidheal** the Festivals of the Gaels (org)

feis(e) n -e f sexual intercourse, copulation

fèist n -e, -ean f feast, banquet Formerly **fèisd**

fèith n -e, -ean f vein, sinew, muscle **fèithean borrach** varicose veins

fèith n -e, -ichean f bog, marsh; channel

feith v -eamh await, wait (for)

fèitheach a -thiche sinewy, muscular

feòcallan n -ain m ferret

feòil n **feòla** f meat **f.-caorach** n mutton **f.-muice** pork **f.-uan** lamb **mairt-fheòil** beef

feòirling n -ean f farthing

feòladair n -ean m butcher

feòlmhor a -a/-oire carnal, sensual

feòrag n -aig, -an f squirrel

feòraich v -ach/-achadh ask, inquire

feuch v -ainn try, test; see **f. ri …** try to … **f. gun tadhail thu** see and call/be sure to call **f. nach tuit thu** watch/see that you don't fall

feudar def v must **'s fheudar gu bheil …** it would seem that … **b' fheudar dhaibh** they had to

feum n -a, -annan f m use, need **a bheil f. agad air?** do you need it/him?

feum def v have to, need to, must **feumaidh mi falbh** I'll have to go **am f. thu sin a dhèanamh?** must you do that?

feumach a -aiche needy **bha sinn f. air** we needed it

feumail a -e/-ala useful

feumalachd n f use, utility, expediency

feur n **feòir** m grass, hay

feurach n -aich m pasture, grazing

feurach a -aiche grassy

feuraich v -achadh graze

feusag n -aig, -an f beard

feusagach a -aiche bearded

feusgan n -ain, -ain m mussel

Insight: fèis

It means a festival, and nowadays most people associate the word with the many *fèisean* set up for young people all over the country at which they learn songs, the playing of instruments, dancing etc. The co-ordinating body is Fèisean nan Gàidheal, based in Portree, Isle of Skye.

fhad is a *conj* while, whilst

fhathast *adv* yet, still

fhèin *pron* self, selves **leatha f.** by herself, alone **math f.** excellent

fhìn *pron Variation on* **fhèin** (*in first person only*)

fhuair *irr v* got (*See irr v* **faigh** *in Grammar*)

fiabhras *n* **-ais, -an** *m* fever **am f. ballach** typhus **am f. breac** typhoid

fiabhrasach *a* **-aiche** feverish

fiacail *n* **fiacla, fiaclan** *f* tooth **fiaclan fuadain** false teeth

fiach *n* **feich, -an** *m* worth, value; debt **fo fhiachaibh** indebted to, owing to **cuir mar fhiachaibh air** *v* oblige, compel **mar fhiachaibh oirnn(e)** incumbent upon us

fiach *a* **-a** worthwhile, worth **cha d' fhiach e** it's useless **is fhiach dhut seo fhaicinn** you should see this **'s fhiach e an t-saothair** it's worth the effort

fiach *v See* **feuch**

fiaclair *n* **-ean** *m* dentist

fiadh *n* **fèidh, fèidh** *m* deer

fiadhaich *a* **-aiche** wild, fierce; angry, furious

fialaidh *a* **-e** generous, liberal

fialaidheachd *n f* generosity, liberality

fiamh *n* **-a** *m* tinge, hue; fear; expression **f. a' ghàire** a hint of a smile

fianais *n* **-ean** *f* witness, evidence, testimony **tog f.** *v* give evidence; profess faith publicly **thoir f.** *v* witness, testify **am f.** in sight/view

fiar *a* **-a** crooked, bent, squint, slanted **f.-shùileach** squint-eyed

fiaradh *n* **-aidh** *m* bend, squint, slant **air f.** slanting, askew

fiathachadh *n* **-aidh, -aidhean** *m* invitation

fiathaich *v* **-achadh** invite

fichead *n* **fichid, -an** *m* twenty (+ *sg*) **trì f.** sixty

ficheadamh *a* twentieth

fideag *n* **-eig, -an** *f* whistle

fideis *n f* fidgeting *vn* **a' f.** fidgeting

fideiseach *a* **-aiche** fidgety

fidheall *n* **fidhle, fidhlean** *f* fiddle, violin

fidhlear *n* **-eir, -an** *m* fiddler, violinist; sandpiper

fidhlearachd *n f* fiddling

fige *n* **-an** *f* fig

figear *n* **-eir, -an** *m* figure (*arithmetic*)

figh *v* **-e** knit; weave

fighe *n f* knitting; weaving

figheadair *n* **-ean** *m* knitter; weaver

fighte *a* knitted; woven

fileanta *a* fluent

fileantach *n* **-aich, -aich** *m* fluent speaker

fileantachd *n f* fluency

filidh *n* **-ean** *m* poet

fill *v* **-eadh** fold; wrap

filleadh *n* **-lidh, -lidhean** *m* fold, plait

fillte *a* folded, plaited; compound

fine *n* **-achan** *f* clan, tribe, kindred

fineachail *a* **-e** tribal; fierce

finealta *a* fine, elegant

finn-fuainneach *a* all, entire **fad f. an latha** the livelong day, all day long

fiodh *n* **-a** *m* wood, timber

fiogais *n* **-ean** *f* fig

fiolan *n* **-ain, -an** *m* beetle, earwig **f.-gòbhlach** earwig

fìon *n* **-a** *m* wine **f. dearg** red wine **f. geal** white wine **f.-dhearc** *f* grape **f.-geur** vinegar **f.-lios** *m* vineyard

fìonan *n* **-ain, -ain/-an** *f m* vine

fionn *a* **-a** white, fair

fionnach *a* **-aiche** hairy

fionnadh *n* **-aidh** *m* hair (*of animals*)

fionnairidh *n* **-ean** *f* evening **air an fhionnairidh** in the evening

fionnan-feòir *n* **fionnain-, fionnain-** *m* grasshopper

fionnar *a* **-aire/-a** cool (*temp*)

fionnarachadh *n* **-aidh** *m* refrigeration

fionnarachd *n f* coolness (*temp*)

fionnaradair *n* **-ean** *m* refrigerator

fionnaraich *v* **-achadh** cool, refrigerate

fionnsgeul *n* **-eil/-eòil, -an** *m* legend

fìor *a* **-a/fìre** (*precedes & lenites n*) true, real, genuine, actual; very/really **f. mhath** very good **f. amadan** a real fool

fios *n* **-a** *m* knowledge, information **tha f. aice** she knows **cò aige tha f.?** who knows? **fhuair sinn f.** we got word **gun fhios nach ...** in case, lest ... **cuir f. thuca** *v* send them word **tha f. gun tadhail iad** surely they'll call

fiosaiche *n* **-an** *m* fortune-teller, seer

fios-naidheachd *n* **fiosan-** *m* press release

fiosrach *a* **-aiche** knowledgeable, well-informed

fiosrachadh *n* **-aidh, -aidhean** *m* information; experience

fiosraich *v* **-achadh** experience

fiosraichte *a* knowledgeable, informed

fir chlis *n m pl* **na F.** the Aurora Borealis, Northern Lights

fìreanachadh *n* **-aidh** *m* justification

fìreanaich *v* **-achadh** justify

fireann *a* male, masculine

fireannach *n* **-aich, -aich** *m* man, male

fìreantachd *n f* righteousness

fìr-eun *n* **-eòin, -eòin** *m* eagle

fìrinn *n* **-e, -ean** *f* truth, fact **an fhìrinn a th' agam** I'm telling the truth, it's true **a dh'innse na f.** to tell the truth **an Fhìrinn** the Bible

fìrinneach *a* **-niche** truthful, factual

fitheach *n* **fithich, fithich** *m* raven

fiù *n m* worth, value **gun fhiù** worthless, useless

fiù *a* worth **fiù is/'s** even **cha robh fiù 's sèithear ann** there wasn't even a chair there

fiùdalach *a* **-aiche** feudal

fiùdalachd *n f* feudalism

flaitheanas *n* **-ais** *m* heaven, paradise

flaitheas *n* **-eis** *m* heaven, paradise

flat *n* **-aichean** *f m* flat; saucer (*Lewis*)

flath *n* **flaith, -an/flaithean** *m* prince, chief

flathail *a* **-e** princely, noble

fleadh *n* **-a, -an** *m* feast, banquet

fleasgach *n* **-aich, -aich** *m* bachelor, youth; best man (*at wedding*)

fleòdradh *n* **-aidh** *m* floating, buoyancy **air f.** afloat

fleòdraich *v* **-radh** float

flin(ne) *n* **-(e)** *m* sleet

fliuch *a* **fliche/fliuiche** wet

fliuch *v* **-adh** wet, moisten

flod *n* **-a** *m* floating, flotation **air f.** floating, afloat

flodach *a* **-aiche** lukewarm (*liquid*)

flùr *n* **flùir, -aichean** *m* flower

flùr *n* **flùir** *m* flour

flùranach *a* **-aiche** flowery

fo *prep* (+ *dat*) under, below, beneath; under the influence of **fon bhòrd** under the table **fo uallach** worried

fo-aodach *n* **-aich** *m* underclothes, underwear

fochann *n* **-ainn** *m* corn in blade

fo-cheumnaiche *n* **-an** *m* undergraduate

fo-chomataidh *n* **-ean** *f* sub-committee

fod *aug prep* under your (*sg*)

fòd/fòid *n* **fòide, -ean** *f* turf, peat, clod **fon fhòid** underground, buried

fodar *n* **-air** *m* fodder, straw

fodha *adv* underneath, sunken **chaidh am bàta f.** the boat went down/sank

fodha(san) *prep pron* under him/it; below him/it

fodhad(sa) *prep pron* under/below you (*sg*)

fodhaibh(se) *prep pron* under/below you (*pl & pol*)

fodhainn(e) *prep pron* under/below us

fodham(sa) *prep pron* under/below me

fòdhpa(san) *prep pron* under/below them

fògair *v* **fògradh/-t** expel, banish

fògairt *n f* expelling, expulsion, banishing, banishment

fògarrach *n* **-aich** *m* exile, refugee

foghain *v* **fòghnadh** suffice **fòghnaidh sin** that will suffice **fòghnaidh na dh'fhòghnas!** enough is enough!

foghainteach *a* **-tiche** strong, powerful; (*met*) outstanding, impressive

foghar *n* **-air** *m* autumn, harvest **am f.** autumn **as t-fhoghar** in autumn

foghlaim *v* **-am** educate, learn

foghlaim(ich)te *a* educated, learned

foghlam *n* **-aim** *m* education **f. tron Ghàidhlig** Gaelic-medium education

fòghnan *n* **-ain** *m* thistle **F. na h-Alba** the Thistle of Scotland

fògradh *n* **-aidh** *m* expelling, expulsion, banishing, banishment

fòidhpe(se) *prep pron* under/below her

foighidinn *n* **-e** *f* patience

foighidneach *a* **-niche** patient

foileach *a* **-liche** over-hasty, blundering

foileag *n* **-eig, -an** *f* pancake

foill *n* **-e** *f* deceit, fraud, treachery

foillseachadh *n* **-aidh, -aidhean** *m* publishing, publication; revealing

foillsich *v* **-seachadh** publish; reveal

foillsichear *n* **-eir, -an** *m* publisher

foinne *n* **-an/-achan** *f m* wart

foirfe *a* perfect **dèan f.** *v* perfect

foirfeach *n* **-fich, -fich** *m* church elder

foirfeachd *n* *f* perfection

foirm *n* **-ean** *m* form (*document*)

foirmeil *a* **-e/-eala** formal

fòirneart *n* **-eirt** *m* violence, oppression

fois *n* **-e** *f* rest, leisure

follais *n* *f* openness, display, view, publicity **am f.** visible, displayed **thàinig e am f.** it became evident/public, it came to light

follaiseach *a* **-siche** obvious, evident, public

fom *aug prep* under my/their; below my/their

fòn *n* **-aichean** *f m* telephone

fòn/fònaig *v* **-adh/-eadh** telephone

fon *aug prep* under their, under the; below their, below the

fonn *n* **fuinn, fuinn** *m* tune, air; mood **dè 'm fonn a bh' air?** what form was he in?

fonnmhor *a* **-oire** *a* tuneful, melodious

for *aug prep* under/below our; under/below your

for *n* **foir** *m* awareness, alertness, attention **cha robh for aca gu ...** they had no idea that ...

forail *a* **-e** aware, alert

fo-rathad *n* **-aid/-rothaid, -an/-ròidean** *m* subway, underground route

forc(a) *n* **-a, -an/-aichean** *f* fork

fòr-chàin *n* **-e, -ean** *f* surtax

fòr-chìs *n* **-e, -ean** *f* surcharge

fòrladh *n* **-aidh** *m* leave, furlough

fo-roinn *n* **-e, -ean** *f* sub-division

forsair *n* **-ean** *m* forester

forsaireachd *n* *f* forestry

fortan *n* **-ain** *m* fortune, luck

fortanach *a* **-aiche** fortunate, lucky

fosgail *v* **-gladh** open

fosgailte *a* open, frank

fosgailteachd *n* *f* openness, frankness

fosgarra *a* open, frank, forthcoming, candid

fosgarrachd *n* *f* candour, openness

fo-sgiorta *n* **-ichean** *f* underskirt

fosgladh *n* **-aidh, -aidhean** *m* opening, aperture; opportunity

fosglair *n* **-ean** *m* opener (*implement*)

fo-thaghadh *n* **-aidh, -aidhean** *m* by-election

fo-thiotal *n* **-ail, -alan** *m* subtitle

fo-thìreach *a* subterranean

fradharc *n* **-airc** *m* eyesight, vision

Fraingis *n* *f* French (*lang*)

Frangach *n* **-aich, -aich** *m* French person *a* French

fraoch *n* **-oich** *m* heather

fras *n* **froise, -an** *f* shower (*of rain*)

fras *v* **-adh** shower

frasach *a* **-aiche** showery

frasair *n* **-ean** *m* shower (*in bathroom*)

freagair *v* **-t/-gradh** answer, reply, respond, suit

freagairt *n* **-ean** *f* answer, reply, response

freagarrach *a* **-aiche** suitable, appropriate

frèam *n* **-a, -aichean** *m* frame, framework **f. streap** climbing frame

freastal *n* **-ail** *m* providence; service *Formerly* **freasdal**

freiceadan *n* **-ain, -ain/-an** *m* guard, watch

freumh *n* **-a, -an/-aichean** *m* root, source

freumhaich *v* **-achadh** root

frìde *n* **-an** *f* insect

frids *n* **-ichean** *m* fridge, refrigerator

frioghan *n* **-ain, -ain** *m* bristle, barb

frionas *n* **-ais** *m* touchiness; fretfulness, vexation

frionasach *a* **-aiche** touchy; fretful, vexed

frìth *n* **-e, -ean** *f* deer forest

frith-ainm *n* **-e, -ean** *m* nickname

frith-bhaile *n* **-ltean** *m* suburb

frithealadh *n* **-aidh** *m* service (*catering*); attendance

fritheil *v* **-ealadh** attend, serve, wait on, minister (to)

frith-rathad *n* **-aid, -ròidean/-an** *m* lane, path

fròg *n* **fròige, -an** *f* hole, chink, niche, nook, den

froga *n* **-ichean** *m* frock

frogail *a* **-e** lively, cheerful

frois *v* **-eadh** scatter seed, thresh

fuachd *n* **-an** *m* cold (*atmos, med*) **bha am f. orm** I had the cold

fuadach *n* **-aich, -aichean** *m* banishment, expulsion **na Fuadaichean** the (Highland) Clearances

fuadaich *v* **-ach(adh)** expel, banish, chase away

fuadain *a* **-e** false, artificial

fuaigheal *n* **-eil** *m* seam, sewing

fuaigheil *v* **-eal** sew, stitch

fuaim *n* **-e, -ean** *f m* sound, noise

fuaimneach *a* **-niche** noisy

fuaimneachadh *n* **-aidh, -aidhean** *m* pronunciation

fuaimreag *n* **-eig, -an** *f* vowel

fuamhaire *n* **-an** *m* giant

fuar *a* **fuaire** cold

fuarachd *n f* dampness, mouldiness

fuaradair *n* **-ean** *m* refrigerator, fridge

fuaraich *v* **-achadh** cool, chill

fuaraidh *a* **-e** damp, chilly, mouldy

fuaralachd *n f* frigidity

fuaran *n* **-ain, -ain/-an** *m* spring (*water*), fountain

fuasgail *v* **-gladh** loosen, untie, release; solve, resolve

fuasgladh *n* **-aidh, -aidhean** *m* solution; release

fuath *n* **-a, -an** *m* hate, hatred, antipathy

fuathaich *v* **-achadh** hate, loathe, detest

fùc *v* **-adh** full (cloth), press, squeeze tightly

fùdar *n* **-air, -an** *m* powder

fùdaraich *v* **-achadh** powder

fuidheall *n* **-dhill** *m* remainder, financial balance

fuigheall *n See* **fuidheall**

fuil *n* **fala** *f* blood, gore **f.-mìos** period (*menstrual*)

fuilear *n* too much **chan fhuilear dhuinn** we need to **cha b' fhuilear dhaibh uile e** they would need it all

fuiling *v* **fulang** suffer, bear, endure

fuilteach *a* **-tiche** bloody

fuiltean *n* **-ein, -an** *m* single hair

fuin *v* **-e(adh)** bake

fuineadair *n* **-ean** *m* baker

fuireach *n* **-rich** *m* waiting, staying, dwelling

fuirich *v* **-reach** wait; stay, live **f. rium** wait for me **tha iad a' f. ann an Dùn Èideann** they live in Edinburgh

fùirneis *n* **-ean** *f* furnace

fulang *n* **-aing** *m* endurance, suffering

fulangach *a* **-aiche** suffering, patient; passive (*gram*) **fad-fhulangach** long-suffering

fulangas *n* **-ais** *m* suffering, passion (*of Christ*)

fulmair *n* **-e, -ean** *m* fulmar

furachail *a* **-e** watchful, vigilant, alert, attentive

furan *n* **-ain** *m* welcome, hospitality **fàilte is f.** a warm welcome

furasta *a* **fasa** easy **nas fhasa** easier *Formerly* **furasda**

furm *n* **fuirm, fuirm/furman** *m* form, bench; stool

furtachd *n f* relief, help, deliverance, solace

furtaich *v* **-achadh** relieve, aid, console

G

ga *aug prep* at his/its (+ *len*), at her/its **a bheil thu ga fhaicinn?** do you see him/it? **chan eil mi ga tuigsinn** I don't understand her

gabh *v* **-ail** take, hold; be possible **an do ghabh sibh biadh?** have you eaten? **g. brath air** take advantage of, exploit **g. os làimh** undertake **g. mo leisgeul**

excuse me **g. ri** accept, adopt, approve
g. a-steach include, encompass **g. òran**
sing a song **cha ghabh e (a) chreidsinn**
it's incredible **cho luath 's a ghabhas**
as soon as possible **gabhaidh e ceud**
it will hold a hundred
gàbhadh *n* **-aidh, -aidhean** *m* peril,
danger
gàbhaidh *a* **-e** perilous, dangerous
gabhail *n* **-alach, -alaichean** *m* lease,
tenure
gabhaltach *a* **-aiche** infectious,
contagious
gabhaltas *n* **-ais** *m* tenancy, tenure
gach *a* each, every
gad *n* **goid, goid/-an** *m* withe; goad
gad èisg a number of fish carried by
a withe, wire or string
gad *aug prep* at your **chan eil mi gad**
chreidsinn I don't believe you
gadaiche *n* **-an** *m* thief
gadhar *n* **-air, -air** *m* hound
gàg *n* **gàige, -an** *f* chink, fissure, chap
in skin
gagach *a* **-aiche** stuttering, stammering
Also **sgagach**
gàgail *n* **-e** *f* cackling
Gàidheal *n* **-eil, -eil** *m* Gael, Highlander
Gàidhealach *a* **-aiche** Highland **croan**
G. *m* Highland cattle
Gàidhealtachd *n* *f* **a' Ghàidhealtachd**
the Highlands
Gàidhlig *n* **-e** *f* Gaelic **a bheil G. agad?**
do you speak Gaelic? *a* Gaelic
gailbheach *a* **-bhiche** stormy
gailearaidh *n* **-ean** *f m* gallery
gaileis *n* *f* braces *pl* **-ean** *Also* **galais**
gailleann *n* **-linn, -an** *f* storm,
tempest
gainmheach *n* **-mhich/**
gainmhche(adh) *f* sand
gainne *n* *f* scarcity, shortage, want
gainnead *n* **-nid** *m* scarcity, shortage,
want
gain(n)eamh *n* **-eimh** *f* sand
gàir *n* **-e, -ean** *m* shout, roar
gàir *v* **-eachdainn/-eachdaich** laugh
gairbhe *n* *f* thickness; roughness

gàirdeachas *n* **-ais** *m* rejoicing, joy
dèan g. *v* rejoice
gàirdean *n* **-ein, -an** *m* arm
gàire *n* *f m* laugh **dèan g.** *v* laugh
gàireachdainn *n* *f* laughter, laughing
Also **gàireachdaich**
gairm *n* **-e, -ean/-eannan** *f* call, cry,
proclamation **g. coilich** cockcrow
gairm *v* call (out), cry (out), crow
(*as cockerel*); summon **g. coinneamh**
convene meeting
gairmeach *a* vocative **an tuiseal g.**
the vocative case
gàirnealair *n* **-ean** *m* gardener
gàirnealaireachd *n* *f* gardening
gaiseadh *n* **-sidh, -sidhean** *m* defect
in crops, blight **g. a' bhuntàta** potato
blight
gaisgeach *n* **-gich, -gich** *m* hero, warrior,
champion
gaisge(achd) *n* *f* heroism, bravery, valour
gaisgeil *a* **-e** heroic, brave, valorous
galan *n* **-ain, -an** *m* gallon
galar *n* **-air, -an** *m* disease **an g.**
roilleach/ronnach foot and mouth
disease *Also* **galair**
Gall *n* **Goill, Goill** *m* Lowlander, stranger
Innse G. the Hebrides
galla *n* **-chan** *f* bitch
gallan *n* **-ain, -ain/-an** *m* stalk; (*met*)
lad, hero
gallta *a* foreign, strange **G.** Lowland
a' Mhachair Ghallta the Lowlands *f*
Galltachd *n* *f* **a' Ghalltachd** the
Lowlands
gam *aug prep* at my **a bheil thu gam**
chluinntinn? do you hear me?
gamhainn *n* **gamhna/gaimhne,**
gamhna/gaimhne/gamhnaichean
m stirk, year-old calf
gamhlas *n* **-ais** *m* malice, hatred,
revenge
gamhlasach *a* **-aiche** malicious,
malevolent, vindictive
gan *aug prep* at their **cuin a tha thu**
gan coinneachadh? when are you
meeting them?
gann *a* **gainne** scarce, limited

gànraich v **-achadh** dirty, soil, besmirch
gaoid n **-e, -ean** f blemish, defect, flaw
gaoir n **-e, -ean** f noise, cry (of pain); thrill **chuir e g. nam fheòil** it made my flesh creep
gaoisid n **-e, -ean** f a hair
gaoisnean n **-ein, -einean** m a hair Also **gaoistean**
gaol n **gaoil** m love **tha g. agam ort** I love you **A ghaoil!** Love!
gaolach a **-aiche** loving, dear
gaoth n **gaoithe, -an** f wind **g. an iar** a westerly wind
gaothach a **-aiche** windy
gar v **-adh** warm, heat (especially self)
gar aug prep at our **chan eil e gar faicinn** he's not seeing us
gàradh See **gàrradh**
garaidh n **-ean** m den
garaids n **-ean** f garage
garbh a **gairbhe** rough, rugged, coarse; thick; wild (of weather) adv extremely **g. trang** very busy
garbhlach n **-aich, -aichean** m rugged terrain
garg a **gairge** fierce, ferocious
ga-rìribh adv See **dha-rìribh**
gàrlach n **-aich** m nyaff, impudent fellow
gàrradair n **-ean** m gardener
gàrradaireachd n f horticulture
gàrradh n **-aidh, -aidhean** m garden, wall, dyke **g. margaidh** market garden
gartan n **-ain, -ain/-an** m tick (insect); garter
gas n **-an** m gas
gas n **gaise, -an/gaisean** f stalk, stem
gasta a fine, splendid Formerly **gasda**
gath n **-a, -an/annan** m sting, dart; ray, beam (of light) **g. grèine** sunbeam
ge conj although **ge b' e** whoever, whatever
gèadh n **geòidh, geòidh** f m goose
geal a **gile** white
gealach n **-aich, -aichean** f moon **g. ùr** new moon
gealag n **-aig, -an** f sea trout
gealag-làir n **gealagan-** f snowdrop
gealagan n **-ain, -ain** m white of egg

gealbhonn n **-bhuinn, -an** m sparrow
geall n **gill, gill** m promise, pledge, bet, wager **cuir g.** v bet, wager
geall v **-tainn** promise, pledge; wager
gealladh n **-aidh, -aidhean** m promise, pledge **g.-pòsaidh** engagement (to marry), betrothal
gealltanach a **-aiche** promising, hopeful
gealltanas n **-ais, -ais** m promise, pledge
gealtach a **-aiche** cowardly, timorous, timid
gealtaire n **-an** m coward
gèam n **geama, geamannan/ geamachan/geamaichean** m game, match
geamair n **-ean** m gamekeeper
geamhrachail a **-e** wintry
geamhradh n **-aidh, -aidhean** m winter
geamhraich v **-achadh** winter, feed during winter
gean n **-a** m mood, humour **g. math/deagh ghean** goodwill
geanail a **-e** cheerful, pleasant
geanm-chnò n **-chnotha, -chnothan** f chestnut
geansaidh n **-ean** m jersey, sweater, jumper
gearain v **-an** complain, grumble, moan
gearan n **-ain, -an** f m complaint, moan, objection **dèan g.** v complain Also **gearain**
gearanach a **-aiche** complaining, grumbling, moaning Also **gearaineach**
gearastan n **-ain, -ain** m garrison Formerly **gearasdan**
geàrd n **geàird, -an** m guard
Gearmailteach n **-tich, -tich** m German a German
Gearmailtis n f German (lang)
geàrr n **-a, -an** f hare
geàrr a **giorra** short
geàrr v **gearradh** cut
gearradh n **-aidh** m cut, cutting **g. cainnte** sharp wit
geàrraidh n **-ean** m common grazing, pasture land
gearra-mhuc n **-mhuic, -mhucan** f guinea pig

Gearran n **-ain** m an G. February
geàrr-chunntas n **-ais, -an** m minute
(*of meeting*), summary
geas n **-a/geis, -an** f charm, spell **fo**
gheasaibh under a spell, spellbound
geasachd n **-an** f enchantment, charm
geata n **-ichean/-chan** m gate
ged conj though, although
ged-thà adv though
gèile n **-achan/-an** m gale
gèill v **-eadh** submit, yield, give in/way
geilt n **-e** f terror, fear
geimheal n **-eil, -mhlean** m fetter
geimhleag n **-eig, -an** f crowbar, lever
geir n **-e** f tallow, suet; fat
gèire n f sharpness, acuteness; bitterness
geòcach a **-aiche** gluttonous, voracious
geòcaire n **-an** m glutton
geòcaireachd n f gluttony
geodal n **-ail** m flattery
geodha n **-chan/-ichean** f m creek,
cove Also **geò**
geòla n **(-dh), -chan** f yawl, small boat
ge-tà adv though
geug n **gèige, -an** f branch (*of tree*)
geum n **-a/gèime, -an** m low, lowing,
bellow
geum v **-naich** low, bellow
geur a **gèire** sharp. sharp-witted,
discerning; bitter
geuradair n **-ean** m sharpener
geuraich v **-achadh** sharpen
geur-amhairc v **-amharc** scrutinize,
study closely
geurchuiseach a **-siche** perceptive,
discerning, shrewd
geur-leanmhainn n **-ean** m persecution
dèan g. v persecute
gheat n **-aichean** f yacht Also **geat**
gheibh irr v will get (*See* irr v **faigh**
in Grammar)
ghia exclam Yuch!
giall n **-a/gèille, -an** f jaw, jowl
gibearnach n **-aich** f m squid Also
gibneach
gibht n **-ean** f gift
Giblean n **-ein** m an G. April
gidheadh adv nevertheless, yet

gilb n **-e, -ean** f chisel Also **geilb**
gilead n **gilid** m whiteness
gille n **-an** lad, boy; servant **g.-cruidh**
cowboy **g.-frithealaidh** waiter, servant
g.-Caluim sword dance
gille-brìghde n **-bhrìghde, gillean-**
m oystercatcher
gille-mirein n **gillean-** m whirlygig
gin v **-eadh/-eamhainn** beget, generate,
reproduce
gin pron any, anyone, anything **a bheil**
g. agad? do you have any?
gine n **-achan** f gene
gineachas n **-ais** m genesis, beginning
gineadh n **ginidh** m conception
gineal n **-eil, -an** m offspring
ginealach n **-aich, -aich** m generation
gineamhainn n m conception, begetting
ginideach a genitive **an tuiseal g.**
the genitive case
ginidh n **-ean** m guinea
gintinn n m reproduction
gintinneachd n f genetics
giobach a **-aiche** hairy, shaggy
gìodhar n **-air, -dhraichean** m gear
(*in engine*)
gìogan n **-ain, -ain/-an** m thistle
giomach n **-aich, -aich** m lobster
gionach a **-aiche** greedy
giorna-giùirne n **-giùirnean**
f helter-skelter (*slide*)
giorra a See **goirid, geàrr**
giorrachadh n **-aidh** m shortening,
abbreviation; synopsis
giorrad n **-aid** m shortness, brevity
giorraich v **-achadh** shorten, abbreviate
gìosg n **-an** m creaking, gnashing
gìosg v **-ail** creak, gnash
giotàr n **-àir, -an** m guitar
giùlain v **-an** carry, bear; comport,
conduct (*oneself*)
giùlan n **-ain, -an** m carrying, carriage;
conduct, behaviour; bier
giullachd n f handling, treatment **droch**
ghiullachd maltreatment, being treated
badly
giuthas n **-ais** m fir, pine
g. Lochlannach spruce

glac *n* **glaice**, **-an** *f* hollow (*in land or hand*); narrow valley, defile

glac *v* **-adh** catch, seize, grasp

glag *n* **glaig** *m* thud, noise of something falling

glag *n See* **clag**

glagadaich *n* **-e** *f* rattling; prattling, loud talk

glaine *n f* cleanliness, purity

glainne *n* **-achan/-nichean** *f* glass **g.-sìde** barometer

glainnichean *n f pl* spectacles, glasses *Also* **glainneachan**

glaisean *n* **-ein**, **-an** *m* sparrow

glaiste *a* locked

glamh *v* **-adh** gobble, devour

glan *a* **glaine** clean, pure; splendid, fine

glan *adv* completely, totally **g. às a chiall** absolutely crazy

glan *v* **-adh** clean, wash

glaodh *n* **-oidh**, **-an** *f m* cry, call, shout

glaodh *v* **-ach/-aich** call, shout

glaodh *n* **-oidh** *m* glue

glaodh *v* **-adh** glue

glaodhaich *n m* shouting, calling, bawling

glaodhan *n* **-ain** *m* pith, pulp

glaoic *n See* **gloidhc**

glas *n* **glaise**, **-an** *f* lock **g.-làmh** handcuff

glas *a* **glaise** grey; (*of land*) green

glas *v* **-adh** lock

glas- *pref* grey-coloured

glasach *n* **-aich**, **-aichean** *m* green field

glasraich *n f* greens, vegetables

glè *adv* very, fairly (+ *len*) **g. mhath** very good/well, fairly good/well

gleac *v* **-adh** struggle, wrestle

gleadhraich *n f m* din, excessive noise

gleann *n* **glinne**, **glinn/-tan** *m* glen

gleans *n* **-a**, **-an** *m* shine **bha g. às** it shone

glèidh *v* **gleidheadh** keep, retain, preserve, observe

glèidhte *a* preserved, reserved, kept

glèidhteachas *n* **-ais** *m* conservation, preservation **neach-glèidhteachais** *m* conservationist

gleoc *n* **-a**, **-aichean** *m* clock

gleus *n* **-a**, **-an** *f m* order, trim; tune, key **air ghleus** in tune

gleus *v* **-adh** prepare; adjust; tune

gleusta *a* prepared; tuned; skilled; shrewd *Formerly* **gleusda**

glic *a* **-e** wise, prudent, sensible

gliocas *n* **-ais** *m* wisdom, prudence

gliog *n* **-a**, **-an** *m* click, tick, tinkle

gliong *n* **-a**, **-an** *m* clink, clang, jingle

gliongarsaich *n f* clinking, clanging

gloc *v* **-ail** cluck (*as of hen*), cackle

gloidhc *n* **-e**, **-ean** *f* fool, idiot **chan eil ann ach g.** he's just a fool

gloine *n See* **glainne**

glòir *n* **-e/glòrach** *f* glory; speech **droch ghlòir** bad language

glòir-mhiann *n* **-a** *f m* ambition

glòir-mhiannach *a* **-aiche** ambitious

glòraich *v* **-achadh** glorify

glòrmhor *a* **-oire** glorious

gluais *v* **gluasad** move

gluasad *n* **-aid**, **-an** *m* movement, motion; gait, carriage

gluasadach *a* **-aiche** moving, mobile

glug *n* **gluig**, **-an** *m* glug, gurgle; gulp

glugan *n* **-ain** *m* bubbling, gurgling

glumag *n* **-aig**, **-an** *f* small pool, puddle; mouthful of bile

glùn *n* **glùine**, **glùinean/glùintean** *f* knee **bean-ghlùine** *f* midwife *Also* **glùin**

glutach *a* **-aiche** gluttonous

glutaire *n* **-an** *m* glutton

gnàth *n* **-a**, **-an/-annan** *m* habit, custom, practice **a-ghnàth** always

gnàth *a* usual, habitual, common

gnàthach *a* **-aiche** customary, habitual, usual

gnàthasach *a* **-aiche** idiomatic

gnàthas-cainnt *n* **-e**, **gnàthasan-** *m* idiom

gnàth-fhacal *n* **-ail**, **-clan** *m* proverb

gnàths *n m* usage, habits

gnè *n f* kind, type, nature; sex, gender

gnìomh *n* **-an/-aran** *m* action, act, deed **cuir an g.** *v* put into practice, carry out

gnìomhach *a* **-aiche** active, industrious; executive

gnìomhachas *n* **-ais** *m* industry

gnìomhair *n* **-ean** *m* verb

gnoban *n* **-ein**, **-an** *m* little hill or knoll

gnog *n* **gnoig**, **-an** *m* knock

gnog *v* **-adh** knock
gnogadh *n* **-aidh, -aidhean** *m* knock, knocking
gnòsad *n* **-aid, -an** *f* grunt
gnòsadaich *n f* grunting *Also vn*
gnothach *n* **-aich, -aichean** *m* business, matter **a dh'aon ghnothach** on purpose, deliberately **an dèan siud an g.?** *v* will that do? **na gabh g. ris** *v* don't have anything to do with it **rinn iad an g.** *v* they managed; they won *Also* **gnothaich**
gnù *a* surly, sullen
gnuadh *a* **-aidhe** surly, gruff
gnùis *n* **-e, -ean** *f* countenance, face
gò *n m* blemish, defect, fault **gun ghò** faultless, without guile
gob *n* **guib, guib/-an** *m* beak, bill (*of bird*); sharp point (*of object*); (*colloq*) gob, mouth
gobach *a* **-aiche** nebby, brash; beaked
gobag *n* **-aig, -an** *f* nebby/brash female
gobha *n* **-nn/-inn, goibhnean** *m* smith, blacksmith
gobhal *n* **-ail/goibhle, goibhlean** *m* fork (*in road*); crotch
gobhar *n* **-air/goibhre, -air/goibhrean** *f m* goat
gòbhlach *a* forked; astride
gòbhlag *n* **-aig, -an** *f* earwig, forkie; (*implement*) fork
gòbhlan-gainmhich *n* **gòbhlain-, gòbhlanan-/gòbhlain-** *m* sand martin, swift

gog *n m* cluck, cackle
gogaid *n* **-e, -ean** *f* coquette, flirt
gogail *n f* clucking, cackling
goid *n* **-e** *f* theft, stealing
goid *v* steal
goil *v* boil **air ghoil** boiling
goile *n* **-an/-achan** *f* stomach; appetite
goileach *a* **-liche** boiling **uisge g.** *m* boiling water
goir *v* **-sinn** call
goireas *n* **-eis, -an** *m* facility, amenity, resource, convenience
goireasach *a* **-aiche** convenient
goirid *a* **giorra** short, brief *adv* shortly **o chionn ghoirid** recently *prep* near **g. dhan bhaile** near the town
goirt *a* **-e** sore, painful; sour
goirtean *n* **-ein, -an** *m* small field, enclosure
goirtich *v* **-teachadh** hurt *Also* **gortaich**
goistidh *n* **-ean** *m* sponsor, godfather; gossip (*person*)
gonadh *n* **-aidh** *m* wounding, stinging **g. ort!** blast you!
gòrach *a* **-aiche** foolish, silly, daft, stupid
gòraiche *n f* folly, silliness, stupidity
gorm *a* **guirme** blue; green (*of grass*); (*met*) green, naive
gort *n* **-a** *f* famine, starvation
gràbhail *a* **-e** disgusting *Also* **grobhail**
gràbhail *v* **-al/-aladh** engrave
gràbhalaiche *n* **-an** *m* engraver
grad *a* **graide** sudden, quick, swift, immediate **gu g.** suddenly, quickly

---

Insight: gorm

The Gaelic colour scheme is different! Referring to eyes, the sea, the sky, paint, *gorm* means blue or dark blue. Of grass, though, it means green! And in the slang *Chan eil thu cho gorm* – You're not so green (i.e., naive). In some areas, however, *liath* does duty for *gorm*.

---

gòbhlan-gaoithe *n* **gòbhlain-, gòbhlanan-/gòbhlain-** *m* swallow
goc *n* **-a, -an/-aichean** *m* tap, faucet, stopcock
gocan *n* **-ain, -an** *m* acolyte, pert little person; whinchat **g. cuthaige** cuckoo's follower, titlark

gràdh *n* **gràidh** *m* love **thugainn, a ghràidh** come on, love/dear
gràdhach *a* **-aiche** loving, dear, beloved
gràdhaich *v* **-achadh** love
gràdhag *n* **-aig** *f* love (*term of endearment applied to a woman*)
gràdhmhor *a* **-oire** loving

graf *n* **-a, -aichean** *m* graph
gràin *n* **-e** *f* loathing, abhorrence
  bha g. aice air she hated him/it
gràin-cinnidh *n* **gràine-cinnidh** *f* racism
gràineag *n* **-eig, -an** *f* hedgehog
gràineil *a* **-e** loathsome, abhorrent, disgusting, heinous
gràinich *v* **-neachadh** scunner, put one off, cause to hate/loathe
gràinne *n* **-an** *f* grain
gràinnean *n* **-ein, -an** *m* granule
gràisg *n* **-e, -ean** *f* rabble, mob
gram *n* **-a, -an/-aichean** *m* gram
gràmar *n* **-air** *m* grammar
gràn *n* **gràin, gràin** *m* grain, cereal
grànda *a* **gràinde** ugly
grannda *a* See **grànda**
gràpa *n* **-n** *m* graip, fork (*agric*)
gràs *n* **gràis, -an** *m* grace
gràsmhor *a* **-oire** gracious
greabhal *n* **-ail** *m* gravel
greadhnach *a* **-aiche** joyful, convivial; majestic
greadhnachas *n* **-ais** *m* joy, conviviality; pomp, majesty
greallach *n* **-aiche** *f* entrails, intestines
greann *n* **greinn** *m* scowl, irritation
  bha g. air he was scowling
greannach *a* **-aiche** wild, rough (*weather*); surly, crabbit, ill-tempered
greannmhor *a* **-oire** amusing, agreeable; comely
greas *v* **-ad** hasten, hurry **g. ort!** hurry up!
grèata *n* **-ichean** *m* grate
greideal *n* **-eil/-ach, -an** *f* griddle, girdle (*baking*)
grèidh *v* **-eadh** grill; groom (*eg horses*)
  droch ghrèidheadh bad treatment
greigh *n* **-e, -ean** *f* herd, stud
grèim *n* **-e, -ean/-eannan** *m* hold, grip, grasp; custody; morsel; stitch (*of clothing*) **g. làimhe** handshake
  g. bìdh a bite of food **an g. aig a' phoileas** in police custody
greimeil *a* **-e** resolute, firm, persistent
greimich *v* **-meachadh** grip, grapple, grasp
greis *n* **-e, -ean** *f* a while, spell (*of time*)

grèis *n* **-e** *f* embroidery **obair-ghrèis** *f* embroidery
greiseag *n* **-eig** *f* a short while
Greugach *n* **-aich, -aich** *m* Greek
  a Greek, Grecian
Greugais *n* *f* Greek (*lang*)
greusaiche *n* **-an** *m* shoemaker, cobbler
grian *n* **grèine** *f* sun **èirigh na grèine** sunrise *f* **dol fodha na grèine** *m* sunset
grianach *a* **-aiche** sunny
grinn *a* **-e** fine, elegant; neat; pretty
grinneal *n* **-eil** *m* gravel
grinneas *n* **-eis** *m* elegance
grìob *n* **-a, -an** *m* coastal precipice
grìogag *n* **-aig, -an** *f* bead
Grioglachan *n* **-ain** *m* **an G.** Pleiades, constellation
Griomasach *n* **-aich, -aich** *m* someone from Grimsay *a* from, or pertaining to, Grimsay
grìos *n* **-a, -achan** *m* grill
grìos *v* **-ad/-adh** blaspheme, swear
grìosad *n* **-aid** *m* blasphemy, swearing
grìosaich *v* **-achadh** grill
grìuthrach *n* **-aich** *f* **a' ghrìuthrach** measles *Also* **grìuthlach**
grod *a* **-a/groide** rotten, putrid
grod *v* **-adh** rot, putrefy
gròiseid *n* **-e, -ean** *f* gooseberry
gruag *n* **gruaig, -an** *f* hair; wig
gruagach *n* **-aiche, -aichean** *f* young woman, maiden
gruagaire *n* **-an** *m* hairdresser
gruaidh *n* **-e, -ean** *f* cheek (*of face*)
gruaim *n* **-e** *f* gloom, sullenness
gruamach *a* **-aiche** gloomy, sullen, stern
grùdadh *n* **-aidh** *m* brewing; distilling
  taigh-grùdaidh *m* brewery; distillery
grùdaire *n* **-an** *m* brewer; distiller
grùdaireachd *n* **-an** *f* brewing; distilling
grùid *n* **-e** *f* dregs
grunn *n* **gruinn** *m* several, a good number
grunnaich *v* **-achadh** wade, paddle (*in water*)
grunnan *n* **-ain, -annan** *m* a few, small group
grunnd *n* **gruinnd/-a, -an** *m* ground; bottom (*of sea*)

gruth *n* **-a** *m* crowdie, curds
grùthan *n* **-ain, -an** *m* liver
gu *adv pref* (*equivalent to* -(*i*)*ly in English adverbs*) *eg* **gu snog** nicely
gu *conj* that (*used to introduce positive subordinate clauses*) **chì mi gu bheil thu trang** I see that you're busy
gu *conj* so that; until **fuirich gu sia uairean** wait till six o'clock
gu *prep* to, towards
gual *n* **guail** *m* coal
gualaisg *n* **-e, -ean** *m* carbohydrate
gualan *n* **-ain, -an** *m* carbon
gualann *n* **-ainn/guailne, guailnean/guaillean** *f* shoulder *Also* **guala, gualainn**
guàna *n m* fertilizer
guanach *a* **-aiche** light, giddy
gu bràth *adv* forever
gucag *n* **-aig, -an** *f* bud, bubble
gucag-uighe *n* **gucaig-, gucagan-** *f* egg-cup
gud *aug prep* to your (*sg*)
gu dè? *interr pron* what?
gu dearbh *adv* indeed
gu deimhinn(e) *adv* certainly
guga *n* **-ichean** *m* young solan goose or gannet
guidh *v* **-e** wish; entreat, pray, implore
guidhe *n* **-achan** *f m* wish; entreaty; swear-word
guil *v* **gul** cry, weep *Also* **a' gal**
guilbneach *n* **-nich, -nich** *f m* curlew
guin *n* **-ean** *m* sting, pang, dart
guin *v* **-eadh** sting, wound
guineach *a* **-niche** stinging, venomous, wounding
guir *v* **gur** hatch, breed
guirean *n* **-ein, -an** *m* pimple, pustule
guirmean *n* **-ein** *m* indigo **g. an fhraoich** bluebell

guiseid *n* **-e, -ean** *f* gusset
gul *n* **guil** *m* crying, weeping
gu lèir *adv* altogether, completely, entirely
gu leòr *adv* enough, plenty, galore
gu leth *adj phr* and a half **uair gu l.** an hour and a half
gum *conj* that (*used to introduce positive subordinate clauses where verb begins in b, f, m, p*)
gum *aug prep* to my; to their
gùn *n* **gùin, gùintean** *m* gown
gùn-oidhche nightgown, nightie
gun *conj* that (*used to introduce positive subordinate clauses*)
gun *prep* (+ *len*) without
gun *aug prep* to the; to their
gun fhios nach *conj* in case, lest
gun fhiosta *adv* unawares, inadvertently
gunna *n* **-ichean/-chan** *m* gun
gur *n* **guir** *m* brood, hatch, incubation
gur *aug conj* that (*used to introduce positive subordinate clauses before nouns and adjectives*)
gur *aug prep* to you (*pl & pol*)
gur *aug prep* at your (*pl & pol*)
gur *aug prep* to our; to your (*pl & pol*)
gurraban *n* **-ain** *m* crouching, hunkering **bha e na ghurraban** he was crouching
gu ruig(e) *prep* up to, as far as, until
gus *prep* so that, in order to
gus *prep* to, until
gus *conj* so that, until
guth *n* **-a, -an** *m* voice; word, mention **cha chuala mi g.** I didn't hear anything **gun ghuth air ...** not to mention ..., to say nothing of ...
gu tur *adv* entirely, completely, totally, altogether

H

h- *part* (*used before words beginning in a vowel when preceded by* **a**)
hàidridean *n, a* **-ein** *m* hydrogen
hallò *exclam* hello

ham(a) *n m* bacon
hamstair *n* **-ean** *m* hamster
hangair *n* **-ean** *m* hangar; hanger
heactair *n* **-ean** *m* hectare

Hearach *n* **-aich**, **-aich** *m* someone from Harris *a* from, or pertaining to, Harris *Also* **Tearach**
heileacoptair *n* **-ean** *m* helicopter
Hiortach *n* **-aich**, **-aich** *m* someone from St Kilda *a* from, or pertaining to, St Kilda *Also* **Tiortach, Hirteach, Tirteach**
hocaidh *n* *m* hockey
hòro-gheallaidh *n* *f* *m* celebration, fling, rave
hù-bhitheil *n* *f* *m* stramash

Insight: Hiort

A common letter in Gaelic, h is normally used only in lenition or aspiration, and not many words start with it. Those that do are often place names, such as Hiort/Hirt, St Kilda, the famous remote group of islands evacuated in 1930, or Na Hearadh, Harris in the Hebrides.

I

i *pron* she, her, it
iad *pron* they, them **iad seo** these **iad sin** those
iadh-shlat *n* **-shlait** *f* honeysuckle
iadsan *emph pron* they, them
iall *n* **èill**, **-an** *f* thong, leash, strap; shoelace
ialtag *n* **-aig**, **-an** *f* bat (*mammal*)
Iapanach *n*, *a* **-aich**, **-aich** *m* Japanese
iar *n* *f* west **an taobh an i.** the west side **i.-dheas** south-west **i.-thuath** north-west
iar- *pref* deputy, vice-, assistant **i.-cheann-suidhe** *m* vice-president
iarainn *a* iron
iarann *n* **-ainn**, **-an** *m* iron (*metal, impl*) **a bheil an t-i. air?** is the iron on?
iar-cheumnach *a* postgraduate
iar-cheumnaiche *n* **-an** *m* postgraduate
iargain *n* *f* sorrow, grief, pain
iargalt(a) *a* **-ailte/-alta** surly, forbidding
iarla *n* **-n/-chan** *m* earl
iarlachd *n* *f* earldom
iar-leasachan *n* **-ain** *m* suffix
iarmad *n* **-aid**, **-an** *m* remnant; offspring, race
iarmailt *n* **-e**, **-ean** *f* sky, firmament
iarnaig *v* **-eadh** iron
iar-ogha *n* **-chan/-ichean** *m* great-grandchild **tha iad anns na h-iar-oghachan** they are second cousins

iarr *v* **-aidh** ask (for), request, seek, want **i. orra tadhal** ask them to call (in)
iarraidh *n* *f* demand; yearning
iarrtach *a* demanding
iarrtas *n* **-ais**, **-an** *m* request, demand, application
iasad *n* **-aid**, **-an** *m* loan **air i.** on loan **am faigh mi i. dhen pheann agad?** may I borrow your pen?
iasg *n* **èisg**, **èisg** *m* fish **i. locha** freshwater fish **i. mara** seafish
iasgach *n* **-aich** *m* fishing, angling **bha e ris an i. fad a bheatha** he was a fisherman all his life
iasgaich *v* **-ach** fish, angle
iasgair *n* **-ean** *m* fisherman, angler
iath *v* **-adh** surround, envelop, encircle
iathaire *n* **-an** *m* aerial
'ic *contr* short for **mhic** of the son **mac Iain 'ic Sheumais** the son of John son of James
idir *adv* at all
idrisgeach *a* **-giche** restless, fidgety
ifrinn *n* **-e**, **-ean** *f* hell
Ìleach *n* **Ìlich**, **Ìlich** *m* someone from Islay *a* from, or pertaining to, Islay
im *n* **ime** *m* butter **i. ùr** fresh butter **i. saillte** salted butter
imcheist *n* **-ean** *f* anxiety, perplexity, doubt **fo i.** anxious **bha i. oirre mu dheidhinn** she was worried about it

imich *v* imeachd go, depart, leave
imleag *n* -eige, -an *f* navel
imlich *v* lick
impidh *n* -e, -ean *f* entreaty, petition,
 persuasion **chuir e i. oirnn fuireach**
 he implored us to stay/wait
impire *n* -ean *m* emperor *Also* iompaire
impireachd *n* -an *f* empire *Also*
 iompaireachd
impis *n f* imminence **an i.** on the point
 of, about to

innleadair *n* -ean *m* engineer, inventor
 i. dealain electrical engineer
innleadaireachd *n f* engineering
innlich *v* -leachadh invent, devise,
 engineer
inns *v* -e(adh) (+ **do**) tell, relate **i. dhi**
 tell her
Innseanach *n* -aich, -aich *m* Indian *a*
 Indian
innte(se) *prep pron* in her(self), in it(self)
 's e cleasaiche a th' i. she's an actress

Insight: Innse Gall

The commonest word for island is *eilean: Na h-Eileanan Siar* – the
Western Isles. But *innis*, plural *innse*, is used in another name: *Innse
Gall* – the Islands of Strangers. The Vikings had invaded and settled
there, and this name indicates the view of the Hebrides then taken
by mainland Gaels.

imprig *n* -ean *f* removal (*house*), flitting
 rinn iad i. they flitted
imrich *n* -e, -ean *f* removal (*house*), flitting
inbhe *n* -an *f* rank, status, prestige
inbheach *n* -bhich, -bhich *m* adult
inbheach *a* -bhiche adult, mature
inbhir *n* -e, -ean *m* confluence, inver
inc *n f m* ink
ine *n* -an *f* nail (*on finger*); claw, talon
in-imrich *n* -e *f* immigration
in-imriche *n* -ean *m* immigrant
inneal *n* -eil, -an *m* machine,
 instrument, engine **i.-ciùil** musical
 instrument **i.-fighe** knitting
 machine **i.-measgachaidh** mixer
 i.-nigheadaireachd washing machine
innean *n* -ein, -an *m* anvil
innear *n* -arach *f* dung, manure *Also* inneir
innidh *n f* bowel
innis *n* innse, innsean *f* island;
 meadow, pasture
innis *v See* inns
Innis-Tileach *n* -Tilich, -Tilich
 m Icelander *a* Icelandic
innleachd *n* -an *f* invention, device,
 mechanism, scheme; ingenuity; wile,
 tactic
innleachdach *a* -aiche ingenious,
 inventive; cunning, tactical

inntinn *n* -e, -ean *f* mind, intellect
inntinneach *a* -niche interesting;
 encouraging, positive-minded
inntleachd *n* (-a) *f* intelligence, intellect
inntleachdail *a* -e intellectual
inntrig *v* -eadh enter
iobair *v* iobradh/-t sacrifice
iobairt *n* -e, -ean *f* sacrifice, offering
ioc *v* -adh pay, render
iochd *n f* mercy, clemency, compassion
iochdar *n* -air, -an *m* bottom, lower part
iochdaran *n* -ain, -an *m* subject, inferior,
 subordinate
iochdmhor *a* -oire merciful, clement,
 compassionate
iocshlaint *n* -e, -ean *f* medicine, balm
iodhal *n* -ail, -an *m* idol **i.-adhradh**
 idolatry
iodhlann *n* -ainn, -an *f* stackyard,
 cornyard
iogad *n* -aid, -an *m* ages, long time,
 yonks
iogart *n* -airt, -an *f m* yoghurt
ioghnadh *n See* iongnadh
iolach *n* -aich, -aich *m* shout, roar
 (*of triumph*)
iolair(e) *n* -(e)an *f* eagle **i.-uisge** osprey,
 sea eagle
iolra *n* -n *m* plural *a* plural

iomadach *a* (*precedes n*) many, many a, numerous

iomadh *a* (*precedes n*) many, many a, numerous

ioma-dhathach *a* **-aiche** multi-coloured

iomadh-fhillte *a* complex, compound, manifold

iomagain *n* **(-e)**, **-ean** *f* worry, concern, anxiety **fo i.** worried, concerned

iomagaineach *a* **-niche** worried, concerned, anxious

ioma-ghaoth *n* **-ghaoith**, **-an** *f* whirlwind

iomain *n* **-e** *f* shinty; driving (*as of cattle*)

iomain *v* play shinty; drive (*as of cattle*)

iomair *n* **-e**, **-ean** *m* ridge (*ploughed*), piece of land

iomair *v* **iomradh** row (*boat*)

iomairt *n* **-e**, **-ean** *f* enterprise, initiative; campaign, venture **dèan i.** *v* campaign

iomall *n* **-aill**, **-aill** *m* border, limit, edge, margin, periphery **i. a' bhaile** the suburbs

iomallach *a* **-aiche** remote, isolated, peripheral

iomarra *a* plural

ioma-shruth *n* **-a**, **-an** *m* cross-current, eddying stream or tide

iomchaidh *a* **-e** suitable, appropriate, proper, fitting

iomchair *v* **-ar** carry, bear

ìomhaigh *n* **-ean** *f* image, statue; countenance

iomlaid *n* **-e**, **-ean** *f* change, exchange

iomlan *a* **-aine** complete, whole, total **gu h-i.** altogether, entirely

iomnaidh *n f* concern, anxiety **chuir e i. oirnn** it worried us

iompachadh *n* **-aidh**, **-aidhean** *m* religious conversion

iompachan *n* **-ain**, **-ain** *m* convert (*relig*)

iompaich *v* **-achadh** convert (*relig*) **chaidh a h-iompachadh** she was converted

iomradh *n* **-aidh**, **-aidhean** *m* mention, report, reference; rowing (*boat*) **dèan i. air** *v* mention

iomraiteach *a* **-tiche** famous, renowned, celebrated

iomrall *n* **-aill**, **-an** *m* wandering, straying; error **chaidh sinn (air) i.** *v* we got lost

iomrallach *v* wandered, confused, mistaken

ionad *n* **-aid**, **-an** *m* place **i.-fàilte** reception (*area*) **i.-fiosrachaidh turasachd** tourist information centre **i.-slàinte** health centre

ionadail *a* **-e** local **riaghaltas i.** *m* local government

ionaghailt *n* **-e**, **-ean** *f* pasture, grazing

ionaltair *v* **-tradh** pasture, graze

ionaltradh *n* **-aidh**, **-aidhean** *m* pasture, grazing

ionann *a* same, equal, alike, identical **chan i. iad idir** they are not at all alike

iongantach *a* **-aiche** surprising; wonderful

iongantas *n* **-ais**, **-an** *m* surprise; wonder

iongar *n m* pus *Also* **ionghar**

iongarach *a* **-aiche** septic

iongnadh *n* **-aidh**, **-aidhean** *m* surprise, wonder **chuir e i. orm** it surprised me **is beag an t-i.** little wonder

ionmhainn *a* **-e/annsa** beloved, dear

ionmhas *n* **-ais**, **-an** *m* finance, riches, treasure **Roinn an Ionmhais** the Finance Dept

ionmhasail *a* **-e** financial

ionmhasair *n* **-ean** *m* treasurer

ion-mhiannaichte *a* highly desirable

ionmholta *a* praiseworthy, laudable, commendable

ionnan *See* **ionann**

ionndrainn *n f m* missing, longing (for)

ionndrainn *v* miss, long (for)

ionnlaid *v* **-ad** wash, bathe **seòmar/rùm i.** *m* bathroom

ionnsachadh *n* **-aidh** *m* learning; instruction

ionnsaich *v* **-achadh** learn; (+ *do*) teach

ionnsaichte *a* learned, educated

ionnsaigh *n* **-ean** *f m* attack, assault, onslaught, invasion **thug iad i. oirnn** *v* they attacked us **a dh'i.** (+ *gen*) to, towards

ionnsramaid *n* **-e**, **-ean** *f* instrument

ionracas *a* **-ais** *m* righteousness, integrity, probity
ionraic *a* **-e** righteous, honest, just
iorghail *n* **-ean** *f* tumult, uproar
iorram *n* **-aim, -aim** *m* rowing song; repetitive song or remarks
ìosal *a* **ìsle** low, lowly **gu h-ì.** down below
ire *n* **-an** *f* level, stage, grade, rate; maturity **an Ì. Choitcheann** Standard Grade (*exam*) **an Ard Ì.** Higher Grade (*exam*) **an ì. mhath** quite; almost **gu ì. mhòir** to a large extent **air tighinn gu ì.** having reached maturity
iriosal *a* **-aile** humble, lowly
irioslachd *n* *f* humility, lowliness
irioslaich *v* **-achadh** humble, humiliate
iris *n* **-e, -ean** *f* magazine, periodical
is *irr v* (*copula of verb* **to be**) am, is, are (*often abbreviated to* **'s**) **'s e oileanach a th' ann** he's a student
is *conj* and (*contr of* **agus**)
isbean *n* **-ein, -an** *m* sausage
ise *emph pron* she, her, it
ìseal *a See* **ìosal**
isean *n* **isein, -an** *m* chick, chicken; bird; young **droch i.** a bad egg (*colloq*), brat **i. deireadh linn** a tail-end baby
ìslich *v* **ìsleachadh** lower; humble

is mathaid *adv* perhaps, maybe
Israelach *n* **-lich, -lich** *m* Israeli *a* Israeli *Also* **Iosaraileach**
ist *interj* wheest, hist!, hush!, quiet!
ite *n* **-an** *f* feather; fin
iteach *n* **itich** *m* plumage
iteach *a* **itiche** feathered, feathery
iteachan *n* **-ain, -ain/-an** *m* weaver's bobbin
iteag *n* **-eig, -an** *f* small feather; flight **air (an) iteig** flying
iteagach *a* **-aiche** feathered, feathery
itealaich *v* **-achadh** fly
itealan *n* **-ain, -ain** *m* aeroplane
iteileag *n* **-eig, -an** *f* kite (*sport*)
ith *v* **-e** eat
iubailidh *n* **-ean** *f* jubilee
iubhar *n* **-air, -an** *m* yew
iuchair *n* **iuchrach, iuchraichean** *f* key; roe of fish
Iuchar *n* **-air** *m* **an t-I.** July
Iùdhach *n* **-aich, -aich** *m* Jew *a* Jewish
iùil-tharraing *n* **-e, -ean** *f* magnetism
iùil-tharraingeach *a* **-giche** magnetic
iùl *n* **iùil, iùilean** *m* guidance, direction **neach-iùil** *m* guide
Iupatar *n* **-air** *m* Jupiter
iutharn(a) *n* *f* hell

L

là *n* **làithean/lathaichean** *m* day
làbha *n* *f* lava
labhair *v* **-t** speak, talk
labhairt *n* *f* speaking, talking **neach-l.** *m* spokesperson
lach *n* **-a, -an/-ain** *f* wild duck
lachan *n* **-ain, -ain** *m* guffaw **l.-gàire** hearty laugh
lachanaich *n* *f* laughing heartily
lachdann *a* **-ainne** dun, tawny, swarthy, sallow
ladar *n* **-air, -an** *m* ladle
ladarna *a* bold, shameless, blatant, presumptuous
ladarnas *n* **-ais** *m* boldness, shamelessness, presumptuousness
ladhar *n* **-air/-dhra, -dhran** *m* hoof

lag *n* **laig/luig, -an** *f m* hollow; dent
lag *a* **laige** weak, feeble, faint
lagaich *v* **-achadh** weaken, undermine *Also intrans*
lagais *n* **-ean** *f* rubbish dump, slag heap
lagan *n* **-ain, -an** *m* small hollow
lagchuiseach *a* **-siche** faint-hearted, unenterprising, weak-willed
lagh *n* **-a, -annan** *m* law **dèan l.** *v* legislate **l. baile** bye-law
laghach *a* **-aiche** nice, pleasant, fine
laghail *a* **-e** lawful, legal
laghairt *n* **-ean** *f m* lizard
Laideann *n* **-dinn(e)** *f* Latin
làidir *a* **-e** strong, robust
laige *n* *f* weakness, faintness

laigh v -e lie (down) **a' dol a laighe** going to bed

laigse n -an/-achan f weakness, defect **chaidh e ann an l.** he fainted

làimh ri adv near, close to

làimhsich v -seachadh handle, treat

laimrig n -e, -ean f landing-place, small harbour Also **laimhrig**

lainnir n -e f radiance, glitter

lainnireach a -riche radiant, glittering, gleaming

làir n -e/làrach, -ean/-idhean/-ichean f mare **l.-bhreabaidh** rocking-horse **l.-mhaide** see-saw

laiste a lit

làitheil a daily

làmh n làimhe, -an f hand **l. ri làimh** hand in hand **an l. dheas/cheart** the right hand **an l. chlì/cheàrr** the left hand **l.-an-uachda(i)r** the upper hand **gabh os làimh** v undertake **ri làimh** at hand **obair-làimhe** f manual work **rug e air làimh oirre** he shook hands with her

làmhachas-làidir n **làmhachais-** m force

làmhagh n -aigh, -aighean f hand-axe Also **làmhag**

làmhchair a -e handy, dexterous

làmh-sgrìobhadh n -aidh m handwriting

làmh-sgrìobhainn n -e, -ean f manuscript

lampa n -ichean f m lamp

làn a làine full, complete **tha mi l.-chinnteach** I'm quite sure/certain **tha l.-earbs' agam ann** I have complete confidence in him **tha a l.-thìd' agad ...** it is high time you ... **làn-ùine** full-time

làn n làin, làin m tide **l. àrd** a high tide **l.-mara** (high) tide

langa n -an/-annan f ling (*fish*)

langan n -ain, -an m bellowing (*of deer*), bellow

langanaich n -e f lowing, bellowing (*of deer*)

langasaid n -e, -ean f sofa, couch, settee

lann n lainn, -an f enclosure, repository

lann n -a/lainne, -an f blade, sword; scale (*on fish*)

lannsa a -ichean f lance, lancet

lannsair n -ean m surgeon

lanntair n -ean m lantern Also **lainntear** f

laoch n laoich, laoich m hero, warrior, champion

laochan n -ain, -ain m little hero (*term of endearment*) **sin thu fhèin, a laochain** well done, my lad/little pal

laogh n laoigh, laoigh m calf

laoidh n -e, -ean f m hymn, anthem, lay

laoidheadair n -ean m hymnbook

lapach a -aiche weak, feeble, frail

làr n làir, làir/-an m floor, ground

làrach n -aich, -aichean f m site; ruin **l.-lìn** website **an l. nam bonn** on the spot, immediately

làraidh n -ean f lorry **l. an sgudail** the bin/refuse lorry

làrna-mhàireach adv the next day

las v -adh light

lasachadh n -aidh, -aidhean m slackening; discount, rebate

lasadair n -ean m match (*to light*)

lasadh n -aidh, -aidhean m lighting; flash

lasaich v -achadh slacken, ease off

lasair n lasrach, lasraichean f flame

Insight: làn

As an adjective, it means full. *Tha e làn* – It's full. As an adverb, fully – *làn-chinnteach*, quite certain. As a noun, it can mean fullness, but very commonly it refers to the tide: *làn àrd* – a high tide, *làn reothairt* – a spring-tide. Notice also *loma-làn* – completely full, packed.

lasgan *n* -ain, -ain *m* outburst **l. gàire**
hearty laugh, peal of laughter
lasganaich *n* -e *f* hearty laughter
lasrach *a* -aiche flaming
lastaig *n*, *a f* elastic
lath *v* -adh numb **theabadh mo**
lathadh I was nearly frozen
latha *n* làithean/-ichean *m* day
Latha na Sàbaid the Sabbath, Sunday
l.-breith birthday **latheigin** *adv* some
day **l.-fèille** public holiday, fair day
L. Luain Doomsday **làithean-saora/**
saor-làithean holidays **l. brèagha air**
choreigin some fine day **nach ann**
oirnn a thàinig an dà l.! how our
circumstances have changed!
làthach *n* -aich/làthcha *f* mire, clay
làthair *n* -e *f* presence **an l.** present
le *prep* (+ *dat*) with, by **'s ann le Iain**
a tha e it belongs to John **le chèile**
both, together
lèabag *n* -aig, -an *f* flounder
leabaidh *n* leapa, leapannan *f* bed
Also **leaba**
leabhar *n* -air, leabhraichean *m* book
L. Aithghearr nan Ceist the Shorter
Catechism **l.-iùil** guidebook **l. latha**
diary **l.-seòlaidh** address book
l.-sgrìobhaidh notebook
leabharlann *n* -ainn, -an *f m* library
leabharlannaiche *n* -an *m* librarian
leabhrachan *n* -ain, -ain *m* pamphlet,
brochure
leabhran *n* -ain, -ain/-an *m* booklet
leac *n* lic/lice, -an *f* flagstone, slab,
flat stone; tombstone
leag *v* -ail knock down, fell, demolish
l. boma drop a bomb
leagh *v* -adh melt, dissolve, smelt;
liquidate
leaghadair *n* -ean *m* smelter
leam(sa) *prep pron* with me; by me **leam**
fhìn alone **'s ann leamsa**
a tha e it's mine **leam-leat** fickle,
non-committal
leamh *a* -a vexing; sarcastic; importunate
leamhaich *v* -achadh vex, irk, irritate;
importune

leamhan *n* -ain *m* elm
leamhnagan *n* -ain, -an *m* stye (*in eye*)
lean *v* -tainn/-tail follow, continue,
pursue **l. ort!** continue!, keep going!
ri leantainn to follow/be continued
leanabachd *n f* childhood, infancy,
childishness
leanabail *a* -e childish, juvenile
leanaban *n* -ain, -an *m* infant,
small child
leanabh *n* -aibh, -an/leanaban
m child, infant, baby
lèanag *n* -aig, -an *f* little meadow, lawn
leanailteach *a* -tiche continuous,
lingering
leann *n* -a, -tan *m* beer, ale; (*any*) liquid
leannan *n* -ain, -ain *m* lover, sweetheart
leannanachd *n f* courtship
leann-dubh *n* -duibh *m* melancholy
leantail/leantainn *n f m* following,
continuing
leantainneach *a* -niche continuous,
lingering; sticky
leantainneachd *n f* continuity
Also **leantalachd**
learag *n* -aige, -an *f* larch
learg *n* -a *f* black-throated diver
leas *n m* benefit, advantage **cha**
leig/ruig thu l. *v* you needn't (bother)
leas- *pref* depute, deputy **l.-stiùiriche**
m deputy director
leasachadh *n* -aidh, -aidhean
m development, improvement,
reformation, supplement **an t-Ath-L.**
the Reformation **l.-fala** blood
transfusion
leasaich *v* -achadh develop, improve,
rectify; fertilize
leasaichte *a* developed, improved,
rectified; fertilized
leasan *n* -ain, -ain/-an *m* lesson
leat(sa) *prep pron* with/by you (*sg*)
leatas *n* -ais, -an *m* lettuce
leatha(se) *prep pron* with/by her
leathad *n* -aid/leothaid, -an/leòidean
m slope, brae
leathann *a* leatha/leithne broad, wide
Also **leathainn**

leathar *n* **-air** *m* leather
led *aug prep* with/by your (*sg*)
leibh(se) *prep pron* with/by you
  (*pl & pol*)
leibideach *a* **-diche** inept, defective;
  accidental, unfortunate
leig *v* **-eil** let, allow, permit **l. anail** draw
  breath, take a breather **l. leatha** leave
  her alone **na l. dad ort** don't let on
  l. ort nach eil fhios agad pretend you
  don't know **l. mu sgaoil** release **l. ris**
  reveal, show
leigeadh *n* **-gidh** *m* letting, allowing;
  discharge (*from boil etc*)
leigeil *n* **-ealach** *m* letting, allowing
  l. fala blood-letting
lèigh *n* **-e, -ean** *m* surgeon, physician
  l.-lann *f m* surgery
leigheas *n* **-eis, -an** *m* cure, remedy,
  healing **l.-inntinn** psychiatry
lèigh-eòlas *n* **-ais** *m* medicine (*science*)
leighis *v* **-gheas** cure, heal
lèine *n* **lèintean** *f* shirt **l.-mharbh** shroud
leinn(e) *prep pron* with/by us
lèir *a* visible, clear
lèir *a* altogether **gu l.** altogether, in total
lèir *v* **-eadh** torment, pain
lèirmheas *n* **-eis, -an** *m* review (*liter*),
  overview
lèirsgrios *n* **-an** *m* total destruction,
  utter ruin
lèirsinn *n* **-e** *f* vision, sight; insight,
  perception
lèirsinneach *a* **-niche** discerning,
  perceptive, enlightened, visionary;
  visible
leis *prep* with, by (+ *def art*); his;
  downwards **l. an droch shìde** because
  of the bad weather **l. a' bhrutha(i)ch**
  down the brae/hill
leis(-san) *prep pron* with/by him; his
  an ann leis-san a tha e? is it his?
leisg *a* **-e** lazy, slothful; reluctant
leisg(e) *n f* laziness, sloth, reluctance
  bha l. air faighneachd he was reluctant
  to ask
leisgeadair *n* **-ean** *m* lazy person,
  lazybones

leisgeul *n* **-eil, -an** *m* excuse, apology
  (*for absence*) **gabh mo l.!** excuse me!,
  pardon me!
leiteachas *n* **-ais** *m* partiality, bias
leithid *n* **-e, -ean** *f* such, the like **chan**
  fhaca duine riamh a l. no one has ever
  seen the like
leitir *n* **-e/leitreach, -ean/leitrichean**
  f hillside, slope
lem *aug prep* with/by my
len *aug prep* with/by their
leòbag *n f See* **lèabag**
Leòdhasach *n* **-aich, -aich** *m* someone
  from Lewis *a* from, or pertaining to,
  Lewis
leòinteach *n* **-tich, -tich** *m* wounded
  person, casualty
leòm *n* **leòim(e)** *f* pride, conceit
leòmach *a* **-aiche** well-dressed,
  smart (*dress*); conceited
leòman *n* **-ain, -ain** *m* moth
leòmhann *n* **-ainn, -ainn** *m* lion
  l.-mara sea lion
leòn *n* **leòin, -tan** *m* wound
leòn *v* **leòn/-adh** wound
leònte *a* wounded, afflicted
leòr *n f* enough, sufficiency **an d' fhuair**
  thu do l.? did you get enough/your fill?
  gu l. plenty, enough **ceart gu l.** OK
l(e)òsan *n* **-ain, -ain** *m* window pane
leotha(san) *prep pron* with/by them
ler *aug prep* with/by our; with/by your
leth *n m* half *a* separate **air l.** exceptional
  às l. on behalf of **fa l.** each one,
  individually **gu l.** and a half **l. mar l.** half
  and half, share and share alike
leth- *pref* half-, semi-
leth-aon *n* **-aoin, -an** *m* twin
lethbhreac *n* **-ric, -ric** *m* copy,
  photocopy, duplicate **dèan l.** *v* duplicate
leth-bhreith *n* **-e** *f* partiality,
  discrimination **dèan l.** *v* discriminate
leth-bhruich *v* (**-eadh**) parboil, half-boil
lethchar *adv* somewhat
leth-chas *n* **-choise, -an** *f* (only) one foot
  air leth-chois on one foot
lethcheann *n* **-chinn, -chinn** *n* temple,
  side of head, cheek (*phys*)

leth-chearcall n -aill, -aill/-an m
semi-circle
leth-cheud n -an m fifty (+ sg)
l. bliadhna fifty years
lethchiallach n -aich, -aich m half-
witted person
leth-chruinne n -an m hemisphere
leth-chrùn n -chrùin, -chrùin/-
chrùintean m half-crown
leth-chuairt n -e, -ean f semi-circle
letheach a half **l. slighe** half-way
leth-fhacal n -ail, -ail/-fhaclan m
byword
leth-làmh n -làimhe, -an f (only) one
hand
leth-mhìle n -mhìltean m half-mile;
five hundred
lethoireach a isolated, remote
leth-phinnt n -ean m half pint
leth-phunnd n -phuinnd, -phuinnd
m half pound
leth-shùil n -shùla, -ean f (only) one eye
leth-uair n -uarach, -ean f half-hour
l. an dèidh uair half past one
leud n leòid, -an m breadth, width
leudaich v -achadh broaden, widen,
expand, enlarge
leug n lèig, -an f jewel, precious stone
leugh v -adh read
leughadair n -ean m reader
leughadh n -aidh m reading
leum n lèim/-a, -annan f m leap,
jump, spring **l.-àrd** high jump **l. droma**
lumbago **l.-fhada** long jump
leum v leum/-adaich leap, jump, spring
l. a sròn she had a nosebleed
leumadair n -ean m jumper (sport);
dolphin
leus n leòis, leòis m ray, light; blister
lì n lighe, lighean f tinge, hue; surface
film
liac v -radh smear, spread
liagh n lèigh, -an f ladle; blade of oar
liath a lèithe grey, blue-grey, blue;
grey-haired
liath v -adh make grey, become grey
tha fhalt air liathadh his hair has
gone grey

liath- pref grey-tinted
liath-reothadh n -reothaidh m
hoar-frost
lìbhrig v -eadh deliver
lìbhrigeadh n -gidh, -gidhean m
delivery (not phys)
lideadh n lididh, lididhean m syllable
Also **lide**
lighiche n -an m doctor, physician
l.-inntinn psychiatrist **l.-sprèidh**
veterinary surgeon
lilidh n -ean f lily
lìnig v -eadh line (clothes etc)
lìnigeadh n -gidh, -gidhean m lining
(in clothes) Also **lìnig**
linn n -e, -tean f m century, age,
generation, era **ri l.** because of (+ gen)
linne n -achan/linntean f pool, pond
liobasta a unwieldy, ungainly
liodraig v -eadh beat up, leather
liogach a -giche sly, cunning
liomaid n -e, -ean f lemon Also **liomain**
lìomh n -a f polish, gloss
lìomh v -adh polish
lìomharra a polished, glossy
lìon n lìn, lìn, -tan m net, web **l. iasgaich**
fishing net **lìn-mhòra** long-lines
lìon n lìn m flax, lint
lìon v -adh fill, replenish
lìonadh n -aidh m filling, replenishing;
incoming tide
lìonmhor a -a numerous, plentiful
lionn n -a, -tan m (any) liquid Also **leann**
lios n -a/lise, -an f m garden
Liosach n -aich, -aich m someone from
Lismore a from, or pertaining to, Lismore
liosta n -ichean f list (written)
liotach a -aiche lisping, slurring
liotair n -ean m litre
lip n -e, -ean f lip
lite n f porridge
litir n litreach, litrichean f letter
litreachadh n -aidh m spelling,
orthography
litreachas n -ais m literature
litrich v -reachadh spell
liubhair v -t (not phys) deliver
liùdhag n -aig, -an f doll

liùg v **-adh** creep, steal, sneak a look at
liùgach a **-aiche** creeping, sneaking
liùgh n **-a, -achan** f lythe Also **liugha**
liut n **liuit** f knack, aptitude **l. air ...** aptitude for ...
liuthad a so many (precedes n)
lobh v **-adh** rot, putrefy
lobhadh n **-aidh** m rot
lobhar n **-air, -air** m leper
lobhta n **-ichean** m loft; storey Also **lobht**
lobhte a rotten, putrid Also **loibh(t), leath**
locair n **-ean/locraichean** f carpenter's plane
locair v **locradh** plane
loch n **-a, -an** f m loch, lake **l.-mara** sea loch
loch-bhlèin n f groin
lochan n **-ain, -ain** m small loch
lochd n **-a, -an** m fault, defect, malice
lochdach a **-aiche** faulty, harmful, malicious
Lochlannach n **-aich, -aich** m Scandinavian, Viking a Scandinavian, Viking
lòchran n **-ain, -ain** m lantern, lamp
lod n **-a, -an** m load
lof n **-a, -aichean** f m loaf
logaidh n **-ean** m forelock, fringe (of hair), mane
loidhne n **-nichean** f line **l.-taice** helpline
loidse n **-achan** f m lodge
loidseadh n **-sidh, -sidhean** m lodging
loidsear n **-eir, -an** m lodger
loineadh n **-nidh** m rubbing; drubbing
lòineag n **-eige, -an** f flake, snowflake; small tuft of wool
loingeas n **-eis** m ship; fleet, navy **l.-cogaidh** warship Also **luingeas**
loinid n **-e, -ean** f churn, whisk
lòinidh n f m **an l.** rheumatism, sciatica
loinn n **-e** f elegance, comeliness, fine finish **tha l. air** it is elegant
loinneil a **-e** elegant, comely
loireach a **-riche** soiled, bedraggled, messy

loireag n **-eig, -an** f untidy or messy female
loisg v **losgadh** burn, inflame, fire
loisgte a burnt
lom a **luime** bare, naked; thin, threadbare
lom v **-adh** make bare, shear, shave
lomadair n **-ean** m shears; shearer, shaver, mower
lomadh n **-aidh** m making bare, shearing, fleecing, shaving, mowing
lomair v **lomradh** mow, shear, fleece
lomaire n **-an** m mower, shearer
loma-làn a brimful, completely full
lomnochd a naked, bare, undressed n f nakedness, nudity
lon n **loin, loin** m elk
lòn n **lòin, lòintean** m pool; meadow
lòn n **lòin** m food, provisions, lunch; livelihood
lon-dubh n **loin-duibh, loin-dubha** m blackbird
long n **luinge, -an** f ship **l.-bhriseadh** m shipwreck **l.-chogaidh** warship **l.-fànais** spaceship **l.-fo-mhuir** submarine
lorg n **luirge, -an** f track, trace; staff, stick **a bheil l. agad air?** do you know where it/he is?
lorg v find, discover; trace, search for
los conj so that, because **air l.** for, on account of
losgadh n **-aidh, -aidhean** m burn, burning, combustion, firing **l.-bràghad** heartburn
losgann n **-ainn, -an** m toad; frog
lot n **-a, -aichean** f allotment, croft
lot n **-a, -an** m wound
lot v **-adh** wound
loth n **-a, -an** f m filly, colt
luach n m value, worth
luachair n **luachrach** f rushes
luachmhor a **-oire** valuable, precious
luadh n **luaidh, luaidh(ean)** m waulking (of tweed), fulling (cloth) **òran luaidh** waulking song Also **luadhadh**
luaidh v **luadh** waulk, full (tweed)
luaidh n f m mention; praise; beloved person **dèan l. air** v make mention of **mo l.** my dear

luaidh v mention, praise
luaidh(e) n -e f m lead
luaineach a -niche restless, fickle
luaireag n -eig, -an f storm petrel
luaisg v **luasgadh** shake, toss, rock, wave, swing
luaisgeanach a -aiche shaking, tossing, swaying, unsettled
luamhan n -ain, -an m lever
luasgan n -ain, -an m shaking, tossing, swaying
luath n **luaith/-a** f ash, ashes *Also* **luaithre**
luath a **luaithe** fast, swift, speedy
luathaireach a -riche mischievous, high-spirited (*of child*)
luaths n **luaiths** m speed, swiftness, velocity
lùb n **lùib, -an** f bend, curve
lùb v -adh bend
lùbach a -aiche bending, winding; pliant
lùbte a bent
luch n -a, -ainn/-an f mouse **l.-fheòir** fieldmouse
luchag n -aig, -an f little mouse
lùchairt n -e, -ean f palace
lucharan n -ain, -ain f dwarf
luchd n m people *used to form collective nouns for groups of people eg* **neach-cunntais** accountant **l.-cunntais** accountants
luchd n -a, -an m load, cargo
luchdaich v -achadh load
luchd-aideachaidh n m professing Christians
luchd-amhairc n m spectators
luchd-casaid n m accusers, prosecution **l.-c. a' Chrùin** the Crown prosecutors
luchd-ceanna(i)ch n m buyers
luchd-ciùil n m musicians
luchd-coimhid n m spectators, observers
luchd-dàimh n m kindred
luchd-ealain n m artist(e)s
luchd-èisteachd n m audience, listeners
luchd-eòlais n m acquaintances
luchd-foillseachaidh n m publishers
luchd-fòirneirt n m terrorists, oppressors

luchd-frithealaidh n m attendants; waiters, waitresses
luchd-leughaidh n m readers, readership
luchd-naidheachd n m journalists, reporters
luchd-obrach n m workers, staff
luchd-riaghlaidh n m rulers
luchd-sàbhalaidh n m rescuers
luchd-seinn n m singers
luchd-sgrùdaidh n m inspectors **l.-s. nan sgoiltean** school inspectors
luchd-siubhail n m travellers
luchd-smàlaidh n m firefighters
luchd-stiùiridh n m directors
luchd-tagraidh n m pleaders, advocates
luchd-trusaidh n m collectors **l.-t. nam fiach** debt collectors
luchd-turais n m tourists
lùdag n -aig, -an f (the) little finger, pinkie; hinge
luga n -n/-ichean f lugworm, sandworm
lugha a less, least **is l. orm e** I can't stand it/him
lùghdachadh n -aidh m decrease, reduction, lessening, diminution, downturn
lùghdaich v -achadh decrease, reduce, lessen, diminish
luibh n -e, -ean f m plant, herb; weed **l.-eòlaiche** m botanist **l.-eòlas** m botany
Lugsamburgach a -aich, -aich m someone from Luxemburg a from, or pertaining to, Luxemburg
luibhre n f an **l.** leprosy
luid n -e, -ean f slovenly person; clumsy person
luideach a -diche silly, daft; shabby, untidy
luideag n -eig, -an f rag
luidhear n -eir, -eirean f vent, chimney; ship's funnel
Luinneach n -nich, -nich m someone from Luing a from, or pertaining to, Luing
luinneag n -eig, -an f ditty, song
Lùnastal n -ail m an **L.** August *Formerly* **an Lùnasdal**

lurach *a* **-aiche** lovely, beautiful, pretty, attractive

lurgann *n* **-ainn, -an** *f* shin

lurmachd *a* *See* **lomnochd**

lus *n* **-a/luis, -an** *m* plant, herb **l. a' chrom-chinn** daffodil **l. an rìgh** thyme **l. nam ban-sìth** foxglove **l. nan cluas** saxifrage

luthaig *v* **-eadh** wish, desire *Also* **lùig**

lùth-chleas *n* **-a, -an** *m* athletics, sport

lùth-chleasachd *n f* athletics, sport

lùth-chleasaiche *n* **-an** *m* athlete, sportsman, sportswoman

lùthmhor *a* **-oire** strong, powerful, athletic, vigorous

lùth(s) *n* **lùith(s)** *m* strength, power, vigour, energy **cion lùith(s)** lack of power/energy **gun l.** unable to move

M

m' *poss pron* my (*used before words beginning in vowels or* **fh**)

ma *conj* if

ma *aug prep* about his/her/its

màb *v* **-adh** abuse, vilify

mabach *a* **-aiche** stammering, stuttering, lisping

mac *n* **mic, mic** *m* son **m. bràthar/ peathar** nephew

mac-an-aba *n m* ring finger

macanta *a* meek, gentle, mild

macantas *n* **-ais** *m* meekness, mildness

mach *adv* out (*used of motion*) **m. à seo!** let's be off!; out you go! **m. air a chèile** at odds

machair *n* **e-/machrach, machraichean** *f m* machair, sandy arable land near coast

machlag *n* **-aig, -an** *f* uterus, womb, matrix

mac-meanmna *n* **mic-** *m* imagination *Also* **mac-meanmainn**

mac-samhail *n* **mic-** *m* replica, facsimile, duplicate; likeness

mac-talla *n* **mic-** *m* echo

madadh *n* **-aidh, -aidhean** *m* hound, dog **m.-allaidh** wolf **m.-ruadh** fox

madainn *n* **maidne, maidnean** *f* morning **M. mhath!** Good morning!

mag *v* **-adh** mock, scoff, laugh at, jeer

magadh *n* **-aidh** *m* mocking, scoffing **cùis-mhagaidh** *f* object of ridicule

magail *a* **-e** scoffing, mocking; apt to mock

magairle *n* **-an** *f m* testicle

màgaran *n* **-ain** *m* crawling on all fours **air mhàgaran** on all fours

maghar *n* **-air, -airean** *m* bait (*fishing*), artificial fly *vn* **a' m.** fishing while moving

maide *n* **-an** *m* stick, wood **m.-tarsainn** beam, cross-beam

maids *v* **-eadh/-igeadh** match

maids(e) *n* **-sichean** *m* match (*light*); match (*game*)

màidsear *n* **-eir, -an** *m* major **M. na Pìoba** Pipe Major

Màigh *n* **-e** *f* **a' Mhàigh** May

maighdeann *n* **-dinn, -an/-dinnean** *f* maiden **m.-phòsaidh** bridesmaid **m.-mhara** mermaid

maigheach *n* **-ghiche, -ghichean** *f* hare

maighstir *n* **-ean** *m* master **Mgr MacÌomhair** Mr MacIver **m.-sgoile** schoolmaster, headmaster

màileid *n* **-e, -ean** *f* bag, suitcase

maill(e) *n f* slowness, tardiness, delay **chuireadh maill oirnn** we were delayed

maille ri *prep* (along) with

mair *v* **-sinn/-eachdainn** last, endure

maireann *a* living, extant **... nach m.** the late **... ri do mhaireann** during your lifetime, as long as you live

maireannach *a* **-aiche** lasting, enduring, everlasting, permanent

mairg *a* woeful, pitiable

màirnealach *a* **-aiche** dilatory, slow

màirnealachd *n f* slowness, delay

mairsinneach *a* **-niche** lasting, long-lasting

mairtfheòil *n* **-òla** *f* beef

maise *n f* beauty, loveliness, comeliness **ball-m.** beauty spot (*on face*); ornament

maiseach *a* **-siche** beautiful, lovely, comely

maistreadh *n* **-ridh** *m* churning (*making butter*)

maith *v See* **math**

màl *n* **màil**, **màil** *m* rent **air mhàl** rented

mala *n* **-idhean/-ichean/mailghean** *f* eyebrow; brow

malairt *n* **-ean** *f* trade, exchange, commerce, business

màlda *a* modest, coy; gentle, mild

mall *a* **maille** slow, tardy

mallachd *n* **-an** *f* curse

mallaich *v* **-achadh** curse

mallaichte *a* cursed, accursed

màm *n* **màim**, **-an** *m* large round hill

mamaidh *n* **-ean** *f* mammy, mummy

màm-slèibhe *n* **màim-**, **màman-** *m* avalanche

manach *n* **-aich**, **-aich** *m* monk

manachainn *n* **-e**, **-ean** *f* monastery

manadh *n* **-aidh**, **-aidhean** *m* omen, warning (*supernatural*), apparition; prophecy **cuir air mhanadh** *v* prophesy

manaidsear *n* **-eir**, **-an** *m* manager

Manainneach *n* **-nich**, **-nich** *m* Manx person *a* Manx

mang *n* **mainge**, **-an** *f* fawn

manran *n* **-ain**, **-an** *m* tuneful sound, melody, crooning

mànranach *a* **-aiche** tuneful, melodious, crooning

maodal *n* **-ail**, **-an** *f* stomach, paunch

maoidh *v* **-eadh** threaten, reproach

maoidheadh *n* **-dhidh**, **-dhidhean** *m* threat, threatening

maoil *n* **-ean** *f* forehead, brow

maoin *n* **-e**, **-ean** *f* wealth, riches, fund

maoineachas *n* **-ais** *m* finance

maoinich *v* **-neachadh** finance, fund

maoiseach *n* **-sich**, **-sichean** *f* doe

maol *n* **maoil**, **maoil** *f m* rounded headland, mull; promontory **M. Chinn Tìre** Mull of Kintyre

maol *a* **maoile** blunt; bald; hornless; stupid

maor *n* **maoir**, **maoir** *m* bailiff, steward, constable **m.-cladaich** coastguard

maorach *n* **-aich** *m* shellfish

maoth *a* **maoithe** soft, tender

maothaich *v* **-achadh** soften; mitigate

mapa *n* **-ichean** *m* map

mar *a, adv, prep* (+ *len*), *conj* as, like **mar seo** *adv* like this, thus **mar sin** *adv* like that, therefore **mar sin leat/leibh** *adv* goodbye **mar a** *conj* as

mar *aug prep* about our

marag *n* **-aig**, **-an** *f* blood-pudding **m. dhubh** black pudding **m. gheal** white pudding

maraiche *n* **-an** *m* seaman, mariner

mar an ceudna *adv* also, likewise, too

mar-aon *adv* together, as one, in concert

marbh *n* **mairbh**, **mairbh** *m* dead person **na mairbh** the dead **marbh(an) na h-oidhche** the dead of night

marbh *a* **mairbhe** dead

marbh *v* **-adh** kill

mar-bhith *n f* fault **gun m.** without fault

marbhrann *n* **-ainn**, **-an** *m* elegy

marbhtach *a* **-aiche** deadly; mortal

marcachd *n f* riding, horsemanship

marcaich *v* **-achd** ride

marcaiche *n* **-an** *m* rider, horseman

marcan-sìne *n* **marcain-** *m* seaspray

marc-shluagh *n* **-aigh** *m* cavalry, horsemen

mar eisimpleir *adv* for example

margadh *n* **-aidh**, **-aidhean** *f m* market **m. nan earrannan** stock exchange

margaid *n* **-e**, **-ean** *f* market

màrmor *n* **-oir** *m* marble

màrsail *n* **-e** *f* marching, march

marsanta *n* **-n** *m* merchant

mart *n* **mairt**, **mairt** *m* cow, steer

Màrt *n* **Màirt** *m* am **M.** March

mar-thà *adv* already

màs *n* **màis**, **-an** *m* buttock, bottom, posterior

mas *conj See* **mus**

maslach *a* **-aiche** disgraceful, shameful

masladh *n* **-aidh**, **-aidhean** *m* disgrace, reproach

maslaich *v* **-achadh** disgrace, put to shame

mastaig *n* **-e**, **-ean** *f* mastiff; (*met*) rotter

ma-tà *adv* then, in that case
matamataig *n m* mathematics
math *n* **maith** *m* good, benefit
 m. a' phobaill the public interest/good
 dè (am) m. a bhith a' bruidhinn?
 what's the use of talking?
math *a* **feàrr** good **gu m.** well **m. air ...**
 good at ... **gu m. fuar** quite cold **chan**
 eil m. dhut ... you must not ... **mas m.**
 mo bharail if I am not mistaken **'s m.**
 sin that's good **m. dha-rìribh** very good
 indeed, excellent
math *adv* well
math *v* **-adh** forgive, pardon **m. dhuinn**
 ar peacaidhean forgive us our sins
ma-thà *adv* then, in that case
mathachadh *n* **-aidh** *m* manure,
 manuring, fertilizer; insistence
mathaich *v* **-achadh** manure;
 (*in argument*) insist
màthair *n* **-ar**, **màthraichean** *f* mother
 m.-chèile mother-in-law
mathan *n* **-ain**, **-an** *m* bear **m.-bàn**
 polar bear
mathanas *n* **-ais** *m* forgiveness, pardon
 Also **maitheanas**
mathas *n* **-ais** *m* goodness, virtue
 Also **maitheas**
math dh'fhaodte *adv, conj* perhaps,
 maybe
meaban *n* **-ain**, **-ain** *m* upstart;
 something damaged
meacan-ruadh *n* **meacain-ruaidh**,
 meacanan-ruadha *m* radish
meadhan *n* **-ain**, **-an** *m* middle, centre;
 medium, means **na meadhanan**
 the media **an teis-m.** the very centre
 m.-aois middle age **na M.-Aoisean** the
 Middle Ages **m.-chearcall** equator
meadhanach *a* **-aiche** middling, so-so;
 intermediate, central
meadhan-là/latha *n* **meadhain-**
 m midday
meadhan-oidhche *n* **meadhain-**
 m midnight
meadh-bhlàth *a* lukewarm
meadhrach *a* **-aiche** glad, joyous,
 merry

meal *v* **-tainn/-adh** enjoy, relish **m. do**
 naidheachd! congratulations! **m. is**
 caith e enjoy it and make good use of it
meal-bhuc *n* **-bhuic**, **-bhucan** *f* melon
meall *n* **mill**, **mill** *m* lump; round hill;
 large number; shower (*of rain*)
 m.-sgòrnain Adam's apple
meall *v* **-adh** deceive **... mura h-eil**
 mi air mo mhealladh ... if I'm not
 mistaken
mealladh *n* **-aidh** *m* deception,
 deceiving
meallta *a* deceptive, deceitful,
 misleading
meamhran *n* **-ain** *m* membrane
mean *a* little **m. air mhean** little by
 little, gradually
mèanan, mèananaich *n See* **mèaran,**
 mèaranaich
meanbh *a* **-a** minute, diminutive
meanbhchuileag *n* **-eig**, **-an** *f* midge
meang *n* **-a/ming**, **-an** *f* blemish, flaw,
 abnormality **gun mheang** faultless
meang(l)an *n* **-ain**, **-an** *m* branch
 (*of tree*), bough
meanmnach *a* **-aiche** spirited, lively
meann *n* **minn**, **minn** *m* kid (*animal*)
meannt *n* **-a** *m* mint
meantraig *v* **-eadh** venture, dare
mear *a* **-a** merry, playful
mearachd *n* **-an** *f* mistake, error
mearachdach *a* **-aiche** mistaken,
 erroneous, inaccurate
mèaran *n* **-ain**, **-an** *m* yawn
mèaranaich *n* **-e** *f* yawning *Also vn* **a' m.**
mèarrs *v* **-adh/-ail** march
mèarrsadh *n* **-aidh** *m* march, marching
meas *n m* esteem, respect; evaluation,
 assessment **le m.** yours sincerely
 (*in letter*)
meas *n* **-a**, **-an** *m* fruit
meas *v* **meas/-adh** consider, esteem;
 reckon, estimate, value
measadh *n* **-aidh**, **-aidhean** *m*
 assessment, evaluation, appraisal,
 reckoning
measail *a* **-e** fond; respected, esteemed
 m. air ... fond of ...

measarra *a* temperate, moderate, sober
measarrachd *n f* temperance, restraint
measg *n* **am m.** (+ *gen*) among, amongst
measgachadh *n* **-aidh, -aidhean** *m* mixture, combination
measgaich *v* **-achadh** mix, mingle
meata *a* timid, faint-hearted, feeble
meatailt *n, a* **-e, -ean** *f* metal
meatair *n* **-ean** *m* metre (*length*)
meidh *n* **-e, -ean** *f* balance, scales **air mheidh** in the balance
meigeadaich *n f* bleating (*of goat or kid*)
meil *v* **-ich/-eadh** grind
mèil *v* **-ich** bleat
meileabhaid *n f* velvet
mèilich *n f* bleating
meilich *v* **-leachadh** chill, benumb
mèinn *n* **-e, -ean** *f* mine (*mil, ind*)
mèinn *n* **-e** *f* disposition, temperament
mèinneadair *n* **-ean** *m* miner
mèinnear *n* **-eir, -an** *m* mineral; miner
mèinnearachd *n f* mining, mineralogy
mèinnearach *a* **-aiche** mineral, mineralogical
mèinneil *a* **-e** placid, gentle, refined
meirg *n* **-e** *f* rust
meirg *v* **-eadh** rust, corrode
meirgeach *a* **-giche** rusty
mèirle *n f* theft, thieving **ri m.** thieving **dèan m.** *v* thieve, steal
mèirleach *n* **-lich, -lich** *m* thief
meòrachadh *n* **-aidh, -aidhean** *m* meditation, deliberation
meòraich *v* **-achadh** meditate, deliberate, reflect *Also* **meòmhraich**
meòrachan *n* **-ain, -ain** *m* memorandum
meud *n* **-an** *m* size, extent, amount
meudachd *n f* size, bulk
meudaich *v* **-achadh** increase, enlarge
meug *n* **meòig** *m* whey
meur *n* **meòir, meòir/-an** *f m* finger, digit; branch (*org*); knot (*in wood*) **m.-lorg** fingerprint **m.-chlàr** keyboard *Also* **meòir**
meuran *n* **-ain, -ain/-an** *m* thimble; knot (*in wood*)
mì- *neg pref* not, dis-, ill-, in-, mis-, -less

mi(se) *pron* I, me
miadhail *a* **-e** respected, esteemed; fond **m. air ...** fond of ...
miag *v* **-ail** mew
mial *n* **-a, -an** *f* louse; tick
mial-chù *n* **-choin, -choin** *m* greyhound
mia(tha)laich *n f* mewing *Also vn* **a' m.**
miann *n* **-an** *f m* desire, wish **bu mhiann leam** I would like
miannaich *v* **-achadh** desire
mias *n* **mias/mèise, -an** *f* basin
miast(r)adh *n* **-aidh** *m* havoc, vandalism
mì-bheusachd *n f* indecency, impropriety
mì-chàilear *a* unpleasant, disagreeable, distasteful
mì-chiatach *a* **-aiche** unseemly, improper; outrageous
mì-chinnt *n f* uncertainty
mì-chinnteach *a* **-tiche** uncertain
mì-chliù *n* disrepute, dishonour
mì-chofhurtail *a* **-e** uncomfortable
mì-chùramach *a* **-aiche** careless
mì-dhòigh *n f* lack of method, lack of care; deprivation
mì-dhòigheil *a* **-e** unmethodical, disorganized
mì-fhaiceallach *a* **-aiche** careless
mì-fhallain *a* **-e** unhealthy, unwholesome
mì-fhoighidneach *a* **-niche** impatient
mì-fhortanach *a* **-aiche** unfortunate, unlucky
mì-fhreagarrach *a* **-aiche** unsuitable
mì-ghean *n* **-a** *m* discontent, melancholy
mì-ghnàthaich *v* **-achadh** abuse
mì-ghoireasach *a* **-aiche** inconvenient
mì-iomchaidh *a* **-e** improper
mì-laghail *a* **-e** unlawful, illegal
mil *n* **meala/mealach, mealan** *f* honey
mìle *n* **mìltean** *f m* thousand; mile
milis *a* **mìlse** sweet; harmonious (*mus*)
mill *v* **-eadh** spoil, mar, ruin
milleadh *n* **-lidh** *m* spoiling, marring, ruining
millean *n* **-ein/-an** *m* million
millteach *a* **-tiche** destructive, ruinous, prodigal, detrimental

milseachd n f sweetness
milsean n -ein, -ein/-an m sweet, dessert
mì-mhisneachadh n -aidh m
discouragement
mì-mhisneachail a -e discouraging,
disheartening
mì-mhisnich v -neachadh discourage,
dishearten
mì-mhodh n -mhoidh, -a m
impoliteness, misbehaviour,
impertinence **na bi ri m.**! don't
misbehave!
mì-mhodhail a -e impolite, misbehaved,
rude, discourteous
min n -e meal f **m.-choirce** oatmeal
m.-fhlùir white flour **m.-sàibh** sawdust
mìn a -e smooth, soft, delicate
mì-nàdarrach a -aiche unnatural
mìneachadh n -aidh, -aidhean
m interpretation, explanation
mìnich v mìneachadh interpret, explain
minig a often, frequent
minig v -eadh mean
ministear n -eir, -an m minister **M. na**
Còmhdhail the Transport Minister
ministrealachd n f ministry (relig, polit)
M. an Dìon the Ministry of Defence
miogadaich n See **meigeadaich**
mion a -a minute, small, on a small scale
m.-chunntas f m detailed account
m.-eòlach (+ **air**) fully conversant with,
expert in **m.-sgrùd** v scrutinize, analyze
mionach n -aich, -aichean m stomach,
intestines, entrails
mionaid n -e, -ean f minute **fuirich m.**
bheag wait a second
mionaideach a -diche precise, detailed,
exact **gu m.** minutely, in detail
mì-onarach a -aiche dishonest,
dishonourable
mion-chànan n -ain, -an f m minority
language
mionn n -a, -an f m oath **mo mhionnan!**
I swear! vn **a' mionnan** swearing
mionnachadh n -aidh m swearing
mionnaich v -achadh swear; curse
mionnaichte a convinced, certain
mions n -a m mince

mìorbhail n -e, -ean f marvel, miracle
mìorbhaileach a -liche marvellous
mìos n -a, -an f m month **m. nam pòg**
honeymoon
miosa a See **dona**
mìosachan n -ain, -ain m calendar
mìosail a monthly
miotag n -aig, -an f glove, mitten
mìr n -e, -ean m bit, piece, fragment
mire n f merriment, mirth, frolic
mìrean n -ein, -ein/-an m particle,
small piece
mì-reusanta a unreasonable
mì-riaghailt n -e, -ean f disorder,
irregularity
mì-riaghailteach a -tiche disorderly,
unruly, irregular
mì-rian n f disorder, disorganization
mì-rianail a -e disordered, disorderly
mì-riaraichte a dissatisfied
mì-rùn n -rùin m malice, ill will
miseanaraidh n -ean m missionary
misg n -e f drunkenness, intoxication
air mhisg drunk
misgear n -eir, -an m drunkard, boozer
mì-sgiobalta a untidy
mì-shealbh n -sheilbh m misfortune,
ill-luck **gheibh thu do mhì-shealbh**
you'll catch it (met)
mì-shealbhach a -aiche unfortunate,
unlucky
mì-shona a unhappy, discontent
misneachail a -e courageous,
encouraging; confident
misneachd n f courage, encouragement,
boldness; confidence Also **misneach**
misnich v -neachadh encourage,
embolden
miste a worse **cha bu mhiste tu sin**
you would be none the worse of that
mì-thaingealachd n f ingratitude
mì-thaingeil a -e ungrateful
mì-thaitneach a -niche unpleasant,
disagreeable
mì-thlachdmhor a -oire unpleasant,
disagreeable
mì-thoileachas a -ais m displeasure,
unhappiness, discontent

mì-thoilichte *a* unhappy, displeased, discontent

mì-thuarail *a* **-e** ill-looking, looking off-colour

mo *poss pron* my, mine (+ *len*) **mo chreach!** Alas! **mo thogair!** who cares? (**m'** *before vowels or* **fh**)

moch *a* **moich(e)** early **o mhoch gu dubh** from dawn till dusk

mocheirigh *n f* rising early

mòd *n* **mòid, -an** *m* mod, assembly, court **am Mòd Nàiseanta** the National Mod

monadh *n* **-aidh, -aidhean** *m* moor, hill, mountain **am M. Ruadh** the Cairngorms

monaiseach *n* **-siche** slow, dull; self-effacing

monmhar *n* **-air, -an** *m* murmur

mòr *a* **motha/mò** big, great, large **tha iad mòr aig a chèile** they are great friends **cha mhòr gum faca sinn iad** we hardly saw them **cha mhòr nach do thuit mi** I almost fell **bha e mòr leam faighneachd** I was reluctant to ask **mòr às fhèin** haughty

Insight: mòd

Although Norse in origin and a cousin of the English 'moot', this word has a particular association in Gaeldom. The National Mod is held each October and features a wide range of competitions for Gaelic singing – children, adult, choral – and recitation, plus drama, exhibitions, fringe events and many impromptu ceilidhs.

modail *n* **-e, -ean** *f* model

modal *n* **-ail, -an** *m* module

modh *n* **-a, -an/-annan** *f m* manner, mode, behaviour; procedure, process; mood (*gram*)

modhail *a* **-e** polite, mannerly, courteous

mogal *n* **-ail, -ail** *m* mesh (*of net*)

mogan *n* **-ain, -an** *m* stash (*of money*); slipper

mòine *n* **mòine/mòna(dh)/mònach** *f* peat, moss **buain na mòna** cutting peat

mòinteach *n* **-tich, -tichean** *f* moor, moorland

moit *n* **-e** *f* pride

moiteil *a* **-e** proud

mol *n* **moil/-a, -an** *m* shingle, shingle beach

mol *v* **-adh** praise; recommend, propose

molach *a* **-aiche** hairy, shaggy, rough

moladh *n* **-aidh** *m* praise; recommendation

molag *n* **-aig, -an** *f* pebble

moll *n* **muill** *m* chaff

molldair *n* **-ean** *m* mould

molt *n* **muilt, muilt** *m* wedder (*sheep*)

moltach *a* **-aiche** (+ **air**) praising, laudatory

mòmaid *n* **-e, -ean** *f* moment

monadail *a* **-e** hilly, mountainous

mòrachd *n f* greatness, majesty

morair *n* **-ean** *m* lord, peer **Taigh nam Morairean** the House of Lords

moralta *a* moral

moraltachd *n f* morality

mòran *n* **-ain** *m* many, much, a lot *adv* much

mòr-bhùth *n* **-a, -an/-bhùithtean** *f* supermarket

mòr-chuid *n f* majority

mòrchuis *n* **-e** *f* pride, haughtiness, conceit

mòrchuiseach *a* **-siche** haughty, conceited, pompous

mòr-chuisle *n* **-an** *f* artery

mòr-dhail *n* **-ean** *m* convention, assembly, congress

morgaids(e) *n* **-an** *m* mortgage

morghan *n* **-ain** *m* gravel, shingle

mòr-ghath *n* **-a, -an** *m* harpoon, trident

mòr-roinn *n* **-e, -ean** *f* continent

mòr-shluagh *n* **-aigh, -an** *m* populace, host, multitude

mòr-thìr *n* **-e, -ean** *f* mainland

mosach *a* **-aiche** miserable, nasty, inclement (*weather*); mean (*person*)

mosgaideach *a* **-diche** dilatory, slow, unreliable

mosgail v **-gladh** arouse, waken

motair n **-ean** m motor **m.-baic** motorbike **m.-baidhsagal** motorbicycle

motha a See **mòr**

mothachadh n **-aidh, -aidhean** m consciousness, awareness; sensation **gun mhothachadh** unconscious

mothachail a **-e** conscious, aware

mothaich v **-achadh** notice, perceive

mothar n **-air, -air** m loud shout Also **mòthar**

mu prep about, around

muasgan-caol n m prawn

muasgain-chaola n m pl scampi

muc n **muice, -an** f pig, sow

mùch v **-adh** stifle, suppress, smother, extinguish

mu choinneamh prep phr (+ gen) opposite **mu ch. na bùtha** opposite the shop

mu chuairt adv, prep phr (+ gen) around **mu ch. an t-saoghail** around the world

muc-mhara n **muic-mhara/muice-mara, mucan-mara** f whale

mud aug prep about your (sg)

mu dheidhinn prep phr (+ gen) about, concerning **mu dh. na coinneimh** about the meeting

mu dheireadh adv eventually, finally, at last **mu dh. thall** at long last

muga n **-nnan** f m mug

mùgach a **-aiche** sullen, surly; gloomy

muicfheòil n **-òla** f pork

muigh adv **a-muigh** out, outside

Muileach n **-lich, -lich** m someone from Mull a from, or pertaining to, Mull

muileann n **muilne/-linn, muilnean/-an** f m mill **m.-gaoithe** windmill

muile-mhàg n **muileacha-màg** f toad Also **muile-mhàgag**

muilicheann n **-chinn, -chinnean** f m sleeve (clothing) Also **muinichill**

muillear n **-eir, -an** m miller

muiltfheòil n **-òla** f mutton

muime n **-achan** f step-mother, foster mother

muin n f back **air m.** (+ gen) on top of **dèan m.** v have sexual intercourse

mùin v **mùn** urinate

muineal n **-eil, -an** m neck

muing n **-e, -ean** f mane

muinighin n **-e** f trust, confidence

muinntir n **-e** f people, folk

muinntireas n **-eis** m domestic service **air mhuinntireas** in service

muir n **mara, marannan** f m sea, ocean **m.-làn** high tide **m.-tiachd** jellyfish **m.-tràigh** low water

mùirn n **-e** f cheerfulness, joy; affection

mùirneach a **-niche** cheerful, joyful; beloved, precious

muirsgian n **-sgein, -an** f razorfish

mulad n **-aid** m sadness, sorrow **fo mhulad** sad, sorrowful

muladach a **-aiche** sad, sorrowful; pitiful

mu làimh adv so-so

mullach n **-aich, -aich/-aichean** m top, summit

mum aug prep about my; about their

mùn n **mùin** m urine

mun aug prep about the; about their

muncaidh n **-ean** m monkey

mun cuairt adv around

mur(a) conj unless, if not

mur aug prep about our; about your (pl & pol)

mura-bhith n f exception

muran n **-ain** m marram grass, sea-bent, bent-grass

murt n **muirt, muirt** m murder

murt v **murt/-adh** murder

murtaidh a **-e** sultry

murtair n **-ean** m murderer

mus conj before

mu seach adv alternately; aside **tè mu s.** one after the other

mu sgaoil adv loose, at large **leig mu s.** v set free, release

mùth v **-adh** change, alter, mutate

mu thimcheall prep phr (+ gen) about, around, concerning

mu thràth adv already, before

N

na *def art* the (*used before pl forms not in gen case*), of the (*used before sg forms of feminine nouns in gen case*) **na h-ùbhlan** the apples **na h-uinneige** of the window

na *neg part* do not (*used in negative commands*) **na bi (cho) gòrach!** don't be (so) silly! **na can an còrr!** don't say any more, say no more!

na *conj* than (*used in comparison of two items*) **tha an tè seo nas motha na an tè sin** this one is bigger than that one

na *rel pron* what, that (which), as much **sin na ghabhas e** that is as much as/all (that) it will take

na *aug prep* in her, in his (+ *len*), in it **na baga** in her bag **na bhaga** in his bag **tha i na dotair** she's a doctor **tha e na shaor** he's a joiner **bha i na cadal** she was asleep **bha e na chadal** he was asleep

na *contr of* **an do** **seo far na thachair e** this is where it happened

nàbachd *n f* neighbourhood

nàbaidh *n* **-ean** *m* neighbour; (*colloq*) mate

nach neg conj whom, that/those ... not **an fheadhainn n. robh an làthair** those who were not present

nad *aug prep* in your (+ *len*) **nad phòcaid** in your pocket **a bheil thu nad dhùisg?** are you awake?

nàdar *n* **-air** *m* nature; type **bha n. de dh'eagal orm ...** I was somewhat afraid to ...

nàdarrach *a* **-aiche** natural

naidheachd *n* **-an** *f* news; story, anecdote **dè do n.?** what's your news?

naidhlean *n* **-ein** *m* nylon

nàimhdeas *n* **-eis** *m* enmity, hostility

nàimhdeil *a* **-e** hostile

nàire *n f* shame, embarrassment **an robh nàir' ort idir?** were you not ashamed? **duine gun n.** a brazen man **mo nàir' ort!** shame on you!

nàisean *n* **-ein, -an** *m* nation

nàiseanta *a* national **Partaidh N. na h-Alba** the Scottish National Party **Dualchas N. na h-Alba** Scottish National Heritage

nàiseantach *n* **-aich, -aich** *m* nationalist

nàiseantachd *n f* nationalism, nationality

naisgear *n* **-eir, -an** *m* conjunction (*gram*)

nall *adv* See **a-nall**

nam *def art* of the (*used before words beginning in b, f, m, p in gen pl*)

nam *conj* if (*followed by the conditional form of verbs beginning in b, f, m, p*) **nam bruthadh tu am putan** if you were to press the button

nam *aug prep* in my (+ *len*) **nam thaigh fhèin** in my own house **bha mi nam chadal** I was asleep

nàmhaid *n* **-ad, -ean/nàimhdean** *m* enemy, foe

nan *def art* of the (*used before words other than those beginning in b, f, m, p in gen pl*)

nan *conj* if (*followed by the conditional form of the verb*) **nan innseadh tu dhomh dè tha dhìth ort** if you a tell me what you want

nan *aug prep* in their **nan obraichean** in their jobs **bha iad nan seasamh** they were standing

naochad *n* **-aid, -an** *m* ninety

naoi *n, a* nine Also **naodh**

naoi-deug *n, a* nineteen **naoi nota deug** nineteen pounds Also **naodh-deug**

naoidheamh *a* ninth Also **naodhamh**

naoidheamh-deug *a* nineteenth **an naoidheamh latha deug** the nineteenth day Also **naodhamh-d.**

naoidhean *n* **-ein, -an** *m* infant, baby

naoinear *n f m* nine (people) Also **naodhnar**

naomh *a* **naoimhe** holy, sacred, saintly

naomh *n* **naoimh, naoimh** *m* saint

naomhachadh *n* **-aidh** *m* sanctification

naomhachd n f holiness, saintliness, sanctity
naomhaich v -achadh sanctify
naosg n naoisg, naoisg m snipe
nar aug prep in our **nar cùram** in our care **bha sinn nar sìneadh** we were having a lie-down
nàr a nàire shameful, disgraceful
nàrach a -aiche ashamed, shamefaced; bashful
nàraich v -achadh shame, embarrass, disgrace **bha sinn air ar nàrachadh** we were mortified
nas aug pron (used with comparative forms of adjectives) **nas motha na** bigger than
nathair n nathrach, nathraichean f snake, serpent
neach n m person, individual (**luchd** is used as the pl of **neach**) n. **sam bith** anyone

neach-ionaid n m proxy, agent, substitute
neach-iùil n m guide
neach-labhairt n m spokesperson, speaker
neach-lagha n -a m lawyer, solicitor
neach-obrach n m worker, employee
neach-riaghlaidh n m ruler, governor
neach-sàbhalaidh n m rescuer
neach-sgrùdaidh n m examiner, inspector
neach-stiùiridh n m director
neach-teagaisg n m teacher
neach-togail n m builder
neach-treòrachaidh n m guide
nead n nid, nid/-an f m nest
neadaich v -achadh nest, nestle
nèamh n nèimh, -an m heaven
nèamhaidh a heavenly
neamhnaid n -e, -ean f pearl, jewel
nèapaigin n (-e), -ean f m handkerchief; napkin

Insight: neach

While *duine* can sometimes mean person as well as man, *neach* is the recognised word for person. It often appears with a suffix – *neach-cuideachaidh*, helper, *neach-ciùil*, musician, *neach-labhairt*, spokesperson etc. The plural used is *luchd* – *luchd-cunntais*, accountants, *luchd-gnothaich*, business people, *luchd a' bhròin*, mourners.

neach-casaid n m procurator
  N.-c. a' Chrùin Procurator Fiscal
  pl **Luchd-casaid**
neach-cathrach n m chairperson, chair
neach-ceàirde n m tradesperson
neach-ceasnachaidh n m questioner, interviewer, quizmaster, inquisitor
neach-ciùil n m musician
neach-comhairleachaidh n m adviser
neach-cuideachaidh n m helper, assistant, aide
neach-deasachaidh n m editor
neach-deilbh n m designer
neach-ealain n m artist(e)
neach-frithealaidh n m waiter, attendant
neach-gairm n m convener
neach-gnothaich n m business person

nèapraigear n -eir, -an m handkerchief
  Also **nèapraig(e)**
nearbha(sa)ch a -a(sa)iche nervous
neart n neirt, -an m strength, might, force
neartaich v -achadh strengthen
neartmhor a -oire strong, powerful
neas n -a, -an m weasel, stoat
neasgaid n -e, -ean f boil, ulcer
nèibhidh n -ean m navy
neo conj or
neo- neg pref in-, un-, -less
neo-abaich a -e unripe
neo-àbhaisteach a -tiche unusual, exceptional
neo-airidh a -e unworthy, undeserving
neo-ar-thaing a independent **air do n.** whether you like it or not **n. bruidhinn, ach cha dèan e dad** plenty talk, but no action

neo-ar-thaingeil *a* independent-minded; ungrateful
neo-bhàsmhor *a* immortal
neo-chaochlaideach *a* unchangeable
neochoireach *a* **-riche** innocent, blameless
neo-chumanta *a* uncommon, unusual
neo-chùramach *a* **-aiche** negligent, careless, inattentive
neo-dhiadhachd *n f* atheism
neo-dhiadhaire *n* **-an** *m* atheist
neo-dhìlseachd *n f* infidelity, disloyalty
neo-eisimeileach *a* **-liche** independent
neo-eisimeileachd *n f* independence
neo-fhoirmeil *a* **-e** informal
neo-fhoirmeileachd *n f* informality
neòghlan *a* **-aine** unclean
neòghlaine *n f* uncleanness, uncleanliness
neoichiontach *a* **-aiche** innocent
neoichiontachd *n f* innocence
neòinean *n* **-ein, -ein/-an** *m* daisy
 n.-grèine sunflower
neo-làthaireachd *n f m* absence
neo-mhearachdach *a* **-aiche** unerring, infallible, correct
neònach *a* **-aiche** strange, unusual, curious
neoni *n m* nothing, zero
neo-oifigeil *a* **-e** unofficial
neo-riaghailteach *a* **-tiche** irregular
neo-thruacanta *a* pitiless, unmerciful, implacable
neul *n* **neòil, neòil** *m* cloud; trance; faint
 chaidh e ann an n. he fainted
neulach *a* **-aiche** cloudy
nì *n* **nithean** *m* thing **nì sam bith** anything **air sgàth Nì Math!** for goodness's sake!
nì *irr v* will do, will make (*See irr v* **dèan** *in Grammar*)
nic *n* daughter (of) (*used only in surnames of women*) **Sìne NicDhùghaill** Jean MacDougall
nigh *v* **-e** wash, clean
nigheadair *n* **-ean** *m* washing machine
nigheadaireachd *n f* washing **an do rinn thu an n.?** have you done the washing?

nigheadair-shoithichean *n* **nigheadairean-** *m* dishwasher
nighean *n* **nighinne/ighne, -an/ighnean** *f* girl, daughter **n. bràthar/n. peathar** niece
nighneag *n* **-eig, -an** *f* young girl, little girl *Also* **nìonag**
nimh *n* **-e** *m* poison, venom
nimheil *a* **-e** poisonous, venomous, virulent
Nirribheach *n* **-bhich, -bhich** *m* Norwegian *a* Norwegian
nis *adv* now *See* **a-nis**
nithear *irr v* will be done, will be made (*See irr v* **dèan** *in Grammar*)
nitheigin *pron* something
niùclas *n* **-ais, -an** *m* nucleus
niùclasach *a* nuclear
no *conj* or
nobhail *n* **-e, -ean** *f* novel
nochd *v* **-adh** appear; reveal, show
nodha *a* new **ùr n.** brand new
nòisean *n* **-ein, -ein** *m* notion; attraction **bha n. mòr aige dhi** he was greatly attracted to her
Nollaig *n* **-e, -ean** *f* an **N.** Christmas **N. Chridheil!** Merry Christmas!
norra(dh) *n m* wink of sleep, nap **cha d' fhuair sinn n. cadail** we didn't get a wink of sleep
norradaich *n* **-e** *f* nodding off, dozing *Also vn* **a' n.**
norrag *n* **-aig, -an** *f* nap, snooze, forty winks
nòs *n* **nòis, -an** *m* habit, custom; style **seinn san t-seann n.** traditional style singing *f*
nota *n* **-ichean** *f* note; pound sterling
nuadh *a* **nuaidhe** new **nuadh-bhàrdachd** modern poetry **an Tiomnadh N.** the New Testament
nuair a *conj* when
nuairsin *adv See* **an uair sin**
nuallanaich *n* lowing, bellowing (*of animals*)
nuas *adv* up, upwards *See* **a-nuas**
null *adv* over (*to the other side*) *See* **a-null**
nur *aug prep* in your (*pl & pol*) **a bheil sibh nur dùisg?** Are you awake?
nurs *n* **-aichean** *f* nurse

O

Ò *exclam* O! Oh!

o *prep* from **o cheann gu ceann** from end to end *Also* **bho**

o (a) *conj* since **tha greis o thachair e** there's a while since it happened *Also* **bho**

òb *n* **-a/òib, -an** *m* bay, creek

obair *n* **obrach/oibre, obraichean/ oibrichean** *f* work, job, employment, labour **o.-làimhe** handiwork **o.-taighe** housework **a dh'aon o./mar aon o.** intentionally, deliberately **gun o.** unemployed

ogha *n* **-ichean/-chan** *m* grandchild **tha iad anns na h-oghaichean** they are first cousins

Ògmhios *n* **-ios(a)** *m* **an t-Ò.** June

ogsaidean *n* **-ein** *m* oxygen

oide *n* **-an** *m* step-father; tutor

oideachas *n* **-ais** *m* education, tuition

oidhche *n* **-annan** *f* night **O. mhath** Good night **o. h-Aoine** Friday night **O. Challainn** Hogmanay **O. Shamhna** Halloween **air an o.** at night

oidhirp *n* **-e, -ean** *f* attempt, effort **dèan o.** *v* try

---

Insight: oidhche

The word for night, opposite of *latha*, and also used to denote particular nights: *Oidhche Shamhna*, Halloween; *Oidhche Nollaig*, Christmas Eve. *Oidhche mhòr* is used for an important or very enjoyable night. Notice also *deich uairean as t-oidhche*, ten o'clock at night, and the phrase *air an oidhche*, at night.

òban *n* **-ain, -ain** *m* small bay, little creek

obann *a* **obainne** sudden **gu h-o.** suddenly

obh *exclam* **obh, obh!** Oh dear!

obraich *v* **-achadh/obair** work

obraiche *n* **-an** *m* worker *Also* **oibriche**

och *exclam* Alas! Ah!

ochanaich *n* **(-e)** *f* sighing

ochd *a* eight *n* **a h-ochd**

ochdad *n* **-aid, -an** *m* eighty

ochdamh *a* eighth

ochd-cheàrnach *n* **-aich** *m* octagon

ochd-deug *n, a* eighteen **ochd troighean deug** eighteen feet

ochdnar *n f m* eight (*people*)

o chionn *prep* since, ago **o ch. f(h)ada** a long time ago

od *aug prep* from your (*sg*)

odhar *a* **-air/uidhre** dun-coloured

ofrail *n* **-e, -ean** *f* offering, sacrifice

òg *a* **òige** young, youthful

ògail *a* **-e** youthful, young

òganach *n* **-aich, -aich** *m* youth, youngster

oifig *n See* **oifis**

oifigeach *n* **-gich, -gich** *m* official, officer

oifigear *n* **-eir, -an** *m* officer, official **àrd-o.** chief executive

oifigeil *a* **-e** official

oifis *n* **-e, -ean** *f* office **o. a' phuist** post office

òigear *n* **-eir, -an** *m* youth, youngster

òigh *n* **-e, -ean** *f* virgin, maiden

oighre *n* **-achan** *m* heir

oighreachd *n* **-an** *f* estate, inheritance

òigridh *n f* (*coll*) youth, youngsters

oilbheum *n* **-eim, -an** *m* offence, umbrage

oilbheumach *a* **-aiche** offensive

oileanach *n* **-aich, -aich** *m* student

oilisgin *n* **-ean** *f m* oilskin

oillt *n* **-e, -ean** *f* horror, dread, terror

oillteil *a* **-e** horrific, horrid, dreadful, terrifying

oilltich *v* **-teachadh** horrify, terrify

oilthigh *n* **-ean** *m* university

òinseach n **-siche, -sichean** f fool
(*female*), foolish woman

oir n **-e, -ean** f m edge, border, margin,
fringe **air an o.** at the edge

oir conj for, because

òirbh(se) prep pron on you (*pl & pol*)

òirdheirc a **-e** glorious; illustrious

òirleach n **-lich, -lich** f inch

oirnn(e) prep pron on us

oirre(se) prep pron on her

oirthir n **-e, -ean** f coast, seaboard

oisean n **-ein, -an** m corner *Also* **oisinn**

oiteag n **-eig, -an** f breeze, gust of wind

oitir n **-e/oitreach, -ean** f bank in sea
o. gainmhich sandbank

òl v drink

ola n **-ichean** f oil **clàr o.** oil production
platform

olc n **uilc** m evil, wickedness

olc a evil, wicked, bad

ollamh n **-aimh, -an** m professor
An t-Oll. MacLeòid Professor
MacLeod

om aug prep from my; from their

òmar n **òmair** m amber

on aug prep from their; from the

on a conj since

onair n **-e, -ean** f honour **air m' onair!**
honestly!

onarach a **-aiche** honest,
honourable

onfhadh n **-aidh, -aidhean** m blast,
storm, raging sea

onghail n **-e** f uproar, tumult

ònrachd n f solitude **bha i na h-ò.**
she was alone

opairèisean n **-ein, -an** f m
operation

òr n **òir** m gold

or aug prep from our, from your

òrach a **-aiche** golden

òraid n **-e, -ean** f speech, lecture,
oration, talk **thoir seachad ò./dèan ò.**
v give a talk/lecture

òraidiche n **-an** m speaker, lecturer

orainds a See **orains**

oraindsear n See **orainsear**

orains a **-e** orange

orainsear n **-eir, -an** m orange

òran n **òrain, òrain** m song **gabh ò.**
v sing a song **ò. càraid** duet **ò. luaidh**
waulking song *Also* **amhran**

òr-bhuidhe a golden yellow, auburn

òr-cheàrd n **-chèird, -an** m goldsmith,
jeweller

òrd n **ùird, ùird/-an** m hammer

òrdag n **-aig, -an** f thumb, toe **an ò. mhòr**
the big toe

òrdaich v **-achadh** order, ordain,
decree

òrdail a **-e** orderly, methodical; ordinal

òrdan n **-ain, -ain** m order

òrdugh n **-uigh, -uighean** m
order, command, decree; order
(*arrangement*) **o. cùirte** court order,
injunction **cuir an ò.** arrange v **na**
h-Òrduighean the Communion
services

òr-iasg n **-èisg, -èisg** m goldfish

orm(sa) prep pron on me

orra(san) prep pron on them

ort(sa) prep pron on you (*sg*)

osag n **osaig, -an** f breeze, gust

osan n **osain/-an** m hose, stocking

os cionn prep phr (+ *gen*) above, over
os ar cionn above us

osgarra a audible

os ìosal adv secretly, covertly,
quietly

os-nàdarra(ch) a supernatural

osna(dh) n **osna(idh), -aidhean** f sigh
dèan/leig o. v sigh

osnaich n **-e, -ean** f sighing *Also* vn
ag o.

ospadal n **-ail, -an** m hospital

ostail n **-ean** f hostel **o. òigridh**
youth hostel

òstair n **-ean** m hotelier, innkeeper

Ostaireach n **-rich, -rich** m Austrian
a Austrian

othail n **-e, -ean** f hubbub, tumult,
uproar; rejoicing

othaisg n **-e, -ean/òisgean** f year-old
ewe, hog

òtrach n **-aich, -aichean** m dunghill,
rubbish dump, midden *Also* **òcrach**

P

paca n **-nnan** m pack Also **pac**
pacaid n **-e, -ean** f packet
pacaig v **-eadh** pack
pacaigeadh n **-gidh** m packing Also
  pacadh
pàganach n **-aich, -aich** m pagan,
  heathen a pagan
pàganachd n f paganism, heathenism
paidh n **-ean/-ichean** m pie **p. ubhail**
  apple pie
paidhir n **pàidhrichean** f m pair
  p. bhrògan pair of shoes
paidirean n **-rin, -rinean** m rosary;
  string of beads
paidse n **-sichean** f patch
pàigh v **-eadh** pay
pàigheadh n **-gidh** m pay, payment,
  wages
pàillean n **-ein, -an** m pavilion,
  marquee, tent
pailm n **-e** f palm (tree)
pailt a **-e** plentiful, abundant
pailteas n **-eis** m plenty, abundance
  tha (am) p. againn we have plenty
pàipear n **-eir, -an** m paper; newspaper
  p.-balla wallpaper **p.-gainmhich**
  sandpaper **p.-naidheachd** newspaper
  am P. Beag the West Highland
  Free Press
pàipearaich v **-achadh** paper, wallpaper
pàipeir a paper
pàirc(e) n **-(e), -(e)an** f park **p.
  chàraichean** car park
paireafain n m paraffin Also **parafan**
pairilis n f m paralysis, palsy
pàirt n **-ean** f m part, portion **gabh p. an**
  v take part in, participate
paisean n **-ein, -an** m faint **chaidh
  e ann am p.** v he fainted Also
  paiseanadh
paisg v **pasgadh** fold, wrap
paisgte a folded, wrapped
pàiste n **-an** m infant, child Formerly **pàisde**
pait n **-e, -ean** f lump, swelling (on body)
pàiteach a **-tiche** thirsty, parched
pana n **-ichean** m pan

pannal n **-ail, -an** m panel **P. na Cloinne**
  the Children's Panel
Pàp(a) n **-(a)n/-(a)chan** m Pope
  am Pàp(a) the Pope
Pàpanach n **-aich, -aich** m Roman
  Catholic a Roman Catholic
paraist(e) n **-an** f parish Formerly
  paraisd(e)
pàrant n **-an** m parent
pàrlamaid n **-e, -ean** f parliament **P. na
  h-Alba** the Scottish Parliament **P. na
  h-Eòrpa** the European Parliament
Pàrras n **-ais** m Paradise
parsail n **-ean** m parcel
partaidh n **-ean** f m party
  p. poilitigeach political party
partan n **-ain, -an** m small crab
pasgan n **-ain, -ain/-an** m package, bundle
pathadh n **-aidh** m thirst **a bheil
  am p. ort?** are you thirsty?
pàtran n **-ain, -an** m pattern
peacach n **-aich, -aich** m sinner
peacach a **-aiche** sinful
peacadh n **-aidh, -aidhean** m sin
peacaich v **-achadh** sin
peall n pill, **pillean** m pelt, hide
peallach a **-aiche** hairy, shaggy
peanas n **-ais, -an** m punishment, penalty
peanasaich v **-achadh** punish, penalize
peann n **pinn, pinn/-tan** m pen
peansail n **-ean** m pencil
peant n **-aichean/-an** m paint
peant v **-adh** paint
peantair n **-ean** m painter, decorator
pearsa n **-chan** m person
pearsanta a personal, subjective
pearsantachd n **-an** f personality
pears-eaglais n **pearsan-/pearsachan-**
  m cleric, clergyman
peasair n **-srach, -sraichean** f pea, peas
peasan n **-ain, -an** m brat, imp
peata n **-n/-aichean/-chan** m pet
  p.-ruadh puffin
peatrail n m petrol Also **peatroil**
peighinn n **-e, -ean** f old penny;
  pennyland (topog)

peile *n* **-lichean** *m* pail *Also* **peidhil**

pèileag *n* **-eig, -an** *f* porpoise

peilear *n* **-eir, -an** *m* bullet **dh'fhalbh iad aig p. am beatha** they went off at high speed

pèin *See* **fhèin**

peinnsean *n* **-ein** *m* pension **p. na Stàite** the State pension

peirceall *n* **-cill/-cle, -an/-clean** *m* jaw, jawbone

peitean *n* **-ein, -an** *m* waistcoat, sweater

peitseag *n* **-eig, -an** *f* peach

peucag *n* **-aig, -an** *f* peacock

peur *n* **-a, -an** *f* pear

Pharasach *n* **-aich, -aich** *m* Pharisee

pian *n* **pèin, -tan** *f m* pain, torment

pian *v* **-adh** pain, torment, annoy

piàna *n* **-than** *m* piano

piantach *a* **-aiche** painful *Also* **piantail**

pic *n* **-e, -ean** *m* pickaxe, pick

picil *n* **-e** *f* pickle

pige *n* **-achan** *m* pitcher, earthen jar *Also* **pigidh**

pile *n* **pilichean/-achan** *f m* pill

pillean *n* **-ein, -an** *m* pillion, cushion, saddle

pinc *a* **-e** pink

pinnt *n* **-ean** *m* pint **p. leann(a)** a pint of beer **leth-phinnt** half a pint

pìob *n* **-a, -an** *f* pipe; bagpipe **p.-analach** windpipe **p.-chiùil** bagpipe **p.-mhòr** Highland bagpipe **p.-uisge** water pipe

pìobair(e) *n* **-(e)an** *m* piper

pìobaireachd *n* *f* piping; pibroch

pìoban *n* **-ain, -ain/, -an** *m* tube, small pipe

pìobar *n* **-air** *m* pepper

pìobraich *v* **-achadh** incite, pep up, urge; pepper

pioc *v* **-adh** pick at, nibble

Piocach *n* **-aich, -aich** *m* Pict

piocach *n* **-aich** *m* saithe, coalfish

piocas (am) *n* **-ais** *m* scabies

piorbhaig *n* **-e, -ean** *f* wig

piorna *n* **-chan** *f m* pirn, bobbin, reel

pìos *n* **-an** *m* piece, section; sandwich; (*colloq*) talent **'s e pìos a th' innte** she's a bit of all right, she's a smasher

piseach *n* **pisich** *f* improvement, prosperity **thàinig p. mhòr air** he/it has improved greatly

piseag *n* **-eig, -an** *f* kitten

pit *n* **-e, -ean** *f* female genitalia, vulva

pitheid *n* **-e, -ean** *f* parrot; magpie *Also* **pioghaid**

piullach *a* **-aiche** untidy, unkempt, shabby; wan *Also* **piollach**

piuthar *n* **peathar, peathraichean** *f* sister **p.-athar** aunt (*on father's side*) **p.-chèile** sister-in-law **p.-màthar** aunt (*on mother's side*)

plaide *n* **-an/-achan** *f* blanket

plàigh *n* **-e, -ean** *f* plague **'s e p. a th'ann** he's/it's a pest

plana *n* **-ichean** *m* plan

planaid *n* **-e, -ean** *f* planet

planaig *v* **-eadh** plan

plangaid *n* **-e, -ean** *f* blanket

plannt *n* **-a, -aichean** *m* plant

plaosg *n* **-oisg, -an** *m* husk, peel, shell, pod

plàst *n* **-a, -an/-aidhean** *m* plaster

plastaig *n* **-e, -ean** *f m* plastic *a* plastic

pleadhag *n* **-aig, -an** *f* paddle; dibble *Also* **pleadhan** *m*

pleadhagaich *v* paddle

plèan(a) *n* **-(a)ichean** *f m* aeroplane

plèastar *n* **-an** *m* plaster (*eg wall*)

plèastraig *v* **-eadh** plaster

pleata *n* **-ichean** *m* plait

ploc *n* **pluic, -an** *m* clod; block

plocan *n* **-ain, -an** *m* small clod; small block

plosg *v* **-artaich/-adh** palpitate, throb, gasp, pant

plub *n* **-a, -an** *m* plop (*sound*), splash

plubadaich *n* **-e** *f* plopping, splashing

plubarsaich *n* **-e** *f* plopping, splashing

plubraich *v* plop, splash, slosh, gurgle

plucan *n* **-ain, -an** *m* stopper (*as in bottle*), bung; pimple

pluga *n* **-ichean** *m* plug

pluic *n* **-e, -ean** *f* cheek

pluiceach *a* **-ciche** chubby-cheeked, having large cheeks

plumadaich *n* **-e** *f* plunging, plummeting

plumair *n* **-ean** *m* plumber

plumais n -e, -ean f plum
poball n -aill m people, public

pongail a -e methodical, punctilious; punctual; sensible

Insight: poball

Poball means people or the public and, like these words, derives from Latin. The adjective *poblach* expresses what is public as opposed to private, and the associated noun *poblachd* is used for a political entity where the people (in theory!) rule – a republic. A republican is a *poblachdach*.

---

poblach a -aiche public **gu p.** in public
poblachail a republican
poblachd n f republic **P. na h-Èireann** the Irish Republic
poca n -nnan m bag, sack **p.-cadail** sleeping bag **p.-droma** haversack
pòcaid n -e, -ean f pocket *Also* **pòca**
pòcair n -ean m poker
pòg n pòige, -an f kiss
pòg v -adh kiss
poidhleat n -eit, -an m pilot *Also* **pìleat**
poidsear n -eir, -an m poacher
poileas n -lis, -lis m police officer, police **ban-phoileas** f policewoman
poileasaidh n -ean m policy **p. àrachais** insurance policy
poileasman n -ain, -ain m policeman
poilitigs n f politics *Also* **poileataigs**
poilitigeach a -giche political
poirdse n -an/-achan f m porch
poit n -e, -ean f pot **p. tì/teatha** teapot **p.-dhubh** small whisky still
pòitear n -eir, -an m tippler, drinker, boozer
pòla n -ichean m pole; Pole **am P. a Deas** the South Pole **am P. a Tuath** the North Pole **p. aodaich** clothes-pole *Also* **pòile**
Pòlainneach n -nich, -nich m Pole a Polish
poll n puill, puill m mud, mire, bog; pool
pollag n -aig, -an f small peatbank; small pool; pollock, lythe
poll-mònach n puill-mhònach, puill-mhònach m peatbank *Also* **poll-mòna(dh)**
pònaidh n -ean m pony
pònair n -arach f bean, beans
pong n puing, -an m music note

pòr n pòir, -an m seed; progeny; spore; pore (*in skin*)
pòrach a -aiche porous
port n puirt, puirt m port, harbour **p.-adhair** airport **p.-iasgaich** fishing port
port n puirt, puirt m tune **port-à-beul** mouth music
Portagaileach n -lich, -lich m Portuguese a Portuguese
portair n -ean m porter, janitor; porter (*drink*)
pòs v -adh marry
pòsadh n -aidh, -aidhean m marriage
post(a) n (-a), puist m postman, postwoman
post n puist, puist m post, stake, stob; post, mail **p.-adhair** airmail **p.-dealain** e-mail
pòsta a married **p. aig Eilidh** married to Helen **càraid phòsta** married couple *Formerly* **pòsda**
postachd n f postage; postal work
post-oifis n puist-, puist- m post office
prab n praib, -an m rheum (*in eye*)
praban n -ain, -an m shebeen
prab-shùileach a -liche bleary-eyed
prais n -e, -ean f pot, pan
pràis n -e f brass
pràiseach a brass
pram n -a, -aichean m pram
pràmh n pràimh m sorrow, sadness, dejection; slumber **fo phràmh** dejected, sorrowing
prann *See* **pronn**
preantas n -ais, -an m apprentice
preas n pris, pris/-an m bush, shrub
preas n -a, -an m wrinkle, crease, fold

preas v **-adh** fold, crease; furrow, wrinkle (*of humans*)

preas(a) n **-(a)ichean** m press, cupboard **p.-aodaich** wardrobe, clothes cupboard **p.-leabhraichean** bookcase

preasach a **-aiche** wrinkled, furrowed

preusant n **-an** m present, gift

prìne n **-nichean/-achan** m pin

priob v **-adh** wink, blink, twinkle

priobadh n **-aidh, -aidhean** m wink, winking, blinking **ann am p. na sùla** in the twinkling of an eye

prìobhaideach a **-diche** private **an roinn phrìobhaideach** f the private sector

prìomh a prime, primary, first, chief, principal **p. bhaile** capital city **am P. Mhinistear** the First Minister **p. oifis** head office, headquarters

prìomhaire n **-an** m prime minister, premier

prionnsa n **-n/-ichean** m prince **am P. Teàrlach** Prince Charles

prionnsapal n **-ail, -ail/-an** m principle **ann am p.** in principle *Also* **prionnsabal**

prìosan n **-ain, -ain/-an** m prison

prìosanach n **-aich, -aich** m prisoner, captive **p. cogaidh** prisoner of war

prìs n **-e, -ean** f price **dè (a') phris a tha e?** how much does it cost?

prìseil a **-e** precious, valuable

pròbhaist n **-e, -ean** m provost

prògram n **-aim, -an** m programme

proifeasair n **-ean** m professor

proifeiseanta a professional

pròis n **-e** f pride, haughtiness

pròiseact n **-eict, -an** f m project

pròiseil a **-e** proud, haughty

pronn a **pruinne** pounded, mashed, ground, pulverized **buntàta p.** m mashed potatoes **airgead p.** m loose change

pronn v **-adh** pound, mash, grind, pulverize **chaidh a phronnadh** he was beaten up

pronnasg n **-aisg** m sulphur, brimstone

pronnfheòil n **-òla** f mince

prosbaig n **-ean** f binoculars, telescope

Pròstanach n **-aich, -aich** m Protestant a Protestant *Formerly* **Pròsdanach**

prothaid n **-e, -ean** f profit

puball n **-aill, -an** m marquee, pavilion

pucaid n **-e, -ean** f bucket

pùdar n **-air, -an** m powder

pùdaraich v **-achadh** powder

pudhar n m harm, injury **cha do chuir e p. orm** it didn't put me up or down

puicean n **-ein, -an** m poke, small bag; (*met*) small man

puing n **-e, -ean** f point; degree (*of temperature*)

puinnsean n **-ein, -an** m poison, venom

puinnseanaich v **-achadh** poison

puinnseanta a poisonous, venomous **p. fuar** bitterly cold

pump(a) n **-(a)ichean** m pump

punnd n **puinnd, puinnd** m pound (*weight*); pound (*money*) **p. Sasannach** pound sterling

pupaid n **-ean** f m puppet

purgadair n **-e** m purgatory; purifier

purgaid n **-e, -ean** f purge, purgative

purgaideach a **-diche** purgative

purpaidh a **-e** purple

put(a) n **-a/-(a)ichean** m buoy

put v **-adh** push, shove, jostle

putan n **-ain, -an** m button

R

rabaid n **-e, -ean** f rabbit

rabhadh n **-aidh, -aidhean** m warning, alarm

rabhd n **-a, -an** m idle or far-fetched talk, spiel

ràc n **ràic, -an** m rake (garden); drake

ràc v **-adh** rake

racaid n **-e, -ean** f racket, noise; racquet; skelp

ràcan n **-ain, -ain/-an** m rake (*garden*); drake

ràc an t-sìl n **ràic-, ràcain-** m corncrake

rach *irr v* **dol** go (*See irr v* **rach** *in Grammar*) **r. an sàs an** tackle, get involved in **r. an urras do** assure **r. às àicheadh** deny **an rachadh agad air?** could/would you be able to do it?

radan *n* **-ain, -ain** *m* rat

ràdh *n* **-an** *m* saying, adage

rag *a* **raige** stiff, rigid; stubborn, obstinate, inflexible **r.-mharbh** stone dead

rag *v* **-adh** stiffen, benumb **bha sinn air ar ragadh leis an fhuachd** we were numb with the cold

rag-mhuinealach *a* **-aiche** obstinate, stubborn

raidhfil *n* **-ean** *f m* rifle

raige *n f* stiffness, rigidity; obstinacy, stubbornness

raighd *v* **-eadh** ride

raighdeadh *n* **-didh** *m* riding **sgoil raighdidh** *f* riding school

raineach *n* **-nich** *f* fern, bracken *Also* **fraineach**

ràinig *irr v* came, reached, arrived (*See irr v* **ruig** *in Grammar*)

raip *n* **-e** *f* dribble, traces of food round mouth; refuse

ràith(e) *n* **-(e)an/-(e)achan** *f* quarter (*of year*), season

ràitheachan *n* **-ain, -ain** *m* quarterly (*magazine*)

ràmh *n* **ràimh, ràimh** *m* oar

ràn *n* **ràin, ràin** *m* cry; roar, yell

ràn *v* **-aich/-ail** cry; roar, yell

rang *n* **-a, -an/-annan** *f m* row (*tier*)

rann *n* **rainn, -an/rainn** *m* verse, stanza

rannsachadh *n* **-aidh, -aidhean** *m* research, investigation, survey

rannsaich *v* **-achadh** research, search, scrutinize, investigate, explore

raon *n* **raoin, -tan/raointean** *m* plain, field; area **r.-cluiche** playing field **r.-laighe** runway **r. ola** oilfield

rapach *a* **-aiche** slovenly, scruffy; inclement, dirty (*weather*)

ràsair *n* **-ean** *m* razor

ràsanach *a* **-aiche** tedious

ràth *n* **-a, -an** *m* raft

rath *n* **-a** *m* prosperity, fortune, luck

rathad *n* **-aid/rothaid, -aidean/ròidean** *m* road, route, way **r.-mòr** main road, trunk road, highway **r.-iarainn** railway, railroad **an r. sin** that way **tog às mo r.!** get out of my way! **chan eil e às an r.** it's not too bad **chaidh e às an r.** he perished

Ratharsach *n* **-aich, -aich** *m* someone from Raasay *a* from, or pertaining to, Raasay

rè *prep* (+ *gen*) during, throughout **rè na h-oidhche** during the night

rèaban *n* **-ain, -an** *m* beard, whiskers

reachd *n* **-an** *m* statute, law, ordinance

reamhar *a* **reamhra/reaimhre** fat, plump

reamhraich *v* **-achadh** fatten

reic *n m* sale **fèill-reic** *f* sale of work

reic *v* sell *Also* **creic**

reiceadair *n* **-ean** *m* seller, salesman, vendor, auctioneer

rèidh *a* **-e** level, even, smooth; ready

rèidhleach *n* **-lich** *m* space, expanse

rèidhlean *n* **-ein, -an** *m* lawn, sward, green

rèidio *n* **-than** *m* radio

rèile *n* **-lichean** *f m* rail

rèilig *n* **-e, -ean** *f* grave, lair, graveyard, crypt *Also* **roilig**

reimhid *adv See* **roimhe**

rèis *n* **-e, -ean** *f* race (*sport*); span, lifetime

rèis *v* **-eadh** race

rèisimeid *n* **-e, -ean** *f* regiment

rèite *n* **-an** *f* accord, agreement, reconciliation

rèiteach *n* **-tich, -tichean** *m* betrothal; agreement, settlement

reithe *n* **-achan** *m* ram (*male sheep*)

rèitich *v* **-teachadh** reconcile, conciliate, arbitrate; settle, sort out

rèitire *n* **-an** *m* referee

reodh *v See* **reoth**

reòiteag *n* **-eig, -an** *f* ice cream

reoth *v* **-adh** freeze, become frozen

reothadair *n* **-ean** *m* freezer

reothadh *n* **-aidh** *m* frost, freezing

reothart *n* **-airt, -an** *f m* spring tide

reòthte *a* frozen *Also* **reòthta**

reub *v* **-adh** tear, rend, rip

reubal(t)ach *n* **-aich, -aich** *m* rebel

reubaire *n* **-an** *m* pirate, plunderer *Also* **reubadair**

reubte *a* riven, rent

reudan n **-ain, -an** m timber moth, woodlouse; dry rot

reul n **rèil, -tan** f star **r.-bhad** m constellation **r.-chearbach** f comet **r.-eòlas** m astronomy **r.-iùil** guiding star, Pole Star

reuladair n **-ean** m astronomer

reultag n **-aig, -an** f asterisk

reusan n **-ain** m reason, cause; sanity

reusanaich v **-achadh** reason

reusanta a reasonable, rational **r. math** reasonably good

ri prep to; engaged in **tha i ri bàrdachd** she composes poetry **bheil cus agad ri dhèanamh?** do you have a lot to do?

riabhach a **-aiche** brindled

riadh n **rèidh** m interest (fin) **chuir e r. mòr dheth** it returned high interest

riaghail v **-ghladh** rule, govern, regulate

riaghailt n **-e, -ean** f rule, regulation

riaghailteach a regular, orderly **r. bitheanta** fairly common

riaghaltas n **-ais, -an** m government **r. ionadail** local government **R. na h-Alba** Scottish Government

riaghladair n **-ean** m ruler, governor, regulator

riaghladh n **-aidh** m ruling, governing

riamh adv ever, before Also **a-riamh**

rian n **-an** m order, method, organization; arrangement (mus) **tha e às a r.** he is mad, crazy **cuir r. air** v organize

rianachd n f administration

rianail a **-e** methodical, orderly; reasonable

riaraich v **-achadh** satisfy, please; share (out), distribute, allocate **doirbh a riarachadh** hard to please

riaraichte a satisfied

riasg n **rèisg** m sedge, dirk-grass, coarse grass, peat moss

riaslach a **-aiche** hectic, extremely busy

riasladh n **-aidh** m struggle, busy toing and froing **bha r. air a' bhoin** the cow was in heat

riatanach a **-aiche** necessary, essential; appropriate

ribe n **-achan** f m snare, trap

ribh(se) prep pron to you (pl & pol)

ribheid n **-e, -ean** f reed (mus)

rìbhinn n **-e, -ean** f maiden

rid aug prep to your (sg)

ridire n **-an** m knight, sir **An R.** Sir

rìgh n **-rean** m king **r.-chathair** f throne

righinn a **rìghne** tough, tenacious, durable

rim aug prep to my

rin aug prep to their

rinn irr v did, made (See irr v **dèan** in Grammar)

rinn(e) prep pron to us

rioban n **-ain, -an** m ribbon **r.-tomhais** measuring tape Also **ribinn** f

riochd n **-a, -an** m appearance, form

riochdaich v **-achadh** represent; produce (eg programme)

riochdail a **-e** beautiful, handsome

riochdair n **-ean** m pronoun

riochdaire n **-an** m representative, delegate; producer (artistic)

rìoghachd n **-an** f kingdom, country **an R. Aonaichte** the United Kingdom

rìoghaich v **-achadh** reign

rìoghail a **-e** royal, regal

rìomhach a **-aiche** beautiful, lovely, fine

rìomhachas n **-ais** m finery, beauty

rionnach n **-aich, -aich** m mackerel

rionnag n **-aige, -an** f star **r. (an) earbaill** shooting star

rionnagach a **-aiche** starry

rir aug prep to our; to your

ris prep to **dè tha thu ris?** what are you doing/up to?

ris adv exposed (to view) **bha a còta-bàn ris** her slip was showing

ris(-san) prep pron to him/it

ri taobh prep phr (+ gen) beside

rithe(se) prep pron to her/it

rium(sa) prep pron to me

riut(sa) prep pron to you

riutha(san) prep pron to them

ro adv too; very (+ len) **ro bheag** too small

ro prep, adv before **ro-làimh** beforehand **ro-ainmichte** a aforementioned, aforesaid Formerly **roimh**

ro-aithris a **-ean** f forecast (weather); prediction

robach a **-aiche** slovenly, untidy, unkempt, squalid

robair(e) n **-(e)an** m robber

robh *irr v* was, were (*never used on its own*) (*See verb* **to be** *in Grammar*)
roc *n* **ruic/-a, -an** *f* wrinkle, crease; entanglement
roc *v* **-adh** wrinkle, crease
rocach *a* **-aiche** wrinkled, creased
rocaid *n* **-e, -ean** *f* rocket
ròcail *n* **-e** *f* croaking, croak
rocail *v* **rocladh** tangle, entangle
ròcais *n* **-ean** *f* rook **bodach-r.** scarecrow
rocladh *n* **-aidh** *m* tangle *Also* **ropladh**
rod *aug prep* before your (*sg*)
rògach *a* **-aiche** (*of an evening*) louring, gloomy
roghainn *n* **-ean** *f m* choice, selection, option **chan eil r. eile ann** there is no alternative **gheibh thu do r.** you can have your pick
roghnaich *v* **-achadh** choose, select
roid *n* **-e, -ean** *f* run before a leap **dh'fhalbh e aig r.** he went off at speed **thug iad r. a-steach dhan bhaile** they nipped into town
roile *n* **-lichean** *f m* roll (*bread*)
roilear *n* **-eir, -an** *m* roller **roilearan-spèilidh** roller blades
roilig *v* **-eadh** roll
roimh *prep See* **ro**
roimhe *adv* before, formerly
roimhe(san) *prep pron* before him/it
roimhear *n* **-eir, -an** *m* preposition
roimhpe(se) *prep pron* before her/it
roimh-ràdh *n See* **ro-ràdh**
ròineag *n* **-eig, -an** *f* a single hair
roinn *n* **-e, -ean** *f* share, portion, division, department; region **an R. Eòrpa** Europe

ròiseid *n* **-e, -ean** *f* resin
ròist *v* **ròstadh** roast
ro-leasachan *n* **-ain, -ain** *m* prefix
rola *n See* **roile**
ròlaist *n* **-e, -ean** *m* exaggeration, fanciful tale
ròlaisteach *a* **-tiche** prone to exaggeration or invention
rom *aug prep* before my
ròmach *a* **-aiche** hairy, shaggy, rough
Ròmàinianach *n* **-aich, -aich** *m* Romanian *a* Romanian
romhad(sa) *prep pron* before you
romhaibh(se) *prep pron* before you (*pl & pol*)
romhainn(e) *prep pron* before us
romham(sa) *prep pron* before me
romhpa(san) *prep pron* before them
ròn *n* **ròin, ròin** *m* seal
ron *aug prep* before the; before their
rong *n* **-a/roinge, -an** *f* rung, spar; boat-rib
rongach *a* **-aiche** dilatory
ronn *n* **roinn** *m* mucus, slaver, spittle
ròp(a) *n* **-(a), -(a)n/-(a)ichean** *m* rope **r.-anairt/-aodaich** clothes-line
ror *aug prep* before our, before your
ro-ràdh *n* **-ràidh, -an** *m* preface, preamble, prologue, introduction
ros *n* **rois, -an** *m* headland, promontory, peninsula
ròs *n* **ròis, -an** *m* rose
ròs *n* **ròis** knowledge **cha d' fhuair mi ròs air riamh** I never found any trace of him/it
ro-shealladh *n* **-aidh, -aidhean** *m* preview
rosg *n* **ruisg, -an** *m* prose

Insight: roinn

A multi-purpose noun and verb, meaning share, but also division, department, section etc. *Roinn an Fhoghlaim*, the Department of Education; *an roinn phoblach*, the public sector. *Roinn mhic is athar* (father's and son's share) means equal sharing, equal distribution. *Roinn mi an t-airgead orra* – I shared out the money among them.

---

roinn *v* divide, share (out)
roinneil *a* departmental, regional
ro-innleachd *n* **-an** *f* strategy

rosg *n* **ruisg, -an** *m* eyelash, eyelid
rosgrann *n* **-ainn, -an** *m* sentence
ròst *n* **-aichean** *f m* roast, roast meat

ròsta *a* roasted, roast
roth *n* **-a, -an** *f m* wheel **r. mun
ghealaich** a halo round the moon
rothaig *v* **-eadh** wind (*as clock*)
rothar *n* **-air, -an** *m* bicycle, cycle
ruadh *a* **ruaidhe** reddish-brown, ruddy,
ginger **falt r.** red hair
ruaig *n* **-e, -ean** *f* chase, pursuit, flight,
rout **chuireadh r. orra** *v* they were
routed/put to flight
rua(i)g *v* **ruagadh/ruagail** chase,
pursue, rout
ruamhair *v* **-ar** dig, delve; rummage
rubair *n* **-ean** *m* rubber
rùbarab *n* **-aib** *m* rhubarb
rubha *n* **-ichean** *m* point (*of land*),
promontory, headland
rùchd *n* **-a, -an** *m* stomach rumble,
belch **dèan r.** *v* belch *Also* **rùchdail**
rùchd *v* **-ail** rumble (*in stomach*)
rud *n* **-an** *m* thing **rud sam bith** anything
rùda *n* **-aichean/-n** *m* ram
rùdan *n* **-ain, -an** *m* knuckle
rudeigin *pron, adv* something, somewhat
tha i r. fuar it's somewhat cold
rudhadh *n* **-aidh** *m* blush, blushing, flush
bha r. na gruaidh she was flushed, she
was blushing
rùdhan *n* **-ain, -ain** *m* small stack of
peat, hay or corn
rug *irr v* caught, seized (*See irr v* **beir**
in Grammar)
ruga *n* **-ichean** *m* rug
rugadh *irr v* was born (*See irr v* **beir**
in Grammar) **r. is thogadh i ann am
Barraigh** she was born and brought up
in Barra

ruibh *prep pron See* **ribh**
r(u)idhil *v* **r(u)idhleadh** reel (*dance*)
r(u)idhle *n* **-an/-achan** *m* reel
ruig *irr v* **-hinn/-sinn/-heachd** reach,
arrive at (*See irr v* **ruig** *in Grammar*)
ruighe *n* **-an** *f m* forearm; slope
(*of hill*), plain
rùilear *n* **-eir, -an** *m* ruler (*measuring*)
ruinn *prep pron See* **rinn**
ruis *n* **-e** *f* elder (*tree*)
Ruiseanach *n* **-aich, -aich** *m* Russian
a Russian
rùisg *v* **rùsgadh** strip, peel; shear, fleece
rùisgte *a* naked, bare; shorn
ruiteach *a* **-tiche** ruddy
ruith *n* **-e, -ean** *f* running, run; rhythm
ruith *v* run, flow **tha 'n ùine air r. oirnn**
we've run out of time
rùm *n* **rùim, rumannan** *m* room; space
rùm-cadail bedroom **rùm-ionnlaid**
bathroom **rùm-suidhe** sitting room
rùm-teagaisg classroom
Rumach *n* **-aich, -aich** *m* someone from
Rum *a* from, or pertaining to, Rum
rùmail *a* **-e** roomy, spacious
rùn *n* **rùin, rùintean** *m* desire, wish,
intention, resolution, secret, love
rùnaich *v* **-achadh** desire, wish,
intend, resolve
rùnaire *n* **-an** *m* secretary **R. na Stàite**
the Secretary of State
rù-rà *a* untidy, topsy-turvy
rùraich *v* **-achadh** search (for); grope
rus *n* **ruis** *m* rice
rùsg *n* **rùisg, -an** peel, rind; bark;
fleece
rùsgadh *n* **-aidh** *m* peeling; shearing

S

's *irr v* is (*See verb* **to be** *in Grammar*)
's *conj* and (*contr of* **agus/is**)
sa *aug prep* in the
-sa *suff* (*used with* **mo, do** my, your
to give emphasis)
sa *suff* this (*equivalent to* **seo**)
Sàbaid *n* **-ean** *f* Sabbath **Latha/Là na S.**
Sunday *Also* **Sàboinn(t)**

sabaid *n* **(-e), -ean** *f* fight, fighting
sabaidich *v* **sabaid** fight
sàbh *n* **sàibh, sàibh/-an** *m* saw
sàbh *v* **-adh** saw
sàbhail *v* **-aladh** save, rescue
sàbhailte *a* safe
sàbhailteachd *n f* safety
sabhal *n* **-ail, -an/saibhlean** *m* barn

sàbhaladh n **-aidh** m saving, rescuing
sabhs n **-a, -an** m sauce
sac n **saic, saic/-an** m burden, load
  an sac asthma
sàcramaid n **-e, -ean** f sacrament
sad v **-ail/-adh** throw
sagart n **-airt, -an** m priest
sàibhear n **-eir, -an** m culvert
saideal n **-eil, -an** m satellite
saidhbhir a **-e** rich, wealthy
saidhbhreas n **-eis** m riches, wealth
saidheans n **-an** m science
saidhleafòn n **-òin, -an** m xylophone
saighdear n **-eir, -an** m soldier
saighead n **saighde/saighid,
  saighdean** f arrow
sail n **-e, -thean** f beam (as in roof),
  joist, large sawn piece of wood
sàil n **sàlach/sàla, -ean** f heel
sailead n **-eid, -an** m salad
saill n f **-e** fat; pickle, brine
saill v **-eadh** salt
saillear n **-eir, -an** f salt cellar
saillte a salty, salted
saimeant n m cement
sàirdseant n **-an** m sergeant
sàl n **sàil(e)** m salt water **an sàl** the sea
salach a **-aiche/sailche** dirty, filthy, foul
salaich v **-ach/-achadh** dirty, soil
salann n **-ainn** m salt
salchar n **-air** m dirt, filth
salm n **sailm, sailm** f m psalm **Leabhar
  nan S.** the Book of Psalms
salmadair n **-ean** m psalter; psalmist
salmaidh n **-ean** m psalmist
saltair v **-t** trample, tread
sam bith adv phr any **duine s. b.** anyone
  rud s. b. anything
samh n **saimh, -an** m odour, smell
sàmhach a **-aiche** silent, quiet **bi s.!**
  be quiet! **fan s.!** be quiet!, never!
  (in surprise)
samhail n **samhla, -ean** m likeness, like,
  equivalent **chan fhaca mi a shamhail**
  I've not seen his like
Samhain n **Samhna** f **an t-Samhain**
  November **Oidhche Shamhna** f
  Halloween

sàmhchair n **-e** f silence, quietness, quiet
samhla(dh) n **-aidh, -aidhean** m
  resemblance, likeness, allegory, figure;
  apparition
samhlachail a figurative; symbolic
samhlaich v **-achadh** liken, compare
samhradh n **-aidh, -aidhean** m summer
  as t-s. in summer
san aug prep in their
-san suff used with **a** his and **an** their to
  give emphasis **an coire-san** their fault
sanas n **-ais, -an** m notice,
  advertisement; whisper **s.-reic**
  advertisement
sannt n **-a** m greed, avarice, covetousness
sanntach a **-aiche** greedy, avaricious,
  covetous
sanntaich v **-tachadh** covet
saobh a **-a/saoibhe** erroneous, false,
  misguided
saobhaidh n **-ean** m den, fox's den, lair
saobh-chràbhadh n **-aidh, -aidhean** m
  superstition
saobh-chreideamh n **-eimh, -an** m
  heresy
saoghal n **-ail, ail/-an** m world; lifetime
  càit air an t-s. an robh sibh? where on
  earth were you?
saoghalta a worldly, materialistic
saoibhir a See **saidhbhir**
saoil v **-sinn/-tinn** think, suppose
  s. an tig iad I wonder if they'll come
  saoilibh? do you think?
saoithean n **-ein, -an/-ein** m saithe
saor n **saoir, saoir** m joiner, carpenter
saor a **saoire** free; cheap **s. 's
  an-asgaidh** free gratis, free of charge
saor v **-adh** free, liberate, exempt
saoradh n **-aidh** m liberation
saor-chlachair n **-ean** m freemason
saor-latha n **-làithean/-lathaichean** m
  holiday
saorsa n f freedom, liberty **s. chatharra**
  civil liberty
saorsainn n **-e** f freedom, liberty
saorsainneachd n f joinery, carpentry
saorsainneil a **-e** relaxed, at ease
saor-thoil n **-e** f free-will

saor-thoileach *a* voluntary
saothair *n* **saothrach** *f* labour, toil
saothraich *v* **-achadh** labour, toil
sàr *n* **sàir, sàir** *m* hero, excellent person
sàr *a* (*precedes & lenites n*) very, extremely, true **sàr sheinneadair** *a* truly great singer
sàrachadh *n* **-aidh** *m* exhaustion, annoyance, bother, harassment
sàraich *v* **-achadh** exhaust, annoy, bother, harass
sàraichte *a* exhausted, exhausting
sàs *n* **sàis** *m* straits, restraint, hold, grasp **an sàs an** involved in, engaged in **chaidh an cur an sàs** they were arrested
sàsachadh *n* **-aidh** *m* satisfaction
sàsaich *v* **-achadh** satisfy
sàsaichte *a* satisfied
Sasannach *n* **-aich, -aich** *m* English person *a* English
sàsar *n* **-air, -an** *m* saucer
sàth *v* **-adh** thrust
sàth *n* **sàith** *m* plenty, surfeit, satiety, abundance
's e *v* it is, he is (*See verb* **bi** *in Grammar*)
seabhag *n* **-aig, -an** *f m* hawk
seac *v* **-adh** wither
seacaid *n* (**-e**), **-ean** *f* jacket
seach *conj* since, because **s. gu** (+ *v*) since, because
seach *prep* instead of, rather than; compared to
seachad *adv* past **san dol-s.** in passing **thoir s.** *v* give (away)
seachad air *prep phr* past, by
seachain *v* **seachnadh** avoid, shun, abstain from
seachd *n, a* seven; (*also used as intensive*) **tha mi s. sgìth dheth** I'm absolutely fed up of it/him
seachdad *n* **-aid, -an** *m* seventy
seachdain *n* **-e/-donach, -ean** *f* week
seachdamh *a* seventh
seachd-deug *n, a* seventeen **seachd latha deug** seventeen days
seachdnar *n f m* seven (people)

seachnadh *n* **-aidh** *m* avoiding, avoidance, shunning
seachran *n* **-ain** *m* wandering **a' dol air s.** wandering, going astray
seach-rathad *n* **-aid, -aidean** *m* bypass
seada *n* **-n/-ichean** *f m* shed
seadag *n* **-aig, -an** *f* grapefruit
seadh *adv* yes, indeed (*used to confirm or lend emphasis*) **s. dìreach** just so
seagal *n* **-ail** *m* rye
seagh *n* **-a, -an** *m* sense, meaning
seàla *n* **-ichean** *f* shawl
sealastair *n* **-ean** *f m* iris (*plant*) *Also* **seileastair**
sealbh *n* **seilbh, -an** *m* fortune; possession, ownership **Aig an t-S. tha brath** Goodness knows **Gu sealladh S. orm** For goodness's sake
sealbhach *a* **-aiche** fortunate, lucky
sealbhadair *n* **-ean** *m* possessor, owner
sealbhaich *v* **-achadh** possess, own
sealg *n* **seilge, -an** *f* hunt
sealg *v* hunt
sealgair *n* **-ean** *m* hunter
sealgaireachd *n f* hunting
seall *v* **-tainn** look, see; show **s. seo!** look at this! **s. dhomh sin** show me that
sealladh *n* **-aidh, -aidhean** *m* view, sight, vision, show, spectacle **às an t-s.** out of sight **an dà shealladh** second sight
Sealtainneach *n* **-nich, -nich** *m* Shetlander *a* Shetland(ic)
seamrag *n* **-aig, -an** *f* shamrock
sean *a* **sine** old
seanadair *n* **-ean** *m* senator
seanadh *n* **-aidh, -aidhean** *m* senate, synod, assembly
seanailear *n* **-eir, -an** *m* general
seanair *n* **-ar, -ean** *m* grandfather; ancestor
seanchaidh *n* **-ean** *m* storyteller
seancharra *a* old-looking, old-fashioned *Also* **seangarra**
seanchas *n* **-ais, -an** *m* conversation, chat; lore
seanfhacal *n* **-ail, -ail/-aclan** *m* proverb
seang *a* **-a** slim, slender

seangan n **-ain, -ain/-an** m ant
seanmhair n **-ar, -ean** f grandmother
seann a old (precedes & lenites n)
  s. chàr an old car **s. fhear** an old one
  s. nòs traditional style **s. taigh** an old
  house **seann-fhasanta** old-fashioned
seans(a) n **-(a)ichean** m chance
seantans n **-an** f sentence (gram)
sear adv east, eastern
searbh a **-a/seirbhe** bitter, sour, tart
searbhachd n f bitterness
searbhadair n **-ean** m towel
searbhag n **-aig, -an** f acid
searbhant(a) n **-(a)n** f servant
searg v wither, shrivel, decay
seargach a withered, shrivelled,
  deciduous
seargadh n **-aidh** m decay
searmon n **-oin, -an** m sermon
searmonaich v **-achadh** preach
searmonaiche n **-an** m preacher
searrach n **-aich, -aich** m foal, colt
searrag n **-aig, -an** f bottle, flask
seas v **-amh** stand
seasamh n **-aimh, -an** m standing,
  stand, stance
seasg a **-a/seisge** barren, sterile
seasgachd n f sterility
seasgad n **-aid, -an** m sixty
seasgaich v **-achadh** sterilize
seasgair a **-e** snug, comfortable,
  sheltered, protected
seasmhach a **-aiche** steadfast, firm,
  stable; durable
seat v **-adh** set (except of sun)
seic n **-ean** f cheque **leabhar-**
  sheicichean m chequebook
Seiceach n **-cich, -cich** m Czech a Czech
seiche n **-an** f hide, skin, pelt
sèid v **-eadh** blow
seidhs(e) n **(-e), -(e)achan** f settee,
  couch
seilbh n **-e, -ean** f possession **gabh s. air**
  v take possession of
seilbheach a **-bhiche** possessive;
  genitive (gram)
seilbhich v **-bheachadh** possess, own
seilcheag n **-eig, -an** f snail, slug

seile n **-an** m spittle, saliva
seileach n **-lich, -lich** m willow
seillean n **-ein, -an** m bee
sèimh a **-e** gentle, mild, calm **an Cuan S.**
  the Pacific Ocean
sèimheachadh n **-aidh** m lenition,
  aspiration (gram)
sèine n **-nichean** f chain
seinn n f singing **s.-phàirteach** harmony
seinn v sing
seinneadair n **-ean** m singer
seirbheis n **-ean** f service **an t-S.**
  Chatharra the Civil Service
seirbheiseach n **-sich, -sich** m servant
seirc n **-e** f love, charity
seirm n **-e** f ring, chime, musical sound
seirm v ring, chime
seise n **-an** m one's match, one's equal
  thachair a sheise ris he met his match
seisean n **-ein** m session
sèist n **-e, -ean** f chorus, refrain
sèist n **-e, -ean** f m siege
sèitean n **-ein, -an** m panting
sèithear n **-thir, sèithrichean** m chair
  s.-cuibhle wheelchair **s.-putaidh**
  pushchair
seo a this
seo pron this (is); these (are)
seòclaid n **-ean** f m chocolate
seòl n **siùil, siùil** m sail
seòl n **siùil, siùil** m method, way
  s.-beatha way of life, lifestyle
seòl v **-adh** sail, navigate; direct, guide
seòladair n **-ean** m sailor
seòladh n **-aidh, -aidhean** m sailing;
  address, direction
seòl-mara n **siùil-mara, siùil-mhara**
  m tide
seòlta a cunning, crafty
seòltachd n f cunning, craftiness, guile
seòmar n **-air, seòmraichean** m room,
  chamber **s.-bìdh** dining-room **s.-cadail**
  bedroom **s.-còmhnaidh** living-room
  s.-fuirich waiting-room **s.-ionnlaid**
  bathroom **s.-leughaidh** reading-room,
  study **s.-sgeadachaidh** dressing-room
  s.-suidhe sitting-room **s.-teagaisg**
  classroom, lecture room

seòrsa *n* **-chan/-ichean** *m* sort, kind, type, species, brand

seòrsaich *v* **-achadh** sort, classify

seotaire *n* **-an** *m* idler, lazybones

seud *n* **seòid, seòid/-an** jewel, gem; (*met*) hero

seudar *n* **-air** *m* cedar

seula *n* **-chan** *m* seal

seulaich *v* **-achadh** seal

seumarlan *n* **-ain, -ain** *m* chamberlain, factor

seun *n* **-a, -an/-tan** *m* charm (*magical*)

seunta *a* charmed, enchanted

sgadan *n* **-ain, -ain** *m* herring

sgàig *n f* fearful disgust, repulsion

sgàil *n* **-e, -ean** *f* shade, shadow, veil, cover **s.-sùla** eyelid

sgàil *v* **-eadh** shade, screen, mask

sgailc *n* **-e, -ean** *f* slap, sharp blow, skelp, smack **s.-creige** echo

sgailc *v* slap, smack, skelp

sgàilean *n* **-ein, -an** *m* umbrella, screen **s.-grèine** parasol

sgàin *v* **-eadh** split, burst **tha mi gu sgàineadh** I've eaten too much/ I'm over-full (*lit* I'm about to burst)

sgàincadh *n* **-nidh** *m* split, crack, bursting

sgainneal *n* **-eil, -an** *m* scandal

sgainnealaich *v* **-achadh** scandalize

sgàird *n* **-e** *f* **an s.** diarrhoea

sgairt *n* **-e, -ean** *f* yell, loud cry

sgairt *n* **-e, -ean** *f* **an s.** diaphragm, midriff **bhris(t) e a s.** he ruptured himself

sgairteil *a* **-e** vigorous, brisk, energetic

sgait *n* **-e, -ean** *f* skate (*fish*)

sgaiteach *a* **-tiche** sharp, cutting (*as in remark*), sardonic; well-expressed, able; (*slang*) stunning

sgal *n* **-a, -an** *m* yell; blow

sgàl *n* **sgàil, sgàil** *m* tray

sgal *v* **-thart(aich)** howl, yell

sgalag *n* **-aig, -an** *f* servant, skivvy

sgall *n* **sgaill** *m* bald patch, baldness

sgallach *a* **-aiche** bald

Sgalpach *n* **-aich, -aich** *m* someone from Scalpay *a* from, or pertaining to, Scalpay

sgamhan *n* **-ain, -an** *m* lung

sgannan *n* **-ain, -an** *m* film, membrane

sgaoil *v* **-eadh** spread, scatter, disperse, disseminate; become undone **leig mu s.** *v* free, liberate, loosen

sgaoth *n* **-oith/-otha, -an** *m* swarm; multitude

sgap *v* **-adh** scatter

sgar *v* **-adh/-achdainn** separate, sever

sgaradh *n* **-aidh, -aidhean** *m* separation **s.-pòsaidh** divorce

sgarbh *n* **sgairbh, sgairbh** *m* cormorant

sgarfa *n* **-ichean** *f m* scarf

sgàrlaid *a* **-e** scarlet

Sgarpach *n* **-aich, -aich** *m* someone from Scarp *a* from, or pertaining to, Scarp

sgath *n m* anything; part **cha robh s. airgid aice** she hadn't any money **a h-uile s. dheth** every bit of it

sgàth *n* **-a, -an** *m* sake; shade, protection **air s.** on account of, because of (+ *gen*)

sgath *v* **-adh** lop, cut, prune, slash

sgàthan *n* **-ain, -an** *m* mirror

sgeadaich *v* **-achadh** decorate, adorn, embellish; dress

sgeadaichte *a* decorated, dressed

sgealb *n* **sgeilb, -an** *f* splinter

sgealbag *n* **-aig, -an** *f* forefinger, index finger

sgeama *n* **-ichean** *f m* scheme

sgeamhadaich *n f* coughing and spluttering

sgeap *n* **sgeip, -an/-aichean** *f* beehive

sgeig *n* **-e** *f* derision, ridicule

sgeigeil *a* **-e** derisive

sgeilb *n* **-e, -ean** *f* wood chisel *Also* **geilb**

sgeileid *n* **-e, -ean** *f* saucepan, skillet

sgeilp *n* **-ichean** *f* shelf

sgèimhich *v* **-mheachadh** beautify, adorn

sgeir *n* **-e, -ean** *f* skerry, reef

sgeith *n* **-e** *m* vomit, vomiting

sgeith *v* **sgeith/-eadh** vomit, spew

sgèith *n* flying **air s.** flying

sgèith *v* fly

sgeith-rionnaig *n m* meteor

sgeul n **sgeòil, sgeòil** m story, tale; trace **a bheil s. orra?** is there any sign of them? *Also* **sgeula** f

sgeulachd n **-an** f story, tale

sgeulaiche n **-an** m storyteller

sgeunach a **-aiche** shy, timid, easily frightened

sgì n **sgithe, sgithean** f ski

sgì v **-theadh** ski

sgialachd n *See* **sgeulachd**

sgiamh n **-a, -an** f m scream, squeal, shriek **dèan s.** v scream

sgiamh v **-ail** scream, squeal

sgiamhach a **-aiche** beautiful

sgiamhaich v **-achadh** beautify

sgiamhail n f screaming

sgian n **sgeine, sgeinean** f knife

sgiath n **sgèithe, -an** f wing; shield

sgiathach a winged

sgiathaich v **-thadh** fly

sgiathalaich n f flying about, fluttering *Also* **sgiathadaich**

Sgiathanach n, a *See* **Sgitheanach**

sgigean n **-ein** m a tiny amount *Also* **gigean**

sgil n **-ean** f m skill

sgileil a **-e** skilful

sgillinn n **-e, -ean** f penny **deich sg.** 10 pence **chan eil s. ruadh agam** I don't have a single penny

sgioba n **-n/-idhean** f m crew, team

sgiobachd n f personnel, manpower

sgiobair n **-ean** m skipper, captain

sgiobalta a tidy, neat; quick

sgioblachadh n **-aidh** m tidying, tidying-up

sgioblaich v **-achadh** tidy, streamline

sgiorradh n **-aidh, -aidhean** m accident

sgiorrghail n f screaming, shrill crying

sgiort(a) n **(-a), -(a)n/-(a)ichean** f skirt

sgìos n *See* **sgìths**

sgìre n **-an** f district, parish **sgìr-easbaig** diocese

sgìreachd n **-an** f district, parish

sgìreil a **-e** district, parochial

sgìth a **-e** tired

sgitheach n **-thich** m hawthorn

sgitheadair n **-ean** m skier

sgitheadh n **-thidh** m skiing

Sgitheanach n **-aich, -aich** m someone from Skye a from, or pertaining to, Skye

sgìtheil a **-e** tiring, wearisome

sgìthich v **-theachadh** tire, make or become weary

sgìths n f m tiredness, weariness, fatigue

sgiùrs v **-adh** scourge, lash

sgiùrsair n **-ean** m scourge

sglàib n f plaster

sglàibeadair n **-ean** m plasterer

sglàibrich v plaster

sglèat n **-a, -an/-aichean** f m slate

sglèat v **-adh** slate

sglèatair n **-ean** m slater

sgleog n **-oig, -an** f blow, slap

sgoch v **-adh** sprain, strain

sgòd n **sgòid, -an** m (*of sail*) sheet; piece of cloth or garment **cha robh s. aodaich orra** they were completely naked

sgoil n **-e, -tean/-ean** f school **àrd-s.** high school **bun-s.** primary school **s.-àraich** nursery school **s.-fhonn** psalmody class

sgoilear n **-eir, -an** m pupil, scholar

sgoilearach a scholastic

sgoilearachd n f scholarship

sgoilt v **sgoltadh** split, cleave, slit

sgoinneil a **-e** terrific, super, superb, smashing, great; strapping (*of person*)

sgol v **-adh** rinse

sgoladh n **-aidh, -aidhean** m rinse, rinsing; (*met*) telling-off

sgolt v **-adh** split, cleave, slit

sgoltadh n **-aidh** m cleft, slit, split

sgona n **-ichean** f m scone

sgonn n **sgoinn/sguinn, -an** m block, lump **s. mòr de ghille** a big strapping lad

sgor n **sgoir, -an** m notch, cut, mark

sgòr n **sgòir, -an/-aichean** m score (*sport*)

sgorach a **-aiche** notched

sgòrnan n **-ain, -an** m gullet, throat

sgòrnanach a **-aiche** bronchial

sgot n **sgoit** m spot, plot of ground; fragment **cha robh s. aca** they hadn't a clue

sgoth n **-a, -an** f skiff, small boat

sgòth *n* **-a, -an** *f* cloud
sgòthach *a* **-aiche** cloudy
sgraing *n* **-e, -ean** *f* frown **chuir e
s. air** *v* he frowned
sgreab *n* **-a, -an** *f* scab
sgread *n* **-a, -an** *m* shriek, screech
sgread *v* **-ail** shriek, screech **rinn i s.** *v*
she shrieked
sgreadhail *n* **-e, -ean** *f* trowel
sgreamh *n* **-a/-eimhe** *m* disgust, loathing
sgreamhaich *v* **-achadh** disgust,
nauseate
sgreamhail *a* **-e** disgusting, nauseating,
horrible, loathsome
sgreataidh *a* **-e** ugly, horrible
sgreuch *n* **-a, -an** *m* scream, screech
dèan s. *v* scream, screech
sgreuch *v* **-ail/-adh** scream, screech
sgriach *v* See **sgreuch**
sgrìob *n* **-a, -an** *f* scrape, scratch; stripe;
trip **chaidh sinn s. dhan bhaile** we
went on a trip to town
sgrìob *v* **-adh** scrape, scratch
sgrìobach *a* **-aiche** striped
sgrìobag *n* **-aig, -an** *f* note (*written*)
sgrìoban *n* **-ain, -an** *m* hoe, rake
sgrìob-cheangail *n* **sgrìoban-ceangail**
f hyphen
sgrìobh *v* **-adh** write
sgrìobhadair *n* **-ean** *m* writer *Also*
sgrìobhaiche
sgrìobhadh *n* **-aidh, -aidhean** *m*
writing, inscription
sgrìobhte *a* written
sgrìobtar *n* **-air, -an** *m* scripture
sgrìobtarail *a* **-e** scriptural
sgrios *n* **-a, -an** *m* destruction, ruin
sgrios *v* **sgrios/-adh** destroy, ruin
sgriosail *a* **-e** destructive, ruinous;
terrible, awful, dreadful **s. daor** terribly
expensive
sgriubha *n* **-ichean** *f m* screw
sgriubhaire *n* **-an** *m* screwdriver
sgròb *v* **-adh** scratch
sgròbadh *n* **-aidh, -aidhean** *m* scratch,
scratching
sgrùd *v* **-adh** scrutinize, examine,
inspect, audit

sgrùdadh *n* **-aidh, -aidhean** *m*
scrutiny, examination, inspection, audit
dèan s. air *v* scrutinize, examine **neach-
sgrùdaidh** *m* examiner, inspector
sguab *n* **-aibe, -an** *f* broom, brush,
sweep; sheaf **s. arbhair** a sheaf of corn
s.-fhliuch mop
sguab *v* **-adh** sweep, brush
sguabadair *n* **-ean** *m* sweeper
sguad *n* **-aid, -an** *m* squad, bunch
of people
sgud *v* **-adh** lop, chop, cut; (+ **leis** *etc*)
snatch
sgudal *n* **-ail** *m* rubbish, trash, garbage
làraidh an sgudail *f* the refuse lorry
sguilearaidh *n* **-ean** *f m* scullery
sguir *v* **sgur** cease, stop **s. dheth** stop it
s. i a smocadh she stopped smoking
sgùirt *n* **-e, -ean** *f* lap
sgur *n* **sguir** *m* ceasing, stopping **gun s.**
endlessly, constantly, non-stop
sgùr *v* **-adh** scour, cleanse
sgùrr *n* **sgurra, sgurran** *m* steep hill,
peak, pinnacle
shìos *adv* down (*stationary*)
shuas *adv* up (*stationary*)
sia *n, a* six
siab *v* **-adh** blow (away), drift
siaban *n* **-ain** *m* sand-drift, sea-spray
siabann *n* **-ainn, -ainn** *m* soap
sia-cheàrnach *n* **-aich, -an** *m* hexagon
a hexagonal
sia-deug *n, a* sixteen **sia bliadhna
deug** sixteen years
sian *n* **sìne, -tan** *f* weather, storm
na siantan the elements
sian *n* See **sìon**
sianar *n* *f m* six (people)
siar *a* west, western **an Cuan S.**
the Atlantic Ocean
siathamh *a* sixth
sibh(se) *pron* you (*pl & pol*)
sìde *n* *f* weather **deagh shìde** good
weather **droch shìde** bad weather
sil *v* **-eadh** drip, drop, rain **a bheil i a'
sileadh?** is it raining?
sileadh *n* **-lidh, -lidhean** *m* dripping;
rainfall, precipitation

sileagan n **-ain**, **-an** m jar
sìlean n **-ein**, **-an** m grain, tiny drop
silidh n m jam
similear n **-eir**, **-an** m chimney
similidh a **-e** sheepish
sìmplich v **-leachadh** simplify
sìmplidh a **-e** simple, easy
sin a that, those
sin pron that **an sin** there; then
sìn v **-eadh** stretch; pass **sìn a-mach** extend, prolong **sìn dhomh an salann** pass me the salt
sinc n m zinc
sinc(e) n **-(e)achan/-(e)an** f m sink
sine n **-an** f teat, nipple
sineach n **sinich**, **sinich** m mammal
sìneadh n **sìnidh** m stretch, stretching
singilte a single, singular
sinn(e) pron we, us
sinn-seanair n **-ar**, **-ean** m great-grandfather
sinn-seanmhair n **-ar**, **-ean** f great-grandmother
sinnsear n **-sir**, **-sirean** m ancestor, forefather
sinnsearachd n f ancestry
sìnteag n **-eig**, **-an** f hop, bound, stride; stepping-stone
siobhag n **-aig**, **-an** f wick
sìobhalta a civil, courteous, polite
sìobhaltachd n f civility; civilization
sìobra n **-than** m zebra
sìochail a **-e** peaceful, peaceable
sìoda n **-chan** m silk
siogàr n **-àir**, **-an** m cigar
sìol n **sil** m seed; sperm; progeny
sìolag n **-aig**, **-an** f sand-eel
sìolaich v **-achadh** seed; beget, propagate; (intrans) multiply
sìolaidh v subside, settle; filter, strain **s. às** peter out
siolandair n **-ean** m cylinder
sìol-chuir v **-chur** sow
siolp v **-adh** slip away, slink off, skulk
sìol(t)achan n **-ain**, **-ain** m filter, strainer
sìoman n **-ain**, **-an** m rope of straw or hay; line for clothes (indoors)

sìon n anything, something **a h-uile s.** everything
Sìonach n **-aich**, **-aich** m Chinese a Chinese
sionnach n **-aich**, **-aich** m fox
sionnsar n **-air**, **-an** m bagpipe chanter
siopsach n **-aich**, **-aichean** m gypsy
sìor a ever, always, continual **s.-mhaireannach** perpetual, everlasting **s.-uaine** evergreen
sioraf n **-aif**, **-an** m giraffe
siorap n **-aip** f m syrup
siorc n **-a**, **-an** m shark
siorrachd n **-an** f shire, county Also **siorramachd**
siorraidh a ever **gu s.** forever
siorraidheachd n f eternity Also **siorrachd**
siorram n **-aim**, **-an** m sheriff Also **siorraidh**
sìos adv down, downwards
siosacot n **-oit**, **-an** m waistcoat
siosar n **-air**, **-an** f m scissors
siosarnaich n f hissing, hiss
siostam n **-aim**, **-an** m system
siota n **-ichean** f sheet
sir v **-eadh** seek, search for
siris(t) n **-ean** f cherry
sìth n **-e** f peace, reconciliation
sitheadh n **-thidh**, **-thidhean** m speed, onrush, impetuosity
sìthean n **-ein**, **-ein/-an** m hillock, knoll, fairy knoll; flower
sitheann n **sithinn/sìthne** f m venison, game; flesh of fowls
sìtheil a **-e** peaceful, tranquil, peaceable
sìthich v **sìtheachadh** pacify
sìthiche n **-an** m fairy
sitig n **-e**, **-ean** f dunghill, midden; outdoors
sitir n **-e** f neighing, braying
sitrich n **-e** f neighing, braying Also vn **a' s.**
siubhail v **-al** travel, journey; die, pass away
siubhal n **-ail**, **siùbhlaichean** m travel **cosgaisean siubhail** f pl travel expenses **fad an t-siubhail** all the time

siùbhlach n -aiche, -aichean m traveller; nomad

siùbhlach a -aiche swift, speedy; wandering, itinerant; fluent (speech)

siùcar n -air, -an m sugar; sweet

siud pron that **an siud** there, over there

siùdan n -ain, -an m swing (for play)

siuga n -nnan f m jug

siùrsach n -aich, -aichean f prostitute

siuthad def v go on! pl **siuthadaibh/siùdaibh**

slabhraidh n -ean f chain

slaic n -ean f blow **thug iad s. air an Riaghaltas** they hit out at the Government

slaic v -eadh thrash, beat, strike

slaighd v -eadh slide

slaightear m -eir, -an m rogue, fraudster Also **slaightire**

slaightearachd n f roguery, fraud

slàinte n f health **bòrd s.** m health board **Seirbheis na S.** the Health Service **Slàinte!** Cheers! **S. mhath!** Your health! Cheers!

slàinteachail a -e hygienic

slat n slait, -an f rod; yard (length) **s.-iasgaich** fishing rod **s.-t(h)omhais** measuring rod; criterion, yardstick

sleagh n -a, -an f spear, javelin

sleamhainn a -e/-mhna slippery

sleamhnag n -aig, -an f slide

sleamhnagan n -ain m stye

sleamhnaich v -achadh slip, slide

sleids n -ichean m sledge

sleuchd v -adh kneel, prostrate self; submit

sliabh n slèibh(e), slèibhtean m mountain, hillside, moor

sliasaid n -e, -ean f thigh

slige n -an/-achan f shell

sligeach a -giche shelled, having a shell, shelly

sligeanach n -aich m tortoise

slighe n -an f way, path, direction, track, route

slinnean n -ein, -an m shoulder, shoulder-blade

slìob v -adh stroke; (met) flatter

sliochd n -a, -an m offspring, progeny, descendants

Insight: slàinte

Slàn is whole or healthy, and *slàinte* is health. *Slàinte Mhath!* – Good health! or Your health! Or you can simply say *Slàinte!* Other variants are *Slàinte Mhòr and Air do dheagh shlàinte!* The Health Board and the Health Service are *Bòrd na Slàinte* and *Seirbheis na Slàinte*. The opposite is *euslaint*.

---

slàinteachas n -ais m hygiene

slàintealachd n f sanitation

slaman n -ain m curds, curdled milk **s.-milis** jelly

slàn a slàine whole, complete, wholesome **s. leat** goodbye, farewell

slànaich v -achadh heal, cure

slànaighear n -eir m saviour **an S.** the Saviour

slaod n slaoid, -an m sledge, raft

slaod v -adh pull, drag, haul

slaodach a -aiche slow, tardy, sluggish

slaodair n -ean m sluggard

slapag n -aig, -an f slipper

slìogach a -aiche sly, sleekit; dilatory

sliopair n -ean f m slipper

slios n -a, -an m side, slope, flank

slis n -e, -ean f slice, rasher

sliseag n -eig, -an f slice, small slice

slisnich v -neadh slice

sloc n sluic, sluic/-an m pit, cavity, hollow

sloinn v -eadh give/trace genealogy/family tree

sloinneadh n -nidh, -nidhean m surname; genealogy

sloinntearachd n f (act of giving a) genealogy

sluagh n **sluaigh, slòigh** m people, host, crowd

sluagh-ghairm n -e, -ean f war-cry, slogan

sluasaid n -e, -ean f shovel

slugadh n -aidh m swallowing, gulping, devouring; capacity **tha s. mòr aig an talla** the hall has a large capacity

slugan n -ain, -an m gullet

sluig v -eadh/slugadh swallow

slupraich n -e f slurping; splashing through water

smachd n m discipline, authority, control **fo s.** under control **cùm s. air** v keep control of

smachdaich v -achadh discipline

smachdail a -e authoritative, commanding, disciplinary

smal n **smail** m spot, stain **gun s.** without blemish **màireach gun s. dhut** may all your days be happy

smàl v -adh extinguish, quench

smàladair n -ean m firefighter

smalan n -ain m grief, sorrow, melancholy

smaoin n -e, -tean f thought, idea

smaoineachadh n -aidh m thinking

smaoin(t)ich v smaoin(t)eachadh/ smaointinn think

smàrag n -aig, -an f emerald

smèid v -eadh wave, beckon

smeòrach n -aich, -aichean f thrush

smeur n -a, -an f bramble

smeur v -adh smear, daub

smid n -e, -ean f syllable, word **cha tuirt e s.** he didn't utter a word

smig n -ean f m chin

smiogaid n -ean f m chin

smior n smir/-a m marrow, pith; strength, pluck, vigour; best part **'s e s. an duin'-uasail a th' ann** he's a real/true gentleman **s.-caillich** spinal marrow

smiorail a -e/-ala strong, vigorous, doughty, plucky Also **smearail**

smiùr v -adh See smeur

smoc v -adh smoke Also **smocaig**

smocadh n -aidh m smoking

smodal n -ail m fragments, crumbs; smattering **s. airgid** loose change

smuain n -e, -tean f thought, idea

smuainich v -neachadh think

smuairean n -ein m dejection

smug n smuig, -an m phlegm

smugadaich n f spitting

smugaid n -e, -ean f spit, spittle **tilg s.** v spit

smugraich n f drizzle

smùid n -e, -ean f smoke, vapour; intoxication **ghabh e droch s.** v he got very drunk

smuig n -ean f snout, visage

smùirnean n -ein, -ein m mote, atom

smùirneanach a atomic

smùr n smùir m dross, dust

sna aug prep in the (before pl nouns)

snag n snaig, -an m knock, crack

snagadaich n -e f gnashing, grating, chattering (of teeth)

snàgail n -e f crawl, crawling

snàgair n -ean m crawler; reptile

snagan-daraich n snagain-, snagain-/snaganan- m woodpecker

snaidhm n -ean, -eannan m knot **cuir s. air** v tie a knot in it Also **snaoim**

snàig v snàgadh/snàgail creep, crawl

snàigeach a -giche creeping, crawling

snàigeadh n -gidh m creeping, crawling

snaigh v -eadh sculpt, carve, hew

snaigheadair n -ean m sculptor

snaigheadh n -ghidh, -ghidhean m sculpture, carving **bha iad a' s. ris an uair** they were cutting it fine

snàithlean n -ein, -an m thread

snàmh v swim

snaoisean n -ein m snuff

snas n snais m accomplishment, elegance, finesse

snasail a -e accomplished, elegant, well-finished

snasmhor a -oire accomplished, elegant, well-finished

snàth n -a/snàith, snàithean m thread

snàthad n -aid, -an f needle

snàthainn n -e/snàithe, -ean/ snàithean m thread, single thread

snàthlainn n See **snàithlean**
sneachd(a) n m snow **a' cur an t-s.** v snowing **bodach-s.** m snowman
snèap n snèip, **-an** f turnip, neep Also **snèip**
sniag n **-an** m sneak
snigh v **-e** leak, drip, seep
snighe n m rain penetration from roof, seeping, seepage, drip
snìomh n **-a**, **-an** m spinning, twist
snìomh v snìomh/**-adh** spin, twist **shnìomh i a h-adhbrann** she twisted/sprained her ankle
snìomhaire n **-an** m wimble, drill
snìomhan n **-ain**, **-an** m spiral
snodhach n **-aich** m sap
snodha-gàire n snodhan- m smile, quick smile
snog a **snoige** nice, lovely, attractive; likeable
snot v **-adh** smell, sniff
snuadh n **-aidh** hue, complexion, appearance, aspect
so a See **seo**
sòbarra a sober
sòbhrach n **-aich**, **-aichean** f primrose Also **seòbhrach**
socair n **-e/socrach** f ease, rest **gabh air do shocair** take it easy
socair a socraiche, **-c** at ease, quiet, tranquil, mild; comfortable
sochair n **-(e)**, **-ean** f benefit, privilege **s. chloinne** child benefit **s. cion-cosnaidh** unemployment benefit
socharach a **-aiche** laid back, easy-going, bashful
socrach a **-aiche** at ease, comfortable, sedate
socraich v **-achadh** settle; determine, fix
sodal n **-ail** f m flattery, fawning
sòfa n **-than** f sofa
sòghail a **-e** sumptuous, luxurious
soidhne n **-achan** m sign Also **soighne**
soilire n m celery
soilleir a **-e** clear, bright
soilleireachd n f clearness, clarity, clarification, brightness
soilleirich v **-reachadh** clear, clarify, illuminate, brighten

soillse n **-an** m light
soillseach a **-siche** bright, clear, shining
soillsich v **-seachadh** light, enlighten
soirbh a **-e** easy
soirbheachadh n **-aidh**, **-aidhean** m success, prosperity
soirbheachail a **-e** successful, prosperous
soirbheas n **-eis**, **-eis** m success, prosperity; favourable breeze
soirbhich v **-bheachadh** succeed, prosper
soircas n **-ais**, **-an** m circus
sòisealach n **-aich**, **-aich** m socialist
sòisealach a **-aiche** socialist
sòisealachd n f socialism, social work
sòisealta a social **na seirbheisean s.** the social services
sòisealtas n **-ais** m society
soisgeul n **-eil**, **-an** m gospel
soisgeulach a **-aiche** evangelical
soisgeulaiche n **-an** m evangelist
soitheach n **-thich**, **-thichean** f m dish; vessel, ship **nigh na soithichean** wash the dishes **s.-sgudail** rubbish bin
soitheamh a **-eimhe** tame, docile, tractable, gentle
sòlaimte a solemn, dignified
solair v **-ar/-aradh** provide, supply, cater for, procure
solarachadh n **-aidh** m provision, supply, catering, procurement
solaraich v **-achadh** provide, supply, cater for, procure
solas n **-ais**, **-ais** m light; traffic lights
sòlas n **-ais**, **-ais** m happiness, joy, solace
sòlasach a **-aiche** happy, joyful
so-leaghadh a dissoluble
so-leughadh a legible
so-loisgeach a combustible
solt(a) a mild, gentle, placid
so-lùbadh a flexible
somalta a placid, docile; inactive
son n m cause, account **air mo shon-sa** on my behalf
'son prep See **airson**
sona a happy, content
sonas n **-ais** m happiness, contentment

sònraich v **-achadh** specify, stipulate

sònraichte a special, particular, specific; remarkable **gu s.** particularly, especially

sop n **suip**, **suip/-an** m wisp

soraidh n f farewell **s. leibh** farewell (to you) (pl & pol)

sòrn n **sùirn** m flue, vent

so-ruighinn a accessible Also **so-ruigsinn**

so-thuigsinn a intelligible, clear

spàgach a **-aiche** splay-footed

spàgail n f walking awkwardly

spaid n **-e**, **-ean** f spade

spaideil a **-e** well-dressed, smart

spaidsirich v **-searachd** parade, saunter

spàin n **-e**, **-ean/-tean/-eachan** f spoon **s.-ti/teatha** teaspoon

Spàinn(t)each n Spaniard a Spanish

Spàinn(t)is n f Spanish (lang)

spàirn n **-e** f effort, exertion, struggle, stress **rinn e s. mhòr** he made a great effort

spàl n **spàil**, **-an** m shuttle **s.-fànais** space shuttle **s.-ite** shuttlecock

spanair n **-ean** m spanner

spàrdan n **-ain**, **-ain/-an** m roost

spàrr n **sparra**, **sparran** m joist, beam; roost

spàrr v **sparradh** thrust, force

spastach n **-aich**, **-aich** m spastic

spastach a **-aiche** spastic

speach n **-a**, **-an** f wasp; (met) spitfire

speal n **-a**, **-an** f scythe

spealg n **speilg**, **-an** f splinter, fragment

spealg v **-adh** splinter, smash

spèil n **-e**, **-ean** f skate

spèil v **-eadh** skate

spèileabord n **-buird**, **-buird** m skateboard, skateboarding

spèile-deighe n f ice skating

spèiliche n **-an** m skater

speireag n **-eig**, **-an** f sparrow-hawk; spitfire, nippy sweetie

spèis n **-e** f esteem, affection, regard, fondness, attachment **bha s. mhòr aige dhi** he held her in great esteem, he was very fond of her

speisealta a specialist

speuclairean n m pl spectacles, glasses **s.-grèine** sunglasses Also **speuclair** (sg)

speur n **-a**, **-an** m sky **na speuran** the heavens, the firmament **s.-sheòladair** spaceman, astronaut **s.-shiubhal** m space travel

speur(ad)air n **-ean** m astronaut, spaceman

speuradaireachd n f study of space

spìc n **-e**, **-ean** f spike

spìdeag n **-eig**, **-an** f nightingale; nippy female

spìocach a **-aiche** mean, miserly, stingy

spìocaire n **-an** m miser

spìocaireachd n f meanness, miserliness

spìon v **-adh** pluck, tug, snatch, wrench

spionnadh n **-aidh** m strength, vigour

spiorad n **-aid**, **-an** m spirit **an S. Naomh** the Holy Spirit

spioradail a **-e** spiritual

spioradalachd n f spirituality

spìosrach a **-aiche** spicy

spìosradh n **-aidh**, **-aidhean** m spice

spìosraich v **-achadh** spice; embalm

spìosraidh n f spices

spiris n **-e**, **-ean** f roost, perch

spitheag n **-eig**, **-an** f chuckie (small flat pebble), skimmer

splais n **-ean** f splash

splais v **-eadh** splash

splaoid f **-ean** jaunt

spleadhach a **-aiche** splay-footed Also **spliathach**

spleuchd n **-a**, **-an** m smarm; stare, gaze

spleuchd v spread out, plaster all over; stare, gaze

spliùchan n **-ain**, **-an** m tobacco pouch Also **spliuchan**

spliugach a **-aiche** snotty

spòg n **spòig**, **-an** f paw; claw, spoke; hand (of watch/clock)

spong n **spuing**, **-an** m sponge

spor n **spuir**, **-an** m spur; claw, talon; flint

sporan n **-ain**, **-ain** m purse

sporghail n f noisy scramble/scrabble, rustling

spòrs n **-a** f sport, fun

spòrsail a **-e** sporting, sporty; funny, in fun

spot n **-an** f m spot
spoth v **spoth, -adh** castrate, geld
spreadh v **-adh** explode, burst
spreadhadh n **-aidh, -aidhean** m
explosion, burst
sprèidh n **-e** f cattle, livestock
spreig v **-eadh** incite
sprochd n m dejection, sadness
fo s. dejected
sprogan n **-ain** m double chin
sprùilleach n **-lich** m crumbs,
fragments, debris
spuaic n **-e, -ean** f smudge v smudge
spùill v **-eadh** plunder
spùinn v **-eadh** plunder
spùinneadair n **-ean** m plunderer
s.-mara pirate
spuir n **-ean** m claw, talon
spùt n **-a, -an** m spout; very small
particle **chan eil s. aige** he has
no idea
spùt v **-adh** spout, squirt
sràbh n **sràibh, -an** m straw
srac v **-adh** tear, rend
sracadh n **-aidh, -aidhean** m tear,
tearing
sradag n **-aig, -an** f spark **tha s. innte**
she has a quick temper
sràid n **-e, -ean** f street
srainnsear n **-eir, -an** m stranger
srann n **srainn, -an** f snore, hum **dèan**
s. v snore
srath n **-a, -an** m wide valley
(usually with river)
sreang n **-a/sreinge, -an** f string
sreap v **sreap/-adh** climb
sreapadair n **-ean** m climber
sreath n **-a, -an** f m row, series
an s. a chèile in a row, in succession
sreothart n **-airt, -an** m sneeze
dèan s. v sneeze Also **sreathart**
sreothartaich n f sneezing Also
sreathartaich
srian n **srèine, -tan/srèinean** f stripe;
bridle **cùm s. air do theanga** v watch
what you say
srianach a **-aiche** striped
sròl n **sròil, -an** m satin

sròn n **sròine, -an/sròinean** f nose;
promontory **ghabh iad san t-sròin e**
they took offence at it Also **sròin**
sròin-adharcach n **-aich** m rhinoceros
srùb n **srùib, -an** m spout
srùbag n **-aig, -an** f a small drink,
a cuppa
srùban n **-ain, -ain** m cockle
sruth n **-a/sruithe, -an** m stream, burn;
current **leis an t-s.** with the current;
(met) downhill
sruth v **-adh** stream, flow
sruthail v **-thladh/srùthladh** wash, rinse
sruthan n **-ain, -ain** m streamlet,
small stream
stàball n **-aill, -aill/-an** m stable
staca n **-nnan** m stack
stad n m stop, halt, pause **na s.**
stationary **chuireadh s. oirnn** v we
were stopped
stad v stop, halt, pause
stad-phuing n **-e, -ean** f full stop
staid n **(-e), -ean** f state, condition
staidhre n **-richean** f stair **shuas**
an s. upstairs **shìos an s.** downstairs
Also **staidhir**
staigh adv See **a-staigh**
stail n **-e, -ean** f still (for whisky)
stailc n **-ean** f strike (labour)
stàile n **-lichean** f stall
stàilinn n **-e** f steel
staing n **-e, -ean** f difficulty, predicament
ann an s. in a quandary/fix
stàirn n **-e** f loud noise, clamour
stairs(n)each n **-s(n)ich, -s(n)ichean** f
threshold; stone steps/stone path
stais n **-e, -ean** f moustache
stàit n **-e, -ean** f state **na Stàitean**
Aonaichte the United States
stàiteil a **-e/-eala** stately
stàitire n **-an** m statesman
stàitireachd n f statesmanship
stalc n **stailc** m starch
stalla n **-chan** m overhanging rock,
precipice
stamag n **-aig, -an** f stomach
stamh n **staimh** m tangle (on shore)
stamp v **-adh** stamp, trample

stamp(a) *n* -(a)ichean *f* (*postage*) stamp
stampail *a* -e handsome
staoig *n* -ean *f* steak
staoin *n* -e *f* tin, pewter
staoin *a* -e shallow; superficial; awry
stapag *n* -aig, -an *f* mixture of meal and cold water
staran *n* -ain, -an *m* path (*to house*)
starrag *n* -aig, -an *f* hoodie crow
steach *adv See* a-steach
steall *n* still, -an *f* spout, squirt
steall *v* -adh spout, squirt
steallair *n* -e, -ean *m* syringe
steapa *n* -ichean *f m* step
stèarnan *n* -ain *m* tern
steatasgop *n* -oip, -an *f m* stethoscope
stèidh *n* -e, -ean *f* foundation, base, basis
stèidheachadh *n* -aidh, -aidhean *m* foundation, establishment
stèidheachd *n f* foundation, institute
stèidhich *v* -dheachadh found, establish, set up
steigeach *a* -giche sticky
stèisean *n* -ein, -an *m* station **s. peatrail** petrol station **s. rèidio** radio station **s. thrèanaichean** train station
stiall *n* stèill, -an *f* strip, stripe, streak **cha robh s. orra** they hadn't a stitch on
stiall *v* -adh thrash, lash; tear into strips; stripe
stiallach *a* -aiche streaky
stìopall *n* -aill, -aill *m* steeple
stiorap *n* -aip, -an *m* stirrup
stiubha *n f* stew
stiùbhard *n* -aird, -an *m* steward
stiùir *n* -e/stiùrach, -ean/-ichean *f* rudder, helm
stiùir *v* -eadh steer, direct, guide
stiùireadair *n* -ean *m* steersman, helmsman
stiùireadh *n* -ridh, -ridhean *m* steering; direction, guidance, management, supervision
stiùiriche *n* -an *m* director **S. an Fhoghlaim** the Director of Education
stob *n* stuib, -an *m* stump; protrusion **bha mi nam s. a' feitheamh riutha** I was left standing around waiting for them

stob *v* -adh stab, thrust
stobach *a* -aiche prickly, barbed
stòbh(a) *n* -(a)ichean *f m* stove
stoc *n* stuic, stuic *m* trunk, stump (*of tree*); stock, livestock
stoc *n* stuic, stuic *m* scarf
stoc *v* -adh stock
stocainn *n* (-e), -ean *f* stocking
stoc-mhargaid *n* -ean *f* stock-exchange
stoidhle *n* -lichean *f* style
stoighle *n See* stoidhle
stò(i)r *v* stòradh store
stòiridh *n* -ean *f m* story *Also* stòraidh
stoirm *n* -e, -ean *f m* storm
stoirmeil *a* -e stormy
stòl *a* -a/stòil, -an *m* stool
stòlda *a* steady, sedate, settled, staid
stopadh *n* -aidh blockage, stoppage
stòr *n* stòir, -an/-aichean *m* store
   s.-dàta database
stòradh *n* -aidh *m* storage, storing
stòras *n* -ais, -ais *m* riches, wealth, resources
stràiceil *a* -e strutting; insolent
stràc *n* -àic, -an *f m* stroke; accent (*in writing*)
strèan *n* -èin *m* strain, stress
streap *v See* sreap
streapadair *n See* sreapadair
strì *n f* strife, struggle, conflict, contention **dèan s.** *v* strive
strì *v* strive, struggle, compete, contest
strìoch *n* -a, -an *f* streak; line; hyphen
strìochd *v* -adh submit, yield, give in, surrender
strìopach *n* -aich(e), -aichean *f* prostitute, whore
strìopachas *n* -ais *m* prostitution
stròc *n* -a, -an *m* stroke (*med*)
stròdhail *a* -e prodigal, extravagant, lavish *Also* strùidheil
stròdhalachd *n f* prodigality *Also* strùidhealachd
structair *n* -ean *m* structure
structarail *a* -e structural
strùidhear *n* -eir, -an *m* spendthrift
strùpag *n See* srùbag
struth *n* -a, -an *f m* ostrich

stuadh n See **stuagh**
stuagh n **stuaigh, -an/-annan**
f wave; gable
stuaim n **-e** f moderation, temperance,
abstemiousness
stuama a **stuaime** moderate,
temperate, sober, abstemious
stuamachd n f temperance,
abstemiousness
stùc n **stùic, -annan** f stack (geol)
stùirceach n **-ciche** surly, scowling
stuig v **-eadh** incite, prompt
stùr n **stùir** m stour, dust
stuth n **-a, -an** m stuff, matter; material
s.-fhiaclan toothpaste
stuthaigeadh n **-gidh** m starch
sù n **-than** m zoo Also **sutha**
suaicheanta a remarkable, notable,
prominent
suaicheantas n **-ais, -ais** m badge,
emblem
suaimhneach a **-niche** tranquil, quiet
suaimhneas n **-eis** m rest, tranquillity,
quiet
suain n **-e** f deep sleep, slumber
suain v **-eadh** wrap
suainealachadh n **-aidh** m
hypnotism
suainealaiche n **-an** m hypnotist
suainealas n **-ais** m hypnosis
Suaineach n **-nich, -nich** m Swede
a Swedish
suaip n **-e, -ean** f slight resemblance
suairce a affable; gentle, courteous
suairceas n **-eis** m affability; gentility,
courteousness
suarach a **-aiche** insignificant, trifling;
mean, contemptible, despicable
suarachas n **-ais** m insignificance;
meanness, contemptibility
suas adv up, upwards
suath v **-adh** rub, wipe; massage
suathadh n **-aidh, -aidhean** m rub,
rubbing, massage, friction
sùbailte a supple, flexible, pliable, elastic
Also **subailte**
sùbailteachd n f suppleness, flexibility
Also **subailteachd**

sùbh n **sùibh, -an** m berry **s.-craoibh**
raspberry **s.-làir** strawberry Also **subh**
subhach a **-aiche** merry
subhailc n **-e, -ean** f virtue
subhailceach a **-ciche** virtuous
subsadaidh n **-ean** m subsidy
sùgach a **-aiche** joyous
sùgh n **-a/sùigh, -an** m juice, sap
sùgh v **-adh** suck, absorb, soak up
Also **sùigh**
sùghach a **-aiche** absorbent
sùghadh n **-aidh** m absorption, suction
sùghmhor a **-oire** juicy
sùgradh n **-aidh** m mirth **dèan s.** v
make merry
suidh v **-e** sit **dèan suidhe** v take a seat
suidhe n **-an/-achan** m sitting
àite-s. n m seat
suidheachadh n **-aidh, -aidhean**
m situation, site; state, condition,
circumstances
suidheachan n **-ain, -ain** m seat; stook
suidhich v **-dheachadh** settle, place,
situate, set, appoint
suidhichte a situated, settled, set
suidse n **-sichean** f m switch **cuir s.**
ri v set on fire
suids-chlàr n **-chlàir** m switchboard
suigeart n **-eirt** m jollity, cheerfulness,
chirpiness
suigeartach a **-aiche** jolly, cheerful,
chirpy
sùil n **sùla, -ean** f eye **s.-bheag** wink
s.-dhubh black eye **thug e s. air** he had
a look at it **s.-chritheach** quagmire
suilbhir a **-e** cheerful
sùilich v **-leachadh** expect, anticipate
sùim n **suime, suimeannan** f sum,
amount; regard, esteem, interest
cha do ghabh e mòran s. dheth
he didn't pay much regard to it
suimeil a **-e** attentive, conscientious;
worthwhile, considerable
suipear n **-eir/-ach, -an** f supper
suirghe n f courtship, wooing,
love-making
suirghiche n **-an** m suitor, lover
sùist n **-e, -ean** f flail

sùist v **-eadh** flail
suiteas n **-eis, -eis** m sweet Also **suitidh**
sùith n **-e** f m soot
sùlaire n **-an** m gannet
sult n **suilt** m fat; joy
Sultain n **-e** f **an t-S.** September
sultmhor a **-oire** fat, plump; joyful, jolly
sumainn n **-e, -ean** f surge (of sea), billow
sumanadh n **-aidh** m summons
sunnd n m mood, humour **bha iad ann an deagh shunnd** they were in good spirits

sunndach a **-aiche** lively, contented, hearty, in good spirits
sùrd n **sùird** m cheerfulness; eagerness
sùrdag n **-aig, -an** f leap, bound, skip
sùrdail a **-e** energetic
susbaint n **-e** f substance, content
susbainteach a **-tiche** substantial
suth n **-a, -an** m embryo
suthainn a eternal **gu s. sìor** forever and ever, eternally

T

tà conj though, although
tàbh n **tàibh, -an** m spoon net, fishing net
tàbhachd n f efficacy, effectiveness; substance; benefit
tàbhachdach a **-aiche** effectual, effective; substantial; beneficial
tabhainn v **-ann** offer, tender Also **tathainn**
tabhair irr v give, bestow (See irr v **tabhair** in Grammar)
tabhairtiche n **-an** m donor, giver
tabhann n **-ainn** m offer, offering Also **tathann**
tabhannaich v bark, yelp
tabhartach a liberal; dative **an tuiseal t.** the dative case
tabhartas n **-ais** m donation, grant, offering, presentation
tac n **-a/taic, -annan/-aichean** f tack (of land)
tac(a) n f time, season **mun t. seo an-uiridh** about this time last year **an t. ri** in comparison with
tacaid n **-e, -ean** f tack
tacan n **-ain, -an** m a while, a short time
tachair v **-t** happen; meet **t. do** happen to (someone) **t. ri** meet (with)
tachas n **-ais** m itch, itchiness Also **tachais**
tachais v **-as/-ais** scratch
tàcharan n **-ain, -an** m sprite, ghost; changeling
tachartas n **-ais, -an** m event, incident, occurrence

tachasach a **-aiche** itchy
tachd v **-adh** choke, smother, strangle
tacsa n m support **an t. ri balla** leaning against a wall
tadhail v **-al** call (on), visit
tadhal n **-ail, -aichean** m visit, call; goal, hail (in sport)
tagach a **-aiche** stocky
tagair v **-t/tagradh** plead, claim, advocate
tagairt n **-e** f claim
tagh v **-adh** choose, select, elect
taghadh n **-aidh, -aidhean** m choice, selection, election **T. Pàrlamaid** General Election
taghta a splendid, fine, chosen, choice
tagradh n **-aidh, -aidhean** m plea, pleading, claim, submission
tagraiche n **-an** m advocate, applicant, candidate (polit)
tagsaidh n **-ean** f m taxi
taibhs(e) n **-(e)an** f m ghost, apparition
taic n **-e** f support; proximity **t. airgid** financial support **cuir t. ri/thoir t. do** v support
taiceil a **-e** supportive
taidh n **-ean** f tie (necktie)
taidhr n **-ichean** f tyre Also **taidhear**
taigeis n **-e, -ean** f haggis
taigh n **-e, -ean** m house **aig an t.** at home **T. nan Cumantan** the House of Commons **T. nam Morairean** the House of Lords **t.-beag** toilet **t.-bìdh** restaurant **t.-ceàirde** factory **t.-chearc**

henhouse **t.-chon** kennel **t.-cluiche**
theatre **t.-cuibhle** wheelhouse **t.-cùirte** courthouse **t.-dhealbh** cinema **t.-dubh** black-house, thatched cottage **t.-eiridinn** hospital, infirmary **t.-faire** watch-house, vigil; mortuary **t.-fuine** bakery **t.-glainne** glasshouse **t.-grùide** brewery **t.-òsta** hotel **t.-seinnse** bar, inn, hotel **t.-solais** lighthouse **t.-spadaidh** slaughterhouse **t.-staile** distillery **t.-tasgaidh** museum **t.-tughaidh** thatched cottage/house

taisg *v* **tasgadh** deposit, store, hoard
taisich *v* **-seachadh** moisten, dampen
taistealach *n* **-aiche, -aichean** *m* pilgrim
taitinn *v* **taitneadh** please, delight (+ **ri**)
taitneach *a* **-niche** pleasant, pleasing, agreeable
taitneas *n* **-eis, -an** *m* pleasure
tàl *n* **tàil, -an** *m* adze
tàladh *n* **-aidh. -aidhean** *m* lullaby: enticing, attracting; soothing
tàlaidh *v* **-adh** entice, attract; soothe; lull

Insight: taigh

Formerly spelt *tigh*, this means house, as in *taigh-bìdh*, restaurant, *taigh-solais*, lighthouse, and many others. The House of Commons is *Taigh nan Cumantan*, and the word also features very often in place names: Taynuilt *(Taigh an Uillt)*, Tayinloan, Tayvallich, Tighnabruaich (note *tigh* in there) and many others.

---

taigheadas *n* **-ais** *m* housing
tàileasg *n* **-eisg** *m* chess; backgammon
tàillear *n* **-eir, -an** *m* tailor
taing *n* **-e** *f* thanks, gratitude **mòran t.** many thanks, thanks very much
taingealachd *n f* gratitude, thankfulness
taingeil *a* **-e** thankful, grateful
tàinig *irr v* came (See *irr v* **thig** in Grammar)
tàir *n* **-e, -ean** *f* contempt; difficulty **dèan t. air** *v* deride, scoff at, disparage
tairbeart *n* **-eirt, -an** *f* isthmus
tairbhe *n f* profit, advantage, benefit
tàireil *a* **-e** insulting, disparaging; contemptible, mean
tairg *v* **-sinn/-se(adh)** offer, tender
tairgse *n* **-an** *f* offer, tender
tàirneanach *n* **-aich, -aich** *m* thunder
tàirnge *n* See **tarrang**
tais *a* **-e** moist, damp
taisbean *v* **-adh** reveal, show, exhibit, demonstrate, manifest
taisbeanadh *n* **-aidh, -aidhean** *m* exhibition, display, show
taisbein *v* See **taisbean**
taiseachd *n f* moisture, dampness, humidity

talamh *n* **-aimh/talmhainn, -an** *m* (the *gen sg* **talmhainn** *f* is more common) earth, land, soil **t.-àitich** arable land **t. bàn** fallow ground
tàlant *n* **-an** *m* talent *Also* **tàlann**
tàlantach *a* **-aiche** talented
talla *n* **-chan/-ichean** *f m* hall **t. a' bhaile** the town/village hall **t. ciùil** music hall
tallan *n* **-ain, -an** *m* partition (*phys*)
talmhaidh *a* **-e** earthly, terrestrial; worldly (*of person*)
tàmailt *n* **-e, -ean** *f* chagrin, humiliation, shame, embarrassment; offence, insult
tàmailteach *a* **-tiche** humiliating, embarrassing; humiliated, embarrassed; indignant, insulted
tamall *n* **-aill, -aill** *m* a while, length of time
tàmh *n* **tàimh** *m* rest, repose **a bheil i na t. an-dràsta?** is she idle/out of work at present?
tàmh *v* rest; stay, dwell
tamhasg *n* **-aisg, -an** *m* blockhead, fool; ghost
tana *a* **taine** thin, slender, slim; shallow
tanaich *v* **-achadh** thin

tànaiste *n* **-an** *m* regent

tanalach *n* **-aich** *m* shallow water

tanca *n* **-ichean** *f m* tank

tancair *n* **-ean** *m* tanker

tannasg *n* **-aisg, -aisg** *m* apparition, ghost, spectre

taobh *n* **taoibh, -an** *m* side; way **ri t.** (+ *gen*) beside **t. an fhasgaidh** the lee side **t. an fhuaraidh** the windward side **t.-duilleig(e)** page (*in book*) **a thaobh** (+ *gen*) concerning, regarding **tha t. aice ri Ìle** she is fond of Islay

taobh *v* **-adh** (+ **ri**) side with, favour

taod *n* **taoid, taoid** *m* halter

taois *n* **-e, -ean** *f* dough

taoisnich *v* **-neachadh** knead

taom *v* **-adh** pour out; bale

tap *n* **-a, -aichean** *f m* tap

tapachd *n f* boldness, sturdiness

tapadh *n* **-aidh** *m* courage **tapadh leat/leibh** thank you

tapaidh *a* **-e** bold, active; well-built

tapais *n* **-ean** *f* carpet

Tarasach *n* **-aich, -aich** *m* native of Taransay *a* from, or pertaining to, Taransay

tarbh *n* **tairbh, tairbh** *m* bull

tarbhach *a* **-aiche** beneficial, advantageous

tarbh-nathrach *n* **tairbh-, tairbh-** *m* dragonfly

tarcais *n* **-e, -ean** *f* contempt, scorn **dèan t. air** *v* scorn, despise *Also* **tarchais**

tarchaiseach *a* **-siche** contemptuous, scornful

targaid *n* **-e, -ean** *f* target

tàrmachan *n* **-ain, -ain** *m* ptarmigan

tàrmaich *v* originate, derive; breed, propagate

tàrmasach *a* **-aiche** fussy, hard to please

tàrr *v* **-sainn/-adh** flee, take off; be in time for **tàrr às** flee, escape **cha do thàrr sinn an t-aiseag** we didn't make the ferry

tarrag *n* **-aig, -an** *f* nail *Also* **tar(r)aig**

tarraing *v* draw, pull, attract **t. anail** draw breath, breathe **t. dealbh** draw a picture **t. à/às** tease **t. air ais** withdraw **a bheil an tì air t.?** has the tea infused?

tarraing *n* **-ean** *f m* attraction; drawing, drag; mention **thoir t. air** mention, refer to

tarraingeach *a* **-giche** attractive

tarrainn *v See* **tarraing**

tarrang *n* **tàirn(g)e, tàirn(g)ean** *f* nail

tarsaing *adv See* **tarsainn**

tarsainn *adv* across, transversely **t. air** *prep* across, over

tarsannan *n* **-ain, -an** *m* cross-beam, transom

tart *n* **tairt** *m* extreme thirst, parchedness; drought

tartmhor *a* **-oire** *m* thirsty, parched

tasgadh *n* **-aidh** *m* deposit, reserve, hoard

tastan *n* **-ain, -an** *m* shilling *Formerly* **tasdan**

tataidh *v* **-adh** attract

tàth *v* **-adh** join together, cement, weld

tàthag *n* **-aig, -an** *f* pointed remark, dig

tathaich *v* frequent, visit

tàthan *n* **-ain, -an** *m* hyphen

tè *n f* one (*f/female*), woman **tè bheag** a whisky ('*a small one*')

teachd *n m* coming, arrival **t.-a-steach** income, revenue **t.-an-tìr** livelihood, subsistence

teachdaire *n* **-an** *m* messenger, courier

teachdaireachd *n f* message, tidings

teacsa *n* **-ichean** *f m* text

teadaidh *n* **-ean** *m* teddy

teadhair *n* **-dhrach, -dhraichean** *f* tether

teagaisg *v* **-asg** teach, instruct; preach

teagamh *n* **-aimh, -an** *m* doubt **gun t.** without a doubt, undoubtedly, indeed

teagasg *n* **-aisg** *m* teaching, instruction, pedagogy; preaching

teaghlach *n* **-aich, -aichean** *m* family

teagmhach *a* **-aiche** doubtful, dubious

teallach *n* **-aich, -aichean** *m* hearth, fireplace, forge

teampall *n* **-aill, -aill** *m* temple

teanas *n* **-ais** *m* tennis

teanchair *n* **-ean** *m* pincers, tongs; vice

teanga *n* **teanga/-dh, -n/-nnan** *f* tongue

teann *a* **teinne** tight, tense **t. air** near to

teann v **-adh** move; commence, begin
  t. às an rathad get out of the way
  theann iad ri seinn they began to sing
  t. a-nall come over here
teannaich v **-achadh** tighten
teanntachd n **-an** f strait, difficulty,
  austerity
teans(a) n **-(a)ichean** m chance
teant(a) n **-(a)ichean** f m tent
tèarainte a safe, secure
tèarainteachd n f safety, security
tearb v **-adh** separate (eg sheep), part
tearc a **teirce** rare, scarce, few
tèarmann n **-ainn, -ainn** m protection,
  refuge, sanctuary, asylum **t. nàdair**
  nature reserve
teàrn v **-adh** deliver (from), save, rescue
  Also **tèarainn**
teàrr n **tearra(dh)** f tar
teàrr v **tearradh** tar
teas n m heat **t.-mheidh** f thermometer
teasach n **-aich, -aichean** f fever
  t. sgàrlaid scarlet fever
teasadair n **-air, -ean** m heater
teasaich v **-achadh** heat
teasairg v **-inn** save, rescue, deliver
  (from) Also **teasraig**
teatha n f tea **copan t.** m cup of tea
teich v **-eadh** flee, escape, retreat
teicneòlach a **-aiche** technological
teicneòlas n **-ais** m technology
  t. fiosrachaidh is conaltraidh
  information and communication
  technology
teicnigeach a **-igiche** technical
tèid irr v go (See irr v **rach** in Grammar)
tèile pron another one (f/female)
teine n **teintean** m fire **na theine** on fire
  cuir t. ri v set fire to **t.-aighir/t.-èibhinn**
  bonfire
teinn n **-e** f strait, predicament
teinntean n **-ein, -ein** m hearth,
  fireplace
teip n **-ichean** f tape, cassette
  t.-chlàradair m tape recorder
teirig v **-eachdainn/teireachdainn**
  expire, run out
teirinn v **teàrnadh** descend

teirm n **-ichean** f term Also **tearm**
teis-meadhan n **-ain** m very centre,
  epicentre
teist n **-e, -ean** f testimony
teisteanas n **-ais, -an** m testimony,
  testimonial, certificate
telebhisean n **-ein, -an** f m television
teleagram n **-aim, -an** m telegram
teleasgop n **-oip, -an** f m telescope
teò-chridheach a **-dhiche** affectionate,
  warm-hearted
teòclaid n See **seòclaid**
teòma a skilful, expert, ingenious
teòmachd n f skill, expertise
teòth v **-adh** warm, heat Also **teò**
teòthachd n f temperature
teothaich v **-achadh** warm, heat
teth a **teotha** hot
teud n **-a/tèid, -an** m string (mus), chord
tha irr v am, is, are; yes (See verb **to be** in
  Grammar)
thàinig irr v came (See irr v **thig** in
  Grammar)
thairis adv across, over **a' cur t.**
  overflowing **a' toirt t.** becoming
  exhausted
thairis (air) prep pron over him
thairis air prep phr across, over
thairte prep pron over her
thall adv over, yonder, on the other side
  air a' cheann t. in the end, ultimately
  t. 's a-bhos here and there **t. thairis**
  abroad
thalla v go!, away!, be off! **t. seo** come
  here (Islay)
thar prep (+ gen) across, over
tharad(sa) prep pron over you (sg)
tharaibh(se) prep pron over you
  (pl & pol)
tharainn(e) prep pron over us
tharam(sa) prep pron over me
tharta(san) prep pron over them
theab def v nearly (did) **t. mi tuiteam**
  I almost fell **theabadh a bhàthadh** he
  was almost drowned
theagamh adv perhaps
thèid irr v (will) go (See irr v **rach**
  in Grammar)

their *irr v* (will) say (*See irr v* **abair** *in Grammar*)

theirig *irr v* go! (*See irr v* **rach** *in Grammar*)

thig *irr v* (will) come **t. a-steach** come in **t. orra falbh** they will have to go

thoir *irr v* give, bestow, take **t. leat** take away (with you) **t. air** force, compel **t. an aire** take care **t. gu buil** effect, implement **t. seachad duais** present a prize **t. do chasan leat!** clear off! **t. a thaobh** persuade, beguile **t. am follais** reveal, make public **t. breith** judge **t. sùil (air)** look (at)

thu(sa) *pron* you (*sg*)

thubhairt *irr v* said (*See irr v* **abair** *in Grammar*)

thuca(san) *prep pron* to them

thug *irr v* gave; brought (*See irr v* **beir** *in Grammar*)

thugad(sa) *prep pron* to you (*sg*)

thugaibh(se) *prep pron* to you (*pl & pol*)

thugainn *def v* come on! let's go! *pl* **thugnaibh, thugainnibh**

thugainn(e) *prep pron* to us

thugam(sa) *prep pron* to me

thuice(se) *prep pron* to her

thuige(san) *prep pron* to him **thuige seo** to date, until now

thuirt *irr v* said (*See irr v* **abair** *in Grammar*)

tì *n f* tea **cupa tì** a cup of tea

tiamhaidh *a* **-e** plaintive, poignant, melancholy

ticead *n See* **tiogaid**

tìde *n* **-ean** *f* time **fad na t.** all the time **ri t./tro thìde** through time, eventually **uair a thìde** an hour **tha a thìd' agad sgur** it's time you stopped

tìde-mhara *n* **-mara**, **tìdean-mara** *f* tide

tidsear *n* **-eir**, **-an** *f m* teacher

tig *irr v* come (*See irr v* **thig** *in Grammar*)

tìgear *n* **-eir**, **-an** *m* tiger

tigh *n See* **taigh**

tighead *n* **-eid** *m* thickness

tighearna *n* **-n** *m* lord **an T.** the Lord (*God*)

tighearnas *n* **-ais** *m* lordship **T. nan Eilean** the Lordship of the Isles

tighinn *irr v* coming (*See irr v* **thig** *in Grammar*) **Dihaoine seo t.** this coming Friday

tilg *v* **-eil/-eadh** throw, cast **thilg iad air ...** they accused him ...

till *v* **-eadh** return

tìm *n* **-e**, **-ean** *f* time

timcheall *adv* around

timcheall *prep* (+ *gen*) round, around, about **t. an taighe** around the house **t. air** around, about

timcheallan *n* **-ain**, **-ain** *m* roundabout

timcheall-ghearradh *n* **-aidh** *m* circumcision

tinn *a* **-e** sick, ill

tinneas *n* **-eis**, **-an** *m* illness, sickness, disease **an t.-busach** mumps **an t.-mara** seasickness **an t. tuiteamach** epilepsy, dropsy **t. inntinn** mental illness **t. an t-siùcair** diabetes

tiodhlac *n* **-aic**, **-an** *m* gift, present, donation **t. Nollaig** Christmas present

tiodhlacadh *n* **-aidh**, **-aidhean** *m* burial, funeral

tiodhlaic *v* **-acadh** inter, bury

tiogaid *n* **-e**, **-ean** *f* ticket *Also* **tigead, tigeard**

tiomnadh *n* **-aidh** *m* will, bequest, testament **an Seann T.** the Old Testament **an T. Nuadh** the New Testament

tiompan *n* **-ain**, **-ain/-an** *m* cymbal

tiona *n* **-ichean** *m* tin, can

tionail *v* **-al** gather, collect, assemble

tional *n* **-ail**, **-an** *m* collection, assembly

tionndaidh *v* **-adh** turn

tionnsgal *n* **-ail/-an** *m* industry; ingenuity, invention

tionnsgalach *a* **-aiche** industrial; inventive

tìoraidh *exclam* cheerio!

tìorail *a* **-e** cosy, sheltered, comfortable

tioram *a* **-a/tiorma** dry

tiormachadh *n* **-aidh** *m* drying **tha t. math ann** there are good drying conditions

tiormachd *n f* dryness, drought

tiormadair *n* **-ean** *m* dryer

tiormaich v -achadh dry
tiota n -n/-idhean m a moment, a short while
tiotal n -ail, -an m title
tiotan n -ain, -ain m a moment, a short while
tìr n -e, -ean f land **Tìr nan Òg** the Land of (Eternal) Youth
Tiristeach n -tich, -tich m someone from Tiree a from, or pertaining to, Tiree *Formerly* **Tirisdeach** *Also* **Tiridheach**
tìr-mòr n m mainland **air t.** on the mainland
titheach a tithiche fond (of) **t. air** keen (on)
tiugainn def v come on!, let's go! pl **tiugnaibh, tiugainnibh**
tiugh a tighe thick, fat, dense
tiùrr(a) n m seaware left by tide, mark of sea on shore; confused heap **bha t. phàipearan air a' bhòrd** there was a heap of papers on the table
tlachd n f pleasure
tlachdmhor a -oire pleasant, pleasing
tlàth a tlàithe mild, mellow, soft
toban n -ain, -an m tuft (of hair, wool etc)
tobar n -air/tobrach, tobraichean f m well, source (gen sg **tobrach** is f)
tobhaig v -eadh tow *Also* **tobh**
tobhta n -ichean f roofless walls, ruin; thwart (in boat)
todha n -ichean m hoe *Also* **tobha**
todhaig v -eadh hoe
todhar n -air m fertilizer, manure, dung **cuir t. air** v fertilize, manure
tofaidh n -ean m toffee
tog v -ail lift, raise, build, construct **thog iad taigh ùr** they built a new house **thogadh i ann an Lios Mòr** she was brought up in Lismore **thog iad orra** they set off **tog às an rathad!** get out of the way! **thog e a' Ghàidhlig ann am Barraigh** he acquired Gaelic in Barra **thog mi ceàrr e** I misunderstood him/it
togail n f lifting; upbringing
togair v togradh/-t wish, desire **a' dèanamh mar a thogras e** doing as he pleases

togalach n -aich, -aichean m building
togarrach a -aiche keen, willing, enthusiastic
togsaid n -ean f cask, drum *Also* **tocasaid**
toibheum n -eim, -an m blasphemy
toidh n -ean m toy
toigh a agreeable, pleasing **is t. leam ...** I like ...
toil n -e, -ean f will, wish **mas e do thoil e** please, if it is your will
toileach a -liche willing, voluntary
toileachadh n -aidh m pleasure, satisfaction
toileachas n -ais m pleasure, contentment **t.-inntinn** pleasure, contentment
toilich v -leachadh please
toilichte a pleased, happy, glad
toil-inntinn n -(e), f pleasure, contentment, satisfaction
toill v -sinn/-tinn deserve, merit; be contained in **cha toill e sa bhaga** it's too big for the bag
toillteanas n -ais, -an m deserts, merit
tòimhseachan n -ain, -ain m riddle, puzzle **t.-tarsainn** crossword puzzle
toimhsean n pl scales, balances, measures
toinisg n -e f sense, common sense, wit
toinisgeil a -e sensible
toinn v -eadh/-eamh twist, twine
toinneamh n -eimh m twist, twisting
toinnte a twisted, complex
tòir n -e/tòrach, -ean/-ichean f pursuit **an t. air** (+ gen) in pursuit of
toir irr v give (See irr v **thoir** in Grammar)
toirds n -ichean f m torch
toirm n -e, -ean f loud murmuring sound, hubbub; hum
toirmeasg n -misg m prohibition, ban; harum-scarum **'s e t. cianail a th' ann** he's a terrible harum-scarum
toirmisg v -measg forbid, prohibit, ban, proscribe
toirmisgte a forbidden, prohibited, banned, proscribed

toirsgeir n **-ean** f peat iron, peatcutter
Also **troidhsgeir**

toirt irr v giving, bestowing, taking
(See irr v **thoir** in Grammar)

toiseach n **-sich**, **-sichean** m beginning,
start, front **an t.** at first **air thoiseach** in
front **t. tòiseachaidh** the very
beginning

tòiseachadh n **-aidh** m beginning,
starting, start

tòisich v **-seachadh** begin, start,
commence, initiate **t. air** begin to

toit n **-e**, **-ean** f smoke, vapour

toitean n **-ein**, **-ein/-an** m cigarette

toll n **tuill**, **tuill** m hole, perforation,
cavity

toll v **-adh** hole, bore, pierce, perforate

tom n **tuim**, **-annan** m round hillock/knoll

tomadach a **-aiche** bulky, large

tomàto n **-than** m tomato

tombaca n m tobacco

tomhais v **-as/-ais** measure; guess

tomhas n **-ais**, **-an/toimhsean** m
measure, measurement, gauge
t.-teas thermometer

tòn n **tòine**, **-an/tòinean** f buttocks,
bottom Also **tòin**

tonn n **tuinn/tuinne**, **tuinn/-an**
f m wave (in sea)

topag n **-aig**, **-an** f skylark

toradh n **-aidh**, **-aidhean** m produce,
fruit(s); result, outcome, consequence
a thoradh sin because of that

torc n **tuirce**, **tuirc** m boar

torman n **-ain**, **-an** m murmur, hum,
rumbling

tòrr n **torra**, **torran** m mound, heap,
conical hill; large quantity or number

torrach a **-aiche** fertile, fruitful; pregnant

tòrradh n **-aidh**, **-aidhean** m burial,
funeral

tosgaire n **-an** m ambassador, envoy

tosgaireachd n f embassy

tost n **-a** m toast (bread)

tost n m silence **bha i na t.** she was silent
Formerly **tosd**

tostair n **-ean** m toaster

tràchdas n **-ais**, **-ais** m thesis, treatise

tractar n **-air**, **-an** m tractor

trafaig n **-e** f traffic

traidhfeal n **-fil**, **-filean** m trifle

traidhsagal n **-ail**, **-an** m tricycle

traidiseanta a traditional

tràigh n **-e/tràghad**, **-ean/tràghannan**
f beach, strand **bha t. mhòr ann an-dè**
there was a very low tide yesterday

tràigh v **tràghadh** ebb

tràill n **-ean** f m slave; addict; scoundrel
's e t. a th' ann he's a rotter/nasty
piece of work

tràillealachd n f slavery, servitude,
servility

tràilleil a slavish, servile

traisg v **trasgadh** fast

tràlair n **-ean** m trawler

tramasgal n **-ail** m trash; (met)
confused mess

trang a **trainge** busy

trannsa n **-ichean** f corridor, passage,
lobby, aisle, hallway

traogh v **-adh** subside, abate; drain

traon n **traoin**, **traoin** m corncrake

trasg n **traisg**, **-an** f fast **latha traisg** m
fast day

trasgadh n **-aidh** m fasting

trasta a diagonal

trastan n **-ain**, **-ain** m cross-beam,
diagonal

tràth a, adv **tràithe** early

tràth n **-a/tràith**, **-an** m time, season;
tense **mu thràth** already **an t. caithte** the
past tense **an t. làthaireach** the present
tense **an t. teachdail** the future tense

tre prep through

treabh v **-adh** plough

treabhaiche n **-an** m ploughman

trealaich n **-ean** f lumber, bits and
pieces; trash **bha t. aig a' choinneimh**
there were quite a few at the meeting

treamhlaidh n **-ean** f bug, virus

trèan(a) n **-(a)ichean** f train

trèanadh n **-aidh** m training

trèanaig v **-eadh** train

treas a third

treibhdhireach a **-riche** sincere,
upright, honest

treibhdhireas *n* **-eis** *m* sincerity, uprightness, honesty

trèicil *n m* treacle

treidhe *n* **-achan** *f m* tray

trèig *v* **-sinn** forsake, quit, desert

trèilear *n* **-eir, -an** *m* trailer

treis *n* **-ean** *f* a while

treiseag *n* **-an** *f* a short while

treòrachadh *n* **-aidh** *m* guidance, direction, leading

treòraich *v* **-achadh** guide, direct, lead

treubh *n* **-a/trèibh, -an** *f* tribe

treubhach *a* **-aiche** valiant

treud *n* **-a/trèid, -an** *m* flock, herd

treun *a* **treasa/treise** strong, brave, valiant

trì *n, a* three

triall *v* go, journey, depart

trian *n m* third (*part*)

Trianaid *n f* Trinity

triantan *n* **-ain, -ain/-an** *m* triangle

triath *n* **-a, -an** *m* lord, chief

trì-bhileach *n* **-lich, -lichean** *m* trefoil

tric *a, adv* **-e** often, frequent

trì-cheàrnach *a* triangular

trì-cheàrnag *n* **-aig, -an** *f* triangle

trìd *prep* (+ *gen*) through, by

trì-deug *n, a* thirteen **trì coin dheug** thirteen dogs

trì-dhualach *a* three-ply

trìd-shoilleir *a* **-e** transparent

trì fichead *n, a* sixty

trì-fillte *a* threefold, triple, treble

trilleachan *n* **-ain, -ain** *m* oystercatcher

trioblaid *n* **-e, -ean** *f* trouble, tribulation

triom *n* **-a** *f* mood

trì-rothach *a* three-wheeled

trithead *n* **-eid, -an** *m* thirty

trìtheamh *a* third

triubhas *n* **-ais, -an** *m* trews, trousers

triùir *n f m* three (people) **t. ghillean** three boys

triuthach *n* **-aich** *f* **an t.** whooping cough

tro *prep* through

trobhad *def v* come, come on, come here

tròcair *n* **-e, -ean** *f* mercy

tròcaireach *a* **-riche** merciful

trod *n* **troid, troid/-an** *f m* quarrel; reproof

trod *aug prep* through your (*sg*)

troich *n* **-e, -ean** *f m* dwarf

troid *v* **trod** quarrel; scold

troigh *n* **-e, -ean** *f* foot (*on body & in length*)

troilidh *n* **-ean** *f* trolley

troimh *prep* See **tro**

troimh-a-chèile *adv* mixed-up, confused

troimh-a-chèile *n f* mix-up, confusion

troimhe(san) *prep pron* through him/it

troimhpe(se) *prep pron* through her/it

trom *a* **truime** heavy, onerous; pregnant

trom *aug prep* through my; through their

tromalach *n* **-aich** *f* preponderance, majority

tromb *n* **-a, -an** *f* jew's harp

trombaid *n* **-e, -ean** *f* trumpet

tromhad(sa) *prep pron* through you (*sg*)

tromhaibh(se) *prep pron* through you (*pl & pol*)

tromhainn(e) *prep pron* through us

tromham(sa) *prep pron* through me

tromhpa(san) *prep pron* through them

trom-inntinn *n* **-e** *f* depression, melancholy

trom-inntinneach *a* **-niche** depressed, melancholy

trom-laighe *n* **-an** *f m* nightmare

trom-neul *n* **-neoil, -neoil/-an** *m* coma

tron *aug prep* through the; through their

tror *aug prep* through our; through your

trosg *n* **truisg, truisg** *m* large cod

trotan *n* **-ain** *m* trot, trotting **dèan t.** *v* trot

truacanta *a* compassionate, merciful, pitying

truacantas *n* **-ais** *m* pity, compassion

truagh *a* **-aighe** miserable, wretched, pitiful, poor (*unfortunate*)

truaghag *n* **-aig, -an** *f* wretch (*female*), poor soul **A thruaghag bhochd!** You poor soul!

truaghan *n* **-ain, -ain/-an** *m* wretch (*male*), poor soul

truaighe *n* **-an** *f* misery, woe
  mo thruaighe! Oh dear!, Alas!
truaill *n* **-e**, **-ean** *f* scabbard
truaill *v* **-eadh** pollute, contaminate,
  defile; corrupt
truailleadh *n* **-lidh** *m* pollution,
  contamination; corruption
truaillte *a* polluted, contaminated,
  defiled; corrupt
truas *n* **truais** *m* pity, compassion,
  sympathy **gabh t. ri** *v* pity **tha t.
  agam rithe** I am sorry for her
truasail *a* **-e** compassionate,
  sympathetic
truileis *n* *f* trash, junk
truinnsear *n* **-eir**, **-an** *m* plate
trus *v* **-adh** gather, collect
trusgan *n* **-ain**, **-an** *m* garb, clothes,
  clothing, apparel, garment
trustar *n* **-air**, **-airean** *m* rotter, scoundrel
tu(sa) *pron* you
tuagh *n* **tuaigh(e)**, **-an** *f* axe
tuaileas *n* **-eis**, **-an** *m* scandal, slander
tuaileasach *a* **-aiche** defamatory,
  slanderous, scurrilous
tuaineal *n* **-eil** *m* dizziness, giddiness
tuainealach *a* **-aiche** dizzy, giddy
tuainealaich *n* **-e** *f* dizziness, giddiness
tuaiream *n* **-eim**, **-an** *f* guess, conjecture
  air thuairam at random **mu
  thuaiream** about
tuairisgeul *n* **-eil**, **-an** *m* description, report
tuairisgeulach *a* **-aiche** descriptive
tuairmeas *n* **-eis**, **-an** *m* guess, conjecture
tuairmse *n* **-an** *f* guess, estimate,
  conjecture **dèan t.** *v* guess
tuam *n* **tuaim**, **-an** *m* tomb
tuar *n* **tuair**, **-an** *m* hue, complexion
tuarastal *n* **-ail**, **-ail/-an** *f* wages, salary,
  earnings *Formerly* **tuarasdal**
tuasaid *n* **-e**, **-ean** *f* quarrel, squabble, fight
tuath *n* **-a** *f* tenantry, country people
  air an t. in the countryside
tuath *n*, *a* north, northern **t. air ...** north
  of ... **mu thuath** in the north, northwards
  an ceann a tuath the north end
tuathal *a* **-aile** anti-clockwise; confused
tuathanach *n* **-aich**, **-aich** *m* farmer

tuathanachas *n* **-ais** *m* agriculture,
  farming
tuathanas *n* **-ais**, **-an** *m* farm
tuba *n* **-nnan** *f m* tub
tubaist *n* **-e**, **-ean** *f* accident, mishap
tubhailt(e) *n* **-an** *f m* towel; tablecloth
  t.-shoithichean dish towel **t.-bùird**
  tablecloth
tùchadh *n* **-aidh** *m* hoarseness **tha
  an t. air** he is hoarse
tùchan *n* **-ain** *m* hoarseness; cooing
tùchanach *a* **-aiche** hoarse
tud *interj* tut!
tug *irr v* gave, brought (*See irr v* **thoir**
  in Grammar)
tugainn *def v* come, come on
  pl **tiugainnibh**
tugh *v* **-adh** thatch
tughadair *n* **-ean** *m* thatcher
tughadh *n* **-aidh** *m* thatch, thatching
tuig *v* **-sinn** understand, comprehend
tuigse *n* *f* understanding, insight
tuigseach *a* **-siche** understanding,
  perceptive
tuil *n* **-e**, **-ean/-tean** *f* flood, deluge,
  downpour
tuilleadh *adv* more, any more; again **a
  thuilleadh air** in addition to, as well as
tuilleadh *n m* more, additional
  quantity/number **t. 's a' chòir** too much
tuireadh *n* **-ridh**, **-ridhean** *m* lament,
  mourning
tui(r)neap *n* **-an** *m* turnip
tuirt *irr v* said (*See irr v* **abair** *in Grammar*)
tùis *n* **-e**, **-ean** *f* incense
tuiseal *n* **-eil**, **-an** *m* case (*gram*) **an t.
  ainmneach** the nominative case
  an t. ginideach the genitive case **an t.
  tabhartach** the dative case
tuisleadh *n* **-lidh**, **-lidhean** *m* stumbling,
  stumble, fall; (*met*) mistake, lapse
tuislich *v* **-leachadh** stumble, fall; (*met*)
  make a mistake, lapse
tuit *v* **-eam** fall
tuiteamach *a* **-aiche** fortuitous,
  contingent; epileptic
tuiteamas *n* **-ais**, **-an** *m* chance
tulach *n* **-aich**, **-aichean** *m* hillock, knoll

tulg *v* **-adh** rock (to and fro)
tulgach *a* **-aiche** rocking
tum *v* **-adh** dip, immerse, plunge
tunail *n* **-ean** *f m* tunnel
tungaidh *a* **-e** musty, damp
tunna *n* **-chan** *m* ton
tunnag *n* **-aig, -an** *f* duck
tùr *n* **tùir, tùir** *m* sense **duine gun t.** *a* reckless man
tùr *n* **tùir, tùir** *m* tower
tur *a* complete, whole, absolute **gu t.** entirely, completely, absolutely
turadh *n* **-aidh** *m* dry weather, dry spell **tha t. ann** it's dry **tha i air t. a dhèanamh** the rain has stopped
turaid *n* **-e, -ean** *f* turret

tùrail *a* **-e** sensible
turas *n* **-ais, tursan/-an** *m* journey, trip; time, occasion **t. malairt** trade mission **aon t.** once **t. eile** another time
turasachd *n* *f* tourism
Turcach *n* **-aich, -aich** *m* Turk *a* Turkish
tursa *n* **-chan** *m* standing stone **Tursachan Chalanais** the Callanish Stones
tùrsach *a* **-aiche** sad, sorrowful
turtar *n* **-air** *m* thud
tùs *n* **tùis** *m* start, beginning, origin **(bh)o thùs** from the beginning, originally
tùsaire *n* **-an** *m* pioneer, innovator
tùsanach *n* **-aich** *m* aborigine
tuthag *n* **-aig, -an** *f* patch

U

uabhar *n* **-air** *m* pride, haughtiness
uabhas *n* **-ais** *m* a lot; terror, dread, horror **bha an t-uabhas dhaoine ann** there were an awful lot of people there
uabhasach *a* **-aiche** terrible, dreadful *adv* very, terribly **u. math** very/terribly good
uachdaran *n* **-ain, -ain** *m* landlord, laird; governor, superior
uachdranachd *n* *f* landlordism; sovereignty, superiority, presidency
uachdranas *n* **-ais** *m* sovereignty, jurisdiction
uaibh(se) *prep pron* from you (*pl & pol*)
uaibhreach *a* **-riche** proud, haughty
uaibhreas *n* **-eis** *m* pride, haughtiness
uaigh *n* **-e/uaghach, -ean** *f* grave, tomb
uaigneach *a* **-niche** lonely, solitary, remote, secret
uaigneas *n* **-eis** *m* loneliness, solitude, secrecy, privacy
uaill *n* **-e** *f* pride, vanity; dignity
uaim *n* **-e** *f* alliteration
uaimh *n* **-e/uamha, -ean/uamhan** *f* cave
uaine *a* green
uainn(e) *prep pron* from us
uaipe(se) *prep pron* from her
uair *n* **uarach, -ean** *f* hour, time **u. an uaireadair** an hour **tha e u.** it is one

o'clock **u. is u.** time and time again, repeatedly **u. dhan robh saoghal** once upon a time
uaireadair *n* **-ean** *m* watch **u.-grèine** sundial
uaireannan *adv* sometimes, at times
uaireigin *adv* sometime
uaisle *n* *f* nobility (*of nature*)
uaithe(san) *prep pron* from him
uallach *n* **-aich, -aichean** *m* concern, worry, burden; responsibility (*duty*) **na gabh u.** don't be concerned
uàlras *n* **-ais, -asan** *m* walrus
uam(sa) *prep pron* from me
uamh *n* See **uaimh**
uamhann *n* **-ainn** *m* dread, terror, horror
uamhas *n* See **uabhas**
uamhasach *a* See **uabhasach**
uan *n* **uain, uain** *m* lamb
uanfheòil *n* **-òla** *f* lamb (*meat*)
uapa(san) *prep pron* from them
uasal *a* **uaisle** noble
uasal *n* **-ail, uaislean** *m* nobleman, gentleman **na h-uaislean** the nobility, aristocracy
uat(sa) *prep pron* from you (*sg*)
ubhal *n* **-ail, ùbhlan** *f m* apple
ubhalghort *n* **-oirt, -an** *m* orchard
ucas *n* **ucais, ucais** *m* coalfish

uchd *n* **-a, -an** *m* chest, breast, bosom; brow of … **ri u. bàis** at the point of death **u.-leanabh** *m* adopted child

uchd-mhacachd *n f* adoption

uchd-mhacaich *v* **-achadh** adopt

ud *dem a* that, yon, yonder

ud *exclam* away!, get away! (*dismissive*)

udalan *n* **-ain** *m* swivel **air u.** moving to and fro

ùdlaidh *a* **-e** gloomy

uèir *n* **-ichean** *f* wire **u.-bhiorach** barbed wire

ugan *n* **-ain, -nan** *m* upper breast

ugh *m* **uighe, uighean** *m* egg

ughach *m* **-aiche** oval

ughagan *n* **-ain** *m* custard

ùghdar *n* **-air, -an** *m* author

ùghdarras *n* **-ais, -an/-ais** *m* authority, mandate **u. ionadail** local authority

ùghdarrasail *a* **-e** authoritative

Uibhisteach *n* **-tich, -tich** *m* someone from Uist *a* from, or pertaining to, Uist

ùidh *n* **-e, -ean** *f* interest, desire

uidh *n* **-e** *f* degree, gradation **u. air n-u.** bit by bit, gradually

uidheam *n* **-eim, -an** *f* machine, utensil; gear, apparatus, equipment

uill *interj* well, indeed

uime(san) *prep pron* about him

uime sin *adv* therefore, thereupon

uimhir *n f* number, quantity; certain amount, measure

uimpe(se) *prep pron* about her

ùine *n* **ùinichean/-achan** *f* time (*span of*), period **anns an u. fhada** in the long term

uinneag *n* **-eige, -an** *f* window

uinnean *n* **-ein, -an** *m* onion

uinnseann *n* **-sinn, -an** *m* ash tree

ùir *n* **-e/ùrach** *f* soil, earth

uircean *n* **-ein, -an** *m* piglet

uiread *n f* a certain amount, measure, so much, as much

uireasbhach *a* **-aiche** suffering discomfort, sore; defective, inadequate

uireasbhaidh *n* **-ean** *f* deficiency, want, need, lack, inadequacy

uirsgeul *n* **-eil, -an** *f m* fable, legend; novel

uirsgeulach *a* **-aiche** fabulous, legendary

uiseag *n* **-eig, -an** *f* lark, skylark

uisge *n* **-achan/-gichean** *m* water; rain **a bheil an t-u. ann?** is it raining?

uisge-beatha *n m* whisky

Insight: uisge

Water or rain. *Uisge-beatha* (water of life) has been shortened in English to yield whisky. It sometimes appears in river names, as in *Uisge Spè* (the Spey). But in some areas the word for water or rain is *bùrn*, and sometimes *bùrn* is used for water but *uisge* for rain!

---

uidheamachd *n* **-an** *f* equipment, apparatus

uidheamaich *v* **-achadh** equip; get ready

uidheamaichte *a* equipped, geared up

ùidheil *a* **-e** interesting, interested

uile *a* every, each, all **u.-gu-lèir** *adv* all, altogether, completely **a h-uile duine** everyone **na h-eòin uile** all the birds

uilebheist *n* **-ean** *f m* monster

uile-chumhachdach *a* **-aiche** all-powerful, almighty, omnipotent

uilinn *n* **uilinn/uilne, uilnean** *f* elbow *Also* **uileann**

uisgich *v* **-geachadh** water, irrigate

ulaidh *n* **-e, -ean** *f* treasure **m' u.** my dear, my precious one

ulbhag *n* **-aig, -an** *f* boulder

ulfhart *n* **-airt** *m* howl (*as dog*)

ullachadh *n* **-aidh** *m* preparation

ullaich *v* **-achadh** prepare

ullamh *a* ready, prepared; finished

ultach *n* **-aich, -aichean** *m* armful, lapful, load

umad(sa) *prep pron* about you (*sg*)

umaibh(se) *prep pron* about you (*pl & pol*)

ùmaidh *n* **-e, -ean** *m* blockhead, dolt, boor
umainn(e) *prep pron* about us
umam(sa) *prep pron* about me
umha *n m* brass; bronze **Linn an U.** the Bronze Age
umhail *a* **-e** obedient; humble
ùmhlachd *n f* obedience; humility; obeisance, homage **dèan u.** *v* pay homage
ùmhlaich *v* **-achadh** (*intrans*) obey, submit; (*trans*) humble, subdue
umpa(san) *prep pron* about them
uncail *n* **-ean** *m* uncle
ung *v* **-achadh/-adh** anoint
ungadh *n* **-aidh** *f* anointing, unction, ointment
Ungaireach *n* **-rich** *m* Hungarian *a* Hungarian
unnsa *n* **-chan/-idhean** *m* ounce
ùpag *n* **-aig, -an** *f* push, elbowing
ùpraid *n* **-e, -ean** *f* uproar, confusion, bustle
ùr *a* **ùire** new, fresh **a bheil càil às ùr?** anything fresh? **tòisich às ùr** *v* start again **talc-ùr** brand new
ur *poss pron* your (*pl & pol*)
ùrachadh *n* **-aidh** *m* renewal, refreshment; modernization
ùraich *v* **ùrachadh** renew, refresh; modernize
urchair *n* **-e/urchrach, -ean** *f* bullet, shot, report of gun

urchasg *n* **-aisg, -an** *m* antibiotic, antidote
ùr-fhàs *n* **-ais** *m* bloom, fresh growth
ùr-fhàs *v* **ùr-fhàs** grow afresh
ùr-ghnàthach *a* **-aiche** innovative
ùr-ghnàthaich *v* **-achadh** innovate
ùrlar *n* **-air, -an** *m* floor
ùrnaigh *n* **-ean** *f* prayer **Ù. an Tighearna** the Lord's Prayer **dèan ù.** *v* pray *Also vn* **ag ù.**
urra *n* **-cha(n)** *f* person **not an u.** a pound each **tha sin an u. riut fhèin** that is up to you **na h-urracha mòra** those and such as those, the high heid yins **gun u.** anonymous
urrainn *n* ability **is u. dhomh** I can
urram *n* **-aim** *m* honour, respect, reverence **cuir u. air** *v* honour
urramach *a* **-aiche** honourable, revered, venerable **an t-Urr** the Rev
urras *n* **-ais, -an** *m* surety, security, bond; trust **cha rachainn an u.** *v* I wouldn't bet against it, I bet
urrasair *n* **-ean** *m* trustee; sponsor
ursainn *n* **-ean** *f* doorpost, jamb
ùruisg *n* **-e, -ean** *m* water spirit; diviner
usgar *n* **-air/-grach, -an/usgraichean** *m* bracelet, necklace, ornament, jewel
uspag *n* **-aig, -an** *f* light gust
ùth *n* **-a, -an/-annan** *m* udder
ùtraid *n* **-e, -ean** *f* access road, track

A

abandon *v* trèig, fàg

abate *v* lùghdaich, sìolaidh, lasaich

abbey *n* abaid *f*

abbot *n* aba *m*

abbreviation *n* giorrachadh *m*

abdicate *v* leig dheth/dhith *etc*, dìobair

abdomen *n* brù *f*, balg *m*

abduct *v* goid air falbh

abhor *v* **she abhors it** is lugha oirre e/ tha dubh-ghràin aice air

abhorrent *a* gràineil, sgreamhail

abide *v* fuirich; (*tolerate*) fuiling

ability *n* comas *m*

abject *a* truagh, dìblidh

able *a* comasach **are you a. to ...?** an urrainn dhut ...? an tèid agad air ...?

abnormal *a* mì-nàdarra; (*unusual*) neo-àbhaisteach, às a' chumantas, annasach

abnormality *n* mì-ghnàthas *m*, meang *f*

aboard *adv* air bòrd

abolish *v* cuir às (do)

abolition *n* cur às (do) *m*

aborigine *n* tùsanach *m*

abortion *n* casg-breith *m*

about *prep* mu, mu dheidhinn (+ *gen*), mu thimcheall (+ *gen*) mun cuairt air, timcheall air *adv* timcheall, mun cuairt **a. to** gus

above *prep* os cionn (+ *gen*) **a. all** gu seachd àraidh *adv* shuas, gu h-àrd

abrasive *a* sgrìobach; (*nature*) ceacharra, amh

abreast *adv* gualainn ri gualainn

abroad *adv* thall thairis **going a.** a' dol a-null thairis

abrupt *a* cas, aithghearr

abscess *n* neasgaid *f*

absence *n* neo-làthaireachd *f* **in the a. of** às aonais (+ *gen*)

absent *a* neo-làthaireach, nach eil an làthair

absolute *a* làn- (*precedes & len n*), iomlan

absolutely *adv* gu tur, gu h-iomlan

absolve *v* math, saor (o)

absorb *v* sù(i)gh, deothail; (*met*) gabh a-steach

abstain (from) *v* seachain; (*eg drink*) na gabh

abstemious *a* stuama

abstinence *n* stuamachd *f*, seachnadh *m*

abstract *a* eas-chruthach

absurd *a* gun toinisg/chiall

abundance *n* pailteas *m*, (*in numbers*) lìonmhorachd *f*

abundant *a* pailt, lìonmhor

abuse *n* mì-bhuileachadh *m*, ana-caitheamh *f m*; (*phys*) droch dhìol *f*, (*verbal*) càineadh *m*, droch bheul *m v* mì-bhuilich; (*phys*) dèan droch dhìol air; (*verbally*) càin, thoir droch bheul do

abysmal *a* sgriosail, muladach

academic *a* sgoilearach

academy *n* acadamaidh *f*, acadamh *f*

accelerate *v* luathaich, greas

accent *n* (*voice*) blas *m*; (*stress*) buille *f*; (*speech mark*) stràc *f m*

accept *v* gabh ri

acceptable *a* iomchaidh, furasta gabhail ris

access *n* (*phys*) rathad *m*, slighe *f*; (*opportunity*) cothrom (air) *m v* ruig air

accessible *a* ruigsinneach, so-ruigsinn, fosgailte

accident *n* tubaist *f*, sgiorradh *m*; (*chance*) tuiteamas *m*

accidental *a* tuiteamach

accidentally *adv* gun fhiosta

accommodate *v* thoir àite-fuirich do; (*hold*) gabh

accommodation *n* àite-fuirich *m*, rùm *m*; (*abstr*) còrdadh *m*

accompany *v* rach còmhla ri; (*mus*) thoir taic do

accompanying *a* an cois (+ *gen*) **a. the letter** an cois na litreach

accomplish *v* coilean, thoir gu buil

accomplished *a* coileanta, deas

accord *n* aonta *m*, co-chòrdadh *m* **in a. with** a rèir (+ *gen*)

accordingly *adv* mar sin, uime sin

according to prep phr a rèir (+ gen)
accordion n bogsa(-ciùil) m
account n iomradh m; (fin) cunntas f m
accountable a cunntachail
accountant n cunntasair m, neach-cunntais m
accumulate v cruinnich
accurate a neo-mhearachdach, ceart
accusation n casaid f
accuse v tog casaid an aghaidh, cuir às leth, fàg air
accused a fo chasaid
accustomed a gnàthach, àbhaisteach
  a. to cleachdte ri
ace n an t-aon m a (colloq) sgoinneil
ache n cràdh m, goirteas m, pian f m
  v **it aches** tha cràdh ann **my back aches** tha cràdh nam dhruim
achieve v coilean, thoir gu buil
achievement n euchd m
acid n searbhag f **a. rain** uisge-searbhaig m, uisge searbhagach m a searbh, geur
acknowledge v aithnich; (admit) aidich, gabh ri
acknowledgement n aithneachadh m; (admission) aideachadh m; (reply) freagairt f, fios-freagairt m
acquaint v cuir eòlas air, thoir eòlas do
acquainted a eòlach **a. with** eòlach air
acquire v faigh
acre n acair(e) f m
across adv tarsainn, thairis, a-null prep tarsainn air, thairis air, thar (+ gen)
act n gnìomh m; (legal) achd f; (in play) earrann f v obraich, dèan gnìomh; (conduct oneself) giùlain thu fhèin etc; (in a play) cluich
action n gnìomh m; (legal) cùis-lagha f
  a. plan plana-gnìomha m
active a gnìomhach, dèanadach; (gram) spreigeach
activity n gnìomhachd f, obair f; (pastime) cur-seachad m
actor n cleasaiche m, actair m
actress n bana-chleasaiche f, ban-actair f
actual a dearbh, fìor (both precede & lenite n)

acute a geur; (intense) dian **a. accent** stràc gheur f m
adapt v atharraich, ceartaich, dèan freagarrach **a. to** fàs suas ri
add v cuir ri, meudaich
adder n nathair(-nimhe) f
addict n tràill f m
addicted a (to) fo smachd, na t(h)ràill do etc
addiction n tràilleachd f
addition n meudachadh m; (sum) cur-ris m **in a. to** a bharrachd/thuilleadh air
additional a a bharrachd, a thuilleadh
address n seòladh m; (talk) òraid f v cuir seòladh air; (talk) dèan òraid, labhair ri; (tackle) cuir aghaidh air
adept a sgileil, ealanta, teòma
adequate a gu leòr, iomchaidh
adhesive n tàthair m a leanailteach
  a. tape teip-tàthaidh f
adjacent (to) a faisg (air), dlùth (do/ri), ri taobh (+ gen)
adjective n buadhair m
adjourn v cuir dàil an, sgaoil, sguir de
adjust v ceartaich, rèitich, atharraich
administration n rianachd f **this A.** an Riaghaltas seo
administrator n rianadair m, rianaire m, neach-riaghlaidh m
admirable a ionmholta
admiration n meas m, sùim f
admire v saoil mòran de **I a. her** tha mi saoilsinn mòran dhith **I a. them** tha meas agam orra
admission n leigeil a-steach m; (confession) aideachadh m
admit v leig a-steach; (confess) aidich
adolescent n òigear m
adopt v uchd-mhacaich; (policy) gabh ri
adoption n uchd-mhacachd f; (policy) gabhail ri m
adore v bi fo throm-ghaol; (relig) dèan adhradh do **she adored him** bha gaol a cridhe aice air
adult n, a inbheach m
adultery n adhaltranas m **commit a.** dèan adhaltranas

advance n dol air adhart m, ceum air thoiseach m; (of money) eàrlas m v rach air adhart; (rank) àrdaich; (money) thoir eàrlas

advanced a adhartach

advantage n buannachd f **she took a. of me** ghabh i brath orm

advantageous a buannachdail

adventure n dàn'-thuras m

adventurous a dàna

adverb n co-ghnìomhair m

adverse a mì-fhàbharach, calltach

adversity n cruaidh-chàs m, teinn f

advertise v cuir sanas, sanasaich

advertisement n sanas m, sanas-reic m

advice n comhairle f

advise v comhairlich, earalaich **be advised** gabh comhairle

adviser n comhairleach m, neach-comhairleachaidh m

advocate n neach-tagraidh m v mol

aesthetic a (bh)o thaobh tlachd

affable a aoigheil, ceanalta

affair n gnothach m, cùis f **he had an a.** bha e a' falbh le tèile

affect v thoir buaidh air, drùidh air; (pretend) leig air/oirre etc

affection n gaol m, spèis f

affectionate a gaolach, teò-chridheach

affirm v dearbh, daingnich

affliction n doilgheas m, àmhghar f m

affluent a beairteach, saidhbhir

afford v ruig air; (provide) builich **I can't a. the time** chan urrainn dhomh ùine a chosg air

afloat adv air bhog, air flod

afraid a fo eagal, eagalach

African n, a Afraganach m, (female) ban-Afraganach f

after prep (+ gen) an dèidh, às dèidh adv an dèidh làimhe **a. all** an dèidh a h-uile rud/càil

afternoon n feasgar m **in the a.** feasgar **Friday a.** feasgar Dihaoine

afterwards adv an dèidh sin

again adv a-rithist

against prep an aghaidh (+ gen)

age n aois f; (period) linn f m **it took ages** thug e ùine chianail v fàs sean/aosta

aged a sean, aosta

agency n (body) buidheann f m

agenda n clàr-gnothaich m

agent n àidseant m, neach-ionaid m; (means) dòigh f

aggravate v dèan nas miosa

aggregate n iomlan m v cuir còmhla

aggression n ionnsaigh f m

aggressive a ionnsaigheach

agile a sùbailte, subailte

agitate v cuir troimh-a-chèile, luasganaich; (polit) piobraich

ago adv o chionn; ... air ais **five years ago** o chionn c(h)òig bliadhna **long ago** o chionn f(h)ada **a short time ago** o chionn ghoirid

agony n dòrainn f

agree v aontaich, còrd, rach le

agreeable a taitneach, ciatach

agreement n aonta m, còrdadh m, cùmhnant m

agriculture n àiteachas m

aground adv air tìr

ahead adv air adhart **a. of** prep phr air thoiseach air

aid n cobhair f, cuideachadh m, còmhnadh m v cuidich, dèan cobhair air **First Aid** Ciad Fhuasgladh m

aim n cuimse f; (intention) amas m, rùn m v cuimsich (+ air); (intend) amais

air n àile m, èadhar f; (breath of) deò f; (mus) fonn m v leig an t-àile gu; (opinion) cuir an cèill

airline n companaidh phlèanaichean f m

airmail n post-adhair m

airport n port-adhair m

aisle n trannsa f

ajar adv leth-fhosgailte

alarm n rabhadh m **a. clock** cloc-rabhaidh m

alarming a eagalach, draghail

alas exclam Och!, Mo chreach!, Mo thruaighe!

alcohol n alcol m, deoch-làidir f

alcoholic n alcolach m tràill dibhe f m
a alcolach
ale n leann m
alert a furachail, forail, deas v **(to)** cuir
na f(h)aireachadh (mu)
alien n coigreach m, neach-fuadain m a
coimheach
alienate v gràinnich
alight a na t(h)eine
alike adv co-ionann, coltach ri chèile
alive a beò
all a uile, iomlan, gu h-iomlan, gu lèir
allegation n cur às leth m **a serious a.**
casaid chudromach f
allege v cuir às leth, fàg air
alleviate v aotromaich, lùghdaich
alliance n caidreachas m, co-chòrdadh m
allocate v suidhich, sònraich; (distribute)
riaraich
allow v leig le, ceadaich
allowance n cuibhreann f m
allude (to) v thoir tarraing/iomradh (air)
ally n caraid m, caidreabhach m; (mil)
co-chòmhragaiche m
almost adv gu bhith, an ìre mhath, gu
ìre bhig, cha mhòr nach, theab **it is a.
finished** tha e gu bhith ullamh, tha e
an ìre mhath ullamh, cha mhòr nach eil
e ullamh **I a. fell** cha mhòr nach do thuit
mi, theab mi tuiteam
alone a na (h-)aonar, leis/leatha fhèin
etc
along (with) adv còmhla ri, cuide ri,
maille ri, le, an cois (+ gen)
aloud adv gu h-àrd-ghuthach **read a.**
leugh a-mach
alphabet n aibidil f
alphabetical a a rèir na h-aibideil **in a.
order** an òrdugh na h-aibideil
already adv mar-thà, mu thràth, cheana
also adv cuideachd, mar an ceudna
alter v atharraich; (intrans) caochail
alteration n atharrachadh m
alternate a mu seach
alternative n roghainn eile f a eile,
eadar-roghnach
alternatively adv air an làimh eile
although conj ged; (before a) ge

altitude n àirde f
altogether adv gu lèir, uile-gu-lèir, gu
h-iomlan, gu tur
always adv an-còmhnaidh, daonnan
am v tha **am not** chan eil (See verb **to be**
in Grammar)
amalgamate v cuir ri chèile, amalaich,
measgaich; (intrans) rach còmhla
amateur n neo-dhreuchdair m a neo-
dhreuchdail
amaze v cuir iongnadh air
amazement n iongantas m, iongnadh m
amazing a iongantach **amazingly good**
iongantach fhèin math
ambassador n tosgaire m
ambiguous a dà-sheaghach
ambition n glòir-mhiann f m, miann-
adhartais f m **I have an a. to ...** tha
miann agam ...
ambitious a glòir-mhiannach, miannach
air adhartas
ambulance n carbad-eiridinn m,
ambaileans f
ambush n feall-fhalach m v dèan feall-
fhalach
amenable a fosgailte (ri, do)
amend v atharraich, leasaich
amendment n atharrachadh m
leasachadh m
amenity n goireas m
American n, a Ameireaganach m,
(female) ban-Ameireaganach f
amiable a càirdeil, bàidheil, ceanalta
amicable a càirdeil, suairce, geanail
amid(st) prep am measg, am meadhan
(both + gen)
amiss adv gu h-olc, ceàrr
ammunition n connadh làmhaich m;
(met) cothrom-losgaidh m
among(st) prep am measg, air feadh
(both + gen)
amount n meud m, uimhir f; (money)
sùim f
ample a pailt; (in size etc) mòr,
tomadach
amplify v meudaich, leudaich air
amputate v geàrr dheth etc, sgath
amuse v toilich, thoir gàire air

amusing *a* èibhinn, ait
anaesthetic *n* an-fhaireachair *m*
analyze *v* mion-sgrùd, sgrùd
analysis *n* mion-sgrùdadh *m*, sgrùdadh *m*, anailis *f*
anarchy *n* ain-riaghailt *f*, ceannairc *f*
anatomy *n* (*body*) bodhaig *f*; (*science*) eòlas bodhaig *m*, corp-eòlas *m*
ancestor *n* sinnsear *m*
anchor *n* acair(e) *f m* **at a.** air (an) acair(e) *v* acraich
anchorage *n* acarsaid *f*
ancient *a* àrsaidh
and *conj* agus, is, 's
anecdote *n* naidheachd *f*, sgeula *f*
angel *n* aingeal *m*
anger *n* fearg *f*, corraich *f v* cuir fearg air
angle *n* uilinn *f*, ceàrn *f m*
angry *a* feargach **he was a.** bha an fhearg air
anguish *n* àmhghar *f m*, dòrainn *f*
animal *n* ainmhidh *m*, beathach *m*
animated *a* beothail, meanmnach
animosity *n* gamhlas *m*, mì-rùn *m*
ankle *n* adhbrann *f m*
annex *v* cuir ri, ceangail ri
annihilate *v* sgrios, cuir às do
anniversary *n* ceann-bliadhna *m*, cuimhneachan bliadhnail *m*
announce *v* ainmich, cuir an cèill, leig fhaicinn
announcement *n* teachdaireachd *f*, fios *m*
annoy *v* cuir dragh air, leamhaich
annoyance *n* dragh *m*, buaireas *m*
annoyed *a* diombach, mì-thoilichte
annoying *a* leamh, buaireanta
annual *a* bliadhnail **a. report** aithisg bhliadhnail *f* **A. General Meeting** Coinneamh Choitcheann Bhliadhnail *f*
annually *adv* gach bliadhna
anonymous *a* gun ainm, gun urra(inn)
another *pron* neach/tè eile *a* eile **one a.** a chèile
answer *n* freagairt *f v* freagair, thoir freagairt (do)
ant *n* seangan *m*
antagonize *v* dèan nàmhaid de

anthem *n* laoidh *f m* **national a.** laoidh nàiseanta/na rìoghachd
antibiotic *n* antibiotaig *f*, urchasg *m*
anticipate *v* sùilich; (*prepare for*) deasaich airson
anti-clockwise *a* tuathal
antidote *n* urchasg *m*
antipathy *n* fuath *m*
antique *n* seann rud *m a* àrsaidh
antler *n* cabar (fèidh) *m*
anxiety *n* dragh *m*, iomagain *f*, imcheist *f*
anxious *a* draghail, iomagaineach, fo imcheist
any *a* sam bith, air bith; (*pron*) aon/fear/tè sam bith, aon, gin **any at all** gin idir
any other business gnothach sam bith eile
anyone *n* neach/duine sam bith *m*
anything *n* dad/sìon/rud/nì (sam bith) *m*, càil (sam bith) *f*
anywhere *adv* àite sam bith
apart *adv* air leth; (*distance, motion*) (bh)o chèile
apartment *n* (*suite of rooms*) seòmraichean *m pl*; (*residence*) flat *f m*
apathy *n* cion ùidh *m*
ape *n* apa *f*
apologize *v* dèan leisgeul, iarr do/a *etc* leisgeul a ghabhail
apology *n* leisgeul *m*
apostrophe *n* asgair *m*
appal *v* cuir uabhas air
appalling *a* sgriosail, cianail, eagalach
apparent *a* soilleir, follaiseach, faicsinneach
appeal *n* tarraing *f*; (*leg*) ath-agairt *m*, ath-thagradh *m v* tarraing; (*leg*) ath-agair **a. against** tagair an aghaidh
appear *v* nochd, thig am fianais/follais
appearance *n* (*phys*) coltas *m*, dreach *m*, aogas *m*
appendicitis *n* an grèim mionaich *m*
appendix *n* (*annexe*) eàrr-ràdh *m*
appetite *n* càil *f*, càil bìdh *f*; (*desire*) miann *f m*
applause *n* bualadh bhas *m*; (*met*) moladh *m*

apple *n* ubhal *f* **a. of eye** dearc na sùla *f* **a.-tree** craobh-ubhail *f*

appliance *n* uidheam *f*, inneal *m*

applicant *n* tagraiche *m*

application *n* iarrtas *m*, tagradh *m*; (*use*) cur an sàs *m* **a. form** foirm/clàr-iarrtais *m*

apply (for) *v* cuir a-steach (airson); (*use*) cuir gu feum, cuir an gnìomh **a. to/with** (*phys*) cuir air

appoint *v* suidhich, cuir an dreuchd

appointment *n* coinneamh *f*, àm suidhichte *m*; (*to post*) cur an dreuchd *m*

apposite *a* freagarrach, iomchaidh

appraise *v* meas, dèan measadh air, thoir beachd air

appreciate *v* cuir luach air; (*understand*) tuig gu math; (*fin*) meudaich, rach suas an luach

apprehensive *a* gealtach, draghail

apprentice *n* preantas *m*, foghlamaiche-ciùird *m*

approach *n* dòigh *f*; (*entry*) slighe *f v* dlùthaich ri, teann ri

appropriate *a* freagarrach, iomchaidh, cubhaidh

approval *n* riarachadh *m*, toileachadh *m*; (*official*) aonta *m*, ceadachadh *m* **win a. of ...** riaraich

approve *v* gabh beachd math air; (*of plan etc*) aontaich ri, ceadaich

approximately *adv* timcheall air, mu thuairmeas, faisg air

April *n* an Giblean *m*

apron *n* aparan *m*

apt *a* deas **a. to** buailteach ri/do

aptitude *n* alt *m*, sgil *m* **an a. for ...** alt air ...

Arab *n* Arabach *m*, (*female*) ban-Arabach *f*

Arabic *a* Arabach **a. numerals** figearan Arabach *n m pl*; (*lang*) Arabais *f*

arable *a* àitich **a. land** talamh àitich *m*

arbitrary *a* neo-riaghailteach, neo-chunbhalach

arbitration *n* eadar-bhreith *f*, breith-rèite *f*

arch *n* stuagh *f*, bogha *m*

archaeologist *n* arc-eòlaiche *m*

archaeology *n* arc-eòlas *m*

architect *n* ailtire *m*

architecture *n* ailtireachd *f*

archive(s) *n* tasglann *f*

arduous *a* doirbh, cruaidh, spàirneil

are *v* tha **are not** chan eil (*See verb* **to be** *in Grammar*)

area *n* farsaingeachd *f*; (*topic*) raon *m*; (*geog*) ceàrnaidh *f*

argue *v* dèan argamaid, connsaich *Also vn* ag argamaid

argument *n* argamaid *f*, connsachadh *m*

argumentative *a* connspaideach, connsachail, aimhreiteach

arise *v* èirich

aristocracy *n* na h-uaislean *m pl*, na maithean *m pl*

arithmetic *n* àireamhachd *f*, cunntas *m*

arm *n* gàirdean *m*

armed *a* fo armachd, armaichte

armful *n* achlasan *m*, ultach *m*

armour *n* armachd *f*

armpit *n* achlais *f*, lag na h-achlaise *f*

army *n* arm *m*, armailt *m*, feachd *f m*

aroma *n* boladh *m*

around *prep* timcheall, mu chuairt, mu thimcheall (*all + gen*) *adv* mun cuairt

arouse *v* dùisg

arrange *v* suidhich, cuir air dòigh; (*put in order*) cuir rian air

arrangement *n* òrdachadh *m*; (*met*) aonta *m*; (*mus*) rian *m*

arrest *v* cuir an grèim, cuir an sàs

arrival *n* teachd *m*, tighinn *m*, ruighinn *m* **on my a.** nuair a ràinig mi, air dhomh ruighinn

arrive *v* ruig, thig

arrogance *n* àrdan *m*, ladarnas *m*

arrogant *a* àrdanach, ladarna

arrow *n* saighead *f*

art *n* ealain *f*; (*pictorial*) dealbhadaireachd *f* **the arts** na h-ealain(ean)

artery *n* cuisle *f*

arthritis *n* tinneas nan alt *m*

article *n* (*lit, gram*) alt *m*, artaigil *m*; (*of clothing*) ball aodaich *m*; (*leg*) bonn *m*

articulate *a* pongail, deas-bhriathrach, siùbhlach

artificial *a* brèige, fuadain
artist *n* dealbhadair *m*; (*performer*) neach-ealain *m*
artistic *a* ealanta
as *adv* cho ... ri (+ *n*), cho ... (+ *v*) is
  as white as snow cho geal ris an t-sneachda **as long as you like** cho fad' 's a thogras tu *conj* mar; (*time*) nuair
ascend *v* dìrich, sreap, rach suas
ascent *n* dìreadh *m*
ascertain *v* faigh a-mach, fiosraich
ash(es) *n* luath *f*, luaithre *f*
ashamed *a* air mo/a *etc* nàrachadh, nàraichte
ashore *adv* air tìr
ashtray *n* soitheach-luaithre *f m*
Asian *n*, *a* Àisianach *m*, (*female*) ban-Àisianach *f*
aside *adv* gu aon taobh, an dàrna taobh, air leth
ask *v* (*request*) iarr; (*enquire*) faighnich, feòraich, farraid
asleep *adv* nam chadal, na c(h)adal *etc*
aspect *n* snuadh *m*, aogas *m*; (*of topic*) taobh *m*; (*view*) sealladh *m*
aspiration *n* miann *f m*, rùn *m*; (*ling*) analachadh *m*
aspire *v* rùnaich, miannaich
ass *n* asal *f m*

assiduous *a* dìcheallach, dìoghrasach
assign *v* cuir air leth, sònraich
assignment *n* obair shònraichte *f*, dleastanas sònraichte *m*; (*educ*) pìos-obrach
assist *v* cuidich, dèan cobhair air
assistance *n* cuideachadh *m*, cobhair *f*
assistant *n* neach-cuideachaidh *m*
association *n* comann *m*, caidreabh *m*
assume *v* bi dhen bheachd; (*take control*) gabh sealbh air
assurance *n* dearbhachd *f*, cinnt *f*; (*insurance*) àrachas *m* **self-a.** dànachd *f*
assure *v* dearbh, dèan cinnteach do **I a. you he'll come** thèid mi an urras dhut gun tig e
asthma *n* a' chuing *f*, an sac *m*
astonish *v* cuir iongnadh air
astonishment *n* mòr-iongnadh *m*, mòr-iongantas *m*
astray *adv* air seachran, air iomrall
astride *adv* casa-gòbhlach
astrologer *n* reuladair *m*
astrology *n* reuladaireachd *f*
astronaut *n* speuradair *m*, speurair *m*
astronomer *n* reul-eòlaiche *m*
astronomy *n* reul-eòlas *m*
asylum *n* comraich *f*, tèarmann *m*; (*instit*) ospadal inntinn *m*

Insight: asleep

To say that someone is in a certain state such as being asleep, you place the word *na* before the state they are in as in *tha e na chadal* (he is asleep) or *tha i na cadal* (she is asleep). Notice that *na* referring to a male lenites the following word. *Tha i na dùisg* gives the opposite meaning: she is awake.

assassinate *v* murt
assault *n* ionnsaigh *f m v* thoir ionnsaigh air
assemble *v* cruinnich
assembly *n* co-chruinneachadh *m*, tional *m*; (*eccl*) àrd-sheanadh *m*; (*polit*) seanadh *m*
assent *n* aonta *m*, aontachadh *m*
assess *v* meas
assessment *n* meas *m*, measadh *m*
asset *n* maoin *f*

at *prep* aig **at all** idir
atheism *n* neo-dhiadhachd *f*
atheist *n* neo-dhiadhaire *m*, ana-creidmheach *m*
athlete *n* lùth-chleasaiche *m*
athletic *a* (*person*) lùthmhor; (*game, feat*) lùth-chleasach
athletics *n* lùth-chleasachd *f*
atlas *n* atlas *m*
atmosphere *n* àile *m*; (*met*) faireachdainn *f*

atom n dadam m, smùirnean m, atam m
atomic a dadamach, smùirneach, atamach
atrocious a uabhasach, eagalach, cianail, sgriosail
atrocity n buirbe f
attach v ceangail, greimich air/ri
attached a ceangailte, an lùib (+ gen), an cois (+ gen) **very a. to ...** fìor mheasail air ...
attachment n dàimh f m, ceangal m; (document) ceanglan m, faidhle m
attack n ionnsaigh f m **she had an attack of ...** bhuail ... i v thoir ionnsaigh (air)
attain v ruig, coisinn, faigh
attainable a ruigsinneach, so-ruighinn, a ghabhas f(h)aighinn
attempt n oidhirp f v dèan oidhirp, feuch ri
attend v fritheil **a. to** dèan, gabh os làimh
attendant n neach-frithealaidh m
attention n aire f, feairt f **pay a. to** thoir an aire do
attentive a furachail, suimeil
attic n seòmar-mullaich m
attitude n seasamh m, beachd m
attract v tarraing, tàlaidh
attraction n tarraing f, tàladh m
attractive a tarraingeach, tlachdmhor, bòidheach
auburn a buidhe-ruadh
auction n rup f **up for a.** ga reic
audible a osgarra, ri chluinntinn
audience n luchd-èisteachd m; (a hearing) èisteachd f
audit n sgrùdadh m v sgrùd, dèan sgrùdadh air
auditor n sgrùdaire m, neach-sgrùdaidh m
August n an Lùnastal m

aunt n piuthar-athar/màthar f, antaidh f **my a.** piuthar m' athar/mo mhàthar, m' antaidh
auspicious a gealltanach, fàbharach, rathail
austere a (of person) cruaidh
austerity n (financial) teanntachd f
Australian n, a Astràilianach m, (female) ban-Astràilianach f
authentic a fìor (+ len), cinnteach, dearbhte, dhà-rìribh
author n ùghdar m
authority n ùghdarras m, smachd m; (warrant) barantas m **the Local A.** an t-Ùghdarras Ionadail
authorize v thoir ùghdarras, ceadaich
autobiography n fèin-eachdraidh f
automatic a fèin-ghluasadach
autonomous a neo-eisimeileach
autumn n am foghar m
auxiliary n neach-cuideachaidh m, neach-taic(e) m a taiceil
available a ri fhaighinn/fhaotainn
avenge v dìol
average n cuibheas m, meadhan m a cuibheasach, gnàthach **on a.** anns a' chumantas
avoid v seachain
await v fuirich ri
awake a na d(h)ùisg etc
award n duais f v thoir duais
aware a mothachail, forail
awareness n mothachadh m
away adv air falbh
awesome a àibheiseach
awful a eagalach, uabhasach, sgràthail
awkward a leibideach, clobhdach
axe n tuagh f, làmhag f, làmhagh f
axle n aiseal f m
aye interj seadh, aidh!

B

baby n leanabh m, bèibidh m
bachelor n baidsealair m, fleasgach m, seana-ghille m
back n cùl m, cùlaibh m v rach air ais; (support) seas, cuidich; (bet on) cuir airgead air adv air ais

background n cùl-raon m, bun-fhiosrachadh m
backside n tòn f, màs m Also tòin
backward(s) adv an comhair a c(h)ùil etc
backward a fad' air ais

bacon m muicfheòil f
bad a dona, droch (*precedes & len n*), olc
  bad-tempered a greannach, eangarra
badge n suaicheantas m, baidse m
badger n broc m
baffle v dubh-fhaillich air, fairtlich air
  b. someone dèan a' chùis air
bag n baga m, màileid f; (*sack*) poca m
baggage n bagaichean m pl
bagpipe n pìob f **great Highland**
  b. pìob-mhòr

bandage n bann m
bang n brag m v thoir brag air, buail
banish v fuadaich, fògair
bank n banca m; (*topog*) bruach f m;
  (*peat*) bac m
bank v cuir dhan bhanca **b. on** theirig an
  urras air
banker n bancair m
bankrupt a briste **the company went
  b.** bhris(t) air a' chompanaidh
banned a toirmisgte

Insight: bagpipes

The bagpipe, *a' phìob-mhòr*, literally the big pipe, is an emblem
of Scottish culture and originates in the country's Gaelic heritage.
There are two strands of bagpipe music, *ceòl-mòr* (big music) and
ceòl-beag (small music). The former, also called pibroch, is the
classical music of the pipes and is highly intricate and ornamented.
Ceòl-beag is the lighter music such as marches, strathspeys and reels.

bail n urras m **on b.** air urras v fuasgail
  air urras, thoir urras air
baillie n bàillidh m
bait n biathadh m, baoit f, maghar m
  v biadh, cuir biathadh/maghar air;
  (*taunt*) leamhaich, mag air
bake v fuin; (*in oven*) bruich san àmhainn
baker n bèicear m, fuineadair m
bakery n taigh-fuine m
baking n bèicearachd f, fuine m
  b. powder pùdar/fùdar-fuine m
balance n meidh f; (*abstr*) cothrom m,
  co-chothrom m; (*fin*) còrr m **b. sheet**
  clàr cothromachaidh m v cuir air
  mheidh; (*abstr*) cothromaich
balanced a cothromach
balcony n for-uinneag f
bald a maol, le sgall
ball n ball m, bàl(l)a m; (*wool*) ceirtle
  f; (*dance*) bàl m
ballast n balaist(e) f m
balloon n bailiùn m
ballot n baileat m, bhòtadh m
ban n toirmeasg m, casg m, bacadh m
  v toirmisg, caisg, bac
band n bann m; (*of people*) buidheann
  f m; (*mus*) còmhlan-ciùil m

banner n bratach f
banquet n fèist f, fleadh m, bangaid f
banter n tarraing-às f
baptism n baisteadh m
Baptist n, a Baisteach m
baptize v baist
bar n crann-tarsainn m; (*pub*) bàr m,
  taigh-seinnse m; (*hindrance*) bacad h
  m **b. chart** clàr-cholbhan m **b. graph**
  graf-cholbhan m
barbaric a borb
barbed a gathach **b. wire** uèir bhiorach/
  stobach f
barber n borbair m, bearradair m
bard n bàrd m, filidh m
bare a lom, rùisgte
bargain n bargan f m; (*agreement*)
  cùmhnant m
barge n bàirdse f
bark n rùsg m; (*of dog*) comhart m
barking n comhartaich f Also vn
  a' comhartaich
barley n eòrna m
barn n sabhal m
barnacle n giùran m, bàirneach f
barometer n glainne-sìde f
barrel n baraille m Also barailte

barren *a* neo-thorrach, seasg; (*land*) fàs
barrier *n* bacadh *m*, cnap-starra *m*
barrow *n* bara *m*
barter *n* malairt *f v* dèan malairt/iomlaid, malairtich
base *n* stèidh *f*, bonn *m*, bun *m*, bunait *f m*
bashful *a* nàrach, diùid
basic *a* bunaiteach, bunasach
basin *n* mias *f*
basis *n* bun *m*, bunait *f m*, bun-stèidh *f*
bask *v* blian
basket *n* basgaid *f*
bass *a* beus
bat *n* slacan *m*, bat *m*; (*mammal*) ialtag *f*
batch *n* baidse *m*, grunn *m*, dòrlach *m*
bath *n* amar *m*
batter *v* liodraig, pronn
battery *n* bataraidh *f m*
battle *n* cath *m*, blàr *m*, batail *m*
bay *n* bàgh *m*, camas *m*, òb *m*
be *v* bi (*See verb* **to be** *in Grammar*)
beach *n* tràigh *f* **shingle b.** mol *m*
bead *n* grìogag *f* **beads** (*relig*) paidirean *m*
beak *n* gob *m*
beam *n* (*of wood*) sail *f*; (*of light*) gath *m*, boillsgeadh *m*; (*apparatus*) crann *m*
bean *n* pònair *f* (*normally used as coll*) **beans** pònairean
bear *n* mathan *m*
bear *v* giùlain; (*suffer*) fuiling; (*a child*) beir
beard *n* feusag *f*
beast *n* beathach *m*, ainmhidh *m*; (*pej*) biast *f*
beat *n* buille *f v* dèan an gnothach air
beautiful *a* brèagha, bòidheach, maiseach, riochdail
beauty *n* bòidhchead *f*, maise *f*, sgèimh *f*, àilleachd *f* **b. spot** ball-seirce *m*
because *conj* airson, a chionn, seach, ri linn **b. of** air sàillibh (+ *gen*)
become *v* fàs, cinn **b. a ...** rach na ... *etc*
bed *n* leabaidh *f* **bed and breakfast** leabaidh is bracaist **bedroom** rùm/seòmar-cadail *m*
bee *n* seillean *m*, beach *m*
beef *n* mairtfheòil *f*

beer *n* leann *m*
beetle *n* daolag *f*
beetroot *n* biotais *m*
before *prep* ro; (*in front of*) air beulaibh (+ *gen*) *adv* roimhe *conj* mus
beforehand *adv* ro-làimh
beg *v* guidh; (*for money etc*) iarr dèirc (air)
beggar *n* dèirceach *m*
begin *v* tòisich
beginner *n* neach-tòiseachaidh *m*
beginning *n* toiseach *m*, tòiseachadh *m*, tùs *m* **the very b.** toiseach tòiseachaidh
behalf *n* **on b. of** às leth (+ *gen*) **on my b.** às mo leth(-sa)
behave *v* bi modhail
behaviour *n* giùlan *m*
behind *adv* air d(h)eireadh *prep* air cùlaibh, air c(h)ùl (*both* + *gen*) **b. them** air an cùlaibh
belch *v* dèan brùchd
belief *n* (*relig*) creideamh *m*
believe *v* creid, thoir creideas do
bell *n* clag *m*
bellow *v* beuc, geum, dèan geum, bùir
belly *n* brù *f*, broinn *f*
belong *v* buin **b. to** buin do **that belongs to me** 's ann leamsa a tha sin
beloved *a* ionmhainn, gràdhach, gràdhaichte
below *adv* shìos; (*down here*) a-bhos; (*downwards*) sìos *prep* fo (+ *len*)
belt *n* crios *m*, bann *m*
bench *n* being(e) *f*
bend *n* lùb *m*, fiaradh *m v* lùb, aom, fiaraich; (*stoop*) crom
beneath *prep* fo (+ *len*)
beneficial *a* feumail, buannachdail
benefit *n* feum *m*, buannachd *f*, tairbhe *f*
benevolent *a* coibhneil, le deagh-ghean
benign *a* coibhneil, fial; (*med*) neo-aillseach, neo-chronail
bent *a* lùbte, fiar, cam; (*stooped*) crom
bequest *n* dìleab *f*
berry *n* dearc *f*, dearcag *f*, sùbh *m*
beseech *v* guidh, dèan guidhe (ri)
beside *prep phr* ri taobh (+ *gen*), làimh ri

besides *adv* a bhàrr air, a bharrachd air, a thuilleadh air; (*anyway*) co-dhiù
best *a, adv* (as) fheàrr
bestow *v* builich
bet *n* geall *m v* cuir geall
betray *v* brath; (*feelings*) leig ris
better *a* nas fheàrr, (*past*) na b' fheàrr
between *prep* eadar *adv* eadar
beware *v* thoir an aire, bi air d' fhaiceall
beyond *prep* air taobh thall, thar (*both + gen*); (*time*) seachad air; (*exceeding*) os cionn (+ *gen*)
bias *n* leiteachas *m*; claon-bhàidh *f*; (*phys*) claonadh *m*
Bible *n* Bìoball *m*
bibliography *n* leabhar-chlàr *m*; (*activity*) leabhar-chlàradh *m*
bicycle *n* baidhsagal *m*, rothair *m*
bid *n* tairgse *f*, iarrtas *m* **bid for** dèan tairgse airson, cuir a-steach airson
big *a* mòr, tomadach
bigot *n* dalm-bheachdaiche *m*
bigotry *n* dalm-bheachd *m*
bile *n* domblas *m*
bilingual *a* dà-chànanach
bill *n* cunntas *f m*; (*of a bird*) gob *m*; (*leg*) bile *m*
billion *n* billean *m*
bin *n* biona *f m*
bind *v* ceangail, naisg; (*fetter*) cuibhrich
binoculars *n* prosbaig *f*, glainneachan *f pl*
biography *n* eachdraidh-beatha *f*
biology *n* bith-eòlas *m*
birch *n* beithe *f*
bird *n* eun *m*
birth *n* breith *f* **b. certificate** teisteanas-breith *m* **birthday** co-là-breith *m*, ceann-bliadhna *m*
biscuit *n* briosgaid *f*
bishop *n* easbaig *m*
bit *n* bìdeag *f*, mìr *m*, pìos *m*, criomag *f*; (*horse's*) cabstair *m*, mìreanach *m*
bitch *n* galla *f*, saigh *f*
bite *n* bìdeadh *m*, bìdeag *f*; (*of food*) grèim *m v* bìd, thoir grèim/bìdeag à
bitter *a* geur, searbh (*also met*)

black *a* dubh, dorch(a); (*mood*) gruamach **blackbird** lon-dubh *m*
blackboard bòrd-dubh *m*
blacken *v* dubh, dèan dubh; (*reputation*) mill cliù
blacksmith *n* gobha *m*
bladder *n* aotroman *m*
blade *n* (*of knife*) lann *f*; (*on tool*) iarann *m*; (*of grass*) bileag *f*
blame *n* coire *f v* cuir coire air, coirich, faigh coire/cron do
blameless *a* neoichiontach, gun choire
bland *a* tlàth, staoin
blank *a* bàn, falamh
blanket *n* plaide *f*, plangaid *f*
blatant *a* dalma, gun chleith
blaze *n* teine lasrach *m*, caoir *f*; (*domestic*) braidseal *m*
bleak *a* lom, aognaidh; (*met*) gun dòchas
bleat *v* dèan mèilich, dèan meigeadaich *Also vn* a' mèilich, a' meigeadaich
bleed *v* caill/sil fuil; (*drain*) leig
blemish *n* gaoid *f*, smal *m*
blend *n* coimeasgadh *m v* coimeasgaich
bless *v* beannaich
blessing *n* beannachd *f*, beannachadh *m*
blethering *n* bleadraich *f*, bleadaireachd *f*
blight *n* gaiseadh *m*
blind *n* sgàil(e) *f*
blind *a* dall **the b.** na doill *n m pl*
blindness *n* doille *f*
blink *v* caog, priob
bliss *n* sòlas *m*, sonas *m*, làn-aoibhneas *m*
blissful *a* sòlasach, sona, làn-aoibhneach
blister *n* builgean *m*, balg *m*, leus *m*
blizzard *n* cathadh-sneachda *m*
block *n* bloc *m*, sgonn *m*, ceap *m v* caisg, cuir bacadh air, dùin
blog *n* bloga *m*
blogger *n* blogaire *m*
blond(e) *a* bàn *n* tè bhàn *f*, fear bàn *m*
blood *n* fuil *f* **b. pressure** bruthadh-fala *m* **b. transfusion** leasachadh-fala *m*
bloodshed dòrtadh-fala *m*
bloody *a* fuilteach **you b. idiot!** amadain na mallachd/croiche! *m*

bloom n blàth m, ùr-fhàs m v thig fo bhlàth

blossom n blàth m

blouse n blobhs(a) f m

blow n buille f, bualadh m, beum m; (weather) sèideadh m v sèid

blue a gorm **light blue** liath

bluff v meall, thoir an car à(s)

blunder n mearachd mhòr f

blunt a maol

blurred a doilleir, a-mach à fòcas

blush n rudhadh (gruaidhe) m v fàs dearg **she blushed** thàinig rudhadh na gruaidh

blushing a rudhach, ruiteach

boar n torc m

board n bòrd m, clàr m; (plank) dèile f v rach air bòrd

boast n bòst m v dèan bòst, bòstaich

boasting n bòstadh m

boat n bàta m; (open) eathar f m **fishing b.** bàt'-iasgaich **sailing b.** bàta-siùil

body n corp m, bodhaig f; (of people) buidheann f m, còmhlan m

bog n bog(l)ach f, fèithe f

boil n neasgaid f

boil v goil; (food) bruich **it's on the b.** tha e a' goil

boiled a bruich

boisterous a gailbheach; (person) iorghaileach

bold a dàna, tapaidh, dalma **b. type** (liter) clò trom m

boldness n dànadas m, dànachd f, tapachd f

bolster v cùm taic ri, misnich

bolt n bolt(a) m

bomb n bom(a) m v leag bom air, bom(aig)

bond n ceangal m, bann m, gealladh m

bone n cnàimh m

bonfire n tein-aighir m, tein-èibhinn m

bonnet n bonaid f m

bonny a bòidheach, brèagha, buaidheach

bonus n leasachadh (duaise) m **it was a real b.** 's e fìor bhuannachd a bh' ann

book n leabhar m **bookshop** bùth leabhraichean f

booklet n leabhran m

boot n bròg f

booth n bùth f, bothan m

booze n deoch-làidir f v òl, gabh steall

border n crìoch f; (edge) oir f m, iomall m

bore v cladhaich, dèan toll; (met) bòraig, sàraich

boring a ràsanach, sàraichte

borrow v faigh (air) iasad

bosom n broilleach m

boss n ceannard m

botany n luibh-eòlas m

both a dà; (of people) dithis **with b. hands** leis an dà làimh **b. sons** an dithis mhac adv le chèile **b. great and small** eadar bheag is mhòr

bother n bodraigeadh m, dragh m v bodraig, cuir dragh air

bottle n botal m

bottom n ìochdar m, bonn m; (sea) aigeann m, grunnd m; (of person) màs m, tòn f **b. up** bhon bhonn suas

bounce v bunsaig, buns

bound n sìnteag f, cruinn-leum f m

boundary n crìoch f

bow n bogha m; (ship) toiseach m; (bending) cromadh-cinn m v (bend) crom, lùb

bowel(s) n innidh f

bowl n bobhla m, cuach f

bowling n bòbhladh m **b. alley** ionad bòbhlaidh m

box n bogsa m, bucas m; (blow) buille f v cuir am bogsa; (fight) bogs(aig)

boxer n bogsair m

boxing n bogsadh m

boy n balach m, gille m

boycott v seachain, na gabh gnothach ri

boyfriend n carabhaidh f m, bràmair m

brace n uidheam-teannachaidh m; (pair) dithis m, càraid f, caigeann f

bracelet n bann-làimhe m

braces n gaileis f

bracken n raineach f

bracket n bracaid f; (in writing) camag f

brae n bruthach f m, leathad m

brag v bòst, dèan bòst

brain n eanchainn f

brake *n* brèig *f*, casgan *m*

bramble *n* (*berry*) smeur *f*; (*bush*) dris *f*

branch *n* geug *f*, meangan *m*; (*abstr*) meur *f*

brand *n* seòrsa *m*; (*of fire*) aithinne *m* **b. new** talc-ùr, ùr nodha

brandy *n* branndaidh *f*

brass *n* pràis *f*

brat *n* isean *m*, peasan *m*

brave *a* gaisgeil, calma

bravery *n* gaisge *f*, gaisgeachd *f*, misneachd *f*

brawl *n* tuasaid *f*, còmhrag *f*

brazen *a* ladarna, gun nàire; (*metal*) pràiseach

breach *n* bris(t)eadh *m*, bealach *m*, beàrn *f m*

breach *v* dèan bris(t)eadh/beàrn

bread *n* aran *m*

breadth *n* leud *m*, farsaingeachd *f*

break *n* bris(t)eadh *m*; (*abstr*) fois *f v* bris(t); (*of word, promise*) rach air ais air

breakfast *n* bracaist *f*

breast *n* broilleach *m*, uchd *m* **a b.** cìoch *f*

breath *n* anail *f*, deò *f*

breathe *v* tarraing anail

breathless *a* gun anail, goirid san anail

breed *n* seòrsa *m*, gnè *f*, sìol *m v* gin, tàrmaich, briod(aich)

breeding *n* briodachadh *m*; (*met*) togail *f*, modh *f*

breeze *n* oiteag *f*, osag *f*, soirbheas *m*

brew *v* dèan grùdaireachd; (*tea*) tarraing

brewery *n* taigh-grùide *m*

bribe *n* brìb *f v* brìb

brick *n* breige *f m*

bride *n* bean-bainnse *f* **the b.** bean na bainnse

bridegroom *n* fear-bainnse *m* **the b.** fear na bainnse

bridesmaid *n* maighdeann-phòsaidh *f*, bean-chomhailteachd *f*

bridge *n* drochaid *f*

bridle *n* srian *f*

brief *v* leig brath gu, thoir fiosrachadh do

brief *a* goirid, geàrr

bright *a* soilleir; (*clever*) comasach

brighten *v* soillsich, soilleirich

brilliant *a* boillsgeach, lainnireach; (*very clever*) air leth comasach

brim *n* oir *f m*, bile *f* **full to the b.** làn gu bheul

bring *v* thoir, bheir **b. up** (*family*) àraich, tog (teaghlach)

brink *n* oir *f m*, bruach *f m*

brisk *a* beothail, sunndach, clis

bristle *n* calg *m*, frioghan *m v* cuir calg air, tog frioghan air

British *a* Breatannach

Briton *n* Breatannach *m*, (*female*) ban-Bhreatannach *f*

brittle *a* pronn, brisg

broad *a* leathan(n), farsaing

broadcast *n* craoladh *m v* craobh-sgaoil, craol

broadcaster *n* craoladair *m*

broadcasting *n* craoladh *m*

brochure *n* leabhran(-shanas) *m*

broken *past part* briste

bronchitis *n* at-sgòrnain *m*

bronze *n* umha *m* **B. Age** Linn an Umha *f m*

brooch *n* bràiste *f*, broidse *m*

brood *n* àl *m*, sìol *m*

brook *n* sruthan *m*, alltan *m*

broom *n* sguab *f*; (*bot*) bealaidh *m*

broth *n* brot *m*, eanraich *f*

brothel *n* taigh-siùrsachd *m*

brother *n* bràthair *m* **b.-in-law** bràthair-cèile *m*

brow *n* mala *f*, bathais *f*, maoil *f*; (*topog*) bruach *f m*

brown *a* donn, ruadh

bruise *n* bruthadh *m*, pat *m v* brùth

brunette *a* donn *n* tè dhonn *f*

brush *n* sguab *f*, bruis *f v* sguab, bruis(ig)

brutal *a* brùideil, garg

brutality *n* brùidealachd *f*

brute *n* brùid *f m*, beathach *m*

bubble *n* builgean *m*, gucag *f*

bucket *n* bucaid *f*, cuinneag *f*

buckle *n* bucall *m*

bud *n* gucag *f*

budge *v* caraich, gluais

budget *n* buidseat *m* **the B.** am Buidseat **b. for** comharraich ionmhas (airson)

budgie n buidsidh m
bug n (illness) treamhlaidh f; (computer) biastag f
build v tog
builder n neach-togail m
building n togalach m, aitreabh m
  b. society comann thogalach m
bulb n bolgan m; (bot) meacan m
bulge v brùchd a-mach
bulky a mòr, tomadach
bull n tarbh m
bullet n peilear m
bullock n damh m
bully n burraidh m
bullying n burraidheachd f
bungalow n bungalo m
buoy n puta m
burden n eallach m
bureaucracy n biurocrasaidh m
bureaucratic a biurocratach
burgh n baile m, borgh m
burglar n gadaiche m
burial n adhlacadh m, tiodhlacadh m, tòrradh m
burly a tapaidh, dòmhail
burn n losgadh m; (stream) sruthan m, ullturn m v losg they suffered burns chaidh an losgadh
bursary n bursaraidh m
burst v spreadh, sgàin
bury v adhlaic, tiodhlaic
bus n bus m **b. stop** stad-bus m **b. station** stèisean bhusaichean m
bush n preas m, dos m
business n gnothach m, gnothachas m, malairt f **it's none of your b.** chan e do ghnothach-sa e

businessman n neach-gnothaich m
bustle n drip f, trainge f
busy a trang, dripeil
but conj, prep ach **b. for that** mura b' e sin
butcher n bùidsear m, feòladair m
butler n buidealair m
butter n ìm m v cuir ìm air
buttercup n buidheag an t-samhraidh f
butterfly n dealan-dè m
buttermilk n blàthach f
buttock n màs m
button n putan m v dùin na putanan, putanaich
buy v ceannaich
buyer n ceannaiche m, neach-ceanna(i)ch m
buzz n srann f, crònan m **it gave me a real b.** thug e fìor thogail dhomh
buzzard n clamhan m
by prep le; (near) faisg air, ri taobh (+ gen) **by herself** leatha fhèin **by degrees** mean air mhean **by night** tron oidhche **by now** thuige seo **a picture by Picasso** dealbh le Picasso
by adv an dara taobh, seachad **we'll need to put a little money by** feumaidh sinn beagan airgid a chur an dara taobh **she went by** chaidh i seachad **by and by** an ceann ùine, ri ùine
by-election n fo-thaghadh m
bypass n seach-rathad m
by-product n far-stuth m, far-bhathar m
byre n bàthach f
byway n frith-rathad m

C

cab n caba m; (taxi) tagsaidh f m
cabbage n càl m
cabin n bothan m; (on ship) cèaban m
cabinet n caibineat m, preasa m **the C.** an Caibineat
cable n càball m
cackle n glocail f
café n cafaidh f m

cage n cèidse f, eunlann f
cairn n càrn m
cajole v coitich, breug
cake n cèic f m
calamity n dosgainn f, mòr-chall m, truaighe f
calculate v meas, tomhais, obraich a-mach

calculator n àireamhair m
calendar n mìosachan m
calf n laogh m; (of leg) calpa m
calibre n cailibhear m, meudachd baraille f; (of person) stuth m, feartan f pl
call n èigh f, gairm f, glaodh m v èigh, glaodh, gairm; (visit) tadhail air; (send for) cuir fios air **they called her Jean** thug iad Sìne (mar ainm) oirre
calling n èigheach f; (vocation) dreuchd f, gairm f
callous a cruaidh(-chridheach), an-iochdmhor
calm a ciùin, sèimh n ciùine f; (weather) fèath f m
calorie n calaraidh m
calve v beir laogh
camel n càmhal m
camera n camara m
camp n campa m **c. site** àite-campachaidh m v campaich
campaign n iomairt f; (in war) còmhrag f v dèan iomairt
can n cana m, crogan m
can v is urrainn do; (may) faod **can you do that?** an urrainn dhut sin a dhèanamh? **can she go?** am faod i a dhol ann?
Canadian n, a Canèidianach m, (female) ban-Chanèidianach f
canal n clais-uisge f, canàl m, faoighteach m
cancel v dubh a-mach/às; (event) cuir dheth
cancer n aillse f **breast c.** aillse broillich
candid a fosgarra
candidate n tagraiche m
candle n coinneal f **candlestick** coinnlear m
candy n candaidh m, suiteis m pl
cane n cuilc f; (stick) bata m
canister n canastair m
canker n cnuimh f, cnàmhainn f
cannabis n cainb f, cainb-lus m
cannon n gunna-mòr m, canan m
canny a cùramach, gleusta
canoe n curachan m, curach Innseanach f
canopy n sgàil-bhrat m

canteen n biadhlann f, ionad bìdh m
canter n trotan m
canvas n canabhas m
canvass v (views) sir beachdan; (votes) sir bhòtaichean; (support) sir taic
cap n currac m, ceap m, bonaid f m; (limit) cuibhreachadh m, cuingealachadh m v (cover) còmhdaich; (limit) cuibhrich, cuingealaich; (surpass) thoir bàrr air
capability n comas m
capable a comasach
capacity n na ghabhas rud/ionad; (role) dreuchd f; (mental) comas m
cape n rubha m, maol m; (cloak) cleòc(a) m, guailleachan m
capital n prìomh-bhaile m, ceanna-bhaile m; (fin) calpa m; (profit) buannachd f a (fin) calpa **c. expenditure** caiteachas calpa m **c. letter** litir mhòr f
capitalism n calpachas m
capitalist n calpaire m
capsize v còp, cuir thairis
captain n caiptean m, sgiobair m
caption n fo-thiotal m, tiotal m
captive n prìosanach m, ciomach m, bràigh f m
captivity n ciomachas m, braighdeanas m
capture n glacadh m
car n càr m **car ferry** aiseag chàraichean m **car park** pàirc(e)-chàraichean f
caramel n carra-mheille f, caramail m
caravan n carabhan f m **c. site** ionad charabhanaichean m
caraway n lus MhicCuimein m, carbhaidh f
carbohydrate n carbohaidreat m, gualaisg m
carbon n carbon m, gualan m **c. dioxide** carbon/gualan dà-ogsaid m
carbuncle n guirean m
carcase n closach f, cairbh f
card n cairt f **cardboard** cairt-bhòrd m
cardiac a cridhe **c. arrest** stad cridhe m
cardigan n càrdagan m, peitean m
cardinal n càirdineal m
cardinal a prìomh **c. number** bun-àireamh f

care n cùram m, aire f, faiceall f **in my c.** air mo chùram(-sa) **take c.** thoir an aire **c. for** v gabh cùram (+ gen), gabh sùim (do)

career n cùrsa-beatha m, dreuchd f **careers convention** fèill dhreuchdan f

careful a cùramach, faiceallach, furachail

careless a mì-chùramach, mì-fhaiceallach; (indifferent) coma

carelessness n mì-chùram m, cion cùraim m, dìth cùraim f m

caress v cnèadaich, cionacraich

caretaker n neach-aire m

cargo n luchd m, cargu m **c. boat** bàta cargu/bathair m

carnage n àr m, casgradh m

carnal a feòlmhor, corporra

carnation n càrnaid f

carnival n càrnabhail m, àrd-fhèill f

carol n laoidh f m, coireal m

carpenter n saor m

carpentry n saorsainneachd f

carpet n brat-ùrlair m, tapais f

carriage n (person) giùlan m; (vehicle) carbad m

carrier n neach-giùlain m; (company) buidheann giùlain f m

carrot n curran m

carry v giùlain, iomchair **c. out** (fulfil) coilean **c. over** thoir air adhart

cart n cairt f

cartilage n maoth-chnàimh m

carton n cartan m

cartoon n cartùn m, dealbh-èibhinn f m

cartridge n catraids(e) f

carve v snaigh; (meat) geàrr

carving n gràbhaladh m, snaigheadh m; (meat etc) gearradh m

case n màileid f, ceas m; (abstr) staid f, cor m; (leg) cùis(-lagha) f; (gram) tuiseal m **nominative c.** an tuiseal ainmneach **gen c.** an tuiseal ginideach **dat c.** an tuiseal tabhartach **if that is the c.** mas ann mar sin a tha **in any c.** co-dhiù

cash n airgead ullamh m, airgead làimhe m

cask n buideal m, baraille m

cassette n cèiseag f **c. recording** clàradh cèiseig m

cast n (performers) sgioba f; (plaster) còmhdach plàsta v caith/tilg (air falbh); (moult) cuir; (mould) molldaich **c. lots** tilg croinn

castigate v cronaich

castle n caisteal m

castrate v spoth

casual a tuiteamach; (employment) sealach

casualty n leòinteach m

cat n cat m

catalogue n catalog f m

catapult n tailm f, lungaid f

cataract n eas m; (on eye) meamran sùla m

catarrh n an galar smugaideach m

catastrophe n mòr-chreach f, lèirsgrios m

catch n glacadh m; (latch) claimhean m **a good c.** deagh mhurrag f, deagh iasgach m v glac, beir air, greimich air

catchy a tarraingeach, fonnmhor

categorical a deimhinnte, mionnaichte

category n gnè f, seòrsa m

cater v thoir biadh do, solair, ullaich

catering n solarachd f

caterpillar n burras m, bratag f

cathedral n cathair-eaglais f, àrd-eaglais f

Catholic n, a Caitligeach m, (female) ban-Chaitligeach f

catholic a coitcheann

cattle n crodh m, sprèidh f **c. grid** cliath chruidh f **c. show** fèill-chruidh f

cauliflower n colag f, càl-colaig m

cause n adhbhar m v adhbhraich

causeway n cabhsair m

caustic a loisgeach; (wit) geur, guineach

caution n faiceall f, cùram m; (warning) rabhadh m v thoir rabhadh, cuir air etc fhaicill, earalaich

cautious a faiceallach, cùramach

cavalry n eachraidh m, marc-shluagh m

cave n uaimh f

cavern n uaimh f, talamh-toll m

cavity n sloc m, toll m, lag f m

cease v sguir, stad
cease-fire n fois-losgaidh m
ceaseless a gun sgur/stad/abhsadh
ceiling n mullach m, mullach rùm/
seòmair
celebrate v dèan subhachas; (mark)
comharraich, cùm; (laud) cuir an cèill
cliù; (sacrament) cuartaich
celebrated a iomraiteach, cliùiteach
celebration n subhachas m; (marking)
comharrachadh m
celebrity n neach iomraiteach m; (fame)
iomraiteachd f
celery n soilire m
celestial a nèamhaidh
cell n (church) cill f; (biol) cealla f; (prison)
cealla prìosain f
cellar n seilear m
cello n beus-fhidheall f
cellular a ceallach
Celt n Ceilteach m
Celtic a Ceilteach
cement n saimeant m v tàth, cuir ri
chèile; (met) neartaich
cemetery n cladh m
censor v caisg
censorious a achmhasanach, coireachail,
cronachail
censure n achmhasan m, cronachadh
m v cronaich, coirich
census n cunntas m; (pop) cunntas-
sluaigh m
cent n seant m **it didn't cost me a c.**
cha do chosg e sgillinn (ruadh) dhomh
centenary n ceud m, ceud bliadhna f,
cuimhneachan ceud m
centimetre n ceudameatair m
centipede n ceud-chasach m
central a meadhain, meadhanach, anns
a' mheadhan
centralize v cuir/thoir dhan mheadhan
centre n meadhan m; (premises)
ionad m
century n linn f m, ceud m, ceud
bliadhna f
cereal n gràn m; (food) biadh
grànach m
cerebral a eanchainneach

ceremony n deas-ghnàth m; (event)
seirbheis f
certain a cinnteach, deimhinnte
absolutely c. mionnaichte
certainly adv gu cinnteach, gu deimhinn,
dha-rìribh
certainty n cinnt f, dearbhadh m
certificate n teisteanas m, barantas m
certify v teistich, dearbh
chaff n moll m, càth f
chain n sèine f, slabhraidh f, cuibhreach
m v cuibhrich, cuir slabhraidh air
chair n cathair f, sèithear m; (person)
cathraiche m **chairlift** beairt-dhìridh
f **chairman** fear-cathrach m, fear na
cathrach m **chairperson** neach-cathrach
m, cathraiche m **chairwoman** bean-
chathrach f, bean na cathrach f v gabh
cathair
chalk n cailc f
challenge n dùbhlan m v thoir dùbhlan
do; (oppose) cuir an aghaidh
chamber n seòmar m
champion n gaisgeach m, curaidh m,
laoch m; (winner) buadhaiche m
chance n cothrom m, seans(a)/teans(a)
m **c. event** tuiteamas m **by c.** le
turchairt/tuiteamas
chancellor n seansailear m
change n atharrachadh m, caochladh m;
(money) iomlaid f, airgead pronn m
v atharraich, caochail, mùth
changeable a caochlaideach
channel n cladhan m, clais f; (topog)
caolas m; (means) modh f m
chant v seinn
chanter n (of pipes) feadan m,
sionnsar m
chaos n mì-riaghailt f
chapel n caibeal m
chaplain n seaplain m; (mil) ministear-
feachd m
chapter n caibideil f m
character n beus f, mèinn f, nàdar m;
(liter) caractar m, pearsa m; (typ) litir f
he's a real c. 's e cinneach a th' ann
characteristic n feart m, dual-nàdair m a
coltach, samhlachail

charge n (cost) prìs f, cosgais f; (attack) ionnsaigh f m; (accusation) casaid f **in c. of** air ceann (+ gen) v (attack) dèan/ thoir ionnsaigh; (accuse) cuir às leth, fàg air **how much did they c. for it?** dè na chuir iad ort e? **take c. of** gabh os làimh

charisma n tarraing pearsa f

charitable a carthannach, coibhneil

charity n carthannas m, coibhneas m; (alms) dèirc f; (agency) buidheann carthannais f m

charm v cuir seun air, cuir fo dhraoidheachd

charming a taitneach, tarraingeach, grinn

chart n cairt-iùil f; (mus) clàr m

charter n cairt f, còir-sgrìobhte f; (hire) fastadh m v fastaidh

chase n sealg f, tòir f, faghaid f v ruith (às dèidh) **c. away** ruaig, fuadaich

chasm n mòr-bheàrn m

chat n còmhradh m, crac m v dèan còmhradh/crac/conaltradh

cheap a saor; (remark) suarach

cheat n mealltair m v meall, thoir an car à, dèan foill air

check v dèan cinnteach, thoir sùil air; (stop) caisg, bac; (reprove) cronaich

checklist n liosta-sgrùdaidh f

cheek n gruaidh f, lethcheann m; (met) mì-mhodh m **some cheek!** abair aghaidh!

cheeky a aghach, mì-mhodhail

cheer v tog spiorad, dèan sunndach **c. on** brosnaich, misnich

cheerful a sunndach, aighearach, ait

cheers (exclam) Slàinte (mhath)!

cheese n càise f m; (one) mulchag f **cheesecake** càis-chèic f

chef n còcaire m

chemical n ceimig f a ceimigeach

chemist n ceimigear m; (pharmacist) cungaidhear m **c.'s shop** bùth-cungaidheir f

chemistry n ceimigeachd f, ceimig f

cheque n seic f **c.-book** leabhar-sheicichean m

cherry n siris(t) f

chess n tàileasg m, fidhcheall m

chest n ciste f; (human) cliabh m, broilleach m, bràigh m **c. of drawers** ciste-dhràthraichean f

chestnut n geanm-chnò f

chew v cagainn, cnàmh

chick(en) n isean m; (pullet) eireag f; (food) cearc f, sitheann f m

chickenpox n a' bhreac-òtraich f

chief n ceannard m; (clan) ceann-feadhna m **c. executive** àrd-oifigear m a prìomh, àrd (precedes n)

chieftain n ceann-feadhna/cinnidh m

child n leanabh m, pàiste m **c. benefit** sochair chloinne f **c. care** cùram-chloinne m

childhood n leanabas m

childish a leanabail, leanabaidh

children n clann f

chill(y) a fuar, aognaidh

chimney n similear m, luidhear m

chin n smig f m, smiogaid f m

Chinese n, a Sìonach m, (female) ban-S(h)ìonach f

chip n mìr m, sgealb f, sliseag f **chips** sliseagan (buntàta) f pl v sgealb, snaigh

chisel n (s)geilb f, sgathair(e) m

chlorine n clòrain m

chocolate n seòclaid f m

choice n roghainn f m, taghadh m

choir n còisir(-chiùil) f

cholesterol n coileastarail m

choke v tachd, mùch

choose v tagh, roghnaich

chop v sgud

chord n còrd(a) m

chore n car-obrach m

chorus n sèist f, co-sheirm f

Christ n Crìosd(a) m

christen v baist

christening n baisteadh m

Christian n Crìosdaidh m a Crìosdail **C. name** ainm baistidh m

Christianity n Crìosdaidheachd f, Crìosdalachd f, an creideamh Crìosdaidh/Crìosdail m

Christmas n Nollaig f **C. Day** Là/Latha na Nollaig(e) m **C. Eve** Oidhche Nollaig f **Merry C.!** Nollaig Chridheil!

chronic a fìor dhona, trom; (med) buan, leantalach; (slang) cianail

chum n companach m, caraid m

chunk n caob m, cnap m
church n eaglais f **C. of Scotland**
Eaglais na h-Alba **Catholic C.** an Eaglais
Chaitligeach **Episcopal C.** an Eaglais
Easbaigeach **Baptist C.** an Eaglais
Bhaisteach **Free C.** an Eaglais Shaor
Free Presbyterian C. an Eaglais Shaor
Chlèireach **churchyard** cladh m, cill f

t-Seirbheis Chatharra f **c. servant**
seirbheiseach catharra m **c. rights**
còraichean catharra f pl **c. war** cogadh
catharra m
civilian n sìobhaltach m, neach nach eil
san Arm m a sìobhaltach
civilization n sìobhaltachd f
civilize v sìobhailich, cuir fo rian

Insight: church

The modern word for church is *eaglais*, which has a similar
etymology to the French *eglise*. An older word, *cill*, refers to the
monastic cells of the early Celtic Church and gives rise to the
ubiquitous Scottish and Irish initial place name element Kil- found
in Kilmarnock, Kildare, Kilsyth and Kilmuir.

---

churlish a doicheallach, mosach, neo-
fhialaidh
churn n crannachan m, muidhe m
cider n leann-ubhal m
cigar n siogàr m
cigarette n toitean m, siogarait f
cinder n èibhleag f
cinema n taigh-dhealbh m
cinnamon n caineal m
circle n cearcall m, cuairt f, buaile f v
cuairtich, cuartaich, iadh
circuit n cuairt f
circular n cuairt-litir f a cruinn, cearclach,
cuairteagach
circulate v cuir mun cuairt, cuir timcheall,
cuairtich
circumference n cearcall-thomhas m
circumspect a faiceallach, aireach
circumstance n cùis f, cor m, staid f,
suidheachadh m
circus n soircas m
cistern n tanca f m
cite v ainmich, tog; (leg) thoir sumanadh
do, gairm
citizen n saoranach m, neach-
àiteachaidh m, neach-dùthcha m
city n cathair-bhaile f, cathair f,
baile-mòr m
civic a cathaireach, catharra
civil a catharra; (behaviour) sìobhalta,
modhail, rianail **the Civil Service** an

claim n tagradh m, còir f **c. form** foirm-
tagraidh m v (t)agair
clam n creachan(n) m
clamour gleadhraich f, othail f
clan n fine f, cinneadh m **clansman** fear-
cinnidh m
clap n bas-bhualadh m; (of thunder) brag
m v buail boisean, bas-bhuail
clarify v soilleirich, dèan soilleir
clarinet n clàirneid f
clarity n soilleireachd f
clash n (dispute) connsachadh m;
(sound) glagadaich f
clasp n cromag f, dealg m; (embrace)
cnèadachadh m
class n (educ) clas m; (type) seòrsa m
social c. eagar sòisealta m **classroom**
rùm/seòmar-teagaisg m
classic(al) a clasaigeach
classified a (information) dìomhair, glaiste
classify v seòrsaich
clause n (gram) clàs m; (condition)
cumha m
claw n spuir m, ionga f
clay n crèadh f, crè f
clean a glan v glan
cleaner n glanadair m, neach-glanaidh m
cleanliness n glainead m
cleanse v glan, ionnlaid
clear v (clarify) soilleirich; (tidy) rèitich,
sgioblaich; (free) saor a soilleir

clearance n fuadach m **the Highland Clearances** na Fuadaichean
cleg n creithleag f
clemency n tròcair f, iochd f
clench v teannaich, dùin
clergy n clèir f **clergyman** pears-eaglais m
clerk n clèireach m **township c.** clàrc a' bhaile m
clever a deas, clis
click v gliog; (met) thig air a chèile
client n neach-dèiligidh m
cliff n creag f, bearradh m
climate n gnàth-shìde f
climax n àirde f
climb v dìrich, sreap
climber n sreapadair m
climbing n dìreadh m, sreap m
clinch v daingnich, teannaich, dùin
cling v claon (ri)
clinic n clionaig f
clink v dèan gliong
clip n cliop m v geàrr, beàrr; (sheep) rùisg; (shorten) giorraich
cloak n cleòc(a) m, fallainn f
clock n cloc m
clockwise a deasail, deiseil
close n (closure) dùnadh m, crìoch f, ceann m; (in tenement) clobhsa m v dùin; (end) crìochnaich
close a faisg, teann, dlùth; (atmos) dùmhail, murtaidh
closed a dùinte
closing n dùnadh **c. date** ceann-latha m
cloth n aodach m **dish-c.** searbhadair-shoithichean m, tubhailt(e)-shoithichean f m **table-c.** tubhailt(e)-bùird f m
clothe v còmhdaich, èid
clothes n aodach m **c.-peg** bioran-anairt m, cnag-aodaich f
clothing n aodach m, èideadh m, trusgan m
cloud n sgòth f, neul m
cloudy a sgòthach, neulach
clover n clòbhar m; (single plant) seamrag f
clown n tuaistear m; (met) amadan m

club n cuaille m; (in sport) caman m; (association) club m **clubhouse** taigh-club m
cluck v dèan gogail
clue n tuairmse f **he hasn't a c.** chan eil sgot/poidhs aige
clump n bad m
clumsy a cliobach, cearbach, liobasta
cluster n bagaid f, cluigean m
clutch v greimich (air), glac
clutter n frachd m
coach n coidse f, bus m; (instructor) oide m v oidich, teagaisg, ionnsaich
coal n gual m **c. mine** mèinn(e)-guail f, toll-guail m
coalition n co-bhanntachd f; aonachadh m, tàthadh m **c. government** riaghaltas co-bhanntachd m
coarse a (texture) garbh; (manners) curs, neo-fhìnealta, amh
coast n oirthir f, costa m
coastguard n maor-cladaich m
coat n còta m **c. of arms** gearradh arm m v còmhdaich, cuir còta air
coax v coitich, tàlaidh
cobweb n eige f, lìon damhain-allaidh m
cocaine n coicèan m
cock n (bird) coileach m **c.-crow** gairm coilich f **haycock** coc fheòir f
cockle n coilleag f, srùban m
cocktail n earball a' choilich m, geinealag f
cocky a bragail
cocoa n còco m
coconut n cnò-còco f
cod n bodach(-ruadh) m, (large) trosg m
code còd m, riaghailt f; (rule) **c. of conduct** riaghailt obrach f
coerce v èignich, ceannsaich
co-exist v bi beò le
coffee n cofaidh f m
coffin n ciste(-laighe) f
cog n fiacail f, roth f m
cogent a làidir, cumhachdach, diongmhalta
coherent a rianail, pongail, òrdail
cohesion n co-cheangal m, leantalachd f, co-thàthadh m

cohesive *a* co-cheangailte, leantalach, co-thàthach
coil *n* cuibhle *f*, cuairteag *f*
coin *n* bonn (airgid) *m*
coincide *v* co-thuit; (*agree*) co-aontaich, thig ri chèile
coincidence *n* tuiteamas *m*, co-thuiteamas *m*; (*agreement*) co-aontachadh *m*
coke *n* còc *m*
cold *n* fuachd *m*; (*common*) cnatan *m* **she had the c.** bha an cnatan oirre *a* fuar
colic *n* grèim-mionaich *m*
collaborate *v* co-obraich
collaboration *n* co-obrachadh *m*
collapse *v* tuit (am broinn a chèile); (*of person*) rach ann an laig(s)e
collar *n* coilear *m*; (*on horse*) braighdean *m* **c.-bone** ugan *m*, cnàimh an uga *m*
collate *v* cuir ri chèile
colleague *n* co-obraiche *m*, companach *m*
collect *v* cruinnich, tionail, trus; (*money*) tog
collection *n* cruinneachadh *m*, tional *m*
collector *n* cruinniche *m*, neach-tionail *m*
college *n* colaiste *f m*
collision *n* bualadh *m*, sgleog *f*
colon *n* caolan mòr *m*; (*gram*) còilean *f*
colonel *n* còirneal *m*, còirnealair *m*
colonial *a* colòiniach
colony *n* coloinidh *m*, eilthir *f*
colossal *a* àibheiseach
colour *n* dath *m* **c.-blind** dath-dhall *v* dath, cuir dath air; (*blush*) rudhadh *m*
coloured *a* dathte
colourful *a* dathach
column *n* colbh *m*; (*rock formation*) stac *m*
coma *n* trom-neul *m*, còma *m*
comb *n* cìr *f*; (*coxcomb*) cìrean *m* **honeycomb** cìr-mheala *f v* cìr
combine *v* cuir/rach còmhla
come *v* thig, ruig **where do you c. from?** cò às a tha thu? **if it comes to the bit** ma thig e gu h-aon 's gu dhà **c. on!** trobhad! t(h)ugainn! **c. to pass** tachair
comedy *n* comadaidh *m*, mear-chluich *f m*

comet *n* reul chearbach *f*, rionnag an earbaill *f*
comfort *n* cofhurtachd *f v* cofhurtaich
comfortable *a* cofhurtail, socair
comic *n* comaig *f m*
comic(al) *a* èibhinn, ait, comaig
comma *n* cromag *f* **inverted commas** cromagan turrach
command *n* òrdugh *m*; (*authority*) ùghdarras *m*, smachd *f v* thoir òrdugh (seachad), òrdaich, àithn, bi an ceann; (*eg respect*) dleas
commander *n* ceannard *m*
commandment *n* òrdugh *m*; (*Bibl*) àithne *f*
commemorate *v* cuimhnich, comharraich
commence *v* tòisich
commend *v* mol
commendable *a* ionmholta, ri mholadh, airidh air moladh
comment *n* iomradh *m*, facal *m*, luaidh *m*, aithris *f v* thoir tarraing (air), dèan luaidh/aithris (air)
commentary *n* cunntas *m*, aithris *f*
commentator *n* neach-aithris *m*
commerce *n* malairt *f*
commercial *a* malairteach
commiserate *v* nochd co-fhaireachdainn/truas ri
commission *n* coimisean *m*; (*warrant*) barantas *m* **the European C.** an Coimisean Eòrpach *m v* barantaich
commissioner *n* coimiseanair *m*
commit *v* cuir an gnìomh; (*undertake*) cuir roimhe/roimhpe *etc*; (*entrust*) earb (ri)
committed *a* dealasach, daingeann **c. to/for ...** (*fin*) air a chur mu choinneamh ...
commitment *n* dealas *m*
committee *n* comataidh *f* **sub-c.** fo-chomataidh
common *a* cumanta, coitcheann
common sense *n* toinisg *f*
commonwealth *n* co-fhlaitheas *m*
commotion *n* ùpraid *f*
communal *n* coitcheann

communicant *n* comanaiche *m*, neach-comanachaidh *m*
communicate *v* com-pàirtich, aithris, cuir an cèill, dèan conaltradh
communication *n* com-pàirteachadh *m*, conaltradh *m*
communion *n* co-chomann *m*; (*relig*) comanachadh *m*, comain *m* **take c.** comanaich *v*
communism *n* comannachas *m*, co-mhaoineas *m*
communist *n* comannach *m*, co-mhaoineach *m* *a* comannach, co-mhaoineach
community *n* coimhearsnachd *f*, co-chuideachd *f* **c. centre** ionad-coimhearsnachd *m* **c. council** comhairle coimhearsnachd *f* **c. service** seirbheis coimhearsnachd *f*
commute *v* (*travel*) siubhail
compact *a* teann, dùmhail, daingeann
compact disc *n* meanbh-chlàr *m*
companion *n* companach *m*
company *n* cuideachd *f*, comann *m*; (*firm*) companaidh *f m*
comparable *a* cosmhail, a ghabhas coimeas **they're not c.** chan ionann iad
compare *v* coimeas, dèan coimeas (ri/eadar)
comparison *n* coimeas *m*
compartment *n* earrann *f*; (*room*) seòmar *m*
compass *n* combaist *f*, cairt-iùil *f*; (*ambit*) raon *m*
compassion *n* truas *m*, iochd *f*
compassionate *a* truasail, iochdmhor
compatible *a* co-chòrdail, co-fhreagarrach
compel *v* co-èignich, thoir air
compensate *v* dìol, ìoc, cuidhtich
compensation *n* dìoladh *m*, cuidhteachadh *m*
compete *v* strì, dèan farpais
competent *a* comasach
competition *n* co-fharpais *f*, farpais *f*
competitive *a* farpaiseach, strìtheil **c. tendering** tairgseachadh farpaiseach *m*
competitor *n* farpaiseach *m*

compile *v* cuir ri chèile, co-chruinnich
complacency *n* somaltachd *f*
complacent *a* somalta
complain *v* gearain, dèan gearan, dèan casaid
complaint *n* gearan *f m*, casaid *f*; (*med*) treamhlaidh *f*
complement *n* làn *m* **a full c. of staff** làn-sgioba *f m*
complete *v* crìochnaich; (*form etc*) lìon *a* iomlan, coileanta
completely *adv* gu h-iomlan, gu tur, buileach
complex *a* iomadh-fhillte, casta
complexion *n* tuar *m*, dreach *m*
complicated *a* toinnte
compliment *n* moladh *m* **with compliments** le dùrachd *f* *v* mol, dèan moladh
comply *v* thig/dèan a rèir, cùm ri
component *n* pàirt *f m*, pìos *m*
compose *v* dèan, cuir ri chèile, sgrìobh; (*oneself*) socraich/stòldaich (e/i *etc* fhèin)
composed *a* socraichte, ciùin, stòlda
composer *n* (*mus*) sgrìobhaiche ciùil *m*; (*liter*) ùghdar *m*
composition *n* sgrìobhadh *m*, (*essay*) aiste *f*
compost *n* todhar gàrraidh *m*
composure *n* suaimhneas *m*, socrachd *f*
compound *n* coimeasgadh *m*, co-thàthadh *m*
comprehend *v* tuig
comprehension *n* tuigse *f*
comprehensive *a* coitcheann, farsaing, iomlan, ioma-chuimseach **c. education** foghlam coitcheann *m* **c. school** sgoil choitcheann *f*
compromise *n* co-rèiteachadh *m*
compulsory *a* do-sheachanta, èigneachail **c. purchase** ceannach èigneachail *m*
compute *v* coimpiut, àireamhaich
computer *n* coimpiutair *m*
computing *n* coimpiutaireachd *f*
comrade *n* companach *m*
concave *a* fo-chearclach
conceal *v* ceil, cleith, falaich

concede v gèill, aidich, strìochd
conceit n fearas-mhòr(a) f, mòrchuis f
conceited a baralach, mòrchuiseach
conceive v fàs torrach/trom; (*think*) gabh a-steach, tuig
concentrate v thoir dlùth-aire do
concentration n (*heed*) dlùth-aire f; (*density*) dùmhlachd f
concentric a co-mheadhanach
concept n bun-bheachd m, smaoineas m
conception n gineamhainn m; (*thought*) beachd m
concern n cùram m, iomagain f; (*business*) gnothach m v cuir uallach/iomagain air; (*oneself with*) gabh gnothach ri
concerning prep mu, mu thimcheall (+ *gen*), mu dheidhinn (+ *gen*)
concert n cuirm-chiùil f, consairt f m **c.-hall** talla-ciùil m
concession n strìochdadh m; (*fin*) lasachadh m; (*licence etc*) ceadachd f
conciliation n rèiteachadh m
concise a goirid, geàrr, sgiobalta
conclude v co-dhùin; (*finish*) crìochnaich
conclusion n co-dhùnadh m; (*finish*) crìoch f
concoct v dèan suas; (*mix*) measgaich
concord n còrdadh m, co-chòrdadh m
concrete n cruadhtan m, concrait f m a rudail, nitheil, susbainteach; (*substance*) concrait, de chruadhtan
concur v aontaich
concurrent a co-cheumnach, co-ruitheach
concussion n criothnachadh-eanchainn m
condemn v dìt
condensation n (*moisture*) taise f
condense v co-dhlùthaich, sùmhlaich
condescend v deònaich, irioslaich; (*be patronizing*) bi mòrchuiseach
condescending a neo-uallach; (*patronizing*) mòrchuiseach
condition n cùmhnant m, cumha m; (*state*) cor m, staid f **on c. that** air chùmhnant gu
conditional a air chùmhnant; (*gram*) cumhach **c. tense** an tràth cumhach m
condom n casgan-gin m

condone v leig seachad
conduct n giùlan m, dol-a-mach m v stiùir, treòraich; (*oneself*) giùlain
conductor n stiùiriche m; (*agent*) stuth-giùlain m
conduit m cladhan-uisge m
cone n còn m; (*pine*) durcan m
confederation n co-chaidreachas m
confer v cuir comhairle ri; (*grant*) builich
conference n co-labhairt f
confess v aidich; (*relig*) faoisidich
confession n aideachadh m, aidmheil f; (*relig*) èisteachd f, faoisid f
confide v leig rùn ri
confidence n misneachd f, dànadas m, earbsa f
confident a misneachail, dàna, bragail
confidential a dìomhair, fo rùn
confine v cùm a-staigh, cuir crìochan ro
confinement n cùbadh m, braighdeanas m; (*pregnancy*) ùine air leabaidh-shiùbhla f
confirm v daingnich, dearbh
confirmation n daingneachadh m; (*relig*) dol fo làimh easbaig m
conflict n strì f, còmhstri f, còmhrag f
conform v rach le, co-fhreagair, gèill, dèan/rach a rèir
confront v seas mu choinneamh, còmhlaich, cuir aghaidh air
confrontation n cur aghaidh air m
confuse v cuir troimh-a-chèile
confused a troimh-a-chèile
confusion n breisleach m, troimh-a-chèile f
congeal v reoth
congenial a taitneach, ri a c(h)àil etc
congestion n dùmhlachd f
congratulate v cuir meal-a-naidheachd air
congratulation(s) n co-ghàirdeachas m **c.!** meal do naidheachd!
congregate v cruinnich
congregation n coitheanal m, co-chruinneachadh m
congress n còmhdhail f
conifer n craobh-durcain f
conjecture n barail f, tuairmeas m

connect v ceangail
connected a ceangailte
connection n ceangal m, co-bhann f **in c. with** a thaobh (+ gen)
conquer v ceannsaich, cìosnaich
conquest n buaidh f, ceannsachadh m
conscience n cogais f, cuinnseas f
conscientious a cogaiseach
conscious a mothachail
consecrate v coisrig
consecration n coisrigeadh m
consecutive a co-leantaileach, às dèidh a chèile
consensus n co-aontachd f
consent n aonta m, cead m v aontaich
consequence n buil f, buaidh f, toradh m
consequently adv uime sin, ri linn sin
conservation n glèidhteachas m, gleidheadh m, dìon m
conservationist n neach-glèidhteachais m
Conservative n Tòraidh m **the C. Party** am Partaidh Tòraidheach m
conservative a caomhnach, glèidhteach, stuama
conserve v glèidh, taisg, dìon
consider v smaoinich, beachdaich, meòraich
considerable a cudromach, fiùghail
considerate a suimeil, mothachail, coibhneil
consideration n suimealachd f, coibhneas m; (of matter) beachdachadh m
consistency n cunbhalachd f
consistent a cunbhalach **c. with** co-chòrdail (ri)
consolation n furtachd f
consolidate v daingnich, neartaich
consonant n connrag f
consortium n co-bhanntachd f
conspicuous a follaiseach, nochdte
conspiracy n co-fheall f, gùim m
conspire v dèan co-fheall/gùim
constable n constabal m, maor-sìthe m
constant a seasmhach, daingeann, cunbhalach, dìleas
consternation n clisgeadh m, uabhas m

constituency n roinn-phàrlamaid f
constitution n (phys) aorabh m, dèanamh m; (org) bonn-stèidh m; (polit) bun-reachd m
constrain v co-èignich, thoir air
constrict v teannaich, tachd
construct v dèan, tog, cuir ri chèile
construction n cur ri chèile m; (building) togail f, togalach m **under c.** ga t(h)ogail, gan togail
constructive a cuideachail, adhartach
consul n consal m
consult v cuir comhairle ri, gabh comhairle
consultant n co-chomhairliche m
consultation n co-chomhairle f **c. paper** pàipear co-chomhairleachaidh m
consultative a co-chomhairleachaidh **c. committee** comataidh co-chomhairleachaidh f
consume v (use) caith; (food) ith; (burn) loisg
consumer n neach-cleachdaidh m, caitheadair m pl luchd-caitheimh/cleachdaidh
consummate a barraichte
consumption n caitheamh f; (med) a' chaitheamh f
contact n (abstr) co-cheangal m; (phys) suathadh m, beantainn m v cuir fios gu, bi an tobha ri
contagious a gabhaltach
contain v cùm; (keep in check) bac, caisg
container n soitheach f m; (for cargo) bogsa-stòraidh m
contaminate v truaill, salaich, gànraich
contemplate v beachd-smaoinich, meòraich, gabh beachd air
contemporary a co-aimsireil; (in age) co-aoiseach n comhais m
contempt n tàir f, tarcais f **he was held in c.** bha e air a chur ann an suarachas
contemptible a suarach
contemptuous a tàireil, tarcaiseach
contend v cathaich, dèan strì an aghaidh (+ gen); (maintain) cùm a-mach
content n susbaint f
content(ed) a riaraichte, toilichte

contention n còmhstri f, connspaid f, aimhreit f, argamaid f

contentious a connspaideach

contentment n toileachas (-inntinn) m, riarachadh m

contents n na tha ann, na tha am broinn ... **list of c.** clàr-innse m

contest n strì f, farpais f v dèan strì; (election) seas

contestant n farpaiseach m

context n co-theacs(a) m

continent n mòr-roinn f

continually adv gun sgur, a-ghnàth **c. asking** a' sìor fhaighneachd

continue v lean (air)

continuing a leantainneach, a' leantainn

continuity n leantalachd f

continuous a leantainneach **c. assessment** measadh leantainneach m

contraception n casg-gin(eamhainn) m

contraceptive a casg-gineamhainneach

contract n cùmhnant m, cunnradh m **c. of employment** cùmhnant-obrach m v (lessen) lùghdaich; (enter into) dèan cùmhnant; (illness) gabh

contraction n teannachadh m, crìonadh m, giorrachadh m, lùghdachadh m

contractor n cunnradair m

contradict v cuir an aghaidh (+ gen)

contrary a an aghaidh (+ gen)

contrast n eadar-dhealachadh m, ao-coltas m v cuir an aghaidh a chèile, dèan iomsgaradh eadar

contravene v bris(t), rach an aghaidh

contribute v cuir ri, cuidich le **c. to** thoir ... do

contribution n tabhartas m, cuideachadh m

contrite a fo aithreachas

control n (abstr) smachd m, ùghdarras m **controls** uidheam-stiùiridh f v ceannsaich **gain c.** faigh smachd air

controller n neach-riaghlaidh m, rianadair m

controversial a connspaideach, connsachail

controversy n connspaid f, connsachadh m

conundrum n tòimhseachan (toinnte) m

convene v tionail, cruinnich, gairm

convener n neach-gairm m

convenience n goireas m **public c.** goireasan poblach

convenient a goireasach

convent n taigh-cràbhaidh m, clochar m

convention n (norm) cleachdadh m, gnàthas m; (body) co-chruinneachadh m, còmhdhail f; (agreement) cùmhnant m

conventional a gnàthach

conversant with a fiosrach (mu), eòlach (air)

conversation n còmhradh m

converse v dèan còmhradh

conversion n (relig) iompachadh m; (building) atharrachadh m

convert n iompachan m

convert v (relig) iompaich; atharraich

convex a os-chearclach

convey v giùlain, iomchair

convict v dìt

conviction n dìteadh m; (feeling) faireachdainn làidir f

convince v dearbh (do)

convivial a cuideachdail

convoy n comhailteachd f; (naut) luing-dhion f pl

coo v dèan dùrdail/tùchan

cook n còcaire m v còcairich, deasaich biadh, bruich

cooker n cucair m

cookery, cooking n còcaireachd f

cool a fionnar; (colloq) smodaig v fuaraich, fionnaraich

co-operate v co-obraich

co-operation n co-obrachadh m

co-operative a co-obrachail, cuideachail

co-opt v co-thagh

co-opted a co-thaghte

co-option n co-thaghadh m

co-ordinate v co-òrdanaich

co-ordinated a co-òrdanaichte

co-ordination n co-òrdanachadh m

co-ordinator n co-òrdanaiche m

cope v dèan an gnothach/a' chùis, cothaich

copious a lìonmhor, pailt

copper n copar m
copse n badan m, frith-choille f
copulate v cuplaich
copy n lethbhreac m, copaidh f m v copaig, dèan lethbhreac, ath-sgrìobh
copyright n còraichean (foillseachaidh) f pl, dlighe-sgrìobhaidh f
coral n corail m
cord n còrd m, bann m
cordial a cridheil, càirdeil
core n cridhe m, eitean m
cork n àrc f, corcais f
corkscrew n sgriubha-àrc m
cormorant n sgarbh m
corn n arbhar m; (on foot) còrn m **c. on the cob** dias Innseanach f
corncrake n traon m, ràc an arbhair m
corner n oisean m, cùil f, còrnair m **c. kick** breab-oisein f **c. stone** clach-oisein/-oisne f
cornflakes n bleideagan coirce f
Cornish a Còrnach **C. person** n Còrnach m, (female) ban-Chòrnach f
coronation n crùnadh m
corporal n corpailear m
corporal a corporra, bodhaige
corporate a corporra
corporation n corporaid f, comhairle baile-mòr f
corpse n corp m, marbhan m
correct v ceartaich a ceart
correction n ceartachadh m
correlation n co-dhàimh f
correspond v co-fhreagair; (write) sgrìobh
correspondence n litrichean f pl, sgrìobhadh m; (match) co-fhreagradh m
corridor n trannsa f
corroborate v daingnich, co-dhearbh
corrode v meirg
corrosion n meirg f, meirgeadh m
corrugated a preasach **c. iron** iarann liorcach m **c. paper** pàipear preasach m
corrupt a coirbte, breun, truaillte v coirb, truaill
corrupted a coirbte, truaillte
corruption n coirbeachd f, truaillidheachd f

cosmetic n cungaidh maise f **c. surgery** lannsaireachd cruth f a (met) air an uachdar
cosmonaut n speur(ad)air m
cosmopolitan a os-nàiseanta
cost n cosgais f **c. of living** cosgais bith-beò f v cosg
costly a cosgail, daor
costume n culaidh f
cosy a seasgair
cot n cot m
cottage n taigh-còmhnaidh beag m
cotton n cotan m **bog-c.** an canach m **c.-wool** snàth-cotain m a cotain
couch n seidhs(e) f, langasaid f
cough n casad m v dèan casad
coughing n casadaich f Also vn a' casadaich
council n comhairle f **C. of Europe** Comhairle na h-Eòrpa f **C. Tax** Cìs Comhairle f
councillor n comhairliche m
counsel v comhairlich
counsellor n neach-comhairle m, comhairleach m
count v cunnt, cunntais, àireamh(aich)
countenance n gnùis f
counter n cuntair m
counter v rach an aghaidh (+ gen)
countess n ban-iarla f
counting n cunntadh m, cunntais f m
countless a gun àireamh, do-àireamh
country n dùthaich f, tìr f, rìoghachd f
countryside n dùthaich f **in the c.** air an dùthaich/tuath
county n siorrachd f, siorramachd f
couple n càraid f, dithis f **a c. of hours** dà uair
courage n misneach(d) f, smior m
courageous a misneachail, smiorail, tapaidh
courier n teachdaire m
course n cùrsa m; (route) slighe f, cùrsa m
court n cùirt f **courthouse** taigh-cùirte/ cùrtach m
court v dèan suirghe vn a' suirghe
courteous a cùirteil, modhail, suairce
courtesy n modh f m, modhalachd f

courtship *n* suirghe *f*, leannanachd *f*
cousin *n* co-ogha *m*
covenant *n* cùmhnant *m*
cover *n* còmhdach *m*, brat *m*; (*for bed*) cuibhrig(e) *f m v* còmhdaich; (*deal with*) dèilig ri
covering *n* còmhdach *m*, brat *m*
covert *a* dìomhair, falaichte, os ìosal
covet *v* sanntaich
cow *n* bò *f*, mart *m*
coward *n* gealtaire *m*, cladhaire *m*
cowardice *n* gealtachd *f*, cladhaireachd *f*
coy *a* nàrach, màlda
crab *n* crùbag *f*, partan *m*
crabbed/crabbit *a* greannach
crack *n* sgàineadh *m*, sgoltadh *m v* sgàin, sgoilt
cradle *n* creathail *f*
craft *n* ceàird *f*; (*cunning*) seòltachd *f*; (*boat*) bàta *m* **craftsman** neach-ceàirde *m*
crafty *a* seòlta, carach
crag *n* creag *f*, stalla *f*, carraig *f*
cram *v* dinn
crammed *a* dinnte, dùmhail
cramp *n* an t-orc *m*, cramb *f*
crane *n* crann *m*; (*bird*) corra-mhonaidh *f*
cranny *n* cùil *f*, fròg *f*
crash *n* stàirn *f*, bualadh *m v* buail na chèile, craisig
crate *n* cliath-bhogsa *m*, creat *m*
craving *n* cìocras *m*, miann *f m*
crawl *v* snàig, crùb
crayon *n* creidhean *m*, cailc dhathte *f*
craze *n* cruaidh-fhasan *m*, annas *m*
crazy *a* cracte, às a c(h)iall *etc*
creak *n* dìosgan *m v* dìosg, dèan dìosgan *Also vn* a' dìòsganaich
cream *n* uachdar *m*, bàrr *m*; (*cosmetic*) cè *m*
crease *n* filleadh *m*, preas *m v* preas(aich)
create *v* cruthaich
creation *n* cruthachadh *m* **Creation** an Cruthachadh *m*, a' Chruthaidheachd *f*
creative *a* cruthachail
creator *n* neach-cruthachaidh *m* **the C.** an Cruthaidhear *m*
creature *n* creutair *m*

credibility *n* creideas *m*
credible *a* creideasach, a ghabhas creidsinn
credit *n* creideas *m* **c. card** cairt-creideis *f* **that's to his c.** tha e ri mholadh airson sin *v* creid
creditable *a* teisteil, measail
creditor *n* neach-fiach *m*, creideasaiche *m*
creed *n* creud *f*, creideamh *m*
creek *n* geodha *m*, òb *m*, òban *m*
creel *n* cliabh *m*
creep *v* snàig, èalaidh, liùg
cremate *v* luaithrich
crematorium *n* luaithreachan *m*
crescent *n* corran *m*; (*of moon*) corran-gealaich *m*
cress *n* biolair *f*
crest *n* suaicheantas *m*; (*bird*) cìrean *m*; (*topog*) mullach *m*, bàrr *m*
crevice *n* sgoltadh *m*, sgàineadh *m*
crew *n* sgioba *f m*, criutha *m*
cricket *n* (*game*) criogaid *m*
crime *n* eucoir *f*
criminal *n*, *a* eucorach *m*
crimson *n*, *a* crò-dhearg *m*
cringe *v* crùb, gìog
cripple *n* crioplach *m*, bacach *m*
crippled *a* bacach, na c(h)rioplach *etc*
crisis *n* càs *m*, èiginn *f*, gàbhadh *m*
crisp *n* brisgean *m pl* brisgeanan *a* brisg
criterion *n* slat-t(h)omhais *f*
critic *n* sgrùdair *m*, breithniche *m*
critical *a* (*vital*) deatamach, èiginneach; (*liter*) sgrùdail, breitheach; (*adversely*) beumach
criticism *n* càineadh; (*liter*) sgrùdadh *m*, breithneachadh *m*
criticize *v* càin
croak *v* dèan gràgail
crockery *n* soithichean *m pl*
crocodile *n* crogall *m*
croft *n* croit *f*, lot(a) *m*
crofter *n* croitear *m* **Crofters Commission** Coimisean nan Croitearan
crony *n* seann charaid *m*, dlùth-chompanach *m*
crook *n* cromag *f*; (*person*) rògaire *m*
crooked *a* cam, crom, fiar

crop n (*harvest*) bàrr m; (*of bird*) sgròban m; (*haircut*) bearradh m v geàrr, buain; (*hair etc*) beàrr

cross n crois f; (*crucifixion*) crann-ceusaidh m **the Red C.** a' Chrois Dhearg a crosta v rach tarsainn/thairis **c. oneself** dèan comharra na croise **c. a cheque** cros seic

cross-beam n spàrr f, trastan m

cross-examine v cruaidh-cheasnaich

cross-eyed a cam, cam-shùileach, fiar-shùileach

crossfire n eadar-theine m

cross-legged a casa-gòbhlach

crossroads n crois (an) rathaid f

crossword n tòimhseachan-tarsainn m

crotch n gobhal m

crouch v crom, crùb

crow n feannag f, starrag f

crowbar n geimhleag f

crowd n sluagh m; (*pej*) gràisg f

crowded a dùmhail

crowdie n gruth m

crown n crùn m; (*of head*) mullach a' chinn m, bàrr a' chinn m v crùn

crucial a deatamach

crucifix n crois f

crucify v ceus

crude a amh; (*met*) drabasta, curs(a)

cruel a an-iochdmhor, neo-thruacanta

cruelty n an-iochd f, neo-thruacantachd f

cruise n cuairt-mara f, turas-cuain m

crumb n criomag f, sprùilleag f, mìr m **crumbs** sprùilleach m

crumple v rocaich

crunch n **when it comes to the c.** nuair a thig e gu h-aon 's gu dhà

crusade n iomairt f **the Crusades** Cogaidhean na Croise m pl

crush n bruthadh m v pronn; (*met*) ceannsaich, mùch

crust n rùsg m, plaosg m

crutch n crasg f, croitse f

crux n cnag (na cùise) f

cry n èigh f, glaodh f m, gairm f; (*tears*) ràn m v èigh, glaodh, gairm; (*shed tears*) caoin, guil

crying n èigheach(d) f, glaodhaich f; (*tears*) caoineadh m, gal/gul m, rànaich f

crystal n criostal m a criostail

cube n ciùb m

cubic a ciùbach

cuckoo n cuthag f

cucumber n cularan m

cuddle v dèan cionacraich air

cue n (*sport*) slat-chluiche f, ciù m; (*stage*) cagar m; (*hair*) ciutha m

cuisine n modh còcaireachd m

cull v tanaich

culpable a ciontach, coireach **c. homicide** marbhadh le coire m

culprit n ciontach m

cultivate v àitich

cultivation n àiteach m

cultural a cultarach

culture n cultar m

cumbersome a trom, liobasta

cunning a seòlta, carach

cup n cupa m, copan m **cup final** cuairt dheireannach a' chupa f

cupboard n preas(a) m

curb v ceannsaich, bac, cuir srian air

curdle v binndich

cure n leigheas m; (*specific*) cungaidh-leigheis f v leighis, slànaich; (*fish*) saill, ciùraig

curious a ceasnachail, farraideach, feòrachail; (*odd*) annasach, neònach

curl n dual m, bachlag f, cam-lùb f v bachlaich, caisich

curlew n guilbneach f m

curling n (*sport*) curladh m

curly a dualach, bachlagach, camagach

currant n dearc(ag) thiormaichte f

currency n airgead m

current n sruth m, buinne f **electric c.** sruth-dealain m

current a gnàthaichte, làithreach **c. account** cunntas làitheil m, cunntas-ruith m **c. affairs** cùisean an latha f pl

currently adv an-dràsta, an-ceartuair

curriculum n curraicealam m, clàr-oideachais m **c. vitae** cunntas-beatha m

curry n coiridh m

curse n mallachd f v mallaich;
(swear) mionnaich, bi ri na mionnan/
guidheachan
cursory a cabhagach, gun aire
curtail v giorraich
curtain n cùirtear m, cùirtean m
curve n lùb f, camadh m
curved a lùbte, le camadh
cushion n cuisean f m, pillean m
custard n ughagan m
custody n grèim m, cùram m
custom n cleachdadh m, àbhaist f,
gnàths m, nòs m
customary a àbhaisteach, gnàthach
customer n neach-ceanna(i)ch m
Customs n seirbheis na Cusbainn f **C.
duty** cìs Cusbainn f

cut n gearradh m v geàrr, giorraich **cut
hair** beàrr **his work is cut out for him**
tha a dhìol/leòr aige ri dhèanamh
cutlery n uidheam-ithe f
cycle n cuairt f, cùrsa m; (bicycle)
baidhsagal m, rothair m
cyclist n baidhsaglair m, rothaiche m
cyclone n toirm-ghaoth f, cuairt-
gaoithe f
cygnet n isean eala m
cylinder n siolandair m
cymbal n tiompan m, ciombal m
cynic n sgaitear m, searbh-neach m
cynical a sgaiteachail, searbhasach
cyst n ùthan m, balgan m
Czech n, a Seiceach m, (female) ban-
S(h)eiceach f

D

dab v suath gu luath/aotrom
dad n dadaidh m
daffodil n lus a' chrom-chinn m
daft a gòrach, baoghalta
dagger n biodag f
daily a làitheil adv gach latha, gu làitheil
dainty n grinn, mìn
dairy n taigh-bainne m **d.-farm**
tuathanas bainne m
daisy n neòinean m
dale n dail f, gleann m
dam n dam m
damage n dìol m, dochann m, milleadh
m v dèan dìol air, dèan dochann air, mill
damn! interj daingit!, gonadh!
damnable a damainte, mallaichte
damnation n dìteadh (sìorraidh) m,
sgrios m interj daingit!
damp a tais
dampness n fuarachd f; (weather)
taiseachd f
dance n dannsa m v danns, dèan dannsa
dancer n dannsair m
dancing n dannsa(dh) m
dandelion n beàrnan-bride m
dandruff n sgealpaich f, càrr f
dandy n spaidire m
danger n cunnart m, gàbhadh m

dangerous a cunnartach
dangle v bi air bhogadan/udalan
Dane n Danmhairgeach m, (female)
ban-D(h)anmhairgeach f
Danish a Danmhairgeach
dank a tungaidh
dapper a speiseanta
dare v dùraig; (challenge) thoir dùbhlan
do **don't you d.** na gabh ort
daring a dàna
dark a dorch(a), doilleir **d. blue** dubh-
ghorm
darken v dorchnaich
darkness n dorchadas m
darling n gaol m, gràdh m, eudail f,
luaidh f m **my d.** a ghaoil, m' eudail a
gaolach, gràdhach
darn v càirich
dart n gath m; (move) siorradh m
dash n ruith f, leum m, ruith is leum;
(punct) strìochag f, sgrìob f v ruith, leum;
(break) spealg **d. to pieces** spealt
data n dàta m
date n latha m; (deadline) ceann-latha
m; (appointment) deit f; (fruit) deit
f **up-to-d.** ùr-nòsach **to d.** gu ruige
seo **d. of birth** latha-breith **out-of-d.**
seann-fhasanta **past sell-by d.** seach

an ceann-latha **she had a d. with Allan** bha deit aice fhèin 's Ailean *v* cuir latha air, comharraich an latha; (*intrans*) fàs seann-fhasanta

dative *a* tabhartach **the d. case** an tuiseal tabhartach *m*

daub *v* smeur, buaic

daughter *n* nighean *f* **d.-in-law** ban(a)-chliamhain *f*

dawn *n* camhana(i)ch *f*, beul an latha *m*

day *n* latha *m*, là *m* **the day after tomorrow** an-earar **the day before yesterday** a' bhòn-dè **d. centre** ionad-latha *m* **daybreak** bris(t)eadh an latha *m* **daylight** solas an latha *m*

daze *v* cuir bho mhothachadh

dazzle *v* deàrrs, boillsgich

debauchery *n* neo-mheasarrachd *f*, mì-gheanmnachd *f*, geòcaireachd *f*

debility *n* laige *f*, anfhainneachd *f*

debit(s) *n* fiachan *f pl v* thoir à (cunntas)

debris *n* sprùilleach *m*

debt *n* fiachan *m pl*; (*met*) comain *f* **in d.** ann am fiachan

debtor *n* neach-fhiach *m*

debut *n* ciad nochdadh *m*

decade *n* deichead *m*

decadence *n* claonadh *m*, coirbeachd *f*, mì-bheusachd *f*

decadent *a* coirbte, mì-bheusach

decant *v* taom; (*move*) gluais

decay *n* crìonadh *m*, seargadh *m*, lobhadh *m v* crìon, searg, caith

decayed *a* seargte, crìon, lobhte

Insight: day

There are two forms of the word for a day, the two syllable *latha* which is much the more common and the single syllable, *là*. *Latha math*, Good day, is used to greet someone and as a parting remark. A diary is *leabhar-latha*, literally a day-book.

---

deacon *n* deucon *m*

dead *a* marbh **d. centre** teis-meadhan *m*

deadly *a* marbhtach

deaf *a* bodhar **d.-mute** balbhan *m*

deafen *v* bodhair, dèan bodhar

deafness *n* buidhre *f*

deal *n* cùmhnant *m*, cunnradh *m* **a great d.** (*much*) tòrr *m* **a good d.** deagh bhargan *m v* dèilig (ri); (*in business*) dèan gnothach ri; (*cards*) roinn

dealer *n* neach-malairt *m*; (*of cards*) neach-roinn *m*

dean *n* deadhan *m*

dear *a* ionmhainn, gràdhach, gaolach; (*expensive*) daor *n* luaidh *f m*, gràdh *m*, eudail *m*

dearth *n* gainne *f*, dìth *f m*

death *n* bàs *m*, caochladh *m*, eug *m*, aog *m*

debate *n* deasbad *f*, deasbaireachd *f v* bi a' deasbad, deasbair

debauched *a* neo-mheasarra, stròdhail

decease *n* caochladh *m*, bàs *m* **the deceased** am fear/an tè nach maireann

deceit *n* cealgaireachd *f*, cealg *f*, foill *f*

deceitful *a* cealgach, foilleil

deceive *v* meall, thoir an car à

December *n* an Dùbhlachd *f*

decency *n* beusachd *f*, cubhaidheachd *f*

decent *a* beusach, cubhaidh

decentralize *v* sgaoil a-mach, gluais (bh) on mheadhan

deception *n* mealladh *m*, foill *f*

deceptive *a* meallta

decide *v* socraich/suidhich (air), co-dhùin, cuir romhad

deciduous *a* seargach

decimal *n, a* deicheamh *m*

decipher *v* mìnich, fuasgail, dèan a-mach

decision *n* breith *f*, co-dhùnadh *m*

decisive *a* dearbhachail, cinnteach

deck *n* deic *f m*, clàr-uachdair *m*; (*of cards*) paca *m*

declaration *n* cur an cèill *m*

declare *v* cuir an cèill, inn(i)s

declension n cromadh m, teàrnadh m; (gram) tuisealadh m
decline n cromadh m, crìonadh m, dol air ais m, dol sìos m v crom, crìon, rach air ais, rach sìos; (gram) claoin
decompose v lobh
decorate v sgeadaich, maisich
decoration n sgeadachadh m, maiseachadh m
decorator n sgeadaiche m
decorum n stuaim f, deagh-bheus f
decrease n lùghdachadh m, dol sìos m v lùghdaich, beagaich, rach sìos
decree n òrdugh m, reachd m, breith f v òrdaich, reachdaich, thoir breith
decrepit a breòite, anfhann
decry v cuir sìos air, càin
dedicate v coisrig **d. to** ainmich air
dedicated a coisrigte; (committed) dìcheallach
dedication n coisrigeadh m; (commitment) dìcheall f m
deduce v dèan a-mach, tuig
deduct v thoir air falbh (bh)o
deed n gnìomh m, euchd m; (leg) sgrìobhainn lagha f
deem v meas
deep a domhainn n doimhne f
deep-freeze n cruaidh-reothadair m
deer n fiadh m **d.-forest** frìth f
deface v mill
defamation n tuaileas m, mì-chliù m
defamatory a tuaileasach
defeat n call m v gabh air, faigh buaidh (air)
defect n easbhaidh f, uireasbhaidh f
defective a easbhaidheach, uireasbhach
defence n dìon m, dìdean f; (excuse) leisgeul m **d. mechanism** dòigh dèiligidh (ri) f
defend v dìon
defender n neach-dìon(a) m, dìonadair m
defensive a dìonadach
defer v cuir air dàil, dàilich **d. to** thoir inbhe/urram do
deference n ùmhlachd f, urram m
defiance n dùbhlan m
defiant a dùbhlanach

deficiency n easbhaidh f, dìth f m
deficient a easbhaidheach
deficit n easbhaidh f, call m
defile v salaich, truaill, gànraich
define v seall brìgh, mìnich
definite a cinnteach, deimhinn(t)e
definition n mìneachadh m, comharrachadh m; (audio-visual) gèire f, soilleireachd f
deflate v traogh, leig gaoth às; (met) thoir a' ghaoth à siùil
deflect v cuir air falbh bho; (intrans) aom, claon
deformity n mì-chumadh m, mì-dhealbh f m
defraud v dean foill (air)
deft a ealamh, deas
defunct a à bith, (bh)o fheum
defy v thoir dùbhlan do, cuir gu dùbhlan
degenerate v rach bhuaithe, meath
degrade v ìslich, truaill
degrading a maslach, truaillidh
degree n inbhe f, ìre f; (acad) ceum m; (temp) puing f **to some d.** gu ìre **by degrees** beag air bheag, mean air mhean
dehydration n sgreubhadh m
deity n diadhachd f; (a god) dia m
dejected a fo bhròn/phràmh/sprochd
dejection n sprochd m, smuairean m
delay n dàil f, maill(e) f v cuir dàil/maill(e) an/air, cùm air ais
delayed a (late) fadalach, air dheireadh
delegate n neach-ionaid m, teachdaire m
delegate v thoir ùghdarras do
delegation n buidheann-riochdachaidh m, luchd-tagraidh m
delete v dubh às/a-mach
deliberate v beachdaich, meòraich
deliberate a a dh'aon ghnotha(i)ch; (pace) mall
delicacy n fìnealtas m, grinneas m
delicate a fìnealta, grinn; (health) meata, lag
delicious a fìor bhlasta
delight n aighear m, aoibhneas m, sòlas m v toilich, dèan aoibhneach **d. in** gabh tlachd an

delightful *a* aoibhneach, sòlasach, ciatach

delineate *v* dealbh, dealbhaich, tarrainn crìoch eadar

delinquent *n* eucorach *m*, ciontach *m a* ciontach, coireach

delirious *a* breisleachail, bruailleanach

delirium *n* breisleach *f*, bruaillean *m*

deliver *v* (*save*) saor, fuasgail, teàrn; (*an address, services*) lìbhrig, liubhair; (*child*) asaidich

deliverance *n* saoradh *f*, fuasgladh *m*, teàrnadh *m*

delivery *n* teàrnadh *m*; (*an address, services*) lìbhrigeadh *m*, liubhairt *m*; (*manner of speech*) cainnt *f*, dòigh-labhairt *f*; (*childbirth*) asaid *f*; (*mail*) post *m*

delude *v* meall, thoir an car à

deluge *n* tuil *f*, dìle *f v* cuir fodha

delusion *n* mealladh *m*, dalladh *m*

delve *v* cladhaich, ruamhair, àitich

demand *n* iarrtas *m*, tagradh *m v* iarr, tagair

demanding *a* iarrtach

demean *v* ìslich, dìblich

demeanour *n* giùlan *m*, modh *f m*, beus *f*

demented *a* air bhoil(e), às a *etc* rian

dementia *n* boile *f*; (*senility*) seargadh-inntinn *m*

demise *n* deireadh *m*; (*gradual*) crìonadh; (*death*) bàs *m*

demit *v* leig dheth/dhith *etc*

democracy *n* deamocrasaidh *m*

democrat *n* deamocratach *m*

democratic *a* deamocratach

demolish *v* leag gu làr

demolition *n* leagail (gu làr) *f*

demon *n* deamhan *m*

demonstrate *v* seall, soilleirich, taisbean

demonstration *n* taisbeanadh *m*, soilleireachadh *m*; (*protest*) sluagh-fhianais *f*

demonstrative *a* comharraichte, suaicheanta

demoralize *v* mì-mhisnich gu tur, thoir an cridhe (bh)o

demur *v* cuir an aghaidh (+ *gen*), cuir teagamh an

demure *a* màlda

den *n* saobhaidh *m*, garaidh *m*, faiche *f*, còs *m*

denial *n* àicheadh *m*; (*withholding*) diùltadh *m*

denigrate *v* dì-mol, cuir sìos air

denomination *n* ainm *m*; (*relig*) eaglais *f*, buidheann (creideimh) *f m*

denote *v* comharraich

denounce *v* càin; (*accuse*) tog casaid an aghaidh (+ *gen*)

dense *a* dùmhail, tiugh; (*not intelligent*) maol

density *n* dùmhlachd *f*, dlùths *m*

dent *n* lag *f m v* dèan lag an

dental *a* fiaclach, deudach

dentist *n* fiaclair *m*

dentistry *n* fiaclaireachd *f*

dentures *n* fiaclan fuadain *f pl*

denunciation *n* càineadh *m*; (*accusation*) casaid *f*

deny *v* àich, rach às àicheadh; (*withhold*) diùlt, cùm (bh)o

depart *v* falbh, triall, tog air *etc*

department *n* roinn *f*

departure *n* falbh *m*, fàgail *f*

depend *v* bi an eisimeil/am freastal (+ *gen*) **d. on** (**someone**) cuir earbsa an, earb à **it depends on ...** tha e an crochadh air ... **you can d. on it** faodaidh tu bhith cinnteach às

dependent *a* eisimeileach **d. on** an eisimeil (+ *gen*), an eisimeil air, an crochadh air, an urra ri

depict *v* dealbh, tarraing dealbh de

depleted *a* falmhaichte, falamh

deplorable *a* sgriosail, muladach, maslach

deplore *v* faic/meas maslach **we d. what you've done** tha an rud a rinn sibh a' cur uabhas oirnn

depopulation *n* fàsachadh *m*

deport *v* fuadaich, fògair, cuir às an tìr

deportment *n* giùlan *m*, gluasad *m*

depose *v* cuir à dreuchd

deposit *n* tasgadh *m* **d. account** cunntas tasgaidh *m* *v* taisg
depot *n* ionad-stòraidh *m*
depraved *a* aingidh, coirbte
depravity *n* truaill(idh)eachd *f*, aingidheachd *f*
depreciate *v* ìslich (ann an luach), rach sìos
depreciation *n* ìsleachadh (luach) *m*, tuiteam (ann an luach) *m*
depress *v* cuir trom-inntinn (air); (*phys*) brùth sìos
depressed *a* airtnealach, fo sprochd, dubhach, trom-inntinneach
depression *n* airtneal *m*, sprochd *f*, trom-inntinn *f*, smalan *m*
deprivation *n* easbhaidh *f*, toirt air falbh *m*
deprive *v* thoir (air falbh) (bh)o, cùm (bh)o
depth *n* doimhneachd *f*, doimhne *f*
deputation *n* buidheann-tagraidh *f m*
depute *a* iar- (+ *len*) **d. director** iar-stiùiriche
deputy *n* neach-ionaid *m a* iar- (+ *len*) **d. head** iar-cheannard *m*
derail *v* cuir bhàrr an rèile; (*met*) cuir drithleann
deranged *a* às a c(h)iall *etc*, air/fon chuthach
derelict *a* trèigte, fàs
deride *v* dèan fanaid air
derision *n* fanaid *f*, sgeig *f*
derivation *n* freumhachadh *m*, bun *m*
derive *v* freumhaich, bunaich
derogatory *a* tarcaiseach, suarach
descend *v* teirinn, crom, thig a-nuas
descendant *n* fear/tè de shliochd *f m*
  descendants (*coll*) sliochd *m*, sìol *m*
descent *n* teàrnadh *m*, cromadh *m*
describe *v* thoir tuairisgeul air, dèan dealbh (de)
description *n* tuairisgeul *m*
descriptive *a* tuairisgeulach
desecrate *v* mì-naomhaich, truaill
desert *n* fàsach *f m*
desert *v* trèig, dìobair **d. from** teich à, ruith à

deserter *n* neach-teichidh *m*, neach-trèigsinn *m*
deserve *v* coisinn, toill, bi airidh air
deserving *a* airidh, toillteanach
design *n* dealbh *f*, dealbhadh *m*; (*intent*) rùn *m* **by d.** a dh'aon ghnotha(i)ch
design *v* dealbhaich, deilbh; (*intend*) rùnaich
designate *v* sònraich, ainmich
designer *n* dealbhaiche *m*, neach-deilbh *m*
desirable *a* ion-mhiannaichte
desire *n* miann *f m*, dèidh *f*, toil *f*, iarrtas *m* *v* miannaich
desirous *a* miannach, dèidheil (air)
desk *n* deasg *m*
desolate *a* fàsail, aon(a)ranach
desolation *n* fàsalachd *f*, aon(a)ranachd *f*
despair *n* eu-dòchas *m v* leig/thoir thairis dòchas
despatch *v* cuir air falbh
desperate *a* èiginneach, nam/na èiginn, na h-èiginn *etc*
desperation *n* èiginn *f*
despicable *a* suarach
despise *v* dèan tàir air
despite *prep* a dh'aindeoin (+ *gen*)
despondency *n* eu-dòchas *m*, dubhachas *m*
despondent *a* eu-dòchasach, dubhach
despot *n* aintighearna *m*
despotism *n* aintighearnas *m*
dessert *n* mìlsean *m*
destination *n* ceann-uidhe *m*
destiny *n* dàn *m* **he was destined to …** bha e/sin an dàn dha
destitute *a* falamh, ainniseach *n* dìol-dèirce *m*
destroy *v* mill, sgrios
destruction *n* milleadh *m*, sgrios *m*, lèirsgrios *m*
destructive *a* sgriosail, millteach
detach *v* dealaich, cuir air leth
detached *a* dealaichte, air leth
detail *n* mion-phuing *f v* thoir mion-chunntas air
detailed *a* mionaideach
detain *v* cùm air ais

detect v (*notice*) thoir an aire; (*find*) lorg; (*discover*) faigh a-mach
detective n lorg-phoileas m
detention n cumail air ais m; (*imprisonment*) cumail an grèim m
deter v cuir bacadh ro
detergent n stuth-glanaidh m
deteriorate v rach bhuaithe
deterioration n dol bhuaithe m, dol am miosad m
determination n diongmhaltas m, cruaidh-bharail f
determine v co-dhuin; cuir ro, faigh a-mach; (*decide*) cuir romhad *etc*
determined a diongmhalta, daingeann
deterrent n casg m, bacadh m
detest v fuathaich, dubh-ghràinich **I d. it** tha grain (an) uilc agam air
detonate v leig dheth, spreadh; (*intrans*) spreadh
detour n cam-rathad m
detract v thoir air falbh (bh)o (luach)
detrimental a cronail, millteach
devaluation n lùghdachadh luach m, dì-luachadh m
devalue v lùghdaich luach, dì-luachaich
devastate v lèirsgrios, dèan lèirsgrios air
devastation n lèirsgrios m
develop v (*trans*) leasaich; (*intrans*) fàs
development n leasachadh m; (*growth*) fàs m
deviate v claon (bho)
device n innleachd f, cleas m
devil n diabhal m, deamhan m, donas m
devilish a diabhlaidh, deamhnaidh
devious a carach
devise v dealbh, innlich
devoid (of) a falamh (de), às eugmhais (+ *gen*)
devolution n tiomnadh-cumhachd m
devolved a tiomnaichte
devote v cosg, thoir (ùine) do
devotion n dìlseachd f, ionmhainneachd f; (*relig*) cràbhadh m; (*devotions*) adhradh m
devour v sluig, glamh
devout a cràbhach
dew n dealt f m, dr(i)ùchd m

dewy a dealtach, dr(i)ùchdach
dexterity n deisealachd f, làmhchaireachd f
diabetes n tinneas an t-siùcair m
diabetic n diabaiteach m
diabolical a diabhlaidh, deamhnaidh; (*met*) sgriosail
diagnose v lorg adhbhar
diagnosis n lorg-adhbhair m
diagonal a trasta(nach)
diagram n diagram m
dial n (*watch*) aodann (uaireadair) m **sun-d.** uaireadair-grèine m
dialect n dualchainnt f
dialogue n còmhradh m
diameter n trast-thomhas m
diamond n daoimean m
diaper n badan m
diaphragm n sgairt f
diarrhoea n an spùt m, a' bhuinneach f
diary n leabhar-latha m
dice n dìsinn m pl dìsnean
dictate v deachd, òrdaich
dictator n deachdaire m
dictatorial a ceannsalach, deachdaireach
dictatorship n deachdaireachd f
diction n modh-cainnt f m
dictionary n faclair m
die v caochail, bàsaich, eug, siubhail
diesel n dìosail m
diet n daithead f **regular d.** riaghailt bìdh f
differ v bi eadar-dhealaichte; (*disagree*) eas-aontaich
difference n eadar-dhealachadh m, diofar m, caochladh m
different a eadar-dhealaichte, diofraichte, air leth, air a' chaochladh
differentiate v diofaraich, eadar-sgar, dèan sgaradh eadar
differentiation n eadar-sgarachdainn f, eadar-dhealachadh m
differing a diofraichte
difficult a doirbh, duilich
difficulty n duilgheadas m, dorradas m
diffident a socharach, mì-mhisneachail, eu-dàna

diffuse(d) *a* sgaoilte *v* sgaoil
dig *v* cladhaich, ruamhair
digest *v* cnàmh, cnuasaich
digestion *n* (an) cnàmh *m*
digger *n* ruamhaire *m*, digear *m*
digit *n* meur *f m*; (*number*) figear *m*
digital *a* meurach; (*number*) figearail, didseatach
dignified *a* le uaisleachd
dignify *v* urramaich, àrdaich
dignity *n* urram *m*, inbhe *f*
digress *v* rach a thaobh, rach thar sgeula
digression *n* fiaradh-sgeula *m*
digs *n* taigh/àite-loidsidh *m*
dilapidated *a* air a dhol bhuaithe
dilatory *a* màirnealach, slìogach
dilemma *n* imcheist *f*, ceist *f*
diligence *n* dìcheall *f m*
diligent *a* dìcheallach, dèanadach
dilute *v* tanaich, lagaich
diluted *a* tanaichte, lagaichte
dim *v* doilleirich, duibhrich
dimension *n* tomhas *m*, meud *m*; (*aspect*) modh *f m*, taobh *m*
diminish *v* lùghdaich, beagaich (air); (*intrans*) lùghdaich
diminutive *a* meanbh, bìodach, beag bìodach
dimple *n* lagan-maise *m*
din *n* gleadhraich *f m*, toirm *f*, othail *f*
dine *v* gabh dinnear/biadh
dinghy *n* geòla-bheag *f*
dingy *a* duainidh, gruamach
dining-room *n* seòmar-bìdh *m*
dinner *n* dinnear *f*, diathad *f* **d.-time** àm dinnearach *m*
dinosaur *n* dìneasair *m*
diocese *n* sgìr-easbaig *f*
dip *n* tumadh *m*, bogadh *m*; (*for sheep*) dup *m v* tùm, bog, dup
diploma *n* teisteanas *m*
diplomacy *n* gleustachd *f*; (*polit*) dioplòmasaidh *f m*
diplomat *n* gleustair *m*; (*polit*) riochdaire dioplòmasach *m*
diplomatic *a* gleusta, faiceallach; (*polit*) dioplòmasach

dire *a* eagalach, uabhasach, cianail **in d. straits** ann an cruaidh-chàs
direct *a* dìreach *v* stiùir, seòl
direction *n* stiùireadh *m*; (*point of compass*) àird *f*
directive *n* òrdugh *m*
directly *adv* air ball; dìreach
director *n* stiùiriche *m*, neach-stiùiridh *m*
dirt *n* salchar *m*
dirty *a* salach *v* salaich
disability *n* ciorram *m*
disabled person *n* ciorramach *m*
disadvantage *n* anacothrom *m*, mì-leas *m*
disadvantaged *a* beag cothrom **the d. na feumaich** *m pl*
disaffected *a* diombach, mì-riaraichte
disagree *v* rach an aghaidh, eas-aontaich
disagreeable *a* mì-thaitneach, mì-thlachdmhor
disagreement *n* eas-aonta *f*, mì-chòrdadh *m*
disallow *v* diùlt, na ceadaich
disappear *v* rach à sealladh
disappoint *v* bris(t) dùil, leig sìos
disappointment *n* bris(t)eadh-dùil *m*
disapprove *v* bi an aghaidh **her parents d. of him** chan eil a pàrantan air a shon
disarm *v* dì-armaich
disarmament *n* dì-armachadh *m*
disaster *n* mòr-thubaist *f*, calldachd *f*
disastrous *a* sgriosail
disband *v* (*intrans*) sgaoil; (*trans*) leig mu sgaoil
disbelief *n* eas-creideamh *m*
disburse *v* caith/cuir a-mach airgead
disc *n* clàr *m*
discard *v* cuir dheth, dhith *etc*/bhuaithe, bhuaipe *etc*
discerning *a* lèirsinneach, tuigseach, geurchuiseach
discernment *n* lèirsinn *f*, tuigse *f*
discharge *n* sileadh *m*; (*release*) leigeil mu sgaoil *m*, fuasgladh *m*; (*debt*) ìocadh *m*, pàigheadh *m v* sil; (*release*) leig mu sgaoil, fuasgail; (*debts*) ìoc, pàigh; (*obligation*) coilean; (*cargo*) falmhaich, cuir air tìr

disciple n deisciobal m
discipline n smachd m; (*acad*) cuspair m
v smachdaich
disclose v foillsich, leig ris
disco n diosgo m
discomfort n mì-chofhurtachd f,
anshocair f
disconcerting n buaireasach
disconnect v fuasgail, dealaich (bh)o
chèile
disconsolate a brònach, dubhach,
tùrsach
discontent n mì-riarachadh m,
mì-thoileachadh m
discontented a mì-riaraichte,
mì-thoilichte
discontinue v leig seachad, sguir de, cuir
stad air
discord n mì-chòrdadh m, aimhreit f;
(*mus*) dì-chòrdadh m, eas-aonta m
discount n lasachadh (prìse) m
discourage v mì-mhisnich
discouragement n mì-mhisneachadh m
discourteous a mì-spèiseil, eas-
urramach, gun mhodh
discourtesy n cion modh(a) m, cion
spèis m
discover v faigh a-mach, lorg
discovery n lorg f
discredit v mì-chliùthaich, thoir creideas
(bh)o
discreet a faiceallach, cùramach
discrepancy n diofar m
discrete a air leth
discretion n faiceall f, cùram m;
(*judgement*) toil f, toinisg f **at your d.**
a rèir do thoil (fhèin)
discriminate v dèan dealachadh eadar
d. in favour of dèan leth-bhreith air
discrimination n eadar-dhealachadh m,
leth-bhreith f
discuss v deasbair, bi a' deasbad,
beachdaich (air/mu)
discussion n deasbaireachd f,
deasbad m, cnuasachadh m,
beachdachadh m
disdain n tàir f, dìmeas m
disease n tinneas m, galar m

disembark v rach air tìr, thig bhàrr/far
(+ *gen*)
disengage v dealaich ri, fuasgail
disentangle v fuasgail, rèitich
disfigure v mill (cruth), cuir à cruth
disgrace n masladh m, tàmailt f, cùis-
mhaslaidh f v maslaich, nàraich
disgraceful a maslach, nàr
disgruntled a mì-riaraichte, diombach
disguise n breug-riochd m **in d.** ann an
riochd ... v cuir breug-riochd air/oirre *etc*
disgust n sgreamh m, gràin f
v sgreamhaich, gràinich
disgusting a sgreamhail, gràineil
dish n soitheach f m **washing the dishes**
a' nighe nan soithichean
dishearten v mì-mhisnich
disheartening a mì-mhisneachail
dishevelled a mì-sgiobalta
dishonest a eas-onarach
dishonesty n eas-onair f
dishonour n eas-onair f, eas-urram m,
mì-chliù m
dishwasher n nigheadair-shoithichean m
disillusion n bris(t)eadh-dùil m, fosgladh
sùla m
disinclined a neo-thoileach, leisg (gu)
disinfectant n dì-ghalaran m
disingenuous a carach, neo-fhosgarra
disintegrate v rach às a chèile
disinterested a gun fhèin-chùis
disjointed a (*met*) neo-thàthach, briste
disk n clàr m
dislike v **dislikes** cha toigh/toil (le), cha
chaomh (le), is beag air
dislocate v cuir à(s) àite, cuir às an alt
dislodge v cuir à(s) àite, fuasgail
disloyal a neo-dhìleas
dismal a dubhach, gruamach, duainidh;
(*poor*) truagh, leibideach
dismantle v thoir às a chèile
dismay n uabhas m
dismiss v cuir air falbh; (*employment*)
cuir à dreuchd
dismissal n (*employment*) cur à
dreuchd m
dismount v teirinn (bh)o, thig de
disobedience n eas-ùmhlachd f

disobedient *a* eas-umhail
disobey *v* bi eas-umhail do, rach an
  aghaidh
disorder *n* mì-rian *m*, buaireas *m*, troimh-
  a-chèile *f*
disorderly *a* mì-rianail
disorganized *a* mì-dhòigheil, gun rian
disown *v* diùlt gabhail ri, cuir cùl ri
disparage *v* cuir sìos air, dì-mol
disparate *a* diofraichte, neo-ionann
disparity *n* diofar *m*, neo-ionannachd *f*
dispassionate *a* ceart-bhreitheach,
  neo-chlaon
dispatch *v* cuir air falbh
dispel *v* sgaoil, fògair
dispensary *n* ìoclann *f*
dispense *v* (*issue*) riaraich; (*drugs etc*)
  dèan suas cungaidh **d. with** faigh
  cuidhteas
dispersal *n* sgapadh *m*, sgaoileadh *m*
disperse *v* sgap, sgaoil
dispersed *a* sgapte, sgaoilte
dispirited *a* neo-shunndach, gun
  s(h)unnd
displace *v* cuir à àite, fògair
display *n* taisbeanadh *m*, foillseachadh
  m v taisbean, foillsich
displease *v* mì-thoilich
displeased *a* mì-thoilichte, diombach
displeasure *n* mì-thoileachas *m*, diomb
  f m
disposal *n* toirt seachad *f*, riarachadh *m*
  d. of faighinn cuidhteas *f*
dispose *v* thoir seachad, riaraich **d. of**
  faigh cuidhteas
dispossess *v* cuir à seilbh
disproportionate *a* neo-chuimseach,
  mì-chothromach
disprove *v* breugnaich
dispute *n* connspaid *f*, aimhreit *f*
  v connsaich, tagair
disqualify *v* dì-cheadaich, cuir à (farpais)
disquiet *n* iomagain *f*, iomnaidh *f*
disregard *v* cuir an neo-shùim, dèan
  dìmeas air
disrepair *n* droch c(h)àradh *m* **in a state
  of d.** feumach air a c(h)àradh
disreputable *a* le droch ainm

disrepute *n* droch ainm *m*, mì-chliù *m*
disrespect *n* dìmeas *m*, eas-urram *m*
disrespectful *a* eas-urramach
disrupt *v* cuir troimh-a-chèile; (*break up*)
  bris(t)
disruption *n* cur troimh-a-chèile *m*;
  (*breaking up*) bris(t)eadh *m* **the
  Disruption** Bris(t)eadh na h-Eaglaise
dissatisfaction *n* mì-riarachadh *m*
dissatisfied *a* mì-riaraichte
dissect *v* sgrùd; (*phys*) geàrr às a chèile
disseminate *v* sgaoil
dissent *n* eas-aonta *m*
dissertation *n* tràchdas *m*
disservice *n* cron *m*
dissident *n* eas-aontaiche *m*
dissimilar *a* eu-coltach (ri)
dissimilarity *n* eu-coltas *m*
dissociate *v* sgar, na gabh gnotha(i)ch ri
dissolute *a* stròdhail
dissolution *n* leaghadh *m*, eadar-
  sgaoileadh *m*; (*eg Parliament*)
  sgaoileadh *m*
dissolve *v* leagh, eadar-sgaoil;
  (*eg Parliament*) sgaoil
dissuade *v* thoir à beachd
distance *n* astar *m*, fad *m*
distant *a* fad' air falbh, cian; (*manner*)
  fad' às; (*relationship*) fada a-mach
distaste *n* mì-thlachd *f*
distasteful *a* mì-chàilear, mì-thaitneach
distil *v* tarraing, dèan grùdaireachd
distillery *n* taigh-staile *m*
distinct *a* eadar-dhealaichte; (*clear*)
  soilleir
distinction *n* eadar-dhealachadh *m*;
  (*quality*) cliù *m*, urram *m*
distinctive *a* sònraichte, eadar-
  dhealaichte
distinguish *v* dèan dealachadh eadar,
  aithnich (bh)o chèile
distinguished *a* òirdheirc, cliùiteach
distort *v* fiaraich
distorted *a* fiar
distortion *n* fiaradh *m*
distract *v* tarraing aire (bh)o, buair
distress *n* àmhghar *f m*, teinn *f*,
  sàrachadh *m*

distressing *a* àmhgharach
distribute *v* sgaoil, roinn, riaraich
distribution *n* sgaoileadh *m*, riarachadh *m*
district *n* ceàrn *f*, sgìre *f*
distrust *n* cion earbsa *m*, mì-earbsa *f*, amharas *m*
distrustful *a* mì-earbsach, amharasach
disturb *v* cuir dragh air, buair
disturbance *n* buaireadh *m*, aimhreit *f*
disturbing *a* draghail
disunity *n* eas-aonachd *f*
disuse *n* dìth cleachdaidh *f m* **it fell into d.** chaidh e à cleachdadh
ditch *n* clais *f*, dìg *f*
ditto *adv* mar an ceudna
dive *v* dàibhig, rach fon uisge
diver *n* dàibhear *m*; (*bird*) eun tumaidh *m*
diverge *v* gabh caochladh slighe
diverse *a* eugsamhail, eadar-mheasgte, de chaochladh sheòrsa
diversify *v* eugsamhlaich, sgaoil
diversion *n* claonadh *m*; (*detour*) cam(a)-rathad *m*; (*distraction*) tarraing aire *f*; (*pastime*) cur-seachad *m*
diversity *n* eugsamhlachd *f*, iomadachd *f*
divert *v* claon; (*detour*) gabh cam(a)-rathad
divide *v* roinn, pàirtich
divided *a* roinnte, air a/an roinn *etc*
dividend *n* earrann *f*, roinn *f*
divine *a* (*relig*) diadhaidh **the D. will** toil Dhè *f*
divinity *n* diadhachd *f*
division *n* roinn *f*, earrann *f*; (*act of*) pàirteachadh *m*
divorce *n* sgaradh-pòsaidh *m* *v* sgar o chèile
divot *n* ceap *m*, sgrath *f*
divulge *v* foillsich, leig ris, taisbean
dizziness *n* tuaineal *m*, tuainealaich *f*, luairean *m*
dizzy *a* ann an tuaineal/luairean
do *v* dèan **do away with** cuir às do **do your best** dèan do dhìcheall **do what you can** dèan na 's urrainn dhut
docile *a* soitheamh, solta
dock *n* doca *m*; (*plant*) copag *f*
docken *n* copag *f*, cuiseag ruadh *f*

docker *n* docair *m*
doctor *n* dotair *m*, lighiche *m*; (*acad*) dotair *m*
doctrinaire *a* rag-bharaileach
doctrine *n* teagasg *m*
document *n* sgrìobhainn *f*
documentary *n* aithriseachd *f a* aithriseach
documentation *n* pàipearan *m pl*
dodge *n* cleas *m v* (*avoid*) seachain
doe *n* (*deer*) maoiseach *f*
dog *n* cù *m*, madadh *m* **dog-tired** cho sgìth ris a' chù **dogfish** biorach *f*
dogged *a* leanailteach, ruighinn
doggerel *n* rannghal *m*, rabhd(aireachd) *f*
dogma *n* gnàth-theagasg *m*
dogmatic *a* rag-bharaileach, fada na c(h)eann fhèin
dole *n* dòil *m*
doll *n* liùdhag *f*, doile(ag) *f*
dollar *n* dolair *m*
dolphin *n* leumadair-mara *m*
dolt *n* burraidh *m*, ùmaidh *m*
domain *n* raon *m*
dome *n* cuach-mhullaich *f*
domestic *a* dachaigheil
domesticate *v* callaich
domesticated *a* callaichte
dominance *n* làmh-an-uachda(i)r *f*
dominant *a* ceannasach, smachdail
dominate *v* ceannsaich, smachdaich, faigh làmh-an-uachda(i)r air
domination *n* ceannsachadh *m*, smachdachadh *m*, làmh-an-uachda(i)r *f*
domineering *a* maighstireil, ceannsalach
dominion *n* uachdranachd *f*
donate *v* thoir tabhartas/tiodhlac
donation *n* tabhartas *m*, tiodhlac *m*
donkey *n* asal *f m*
donor *n* tabhartaiche *m*
doom *n* bàs *m*, sgrios *m*; (*judgement*) binn *f*, dìteadh *m*
doomsday *n* Latha Luain *m*
door *n* doras *m* **front d.** doras-aghaidh **back d.** doras-cùil **d.-handle** làmh dorais *f* **doorpost** ursainn *f* **doorstep** maide-buinn *m*, leac an dorais *f*

dormant *n* na c(h)adal *etc*, na t(h)àmh *etc*, falaichte
dormitory *n* seòmar-cadail *m*
dormouse *n* dall-luch *f*
dose *n* dòs *m*; (*measure*) tomhas *m*
dot *n* dotag *f*; (*punct*) puing *f*
dote *v* gabh mòr-mhiadh air
dotted *a* dotagach
double *n* a dhà uimhir *f*, uimhir eile *f*; (*person*) mac-samhail *m* **d. chin** sprogan *m*, sprogaill *f* **d.-decker bus** bus dà-ùrlair *m* **d. glazing** uinneag dhùbailte *f a* dùbailte, dà-fhillte *v* dùblaich
doubt *n* teagamh *m*, imcheist *f v* cuir an teagamh, cuir teagamh an
doubtful *a* teagmhach
doubtless *adv* gun teagamh, gu cinnteach
dough *n* taois *f*; (*slang*) airgead *m*
dour *a* dùr
douse *v* smàl
dove *n* calman *m*
dowdy *a* seann-fhasanta, sgleòideach, duainidh
down *n* clòimhteach *f*
down *prep* shìos; (*motion*) sìos, a-nuas **are they d. there?** a bheil iad shìos an sin? **come d. here** thig a-nuas an seo
downcast *a* smuaireanach, dubhach
downfall *n* tuiteam *m*, leagadh *m* **that was his d.** 's e sin a dh'fhoghain dha
downhill *adv* leis/sìos an leathad, leis a' bhrutha(i)ch
downpour *n* dìle (bhàthte) *f*, deàrrsach *f*
downright *adv* dìreach
downstairs *adv* shìos an staidhre; (*motion*) sìos an staidhre
downward(s) *adv* sìos, a-nuas **going d.** a' dol sìos **coming d.** a' tighinn a-nuas
dowry *n* tochradh *m*
doze *v* dèan norrag/snuachdan
dozen *n* dusan *m*
dozy *a* cadalach
drab *a* duainidh
draft *n* dreach *m*, (*mil*) foireann *m*
drag *v* slaod, dragh, tarraing
dragon *n* dràgon *m*

drain *n* drèana *f*, clais *f v* drèan, sìolaidh, traogh
drainage *n* drèanadh *m*
drake *f n* (d)ràc *m*, ràcan *m*
dram *n* dram(a) *f m*
drama *n* dràma *f m*
dramatic *a* dràmadach
drat (it)! *interj* gonadh air!
draught *n* gaoth *f*; (*of ship*) tarraing-uisge *f* **d.-beer** leann baraille *m*
draughts *n* dàmais *f*
draughtsman *n* neach-tarraing *m*
draw *v* (*pull*) tarraing, dragh, slaod; (*picture*) dèan dealbh **d. lots** cuir croinn
drawer *n* drathair *m*
drawing *n* dealbh *f m*
drawing-pin *n* tacaid *f*
drawl *v* bruidhinn gu slaodach/sgleogach
dread *n* oillt *f*, uamhann *m*, sgàth *m*
dreadful *a* eagalach, cianail
dream *n* aisling *f*, bruadar *m v* bruadair, faic aisling *Also vn* ag aisling
dreary *a* muladach, dorcha, gruamach
dredge *v* sgrìob/glan grunnd
dregs *n* druaip *f*, grùid *f*
drenched *a* bog fliuch
dress *n* dreasa *f m*; (*clothes*) aodach *m*
dress *v* cuir aodach air/oirre *etc*, cuir uime/uimpe *etc*
dresser *n* (*furniture*) dreasair *m*
dressing *n* (*med*) bann lota *m*; (*salad*) sùgh saileid *m*
dressing-table *n* bòrd-sgeadachaidh *m*
dribble *v* dèan roill; (*in football*) drioblaig
drift *n* siabadh *m*; (*argument*) brìgh *f* **sand-d.** siaban *m* **snow-d.** cuithe sneachd(a) *f v* siab, falbh le gaoith; (*of snow*) rach na chuithe
drill *n* (*tool*) snìomhaire *m*; (*mil*) drile *f*; (*veg*) sreath *m v* drilich, drilig
drink *n* deoch *f v* òl, gabh deoch
drinker *n* neach-òil *m*, pòitear *m*
drip *n* boinne *m*, sileadh *m*, snighe *m*
drive *v* dràibh; (*animals*) iomain **d. away** ruaig
drivel *n* sgudal *m*
driver *n* dràibhear *m*; (*of animals*) neach-iomain *m*

driving n dràibheadh m; (of animals) iomain f

drizzle n ciùthran m, ciùthranaich f, smugraich f

droll a neònach; (amusing) ait

droop v crom, aom

drop n boinne f, braon m, drudhag f, deur m; (fall) tuiteam m

drop v leig às; (give up) leig seachad; (fall) tuit; (liquid) sil **d. me a line** cuir sgrìobag thugam **d. in any time** tadhail uair sam bith

dross n (coal) smùr f m; (met) smodal m

drought n mòr-thiormachd f, tartmhorachd f

drove n dròbh f m, treud m

drover n dròbhair m

drown v bàth; (intrans) bi air a b(h)àthadh etc

drowning n bàthadh m

drowsy a cadalach

drudgery n dubh-chosnadh m, tràilleachd f

drug n droga f, cungaidh-leighis f **d. addict** tràill-dhrogaichean f

druid n draoidh m

drum n druma f m

drummer n drumair m

drunk a air an daoraich, air mhisg **he was d.** bha an deoch/daorach air

drunkard n drungair m, misgear m

drunkenness n misg f, daorach f

dry a tioram; (thirsty) pàiteach v tiormaich **dry-clean** tioram-ghlan

dryer n tiormadair m

drying n tiormachadh m **good d. weather** turadh math m

dry-rot n mosgan m

dual a dùbailte **d.-carriageway** rathad dùbailte m

dubious a teagmhach

duchess n ban-diùc f

duck n tunnag f, (wild) lach f

duct n pìob-ghiùlain f

dud n rud gun fheum m

due n còir f, dlighe f a (deserved) dligheach, cubhaidh; (of debt) ri phàigheadh **when is it d.?** cuin a tha dùil ris? **d. back** ri th(i)lleadh etc

duel n còmhrag-dithis f

duet n òran-càraid/dithis m

duke n diùc m

dulcet a binn, fonnmhor

dull a dorch(a), gruamach, doilleir; (of hearing) bodhar; (personality) trom, somalta

dulse n duileasg m

duly adv gu riaghailteach

dumb a balbh **d. person** balbhan m

dumbness n balbhachd f; (silence) tostachd f

dummy n neach-brèige m

dump n òtrach m, lagais f, sitig f v caith air falbh, cuir bhuat

dumpling n turraisg f, duf m

dun a ciar, odhar, lachdann

dung n innear f, buachar m, todhar m **dunghill** sitig f, dùnan m

dungeon n toll-dubh m, sloc m

duodenum n beul a' chaolain m

dupe v meall, thoir an car à

duplicate n lethbhreac m, mac-samhail m

durable a maireannach, buan, seasmhach

duration n ùine f, fad m

during prep rè (+ gen)

dusk n ciaradh (an fheasgair) m, beul na h-oidhche m, eadar-sholas m

dusky a ciar

dust n dust m, duslach m, stùr m; (human remains) dust m v dust(aig)

dustbin n soitheach-sgudail f m

duster n dustair m

dusting n dustadh m

dusty a dustach

Dutch n (lang) Dùitsis f a Dùitseach

Dutchman n Dùitseach m **Dutchwoman** ban-D(h)ùitseach f

duty n dleastanas m; (excise) cìs f **d.-free** saor o chìsean

dux n ducs m

dwarf n troich f m

dwelling n àite/ionad-còmhnaidh m, fàrdach f **d. house** taigh-còmhnaidh m

dye n dath m v dath

dyke n (wall) gàrradh m

dynamic *a* fiùghantach
dynamics *n* daineamaig *f*
dynamite *n* daineamait *m*

dynamo *n* daineamo *m*
dynasty *n* sliochd rìoghail *m*
dysentry *n* a' bhuinneach mhòr *f*

E

each *a* gach *adv* an urra, an duine,
an ceann **e. other** a chèile **each one
is different** tha gach fear/tè eadar-
dhealaichte **they cost £20 each** tha
iad a' cosg £20 am fear/an tè
eager *a* dealasach
eagerness *n* dealas *m*
eagle *n* iolair(e) *f*
ear *n* cluas *f*; (*of corn*) dias *f*
earl *n* iarla *f m*
early *a* tràth, moch
earmark *v* (*met*) comharraich, sònraich;
(*phys*) cuir comharra air
earphone *n* cluasan *m*, fòn-cluaise *f m*
earn *v* coisinn
earnest *a* dùrachdach
earning(s) *n* tuarastal *m*, cosnadh *m*
earring *n* fàinne-cluaise *f m*
earth *n* talamh *m*; (*soil*) ùir *f* **the E.** an
Talamh, an Cruinne-cè *m* **where on e.
were you?** càit air an t-saoghal an robh
thu?
earthly *a* talmhaidh
earthquake *n* crith-thalmhainn *f*
earthworm *n* boiteag *f*
earwig *n* gòbhlag(-stobach) *f*, fiolan-
gòbhlach *m*
ease *n* fois *f*, tàmh *m*
east *n* ear *f*, an àird an ear *f*
Easter *n* a' Chàisg *f* **e. egg** ugh Càisge *m*
easterly *a* an ear, (bh)on ear
easy *a* furasta, soirbh
eat *v* ith
eavesdropping *n* farchluais *f*
ebb *n* tràghadh *m* **ebb-tide** sruth-
tràghaidh *m* *v* tràigh, traogh
eccentric *a* àraid, annasach, neònach
ecclesiastic *a* eaglaiseil
echo *n* mac-talla *m*
eclectic *a* roghainneach
eclipse *n* dubhadh grèine/gealaich *m*
ecology *n* eag-eòlas *m*

economic *a* eaconamach
economical *a* cùramach, caomhnach/
cùmhnach
economics *n* eaconamas *m*,
eaconamachd *f*
economist *n* eaconamair *m*
economize *v* caomhain/cumhain
economy *n* eaconamaidh *f m*
ecstasy *n* àrd-aoibhneas *m*, mire *f*; (*drug*)
eacstasaidh *f m*
ecstatic *a* àrd-aoibhneach, air mhire
ecumenical *a* eadar-eaglaiseil
edge *n* oir *f m*, iomall *m*, bruach *f m*;
(*blade*) faobhar *m*; (*verge*) fàl *m*
edible *a* so-ithe, a ghabhas ithe
edict *n* reachd *m*
edit *v* deasaich
edition *n* deasachadh *m*, eagran *m*
editor *n* neach-deasachaidh *m*,
deasaiche *m*
editorial *n* colbh deasaiche *m*
educate *v* foghlaim, teagaisg, ionnsaich
educated *a* foghlaim(ich)te **a well-e.
person** neach a fhuair deagh fhoghlam
education *n* foghlam *m*, oideachas *m*
e. authority ùghdarras foghlaim *m*
educational *a* oideachail, foghlaim
eel *n* easgann *f*
eerie *a* iargalta, gaoireil
effect *n* buaidh *f*, buil *f*, toradh *m* *v* thoir
gu buil, coilean
effective *a* èifeachdach, buadhach
effectively *adv* gu h-èifeachdach, le
èifeachd
effeminate *a* boireannta
effervescent *a* met beothail,
suigeartach, làn sunnd
efficacy *n* èifeachd *f*
efficiency *n* èifeachdas *f*
efficient *a* èifeachdach, (*person*)
gnothachail
effort *n* oidhirp *f*, dìcheall *f m*, spàirn *f*

effrontery *n* bathais *f*, ladarnas *m*
egg *n* ugh *m* **boiled egg** ugh air a
  bhruich **egg-cup** glainne/gucag-uighe
  f **egg-white** gealagan *m* **egg-yolk**
  buidheagan *m*
ego *n* fèin *f*, an fhèin *f*
egotism *n* fèin-spèis *f*
egotist *n* fèin-spèisiche *m*, fèinear *m*
egotistical *a* fèin-spèiseach
Egyptian *n, a* Èipheiteach *m*, (*female*)
  ban-Èipheiteach *f*
eider duck *n* lach mhòr *f*
eight *n* a h-ochd *a* ochd **e. people**
  ochdnar *f m*
eighth *a* ochdamh
eighteen *n, a* ochd-deug **e. years** ochd
  bliadhna deug
eighty *n* ceithir fichead *m*, ochdad *m*
either *a, pron, conj, adv* **on e. side of it**
  air gach taobh dheth/dhith **e. of them**
  an dara/dàrna fear/tè dhiubh, fear seach
  fear dhiubh, tè seach tè dhiubh **e. go**
  or stay an dara cuid falbh no fuirich
  that's not right e. chan eil sin ceart a
  bharrachd/nas mò
eject *v* cuir/tilg a-mach
elaborate *a* mionaideach, casta
  v leudaich (air)
elapse *v* rach seachad
elastic *n, a* lastaig *f* (*supple*) sùbailte,
  subailte
elation *n* mòr-aoibhneas *m*
elbow *n* uileann *f*, uilinn *f*
elder *n* (*eccl*) èildear *m*, foirfeach *m*; (*tree*)
  droman *m a* nas/as sine, na/a bu shine
elderly *a* sean, aosta
elect *v* tagh
elected *a* air a t(h)aghadh, taghte
election *n* taghadh *m* **e. day** latha
  taghaidh *m*
elector *n* neach-taghaidh *m*, neach-
  bhòtaidh *m*
electorate *n* luchd-taghaidh *m*
electric(al) *a* dealain
electrician *n* dealanair *m*
electricity *n* dealan *m*
electronic *a* dealanta(ch),
  eileagtronaigeach

elegance *n* grinneas *m*, eireachdas *m*,
  snas *m*, loinn *f*
elegant *a* grinn, eireachdail, snasail,
  loinneil
elegy *n* marbhrann *m*, tuireadh *m*,
  cumha *m*
element *n* eileamaid *f*; (*in nature*) dùil *f*
elementary *a* bunasach, sìmplidh
elephant *n* ailbhean *m*
elevate *v* àrdaich, tog suas
elevation *n* àrdachadh *m*; (*height*) àirde
  f; (*plan*) dealbh *f m*
elevator *n* àrdaichear *m*
eleven *n, a* aon-deug **e. men** aon duine
  deug
elf *n* màileachan *m*
elicit *v* faigh/lorg a-mach
eligible *a* airidh air roghainn, iomchaidh,
  dligheach; (*person*) so-thaghte
eliminate *v* cuir às do, geàrr às
elk *n* lon *m*
elm *n* leamhan *m*
elocution *n* deas-chainnt *f*, uirgheall *m*
elongate *v* fadaich, tarraing/sìn a-mach
elope *v* teich, ruith air falbh
eloquence *n* deas-bhriathrachd *f*
eloquent *n* deas-bhriathrach
else *a, adv* eile **or e.** air neo
elucidate *v* soilleirich
elude *v* seachain, èalaidh às
elusive *a* èalaidheach
emaciated *a* reangach, seargte
e-mail *n* post-dealain *m*
emanate *v* sruth/thig (bh)o
embargo *n* bacadh *m*
embark *v* (*board*) rach air bòrd **e. on**
  tòisich air
embarrass *v* nàraich, tàmailtich
embarrassed *a* air mo/a *etc* nàrachadh
embarrassing *a* nàrach, tàmailteach
embarrassment *n* nàrachadh *m*,
  tàmailt *f*
embassy *n* ambasaid *f*
embellish *v* sgeadaich, sgèimhich
ember *n* èibhleag *f*
embezzle *v* dèan foill le airgead
embittered *a* searbh
emblem *n* suaicheantas *m*

embrace v glac nad ghàirdeanan; (*accept*) gabh ri

embroider v cuir obair-ghrèis air

embroidery n obair-ghrèis f

embryo n suth m, tùs-ghinean m

emerald n smàrag f

emerge v thig am bàrr/am follais

emergency a suidheachadh-èiginn m, èiginn f **e. exit** doras-èiginn m

emigrant n eilthireach m

emigrate v fàg an dùthaich, dèan eilthireachd

emigration n eilthireachd f, às-imrich f

eminent a àrd, inbheil, iomraiteach

emit v leig a-mach

emotion n faireachdainn làidir f

emotional a làn faireachdainn

empathy n co-fhaireachdainn f

emperor n ìmpire m

emphasis n cudrom m; (*in speech*) sìneadh m

emphasize v cuir cudrom air; (*in speech*) cuir sìneadh an

emphatic a neartmhor, làidir

empire n ìmpireachd f

employ v fastaidh, thoir obair do; (*use*) cleachd

employee n neach-obrach m, obraiche m, cosnaiche m

employer n fastaiche m

employment n obair f, cosnadh m

empower v thoir comas/ùghdarras do

emptiness n falamhachd f

empty a falamh v falmhaich

emulate v bi a' comharspaidh ri

enable v dèan comasach, thoir comas do

enact v cuir an gnìomh, coilean; (*leg*) dèan lagh de

enamel n cruan m

enchanted a fo gheasaibh, seunta

encircle v cuartaich

enclose v cuartaich, iath mun cuairt; (*in letter etc*) cuir an cois

enclosed a cuartaichte; (*of document etc*) an cois ...

enclosure n crò m, geàrraidh m; (*document etc*) na tha an cois ...

encompass v cuartaich, iath; (*include*) gabh a-steach

encounter n coinneachadh m, tachairt f v coinnich (ri), tachair (ri)

encourage v misnich, brosnaich

encouragement n misneachadh m, brosnachadh m

encouraging a brosnachail

encyclopedia n leabhar mòr-eòlais m

end n deireadh m, crìoch f, ceann m **in the end** aig a' cheann thall **from end to end** (bh)o cheann gu ceann **we will never hear the end of it** cha chluinn sinn a dheireadh (gu bràth/sìorraidh) **come to an end** thig gu ceann/crìch v crìochnaich, cuir crìoch air, thoir gu ceann

endanger v cuir an cunnart

endangered a an cunnart

endear v coisinn meas/spèis

endeavour n spàirn f, oidhirp f v oidhirpich

endless a gun cheann, gun chrìoch, sìorraidh, neo-chrìochnach

endorse v (*support*) cuir aonta ri, thoir taic do; (*sign*) cuir ainm ri

endow v builich, bàirig

endowment n buileachadh m, bàirigeadh m

endurance n fulang(as) m

endure v fuiling; (*last*) seas, mair

enemy n nàmhaid m, eascaraid m

energetic a lùthmhor, sgairteil

energize v cuir brìgh/spionnadh an

energy n lùth m, neart m, spionnadh m, brìgh f

enforce v cuir an gnìomh; (*compel*) spàrr (air)

enforcement n cur an gnìomh m, sparradh m

engage v (*hire*) fastaidh **e. with** rach an sàs an

engaged a (*to be married*) fo ghealladh-pòsaidh; (*of phone*) trang; (*of toilet*) ga c(h)leachdadh **e. in** an sàs an

engagement n (*marriage*) gealladh-pòsaidh m; (*commitment*) dleastanas m

engaging a taitneach, tarraingeach

engine *n* einnsean *m*, inneal *m*, beairt *f*
engineer *n* einnseanair *m*, innleadair
  m **chief e.** prìomh innleadair **civil e.**
  innleadair-togail
engineering *n* einnseanaireachd *f*,
  innleadaireachd *f*

enrol *v* clàraich
en route *adv* air an t-slighe, air an rathad
ensemble *n* (*mus*) co-cheòltairean *m pl*;
  (*dress*) èideadh *m*
ensign *n* (*flag*) bratach *f*
ensue *v* lean, tachair (ri linn)

Insight: English

A person from England is a *Sasannach*, which strictly speaking
refers to an Englishman. An Englishwoman is *ban-S(h)asannach*.
The English language is *Beurla* or *a' Bheurla Shasannach* to
distinguish it from Lowland Scots, known as *a' Bheurla Ghallta*.

English *n* (*lang*) Beurla (Shasannach)
  f a Sasannach
Englishman *n* Sasannach *m*
  Englishwoman ban-S(h)asannach *f*
engrave *v* gràbhail
engrossed *a* beò-ghlacte
enhance *v* leasaich, thoir feabhas air;
  (*add to*) cuir ri
enjoy *v* còrd (ri), gabh tlachd an, meal
  they enjoyed the holidays chòrd
  na làithean-saora riutha
enjoyment *n* tlachd *f*, toileachas *m*,
  toil-inntinn *f*
enlarge *v* leudaich, meudaich
enlargement *n* leudachadh *m*,
  meudachadh *m*; (*phot*) meudachadh *m*
enlighten *v* soilleirich (do), thoir
  soilleireachadh (do)
enlist *v* (*mil*) liost(aig), gabh san Arm;
  (*support*) sir
enliven *v* beothaich
enmity *n* nàimhdeas *m*
enormous *a* ana-mhòr, àibheiseach
enough *n* leòr *f a, adv* gu leòr **did you
  get e.?** an d' fhuair thu do leòr/gu leòr?
  e. is e. fòghnaidh na dh'fhòghnas **do
  you have e. money?** a bheil airgead gu
  leòr agaibh? **I wasn't fast e.** cha robh
  mi luath gu leòr
enquire *v* faighnich, feòraich
enquiry *n* ceist *f*
enrage *v* cuir caoch/fearg air
enrich *v* dèan beairteach; (*soil etc*)
  neartaich

ensure *v* dèan cinnteach
entangle *v* rib, cuir an sàs, amail, rocail
entangled *a* an grèim, air amaladh, air
  rocladh
enter *v* rach/thig a-steach, inntrig
enterprise *n* iomairt *f*
enterprising *a* adhartach, iomairteach
entertain *v* dèan cur-seachad do,
  dèan dibhearsain; (*hospitality*) thoir
  aoigheachd do
entertainer *n* fèistear *m*, aisteach *m*
entertainment *n* fèisteas *m*, cur-
  seachadachd *f*, dibhearsain *m*;
  (*hospitality*) aoigheachd *f*
enthusiasm *n* dealas *m*, dìoghras *m*
enthusiastic *a* dealasach, dìoghrasach
entice *v* tàlaidh, meall, thoir a thaobh,
  breug
enticing *a* tarraingeach, tàlaidheach
entire *a* iomlan, slàn, uile
entirely *adv* gu lèir, gu tur
entitlement *n* còir *f*, làn-chòir *f*
entrails *n* mionach *m*, caolain *m pl*;
  (*animals*) greallach *f*
entrance *n* dol/tighinn a-steach *m*,
  inntrigeadh *m*; (*way in*) slighe a-steach *f*
  main e. doras-mòr *m*, prìomh dhoras *m*
entreat *v* guidh (air)
entreaty *n* guidhe *f m*, achanaich *f*
entrepreneur *n* iomairtiche *m*
entrust *v* fàg an urra ri, cuir air cùram
entry *n* teachd a-steach *m*, inntrigeadh *m*
enumerate *v* àireamh(aich), cunnt
enunciate *v* cuir an cèill, aithris

envelop v còmhdaich, cuartaich
envelope n cèis-litreach f
envious a farmadach
environment n àrainneachd f
environmentalist n neach-àrainneachd m
envoy n tosgaire m
envy n farmad m, eud m v bi ri
farmad **I envied her** bha farmad
agam rithe
epic n euchd-dhàn m, mòr-dhuan m
epidemic n galar sgaoilte m, ruathar m
epilepsy n an tinneas tuiteamach m
episcopal a easbaigeach
Episcopalian n, a Easbaigeach m
episode n pàirt-sgeul m; (occurrence)
tachartas m
epitome n sàr eisimpleir f m **the e. of**
laziness dealbh na leisge f m
equable a cothrom, rèidh, ciùin
equal a ionann, co-ionann
e. opportunities co-ionannachd
chothroman f n seise m v bi co-ionann
equality n co-ionannachd f,
cothromachd f
equalize v dèan co-ionann; (in sport)
co-chothromaich
equation n co-ionannachadh m; (maths)
co-aontar m
equator n meadhan-chearcall (na
talmhainn) m, Crios-meadhain m
equestrian n marcaiche m
equilateral a co-shliosach **e. triangle**
triantan ionann-thaobhach m
equinox n co-fhreagradh nan tràth m
equip v uidheamaich, beairtich
equipment n uidheam f, acfhainn f
equipped a uidheamaichte,
acfhainneach
equivalent a co-ionann
era n linn f
eradicate v cuir às do, spìon à bun
erase v dubh às/a-mach
erect v tog, cuir suas a dìreach
erode v creim, bleith; (intrans) cnàmh,
crìon
erosion n (act) creimeadh m, bleith f;
(state) cnàmh m, crìonadh m
erotic a earotach

err v rach ceàrr, dèan mearachd, rach air
seachran
errand n gnothach m, ceann-gnothaich m
erroneous a mearachdach, iomrallach
error n mearachd f, iomrall m
eruption n brùchdadh m; (volcanic)
spreadhadh m
escalator n streapadan m
escape n teicheadh m, tàrrsainn às m
v teich, tàrr às
escort n coimheadachd f, freiceadan m
v coimheadaich, bi mar chompanach
Eskimo n, a Easgiomach m, (female)
ban-Easgiomach f
especially adv gu h-àraidh, gu sònraichte
espionage n beachdaireachd f
esplanade n àilean m
espouse v nochd/thoir taic do, taobh ri
essay n aiste f
essence n brìgh f, sùgh m
essential a deatamach, riatanach
establish v stèidhich, suidhich, cuir air
bhonn
establishment n stèidheachadh m, cur
air bhonn m **the E.** na h-urracha mòra
m pl
estate n oighreachd f **e. agent** reiceadair
thaighean m
esteem n meas m, spèis f v meas, cuir
luach air
estimate n tuairmse f v thoir tuairmse
air, meas luach
estuary n inbhir m
eternal a sìorraidh, maireannach, bith-
bhuan, suthainn
eternally adv gu sìorraidh, gu bràth
eternity n sìorr(aidhe)achd f, bith-
bhuantachd f, biothbhuantachd f
ether n adhar fìnealta m; èatar m
ethical a beusanta, modhannach;
(of conduct) beusach
ethics n beus-eòlas m; (personal) beusan
m pl
ethnic a cinneachail
ethos n nòs m, feallsanachd f
etiquette n modh f m, dòigh-giùlain f
eulogy n moladh m, òraid-mholaidh f;
(poem) dàn molaidh m

euphemism *m* caomh-ràdh *m*, maoth-fhacal *m*

euro *n* euro *f m*, iùro *f m*

European *n*, *a* Eòrpach *m*
E. Commission an Coimisean Eòrpach *m* **E. Parliament** Pàrlamaid na h-Eòrpa *f* **E. Union** an t-Aonadh Eòrpach *m*

evacuate *v* falmhaich

evade *v* seachain, faigh às

evaluate *v* meas, tomhais luach

evaluation *n* measadh *m*, luachadh *m*, tomhas luach *m*

evangelical *a* soisgeulach

evaporate *v* deataich

evaporation *n* deatachadh *m*

evasion *n* seachnadh *m*

even *a* rèidh, còmhnard **e.-tempered** ciùin **e. number** àireamh chothrom *f*

even *adv* eadhon, fiù 's **he didn't e. have a coat** cha robh fiù 's còta aige **e. the old folk were there** bha na seann daoine fhèin ann

evening *n* feasgar *m* **early e.** fionnairidh *f*

event *n* tachartas *m*

eventually *adv* mu dheireadh thall

ever *adv* uair sam bith; (*past only*) riamh; (*fut only*) gu bràth, gu sìorraidh **he was as stubborn as e.** bha e cho rag 's a bha e riamh

everlasting *a* sìorraidh, bith-bhuan **e. life** a' bheatha mhaireannach *f*

every *a* a h-uile, gach

everyday *a* làitheil; (*routine*) àbhaisteach

everyone *pron* a h-uile duine/neach, gach duine/neach

everything *pron* a h-uile nì/rud, gach nì/rud

everywhere *pron* (anns) a h-uile (h-)àite, (anns) gach àite

evict *v* fuadaich, cuir à seilbh

eviction *n* fuadach *m*, cur à seilbh *m*

evidence *n* fianais *f*, teisteanas *m*

evident *a* soilleir, follaiseach

evil *n* olc *m*, aingidheachd *f a* olc, aingidh

evoke *v* thoir gu cuimhne

evolution *n* mean-fhàs *m*

evolve *v* thoir gu bith; (*intrans*) thig gu bith, mean-fhàs

ewe *n* caora *f*

exacerbate *v* dèan nas miosa

exact *a* ceart, mionaideach, pongail, eagnaidh

exactly *adv* dìreach, gu mionaideach

exaggerate *v* àibheisich, cuir ris (an fhìrinn)

examination *n* deuchainn *f*, ceasnachadh *m*; (*scrutiny*) sgrùdadh *m*

examine *v* ceasnaich; (*scrutinize*) sgrùd, dèan sgrùdadh air

examiner *n* neach-ceasnachaidh *m*; (*scrutineer*) neach-sgrùdaidh *m*, sgrùdaire *m*

example *n* eisimpleir *f m*, ball-sampaill *m*

excavate *v* cladhaich, ruamhair

exceed *v* rach thairis air

exceedingly *adv* glè (+ *len*), anabarrach

excel *v* dèan math (an), bi sònraichte/barraichte air; (*surpass*) thoir bàrr (air) **she excelled at music** bha i sònraichte/barraichte air ceòl

excellence *n* feabhas *m*, sàr-mhathas *m*

excellent *a* sàr-mhath, barrail, sgoinneil

except *prep* ach, a-mach air **e. for one or two** a-mach air fear/tè no dhà

exception *n* mura-bhith *f*, fàgail a-mach *f*, nì eadar-dhealaichte *m* **with the e. of** ach a-mhàin **everyone without e.** a h-uile duine riamh **take e. to** nochd diomb (mu)

exceptional *a* air leth, sònraichte

excess *n* (*surplus*) còrr *m*; (*too much*) anabarr *m*, cus *m*, tuilleadh 's a' chòir *m*

excessive *a* neo-chuimseach, mì-choltach, fada cus

exchange *n* iomlaid *f*, malairt *f* **e. rate** co-luach an airgid *m*, luach-iomlaid *m* *v* dèan iomlaid, malairtich

exchequer *n* stàit-chiste *f* **the E.** Roinn an Ionmhais *f*

excise *v* geàrr às/de

excite *v* brosnaich, gluais

excited *a* air bhioran, air bhoil

excitement *n* brosnachadh *m*, spreagadh *m*, boil *f*
exclaim *v* glaodh
exclamation *n* glaodh *m*, clisgeadh *m*
  e. mark clisg-phuing *f*
exclude *v* cùm a-muigh, dùin a-mach, toirmisg
exclusion *n* cumail a-muigh *m*, dùnadh a-mach *m*, toirmeasg *m*
exclusive *a* toirmeasgach; (*expensive*) fìor chosgail
excruciating *a* creadhnachail, fìor chràiteach
excursion *n* cuairt *f*, sgrìob *f*
excuse *n* leisgeul *m v* gabh leisgeul (+ *gen*)
execute *v* cuir an gnìomh, thoir gu buil; (*person*) cuir gu bàs
execution *n* cur an gnìomh *m*; (*person*) cur gu bàs *m*
executive *n* (*person*) neach-gnìomh *m*, gnìomhaiche *m*; (*body*) roinn-ghnìomha *f*
exemplar *n* eisimpleir *f m*
exemplify *v* bi mar/nad eisimpleir de
exempt *a* saor (bh)o, neo-bhuailteach
exemption *n* saoradh (bh)o *m*
exercise *n* eacarsaich *f* **e. book** leabhar-obrach *m v* gnàthaich, cleachd; (*work out*) dèan eacarsaich
exertion *n* spàirn *f*, dìcheall *f m*
exhaust *v* traogh; (*tire out*) claoidh
exhausted *a* traoghte, air teirigsinn; (*of person*) claoidhte
exhaustion *n* traoghadh *m*; (*of person*) claoidheadh *m*
exhaustive *a* iomlan, mion
exhibit *v* taisbean
exhibition *n* taisbeanadh *m*
exhilarating *a* meanmnach, aighearach
exhort *v* brosnaich, earalaich
exile *n* fògarrach *m*, eilthireach *m v* fògair, fuadaich
exist *v* bi beò, bi ann **it doesn't e.** chan eil e ann/ann am bith
exit *n* dol a-mach *m*; (*way out*) slighe a-mach *f*
exorbitant *a* mì-choltach, ana-cuimseach, thar nam bonnan

exotic *a* cian-annasach, cian-thìreach
expand *v* sgaoil, meudaich, leudaich
expansion *n* sgaoileadh *m*, meudachadh *m*, leudachadh *m*
expect *v* bi an dùil (gu), sùilich
expects tha dùil aig …
expectant *a* dòchasach, fiughaireach
expectation *n* dùil *f*, dòchas *m*, fiughair *f*
expedient *a* freagarrach (san àm); (*unethical*) airson a m(h)aith fhèin
expedite *v* luathaich, cuir cabhag air
expedition *n* turas *m*; (*speed*) cabhag *f*, luaths *m*
expel *v* cuir às, fògair, fuadaich
expend *v* caith, cosg
expenditure *n* caiteachas *m*, cosgais *f*
expense *n* cosgais *f*
expensive *a* cosgail, cosgaiseach, daor
experience *n* eòlas *m*, fiosrachadh *m*, fèin-fhiosrachadh *m v* fiosraich, fairich
experienced *a* eòlach
experiment *n* deuchainn *f*, dearbhadh *m*
expert *n* eòlaiche *m a* fiosrach, eòlach, ealanta, teòma
expertise *n* ealantas *m*, teòmachd *f*
explain *v* mìnich
explanation *n* mìneachadh *m*
explicit *a* soilleir, follaiseach, gun chleith
explode *v* spreadh
exploit *n* euchd *m v* gabh an cothrom air, cleachd airson prothaid **e. unfairly** gabh brath air
exploitation *n* gabhail a' chothruim air *m*, cleachdadh airson prothaid *m*; (*unfair*) gabhail brath air *f*
explore *v* rannsaich, lorg a-mach
explosion *n* spreadhadh *m*
explosive *n* stuth spreadhaidh *m*
  e. device inneal/uidheam spreadhaidh *m*
export *n* às-mhalairt *f*, às-bhathar *m*
  e. market margadh às-mhalairt *m v* cuir a-null thairis, às-mhalairtich
expose *v* leig ris, nochd, thoir am follais
exposed *a* am follais; (*skin*) ris; (*site*) fosgailte
expound *v* mìnich, soilleirich
express *v* cuir an cèill; (*send quickly*) luathaich

express a luath **e. train** trèan-luath
f **with the e. purpose** a dh'aon
ghnotha(i)ch
expression n dòigh/modh-labhairt f;
(phrase) abairt f; (facial) coltas m,
fiamh m
expulsion n fògradh m
exquisite a loinneil, fìor àlainn
extempore a an làrach nam bonn, gun
ullachadh
extend v sìn, leudaich, cuir ri **e. to** ruig (air)
extension n sìneadh m, leudachadh m
   e. work obair-leudachaidh f
extensive a farsaing, leathann
extent n farsaingeachd f, leud m,
meud m
exterior n taobh a-muigh m
exterminate v cuir às do, sgrios
external a (bh)on/air an taobh a-muigh
extinct a à bith; (volcano) marbh
extinguish v cuir às, smàl, mùch
extol v àrd-mhol
extort v foireignich

extra a fìor (+ len), ro (+ len);
(additional) a chòrr adv a bharrachd, a
thuilleadh
extract n earrann f, cuibhreann f m
   v tarraing/thoir/tog à
extraordinary a anabarrach, iongantach
(fhèin)
extravagance n ana-caitheamh m,
stròdhalachd f
extravagant a ana-caitheach, stròdhail
extreme a fìor (+ len), ro (+ len),
anabarrach n iomall m, ceann thall m
extremely adv dha-rìribh **e. good** math
dha-rìribh
extricate v saor, fuasgail
extrovert n neach fosgarra m
eye n sùil f; (of needle) crò (snàthaid) m
   eye-opener fosgladh sùla m, sùileachan
m **eyebrow** mala f **eyelash** fabhra m,
rosg m **eyelid** sgàile sùla f, fabhra m
   eyesight fradharc m, lèirsinn f **eyesore**
cùis sgreamh f
eyrie n nead iolaire m

F

fable n uirsgeul f m, sgeulachd f
fabric n aodach m, eige f; (structure)
dèanamh m
fabulous a uirsgeulach; (wonderful)
iongantach, mìorbhaileach
face n aodann m, aghaidh f; (human
only) gnùis f **f.-cloth** clobhd aodainn m
   v cuir/thoir aghaidh air; (be opposite) bi
mu choinneamh
facet n taobh m
facetious a saobh-spòrsail, magail
facile a furasta; (superficial) staoin
facilitate v dèan nas fhasa do, dèan
comasach, cuidich
facility n goireas m **f. in** alt (air) m
facing adv mu choinneamh (+ gen)
fact n fìrinn f
faction n buidheann f m
factor n adhbhar m, eileamaid f; (agent)
bàillidh m, seumarlan m; (math) factar m
factory n factaraidh f m, ionad ceàirde
m, ionad tionnsgain m

faculty n ciad-fàth f, comas m, bua(i)dh
f; (acad) dàimh m **she had all her
faculties** bha a buadhan uile aice
fade v searg, crìon, meath
fail v fàillig; (intrans) fàilnich, dìobair
failing n fàilligeadh m, fàillinn f
failure n fàilligeadh m, fàilneachadh m
faint n neul m, laigse f, luairean m
   v fannaich, fanntaig, rach an laigse
faint a fann, lag; (unclear) neo-shoilleir
   f.-hearted lag-chridheach, meata
fair n fèill f, faidhir f
fair a bàn, fionn; (beautiful) maiseach;
(just) ceart, cothromach
fairly adv an ìre mhath, gu math
fairness n bàinead f; (beauty)
maisealachd f; (justness) ceartas m,
cothromachd f
fairy n sìthiche m; (female) bean-shìth f
faith n creideamh m; (trust) earbsa f,
muinighin f, creideas m
faithful a dìleas

faithfulness n dìlseachd f
falcon n seabhag f
fall n tuiteam m, leagail m **f. out** dol a-mach air a chèile m v tuit; (in level) sìolaidh
fallow a bàn
false a meallta, brèige; (wrong) ceàrr
  f. teeth fiaclan fuadain f pl
falsehood n breug f
falter v lagaich, tuislich
fame n cliù m, ainm m
familiar a eòlach (air); (manner) faisg
familiarize v cuir eòlas air, cuir aithne air
family n teaghlach m **f. tree** craobh-teaghlaich f
famine n gort(a) f
famous a ainmeil, iomraiteach
fan n gaotharan m
fanatic n eudmhoraiche m, dìoghrasaiche m
fanatical a eudmhorach, dìoghrasach
fanaticism n eudmhorachd f, dìoghrasachd f
fancy a àraid, annasach
fancy v smaoinich, beachdaich; (desire) miannaich
fancy dress n aodach-brèige m, culaidh choimheach f
fank n (agric) faing f, fang m
fantastic a mìorbhaileach; (incredible) do-chreidsinn
fantasy n sgeul mhìorbhail m; (delusion) sgeul gun bhrìgh
far a, adv fada **f. away** fad' air falbh
  f. more tòrr a bharrachd **f.-fetched** ràbhartach **f.-sighted** fad-fhradharcach
farce n baoth-chluich f, sgeig-chluich f
fare n faradh m; (food) biadh m, lòn m
farewell n soraidh f, slàn m, beannachd (le) f
farm n tuathanas m, baile-fearainn m
  farmhouse taigh-tuathanais m
farmer n tuathanach m
farming n tuathanachas m
fart n braidhm m; (soundless) tùt m v dèan braidhm/tùt
farther adv nas fhaide, na b' fhaide a as fhaide, a b' fhaide

fascinate v tog aire/ùidh, tàlaidh
fascinating a tarraingeach, ùidheil
fascism n faisisteachd f
fascist n, a faisisteach m
fashion n fasan m; (habit) cleachdadh m, gnàths m, dòigh f **in f.** san fhasan **out of f.** às an fhasan v cum, dealbh
fashionable a fasanta, nòsail
fast n trasg f, trasgadh m **f.-day** latha-traisg/trasgaidh m v traisg
fast a luath; (firm) daingeann, teann
fasten v ceangail, dùin **f. on to** gabh grèim air
fat n saill f, sult m, geir f, blona(i)g f; (state) reamhrachd f a reamhar, tiugh
fatal a marbhtach, bàsmhor
fate n dàn m
father n athair m **F.** (relig) an t-Athair
  F. Christmas Bodach na Nollaig m
  f.-in-law athair-cèile m
fathom n aitheamh m
fathom v (understand) tuig, dèan a-mach
fatigue n sgìths f m
fatten v reamhraich
fault n coire f, cron m, lochd m; (geog) sgàineadh m v faigh coire do
faultless a neo-choireach, gun mheang
faulty a easbhaidheach
fauna n ainmhidhean m pl
favour n fàbhar m, bàidh f; (decoration) suaicheantas m v bi fàbharach do, nochd fàbhar do
favourable a fàbharach
favourite n annsachd f, neach as annsa/docha (le) m a ... as annsa/docha (le)
fawn n mang f
fax n facs m v cuir facs (gu)
fear n eagal m, fiamh m
fear v gabh eagal, bi fo eagal
fearful a eagalach
fearless a gun eagal, gun athadh
feasibility n comasachd f **f. study** sgrùdadh comasachd m
feasible a comasach, a ghabhas dèanamh
feast n fèist f, fleadh m, cuirm f
feat n euchd m

feather n ite f, iteag f
feature n (aspect) comharra m; (facial features) aogas m; (landscape) feart-tìre m; (article) alt sònraichte m
February n an Gearran m
federal a feadarail
federation n caidreachas m
fee n (payment) duais f; (charge) cìs f
feeble a fann, anfhann, breòite
feed v biadh, beathaich
feedback n fios air ais m
feeding n beathachadh m; (for animals) fodradh m
feel v fairich, mothaich; (touch) làimhsich, feuch
feeling n faireachdainn f, mothachadh m
feign v leig air/oirre etc
fell v leag, geàrr sìos
fellow n companach m, duine m
fellow pref co-
fellowship n comann m, companas m, caidreabh m
felony n eucoir f
felt n teàrr-anart m
female n bean f, boireannach m a boireann
feminine a banail, màlda; (gram) boireannta
feminist n boireannaiche m
fence n feansa f m, callaid f v feans(aig)
ferment n (confusion) troimh-a-chèile f v (alcohol) brach
fern n raineach f
ferocious a garg
ferocity n gairge f
ferret n feòcallan m, neas f
ferry n aiseag m; (boat) bàt'-aiseig m
fertile a torrach
fertility n torrachas m
fertilizer n todhar m, mathachadh m artificial **f.** todhar Gallta
fervent a dùrachdach, dian, eudmhor
fervour n dèine f, dùrachd f, dìoghras m, eud m
fester v lionnraich, grod
festival n fèis f, fèill f

festive a fleadhach, cuirmeach, meadhrach **f. season** àm a' ghreadhnachais m
festivity n subhachas m, greadhnachas m
fetch v faigh, thoir gu
fetching a tarraingeach, taitneach
fetter n cuibhreach m, geimheal m
feu n gabhail m
feud n falachd f, strì f, connsachadh m v connsaich
feudal a fiùdalach
feudalism n fiùdalachd f
fever n fiabhras m, teasach f
few n beagan m, deannan m a ainneamh, gann, tearc
fiance(e) n leannan m
fibre n (textile) snàithleach m; (in diet) freumhag f
fickle a caochlaideach, gogaideach, leam-leat
fiction n uirsgeul f m, ficsean m
fictional a uirsgeulach, ficseanail
fiddle n fidheall f v bi ri fìdhlearachd, cluich air an fhidhill; (be dishonest) bi ri foill **don't f. with it** na bi a' fideis ris
fiddler n fìdhlear m
fidelity n dìleachd f
fidgety a idrisgeach, fideiseach, beag-fois
field n achadh m, raon m **f.-mouse** luch-fheòir f
fiend n deamhan m
fierce a fiadhaich, garg
fiery a teinnteach, loisgeach; (temper) sradagach, aithghearr/cas (san nàdar) **f. cross** crann-tàra m
fifteen n còig-deug **f. pence** còig sgillinn deug
fifth a còigeamh
fiftieth a leth-cheudamh
fifty n leth-cheud m, caogad m **f. pounds** leth-cheud/caogad not
fight(ing) n sabaid f, còmhrag f v sabaidich, dèan sabaid, còmhraig
figure n figear m; (shape) cumadh m, cruth m; (of speech) samhla m, ìomhaigh f

file n (*tool*) eighe f; (*office*) faidhle m
v lìomh; (*papers*) faidhl(ig), cuir ann am
faidhle
filing n faidhleadh m **f. cabinet** preasa
faidhlidh m
fill n lìon m, sàth m v lìon; (*intrans*) lìon,
fàs làn
filling a sàthach
filling-station n stèisean connaidh/
peatrail m
filly n loth f m
film n film m; (*membrane*) sgannan m
f.-star reul m, reultag film f
filter n sìoltachan m
filth n salchar m
filthy a salach
fin n ite f
final a deireannach n; (*sport*) cuairt
dheireannach f
finalize v thoir gu crìch, crìochnaich
finally adv mu dheireadh thall
finance n ionmhas m, maoineachas
m, airgead m **F. Department** Roinn
an Ionmhais f v maoinich, pàigh,
ionmhasaich
financial a ionmhasail, ionmhasach
f. year bliadhna-ionmhais f
financier n maoiniche m
find v faigh, lorg
fine n càin f v cuir càin (air)
fine a (*quality*) grinn; (*smooth*) mìn;
(*weather*) brèagha **that's f.** tha sin
taghta/glan
finesse n snas m, fìnealtachd f
finger n meur f, corrag f **f.-nail** ìne f
f.-print lorg-meòire f v làimhsich, cuir
meur air
finish n crìoch f, ceann m v crìochnaich,
cuir crìoch air
finished a crìochnaichte, deiseil, ullamh
Finn n Fionnlannach m, (*female*) ban-
Fhionnlannach f
Finnish a Fionnlannach
fir n giuthas m
fire n teine m **f. alarm** inneal-rabhaidh
teine m, clag teine m **f.-engine**
einnsean-smàlaidh m **f.-escape**
slighe teichidh f **f.-extinguisher**

inneal-smàlaidh m **firefighter** neach-
smàlaidh m, smàladair m **firework**
teine-ealain m **fireworks** teintean-ealain
firelighter lasadair-teine m **fireside**
teallach m **firewood** fiodh-connaidh m
by the f. an tac an teine v (*weapons*)
loisg **set f. to** cuir teine ri, cuir na
t(h)eine *etc*
firm n companaidh f m
firm a daingeann, cruaidh; (*steadfast*)
seasmhach, diongmhalta
firmness n daingneachd f, cruas
m; (*steadfastness*) seasmhachd f,
diongmhaltas m, cruas m
first a ciad, a' chiad, prìomh **f. thing in
the morning** a' chiad char sa mhadainn
First Minister a' Chiad Mhinistear m
adv an toiseach, anns a' chiad àite
from f. to last bho thùs gu èis
first aid n ciad-fhuasgladh m
firth n linne f, caol m, caolas m
fiscal n fiosgail m a fiosgail; (*fin*)
ionmhasail
fish n iasg m **f.-farm** tuathanas-èisg m
f.-market margadh-èisg m **f.-shop** bùth-
èisg f v iasgaich, bi ag iasgach
fisherman n iasgair m
fishing n iasgach m **f.-line** driamlach f m
f.-rod slat-iasgaich f
fishmonger n reiceadair èisg m
fissure n sgoltadh m, sgàineadh m
fist n dòrn m
fit n cuairt f, taom m **he took a fit**
thàinig cuairt air
fit a fallain; (*suitable*) iomchaidh,
cubhaidh v dèan freagarrach, cuir an
òrdugh; (*suit*) freagair
fitful a plathach
fitness a fallaineachd f; (*suitability*)
freagarrachd f
fitting a iomchaidh, cubhaidh
five n, a còig a còig **f. people** còignear
f m
fix v suidhich, socraich; (*mend*) càirich
that'll fix him bheir siud air
fixture n rud suidhichte m; (*sport*) gèam
m, maids m **f. list** clàr-gheamannan m
flabby a plamach, bog

flag n bratach f **flagpole** brat-chrann m
flagrant a dalma, ladarna
flagship n prìomh long f a suaicheanta
flail n sùist f
flair n liut m, alt m
flake n bleideag f
flame n lasair f
flammable a lasanta
flan n flana m
flank n slios m, taobh m
flap n flapa m **in a f.** na b(h)oil etc
  v crath
flare n lasair-bhoillsg m
flash n lasadh m, boillsgeadh m
  v deàlraich, boillsg, las
flashback n ais-shealladh m
flashing a boillsgeach
flask n flasg m, searrag f, buideal m
flat n còmhnard m; (residence) flat f m
  f. calm fèath nan eun f m a còmhnard,
  rèidh; (met) neo-bheothail; (mus) maol,
  flat
flatten v dèan rèidh; (mus) maolaich
flatter v dèan brosgal/miodal/sodal
flattering a brosgalach, sodalach
flattery n brosgal m, miodal m, sodal m
flatulence n gaoth f
flavour n blas m
flaw n meang f, gaoid f
flax n lìon m
flea n deargann f, deargad f
flee v teich, tàrr às
fleece n rùsg m; (garment) seacaid-
  bhlàth f
fleet n cabhlach m, loingeas m
flesh n feòil f
flex n fleisg f, càball m
flexibility n sùbailteachd f, subailteachd
  f
flexible a sùbailte, subailte, so-lùbach
flicker v priob
flight n (in air) iteag m, iteal(adh) m;
  (on plane) turas-adhair m; (escape)
  teicheadh m, ruaig f; (of imagination)
  ruith-inntinn f
flimsy a tana, lag **f. excuse** leisgeul
  bochd m
flinch v clisg

fling v tilg, caith
flint n ailbhinn f, spor m
flippant a beadaidh
flirt n beadrach f, gogaid f v beadraich,
  dèan beadradh
flit v èalaidh; (move house) dèan imrich
flitting n (moving house) imprig f,
  imrich f
float n puta m, fleòdragan m
float v flod, bi a'/air fleòdradh, bi air
  bhog
flock n treud m, (birds) ealt(a) f
flood n tuil f, dìle f **f.-gate** tuil-dhoras m
  v còmhdaich le uisge
flooded a fo uisge, bàthte
flooding n tuileachadh m
floor n làr m, ùrlar m **f.-board** clàr ùrlair
  m, bòrd an ùrlair m
floppy disc n clàr-bog m
floral a flùr(an)ach, dìtheanach
florid a ruiteach
florist n reiceadair-fhlùraichean m
flounder n lèabag f, leòbag f
flour n flùr m, min-fhlùir f
flourish v fàs, rach gu math le; (brandish)
  steòrn le
flow n sruth m, sileadh m **f. chart** clàr-
  srutha m, clàr-ruith m **f.-tide** sruth-
  lìonaidh v sruth, ruith, sil
flower n flùr m, dìthean m, blàth m
flowery a flùr(an)ach, dìtheanach
flu n an cnatan mòr m
fluctuate v luaisg, atharraich (bho àm
  gu àm)
fluent a fileanta, siùbhlach **f. speaker**
  fileantach m
fluid n lionn m
fluke n (chance) turchairt m, tuiteamas
  m; (of anchor) fliùt m, pliuthan m;
  (worm) cnuimh f, cruimh f
fluoride n fluoraid m
flurry n othail f
flush n (facial) rudhadh m v fàs dearg;
  (toilet) sruthlaich
fluster v cuir an cabhaig, cuir troimh-a-
  chèile
flute n duiseal f, cuisle-chiùil f
flutter v (fly) dèan itealaich, sgiathalaich

flux n sruthadh m, ruith f
fly n cuileag f; (*fishing*) maghar m
fly a carach, seòlta
fly v rach/falbh air iteig, itealaich;
  (*escape*) teich
flying n itealaich f, sgiathalaich f
foal n searrach m, loth f m
foam n cop m, cobhar m
focus n fòcas m v dèan fòcas air,
  cuimsich air
fodder n fodar m
foe n nàmhaid m, eascaraid m
foetus n ginean m, toircheas m
fog n ceò f m
foggy a ceòthach
foible n laigse bheag f
foil v cuir casg air, bac
fold n filleadh m, preas m; (*animal*)
  buaile f, crò m v paisg, fill
folder n pasgan m
foliage n duilleach m
folk n muinntir f, sluagh m, poball m,
  daoine m pl **f. music** ceòl dùthchasach
  m **folksong** mith-òran m **folktale**
  mith-sgeul m, sgeulachd f **folklore**
  beul-aithris f
follow v lean, thig an dèidh **as follows**
  mar a leanas
following a the f. ... an/am/an t-/a' ... a
  leanas **a f. wind** gaoth na c(h)ùl etc
folly n gòraiche f, amaideas m
fond a (*of*) dèidheil/measail/miadhail air
  a f. mother màthair chaomh f
fondle v cnèadaich, tataidh
font n amar(-baistidh) m; (*type*) clò m
food n biadh m, lòn m
fool n amadan m, gloidhc f **female f.**
  òinseach f v meall, thoir an car à
foolish a gòrach, amaideach
foot n cas f, troigh f; (*of hill*) bonn m,
  bun m; (*in length*) troigh f **f. and mouth
  disease** an galar roil(l)each/ronnach m
football ball-coise m **footpath** frith-
  rathad m **footprint** lorg-coise f **footstep**
  cas-cheum m
for prep do, ri, airson (+ gen); (*time*) fad
  he left this for you dh'fhàg e seo dhut
  wait for me fuirich rium **they'll be here**

for a week bidh iad an seo airson/fad
  seachdain **we paid £100 for it** phàigh/
  thug sinn ceud not air
forbearance n foighidinn f
forbid v toirmisg
forbidden a toirmisgte
force n neart m, cumhachd f m **the
  Armed Forces** Feachdan na Dùthcha
  f pl **undue f.** làmhachas-làidir m v co-
  èignich, thoir air, spàrr (air) **she forced
  her to do it** thug i oirre a dhèanamh
forceful a neartmhor, buadhmhor
ford n àth m; (*between islands*) fadhail f
forecast n ro-aithris f, ro-amas m
  weather f. tuairmse sìde f v dèan ro-
  aithris, dèan ro-amas; (*weather*) dèan
  tuairmse air an t-sìde
forefather n sinnsear m
forefathers na h-athraichean m pl
forefront n fìor thoiseach m **in the f. of
  the campaign** air ceann na h-iomairt
forego v leig seachad, dèan às aonais
forehead n bathais f, maoil f, mala f
foreign a coimheach, cian **F. Office** Oifis
  nan Dùthchannan Cèin f
foreigner n coigreach m
forelock n dosan m, logan m
foreman n gafair m
foremost a prìomh adv air thoiseach
forenoon n ro mheadhan-latha m, ro-
  nòin m
forensic a foireansach
foresee v faic ro-làimh
foresight n ro-shealladh m; (*met*) lèirsinn f
forest n coille f **deer f.** frìth f
forester n forsair m, coilltear m
forestry n forsaireachd f, coilltearachd f
  F. Commission Coimisean na Coille m
foretaste n blasad ro-làimh m, ro-aithne f
foretell v fàisnich
forever adv gu bràth, gu sìorraidh,
  a-chaoidh **f. more** gu bràth tuilleadh
forewarn v cuir air earalas
foreword n ro-ràdh m
forfeit v caill (còir air)
forge n teallach m, ceàrdach f v dealbh
  à meatailt; (*document etc*) feall-dheilbh,
  sgrìobh gu fallsa; (*links etc*) stèidhich

forgery *n* fallsaidheachd *f*, meall-sgrìobhadh *m*
forget *v* dìochuimhnich
forgetful *a* dìochuimhneach
forgive *v* math, thoir mathanas
forgiveness *n* mathanas *m*
fork *n* forc(a) *f*, greimire *m*; (*in road*) gobhal *m*
form *n* cumadh *m*, cruth *m*, riochd *m*, dealbh *f m*; (*document*) foirm *m*; (*mood*) cor *m*, triom *f*; (*seat*) furm *m* **in good f.** an deagh shunnd *v* dealbh, cum, cruthaich, cuir ri chèile
formal *a* foirmeil, riaghailteach
formality *n* foirmealachd *f*, deas-ghnàth *m* **a f.** gnàths *m*
format *n* cruth *m*
formation *n* cumadh *m*, eagar *m*
former *a* a chaidh seachad, a bha ann (roimhe)
formidable *a* foghainteach
formula *n* foirmle *f*
formulate *v* riaghailtich, cuir ri chèile
fornication *n* feise neo-dhligheach *f*
forsake *v* trèig, dìobair, cuir cùl ri
fort *n* dùn *m*, daingneach *f*

fortune *n* fortan *m*, sealbh *m*, àgh *m*
forty *n*, *a* dà fhichead *m*, ceathrad *m* **f. winks** norrag *f*
forum *n* fòram *m*
forward *a* iarrtach, aghach
forward(s) *adv* air adhart *v* adhartaich, cuir air adhart
fossil *n* fosail *f* **f.-fuel** connadh-fosail *m*
foster *v* altraim, àraich
foster-father *n* oide *m*
fosterling *n* dalta *m*
foster-mother *n* muime *f*
foul *n* fealladh *m*
foul *a* salach, gràineil, breun *v* salaich, gànraich; (*sport*) dèan fealladh
found *v* stèidhich, suidhich, bunaitich
foundation *n* stèidh *f*, bunait *f m*; (*org*) stèidheachd *f*
founder *v* theirig fodha
foundry *n* leaghadair *m*, ionad-leaghaidh *m*
fountain *n* fuaran *m*
four *n a* ceithir *a* ceithir **f. people** ceathrar *f m*
fourteen *n*, *a* ceithir-deug **f. fish** ceithir iasg deug

Insight: fort

The Gaelic word *dùn* which derives from the ancient Celtic term *dunon*, a hillfort, is often found as the first element in place names in Scotland and Ireland eg Dundee, Dunblane, Dungannon and Dunkeld. It can also appear as *Dum,* as in Dumfries and Dumbarton.

forth *adv* a-mach, air adhart **from this time f.** o seo a-mach/suas
forthcoming *a* a' tighinn, ri teachd; (*open*) fosgarra
forthright *a* dìreach, fosgailte
forthwith *adv* gun dàil
fortieth *a* dà fhicheadamh
fortify *v* daingnich, neartaich
fortitude *n* tapachd *f*, fiùghantachd *f*
fortnight *n* cola-deug *f*, ceala-deug *f*
fortress *n* daingneach *f*
fortuitous *a* tuiteamach
fortunate *a* fortanach, sealbhach

fourteenth *a* ceathramh deug
fourth *a* ceathramh
fowl *n* eun *m*
fox *n* sionnach *m*, madadh-ruadh *m*
foxglove *n* lus nam ban-sìth *m*
foyer *n* for-thalla *m*
fraction *n* mìr *m*, bloigh *f*
fracture *n* bris(t)eadh *m v* bris(t), bloighdich
fragile *a* brisg, lag
fragment *n* fuidheall *m*, bloigh *f*, criomag *f*, mìr *m*
fragmented *a* bìdeagach, às a chèile

fragrance n cùbhraidheachd f
fragrant a cùbhraidh
frail a lag, anfhann
frame n frèam m, cèis f; (of mind) staid-inntinn f
framework n frèam m
franchise n còir f, còrachd f, ceadachd f
frank a faoilidh, fosgailte
frantic a air bhoil(e), air chuthach
fraternal a bràithreil
fraud n foill f
fraudster n neach-foill m, slaightear m
fraudulent a foilleil, fealltach
fray v bleith, sgaoil
freak n cùis-iongnaidh f a f. event fìor thuiteamas m
freckled a breac-bhallach
freckles n breacadh-seunain m
free a saor; (of charge) an-asgaidh v saor, leig fa sgaoil
freedom n saorsa f, saorsainn f, cead m
freelance a ag obair air a c(h)eann fhèin
freemason n saor-chlachair m
freeze n reothadh m v reoth; (stop) cuir casg air
freezer n reothadair m
freight n luchd m; (charge) faradh m
French n the F. na Frangaich m pl a Frangach; (lang) Fraingis f
Frenchman n Frangach m
Frenchwoman ban-Fhrangach f
frenetic a air bhoil(e)
frenzy n boil(e) f
frequent a tric, minig, bitheanta
frequent v tadhail, tathaich
frequently adv gu tric, gu minig
fresh a (produce) ùr; (atmos) fionnar
freshen v ùraich
freshness n ùrachd f, ùralachd f
fret v luaisg, bi frionasach
friction n suathadh (ri chèile) m, bleith f; (discord) eas-aonta m
Friday n Dihaoine m
fridge n fuaradair m, frids m
friend n caraid m female f. banacharaid f
friendly a càirdeil, dàimheil
friendship n càirdeas m, dàimh f m
fright n eagal m, clisgeadh m

frighten v cuir eagal air were you frightened? an robh an t-eagal ort?
frightening a eagalach
frightful a eagalach, oillteil
frigid a fuar
frill n fraoidhneas m without any frills gun spaidealachd sam bith
fringe n fraoidhneas m, oir f m, iomall m; (hair) logaidh f the Festival F. Iomall na Fèise
frisky a mear, mìreagach
frivolous a faoin, luideach
frock n froga m
frog n losgann m
from prep (bh)o, à f. time to time (bh)o àm gu àm f. dawn till dusk o mhoch gu dubh, a man from Uist fear à Uibhist
front n aghaidh f, aodann m, toiseach m, beulaibh m in f. air thoiseach in f. of air beulaibh (+ gen)
frontier n crìoch f
frost n reothadh m
frosty a reòthte a f. reception fàilte glè fhuar
froth n cop m
frown n gruaim f, sgraing f, greann f
frozen a reòthte, reothta
frugal a glèidhteach, caomhntach
fruit n meas m; (produce) toradh m f.-cake cèic-mheasan f m f. juice sùgh mheasan m
fruitful a torrach; (successful) soirbheachail
fruition n buil f come to f. thig gu buil v
fruitless a neo-thorrach; (met) gun tairbhe a f. expedition/exercise siubhal gun siùcar
frustrate v leamhaich; (hinder) cuir bacadh air
fry v fraighig, praighig
frying-pan n aghann f, praigheapan m
fuel n connadh m
fugitive n fògarrach m
fulfil v coilean
fulfilled a coileanta, sàsaichte
full a làn, iomlan f. to the brim loma-làn f. moon gealach (sh)làn f f.-time làn-thìde, làn-ùine

full stop n (*punct*) stad-phuing f
fulmar m fulmair m
fumble v làimhsich gu cearbach, bi cliobach
fumes n deatach f, smùid f
fun n fealla-dhà f, dibhearsain m, spòrs f
function n feum m; (*of person*) dreuchd f; (*event*) cruinneachadh m v obraich
fund n maoin f, stòr m **funds** ionmhas m, airgead m v maoinich
fundamental a bunaiteach
fundraising n togail-airgid f
funeral n tiodhlacadh m, adhlacadh m, tòrradh m
funnel n pìob-tharraing f; (*on ship*) luidhear m
funny a èibhinn, ait
fur n bian m
furious a fiadhaich, air/fon chuthach
furnace n fùirneis f
furnish v cuir àirneis an; (*provide*) thoir do, uidheamaich

furniture n àirneis f **item of f.** ball àirneis m
furrow n clais f, sgrìob f; (*wrinkle*) roc f, preas m
furry a molach, ròmach
further v cuir air adhart, adhartaich a, adv a bharrachd
further education n foghlam adhartach m
furthermore adv rud eile, a thuilleadh air sin, cho math ri sin, a bhàrr/bharrachd air sin
furtive a fàilidh, lìogach
fury n cuthach m
fuse n fiùs(a) m
fusion n leaghadh m, aonadh m
fuss n othail f, ùpraid f
fussy a àilgheasach, tàrmasach
futile a dìomhain, faoin
future n àm ri teachd m a ri teachd, teachdail **f. tense** an tràth teachdail m

G

gadget n uidheam f, magaid f
Gael n Gàidheal m, (*female*) ban(a)-Ghàidheal f
Gaelic n, a Gàidhlig f (*usually with def art*) a' Ghàidhlig

galley n birlinn f; (*kitchen*) cidsin m
galling a leamh, doimheadach
gallon n galan m
gallop v falbh aig roid; (*on horseback*) luath-mharcaich

Insight: Gael

The term Gael or *Gàidheal* denotes a Gaelic speaker and is used in both Scotland and Ireland. The area where Gaels live is called the *Gàidhealtachd* in Scotland and the *Gaeltacht* in Ireland.

---

gag v cuir glas-ghuib air
gain n buannachd f v buannaich, coisinn; (*reach*) ruig
gait n dòigh-gluasaid f
galaxy n Slighe Chlann Uisnich f, reul-chrios m
gale n gèile m, gaoth mhòr f
gallant a (*chivalrous*) flathail; (*spirited*) meanmnach **a g. effort** oidhirp thapaidh
gallery n gailearaidh f m, lobhta m

gallows n croich f
galore adv gu leòr
gamble v cuir airgead air gheall, dèan ceàrrachas
gambler n ceàrraiche m
gambling n ceàrrachas m
game n gèam m, cluiche f; (*food etc*) sitheann f m
gamekeeper n geamair m
gander n gànradh m, gèadh fireann m
gang n buidheann f m, foireann m

gannet n sùlaire m **g. chick** guga m
gap n beàrn f m; (topog) bealach m
garage n garaids f v cuir ann an garaids
garbage n sgudal m
garbled a troimh-a-chèile
garden n gàrradh m, lios m
gardener n gàirnealair m, gàrradair m
gardening n gàirnealaireachd f, gàrradaireachd f
gargle v sruthail
garlic n creamh m
garment n bad aodaich m
garrison n gearastan m
garrulous a cabach, goileamach
gas n gas m **gas cooker** cucair gas m **gas fire** teine gas m v mùch le gas, sgaoil gas
gash n gearradh m, lot domhainn m, beum m v geàrr, sgor
gasp n plosg m, ospag f v plosg
gastric a meirbheach
gastronomic a sògh-itheil
gate n geata m, cachaileith f
gather v cruinnich, tionail, trus; (money) tog
gathering n cruinneachadh m, co-chruinneachadh m
gaudy a bastalach
gauge n tomhas m v tomhais, meas
gaunt a caol, seang, tana, lom
gay a sunndach, sùgach, aighearach; (homosexual) co-ghnèitheach, co-sheòrsach
gaze v dùr-amhairc
gear n uidheam f, àirneis f; (clothes) trusgan m; (in engine) gìodhar f
gem n seud m, neamhnaid f, leug f
gender n gnè f
gene n gine f
genealogical a sloinnteachail
genealogist n sloinntear m
genealogy n sloinntearachd f
general n seanailear m
general a coitcheann, cumanta **in g.** sa bhitheantas, sa chumantas **G. Election** Taghadh Coitcheann m, Taghadh Pàrlamaid m
generalize v coitcheannaich

generally adv am bitheantas, sa bhitheantas
generate v gin, tàrmaich
generation n ginealach m, glùn f; (creation) gineamhainn m **g. gap** sgaradh nan ginealach m
generator n gineadair m
generic a gnèitheach, coitcheann
generosity n còiread f, fialaidheachd f, fiùghantachd f
generous a còir, fialaidh, faoilidh
genesis n gineachas m, toiseach m
genetic a ginteil
genetics n ginntinneachd f
genial a dàimheil, cridheil, aoigheil
genitals n buill-gineamhainn m pl
genitive a ginideach **the g. case** an tuiseal ginideach/seilbheach m
genius n (person) sàr-ghin m; (quality) sàr-ghineachas m, sàr-chomas m
gentle a ciùin, socair, soitheamh
gentleman n duin(e)-uasal m
genuine a fìor, dha-rìribh
geography n cruinn-eòlas m
geologist n clach-eòlaiche m
geology n clach-eòlas m
geometry n geoimeatraidh m
germ n bitheag f
German n, a Gearmailteach m, (female) ban-Ghearmailteach f; (lang) Gearmailtis f
germinate v ginidich, thoir fàs; (intrans) fàs
get v faigh; (grow) fàs **g. away!** thalla! **get dressed** cuir aodach ort **get rid of** faigh cuidhteas **getting on for ...** a' sreap ri ... **get the better of** faigh làmh-an-uachda(i)r air **get used to** fàs cleachdte ri
ghastly a oillteil, sgriosail
ghost n taibhs(e) f m tannasg m, bòcan m **the Holy G.** an Spiorad Naomh m
ghostly a taibhseil
giant n famhair m, fuamhaire m
giddy a tuainealach; (met) guanach, faoin
gift n tiodhlac m, gibht f
gifted a comasach, tàlantach

gigantic *a* àibheiseach mòr
giggle *v* dèan braoisgeil *Also vn*
　a' braoisgeil, a' cireaslaich
gimmick *n* innleachd *f*
gin *n* (*drink*) sine *f*, Sineubhar *f*; (*trap*)
　ribe *m*
ginger *n* dinnsear *m*
gingerbread *n* aran-crì/cridhe *m*
giraffe *n* sioraf *m*
girl *n* caileag *f*, nighean *f*
girlfriend *n* leannan *m*, bràmair *m*
gist *n* brìgh *f*
give *v* thoir, tabhair **g. up** leig seachad/
　thoir thairis
glacier *n* eigh-shruth *m*
glad *a* toilichte, aoibhinn
gladden *v* toilich, dèan aoibhneach
gladness *n* toil-inntinn *f*, aoibhneas *m*,
　toileachas *m*
glamour *n* riochdalachd *f*
glance *n* sùil aithghearr *f v* grad-amhairc
gland *n* fàireag *f*
glare *n* deàrrsadh *m*, dalladh *m*; (*look*)
　sùil fhiadhaich *f*; (*of publicity*) làn-
　fhollais *f v* thoir sùil fhiadhaich
glaring *a* (*obvious*) làn-fhollaiseach
glass *n* glainne *f* **g.-house** taigh-glainne *m*
glasses *n* glainneachan *f pl*, speuclairean
　m pl, speuclair *m*
gleam *n* boillsgeadh *m v* boillsg, soillsich,
　deàrrs
gleaming *a* boillsgeach, deàrrsach
glee *n* mire *f*, cridhealas *m*
glen *n* gleann *m*
glib *a* mìn-chainnteach, cabanta
glide *v* sigh, gluais gu ciùin
glider *n* glaidhdear *m*, plèan-seòlaidh *m*
glimmer *n* fann-sholas *m*
glimpse *n* aiteal *m*, boillsgeadh *m*,
　plathadh *m v* faigh sealladh
　(aithghearr) de
glisten *v* deàlraich, boillsg
glitter *n* lainnir *f v* deàrrs, boillsg, dèan
　lainnir/drithleann
glittering *a* boillsgeach, lainnireach
global *a* domhanta, cruinne, cruinneil
　g. warming blàthachadh na cruinne *m*
globe *n* cruinne *m* (*f in gen*)

gloom *n* duibhre *f*; (*dejection*) gruaim *f*,
　smalan *m*
gloomy *a* doilleir, gruamach; (*dejected*)
　fo ghruaim, smalanach
glorious *a* glòrmhor, òirdheirc
glory *n* glòir *f*
gloss *n* lìomh *f*; (*explanation*)
　mìneachadh *m v* lìomh; (*explain*) mìnich
glossy *a* gleansach, lìomharra
glove *n* miotag *f*
glow *n* lasadh *f*, blàthachadh *m v* deàrrs,
　las
glue *n* glaodh *m v* glaodh, tàth
glum *a* tùrsach, gruamach
glut *n* cus *m*, tuilleadh 's a' chòir *m*
glutton *n* glutaire *m*, geòcaire *m*,
　craosaire *m*
gnarled *a* meallach, plucach
gnash *v* gìosg
gnat *n* corr-mhial *f*
gnaw *v* creim, cagainn
go *v* falbh, imich, rach, theirig **go away!**
　thalla! **let him go** leig às e **go on/ahead**
　siuthad
goad *v* brod, greas; (*met*) stuig, cuir
　thuige
goal *n* ceann-uidhe *m*; (*in sport*) gòil *m*;
　(*score*) tadhal *m*, gòil *m* **goalkeeper**
　neach-gleidhidh *m*
goat *n* gobhar *f m*
God, god *n* Dia, dia *m*
goddess *n* ban-dia *f*
godly *a* diadhaidh
gold *n* òr *m*
gold(en) *a* òir, òrail, òrdha, òr-bhuidhe
golden eagle *n* fìr-eun *m*, iolaire-
　bhuidhe *f*
goldfish *n* òr-iasg *m*
golf *n* goilf *m* **g.-club** caman goilf *m*;
　(*org*) comann goilf *m* **g.-course** raon
　goilf *m*
golfer *n* goilfear *m*
good *a* math, deagh (*precedes & len n*)
　g.-natured dòigheil, mèinneil **g.-looking**
　brèagha, eireachdail *n* math *m*
goodbye *n*, *interj* slàn le, beannachd le
　g. (to you) slàn leat, beannachd leat
　she said g. to them dh'fhàg i slàn aca

Good Friday n Dihaoine na Ceusta/a'
Cheusaidh/na Càisge m
goodness n mathas m, deagh-bheus f
(**My**) **g.!** A chiall!
goods n bathar m, cuid f, maoin f
g. train trèan bathair m
goodwill n deagh-ghean m, deagh
mhèinn f
goose n gèadh m
gorge n (topog) clais mhòr f, mòr-ghil f;
(gullet) slugan m v lìon craos
gorgeous a eireachdail, riochdail, rìomhach
gorse n conasg m
gospel n soisgeul m
gossip n geodal m, fothal m; (person)
goistidh m v bi a' gobaireachd, bi a'
fothal
gouge (out) v buin à, cladhaich à
govern v riaghail, seòl
government n riaghaltas m, riaghladh m
the G. an Riaghaltas m
governor n riaghladair m
gown n gùn m
grab v faigh/gabh grèim air
grace n gràs m; (prayer) altachadh
m; (quality) loinn f, eireachdas m
v sgeadaich, maisich, cuir loinn air
graceful a grinn
grade n ìre f v cuir an òrdugh, rangaich
gradient n àrdachadh m, ìsleachadh m,
caisead m
gradual a beag air bheag, ceum air
cheum, mean air mhean
gradually adv beag air bheag, ceum air
cheum, mean air mhean
graduate v ceumnaich
graft n nòdachadh m; (fin)
slaightearachd f v nòdaich
grain n gràinne f, gràinnean m, sìlean m;
(coll) gràn m, sìol m
gram n gram m
grammar n gràmar m
grammatical a gramataigeach,
gràmarach
grand a mòr, prìomh (precedes & len n)
that's g. tha sin gasta
grandchild n ogha m
grandfather n seanair m

grandmother n seanmhair f
granite n clach-ghràin f, eibhir f
grant n tabhartas m v (allow) ceadaich,
deònaich; (bestow) builich **g. aid** thoir
tabhartas-cuideachaidh
granule n gràinean m, gràineag f
grape n fìon-dhearc f
grapefruit n seadag f
graph n graf m
grasp v dèan grèim air, greimich, glac
grass n feur m
grasshopper n fionnan-feòir m
grassroots n ìre an t-sluaigh f **at the g.**
aig ìre an t-sluaigh
grate n grèata m v sgrìob, thoir sgreuch
air; (met) bi mì-thaitneach
grateful a taingeil
grater n sgrìoban m
gratify v toilich, sàsaich
gratifying a riarachail, sàsachail
grating a sgreuchach, sgreadach
gratitude n taingealachd f,
buidheachas m
grave n uaigh f **graveyard** cladh m
grave a stòlda, suidhichte
grave accent n stràc fhada m
gravel n greabhal m, grinneal m,
morghan m
gravity n (force) iom-tharraing f; (mass)
dùmhlachd f; (seriousness) sòlaimteachd f
gravy n sùgh feòla m, grèibhidh m
graze v feuraich, ionaltraich, bi ag
ionaltradh; (touch) suath (an)
grease n saill f, crèis f
greasy a crèiseach
great a mòr, àrd
great-grandchild n iar-ogha m
great-grandfather n sinn-seanair m
great-grandmother n sinn-seanmhair f
greatness n mòrachd f; (size) meudachd f
greed n sannt m, gionaiche m
greedy a sanntach, gionach
Greek n, a Greugach m, (female) ban-
Ghreugach f; (lang) Greugais f
green a uaine; (of grass) gorm, glas;
(inexperienced) gorm n (dath) uaine m;
(grass) rèidhlean m, faiche f **G. Party** am
Partaidh Uaine m

greenhouse n taigh-glainne m
greet v fàiltich, cuir fàilte air,
　beannaich do
greeting n fàilte f, beannachadh m
grey a glas, liath **g. area** cùis neo-
　chinnteach f **g.-haired** liath
grid n cliath f
grief n bròn m, mulad m
grievance n cùis-ghearain f
grieve v caoidh
grill n (cooking) grìosach f v grìosaich
grim a mùgach, gnù
grimace n drèin f, gruaim f, mùig m
grin n braoisg f v cuir braoisg air/oirre etc
grind v meil, bleith, pronn
grip n grèim m
grisly a oillteil, dèisinneach
grit n grinneal m, garbhan m; (of
　character) tapachd f
groan n cnead m, osann m, osna f m
　v dèan cnead/osna
grocer n grosair m
groin n loch-bhlèin f
groom n gille-each m; (bridegroom) fear
　na bainnse m
groove n clais f, eag f
grope v fairich, rùraich
gross a garbh, dòmhail; (whole) iomlan;
　(disgusting) sgreamhail
grotesque a suaitheanta, mì-
　dhealbhach, mì-nàdarrach
ground n grunnd m, talamh m, fonn m;
　(foundation) (bonn-) stèidh f; (in piping)
　ùrlar m **grounds** adhbhar m **g. floor** làr
　ìosal m a pronn
groundwork n stèidh f, deasachadh m
group n buidheann f m, còmhlan m
　g. work obair-buidhne f
group v cuir am buidhnean
grouse n cearc-fhraoich f, coileach-
　fraoich m; (complaint) gearan f m
grove n doire f m
grovel v snàig, liùg
grow v fàs, cinn, cinnich, meudaich;
　(trans) thoir fàs air
growl n dranndan m, grùnsgal m
　v dèan dranndan
growth n fàs m, cinneas m, toradh m

grudge n diomb f m, doicheall m v sòr,
　talaich
gruff a gnuadh, durg(h)a, neo-aoigheil;
　(voice) greannach
grumble v gearain, talaich, dèan cànran
grumbling n gearan f m
grunt n gnòsail f, gnòsad f v dèan
　gnòsail/gnòsad
guarantee n urras m, barantas m v rach
　an urras, barantaich
guard n (person) geàrd m, freiceadan m;
　(watch) faire f, dìon m v geàrd, glèidh, dìon
guardian n neach-gleidhidh m, neach-
　cùraim m
guess n tomhas m, tuairmse f, tuaiream f
　v tomhais, thoir tuairmse/tuairmeas
guest n aoigh m **g.-house** taigh-
　aoigheachd m
guidance n stiùireadh m, iùl m,
　treòrachadh m, seòladh m **g. teacher**
　tidsear treòrachaidh m
guide n neach-iùil/treòrachaidh m
　guide-book leabhar-iùil m v seòl, stiùir,
　treòraich
guidelines n seòladh m, stiùireadh m
guile n gò m, gleustachd f
guilt n ciont(a) m
guilty a ciontach
guinea-pig n gearra-mhuc f; (met) ball-
　sampaill m
guise n riochd m
guitar n giotàr m
gulf n camas mòr m, bàgh mòr m; (met)
　astar mòr m
gull n faoileag f
gullet n goile f, sgòrnan m, slugan m
gullible a so-mheallta, furasta an car a
　thoirt às/aiste etc
gulp n slugadh m, glacadh m v sluig,
　glac, glut
gum n càirean m, bannas m; (glue)
　glaodh m, bìth f **chewing gum** guma
　cagnaidh m
gumption n ciall f, toinisg f
gun n gunna m
gunwale n beul(-mòr) m
gurgle n glugan m v dèan glugan/
　plubraich

gush v spùt, brùchd
gust n oiteag f, osag f, cuairt-ghaoth f
gusty a oiteagach, gaothar
gut n caolan m **you've got guts** tha misneach(d) agad v cut, thoir am mionach à
gutter n guitear m; (of fish) cutair m

guy n fear m **come on, guys** siuthadaibh, fhearaibh
gymnasium n lann lùth-chleas f, talla spòrs m
gymnast n lùth-chleasaiche m
gymnastics n lùth-chleasachd f
gynaecology n lèigh-eòlas bhan m
gypsy n siopsach m, giofag f, rasaiche m

H

habit n cleachdadh m, fasan m, àbhaist f, nòs m; (clothing) earradh m, èideadh m
habitable a freagarrach airson còmhnaidh
habitat n àrainn f
habitual a gnàthach adv daonnan, gu gnàthach
hack v geàrr, spòlt, sgolt, sgoch
haddock n adag f
haemorrhage n sileadh/dòrtadh-fala m

dozen leth-dusan **h.-bottle** leth-bhotal m **h.-hearted** meadh-bhlàth **h.-pint** leth-phinnt m **halfway** a, adv letheach-slighe **h.-wit** gloidhc f, lethchiallach m **six and a h.** sia gu leth
halibut n lèabag/leòbag leathann f
hall n talla f m; (hallway) trannsa f
hallmark n comharra m
hallow v coisrig, naomhaich
Halloween n Oidhche Shamhna f

Insight: Halloween

Halloween, *Oidhche Shamhna*, originated in the pagan Celtic festival of *Samhain* when the spirits of the Otherworld were said to mingle with this world. *Samhain* was one of four major Celtic festivals. Halloween occurs on the last night of October and *an t-Samhain* is the Gaelic for November.

hag n badhbh f, sgroidhd f
haggis n taigeis f
haggle v barganaich, deasbair mu phrìs
hail n clach-mheallain f, (hailstones) clachan-meallain pl
hair n falt m, gruag f; (one) gaoisnean m, fuiltean m, ròineag f; (of animals) gaoisid f, fionnadh m **h.-brush** bruis-chinn/fhuilt f **h.-dryer** tiormadair gruaige m
haircut n cliop m, bearradh fuilt m
hairdresser n gruagaire m
hairy a gaoisideach, molach, ròmach, fionnach
hale a slàn, fallain **h. and hearty** slàn fallain
half n leth m **h. past one** leth-uair an dèidh uair **h. a pound** leth-phunnd **h. a**

hallucination n mearachadh m, breug-shealladh m
halo n fàinne solais f; (eg round moon) buaile f, roth f, riomball m
halt n stad m v stad
halter n aghastar m
halve v dèan dà leth air
ham n hama f
hamlet n clachan m
hammer n òrd m v buail le òrd
hamper n basgaid f **food h.** basgaid bìdh
hamper v bac, cuir bacadh air
hamster n hamstair m
hamstring n fèith na h-iosgaid f
hand n làmh; (large) cròg f **handloom** beart-làimhe f **the upper h.** làmh-an-uachda(i)r f v sìn (+ do)

handbag *n* baga-làimhe *m*
handcuff *n* glas-làmh *f v* cuir glas-làmh air
handful *n* làn dùirn *m*; (*number*) dòrlach *m*
handicap *n* bacadh *m*; (*phys*) ciorram *m*
handicapped *a* ciorramach, ana-cothromach
handicraft *n* ceàird *f*
handiwork *n* obair-làimhe *f*
handkerchief *n* nèapraigear *f*, nèapraig(e) *f*
handle *n* (*of door etc*) làmh *f*; (*of impl*) cas *f*; (*of cup, dish*) cluas *f v* làimhsich
handless *a* (*met*) cliobach
handshake *n* crathadh-làimhe *m*
handsome *a* eireachdail, maiseach, riochdail
handwriting *n* làmh-sgrìobha(i)dh *m*
handy *a* deas, ullamh; (*good with hands*) làmhchair(each); (*nearby*) deiseil, goirid
hang *v* croch **h. on!** fuirich!, dèan air do shocair!
hanging *n* crochadh *m*
hangover *n* ceann-daoraich *m*, ceann goirt *m*
hanker *v* miannaich
haphazard *a* tuiteamach; (*untidy*) rù-rà
happen *v* tachair
happiness *n* sonas *m*, toileachas *m*, àgh *m*
happy *a* sona, toilichte, àghmhor
harangue *n* òraid-ghearain *f*
harass *v* sàraich, leamhaich
harassed *a* sàraichte
harassment *n* sàrachadh *m* **sexual h.** sàrachadh gnè *m*
harbour *n* caladh *m*, port *m* **h.-master** ceannard-calaidh/puirt *m v* thoir fasgadh do, ceil
hard *a* cruaidh; (*of understanding*) doirbh *adv* cruaidh, dian **h.-hearted** cruaidh-chridheach **h.-working** dìcheallach
harden *v* cruadhaich, fàs cruaidh
hardly *adv* (bi) gann; cha mhòr gu(n) **there was h. any food left** is gann gun robh biadh air fhàgail **she could h. reach it** cha mhòr gun ruigeadh i air

hardship *n* cruadal *m*, cruaidh-chàs *m*, teinn *f*
hardware *n* bathar cruaidh *m*
hardy *a* cruaidh, calma
hare *n* geàrr *f*, maigheach *f*
harm *n* cron *m*, milleadh *m*, beud *m v* mill, dèan cron/milleadh air
harmful *a* cronail, millteach
harmless *a* gun lochd, neo-lochdach, gun chron
harmonious *a* co-sheirmeach, co-chòrdach, leadarra
harmonize *v* cuir an co-chòrdachd, dèan ceòl-rèimeadh
harmony *n* co-sheirm *f*, co-cheòl *m*, ceòl-rèimeadh *m*
harness *n* acfhainn *f*, uidheam *f v* beairtich; (*utilize*) dèan feum de
harp *n* clàrsach *f*
harper *n* clàrsair *m*
harpoon *n* mòr-ghath *m*
Harrisman *n* Hearach *m* **Harriswoman** ban-Hearach *f*
Harris Tweed *n* an Clò Mòr/Hearach *m*
harrow *n* cliath *f v* cliath
harrowing *a* gaoirsinneach
harsh *a* garg, borb; (*sound*) neo-bhinn
harvest *n* buain *f*, foghar *m* **h. moon** gealach an abachaidh *f*
haste *n* cabhag *f*
hasten *v* greas, dèan cabhag; (*trans*) cuir cabhag air
hasty *a* cabhagach, bras, cas
hat *n* ad(a) *f*
hatch *n* gur *m*; (*on ship*) haidse *f v* guir; (*met*) tàrmaich
hatchet *n* làmhagh *f*, làmhag *f*, tuagh *f*
hate *n* fuath *m*, gràin *f v* fuathaich, gràinich **she hated them** bha gràin aice orra
hatred *n* fuath *m*, gràin *f*
haughtiness *n* àrdan *m*, uabhar *m*
haughty *a* àrdanach, uaibhreach
haul *n* tarraing *f* **a big h.** meall mòr *m v* tarraing, slaod
haulage *n* tarraing bathair *f*, gluasad bathair *m*

haunch *n* leis *f*, leth-deiridh *m*, ceathramh *m*

haunt *n* àite-tathaich *m v* tathaich, tadhal

have *v* bi aig, seilbhich; (*take*) gabh; (*must*) feumaidh **do you h. money?** a bheil airgead agad? **will you h. a drink?** an gabh thu deoch? **you'll h. to call** feumaidh tu tadhal

haven *n* caladh *m*, acarsaid *f*

havoc *n* sgrios *m*, miast(r)adh *m*

hawk *n* seabhag *f m*

hawthorn *n* sgitheach *m*

hay *n* feur *m* **haystack** cruach-fheòir *f* **haycock** coc *f*

hazard *n* cunnart *m*, gàbhadh *m*

hazardous *a* cunnartach

haze *n* ceò *f m*, smùid *f*

hazel *n* calltainn *m* **hazelnut** cnò-challtainn *f a* (*colour*) buidhe-dhonn

hazy *a* ceòthach, sgleòthach, culmach

he *pron* e, (*emph*) esan

head *n* ceann *m*; (*person*) ceannard *m a* àrd-, prìomh **h. office** prìomh oifis *f v* stiùir **h. for** dèan air **headfirst** an comhair a c(h)inn *etc* **headlong** an comhair a c(h)inn *etc*; (*met*) (gu) bras **headstrong** fada na c(h)eann (fhèin) *etc*, ceann-làidir, ceannasach

headache *n* ceann goirt *m*

header *n* (*football*) buille-cinn *f*

heading *n* ceann *m*

headland *n* rubha *m*

headline *n* ceann-naidheachd *m*

headmaster *n* maighstir-sgoile *m*, ceannard-sgoile *m*

headmistress *n* bana-mhaighstir-sgoile *f*, ceannard-sgoile *m*

headphone *n* fòn-cluaise *m*

headquarters *n* prìomh-oifis *f*

headsquare *n* beannag *f*

headteacher *a* ceannard-sgoile *m*

headway *n* adhartas *m*

heal *v* leighis, slànaich *Also intrans*

health *n* slàinte *f* **h. board** bòrd slàinte *m* **h. centre** ionad-slàinte *m* **Your h.!** Slàinte mhath!

healthy *a* fallain, slàn

heap *n* tòrr *m*, càrn *m*, dùn *m v* càrn, cruach

hear *v* cluinn, èist

hearing *n* (*faculty*) claisneachd *f*; (*listening*) èisteachd *f* **h.-aid** inneal claisneachd *m*

hearsay *n* fathann *m*, iomradh *m*

hearse *n* carbad-tiodhlacaidh *m*

heart *n* cridhe *m*; (*centre*) meadhan *m*; (*met*) spiorad *m* **h.-attack** grèim-cridhe *m* **heartbreak** bris(t)eadh-cridhe *m* **heartburn** losgadh-bràghad *m* **heartfelt** *a* dùrachdach, (bh)on chridhe, dha-rìribh

hearten *v* misnich, cùm cridhe ri

hearth *n* cagailt *f*, teinntean *m*, leac an teinntein *f*

hearty *a* cridheil, sunndach

heat *n* teas *m v* teasaich

heated *a* teth, air a theasachadh

heater *n* teasadair *m*, uidheam teasachaidh *f*

heath *n* (*topog*) blàr-fraoich *m*; (*bot*) fraoch *m* **h. burning** falaisg *f*

heathen *n* cinneach *m*, pàganach *m a* pàganta

heather *n* fraoch *m*

heating *n* teasachadh *m*

heaven *n* nèamh *m*, flaitheanas *m* **the heavens** na speuran *m pl* **Good heavens!** Gu sealladh orm!

heavenly *a* nèamhaidh

heavy *a* trom; (*of spirit*) airtnealach

Hebrew *n, a* Eabhra(idhea)ch *m*; (*lang*) Eabhra *f*

Hebridean *n, a* Innse-Gallach *m*

heckle *v* buair, piobraich

heckler *n* buaireadair *m*

hectare *n* heactair *m*

hectic *a* riaslach

hedge *n* callaid *f*

hedgehog *n* gràineag *f*

heed *n* feart *f*, aire *f* **pay no h. to him!** na toir feart air! *v* thoir feart/aire

heel *n* sàil *f*, bonn(-dubh) *m v* cuir sàil air **h. (over)** rach air fiaradh

hefty *a* tomadach, garbh, tapaidh

heifer *n* agh *f m*

height n àirde f; (topog) mullach m, binnean m
heighten v àrdaich, tog suas
heinous a aingidh, gràineil
heir n oighre m **heiress** ban-oighre f
heirloom n seud m, ball-sinnsearachd m
helicopter n heileacoptair m
helium n hilium m
hell n ifrinn f, iutharna f
hellish a ifrinneach, iutharnail; (met) diabhlaidh
helm n falmadair m, stiùir f **helmsman** stiùireadair m
helmet n clogad f m
help n cuideachadh m, cobhair f **helpline** loidhne-taice f v cuidich, thoir cobhair (do)
helper n neach-cuideachaidh m, cuidiche m
helpful a cuideachail
helpless a gun chuideachadh, gun taic
helter-skelter n giorna-gùirne m **go h.** rach na ruith 's na leum
hem n fàitheam m v **hem in** crò, druid
hemisphere n leth-chruinne m (f in gen sg)
hemp n cainb f
hen n cearc f **hen-house** bothag-chearc f
hence adv (time) à seo suas; (place) às a seo; (for that reason) air an adhbhar sin, mar sin
henceforth adv o seo a-mach
henpecked a fon spòig
heptagon n seachd-shliosach m, seachd-cheàrnach m
her pron i, (emph) ise poss pron a, a h- (before vowels)
herald n teachdaire m, earraid m
heraldic a suaicheantach, earraideach
heraldry n earraideas m
herb n lus m, luibh f m
herbal a lusragach
herd n treud m, greigh f, buar m; (person) buachaille m v buachaillich
herdsman n buachaille m
here adv an seo, seo
hereafter adv (bh)o seo a-mach, san àm ri teachd

hereby adv le seo, leis a seo
hereditary a dùth, dùthchasach **h. right** còir oighre f
herein adv an seo
heresy n saobh-chreideamh m, eiriceachd f
heretic n saobh-chreidmheach m
heretical a saobh-chreidmheach
herewith adv seo, le seo, leis a seo
heritable n oighreachail
heritage n dualchas m, oighreachd f
hermit n aonaran m, dìthreabhach m
hernia n màm-sic(e) m
hero n laoch m, gaisgeach m, curaidh m
heroic a gaisgeil
heroin n hearoin m
heroine bana-ghaisgeach f, ban-laoch f
heroism n gaisgeachd f
heron n corra-ghritheach f
herring n sgadan m
herself pron ise, i fhèin
hesitate v stad; (mental) bi teagmhach
hesitation n stad f; (mental) teagamh m
heterogeneous a iol-ghnèitheach, ioma-sheòrsach
hew v geàrr, snaigh
hexagon n sia-shliosach m, sia-cheàrnach m
hexameter n sia-chasach m, meadrachd shia-chasach f
hey! interj hoigh!
heyday n treise f **in his/her h.** an trèine a neairt
hiatus n beàrn f, bris(t)eadh m
hibernation n cadal a' gheamhraidh m
hiccup n (an) aileag f
hidden a falaichte, am falach
hide n seiche f, bian m; (place) àite-falaich m v cuir am falach, falaich, ceil, cleith; (intrans) rach am falach
hide-and-seek n falach-fead m
hideous a oillteil, gràineil
hiding n falach m; (beating) liodraigeadh m, loineadh m **in h.** am falach **h.-place** àite-falaich m
hierarchy n rangachd f, siostam rangachaidh m; (eccl) riaghladh eaglais m **the h.** na h-urracha mòra pl

higgledy-piggledy adv dromach-air-thearrach, triomach-air- thearrach, rù-rà
high a àrd **h. and dry** tioram tràighte **h. court** àrd-chùirt f **h. jump** leum-àrd f m **h. tide** làn-àrd/mòr m **at h. tide** aig muir-làn **h.-powered** mòr-chumhachdach **h. priest** àrd-shagart m **h.-profile** follaiseach **h. school** àrd-sgoil f **h.-spirited** aigeannach, sùrdail **h. spirits** àrd-aigne f, sùrd m **h. water** muir-làn f m
Higher n (exam) Àrd Ìre f
Highland a Gàidhealach **the H. Council** Comhairle na Gàidhealtachd f
Highlander n Gàidheal m, (female) ban(a)-Ghàidheal f
Highlands, the n a' Ghàidhealtachd f **H. and Islands Enterprise** Iomairt na Gàidhealtachd is nan Eilean f
highlight v cuir/leig cudrom air, soillsich
highway n rathad-mòr m
hilarity n àbhachd f, àbhachdas m
hill n cnoc m
hillock n cnocan m, tulach m
hillside n taobh cnuic m, slios beinne m, leitir f, leacann f
hilly a cnocach, monadail
him pron e, (emph) esan
himself pron e fhèin
hind n eilid f
hinder v cuir bacadh air, bac
Hindi n (lang) Hindidh f
hindrance n bacadh m
Hindu n, a Hindeach m, (female) ban-Hindeach f
hinge n bann m, lùdag f
hint n sanas m, leth-fhacal m, oidheam m v thoir sanas, thoir tuairmeas
hip n cruachann f m
hippopotamus n each-aibhne m
hippy n hipidh m
hire n fastadh m v fastaidh, tuarastalaich
  hire-purchase ceannach-iasaid m, ceannach air dhàil m
hirsute a molach
his poss pron a (+ len)
Hispanic a Spàinn(t)each
hiss(ing) n siosarnaich f

historian n eachdraiche m, neach-eachdraidh m
historical a eachdraidheil
history n eachdraidh f
hit n buille f; (on target) bualadh m v buail
hitch n (snag) amaladh m, tuisleadh m v ceangail **h.-hike** sir lioft **h. up** slaod suas
hither adv an seo **h. and thither** an siud 's an seo, a-null 's a-nall
hitherto adv gu ruige seo, fhathast
hive n sgeap f, beachlann f
hoard n tasgaidh f; (treasure) ulaidh f v taisg, glèidh
hoar-frost n liath-reothadh m
hoarse a tùchanach **he was h.** bha an tùchadh air
hoarseness n tùchadh m
hoary a liath
hoax n cleas-meallaidh m
hobble v cuagail
hobby n cur-seachad m
hockey n hocaidh m
hoe n todha m, sgrìoban m v todhaig
Hogmanay n a' Challainn f, Oidhche Challainn f, a' Chullaig f
hoist v tog suas
hold n grèim m; (of ship) toll m v cùm, cùm grèim air **h. back** cùm air ais **h. on** (wait) fuirich tiotan
hole n toll m v toll, tollaich
holiday n latha-saor m, saor-latha m, latha-fèille m
holiness n naomhachd f
holistic a iomlanach
hollow n lag f m, còs m a falamh, fàs; (met) gun bhrìgh
holly n cuileann m
holy a naomh, coisrigte
homage n ùmhlachd f
home n dachaigh f **h.-help** cuidiche-taighe m adv dhachaigh
home economics n eaconamas dachaigh m
homeless a gun dachaigh n daoine gun dachaigh m pl
home rule n fèin-riaghladh m

homesick *a* leis a' chianalas **she was h.** bha an cianalas oirre
homesickness *n* cianalas *m*
homespun *a* gun leòm
homicide *n* murt *m*
homogeneous *a* aon-ghnèitheach, aon-sheòrsach
homosexual *n, a* co-ghnèitheach *m*, co-sheòrsach *m*
homosexuality *n* fearas-feise *f*
hone *v* faobhraich
honest *a* onarach, treibhdhireach, ionraic
honesty *n* onair *f*, treibhdhireas *m*, ionracas *m*
honey *n* mil *f* **honeycomb** cìr-mheala *f*
honeymoon *n* mìos nam pòg *f m* **h. period** àm nam pòg *m*
honeysuckle *n* iadh-shlat *f*
honorary *a* urramach
honour *n* onair *f*, urram *m v* onaraich, cuir urram air; (*fulfil*) coilean
honourable *a* onarach, urramach
hoodie-crow *n* feannag *f*
hoodwink *v* meall, thoir an car às
hoof *n* ladhar *m*, crubh *m*
hook *n* dubhan *m*, cromag *f v* glac le/air dubhan
hooligan *n* miastair *m*, ùpraidiche *m*
hooliganism *n* miast(r)adh *m*
hoop *n* cearcall *m*
hoot *v* goir, glaodh; (*vehicle*) seinn dùdach
hoover *n* sguabadair *m*
hop *n* sìnteag *f v* geàrr sìnteag, falbh air leth-chois
hop(s) *n* lus an leanna *m*
hope *n* dòchas *m v* bi an dòchas **I h.** tha dòchas agam
hopeful *a* dòchasach
hopeless *a* eu-dòchasach, gun dòchas
horde *n* dròbh *m*, greigh dhaoine *f*
horizon *n* fàire *f*, am bun-sgòth *m* **on the h.** air fàire
horizontal *a* còmhnard
hormone *n* hòrmon *m*, brodag *f*
horn *n* adharc *f*, cabar *m*; (*drinking, mus*) còrn *m*; (*car*) dùdach *m*
hornet *n* connspeach *f*

horoscope *n* reul-fhrìth *f*
horrible *a* sgreamhail, oillteil
horrid *a* sgreataidh
horror *n* uamhann *m*, oillt *f*, cùis-uabhais *f*
horse *n* each *m* **h. racing** rèiseadh-each *m* **horseshoe** crudha (eich) *m* **on horseback** air muin eich
horse-fly *n* creithleag *f*
horseman *n* marcaiche *m*
horsemanship *n* marcachd *f*
horse-radish *n* meacan ruadh *m*, racadal *m*
horticulture *n* gàrradaireachd *f*, tuathanas gàrraidh *m*
hose *n* (*stocking*) osan *m*, stocainn *f*; (*for water*) pìob-uisge *f*
hospitable *a* aoigheil, fialaidh
hospital *n* ospadal *m*, taigh-eiridinn *m*
hospitality *n* aoigheachd *f*, fàilte 's furan
host *n* fear-an-taighe *m*, neach-aoigheachd *m*; (*of people*) sluagh *m*
hostage *n* bràigh *f m*, giall *m*, neach am bruid *m*
hostel *n* ostail *f*
hostess *n* bean-an-taighe *f*
hostile *a* nàimhdeil
hostility *n* nàimhdeas *m*
hot *a* teth **hot-water bottle** *n* botal-teth *m*
hotch-potch *n* brochan *m*, butarrais *f*
hotel *n* taigh-òsta *m*
hotelier *n* òstair *m*
hound *n* gadhar *m*, cù-seilge *m*
hour *n* uair *f*
hourly *adv* gach uair, san uair
house *n* taigh *m* **H. of Commons** Taigh nan Cumantan **H. of Lords** Taigh nam Morairean *v* thoir/faigh taigh do **housekeeping** banas-taighe *f* **housewife** bean-taighe *f* **housework** obair-taighe *f*
household *n* teaghlach *m*
householder *n* ceann-taighe *m*
housing *n* taigheadas *m* **h. scheme** sgeama-thaighean *f*
hovel *n* bruchlag *f*, bothan *m*
hovercraft *n* bàta-foluaimein *m*

how *adv, int part* ciamar, cionnas (*before a or adv*) dè (cho), cia **how are you?** ciamar a tha thu? **how old is she?** dè an aois a tha i? **how often?** dè cho tric? **how many are there?** cia mheud a th' ann?

however *adv* ge-tà, gidheadh; co-dhiù

howl *n* donnal *m*, ulfhart *m* *v* dèan donnalaich/ulfhart

hubbub *n* othail *f*, coileid *f*

huddle *v* crùb còmhla

hue *n* dath *m*, tuar *m*, snuadh *m*, lì *f* **hue and cry** othail is èigheach

huff *n* stuirt *f* **in the h.** ann an stuirt

hug *v* glac teann thugad

huge *a* ana-mhòr

hulk *n* (*naut*) bodhaig luinge *f*; (*person*) sgonn mòr (duine) *m*, liodar *m*

hull *n* slige soithich *f*

hum *n* srann *f*, crònan *m* *v* dèan torman/crònan

human *a* daonna **h. rights** còraichean daonna *f pl*

humane *a* caomh, truacanta, daonnadach

humanism *n* daonnachas *f*

humanist *n* daonnaire *m*

humanity *n* daonnachd *f*, nàdar a' chinne-daonna *m*

humble *a* iriosal *v* (*oneself*) irioslaich, ùmhlaich; (*subdue*) thoir fo smachd

humbug *n* amaideas *m*; (*person*) buamastair *m*

humid *a* bruthainneach, tais

humidity *n* bruthainneachd *f*, taiseachd *f*

humiliate *v* tàmailtich, nàraich

humiliating *a* tàmailteach

humiliation *n* irioslachadh *m*, ùmhlachadh *m*

humility *n* irioslachd *f*

humorous *a* ait, àbhachdach, èibhinn

humour *n* àbhachdas *m*; (*mood*) sunnd *m*, càil *f* **in good h.** an deagh thriom/shunnd **to h. someone** airson neach a thoileachadh

hump *n* croit *f* **humpbacked** *a* crotach

hunch *n* giùig *f*, meall *m*; (*idea*) beachd *m*

hundred *n*, *a* ceud *m*

hundredth *a* ceudamh

Hungarian *n*, *a* Ungaireach *m*, (*female*) ban-Ungaireach *f*

hunger *n* acras *m* **h.-strike** *n* stailc acrais *f*, diùltadh-bìdh *m*

hungry *a* acrach

hunt *n* sealg *f* *v* sealg

hunter *n* sealgair *m*

hunting *n* sealg *f*, sealgaireachd *f*

hurdle *n* cliath *f*

hurl *v* tilg

hurley/hurling *n* iomain Èireannach *f*

hurly-burly *n* uirle-thruis *f*

hurricane *n* doineann *f*

hurried *a* cabhagach

hurry *n* cabhag *f* **they were in a h.** bha cabhag orra *v* cuir cabhag air, luathaich; (*intrans*) dèan cabhag, greas (ort/air/oirre *etc*)

hurt *n* goirteachadh *m*, leòn *m* *v* goirtich, leòn

hurtful *a* goirt, cronail

husband *n* fear-pòsta *m*, cèile *m*

husbandry *n* àiteachas *m*

hush *v* sàmhaich, tostaich *interj* ist!

husk *n* cochall *m*, plaosg *m*

husky *a* plaosgach; (*voice*) tùchanach

hustle *n* drip *f* *v* cuir cabhag air, spursaig

hut *n* bothan *m*

hutch *n* bothag coineanaich *f*

hydrant *n* tobar-sràide *f m*

hydro-electric *a* dealan-uisgeach

hydro-electricity *n* dealan-uisge *m*

hydrogen *n* haidridean *m*

hyena *n* hièna *m*

hygiene *n* slàinteachas *m*

hygienic *a* slàinteachail

hymn *n* laoidh *f m*, dàn spioradail *m* **hymnbook** laoidheadair *m*

hype *n* haidhp *f*

hyperbole *n* spleadhachas *m*, àibheiseachadh *m*

hypercritical *a* trom-bhreitheach

hyphen *n* sgrìob-cheangail *f*, tàthan *m*

hypnosis *n* suainealas *m*

hypnotic *a* suainealach

hypnotism *n* suainealachadh *m*

hypnotist *n* suainealaiche *m*
hypochondriac *a* leann-dubhach
hypocrisy *n* breug-chràbhadh *m*, cealg *f*, gò *m*
hypocrite *n* breug-chràbhaiche *m*, cealgair(e) *m*

hypocritical *a* breug-chràbhach, dà-aodannach, cealgach
hypothesis *n* beachd-bharail *f*
hypothetical *a* baralach
hysterical *a* r(e)achdail
hysterics *n* r(e)achd *f*, dol bho rian *m*

I

I *pron* mi, (*emph*) mise
ice *n* deigh *f*, eigh *f*, eighre *f* **the Ice Age** Linn na Deighe *f* **iceberg** beinn-deighe *f*, cnoc-eighre *m* **ice-cream** reòiteag *f* **ice-rink** rinc-deighe *f* **ice-skating** spèileadh-deighe *m*
Icelander *n* Innis-Tìleach *m*, (*female*) ban-Innis-Tìleach *f*
Icelandic *a* Innis-Tìleach
icicle *n* caisean-reòthta *m*, stob reòthta *f*
icing *n* còmhdach-siùcair *m*
icon *n* ìomhaigh *f*
icy *a* reòthte, deighe
idea *n* smaoineas *m*, smaoin *f*, smuain *f* **I've no i.!** chan eil càil/sìon a dh'fhios agam!
ideal *a* taghta, sàr, barrail, sàr-inbheach
identical *a* ionann, co-ionann, ceudna
identification *n* aithneachadh *m*, dearbhadh-ionannachd *m*
identify *v* comharraich, dearbh-aithnich
identity *n* dearbh-aithne *f*, ionannachd *f* **i. card** cairt-aithneachaidh *f*
ideology *n* smaoineasachd *f*, creud *f*
idiom *n* gnàthas-cainnt *m*
idiosyncracy *n* nòsarachd *f*
idiosyncratic *a* nòsarach
idiot *n* amadan *m*, gloidhc *f*
idiotic *a* amaideach
idle *a* dìomhain; (*lazy*) leisg; (*at rest*) na t(h)àmh *etc*; (*thought*) faoin
idol *n* iodhal *m*, ìomhaigh *f*
idolize *v* dèan iodhal de, bi ag adhradh do
idyllic *a* eireachdail
if *conj* ma, nan, nam; (*if not*) mur(a); (*whether*) a/an/am **if they come** ma thig iad **if she does not come** mur(a) tig i **if you had come earlier** nan robh sibh air tighinn na bu tràithe **ask him**

if he is playing faighnich dha/dheth a bheil e a' cluich
igloo *n* taigh-sneachda *m*
ignite *v* cuir teine ri, las
ignition *n* lasadh *m*, losgadh *m*; (*car*) adhnadh *m*
ignoble *a* suarach, neo-uasal
ignorance *n* aineolas *m*
ignorant *a* aineolach
ignore *v* leig seachad
ill *a* tinn, bochd, meadhanach; (*bad*) olc, dona **ill-informed** aineolach, beag-fios **ill-natured** droch-nàdarrach **ill-health** euslaint *f* **ill-treatment** droch làimhseachadh *m*
illegal *a* mì-laghail
illegible *a* do-leughadh, nach gabh leughadh
illegitimate *a* neo-dhligheil; (*person*) dìolain
illiberal *a* (*mean*) neo-fhialaidh; (*met*) cumhang
illicit *a* neo-cheadaichte, mì-laghail
illiterate *a* neo-litearra
illness *n* tinneas *m*, euslaint *f*
illogical *a* mì-sheaghach
illuminate *v* soilleirich
illumine *v* soillsich, soilleirich
illusion *n* mealladh *m*, mearachadh *m*
illustrate *v* dealbhaich; (*show*) seall, nochd
illustrated *a* dealbhaichte
illustration *n* dealbh *f m*; (*example*) eisimpleir *f*
illustrator *n* dealbhadair *m*
illustrious *a* cliùiteach, ainmeil
image *n* ìomhaigh *f*; (*liter only*) samhla *m*
imagery *n* ìomhaigheachd *f*

imaginary a mac-meanmnach, ìomhaigheach

imagination n mac-meanmna m, mac-meanmainn m

imaginative a mac-meanmnach

imagine v smaoinich, smuainich (air); (*wrongly*) gabh na c(h)eann *etc*

imbecile n lethchiallach m

imbibe v òl, deothail

imbue v lìon

imitate v (*mimic*) dèan atharrais air; (*follow*) lean (eisimpleir, dòigh *etc*)

imitation n atharrais f, breug-shamhail m; (*copying*) leantainn f m

immaculate a gun smal, fìorghlan

immaterial a coma **it is i.** chan eil e gu diofar; (*without matter*) neo-nitheach

immature a an-abaich; (*person*) leanabail

immaturity n an-abaichead m; (*person*) leanabalachd f

immediate a grad, ealamh

immediately adv gun dàil, anns a' bhad, air ball

immense a àibheiseach, ana-mhòr

immerse v cuir am bogadh, tum, bog

immersion n tumadh m, bogadh m, cur am bogadh m **i. course** cùrsa bogaidh m

immigrant n in-imrich m

immigration n in-imriche f, imrich a-steach f

imminent a gus teachd, an impis (+ vn)

immobile a neo-ghluasadach

immodest a mì-nàrach, mì-bheusach

immoral a mì-mhoralta

immorality n mì-mhoraltachd f

immortal a neo-bhàsmhor

immovable a neo-ghluasadach, nach gabh gluasad

immune a saor (bh)o, air a d(h)ìon (bh)o *etc*

immunisation n banachdach f

immunity n met (*med*) dìonachd f, dìon m; (*leg*) saorsa f

immunize v dìon (bh)o ghalar, cuir a' bhanachdach air

imp n (*met*) peasan m, deamhain m, spealg (dhen donas) f

impact n buaidh f v **i. on** thoir buaidh air

impair v mill, lùghdaich

impart v com-pàirtich

impartial a ceart-bhreitheach, cothromach, gun leth-bhreith

impasse n staing f

impassioned a lasanta, dùrachdach

impassive a do-fhaireachadh, socair, a' cleith faireachdainn

impatience n mì-fhoighidinn f, cion na foighidinn m

impatient a mì-fhoighidneach

impeach v casaidich (às leth na Stàite)

impeccable a gun smal, gun mheang, foirfe

impede v bac, cuir maill air

impediment n bacadh m, cnap-starra m

impenetrable a do-inntrig; (*met*) do-thuigsinn

imperative n (*command*) cruaidh-òrdugh m; (*urgency*) deatamas m **the i. mood** am modh àithneach m a (*urgent*) deatamach; (*gram*) àithneach

imperfect a neo-choileanta, easbhaidheach

imperial a ìmpireil

impersonal a neo-phearsanta

impersonate v gabh riochd (cuideigin)

impertinent a mì-mhodhail, beadaidh, bleideil

imperturbable a ciùin, somalta, sona

impetuous a bras, cas

impetus n gluasad m, sitheadh m

impinge v buail (air), suath (ri)

implacable a do-rèiteachail, neo-thruacanta

implant v suidhich, cuir a-steach

implausible a mì-choltach

implement n inneal m, uidheam f

implement v thoir gu buil, cuir an sàs

implicate v cuir an lùib

implication n (*impact*) buaidh f, buil f

implicit a fillte, ri thuigsinn

implied a fillte, air a chiallachadh

implore v guidh, aslaich

imply v ciallaich, gabh a-steach

impolite a mì-mhodhail

import *n* brìgh *f*, ciall *f*; (*imports*) bathar a-steach *m*, in-mhalairt *f v* thoir a-steach bathar

importance *n* cudrom/cuideam *m*

important *a* cudromach, brìoghmhor

impose *v* cuir air, leag air, spàrr air

in *prep* ann, an, am, ann an/am/a **in the** anns an/a'/na, sa *adv* (*inside*) a-staigh; (*at home*) a-staigh, aig an taigh; (*motion*) a-steach

inability *n* neo-chomas *m*, dìth comais *f m*

inaccessible *a* do-ruigsinn, do-ruighinn

Insight: in

The preposition *ann* is followed by *an* (or *am* before words beginning in b, f, m or p) when there is no definite article involved eg *ann am mionaid*, in a minute. When the definite article, the, features you use *anns an* or *anns a'* as in *anns an taigh-òsta*, in the hotel, *anns a' mhuir*, in the sea.

---

imposition *n* leagail *f*, sparradh *m*

impossible *a* do-dhèanta, eu-comasach

impostor *n* mealltair *m*

impotence *n* eu-comas *m*

impotent *a* eu-comasach

impound *v* punnd

impoverish *v* dèan/fàg bochd

impractical *a* nach obraich; (*person*) mì-dhòigheil

impress *v* (*someone*) fàg làrach air, coisinn deagh bheachd, drùidh air

impression *n* (*view*) beachd *m*; (*mark*) làrach *f m*; (*book*) deargadh *m*

impressive *a* drùidhteach, foghainteach, suimeil

imprison *v* cuir dhan phrìosan

improbable *a* mì-choltach

impromptu *a* gun ullachadh, an làrach nam bonn

improper *a* mì-iomchaidh

improve *v* leasaich, cuir am feabhas, dèan nas fheàrr; (*intrans*) tog air/oirre *etc*, thig air adhart, rach am feabhas

improvement *n* leasachadh *m*, feabhas *m*, piseach *f*

improvise *v* dèan gun ullachadh

impudence *n* beadaidheachd *f*, ladarnas *m*

impudent *a* beadaidh, ladarna

impulse *n* spreigeadh *m*, togradh *m*

impulsive *a* spreigearra, bras

impurity *n* neòghlaine *f*, truailleadh *m*

impute *v* cuir às leth

inaccurate *a* mearachdach

inactive *a* neo-ghnìomhach, na t(h)àmh *etc*

inadequate *a* easbhaidheach

inadvertently *adv* gun fhiosta

inane *a* faoin

inanimate *a* marbh, gun bheatha

inappropriate *a* mì-choltach, mì-fhreagarrach, neo-iomchaidh

inarticulate *a* mabach, gagach

inattention *n* cion aire *m*, neo-aire *f*

inattentive *a* neo-aireil, cion-aireachail

inaudible *a* nach gabh cluinntinn

inaugurate *v* tòisich; (*with ceremony*) coisrig

inauspicious *a* bagarrach

inbred *a* eadar-ghinte; (*ingrained*) nàdarra, dualchasach

incalculable *a* do-àireamh, thar tomhais

incapable *a* neo-chomasach

incapacity *n* neo-chomas *m*

incendiary *a* loisgeach

incense *n* tùis *f*

incense *v* cuir an cuthach/fhearg air

incentive *n* brosnachadh *m*

inception *n* tùs *m*, toiseach *m*

incessant *a* sìor, daonnan, gun sgur/stad

incessantly *adv* gun sgur/stad

incest *n* col *m*

inch *n* òirleach *f*; (*island*) innis *f*

incident *n* tachartas *m*

incinerate *v* dubh-loisg

incision *n* gearradh *m*

incisive *a* geur, geurchuiseach
incite *v* brosnaich, gluais, spreig
incitement *n* brosnachadh *m*,
piobrachadh *m*
incivility *n* mì-shìobhaltachd *f*,
mì-mhodhalachd *f*
inclement *a* an-iochdmhor; (*weather*)
mosach
inclination *n* (*tendency*) aomadh *m*,
claonadh *m*; (*desire*) iarraidh *m*, togradh
m, deòin *f*
incline *n* leathad *m v* aom, claon; (*desire*)
togair
inclined (to) *a* builteach
include *v* gabh/thoir a-steach
inclusion *n* gabhail a-steach *m*,
in-ghabhail *m* **social i.** in-ghabhail
sòisealta
inclusive *a* a ghabhas a-steach,
in-ghabhalach
incoherent *a* neo-leanailteach, sgaoilte;
(*speech*) mabach
income *n* teachd-a-steach *m* **i. support**
taic teachd-a-steach *f* **i. tax** cìs
cosnaidh *f*
incomparable *a* gun choimeas
incompatible *a* nach freagair, nach tig
air a chèile
incompetence *n* neo-chomasachd *f*
incompetent *a* neo-chomasach
incomplete *a* neo-choileanta,
neo-iomlan
incomprehensible *a* do-thuigsinn
inconceivable *a* do-smaoineachaidh,
thar tuigse
inconclusive *a* neo-chinnteach,
neo-dhearbhte
incongruous *a* mì-fhreagarrach,
mì-choltach
inconsiderate *a* beag-diù, neo-shuimeil,
neo-mhothachail
inconsistency *n* neo-chunbhalachd *f*
inconsistent *a* neo-chunbhalach
inconsolable *a* nach gabh
cofhurtachadh
incontinent *a* (*phys*) neo-dhìonach
inconvenience *n* neo-ghoireasachd *f*
inconvenient *a* mì-ghoireasach

incorporate *v* co-cheangail, gabh
a-steach
incorporation *n* co-cheangal *m*, gabhail
a-steach *m*
incorrect *a* mearachdach, ceàrr
incorrigible *a* thar leasachaidh
incorruptible *a* neo-thruaillidh,
do-choirbte, nach gabh coirbeadh/
truailleadh
increase *n* meudachadh *m*, cinntinn *m*
v meudaich, cuir am meud; (*intrans*) fàs
lìonmhor, rach am meud
incredible *a* do-chreidsinn(each)
incredulity *n* cion creidsinn *m*
increment *n* leasachadh *m*,
meudachadh *m*
incremental *a* beag air bheag, mean air
mhean
incriminate *v* cuir ciont(a) air
incubate *v* guir
incubation *n* gur *m*
incumbent (on) *a* mar fhiachaibh (air)
incur *v* tarraing (air/oirre fhèin *etc*), bi
builteach do
incurable *a* do-leigheas, thar leigheas,
nach gabh leigheas
indebted *a* an comain (+ *gen*), fo
fhiachan (do)
indecency *n* mì-chuibheasachd *f*,
mì-bheus *f*, drabastachd *f*
indecent *a* mì-chuibheasach,
mì-bheusach, drabasta
indecision *n* neo-dheimhinnteachd *f*
indecisive *a* neo-dheimhinnte, eadar dà
bheachd
indeed *adv* gu dearbh(a), gu deimhinne
indefensible *a* neo-leisgeulach, nach
gabh dìon
indefinite *a* neo-shònraichte,
neo-chinnteach
indelible *a* nach gabh dubhadh/
suathadh às
indelicate *a* neo-ghrinn, neo-cheanalta
indented *a* eagach, gròbach
independence *n* neo-eisimeileachd *f*;
(*polit*) saorsa *f*
independent *n* neo-eisimeileach *m a*
neo-eisimeileach; (*polit*) saor

indescribable *a* do-aithris **it's i.** cha
ghabh eachdraidh/luaidh dèanamh air
indestructible *a* nach gabh sgrios
indeterminate *a* neo-chinnteach, gun
sònrachadh
index *n* clàr-amais **i. finger**
sgealbag/calgag *f* **i.-card** cairt-
comharrachaidh *f*
Indian *n, a* Innseanach *m, (female)* ban-
Innseanach *f*
indicate *v* comharraich, taisbean
indication *n* comharra *m* **there is every
i. that ...** tha a h-uile coltas gu ...
indicator *n* taisbeanair *m*
indict *v* cuir às leth, tog casaid an
aghaidh (+ *gen*)
indifference *n* neo-shùim *f,* cion-diù *m*
indifferent *a* coma, neo-shuimeil,
coingeis
indigenous *a* dùthchasach
indigent *a* ainniseach
indigestion *n* cion-cnàmh *m,*
dìth-cnàmhaidh *f*
indignant *a* diombach, feargach
indignation *n* diomb *f m,* corraich *f*
indignity *n* tàmailt *f*
indigo *n* guirmean *m*
indirect *a* neo-dhìreach, fiar
indiscipline *n* cion smachd *m,* mì-rian *m*
indiscreet *a* neo-chrìonna, mì-
chùramach
indiscretion *n* neo-chrìonnachd *f*
indiscriminate *a (random)* neo-
chuimsichte; *(jumbled)* am measg a
chèile
indispensable *a* riatanach,
neo-sheachanta
indisposed *a* tinn, bochd
indistinct *a* neo-shoilleir
indistinguishable *a* nach gabh
aithneachadh/dealachadh (bh)o chèile;
(vision) doilleir
individual *n* urra *f,* neach (air leth) *m,*
pearsa *m a* fa leth, air leth, pearsanta
individually *adv* air leth, fa leth
indolent *a* leisg, dìomhain
indomitable *a* do-chlaoidhte
indoor(s) *a, adv* a-staigh

induce *v* adhbhraich, thoir air; *(birth)*
thoir air adhart
inducement *n* brosnachadh *m*
induct *v (educ)* oidich; *(eccl)* pòs (ri
coitheanal)
induction *n (educ)* oideachadh *m,*
inntrigeadh *m; (eccl)* pòsadh *m*
indulge *v* leig le, toilich
indulgence *n* gèilleadh *m,* toileachadh
m; (favour) cead *m* **i. in** tromachadh air
industrial *a* tionnsgalach,
gnìomhachasach **i. estate** raon
gnìomhachais *m*
industrialist *n* tionnsgalaiche *m,* neach-
gnìomhachais *m*
industrious *a* dèanadach, gnìomhach
industry *n* gnìomhachas *m,* tionnsgal *f;
(effort)* saothair *f*
inebriated *a* air mhisg, fo/air dhaorach
inedible *a* nach gabh ithe
ineffective *a* neo-èifeachdach,
neo-bhuadhach
ineffectual *a* neo-tharbhach
inefficiency *n* neo-èifeachdas *m*
inefficient *a* neo-èifeachdach/tharbhach
inelegant *a* mì-loinneil
ineligible *a* neo-cheadaichte,
neo-iomchaidh
inept *a* leibideach
inequality *n* neo-ionannachd *f*
inequitable *a* mì-cheart,
mì-chothromach
inert *a* na t(h)àmh *etc,* marbhanta
inertia *n* tàmhachd *f; (in person)*
leisg(e) *f*
inestimable *a* os cionn luach, nach gabh
a luach
inevitable *a* do-sheachanta
inexcusable *a* neo-leisgeulach
inexpensive *a* saor
inexperience *n* cion eòlais *m*
inexperienced *a* neo-eòlach, gun eòlas,
neo-chleachdte
inexplicable *a* do-thuigsinn, nach gabh
tuigsinn
infallible *a* neo-mhearachdach
infamous *a* maslach, mì-chliùiteach
infamy *n* masladh *m,* mì-chliù *m*

infant n naoidhean m, pàiste beag m, leanaban m
infantry n coisridh f, saighdearan-coise m pl
infatuation n dalladh m, cur fo gheasaibh m **he had an i. for her** bha e air a dhalladh leatha
infect v cuir galar/tinneas air, truaill
infection n galar-ghabhail m
infectious a gabhaltach **i. disease** tinneas gabhaltach m
infer v co-dhùin
inference n co-dhùnadh m
inferior a nas miosa; (in quality) bochd, truagh; (in status) ìochdarach
infertile a neo-thorrach, aimrid
infidel n ana-creidmheach m
infidelity n neo-dhìlseachd f
infiltrate v èalaidh (a-steach)
infinite a neo-chrìochnach, suthainn
infinity n neo-chrìochnachd f
infinitive n neo-fhinideach m **the i. mood** am modh neo-fhinideach f m
infirm a anfhann
infirmary n taigh-eiridinn m
infirmity n laige f, anfhannachd f, breòiteachd f
inflame v (met) fadaidh, cuir suidse ri; (lit) cuir teine ri
inflammable a lasarra, lasanta
inflammation n (med) at m, teas-at m, ainteas m; (lit) lasadh m
inflammatory a (met) buaireasach; (med) le at; (lit) loisgeach
inflate v sèid (suas), cuir gaoth an; (intrans) at
inflated a air at
inflation n sèideadh m; (fin) atmhorachd f
inflexible a rag, neo-lùbach
inflict v leag … air
influence n buaidh f **under the i. of alcohol** fo bhuaidh na dibhe, fon mhisg v thoir buaidh air, buadhaich air
influential a buadhach, aig a bheil buaidh
influenza n an cnatan mòr m
influx n sruth (a-steach) m

inform v innis (do), thoir brath (do), cuir/ leig/thoir fios (gu/do)
informal a neo-fhoirmeil
information n fiosrachadh m, brath m **i.-centre** ionad-fiosrachaidh m **i. and communications technology (ICT)** teicneòlas fiosrachaidh is conaltraidh (TFC) m
informed a fiosrach, fiosraichte
informer n neach-brathaidh m, brathadair m
infrastructure n bun-structair/eagar m
infrequent a ainneamh
infringe v bris(t) a-steach air
infringement n bris(t)eadh a-steach m
infuriate v cuir air bhoil(e), cuir corraich/ cuthach air
infuse v lìon (le), cuir … air feadh
ingenious a innleachdach, teòma
ingenuity n innleachd f, teòmachd f
ingrained a fuaighte
ingratiate v lorg fàbhar
ingredient n tàthchuid f
inhabit v àitich, tuinich, tàmh (an)
inhabitant n neach-àiteachaidh m pl luchd-àiteachaidh, muinntir (an àite) f
inhale v tarraing anail, gabh a-steach leis an anail
inherent a dualach, in-ghnèitheach
inherit v sealbhaich/faigh mar oighreachd
inheritance n oighreachd f, sealbh m; (cult) dualchas m
inhibit v caisg, cùm air ais, cuir stad air
inhibition n casg m, bacadh m, cuing (san nàdar) f **she had no inhibitions about singing on stage** cha robh leisge sam bith oirre seinn air àrd-ùrlar
inhospitable a mosach, neo-fhialaidh
inhuman a mì-dhaonna
inhumane a an-iochdmhor
inhumanity n an-iochdmhorachd f
inimitable a gun choimeas
iniquitous a aingidh
iniquity n aingidheachd f, olc m
initial n ciad litir f **my initials** ciad litrichean m' ainm a ciad, tùsail

initially adv sa chiad dol a-mach, aig toiseach gnothaich

initiate v tòisich, cuir air bhonn/chois; (into an order) gabh a-steach; (into a skill) teagaisg, oidich

initiative n iomairt f, tionnsgnadh m

inject v (med) sàth-steallaich; (met) cuir a-steach do, cuir ri

injection n sàth-stealladh m **i. of** cur a-steach m, cur ris m

injunction n àithne f, òrdugh m

injure v goirtich, ciùrr, dèan dochann air, leòn

injury n goirteachadh m, dochann m, leòn m

injustice n ana-ceartas m

ink n dubh m, inc f m

inland a a-staigh san tìr

inmate n neach fo chùram/ghlais m

inn n taigh-seinnse/òsta m

innate a dualach, nàdarra

inner a as fhaide/a b' fhaide a-staigh

innocence n neoichiontachd f, ionracas m

innocent a neoichiontach, ionraic

innocuous a neo-lochdach, neochoireach

innovation n ùr-ghnàthachadh m, nuadhas m

innovative a ùr-ghnàthach

innovator n ùr-ghnàthadair m, nuadhasair m

innuendo n fiar-shanas m, leth-iomradh m

innumerable a gun àireamh, do-àireamh

inoculate v dìon (bh)o ghalar

inoculation n dìon (bh)o ghalar m

inoffensive a neo-lochdach

inoperable a (med) do-leigheas, nach gabh leigheas

inopportune a mì-thràthail

inordinate a neo-chuimseach **an i. length of time** ùine gun chiall f

input n cur a-steach m v cuir a-steach

inquest n rannsachadh m, sgrùdadh m

inquire v feòraich, faighnich

inquiring a rannsachail

inquiry n rannsachadh m; (query) ceist f **public i.** rannsachadh poblach

inquisitive a ceasnachail, farraideach

insane a às a c(h)iall etc, às a rian etc

insanity n cuthach m, dìth-cèille f m; (slang) crac m

insatiable a nach gabh sàsachadh/riarachadh

inscribe v sgrìobh air

inscription n sgrìobhadh m; (statue etc) snaigheadh m

insect n biastag f, meanbh-fhrìde f

insecure a neo-thèarainte

insecurity n neo-thèarainteachd f

insemination n sìolachadh m

inseparable a do-sgaradh, nach gabh dealachadh

insert v cuir a-steach

inside n an taobh/leth a-staigh m **i.-out** caoin air ascaoin, an taobh a-staigh a-muigh prep am broinn (+ gen) adv a-staigh

insidious a lìogach, sniagach; (dangerous) cunnartach

insight n lèirsinn f

insignia n suaicheantas m

insignificant a suarach, beag-seagh

insincere a neo-threibhdhireach, neo-dhùrachdach

insincerity n neo-threibhdhireas m, neo-dhùrachd f

insinuate v leth-thuaileasaich

insipid a blian, gun bhlas

insist v cùm a-mach **i. on** sìor iarr **he insists on a dram every night** feumaidh e drama fhaighinn a h-uile h-oidhche

insolence n stràicealachd f

insolent a stràiceil

insoluble a do-sgaoilte; (problem) do-rèite, nach gabh rèiteach/f(h)uasgladh

insolvent a briste, air bris(t)eadh air/oirre etc

insomnia n bacadh-cadail m

inspect v sgrùd

inspection n sgrùdadh m

inspector n neach-sgrùdaidh m, sgrùdaire m

inspiration *n* sàr-smaoin *f*; (*source of*) brosnachadh *m*
inspire *v* brosnaich, spreag
inspiring *a* brosnachail, spreagail
instability *n* cugallachd *f*, neo-sheasmhachd *f*
instal *v* (*object*) cuir a-steach; (*person*) cuir an dreuchd, suidhich
installation *n* (*of object*) cur a-steach *m*; (*person*) cur an dreuchd *m*, suidheachadh *m*
instalment *n* cuibhreann *f m*, earrann *f*
instance *n* eisimpleir *f m* **for i.** mar eisimpleir **in the first i.** anns a' chiad àite **in this i.** an turas seo
instant *n* tiota *m a* grad, an làrach nam bonn
instantly *adv* sa bhad, san spot
instead *adv* an àite, an àite sin
instigate *v* cuir air bhonn, tòisich; (*incite*) piobraich
instigation *n* cur air bhonn *m*, tòiseachadh *m*; (*incitement*) piobrachadh *m*
instil *v* teagaisg, cuir an inntinn
instinct *n* gnèithealachd *f*, nàdar *m*
instinctive *a* gnèitheach, nàdarrach, a rèir gnè
institute *n* stèidheachd *f v* cuir air chois, stèidhich
institution *n* (*act of*) stèidheachadh *m*; (*place*) ionad *m*, stèidheachd *f*; (*practice*) riaghailt *f*
instruct *v* teagaisg, ionnsaich
instruction *n* teagasg *m*, ionnsachadh *m*; (*order*) òrdugh *m*, stiùireadh *m*
instructor *n* neach-teagaisg *m*
instrument *n* (*tool*) inneal *m*; (*mus*) ionnsramaid *f*, inneal-ciùil *m*; (*means*) meadhan *m*
instrumental *a* (*mus*) ionnsramaideach **i. in** mar mheadhan air
insubordinate *a* eas-umhail
insufferable *a* doirbh a ghiùlan, doirbh cur suas leis; (*met*) maslach
insufficient *a* goirid, geàrr, gann
insular *a* eileanach; (*met*) cumhang

insulate *v* còmhdaich **i. from** dealaich, cuir air leth
insulated *a* còmhdaichte **i. from** dealaichte, air a chur air leth
insult *n* ailis *f*, beum *m v* ailisich, thoir beum/droch bheul do
insulting *a* beum(n)ach, tàireil
insurance *n* àrachas *m* **i. claim** tagradh àrachais *m* **i. company** companaidh àrachais *f m* **i. policy** poileasaidh àrachais *m*
insure *v* thoir àrachas air, faigh/thoir urras air
insured *a* fo àrachas
insurrection *n* ar-a-mach *m*
intact *a* slàn, iomlan
intake *n* gabhail a-steach *f*
intangible *a* nach gabh làimhseachadh/fhaicinn, do-bheantainn
integral *a* (*intact*) slàn, coileanta, riatanach (*do*)
integrate *v* aonaich **i. with** fill a-steach còmhla ri
integrated *a* aonaichte, fighte-fuaighte
integrity *n* treibhdhireas *m*, ionracas *m*; (*wholeness*) iomlanachd *f*
intellect *n* inntinn *f*
intellectual *a* inntleachdail *n* inntleachdach *m*
intelligence *n* tuigse *f*; (*report*) aithris *f*, fiosrachadh *m*; (*covert*) fàisneis *f*
intelligent *a* inntleachdach, tùrail
intelligible *a* so-thuigsinn
intemperate *a* mì-stuama, ana-measarra
intend *v* dùilich, cuir roimhe/roimhpe *etc*, rùnaich
intended *a* san amharc
intense *a* dian, teann
intensify *v* teinnich, geuraich
intensity *n* dèine *f*, teinne *f*
intensive *a* dian **i. care** dlùth-chùram *m*
intent *n* rùn *m*
intention *n* rùn *m*, dùil *f*
intentional *a* a dh'aon obair/ghnotha(i)ch
intentionally *adv* a dh'aon ghnotha(i)ch
inter *v* adhlaic, tiodhlaic
inter- *pref* eadar-

interaction n eadar-obrachadh m
interactive a eadar-ghnìomhach
intercede v dèan eadar-ghuidhe
intercept v ceap, stad san t-slighe
interchange n iomlaid f, malairt f
interchangeable a co-iomlaideach, co-mhalairteach, a ghabhas iomlaid/malairt
intercourse n (social) co-chomann m, comhluadar m; (sexual) feis(e) f
interdependent a eadar-eisimeileach, an eisimeil a chèile
interdict n toirmeasg/bacadh (lagha) m
interest n ùidh f; (fin) riadh m; (stake) earrann f, pàirt f m **i. rate** ìre an rèidh f v gabh/tog ùidh
interesting a ùidheil, inntinneach
interface n eadar-aghaidh f
interfere v gabh gnotha(i)ch ri, buin ri
interference n gabhail gnotha(i)ch ri m, buntainn ri m; (atmos) riasladh m
interim n eadar-àm m a eadar-amail
In the I. anns an eadar-àm
interior n an leth/taobh a-staigh m
interject v geàrr a-steach, caith a-steach
interlacing a eadar-fhighte
interlink v naisg, ceangail ri chèile
interlocking a co-naisgte, co-cheangailte
interlude n eadar-chluiche f
intermediate a eadar-mheadhanach, meadhanach
interment n adhlacadh m, tiodhlacadh m
interminable a neo-chrìochnach, gun chrìoch
intermittent a (bh)o àm gu àm, air is dheth
internal a a-staigh
international n eadar-nàiseanail m a eadar-nàiseanta
internecine a co-sgriosail
internet n eadar-lìon m **the I.** an t-Eadar-lìon
interpret v mìnich; (translate) eadar-theangaich
interpretation n mìneachadh m; (translation) eadar-theangachadh m

interpreter n neach-mìneachaidh m, mìniche m; (translator) eadar-theangaiche m
interrogate v cruaidh-cheasnaich
interrogation n cruaidh-cheasnachadh m
interrupt v bris(t) a-steach (air); (halt) cuir casg/stad air
interruption n bris(t)eadh a-steach m; (halting) casg m, stad m
intersect v geàrr tarsainn (a chèile), trasnaich
intersperse v sgap am measg
intertwined a eadar-thoinnte
interval n eadar-ùine f, eadar-àm m; (school) àm-cluiche m, pleidhe m
intervene v rach san eadraiginn, thig eadar
intervention n tighinn eadar m
interview n agallamh m v dèan agallamh le
interviewer n agallaiche m, ceasnaiche m, neach-ceasnachaidh m
intestine(s) n caolan(an) m; (animal only) greallach f
intimacy n dlùth-chaidreabh m
intimate a dlùth-chaidreach, fìor eòlach
intimate v ainmich, inn(i)s
intimation n ainmeachadh m, fios m
intimidate v cuir fo eagal
into adv do, a-steach do
intolerable a do-ghiùlan, nach gabh fhulang **i. pain** cràdh eagalach/thar tomhais m
intolerant a neo-fhulangach, cumhang na s(h)ealladh etc
intonation n fonn cainnt m
intoxicated a air mhisg, air an daoraich, fo bhuaidh na dibhe
intoxication n misg f, daorach f
intractable a nach gabh f(h)uasgladh, neo-fhuasglach
intrepid a dàna, gaisgeil, tapaidh
intricate a toinnte, mion
intrigue n cluaineas m, cuilbheart f
intrinsic a gnèitheach, ann fhèin etc
introduce v cuir an aithne; (subject) tog, thoir iomradh air

introduction n cur an aithne m; (of subject) togail f; (in book) ro-ràdh m

introvert a neo-fhosgarra, dùr

intrude v bris(t)/brùth a-steach

intuition n im-fhios m

inundate v cuir fo uisge **we were inundated with requests** bha sinn a' dol fodha le iarrtasan

invade v thoir ionnsaigh air, bris(t) a-steach

invalid n euslainteach m

invalid a neo-bhrìgheil, neo-dhligheach

invalidate v cuir an neo-bhrìgh

invaluable a thar luach, nach gabh luach a chur air

invariably adv an-còmhnaidh, daonnan; (very frequently) mar as trice

invasion n ionnsaigh f m, bris(t)eadh a-steach m

inveigle v meall, thoir a thaobh

invent v innlich, tionnsgail

invention n innleachd f, tionnsgal m

inventive a innleachdach, tionnsgalach

inventor n innleadair m, tionnsgalair m

inventory n cunntas f m, clàr-seilbhe/ stuthan m

invert v cuir bun-os-cionn, tionndaidh

invest v (fin) cuir an seilbh, cuir airgead an

investigate v rannsaich, sgrùd

investigation n rannsachadh m, sgrùdadh m

investment n (fin) cur an seilbh m, airgead-seilbhe/tasgaidh m

investor n neach-tasgaidh m

invidious a fuath-dhùsgach; (unfair) mì-cheart

invigilate v cùm sùil air, bi ri faire

invincible a do-cheannsachail, nach gabh ceannsachadh

invisible a neo-fhaicsinneach

invitation n cuireadh m, fiathachadh m

invite v iarr, thoir cuireadh (do), thoir fiathachadh (do)

inviting a tarraingeach

invoice n cunntas f m, fairdeal m

involuntary a neo-shaor-thoileach, an aghaidh toil

involve v gabh a-steach **were you involved in it?** an robh thusa na lùib/ an sàs ann?

irascible a crosta, feargach, greannach

irate a feargach, fiadhaich

ire n fearg f, corraich f

iris n (of eye) cearcall na sùla m; (plant) sealastair f m, seileastair f m

Irish n (lang) a' Ghaeilge f, Gàidhlig na h-Èireann f a Èireannach

Irishman n Èireannach m **Irishwoman** ban-Eireannach f

irksome a leamh, sàraichte

iron n iarann m a iarainn **I. Age** Linn an Iarainn f **i. ore** clach-iarainn f v iarnaig

ironic(al) a ìoranta

irony n ìoranas m

irrational a neo-reusanta

irreconcilable a do-rèiteachail, nach gabh toirt gu chèile

irregular a neo-chunbhalach, neo-riaghailteach **i. verb** gnìomhair neo-riaghailteach m

irregularity n neo-chunbhalachd f, neo-riaghailteachd f

irrelevant a nach buin dhan/ris a' ghnothach, neo-bhointealach, mì-fhreagarrach

irreparable a nach gabh càradh/ leasachadh

irrepressible a nach gabh casg(adh)

irresistible a nach gabh diùltadh

irrespective adv a dh'aindeoin

irresponsible a neo-chùramach, gun chùram

irresponsibility n cion cùraim m, dìth cùraim f m

irretrievable a nach gabh lorg/sàbhaladh

irreverence n eas-urram m

irreverent a eas-urramach

irreversible a nach gabh atharrachadh

irrevocable a nach gabh tilleadh/ atharrachadh

irrigation n uisgeachadh m

irritable a crosta, frionasach, greannach

irritate v cuir caise/frionas air

irritation n crostachd f, frionas m

is v tha, is (See verb **to be** in Grammar)

Islam n an creideamh Ioslamach m; (people) a' mhuinntir Ioslamach f
Islamic a Ioslamach
island n eilean m, innis f
islander n eileanach m
Islay person n Ìleach m, (female) ban-Ìleach f
isolated a air leth, iomallach, lethoireach
isolation n aonarachd f, lethoireachd f **in i.** leis fhèin
Israeli n, a Israelach/Iosaraileach m
issue n ceist f, cùis f; (offspring) clann f, sliochd m; (liter) iris f v bris(t)/thig/cuir a-mach, lìbhrig

isthmus n tairbeart f, aoidh f
it pron e, i
Italian n, a Eadailteach m, (female) ban-Eadailteach f; (lang) Eadailtis f
italics n clò eadailteach m
itch n tachas m; (desire) miann f m
itchy a tachasach
item n nì m, rud m
itinerant a siùbhlach, siubhail
itinerary n clàr-siubhail m
its poss pron a
itself pron e/i fhèin
ivory n ìbhri f
ivy n eidheann f

J

jackdaw n cathag f
jacket n seacaid f
Jacobite n Seumasach m **J. Rebellion/Rising** Ar-a-mach nan Seumasach m
jade n sèad f
jaded a seachd sgìth
jag n briogadh m; (notch) eag f
jagged/jaggy a eagach
jail n prìosan m
jam n silidh m; (congestion) dùmhlachd f **in a jam** ann an staing **jam-jar** crogan-silidh m v brùth, dùmhlaich **my fingers got jammed** chaidh mo mheòirean a ghlacadh
jangle v dèan gleadhraich/gliongadaich
janitor n dorsair m, neach-cùraim sgoile m
January n am Faoilleach/Faoilteach m
Japanese n, a Iapanach, (female) ban-Iapanach f
jar n crogan m, sileagan m
jargon n ceàird-chainnt f
jaundice n a' bhuidheach f, an tinneas buidhe m
jaunt n sgrìob f, splaoid f
javelin n sleagh f
jaw n peirceall m, giall f
jealous a eudmhor **she was j. of her** bha i ag eudach rithe
jealousy n eud m, eudmhorachd f
jeans n dinichean f pl

jeer v mag (air), dèan magadh (air)
Jehovah n Iehòbhah m
jelly n slaman-milis m
jellyfish n muir-tiachd f m
jeopardy n cunnart m, gàbhadh m
jerk n tarraing obann f, tulgag f v tarraing gu h-obann
jersey n geansaidh m
jest n abhcaid f, fealla-dhà f
jet n steall m; (plane) seit (phlèan) m
jettison v tilg a-mach, cuir bhuat
jetty n cidhe m, laimrig f
Jew n Iùdhach m **Jewess** ban-Iùdhach f
jewel n seud m, leug f, àilleag m
jeweller n seudair m
jewellery n seudraidh f
Jewish a Iùdhach
jig n (tune) port-cruinn m; (dance) sige f
jigsaw n mìrean-measgaichte f pl
jilt v trèig, faigh cuidhteas (leannan)
jingle n gliong m; (ad) rannag f
job n obair f, cosnadh m **job-centre** ionad-obrach m **job description** dealbh-obrach f m
jockey n marcach m, marcaiche m
jocular a spòrsail, abhcaideach
jog v bi a' trotan, ruith; (nudge) put; (memory) brod cuimhne
join v ceangail, aonaich, cuir ri chèile, tàth; (eg club) gabh ballrachd an
joiner n saor m

joinery n saorsainneachd f
joint n alt m; (of meat) spòlt m a co-, coitcheann, co-phàirteach
jointly adv cuideachd, le chèile, an co-bho(i)nn
joist n sail f, spàrr m, cas-ceangail f
joke, joking n abhcaid f, fealla-dhà f **I was only joking** cha robh mi ach ri spòrs
jolly a cridheil, aighearach
jolt n crathadh m, tulgadh m
jostle v put, brùth (a-null 's a-nall)
jotter n diotar m, leabhran-sgrìobhaidh m
journal n (diary) leabhar-latha m; (magazine) iris f
journalism n naidheachdas m
journalist n neach-naidheachd m, naidheachdair m
journey n turas m, cuairt f
jovial a fonnmhor, suilbhir
jowl n giall f, bus m
joy n aoibhneas m, gàirdeachas m, sòlas m
joyful a aoibhneach, ait, sòlasach
jubilant a luathghaireach, sàr-thoilichte
jubilee n iubailidh f
judge n britheamh m v thoir breith, breithnich, meas
judgement n breith f, breithneachadh m, binn f **J. Day** Latha a' Bhreitheanais m, Latha Luain m
judicial a laghail, a rèir an lagha, breitheach
judicious a tuigseach, geurchuiseach
jug n siuga f m

juggle v làmh-chleasaich
jugular n fèith sgòrnain f
juice n sùgh m; (essence) brìgh f
juicy a sùghmhor; (pithy) brìoghmhor
July n an t-Iuchar m
jumble n measgachadh m, brochan m **j. sale** reic treal(l)aich m v cuir troimh-a-chèile, measgaich
jump n leum m, sùrdag f **standing j.** cruinn-leum m f v leum
jumper n (sport) leumadair m; (garment) geansaidh m
junction n snaidhm m, comar m, ceangal m
June n an t-Ògmhios m
jungle n dlùth-choille f
junior a as òige, a b' òige
juniper n aiteann m
junk n smodal m, truileis f; (naut) long Shìonach f
Jupiter n Iupatar m
jury n diùraidh m
just a cothromach, ceart, fìrinneach adv (recently) dìreach; (with difficulty) air èiginn **j. now** an-dràsta, an-ceartuair **it is j. amazing** tha e dìreach iongantach **the shop has j. closed** tha a' bhùth dìreach air dùnadh **they only j. escaped** 's ann air èiginn a thàrr iad às
justice n ceartas m
justifiable a reusanta, a ghabhas seasamh/dìon
justify v seas, dìon; (relig) fìreanaich
juvenile n òganach m a òigridh

Insight: just

Just in the sense 'fair' is *cothromach* or *ceart*, while just in relation to time or to intensity is *dìreach* eg *dìreach mionaid*, just a minute and *dìreach sgoinneil*, just terrific. Just now is *an-dràsta*. Only just is rendered *air èiginn*. *'S ann air èiginn a phasaig mi*, I only just passed.

K

kangaroo n cangarù m
keel n druim m
keen a dian, dealasach; (sharp) geur

keenness n dealas m, eudmhorachd f
keep v cùm, glèidh
keeper n neach-gleidhidh m

keepsake n cuimhneachan m
kelpie n each-uisge m, ùruisg m
kennel n taigh-chon m
kerb n oir a' chabhsair f m, cabhsair m
kernel n eitean m
kestrel n speireag ruadh f, clamhan ruadh m
kettle n coire m
key n iuchair f; (mus) gleus f m; (on keyboard) meur f; (solution) fuasgladh m a cudromach, prìomh (precedes n)
keyboard n meur-chlàr m
kick n breab f m v breab
kid n meann m; (child) pàiste m
kidnap v thoir am bruid
kidney n dubhag f, àra f, àirne f
kill v marbh, cuir gu bàs
killer n murtair m
killing n marbhadh m, spadadh m
kilogram(me) n cileagram m
kilometre n cilemeatair m
kilowatt n cileabhat m
kilt n (f)èileadh m
kin(dred) n dàimhean f m pl, càirdean m pl
kind n gnè f, seòrsa m
kindle v las, fadaich; (met) beothaich, brosnaich
kind(ly) a coibhneil, còir, bàidheil
kindness n coibhneas m, caomhalachd f, bàidhealachd f
kindred a co-aigneach **they were k. spirits** bha iad a dh'aon aigne

kinsman n fear-dàimh m **kinswoman** bean-dàimh f
kipper n ciopair m, sgadan rèisgte m
kirk n eaglais f
kiss n pòg f v pòg, thoir pòg (do)
kit n acfhainn f, uidheam f; (clothes) èideadh m
kitchen n cidsin m
kite n iteileag f; (bird) clamhan m
kitten n piseag f
knack n alt m, liut f
knead v fuin, taoisnich
knee n glù(i)n f **k.-cap** failmean (na glùine) m
kneel v lùb glù(i)n, sleuchd
knickers n drathais/drathars f
knife n sgian f
knight n ridire m
knit v figh **k. together** (after injury) ceangail, slànaich
knitting-needle n bior-fighe m
knob n cnap m, cnag f
knock n buille f, sgailc f, sgleog f; (at door) gnogadh m v (door) gnog **k. down** leag
knocking n gnogadh m
knoll n tom m, tolman m, tulach m **fairy k.** sìthean m
knot n snaidhm/snaoim m; (nautical mile) mìle mara m; (in wood) meuran m v snaidhmich/snaoimich, cuir snaidhm/snaoim air
know v **knows** tha fios aig; (person) is aithne do; (recognize) aithnich **k. well** bi eòlach air
knowledge n eòlas m, aithne f

Insight: know

Tha fios aig ... is the way of saying someone knows something. The preposition *aig* changes according to the person who knows, so *tha fios agam* is I know and *tha fios aige* is he knows. To say you know someone, you use the appropriate form of *is aithne do* ... e.g. *is aithne dhi Cailean,* she knows Colin.

---

kinetic a gluaiseach
king n rìgh m
kingdom n rìoghachd f

knowledgeable a fiosrach
knuckle n rùdan m
kyle n caol(as) m

L

label n bileag f v cuir bileag air

laboratory n obair-lann f, deuchainn-lann f

laborious a saothrachail, deacair

labour n saothair f, obair f; (med) saothair chloinne f **in l.** air leabaidh-shiùbhla **the L. Party** am Partaidh Làbarach m v saothraich, obraich

labourer n obraiche m, dubh-chosnaiche m

labyrinth n ioma-shlighe f

lace n sròl m; (shoe) barrall m v ceangail

lack n easbhaidh f, dìth f m, cion m v bi a dh'easbhaidh **he lacks ...** tha ... a dhìth air

lacklustre a marbhanta, gun spionnadh

laconic a geàrr-bhriathrach

lad n gille m, balach m

ladder n (f)àradh m

ladle n ladar m, liagh f

lady n bean-uasal f, baintighearna f, leadaidh f

ladybird n an daolag dhearg-bhreac f

lager n làgar m

lair n saobhaidh f, garaidh m; (grave) rèilig f

laird n uachdaran m

lake n loch m

lamb n uan m; (meat) uanfheòil f, feòil uain f

lame a cuagach, bacach, crùbach

lament n cumha m, tuireadh m, caoidh f v caoidh, dèan tuireadh

lamentable a cianail, tùrsach, muladach

laminated a lannaichte

lamp n lampa f m **l.-post** post-lampa m **l.-shade** sgàil-lampa f

lampoon n aoir f v aoir

lance n sleagh f; (med) lannsa f v leig fuil, geàrr le lannsa

land n fearann m, talamh m; (country) tìr f, dùthaich f **the L. Court** Cùirt an Fhearainn f v (go ashore) rach air tìr; (of plane) laigh; (goods) cuir air tìr

landlady n bean an taighe f

landlord n (estate) uachdaran m; (property, pub etc) fear an taighe m

landmark n comharra-stiùiridh m

landowner n uachdaran m

landscape n dealbh-tìre f m, cruth tìre m; (picture) sealladh tìre m

landslide n maoim-slèibhe f, maoim-talmhainn f

lane n frith-rathad m, caolshràid f; (on motorway) sreath f m

language n cànan f m; (speech) cainnt f

languid a anfhann, gun sunnd

languish v fannaich, crìon **l. in jail** rìghnich sa phrìosan

lanky a fada caol

lantern n lanntair m, lainntear f m, lòchran m

lap n uchd m, sgùird f; (sport) cuairt f v (slurp) slupairich, bileagaich; (waves) sruthail

lapel n liopaid f, fillteag f

lapse n sleamhnachadh m, tuisleadh m; (in time) beàrn f m v sleamhnaich, tuislich, dèan mearachd; (expire) thig gu ceann **she lapsed into English** thionndaidh i gu Beurla

lapwing n curracag f

larceny n goid f, gadachd f

larch n learag f

lard n blona(i)g f

larder n preas/seòmar-bìdh m

large a mòr, tomadach

lark n uiseag f, topag f; (play) cleas m

larynx n bràigh an sgòrnain m

laser n leusair m **l. beam** gath leusair m **l. printer** clò-bhualadair leusair m

lash v sgiùrs, stiall

lass n nighean f, caileag f

last a deireannach, mu dheireadh **l. week** an t-seachdain seo chaidh **l. night** a-raoir **the night before l.** a' bhòn-raoir **l. year** an-uiridh **the l. person** an duine mu dheireadh adv air deireadh **at (long) l.** mu dheireadh (thall) v mair, seas

lasting a maireannach, buan

latch n clàimhean m, dealan-dorais m

late *a* anmoch, fadalach, air deireadh; (*evening, night*) anmoch; (*deceased*) nach maireann **they arrived l.** bha iad fada gun tighinn

lately *adv* o chionn ghoirid

latent *a* falaichte, neo-fhollaiseach

lateral *a* taobhach, leth-taobhach

lathe *n* beairt-thuairnearachd *f*

lather *n* cop *m*

Latin *n* Laideann *f*

latitude *n* domhan-leud *m*; (*scope*) saorsa *f*

latter *a* deireannach, mu dheireadh

laud *v* àrd-mhol

laudable *a* ionmholta, ri m(h)oladh *etc*

laugh *n* gàire *f m* **loud l.** lachan *m*, lasgan *m v* gàir, dèan gàire

laughing-stock *n* culaidh/cùis-mhagaidh *f*

laughter *n* gàireachdaich *f* **loud l.** lasganaich *f*

launch *n* cur air bhog *m*; (*product*) foillseachadh *m v* cuir air bhog; (*product*) foillsich; (*begin*) tòisich air

laundry *n* taigh-nighe *m*

lava *n* làbha *f*

lavish *a* fialaidh, strùidheil, cosgail

law *n* lagh *m* **lawsuit** cùis lagha *f*

lawful *a* laghail

lawless *a* mì-riaghailteach, gun spèis do lagh

lawn *n* rèidhlean *m*, faiche *f* **l.-mower** lomaire-feòir *m*

lawyer *n* neach-lagha *m*

lax *a* slac, sgaoilte, gun chùram

laxative *n* purgaid *f*

lay *v* càirich, cuir **lay egg** breith ugh **lay foundation** leag stèidh **lay off** (*staff*) leig mu sgaoil **lay wager** cuir geall **lay waste** sgrios, cuir fàs

layer *n* filleadh *m*, sreath *f m*

layout *n* cruth *m*; (*of page*) coltas-duilleig *m*

laziness *n* leisg(e) *f*

lazy *a* leisg

lazybones *n* leisgeadair *m*

lead *n* (*metal*) luaidh(e) *f m*

lead *n* stiùir *f*; (*dog's*) taod *m v* stiùir, treòraich

leader *n* ceannard *m*, ceannbhair *m*

leadership *n* ceannas *m*

leaf *n* duilleag *f*

leaflet *n* duilleachan *m*, bileag *f*

league *n* dionnasg *m*; (*sport*) lìog *f* **the Premier L.** a' Phrìomh Lìog

leak *n* aoidion *m v* leig a-steach/a-mach; (*intrans*) bi aoidionach; (*reveal*) leig mu sgaoil

leaking, leaky *a* aoidionach

lean *v* leig do thaic air, leig cudrom air

lean *a* caol, tana

leap *n* leum *f m* **standing l.** cruinn-leum *m* **l. year** bliadhna-lèim *f v* leum, thoir leum

learn *v* ionnsaich, foghlaim

learned *a* foghlaim(ich)te, ionnsaichte

learner *n* neach-ionnsachaidh *m pl* luchd-ionnsachaidh

lease *n* gabhail *m*, còir *f v* gabh air mhàl

leash *n* iall *f*

least *sup a* as lugha **at l.** co-dhiù, aig a' char as lugha

leather *n* leathar *m a* leathair

leave *n* (*permission*) cead *m*; (*from duty*) fòrladh *m*

leave *v* fàg, trèig **l. alone** leig le **l. off** sguir de

lecherous *a* drùiseil

lecture *n* òraid *f v* dèan òraid, thoir (seachad) òraid; (*tell off*) cronaich

lecturer *n* òraidiche *m*

ledge *n* leac *f*; (*topog*) palla *m*

ledger *n* leabhar-cunntais *m*

lee *n* taobh an fhasgaidh *m*

leek *n* creamh-gàrraidh *m*

leer *v* claon-amhairc

left *n* an taobh clì/ceàrr *m*, an làmh chlì/cheàrr *f* **the l. hand** an làmh chlì *f*, a' chearrag *f* **l.-handed** ciotach, cearragach *a* clì **l. over** air fhàgail

leftovers corran *m pl*

leg *n* cas *f*; (*of meat*) ceathramh feòla *m*

legacy *n* dìleab *f*

legal *a* laghail, dligheach, ceadaichte

legalize *v* dèan laghail

legend *n* uirsgeul *f m*, fionnsgeul *m*

legendary *a* uirsgeulach; (*famous*) iomraiteach

legible *a* so-leughte, a ghabhas leughadh
legislate *v* dèan lagh(an), reachdaich
legislation *n* reachdas *m*
legitimate *a* dligheach
leisure *n* saor-ùine *f* **l. activity**
cur-seachad *m*
lemon *n* liomaid *f* **l. sole** lèabag cheàrr *f*
lemonade *n* liomaineud *m*
lend *v* thoir iasad (de), thoir an iasad
length *n* fad *m*, faid *f*
lengthen *v* cuir fad ri/às, dèan nas
fhaide, sìn; (*intrans*) fàs nas fhaide, sìn
leniency *n* tròcair *f*, iochdalachd *f*, iochd *f*
lenient *a* tròcaireach, iochdail
lenition *n* sèimheachadh *m*
lens *n* lionsa *f*
Lent *n* an Carghas *m*
lentil *n* leantail *m*, peasair nan luch *f*
leopard *n* liopard *m*
leper *n* lobhar *m*
leprosy *n* luibhre *f*
lesbian *n, a* leasbach *f*
less *comp a* nas lugha, na bu lugha
lessen *v* lùghdaich, beagaich (air);
(*intrans*) lùghdaich
lesson *n* leasan *m*
let *v* leig le, ceadaich; (*property*) thoir air
ghabhail **let go** leig às **let on** leig ort/
air/oirre *etc*
lethal *a* marbhtach, bàsmhor
lethargic *a* trom, slaodach
letter *n* litir *f* **capital l.** litir mhòr **l.-box**
bogsa-litrichean *m*
lettuce *n* leatas *f*
leukaemia *n* bànachadh-fala *m*
level *n* còmhnard *m*; (*grade*) inbhe *f*, ìre
f a còmhnard, rèidh *v* dèan còmhnard/
rèidh **l. an accusation at** cuir às leth
(*+ gen*)
lever *n* geimhleag *f*, luamhan *m* **gear l.**
stob nan gìodhraichean *m*
levy *n* cìs *f v* (*tax etc*) leag
lewd *a* draosta
Lewis person *n* Leòdhasach *m*, (*female*)
ban-Leòdhasach *f*
liability *n* (*fin*) fiach *m*; (*tendency*)
buailteachd *f* **it was just a l.** cha robh
ann ach call

liable *a* buailteach (do), dualtach
liaise *v* dèan ceangal (ri)
liaison *n* ceangal *m*, co-cheangal *m*
liar *n* breugaire *m*, breugadair *m*
libel *n* tuaileas *m*, cliù-mhilleadh *m v* cuir
tuaileas air, mill cliù **he libelled me** chuir
e na breugan orm
libellous *a* tuaileasach
liberal *a* fial, fialaidh; (*phil*) libearalach
Liberal *n, a* Libearalach *m* **L. Democratic**
Party am Partaidh Libearalach
Deamocratach *m*
liberate *v* saor, cuir mu sgaoil
liberation *n* saoradh *m*, leigeil/cur mu
sgaoil *m*
liberty *n* saorsa *f*
libidinous *a* ana-miannach, drùiseil
librarian *n* leabharlannaiche *m*
library *n* leabharlann *f m*
licence *n* cead *m*
license *v* ceadaich, thoir cead do/seachad
licensed *a* fo cheadachd, le cead,
ùghdarraichte
licentious *a* mì-bheusach
lick *v* imlich
lid *n* ceann *m*, mullach *m*
lie *n* breug *f* **I had a lie-down** chaidh
mi nam shìneadh *v* (*tell untruth*) inn(i)s
breug; (*phys*) laigh
lieutenant *n* leifteanant *m*; (*associate*)
neach-ionaid *m*
life *n* beatha *f*; (*vitality*) beothalachd *f*
l.-insurance àrachas beatha *m* **l.-style**
dòigh-beatha *f* **lifebelt** crios-teasairginn
m **lifeboat** bàta-teasairginn *m*
lifeguard neach-teasairginn *m* **l.-jacket**
seacaid-teasairginn *f* **lifeline** loidhne-
teasairginn *f*; (*met*) cothrom eile *m*
lifeless *a* marbh, gun deò; (*met*) trom
lifetime *n* rè *f*, beò *m*, saoghal *m*
lift *n* togail *f*; (*elevator*) àrdaichear *m v* tog
ligament *n* ball-nasg *m*, ceanglachan *m*
light *n* solas *m*; (*daylight*) soilleireachd
f **l.-house** taigh-solais *m v* las **l. up**
(*+ met*) soillsich
light *a* aotrom; (*of daylight*) soilleir
l.-headed aotrom, mear **l.-hearted**
sunndach, suigeartach, aighearach

lighten v deàlraich, soillsich; (*weight*) aotromaich

lighter n lasadair m

lightning n dealanach m

like v **likes** is toigh/toil (le), is caomh le **be l.** bi coltach ri

like n leithid f, samhail f, mac-samhail m a coltach (ri), mar (+ *len*) adv mar

likelihood n coltas m

likely a coltach, dòcha

liken v samhlaich, coimeas

likeness n (*similarity*) coltas m, ìomhaigh f; (*picture*) dealbh f m

likewise adv cuideachd, mar an ceudna

lilac n liath-chorcra f a bàn-phurpaidh

lily n lilidh f

limb n ball m

lime n aol m; (*fruit/tree*) teile f

limit n crìoch f, iomall m v cuingealaich, cuir crìoch ri

limited a cuingealaichte, cuibhrichte **l. company** companaidh earranta f m

limp n ceum m **he has a l.** tha ceum ann, tha e cuagach a bog v bi bacach/ cuagach/crùbach

limpet n bàirneach f

line n loidhne f; (*in writing*) sreath f m; (*clothes*) ròp anairt m; (*fishing*) driamlach f; (*geneal*) sìol m, gineal f m **l.-fishing** dorghach m **on-l.** air loidhne v lìnig

linear a sreathach, loidhneach

linen n anart m, lìon-aodach m

ling n (*fish*) langa f

linger v dèan dàil, rongaich, gabh ùine

lingerie n aodach-cneis m

linguistic a cànanach

lining n lìnig(eadh) m

link n ceangal m; (*in chain*) tinne f, dul m **linkspan** alt-aiseig m v dèan co-cheangal

lint n lìon m, caiteas m

lintel n àrd-doras m

lion n leòmhann m **the l.'s share** an ceann reamhar m

lip n bile f, lip f; (*geog*) oir f m **lip-service** beul bòidheach m **lipstick** dath-lipean m, peant bhilean m

liqueur n liciùr m

liquid n lionn m a lionnach, sruthach

liquidate v (*company*) sgaoil; (*kill*) cuir às do

liquidation n (*of company*) sgaoileadh m

liquidize v lionnaich

liquor n deoch(-làidir) f

liquorice n carra-mheille m

lisp n liotaiche m, liotachas m v bi liotach

lisping a liotach

list n liosta f; (*to side*) fiaradh m v dèan liosta; (*of ship*) liost(aig)

listen v èist (ri)

listening n èisteachd f

listless a gun lùths/sunnd

literacy n litearrachd f, litearras m

literal a litireil

literary a litreachail

literate a litearra

literature n litreachas m **oral l.** litreachas beòil

lithe a sùbailte, subailte

litigate v rach gu lagh, agair lagh air

litigation n agartachd f, cùis-lagha f

litre n liotair m

litter n sgudal m; (*of animals*) cuain f, iseanan m pl v fàg na bhùrach **discard l.** fàg sgudal

little n beagan m, rud beag m a beag, meanbh

liturgy n ùrnaigh choitcheann f

live v bi beò

live a beò

livelihood n beòshlaint f, teachd-an-tìr m, bith-beò m

lively a beothail, frogail, sunndach

liver n adha m, grùthan m

livid a (*met*) **he was l.** bha an cuthach dearg air

living n beòshlaint f, teachd-an-tìr m, bith-beò m a beò

lizard n laghairt f m, dearc-luachrach f

load n luchd m, eallach m; (*on mind*) uallach m v luchdaich, lìon; (*gun*) cuir urchair an

loaf n lof f m

loan n iasad m **loanword** facal-iasaid m v thoir iasad do, thoir ... air iasad

loath *a* ain-deònach
loathe *v* fuathaich **I loathed it** bha gràin (an) uilc agam air
loathing *n* gràin uilc *f*, sgreamh *m*
loathsome *a* gràineil, sgreamhail, sgreataidh
lobby *n* lobaidh *f*, trannsa *f*; (*pressure group*) luchd-coiteachaidh *m* *v* coitich
lobster *n* giomach *m* **l.-pot** cliabh-ghiomach *f*
local *a* ionadail **l. authority** ùghdarras ionadail *m* **l. government** riaghaltas ionadail *m*
locality *n* àite *m*, coimhearsnachd *f*, sgìre *f*
locate *v* suidhich, cuir na àite
location *n* suidheachadh *m*, àite *m*
loch *n* loch *m*
lock *n* glas *f*; (*of hair*) dual *m*, ciabh *f*, cuailean *m* *v* glas
locker *n* preasa glaiste *m*
locus *n* lòcas *m*, àite *m*
locust *n* lòcast *m*
lodge *n* loidse *f m*, taigh-geata *m*
lodge *v* (*submit*) cuir a-steach, càirich; (*stay*) gabh còmhnaidh
lodger *n* loidsear *m*
lodging *n* loidseadh *m* **l. house** taigh-loidsidh *m*
loft *n* lobhta *m*
log *n* sail *f*, loga *f m*; (*book*) leabhar-aithris *m*; (*math*) log *m*
logic *n* loidsig *f*
logical *a* loidsigeach
log off *v* log dheth, tarraing às
log on *v* log air, dèan ceangal
loin *n* blian *m* **the loins** an leasraidh *f*
loiter *v* dèan màirneal, rongaich
lollipop *n* loiliopop *f*
Londoner *n* Lunnainneach *m*, neach à Lunnainn *m*
lone *a* aonarach, na (h-)aonar *etc*, leis/leatha fhèin *etc*
loneliness *n* aon(a)ranachd *f*
lonely *a* aon(a)ranach
loner *n* aonaran *m*
long *a* fada **l. ago** o chionn f(h)ada **l.-lasting** buan, maireannach **l.-suffering** fad-fhulangach **l.-term** fad-ùine *v* **l. for** miannaich; (*weary for*) gabh fadachd ri
long division *n* roinn fhada *f*
longing *n* miann *f m*, togradh *m*, fadachd *f*
longitude *n* domhan-fhad *m*
long jump *n* leum-fada *m*, leum-fhada *f*
look *n* sùil *f*; (*appearance*) coltas *m*, fiamh *m* *v* seall, coimhead, amhairc **l. for** coimhead airson, lorg, sir
loom *n* beairt(-fhighe) *f*
loop *n* lùb *f*
loophole *n* beàrn *f m*, dòigh às *f*
loose *a* fuasgailte, sgaoilte, gun cheangal **l. change** airgead pronn *m*
loose(n) *v* fuasgail, cuir/leig mu sgaoil
loot *n* creach *f* *v* creach
lop *v* sgud, sgath, geàrr
lopsided *a* leathoireach, gu aon taobh
loquacious *a* briathrach
lord *n* tighearna *m*, triath *m*, morair *m* **House of Lords** Taigh nam Morairean *m* **the Lord's Prayer** Ùrnaigh an Tighearna *f*
lorry *n* làraidh *f*
lose *v* caill
loss *n* call *m*
lost *a* air chall, caillte
lot *n* (*amount*) mòran *m*, tòrr *m*; (*in life*) crannchur *m* **cast lots** tilg croinn
lotion *n* cungaidh *f*
lottery *n* crannchur *m* **the National L.** an Crannchur Nàiseanta
loud *a* àrd, faramach
loudspeaker *n* glaodhaire *m*
lounge *n* rùm-suidhe *m* *v* sìn
louse *n* mial *f*
lousy *a* grod; (*with lice*) mialach
lout *n* burraidh *m*
love *n* gaol *m*, gràdh *m*; (*tennis*) neoni *m* **my l.** m' eudail *v* gràdhaich, thoir gaol **I l. you** tha gaol agam ort **we l. skiing** 's fìor thoigh leinn sgitheadh, tha sinn fìor dhèidheil/mhiadhail air sgitheadh
lovely *a* bòidheach, àlainn, lurach, maiseach
lover *n* leannan *m*
lovesick *a* an trom-ghaol

Insight: love

There are two main words for love, *gaol* and *gràdh*. To say you love someone, you use *tha gaol agam air ...* I love you is *tha gaol agam ort*. Common terms of endearment are *m' eudail* and *a luaidh*, both meaning my dear.

---

loving *a* gràdhach, ionmhainn
low *a* ìosal, ìseal
low *v* geum, bi a' geumnaich
lower *v* ìslich, lùghdaich
lowing *n* geumnaich *f*
Lowlander *n* Gall *m*, (*female*) bana-Ghall *f pl* Goill
low water *n* muir-tràigh *f*
loyal *a* dìleas
loyalist *n* dìlseach *m*
loyalty *n* dìlseachd *f*
lubricate *v* lìomh, dèan sleamhainn, cuir ola air/an
lucid *a* soilleir
luck *n* sealbh *m*, fortan *m*, rath *m*
  Good l.! Gur(a) math a thèid dhut/ leat!
lucky *a* sealbhach, fortanach
lucrative *a* airgeadach, mòr-bhuannachdail, mòr-phrothaideach
ludicrous *a* amaideach, gòrach
luggage *n* bagaichean *m pl*, màileidean *f pl*
lukewarm *a* meadh-bhlàth, flodach
lull *v* meall; (*to sleep*) cuir a chadal
lullaby *n* tàladh *m*
lumbago *n* leum-droma *m*
lumber *n* trealaich *f*, seann àirneis *f*

luminous *a* soillseach, deàlrach
lump *n* cnap *m*; (*geog*) meall *m* **a l. sum** cnap airgid *m*
lumpy *a* cnapach
lunacy *n* euslaint-inntinn *f*; (*met*) mullach an amaideis *m*
lunatic *n* euslainteach-inntinn *m*
lunch *n* lòn *m*, diathad *f* **l. break** tràth-bìdh *m*, biadh meadhain-latha *m*
lung *n* sgamhan *m*
lurch *n* tulgadh *m*, siaradh *m v* dèan tulgadh/siaradh
lure *v* buair, breug
lurid *a* eagalach, sgràthail, oillteil
lurk *v* falaich, siolp
luscious *a* sòghmhor
lush *a* mèath
lust *n* ana-miann *f m*, drù(i)s *f v* **l. after/ for** sanntaich, miannaich
lustre *n* deàlradh *m*, gleans *m*, lainnir *f*; (*met*) mòr-chliù *m*
luxurious *a* sòghail
luxury *n* sògh *m*, sòghalachd *f*
lying *n* (*phys*) laighe *f*; (*telling lies*) innse bhreug *f a* (*untruthful*) breugach
lynch *v* croch (gun chùirt)
lyric *n* liric *f*, ealaidh *f*
lythe *n* (*fish*) liugha *f*, liùgh *f*

M

machination *n* innleachd *f*
machine *n* inneal *m*
machinery *n* innealradh *m*; (*met*) modhan-obrach *f m pl*
mackerel *n* rionnach *m*
mad *a* às a c(h)iall/rian *etc*; (*slang*) cracte **he was mad** (*angry*) bha an cuthach air
madam *n* bean-uasal *f*
madden *v* (*anger*) cuir an cuthach air

madness *n* dìth-cèille *f m*; (*slang*) crac *m*
magazine *n* iris *f*; (*quarterly*) ràitheachan *m*; (*arms store*) armlann *f*; (*of gun*) cèis-bhiathaidh *f*
maggot *n* cnuimh *f*
magic *n* draoidheachd *f a* draoidheil
magician *n* draoidh *m*
magistrate *n* bàillidh *m*, maighstir-lagha *m*

magnanimous a fial-inntinneach, fialaidh

magnet n magnait m, clach-iùil f

magnificent a òirdheirc

magnify v meudaich; (extol) àrdaich

magpie n pitheid f, pioghaid f

maid(en) n maighdeann f, gruagach f; (servant) searbhanta f

mail n post m, litrichean f pl **m.-order** òrdugh tron phost m v post(aig), cuir sa phost

maim v ciorramaich, leòn, ciùrr

main a prìomh **m. road** rathad-mòr m

mainland n tìr-mòr f m, mòr-thìr f

mainly adv anns a' mhòr-chuid, gu beagnaich

maintain v (keep) glèidh, cùm; (support) cùm suas; (in argument) cùm a-mach, tagair

maintenance n gleidheadh m, cumail suas f; (of person) beathachadh m

maize n cruithneachd Innseanach f m

majestic a flathail

majesty n mòrachd f, rìoghachd f

major n (mil) màidsear m; (sport) prìomh fharpais f

major a mòr, cudromach; (greater) ... as/a bu motha

majority n mòr-chuid f, tromlach f, a' chuid as/a bu motha f

make n seòrsa m **m.-up** rìomhadh (gnùis(e)) m; (met) dèanamh m, nàdar m v dèan; (compel) thoir air, co-èignich; (bed) càirich **m. for** (head for) dèan air **m. believe** leig air/oirre etc **we'll m. it** nì sinn a' chùis

male n fireannach m a fireann

malevolent a gamhlasach, le droch rùn

malice n mì-rùn m, droch rùn m, droch mhèinn f

malicious a droch-rùnach, droch-mhèinneach

malign v mì-chliùthaich

malignant a millteach; (of cancer) cronail, nimheil

mallard n lach riabhach f

malleable a so-chumte, a ghabhas cumadh

malnutrition n dìth beathachaidh f m, cion a'-bhìdh m

malpractice n mì-chleachdadh m, droch ghiùlan m

malt n braich f **m. whisky** mac na braiche m

maltreat v droch-làimhsich, dèan droch ghiullachd air

maltreatment n droch-làimhseachadh m, droch ghiullachd f

mammal n sineach m, mamal m

man n duine m, fear m, fireannach m; (husband) duine m

manage v stiùir, ruith; (be able to) dèan a' chùis

manageable a so-riaghladh, so-stiùireadh, a ghabhas dèanamh

management n stiùireadh m, riaghladh m; (personnel) luchd-stiùiridh m

manager n manaidsear m, ceannbhair m

manageress n bana-mhanaidsear f, bana-cheannbhair f

mandate n òrdugh m, àithne f; (electoral) ùghdarras m

mandatory a do-sheachanta, èigneachail

mane n muing f

manfully adv gu duineil, gu dian

mangle v reub, dèan ablach de

manhood n fearalas m

mania n boile-cuthaich f

maniac n neach-cuthaich m, caochanach m

manic a fon chuthach

manicure n grinneachadh làimhe m v grinnich làmhan

manifest a follaiseach, soilleir v taisbean, nochd, foillsich

manipulate v obraich

mankind n an cinne-daonna m

manliness n duinealas m, fearalachd f

manly a duineil, fearail

manner n modh f m, seòl m, dòigh f

mannerism n cleachdadh m, cleas m, cuinse f

mannerly a modhail

manners n modh f m

manoeuvre n eacarsaich f; (mil) gluasad (airm) m; (met) innleachd f, cleas m

manpower n sgiobachd f

manse n mansa m

mansion n taigh/aitreabh mòr m, àros m

mantlepiece n breus m

manual a làimhe **m. work** obair làimhe f n leabhar-làimhe/mìneachaidh m

manufacture v dèan

manure n todhar m, mathachadh m, innear f

manuscript n làmh-sgrìobhainn f

Manx n Gàidhlig Mhanainneach f a Manainneach

Manxman n Manainneach m **Manxwoman** ban-Mhanainneach f

many n mòran m a iomadh, iomadach **m. people** mòran dhaoine **m. a time ...** 's iomadh uair ... **as m. again** uiread eile **so m.** a leithid de, uiread de **twice as m.** a dhà uimhir

map n map(a) m, clàr-dùthcha m

mar v mill

marble n màrmor m; (ball) marbal m, mìrleag f

March n am Màrt m

march n màrsail f, mèarrsadh m; (tune) caismeachd f v dèan màrsail/mèarrsadh, mèarrs

mare n làir f

margarine n margarain m

margin n oir f m, iomall m

marginal a iomallach, leathoireach

marigold n a' bhile bhuidhe f

marine a mara

mariner n maraiche m

maritime a cuantach

mark n comharra m; (trace) làrach f m, lorg f; (currency) marc m v comharraich; (notice) thoir fa-near, gabh beachd air

market n fèill f, margadh f m, margaid f **m. place** ionad margaidh m

marketing n margaideachd f

marmalade n marmalaid m

marquee n puball m, pàillean m

marquis n marcas m

marriage n pòsadh m

married a pòsta **m. couple** càraid phòsta f

marrow n smior m; (veg) mearag f

marry v pòs

marsh n boglach f, fèith f **m.-marigold** lus buidhe Bealltainn m

marshal v cuir an òrdugh, trus

mart n ionad-margaidh m

martial a gaisgeanta

Martinmas n an Fhèill M(h)àrtainn f, Latha Fhèill Màrtainn m

martyr n martarach ṁ

marvel n iongnadh m, mìorbhail f v gabh iongnadh

marvellous a mìorbhaileach, iongantach

Marxist n, a Marcsach m

mascot n suaichnean m

masculine a fearail; (gram) fireannta

mash v pronn

mashed a pronn

mask n aghaidh-choimheach f, aodannan m

mason n clachair m

masonry n clachaireachd f

mass n tomad m; (great quantity) meall m, tòrr m; (majority) mòr-chuid f; (relig) aifreann f m

massacre n casgradh m v casgair, murt

massage n suathadh/taosgnadh-bodhaig m

massive a tomadach, àibheiseach

mast n crann m

master n maighstir m; (of ship) sgiobair m **m. of ceremonies** fear an taighe m v (subdue) ceannsaich; (become proficient in) fàs suas ri

masterly a ealanta, sgaiteach

masterpiece n sàr obair f, euchd m

mat n brat m

match n maids(e) m, lasadair m; (sport) maids(e) m; (equal) seise m, samhail m **m.-box** bogsa/bucas-mhaidseachan m v freagair, co-fhreagair, maids

mate n cèile m, companach m; (rank) meat(a) m

material n stuth m

materialistic a saoghalta

maternal a màithreachail

maternity *a* màthaireil **m. hospital** ospadal mhàthraichean *m* **m. leave** fòrladh màthaireil *m*

mathematical *a* matamataigeach

mathematics *n* matamataig *m*

matrimony *n* dàimh-pòsaidh *f m*

matrix *n* machlag *f*; (*maths*) meatrags *f*

matron *n* bean-phòsta *f*; (*rank*) ban-cheannard *f*

matter *n* stuth *m*, brìgh *f*; (*affair*) gnothach *m*, cùis *f* **what's the m.?** dè tha ceàrr? *v* **it does not m.** chan eil e gu diofar

mattress *n* bobhstair *m*

mature *a* abaich; (*person*) inbheach, air tighinn gu ìre *v* abaich; (*of person*) ruig ìre

maturity *n* abaichead *m*, ìre *f*

maul *v* pronn, lidrig

mauve *n* liath-phurpaidh *m*

maximize *v* barraich

maximum *a* ... as motha **the m.** a' chuid as motha *n* os-mheud *m*

May *n* an Cèitean *m*, a' Mhàigh *f* **May Day** Latha (Buidhe) Bealltainn *m*

may *v* (*permission*) faod; (*perhaps*) faod, 's dòcha **may I go?** am faod mi falbh? **they may not** chan fhaod iad **she may come** faodaidh i tighinn; (*perhaps*) faodaidh gun tig i, 's dòcha gun tig i

mayday *n* gairm èiginn *f*

mayor *n* àrd-bhàillidh *m*, ceannard baile *m*

maze *n* ioma-shlighe *f*

me *pron* mi, (*emph*) mise

meadow *n* lòn *m*, faiche *f*, dail *f*, lèana *f*

meagre *a* gann, lom

meal *n* biadh *m*; (*flour*) min *f*

mean *a* spìocach; (*of spirit*) suarach, tàireil; (*stat*) meadhanail

mean *v* ciallaich; (*intend*) cuir romhad

meaning *n* ciall *f*, seagh *m*, brìgh *f*

meaningful *a* ciallach, brìoghmhor

meanness *n* spìocaireachd *f*; (*of spirit*) suarachas *m*

meantime *adv* an-dràsta **in the m.** anns an eadar-àm

meanwhile *adv* aig a' cheart àm

measles *n* a' ghriùthrach *f*, a' ghriùthlach *f*

measure *n* tomhas *m*; (*portion*) cuid *f*, roinn *f*; (*action*) ceum *m v* tomhais

measurement *n* tomhas *m*

meat *n* feòil *f*

mechanic *n* meacanaig *f*

mechanical *a* meacanaigeach

mechanism *n* uidheam *f*; (*means*) meadhan *m*, dòigh *f*

medal *n* bonn *m* **gold medal** bonn òir

meddle *v* buin ri, cuir làmh an, gabh gnothach ri

media, the *n* na meadhanan *m pl*

mediate *v* rèitich, rach san eadraiginn, eadar-mheadhanaich

mediation *n* eadraiginn *f*, eadar-ghuidhe *f*

mediator *n* eadar-mheadhanair *m*

medical *a* lèigh, meidigeach

medication *n* cungaidh leighis *f*

medicine *n* ìocshlaint *f*, cungaidh *f*; (*science*) eòlas-leighis *m*

medieval *a* meadhan-aoiseil

mediocre *a* lapach

meditate *v* beachdaich, beachd-smaoinich, meòraich

Mediterranean *n* a' Mhuir Mheadhan-thìreach *f a* Meadhan-thìreach

medium *a* meadhanach **m.-sized** meadhanach mòr **m. wave** bann meadhanach *m* meadhan *m*

meek *a* macanta, ciùin

meet *v* coinnich, tachair; (*gather*) cruinnich; (*fulfil*) coilean

meeting *n* coinneamh *f*; (*act of*) coinneachadh *m*

melancholy *n* leann-dubh *m a* dubhach, fo leann-dubh

mellifluous *a* binn, milis

mellow *a* tlàth, làn-abaich

melodic/melodious *a* binn, fonnmhor

melody *n* fonn *m*

melon *n* meal-bhuc *f m*

melt *v* leagh

member *n* ball *m* **MP** BP (Ball Pàrlamaid) *m* **MSP** BPA (Ball Pàrlamaid na h-Alba) **MEP** BPE (Ball Pàrlamaid Eòrpach)

membership n ballrachd f
membrane n meamran m
memento n cuimhneachan m
memoir(s) n eachdraidh-beatha f
memorable a ainmeil, fada air chuimhne
memorandum/memo n meòrachan m
memorial n cuimhneachan m **m. stone**
  clach-chuimhne f **m. cairn** càrn-cuimhne
  m **m. service** seirbheis cuimhneachaidh f
memorize v cùm air chuimhne
memory n cuimhne f
menace n bagradh m, maoidheadh m
  he's a m. 's e plàigh a th' ann v bagair,
  maoidh
mend v càirich **be on the m.** rach am
  feabhas, thig air adhart
menial a sgalagail, seirbheiseil
meningitis n fiabhras eanchainn(e) m,
  teasach eanchainn f
mental a inntinneil **m. hospital** ospadal
  inntinn m
mention n iomradh m, luaidh m v
  ainmich, thoir iomradh/tarraing air, dèan
  luaidh air
menu n clàr-bìdh m, cairt-bìdh f;
  (computer) clàr-iùil m
mercenary n (mil) amhasg m, buanna m
mercenary a sanntach, miannach air
  airgead
merchandise n bathar m
merchant n ceannaiche m, marsanta m
  the M. Navy an Cabhlach Marsantach m
merciful a tròcaireach, iochdmhor
merciless a gun tròcair, an-iochdmhor
mercury n airgead-beò m
mercy n tròcair f, iochd f
merely adv a-mhàin, dìreach
merge v rach còmhla, coimeasg; (trans)
  aonaich, dèan cothlamadh
merger n coimeasg(adh) m, aonadh m
meringue n mearang m
merit n luach m, airidheachd f v toill, bi
  airidh air
mermaid n maighdeann-mhara f
merriment n aighear m, mire f
merry a aighearach, mear
mesh n mogal m
mesmerize v dian-ghlac, cuir fo gheas

mess n bùrach m, butarrais f; (staff)
  seòmar-comaidh m
message n teachdaireachd f
messenger n teachdaire m
metabolism n meatabolachd f,
  fàs-atharrachadh m
metal n meatailt f **m. work** obair
  mheatailt f
metamorphose v cruth-atharraich
metaphor n meatafor m
metaphorical a meataforach
metaphysical a feallsanachail
meteor n dreag f, rionnag-earbaill f
meteorite n aileag f, sgeith-rionnaig f
meteorological a sìd'-eòlach **Met.**
  Office Oifis na Sìde f
meteorology n eòlas-sìde m
meter n inneal-tomhais m
method n dòigh f, seòl m, modh f m;
  (order) rian m
methodical a òrdail, rianail, pongail
methodology n dòigh-obrach f, modh-
  obrach f m
metre n meatair m; (of poetry)
  rannaigheachd f, meadrachd f
metric a meatrach
metrical a rannaigheachd, meadrachail
metro n trèan fo thalamh f
metropolitan a prìomh-bhailteach
mettle n smioralachd f
mew v dèan miathalaich/miamhail
Michaelmas n an Fhèill M(h)ìcheil f,
  Latha Fhèill Mìcheil m
microbe n bitheag f, meanbhag f
microbiology n meanbh-bhith-eòlas m
microphone n maicreafòn m
microscope n maicreasgop m
microwave n meanbh-thonn f; (oven)
  àmhainn mheanbh-thonnach f
midday n meadhan-latha m
midden n sitig f, òcrach f, òtrach f
middle n meadhan m **m.-aged** sa
  mheadhan-latha **(the) M. Ages**
  na Meadhan-Aoisean f pl **m.-class**
  eagar meadhanach m a meadhan,
  meadhanach
midge n meanbhchuileag f
midnight n meadhan-oidhche m

midriff *n* (an) sgairt *f*
midsummer *n* meadhan (an t-)
samhraidh *m*; (*St John's Day*) Latha
Fèill Eòin *m*
midway *adv* letheach-slighe, sa
mheadhan
midwife *n* bean-ghlùine *f*
midwifery *n* banas-glùine *m*
might *n* cumhachd *f m*, neart *m*,
spionnadh *m*
might *v* faod, 's dòcha; (*ought*) bu choir
dhut **a seat belt m. have saved his life**
dh'fhaodadh gum biodh/gun robh crios-
sàbhalaidh air a chumail beò **you m.**
have apologized to her bha coir agad
a bhith air mathanas iarraidh oirre
mighty *a* cumhachdach, foghainteach
migrate *v* dèan imrich
migration *n* imrich *f*; (*overseas*) imrich
cuain
mild *a* màlda, ciùin, tlàth
mildew *n* clòimh-liath *f*
mile *n* mìle *f m* **mileage** astar mhìltean
m **milestone** clach-mhìle *f*
militant *n* mìleantach *m*, cathach *m a*
mìleanta, cathachail
military *a* cogail, armailteach
militate *v* (*against*) obraich an
aghaidh
militia *n* mailisidh *m*
milk *n* bainne *m v* bleoghain
mill *n* muileann *f m* **millstone** clach-
mhuilinn *f*; (*met*) eallach *m*
millennium *n* mìle bliadhna *f m*
milligram *n* mìlegram *m*
millilitre *n* mìleliotair *m*
millimetre *n* mìlemeatair *m*
million *n* millean *m*
millionaire *n* milleanair *m*
mime *n* mìm *f v* dèan mìm
mimic *v* dèan atharrais (air)
mince *n* mions *m*
mind *n* inntinn *f*, aigne *f*, ciall *f* **keep in**
m. cuimhnich *v* **what did you have in**
m.? dè bh' agad san amharc? **he is out**
of his m. tha e às a chiall *v* thoir an aire,
thoir fa-near; (*remember*) cuimhnich
mindful *a* cuimhneachail, cùramach

mine *n* mèinn *f* **coal m.** toll-guail *m v*
cladhaich; (*plant mines*) cuir mèinnean
(an)
mine *pron* leamsa, agamsa **that's m.** 's
ann leamsa a tha sin **this memory of**
m. a' chuimhne seo agamsa
miner *n* mèinneadair *m*, mèinnear *m*
mineral *n* mèinnir *m a* mèinnireach **m.**
water uisge mèinnireach *m*
mingle *v* measgaich, coimeasg, cuir an
ceann a chèile; (*with people*) rach an
lùib
minibus *n* bus beag *m*, mion-bhus *m*
minimal *a* fìor bheag; (*least*) as/a bu
lugha
minimize *v* lùghdaich, ìslich
minimum *n* a' chuid as/a bu lugha *f*, ìos-
mheud *m a* as/a bu lugha
minister *n* ministear *m v* fritheil,
ministrealaich
ministry *n* ministre(al)achd *f* **the M. of**
Defence Ministre(al)achd an Dìon *f*
mink *n* minc *m*
minor *a* beag, as lugha, fo- *n* òg-aoisear
m
minority *n* mion/beag-chuid *f*; (*age*) òg-
aois *f* **m. language** mion-chànan *f m*
mint *n* meannt *m*; (*place*) taigh-cùinnidh
m **he made a m.** rinn e fortan
minus *prep* às aonais (+ *gen*); (*math*)
thoir air falbh
minute *n* mionaid *f*; (*of meeting*) geàrr-
chunntas *m*, geàrr-aithris *f*
minute *a* meanbh, mion, beag bìodach
miracle *n* mìorbhail *f*
miraculous *a* mìorbhaileach
mirage *n* mearachadh sùla *m*
mire *n* poll *m*, eabar *m*
mirror *n* sgàthan *m*
mirth *n* mire *f*, sùgradh *m*
misadventure *n* mì-shealbh *m*,
sgiorradh *m*
misbehave *v* bi ri mì-mhodh, bi mì-
mhodhail
misbehaviour *n* mì-mhodh *m*, droch
ghiùlan *m*
miscalculate *v* àireamh(aich) ceàrr;
(*met*) dèan co-dhùnadh ceàrr

miscall v càin
miscarriage n (med) asaid anabaich f; (general) dol a dhìth m **m. of justice** iomrall ceartais m
miscarry v asaid an-abaich; (general) rach a dhìth
miscellaneous a measgaichte, eugsamhail
miscellany n measgachadh m
mischief n luathaireachd f; (serious) aimhleas m, miastadh m
mischievous a luathaireach
misconception n mì-thuigsinn f, claon-bheachd m
misconduct n mì-mhodh m, droch ghiùlan m
misdemeanour n eucoir f, mì-ghnìomh m
miser n spìocaire m
miserable a truagh, brònach
misfit n faondraiche m
misfortune n mì-fhortan m, mì-shealbh m
misgiving(s) n teagamh(an) m (pl)
misguided a neo-ghlic, cearbach
mishap n mì-thapadh m, tubaist f
misinform v thoir fios meallta/ceàrr
misinterpret v mì-bhreithnich, tog ceàrr
misjudge v thoir mì-bhreith (air), tuig ceàrr
mislay v caill
mislead v meall, mì-threòraich, cuir ceàrr/air seachran
misleading a meallta
mismatch n neo-ionannachd f

miss v ionndrainn; (train etc) caill; (target etc) ana-cuimsich
missile n tilgean m, astas m
missing a a dhìth, a dh'easbhaidh; (person) air chall, gun lorg
mission n misean f; (purpose) rùn m **m. statement** aithris rùin f
missionary n miseanaraidh m
mist n ceò f m, ceathach m
mistake n mearachd f, iomrall m
Mister (Mr) n Maighstir (Mgr) m
mistletoe n uil-ìoc m
mistress n bana-mhaighstir f; (lover) coimhleapach f m, boireannach eile m
Mrs A' Bh
misty a ceòthach, ceòthar
misunderstand v tog ceàrr
misunderstanding n mì-thuigse f, togail ceàrr f
misuse n mì-bhuileachadh m
mite n fìneag f
mitigating a lasachaidh, maothachaidh
mitigation n lasachadh m, maothachadh m
mix v measgaich, cuir an lùib a chèile, cothlaim
mixed a measgaichte, measgte
mixer n measgaichear m, inneal-measgachaidh m
mixture n measgachadh m
moan n gearan f m; (sound) acain f, osna f v gearain; (sound) dèan acainn/osna
mob n gràisg f

Insight: mo

Mo, my, causes the next word to lenite, as in *mo pheann,* my pen, where *peann* is the standard form of the word. When *mo* is followed by a word beginning in a vowel, it is reduced to *m'* as in *m' athair,* my father. *Do*, your, follows the same pattern.

---

misplace v caill
misprint n mearachd clò f
misrepresent v thoir claon-aithris
misrule n mì-riaghladh m; (anarchy) mì-riaghailt f
Miss n A' Mhaighdeann f (abb) A' Mh.

mobile a gluasadach **m. phone** n fòn-làimhe f m
mobility n gluasadachd f, cothrom gluasaid m
mock v mag (air), dèan fanaid (air)
mockery n magadh m, fanaid f

mod n mòd m **the National Mod** am Mòd Nàiseanta **local m.** mòd ionadail
mode n modh f m, dòigh f, seòl m, rian m
model n modail m, cruth m, samhail m; (make) seòrsa m; (fashion) modail m a **m. employee** brod an obraiche v deilbh, cum, dealbhaich **m. oneself on** lean eisimpleir (+ gen)
modem n mòdam m
moderate a cuibheasach, meadhanach; (disposition) stuama, riaghailteach v (of weather) ciùinich; (exams) co-mheas
moderation n stuaim f, riaghailteachd f; (of exams) co-mheasadh m
moderator n co-mheasadair m; (eccl) modaràtair m
modern a ùr, nuadh, nodha
modernize v ùraich, nuadhaich
modest a nàrach, màlda, socharach
modesty n beusachd f, màldachd f, socharachd f
modify v atharraich, leasaich
module n modal m
moist a tais, bog
moisten v taisich, bogaich
moisture n taiseachd f, fliche f
mole n (animal) famh f; (on skin) ball-dòrain m; (insider) ruamharaiche m **molehill** dùnan-faimh m
molecule n moileciuil m
molest v (accost) thoir ionnsaigh air; (annoy) cuir dragh air
mollify v maothaich, ciùinich
molten a leaghte
moment n tiota(n) m, mòmaid f
momentary a car tiota
momentous a fìor chudromach
momentum n cumhachd gluasaid f m; (velocity) luaths m
monarch n monarc m
monarchist n monarcach m
monarchy n monarcachd f
monastery n manachainn f
Monday n Diluain m
monetary a ionmhasail
money n airgead m
mongol n mongolach m
mongrel n, a eadar-ghnè f

monitor v cùm sùil air, sgrùd
monk n manach m
monkey n muncaidh m
mono- pref aon-
monopolize v lèir-shealbhaich, gabh thairis
monopoly n monopolaidh f m, lèir-shealbhachd f
monotonous a aon-duanach, liosta
monotony n an aon duan m, liostachd f
monster n uilebheist f m
monstrous a sgriosail, oillteil
month n mìos f m
monthly a mìosail
monument n carragh-cuimhne f, càrn-cuimhne m
mood n sunnd m, gleus f m, triom f; (gram) modh f m
moody a caochlaideach; (sulky) gnù, mùgach
moon n gealach f m **moonlight** solas na gealaich m **the man in the m.** bodach na gealaich m
moor n mòinteach f, monadh m **m. fire** falaisg f
moor v acraich
moorhen n cearc-fhraoich f
moose n lon m
mop n mop m, sguab-fhliuch f
mope v bi fo ghruaimean
moral a moralta, beusach n (of story) teagasg m, teachdaireachd f **morals** n beusan f pl
morale n misneachd f, spiorad m
morality n moraltachd f
morass n bog(l)ach f
morbid a mì-fhallain, dubhach
more n tuilleadh m, barrachd f adv **any m.** tuilleadh, nas mò
morning n madainn f
moron n lethchiallach m
morose a gruamach, mùgach
morphia, morphine n moirfin f
morsel n mìr f, criomag f, bìdeag f
mortal a bàsmhor
mortar n aol-tàthaidh m
mortgage n morgaids(e) m
mosaic n breac-dhualadh m

Moslem *n*, *a See* Muslim
mosque *n* mosg *m*
mosquito *n* mosgìoto *f*
moss *n* (*bot*) còinneach *f*; (*topog*) bog(l)ach *f*
most *n* a' mhòr-chuid *f*, a' chuid as motha *f a* as motha/a bu mhotha, a' chuid as motha/a bu mhotha
mostly *adv* mar as trice, sa mhòr-chuid
moth *n* leòmann *m*
mother *n* màthair *f* **m.-in-law** màthair-chèile *f*
motion *n* gluasad *m*; (*at meeting*) moladh *m* **set in m.** cuir a dhol *v*
motivate *v* spreag, brod
motivation *n* togradh *m*
motive *n* adhbhar *m*, ceann-fàth *m*
motley *a* ioma-sheòrsach, ioma-dhathach
motor *n*, *a* motair *m* **m. bicycle** motair-baidhsagal *m* **m.-cycle** motair-rothair *m*
motorist *n* motairiche *m*
motorway *n* mòr-rathad *m*
motto *n* faca(i)l-suaicheantais *m*
mould *n* molldair *m*; (*form*) cruth *m* **blue m.** clòimh-liath *f v* cum, thoir cumadh air
moult *v* cuir/tilg na h-itean, cuir fionnadh/gaoisid
mound *n* tom *m*, tòrr *m*
mount *v* dìrich, streap; (*horse*) rach air muin eich; (*set up*) cuir air dòigh
mountain *n* beinn *f*, monadh *m*
mountaineer *n* sreapadair (beinne) *m*
mountaineering *n* sreapadaireachd *f*, sreap nam beann *m*
mourn *v* caoidh
mournful *a* brònach, tiamhaidh
mourning *n* bròn *m*, caoidh *f*, tuireadh *m* **in m.** a' caoidh, ri bròn
mouse *n* luch *f*
moustache *n* stais *f*
mouth *n* beul *m*; (*large*) craos *m* **m.-music** port-à-beul *m* **m.-organ** òrgan-beòil *m*
mouthful *n* làn-beòil *m*, balgam *m*
move *v* gluais, caraich; (*propose*) cuir air adhart, mol **m. house** dèan imrich/imprig
movement *n* gluasad *m*

moving *a* (*emotion*) drùidhteach
mow *v* geàrr, buain
mower *n* lomaire *m*
much *adv* mòran; (*with a*) fada **as m. again** uimhir eile **as m. as** uiread ri/agus **too m.** cus **that is m. better** tha sin fada/cus/mòran nas fheàrr *n* mòran *m*
muck *n* salchar *m*, eabar *m*; (*manure*) buachar *m*, innear *f*
mucky *a* salach
mucus *n* ronn *m*
mud *n* poll *m*, eabar *m*
muddle *n* bùrach *m*, troimh-a-chèile *f v* cuir troimh-a-chèile
muddy *a* eabarach, fo eabar/pholl
muffle *v* (*wrap up*) còmhdaich; (*deaden*) mùch
mug *n* muga *f m*; (*fool*) gloidhc *f*
mug *v* thoir ionnsaigh goid
mugging *n* ionnsaigh-goid *f*
muggy *a* bruthainneach
Mull person *n* Muileach *m*, (*female*) ban(a)-Mhuileach *f*
multi- *pref* Ioma-
multicoloured *a* ioma-dhathach
multicultural *a* ioma-chultarach
multilateral *a* ioma-thaobhach
multilingual *a* ioma-chànanach
multimedia *n* ioma-mheadhan *m*
multinational *a* ioma-nàiseanta
multiple *a* ioma-sheòrsach, iomadach
multiplication *n* iomadachadh *m*, meudachadh *m*
multiply *v* iomadaich, meudaich; (*genetically*) sìolaich, fàs lìonmhor
multitude *n* mòr-shluagh *m*
mum(my) *n* mamaidh *f*
mumble *v* bi a' brunndail
mumps *n* an t-at-busach *m*, an tinneas-plocach *m*
munch *v* cagainn
mundane *a* àbhaisteach, làitheil
mural *n* dealbh-balla *m*
murder *n* murt *m v* dèan murt
murderer *n* murtair *m*
murmur *n* (*of nature*) monmhar *m*, torman *m*, crònan *m*; (*person*) brunndail *f*

muscle n fèith f
muscular a fèitheach
museum n taigh-tasgaidh m
mushroom n balgan-buachair m
music n ceòl m
musical a ceòlmhor, binn; (*person*) math air ceòl **m. instrument** n inneal-ciùil m
musician n neach-ciùil m
Muslim n, a Muslamach m, (*female*) ban-Mhuslamach f
mussel n feusgan m
must v feumaidh, bi aig … ri …, 's èiginn do, 's fheudar do
mustard n (*bot*) sgeallan m; (*condiment*) mustard m
muster v cruinnich, trus
musty a tungaidh, fuaraidh
mutation n mùthadh m, atharrachadh m

mute a balbh, tostach
mutilate v ciorramaich, geàrr
mutiny n ceannairc f, ar-a-mach m v dèan ceannairc/ar-a-mach
mutter v dèan dranndan/gearan
mutton n muilt-fheòil f, feòil caorach f
mutual a co-aontach, a rèir a chèile
muzzle v cuir glas-ghuib air
my poss pron mo, (*before vowels*) m', agam(sa) **my key** an iuchair agam
myself pron mi fhèin/fhìn
mysterious a dìomhair
mystery n dìomhaireachd f, rùn dìomhair m
mystical a fàidheanta
mystify v cuir an imcheist
myth n miotas m, uirsgeul m
mythical a miotasach
mythology n miotas-eòlas m

N

nag v dèan cànran
nail n tarrag f; (*finger/toe*) ìne f **n.-file** lìomhan-ìnean m **n. varnish** bhàrnais ìnean f
naive a neoichiontach, sìmplidh
naked a lomnochd, rùisgte
name n ainm m; (*reputation*) cliù m v ainmich **give a n. to** thoir ainm air
nap n norrag f, snuachdan m, cadalan m; (*on cloth*) caitean m

nasty a mosach, suarach
nation n nàisean m, dùthaich f, rìoghachd f
national a nàiseanta **n. insurance** n àrachas nàiseanta m **the N. Health Service** Seirbheis Nàiseanta na Slàinte f
nationalism n nàiseantachas m
nationalist n, a nàiseantach m
nationality n nàiseantachd f
nationalize v stàit-shealbhaich, cuir an seilbh na stàite

Insight: name

Ainm is a name. To ask someone their name, you say *dè an t-ainm a th' ort?* what's your name? You reply by stating your name or by saying *is mise* followed by your name eg *is mise Ceit*, I am Kate. The verb to name is *ainmich*.

---

napkin n nèapaigin f m
nappy n badan m
narrate v aithris
narration n aithris f, iomradh m, seanchas m
narrator n neach-aithris m, seanchaidh m
narrow a cumhang, caol **n.-minded** cumhang

native n dùthchasach m **n. of** neach a mhuinntir … m (+ gen) a dùthchasach, san dualchas **n. speaker** fileantach ((bh)o dhùthchas) m
natural a nàdarra(ch)
naturalist n neach-eòlais-nàdair m
naturally adv gu nàdarra(ch)

nature n nàdar m, gnè f, seòrsa m
n. reserve tèarmann nàdair m
naught n neoni m
naughty a dona, mì-mhodhail
nausea n òrrais f, neoshannt m
nautical a seòlaidh, maraireachd
navel n imleag f
navigate v (plot course) tog cùrsa; (make passage) seòl
navigation n mara(irea)chd f
navy n cabhlach m, nèibhidh m
navy-blue a dubh-ghorm
neap-tide n conntraigh f
near a faisg (air), dlùth (air), teann (air)
nearly adv faisg/dlùth air; (almost) cha mhòr nach (+ v)
neat a grinn, sgiobalta, cuimir
necessary a riatanach, deatamach, do-sheachanta
necessity n riatanas m, deatamachd f
dire n. an dubh-èiginn f
neck n amha(i)ch f, muineal m
necklace n seud-muineil m, usgar-bràghad m, paidirean m
need n feum m; (want) dìth f m, easbhaidh f; (poverty) airc f v bi feumach air; (must) feum(aidh); (want) bi a dhìth air **we n. money** tha sinn feumach air airgead **we'll n. to go** feumaidh sinn falbh **what do you n.?** dè tha dhìth ort? **you n. not do that** cha leig/ruig thu a leas sin a dhèanamh
needle n snàthad f
needless a gun adhbhar
needy a ainniseach, easbhaidheach n **the n.** na feumaich m pl
negative a àicheil
neglect n dearmad m v dèan dearmad (air), bi gun diù (mu)
negligence n dearmadachd f, mì-chùram m, cion diù m
negligent a dearmadach, mì-chùramach
negligible a suarach, neonitheach
negotiate v barganaich, dèan gnothach (ri), co-rèitich
negotiation n barganachadh m, co-rèiteachadh m
neigh v dèan sitir/sitrich, sitrich

neighbour n nàbaidh m, coimhearsnach m
neighbourhood n nàba(idhea)chd f, coimhearsnachd f
neither a, pron a h-aon conj cha mhò adv nas mò **n. of them stayed** cha do dh'fhuirich a h-aon aca/fear seach fear aca/tè seach tè aca **she doesn't drive and n. does he** cha dèan ise dràibheadh 's cha mhò a nì esan
neo- pref nuadh-
nephew n mac peathar/bràthar m
nerve n fèith-mhothachaidh f, nearbh f **what a n.!** abair aghaidh! **he lost his n.** chaill e a mhisneachd
nervous a iomagaineach, nearbha(sa)ch
nest n nead f m v neadaich
net n lìon m **the Net** an Lìon
netball n ball-lìn m
nettle n deanntag f, feanntag f
network n lìon m, lìonra m v dèan lìonra; (met) dèan eadar-cheanglaichean
neuter a (gram) neodrach
neutral a neo-phàirteach, gun taobh
never adv (with neg v) a-chaoidh, gu bràth, uair sam bith; (in past) (a-)riamh **n. mind!** interj coma leat!
nevertheless adv an dèidh sin, a dh'aindeoin sin
new a ùr, nuadh **New Year** a' Bhliadhn' Ùr f **N. Year's Day** Latha na Bliadhn' Ùire m **Happy New Year!** Bliadhna Mhath Ùr!
news n naidheachd f, fios m **newspaper** pàipear-naidheachd m
next a an ath (+ len), ... as fhaisge/a b' fhaisge adv a-nis **n. week** an ath sheachdain **what next!** dè nis!, dè an ath rud!
nibble v criom, creim
nice a gasta, laghach, snog
niche n cùil f, oisean m
nick n eag f **in the n. of time** dìreach na uair/ann an tide v eagaich; (steal) goid
nickname n far-ainm m, frith-ainm m
niece n nighean peathar/bràthar f
night n oidhche f **all n.** fad na h-oidhche **at n.** air an oidhche **the n. before last** a' bhòn-raoir **last n.** a-raoir **tonight** a-nochd **tomorrow n.** an ath-oidhch'

nightgown/nightie n gùn-oidhche m
nightmare n trom-laighe f m
nil n neoni m
nimble a clis, sgiobalta
nine n a naoi a naoi, naodh **n. people** naoinear, naodhnar f m
nineteen n, a naoi-deug, naodh-deug **n. points** naoi puingean deug
ninety n, a ceithir fichead 's a deich, naochad m
ninth a naoidheamh, naodhamh
nip n bìdeadh m, teumadh m; (of whisky) tè bheag f v bìd, teum
nit n mial f
no neg response cha/chan plus verb used in question **will you be there? no** am bi thu ann? cha bhi **will she tell him? no** an innis i dha? chan innis a sam bith, gin, sgath **it was of no benefit to him** cha robh buannachd sam bith ann dha **we have no milk** chan eil sgath bainne againn **there were no children** cha robh gin a chloinn ann adv càil/dad nas ... (with neg v) **he is no better** chan eil e càil/dad nas fheàrr
nobility n uaislean m pl, maithean m pl; (quality) uaisleachd f
noble n, a uasal m
nobody/no one n (after neg v) aon m, duine m **there was n. to be seen** cha robh duine/neach (sam bith) ri fhaicinn
nod n gnogadh cinn m v gnog/crom (do cheann) **she nodded off** rinn i norrag
noise n fuaim f m
noisy a fuaimneach, gleadhrach, faramach
nominal a san ainm
nominate v ainmich
nomination n ainmeachadh m
nominative a ainmneach **the n. case** an tuiseal ainmneach m
non- pref neo-
non-stop a, adv ... gun stad
nonchalant a gun chùram
none pron (after neg v) aon duine m, neach (sam bith) m, gin f, sgath m
nonsense n amaideas m
nonsensical a gun chiall, amaideach

nook n cùil f, iùc f
noon n nòin m, meadhan-latha m
nor conj no, cha mhò
norm n àbhaist f
normal a riaghailteach, àbhaisteach, gnàthach
normally adv am bitheantas, anns a' chumantas
Norse a Lochlannach
north n, a (an) tuath m, an àird a tuath f **in the n.** mu thuath **n. of** tuath air **n.-east** (an) ear-thuath m **n.-west** (an) iar-thuath m
Norwegian n, a Nirribheach m, (female) ban-Nirribheach f
nose n sròn f **nosebleed** leum-sròine m
nostalgia n cianalas m
not adv cha, chan, na, nach **we will not go there** cha tèid sinn ann **I will not leave it** chan fhàg mi e **do not move it** na gluais e **he said that he would not do that** thuirt e nach dèanadh e sin
notable a ainmeil, sònraichte
notch n eag f
note n nota f; (letter) sgrìobag f; (mus) pong m v thoir fa-near, comharraich
noted a ainmeil, cliùiteach
nothing n neoni m; (with neg) nì/rud sam bith **she would think n. of it** cha shaoileadh i dad dheth
notice n fios m, brath m; (written) sanas m; (warning) rabhadh m v mothaich, thoir fa-near, thoir an aire
notify v leig fhaicinn do, thoir fios (do)
notion n beachd m, smaoin f; (concept) bun-bheachd m
notorious a suaicheanta, le droch cliù
noun n ainmear m **verbal n.** ainmear gnìomhaireach
nourish v àraich, beathaich, tog
nourishment n beathachadh m
novel n nobhail f, uirsgeul f m
novel a nuadh, annasach
novelty n annas m
November n an t-Samhain f
now adv a-nis(e), an-dràsta, an-ceartuair **now and again** an-dràsta 's a-rithist
nowadays adv an-diugh, san là an-diugh

nowhere adv (after neg v) an àite sam bith
nozzle n soc m, smeachan m
nuclear a niùclasach **n. power** cumhachd niùclasach f m **n. waste** sgudal niùclasach m **n. weapons** armachd niùclasach f
nucleus n niùclas m
nude a rùisgte, lomnochd
nudge v put
nuisance n dragh m
null a gun stàth, gun bhrìgh **n. and void** falamh gun èifeachd
numb a meilichte, rag le fuachd, anns an eighealaich **n. with cold** air a lathadh etc v meilich, ragaich
number n àireamh f **phone n.** àireamh-fòn v cunnt(ais), àireamh(aich)

numeral n figear m
numerate a àireamhachail
numerical a àireamhach
numerous a lìonmhor, iomadach (precedes n)
nun n bean-chràbhaidh f, cailleach-dhubh f
nurse n banaltram f, nurs f v nurs(aig), altraim
nursery n seòmar-altraim m; (school) sgoil-àraich f; (bot) planntlann f
nursing n banaltramachd f, nursadh m; (of child) altramas m **n.-home** taigh-altraim m
nurture v àraich, oileanaich
nut n (food, mech) cnò f
nutrition n beathachadh m, mathas m
nylon n naidhlean m

O

oak n darach m a daraich
oar n ràmh m
oasis n innis-fàsaich f
oatcake n aran-coirce m
oath n bòid f **oaths** mionnan f m pl
oatmeal n min-choirce f
oats n coirce m
obdurate a rag-mhuinealach
obedience n ùmhlachd f
obedient a umhail
obese a reamhar, tiugh, sultmhor
obey v bi umhail (do)
obituary n iomradh-bàis m; (death notice) sanas bàis m
object n nì m, rud m; (objective) adhbhar m **o. of ...** cùis- ... f, cuspair m (+ gen); (gram) cuspair m
object v cuir an aghaidh

objection n cur an aghaidh m, gearan f m
objective n amas m, ceann-uidhe m a cothromach, neo-eisimeileach
obligation n comain f, dleastanas m
oblige v (require) cuir mar fhiachaibh air; (do a favour to) cuir fo chomain
obliging a èasgaidh, deònach
obliterate v dubh a-mach
oblong a cruinn-fhada
obnoxious a gràineil
obscene a draosta, drabasta
obscure a doilleir; (met) dìomhair v dèan doilleir, cuir fo sgleò, falaich
observant a forail, mothachail, aireil
observatory n amharclann f
observe v amhairc, coimhead, thoir an aire; (keep) cùm, glèidh

---

Insight: obscure

Doilleir is the word for obscure. It is one of several pairs of words where a negative meaning is signified by an initial d while the positive is indicated by an initial s. *Soilleir* means clear or bright. Other examples are *soirbh* (easy) and *doirbh* (difficult), *sona* (happy) and *dona* (bad).

observer n neach-coimhid m, neach-amhairc m

obsession n beò-ghlacadh m

obsolete a à cleachdadh, (bh)o fheum

obstacle n cnap-starra m, bacadh m

obstinate a rag-mhuinealach, fada na c(h)eann fhèin etc

obstruct v bac, cuir bacadh air

obstruction n cnap-starra m, bacadh m

obtain v faigh

obvious a follaiseach, soilleir, nochdte

occasion n (event) tachartas m; (reason) adhbhar m; (time) uair f, turas m **on one o.** aon uair/turas

occasionally adv corra uair, an-dràsta 's a-rithist, (bh)o àm gu àm

occupation n obair f, dreuchd f; (of property) gabhail thairis m

occupy v gabh sealbh/còmhnaidh; (space) lìon; (time) cuir seachad tìde; (property) gabh thairis

occur v tachair **o. to** thig a-steach air

occurrence n tachartas m

ocean n cuan m, fairge f

octagon n ochd-shliosach m

octave n ochdad m

October n an Dàmhair f

octopus n ochd-chasach m, gibearnach-meurach m

odd a neònach, àraid; (number) còrr **o. one out** (an) conadal m

odds n còrrlach m; (leftovers) fuidheall m **against the o.** an aghaidh an t-sruth **it makes no o.** is coma, chan eil e gu diofar

ode n duan m

odour n boladh m, boltradh m

of prep de/dhe, à **one of these days** latha dhe na lathaichean **many of us** mòran againn/dhinn **think of it** smaoinich air/mu dheidhinn (often conveyed by gen form) **a sum of money** sùim airgid **of course it is** nach eil fhios gu bheil

off prep de, dhe, bhàrr/far (+ gen) **the car went off the road** chaidh an càr bhàrr an rathaid/dhen rathad adv dheth **he put off the light** chuir e dheth an solas **they made off** rinn iad às **come off it!** thalla is thoir ort! **it's gone off** (gone bad) tha e air a dhol grod

offence n oilbheum m, coire f; (criminal) eucoir f

offend v dèan/thoir oilbheum do; (criminally) dèan eucoir

offender n eucorach m, ciontach m

offensive a oilbheumach; (attacking) ionnsaigheach

offer n tairgse f, tathann m v tairg, dèan/thoir tairgse, tathainn

offhand a coma, beag-sùim

office n oifis f, oifig f; (role) dreuchd f

officer n oifigear m

official n oifigeach m a oifigeil **o. opening** fosgladh oifigeil m

offspring n sliochd m, àl m

often adv (gu) tric, (gu) minig

oil n ola f v cuir ola air **oilfield** raon-ola m **oilrig** crann-ola m **oil-tanker** tancair ola m

oily a olach, ùilleach

ointment n acfhainn f, aolmann m

old a sean, aosta **old-fashioned** seann-fhasanta **old man** bodach m **old woman** cailleach f

olive n (tree) crann-ola m; (fruit) meas a' chroinn-ola m, dearc-ola m **o.-oil** ola a' chroinn-ola f

omen n manadh m

ominous a droch-fhàistinneach

omission n dearmad m

omit v dèan dearmad, fàg às

omnipotent a uile-chumhachdach

on prep air; (after) an dèidh adv air; (onwards) air adhart **off and on** air is dheth, thuige 's bhuaithe

once adv uair, aon uair/turas

one n a h-aon; (person) neach m, fear m, tè f; (one thing) aon(an) m

one a aon **one-way** aon-shligheach, aon-rathad

onerous a trom, sàrachail

onion n uinnean m

on-line n air-loidhne

only a aon **the o. way** an aon dòigh adv a-mhàin conj (after neg v) ach **he o. wanted to help her** cha robh e ach airson a cuideachadh

onus *n* uallach *m*

onward *adv* air adhart

ooze *v* sil

opaque *a* doilleir, do-lèirsinneach

open *v* fosgail *a* fosgailte; (*frank*) fosgarra

opener *n* fosglair *m*

opening *n* fosgladh *m*; (*gap*) beàrn *f m*

openly *adv* gu fosgailte

opera *n* opara *f pl* oparathan

operate *v* obraich; (*med*) dèan opairèisean, cuir fon sgithinn

operation *n* obair *f*, gnìomhachd *f*; (*med*) opairèisean *f m*

opinion *n* barail *f*, beachd *m* **o. poll** cunntas-bheachd *m*

opinionated *a* rag-bharalach, fada na c(h)eann fhèin *etc*

opponent *n* cuspairiche *m*, neach-dùbhlain *m*

opportune *a* fàbharach

opportunity *n* cothrom *m*

oppose *v* cuir an aghaidh

opposite *n* ceart-aghaidh *f prep* (+ *gen*) fa chomhair, mu choinneamh

opposition *n* cur an aghaidh *m*, dùbhlan *m*; (*polit*) **the O.** am Partaidh Dùbhlanach *m*

oppress *v* claoidh, dèan fòirneart air

oppression *n* ainneart *m*, fòirneart *m*

oppressive *a* ainneartach, fòirneartach; (*weather*) trom, murtaidh

opt for *v* tagh **opt out** tarraing a-mach/às

optician *n* fradhairciche *m*, neach nan sùilean *m*

optimism *n* so-aigne *f*

optimistic *a* so-aigneach

option *n* roghainn *f m*

optional *a* roghnach, ri roghnachadh

opulence *n* saidhbhreas *m*, toic *f*

or *conj* no, air neo

oral *a* labhairteach, beòil **o. tradition** beul-aithris *f*

orange *n* orainsear *m* **o. juice** sùgh orains *m a* orains

orator *n* òraidiche *m*

orbit *a* reul-chuairt *f*, cuairt *f*

Orcadian *n, a* Arcach *m*, (*female*) ban-Arcach *f*

orchard *n* ubhal-ghort *m*

orchestra *n* orcastra *f*

ordain *v* socraich, sònraich; (*relig*) cuir an dreuchd

ordeal *n* cruaidh-dheuchainn *f*

order *n* òrdugh *m*, òrdan *m*; (*relig*) riaghailt *f* **in o. that** air chor ('s gu) **out of o.** briste; (*met*) mì-iomchaidh

order *v* òrdaich; (*arrange*) cuir an òrdugh

orderly *a* òrdail, riaghailteach

ordinary *a* àbhaisteach, cumanta

ore *n* clach-meinnir *f*

organ *n* (*body*) ball *m*; (*mus*) òrgan *m*

organic *a* fàs-bheairteach

organist *n* òrganaiche *m*

organization *n* buidheann *f m*; (*act of*) eagrachadh *m*

organize *v* cuir air dòigh, eagraich

organizer *n* neach-eagrachaidh *m*, eagraiche *m*

orgy *n* ruidhtearachd *f*

oriental *a* earach

orifice *n* fosgladh *m*

origin *n* tùs *m*, bun *m*, màthair-adhbhar *f*

original *a* tùsail, prìomh, bun-

originate *v* tàrmaich, tòisich

ornament *n* òrnaid *f*, ball-maise *n*

ornamental *a* òrnaideach

ornate *a* mòr-mhaisichte, mòr-sgeadaichte

ornithology *n* eun-eòlas *m*

orphan *n* dilleachdan *m*

orthodox *a* gnàthach; (*relig*) ceart-chreideach

osprey *n* iolair-uisge *f*

ostrich *n* struth *m*

other *pron* eile **the o. day** an latha roimhe **one after the o.** fear/tè às dèidh fir/tè **the others** càch **they gave each o. gifts** thug iad tiodhlacan dha chèile

otherwise *adv* a chaochladh, air mhodh eile; (*or else*) no

otter *n* biast-dhubh *f*, dòbhran *m*

ouch! *exclam* aobh!, aobhag!

ought *v* is còir, tha còir aig **she o. to do it** is còir dhi a dhèanamh/tha còir aice

a dhèanamh **you o. to have done it** bu
chòir dhut a bhith air a dhèanamh/bha
còir agad a bhith air a dhèanamh
ounce n unnsa m
our poss pron ar, ar n- (before vowels),
againne **our father** ar n-athair **our
house** an taigh againne
ourselves pron sinn fhèin/fhìn
oust v cuir às
out adv a-muigh; (motion outwards)
a-mach **O. you/we go!** Mach à seo!
outcast n dìobarach m
outcome n buil f, toradh m
outcry n iolach f, gàir m
outdoors adv a-muigh, air a' bhlàr
a-muigh
outer a a-muigh, a-mach
outfit n trusgan m, aodach m
outing n splaoid f, cuairt f
outlaw n neach-cùirn m, neach fon choill
m v cuir fon choill
outline n dealbh-iomaill f m; (met)
cnàmhan m pl v thoir cunntas air
outlook n sealladh m
out-of-date a à fasan, às an fhasan;
(past sell-by date) seachad air a'
cheann-latha
output n cur a-mach m, toradh m
outrage n cùis-uabhais f
outrageous a uabhasach
outright adv (gu) buileach, (gu) tur
outset n fìor thoiseach m, ciad dol
a-mach m
outside n an taobh/leth a-muigh
m adv a-muigh; (motion) a-mach
outsize n, a mòr-thomhas m, mòr-mheud
m
outskirts n iomall (baile) m
outspoken a fosgarra, a-mach leis
outstanding a barraichte, air leth ...
outward a air an taobh a-muigh; (met)
faicsinneach
outwardly adv (bh)on taobh a-muigh,
(bh)o shealladh dhaoine
outwit v thoir an car à/às
oval a air chumadh uighe, ugh-chruthach
n ugh-chruth m
ovation n mòr-bhualadh-bhas m

oven n àmhainn f
over prep (above) os cionn (+ gen);
(beyond) thar (+ gen); (across) thairis air,
tarsainn air adv (hither) a-null; (yonder)
a-nall; (past) seachad; (additional) a
bharrachd, a bhàrr air; (left over) a chòrr
pref ro- (+ len)
overall a iomlan
over-anxious a ro chùramach
overcharge v iarr/cuir tuilleadh 's a'
chòir (+ air)
overcome v thoir buaidh air, ceannsaich
overdo v dèan tuilleadh 's a' chòir
overdraft n for-tharraing f
overdue a fadalach
overflow n cur thairis m v cuir thairis
overhead adv os cionn, gu h-àrd
   overheads n cosgaisean a bharrachd
   f pl
overhear v dèan farchluais
overload v an-luchdaich, cuir cus air
overlook v seall thairis air; (forget) dèan
dearmad air
overnight a tron oidhche
overrule v bac, diùlt
overrun v cuir fo smachd; (time) ruith
thairis air ùine
overseas a thall thairis adv thall thairis;
(motion) a-null thairis
overshadow v cuir fo sgàil
oversight n dearmad m; (supervision)
stiùireadh m
overt a nochdte, follaiseach
overtake v beir air, rach seachad air
overthrow v tilg sìos, cuir às do
overtime n ùine a bharrachd f, còrr ùine f
overturn v cuir car de, cuir bun-os-cionn
overweight a ro throm
owe v bi fo fhiachan aig; (gratitude) bi an
comain (+ gen) **I o. him £20** tha fichead
not aige orm **he owes me £20** tha
fichead not agam air
owl n cailleach-oidhche f, comhachag f
own pron fhèin/fèin
own v sealbhaich; (admit) gabh ri, aidich
   she owns it 's ann leatha(se) a tha e
owner n neach-seilbhe m, sealbhadair m
ownership n sealbh m

ox n damh m
oxter n achlais f
oxygen n ogsaidean m

P

pace n ceum m; (*speed*) astar m v
   ceumnaich, spaidsirich
pacifist n sìochantair m
pacify v sìthich, ciùinich
pack n paca m; (*a large number of*)
   dròbh f m **a pack of lies** tòrr bhreug(an)
   v pacaig; (*fill up*) lìon
package n pasgan m, pacras m **p. deal**
   tairgse iomlan f
packaging n pacaigeadh m,
   còmhdach m
packet n pacaid f
packing n pacadh m, pacaigeadh m
pact n cùmhnant m, còrdadh m
pad n pada f; (*residence*) cùil f
paddle n pleadhag f, pleadhan m
   v grunnaich, plubraich; (*boat*)
   pleadhagaich
pagan n, a pàganach m
paganism n pàganachd f
page n duilleag f, taobh-duilleig(e) m;
   (*boy*) gille-frithealaidh m
pageant n taisbeanadh-gluasaid m
pail n peile m, cuinneag f
pain n cràdh m, pian f m
painful a cràiteach, piantach
painstaking a saothrachail,
   mionaideach
paint n peant(a) m v peant
painter n peantair m; (*boat's rope*) ball m
painting n peantadh m; (*a picture*)
   dealbh f m
pair n càraid f, paidhir f m v dèan càraid/
   paidhir
Pakistani n, a Pagastànach m, (*female*)
   ban-Phagastànach f
pal n companach m
palace n lùchairt f
palatable a blasta
palate n càirean m, mullach-beòil m;
   (*met*) càil f
pale a bàn

oyster n eisir m
oystercatcher n trilleachan m
ozone n òson m, àile m

palm n bas/bois f; (*tree*) craobh-phailm f
palpable a follaiseach; (*tangible*)
   faireachdail, a ghabhas fhaireachdainn
palpitation n plosgartaich f
paltry a suarach
pamper v dèan cus de, peataich
pamphlet n duilleachan m, bileag f
pan n pana m **p. loaf** lof(a)-phan(a) f
pan- pref uil(e)-
panacea n uil-ìoc m
pancake n foileag f
pancreas n am brisgean milis m
pandemic n mòr-ghalar m
pander (to) v riaraich
pane n l(e)òsan m, glainne f
panel n pannal m; (*section*) clàr m
pang n biorgadh m, guin m
panic n clisgeadh m, breisleach m
pansy n bròg na cuthaig f
pant v plosg
panther n pantar m
panting n plosgartaich f **he was p.** bha
   anail na uchd, bha aonach air
pantomime n pantomaim m
pantry n stòr-bìdh m, preas(a)-bìdh m
pants n drathais f, pants f pl; (*trousers*)
   briogais f
papal a pàpach
paper n pàipear m **p.-clip** greimear-
   pàipeir m v pàipearaich, boltaig
par n co-ionannachd f; (*golf*) an cuibheas
   m **feeling below par** gun a bhith ann
   an sunnd
parable n cosamhlachd f
parachute n paraisiut m
parade n (*march*) caismeachd f v
   spaidsir
Paradise n Pàrras m
paradox n frith-bharail f, dubh-fhacal m
paraffin n paireafain m
paragon n sàr-eisimpleir f m
paragraph n paragraf m

parallel n (*line*) sgrìob cho-shìnte f; (*met*) samhailt f a co-shìnte; (*met*) ionann
paralysis n pairilis f m
parameter n paraimeatair m, crìoch f
paramount a os cionn gach nì, fìor chudromach
parapet n uchd-bhalla m
paraphrase n ath-innse f; (*relig*) laoidh m
parasite n dìosganach m, faoighiche m
parasol n sgàilean-grèine m
paratrooper n saighdear paraisiuit m
parcel n parsail m, pasgan m, trusachan m
parched a pàiteach, gus tiachdadh/teuchdadh
pardon n mathanas m v math, thoir mathanas **p. me** gabh mo leisgeul
pare v beàrr, snaigh
parent n pàrant m
parish n sgìre f; (*eccl*) paraist(e) f
parity n co-ionannachd f
park n pàirc(e) f **car p.** pàirc(e) chàraichean f v parc; (*set down*) càirich
parking place n ionad/àite-parcaidh m
Parliament n Pàrlamaid f
parochial a sgìreachdail, sgìreil; (*met*) beag-seallaidh
parody n atharrais f
parole n paròil m
parrot n pitheid f, pearraid f
parry v dìon o bhuille; (*met*) cuir seachad
parsimonious a cruaidh, spìocach
parsley n peirsill f
parsnip n curran geal m
part n pàirt f m, cuid f, roinn f, cuibhreann f m; (*in drama*) pàirt f m **for my p.** air mo shon-sa v sgar, dealaich, tearb
partake v com-pàirtich
partial a ann an cuid; (*biased*) leth-bhreitheach **p. to** dèidheil/titheach air
participant n com-pàirtiche m
participate v com-pàirtich, gabh pàirt (an)
particle n gràinean m, mìrean m; (*gram*) mion-fhacal m
particular a àraidh, sònraichte; (*fastidious*) faiceallach

parting n dealachadh m
partisan a aon-taobhach, leth-bhreitheach
partition n balla-tarsainn m, tallan m, cailbhe m; (*polit*) roinn f v roinn
partly adv gu ìre, ann an cuid
partner n companach m; (*in business*) neach-com-pàirt m v rach cuide ri, rach an co-bhonn ri
partnership n companas m, caidreabh m; (*in business*) com-pàirteachas m
partridge n cearc-thomain f
party n partaidh m; (*group*) buidheann f m
pass n (*topog*) bealach m; (*in games*) pas m
pass v rach/gabh seachad; (*in sport*) pas(aig); (*exam*) dèan a' chùis, pas(aig); (*eg salt*) thoir/sìn do; (*law*) dèan lagh **p. away** eug, siubhail **p. the time** cuir seachad ùine
passage n turas m, slighe f; (*text*) earrann f **passageway** trannsa f
passenger n neach-siubhail m pl luchd-siubhail
passing place n àite-seachnaidh m
passion n boile f, dìoghras m; (*of Christ*) fulangas (Chrìosd) m
passionate a dìoghrasach
passive a neo-ghnìomhach; (*gram*) fulangach
passport n cead-siubhail f
password n facal-faire m
past a seachad **p. tense** an tràth caithte m n an t-àm a dh'fhalbh m prep seach, seachad air
paste n taois f; (*glue*) glaodh m v glaodh
pasteurize v paistiuraich
pastime n cur-seachad m
pastor n aoghair m
pastoral a (*relig*) aoghaireil; (*way of life*) treudach
pastry n pastraidh m
pasture n ionaltradh m, feurach m
pat v clapranaich
patch n brèid m, tuthag f v cuir tuthag air, cuir pìos ùr air
patently adv gu follaiseach

paternal *a* athaireil
path *n* starran *m*, ceum *m*, frith-rathad *m*
pathetic *a* truagh; (*awful*) cianail **a p. soul** culaidh-thruais *f*
pathology *n* galar-eòlas *m*
pathos *n* drùidhteachd *f*, truasachd *f*
patience *n* foighidinn *f*
patient *n* euslainteach *m a* foighidneach
patiently *adv* gu foighidneach
patriotism *n* gràdh-dùthcha *m*
patrol *n* freiceadan-faire *m*
patron *n* neach-taice *m*
patronymic *n* sloinneadh *m*
patter *n* briog-brag *m*; (*talk*) goileam *m*
pattern *n* pàtran *m*
paucity *n* gainne *f*
paunch *n* maodal *f*
pauper *n* ainnis *m*, bochd *m*
pause *n* stad *m*, anail *f v* stad, fuirich
pavement *n* cabhsair *m*
pavilion *n* pàillean *m*
paw *n* spòg *f*, màg *f*
pawn *v* cuir dhan phàn
pay *n* pàigheadh *m*, tuarastal *m v* pàigh; (*met*) dìol **p. attention to** thoir aire (*do*) **you'll pay for it yet** dìolaidh tu air fhathast
payable *a* ri p(h)àigheadh
payment *n* pàigheadh *m*
pea *n* peasair *f pl* peasraichean
peace *n* sìth *f*, fois *f*, tàmh *m*
peaceful *a* sìtheil, ciùin
peach *n* peitseag *f*
peacock *n* peucag *f*, coileach-peucaig *m*
peak *n* (*hill*) stùc *f*, binnean *m*; (*summit*) mullach *m*
peal *n* torrann *m*, bualadh *m*
peanut *n* cnò-thalmhainn *f*
pear *n* peur *f*
pearl *n* neamhnaid *f*
peasant *n* neach-tuatha *m*
peat *n* mòine *f*; (*single*) fàd *m* **p.-bank** poll-mòna(ch)/mòna(dh) *m* **p.-stack** cruach-mhòna(ch)/mhòna(dh) *f*
pebble *n* molag *f*
peck *v* pioc; (*kiss*) thoir pògag
peculiar *a* àraid, neònach

pedal *n* casachan *m*, troighean *m*
pedantic *a* rag-fhoghlamach
peddle *v* reic, malairtich
pedestal *n* bun-carraigh *m*, bonn *m*
pedestrian *n* coisiche *m* **p. precinct** àrainn-choisichean *f a* coise; (*uninspiring*) mu làimh **p. way** ceum coise *m*
pedigree *n* sinnsearachd *f*
peel *n* rùsg *m*, plaosg *m v* rùisg
peeled *a* air a rùsgadh
peep *n* caogadh *m*, dìdeadh *m v* caog, dìd
peer *n* (*noble*) morair *m*; (*in age*) comhaois *m*; (*equal*) seise *m*, co-inbheach *m*
peeved *a* leamh, tàmailteach
peewit *n* curracag *f*
peg *n* cnag *f*, ealchainn *f*
pelican *n* peileagan *m*
pellet *n* gràinnean *m*
pelt *n* bian *m*, seiche *f*
pelt *v* caith … air
pen *n* peann *m*; (*fold*) crò *m*, buaile *f*
penalize *v* peanasaich, cuir peanas air
penalty *n* peanas *m* **p. kick** breab peanais *f*
pence *n* sgillinnean *f pl*
pencil *n* peansail *m* **p. sharpener** geuraiche peansail *m*
pendant *n* crochadan *m*
pending *a* a' feitheamh, ri t(h)ighinn
pendulum *n* cudrom-siùdain *m*
penetrate *v* drùidh, faigh tro
penetrating *a* drùidhteach; (*met*) geurchuiseach
penguin *n* ceann-fionn *m*
penicillin *n* peinisilean *m*
peninsula *n* leth-eilean *m*
penis *n* bod *m*
penitence *n* aithreachas *m*
penitent *a* aithreachail
penknife *n* sgian-p(h)òcaid *f*
pennant *n* bratachag *f*
penniless *a* gun sgillinn
penny *n* sgillinn *f*
pension *n* peinnsean *m*
pensioner *n* peinnseanair *m*, neach-peinnsein *m*

pensive *a* fo throm-smaoin
pentagon *n* còig-cheàrnach *m*
Pentecost *n* a' Chaingis *f*
penthouse *n* bàrr-àros *m*
penultimate *a* leth-dheireannach
people *n* sluagh *m*, muinntir *f*
pepper *n* piobar *m*
per capita *adv* gach pearsa/neach
perceive *v* mothaich, thoir fa-near
per cent *adv* sa cheud
percentage *n* ceudad *m*, ìre sa cheud *f*
perceptible *a* nochdte
perception *n* tuigse *f*, lèirsinn *f*
perceptive *a* lèirsinneach, breithneachail, geurchuiseach
perch *n* spiris *f*, spàrr *m*; (*fish*) creagag *f*
  v rach air spiris
percolate *v* sìolaidh
percolator *n* sìol(t)achan *m* coffee p.
  sìol(t)achan cofaidh
percussion *n* bualadh *m*, faram *m*
peremptory *a* obann, sparrail; (*decisive*) do-atharraichte
perennial *a* bliadhnail; (*long-lasting*) maireannach
perfect *a* coileanta, foirfe *v* dèan coileanta/foirfe
perfection *n* foirfeachd *f*, coileantachd *f*
perfectionist *n* foirfiche *m*
perforate *v* toll, cuir tuill an
perform *v* (*carry out*) dèan, coilean; (*in play*) cluich; (*stage*) cuir air àrd-ùrlar
performance *n* (*execution*) coileanadh *m*, cur an gnìomh *m*; (*on stage etc*) cluich *f* p. indicator comharra coileanaidh *m*
performer *n* cluicheadair *m*, cleasaiche *m*
perfume *n* cùbhrachd *f*
perhaps *adv* is dòcha (gu), math dh'fhaodte/is mathaid (gu)
peril *n* gàbhadh *m*
perilous *a* gàbhaidh
perimeter *n* cuairt-thomhas *m*
period *n* ùine *f*; (*era*) àm *m*; (*punct*) stad-phuing *f*; (*menstruation*) fuil-mìos *f*
periodical *n* ràitheachan *m*, iris *f*
periodically *adv* (bh)o àm gu àm

peripheral *a* iomallach, air an oir; (*met*) neo-chudromach
periphery *n* iomall *m*, oir *f m*
periscope *n* pearasgop *m*
perish *v* rach a dhìth, rach às an rathad
perjure *v* thoir fianais-bhrèige/mionnan-eithich
perjury *n* eitheach *m* commit p. *v* thoir fianais-bhrèige/mionnan-eithich
perky *a* bideanach
perm *n* pearm *m*
permanent *a* buan, maireannach
permeate *v* rach air feadh, rach tro
permissible *a* ceadaichte
permission *n* cead *m*
permit *n* bileag-cead *f*, ceadachd *f*
  v ceadaich, leig le
permutation *n* iomlaid *f*, mùthadh *m*
pernicious *a* millteach
perpendicular *a* inghearach, dìreach suas/sìos
perpetrate *v* dèan, cuir an gnìomh
perpetual *a* sìor-mhaireannach
perpetuate *v* cùm a' dol, sìor chleachd
perplex *v* cuir imcheist air
perplexed *a* imcheisteach, an imcheist
perquisite *n* frith-bhuannachd *f*
persecute *v* geur-lean, dèan geur-leanmhainn air
persecution *n* geur-leanmhainn *m*
perseverance *n* leanaltas *m*, cumail aige *f*
persevere *v* lean air, cùm aig/ri
persist *v* lean air/ri, cùm a' dol
persistent *a* leanailteach, sìor-
person *n* neach *m*, pearsa *m*
  spokesperson neach-labhairt *m*
personable *a* tlachdmhor
personal *a* pearsanta
personality *n* pearsantachd *f* a p. pearsa ainmeil *m*
personification *a* pearsachadh *m*
personify *v* pearsaich
personnel *n* luchd-obrach *f*, sgioba *f*, sgiobachd *f* P. Dept Roinn na Sgiobachd *f*
perspective *n* (*standpoint*) sealladh *m*, beachd *m*; (*in art*) buaidh-astair *f* from my p. na mo shealladh-sa

perspiration n fallas m
perspire v cuir fallas de **he was perspiring** bha fallas air/bha e a' cur falla(i)s dheth
persuade v cuir ìmpidh air, thoir … a thaobh, thoir air
persuasion n ìmpidh f, toirt … a thaobh m; (creed) creideamh m; (values) feallsanachd f
persuasive a buadhmhor, a bheir neach a thaobh
pervasive a lìonsgarach, fad' is farsaing
pertain v buin do
pertinent a iomchaidh
perturb v buair, cuir dragh air
perturbed a draghail
peruse v leugh; (scrutinise) sgrùd, rannsaich
pervade v lìon, rach air feadh
perverse a claon
pervert n claonaire m v claon, cuir fiaradh an
pessimism n eu-dòchas m
pessimist n neach gun dòchas m
pessimistic a eu-dòchasach
pest n plàigh f **he's a p**. 's e plàigh a th' ann
pester v cuir dragh air
pesticide n puinnsean bhiastagan m
pet n peata m
petal n flùr-bhileag f
petition n athchuinge f, tagradh m, guidhe f m v dèan athchuinge, guidh, aslaich
petrified a a' dol à cochall mo chridhe, eagal mo bheatha orm etc
petrol n peatrail m **p.-pump** pump(a) peatrail m
petticoat n còta-bàn m
petty a beag, suarach
petulant a bleideil
pew n suidheachan m, treasta m
pewter n feòdar m
phallic a bodail, mar bhod
phantom n taibhs(e) m, tannasg m
pharmacy n eòlas-leigheasan m; (shop) bùth-ceimigeir f

phase n ìre f **p. in** v thoir a-steach mean air mhean **p. out** v cuir às mean air mhean
pheasant n easag f
phenomenon n iongantas m, rud air leth m
phial n meanbh-bhotal m
philanthropy n deagh euchdachd f
philology n eòlas chànan m
philosopher n feallsanach m
philosophical a feallsanachail; (stoical) leagte ri
philosophy n feallsanachd f
phlegm n ronn m
phone n fòn f m v fòn(aig)
phonetic a fogharach
phoney a fallsa, breugach, gun bhrìgh n mealltaire m
phosphate n fosfat m
phosphorescence n caile-biànain m, teine-sionnachain m
phosphorus n fosfor m, sionn m
photocopier n lethbhreacadair m, copaidhear m
photocopy n lethbhreac m, copaidh f v dèan lethbhreac/copaidh
photograph n dealbh camara f m v tog dealbh
photographer n neach-togail-dhealbh m
photography n togail dhealbh f
phrase n abairt f
physical a corporra **p. education** foghlam corporra m
physician n lèigh m, lighiche m
physics n fiosaig f
physiotherapist n anaclair-cuirp m
physiotherapy n anacladh-cuirp m
physique n dèanamh m
pianist n cluicheadair piàna m
piano n piàna m
pibroch n ceòl-mòr m
pick n taghadh m; (pickaxe) pic m, piocaid f v (choose) tagh, roghnaich; (lift) tog; (meat off bones) pioc, spiol
picket n piceid m
pickle n picil f v saill, cuir ann am picil
pickpocket n mèirleach-pòcaid m
picky a àilgheasach

picnic n cuirm-chnuic f
Pict n Cruithneach m
picture n dealbh f m, pioctar m
picturesque a àillidh, mar dhealbh
pie n paidh m **pie chart** clàr-cearcaill m
piece n pìos m, mìr m, earrann f, bìdeag f; (sandwich) pìos m
piecemeal a (unsystematic) bìdeagach adv (gradually) mean air mhean
pier n cidhe m
pierce v toll
piercing a (sound) biorach
piety n cràbhadh m
pig n muc f **piglet** uircean m **pigsty** fail-mhuc f
pigeon n calman m
pig-headed a ceann-dàna, rag
pike n pìc f; (fish) geadas m
pile n dùn m, càrn m, tòrr m v càrn, cruach
pilfer v dèan braide, goid
pilgrim n taistealach m
pilgrimage n taistealachd f, taisteal m
pill n pile f m, gràinnean m
pillage v creach, spùill
pillar n carragh f, colbh m
pillow n cluasag f **p.-case** cuibhrig(e)-cluasaig f m
pilot n neach-iùil m, paidhleat m **p. scheme** sgeama dearbhaidh m v (guide) treòraich, stiùir; (try out) dèan dearbhadh air, feuch
pimple n guirean m, plucan m
pin n prìne m, dealg f **pin cushion** prìneachan m **pins and needles** cadal-deilgneach m
pincers n teanchair m
pinch n bìdeag f, gòmag f; (small quantity) gràinnean m v thoir bìdeag/gòmag à
pine n giuthas m **p. forest** giùthsach m
pine v searg, caith **p. for** gabh fadachd airson
pineapple n anann m
pink a pinc, bàn-dhearg
pinky n lùdag f
pinnacle n binnean m, bidean m

pint n pinnt m **a p. of beer** pinnt leann(a)
pioneer n tùsaire m
pious a cràbhach, diadhaidh
pipe n pìob f v cluich/seinn a' phìob
pipeline n loidhne phìoban f **in the p.** sa bheairt
piper n pìobaire m
piping n pìobaireachd f
pirate n spùinneadair-mara m
pistol n daga m
piston n loinid f
pit n toll m, sloc m
pitch n (tar) bìth f; (sound) àirde f; (sport) raon-cluiche m
pitch v suidhich; (throw) tilg; (target) amais **p. tent** cuir suas teanta
pitfall duilgheadas m
pith n glaodhan m; (met) spionnadh m, brìgh f
pitiful a truagh
pittance n sùim shuarach f
pity n truas m, iochd f, truacantas m **what a p.!** 's mòr am beud! v gabh truas de/ri
pivot n maighdeag f
pizza n piotsa m
placate v ciùinich
place n àite m, ionad m **p. name** ainm-àite m v suidhich, socraich, càirich, cuir
placid a ciùin, sèimh
plagiarism n mèirle-sgrìobhaidh f
plague n plàigh f
plaice n lèabag/leòbag-mhòr f
plaid n breacan m a breacain
plain n còmhnard m, faiche f a rèidh, còmhnard; (clear) soilleir, plèan; (ordinary) plèan
plaintive a tiamhaidh
plait n figheachan m
plan n plana m, innleachd f **development p.** plana leasachaidh m v dealbh, innlich, planaig
plane n plèan(a) m, itealan m; (tool) locair f; (abstr) raon m v locair, locraich
planet n planaid f
plank n clàr m, dèile f
planner n neach-dealbh(ach)aidh m

planning n dealbh(ach)adh m, planadh m **p. permission** cead-dealbh(ach)aidh m

plant n lus m, luibh f m, planntrais f; (mech) uidheam m; (factory) factaraidh f m v cuir, planntaich; (place) suidhich

plantation n (place) ionad-cuir/cura m; (trees etc) planntachas m

plaster n plèastar m, sglàib f; (med) plàst m

plaster v plèastair

plasterer n plèastair m

plastic n plastaig f **p. surgery** n ath-dhealbhadh bodhaig m a plastaig

plasticine n plastasan m

plate n truinnsear m; (sheet) pleit f

platform n àrd-ùrlar m

platter n truinnsear mòr m

plausible a beulach, beulchar

play n cluich(e) f m, cleas m; (stage) dealbh-chluich f m v cluich

player n cluicheadair m

playful a beadrach, sùgrach

playground n raon-cluiche m

playgroup n cròileagan m

playleader n stiùiriche-cluiche m

playwright n sgrìobhaiche dràma m, dràmadaiche m

plea n guidhe f m; (law) tagradh m

plead v guidh air; (in law) tagair; (excuse) thoir mar leisgeul

pleasant a taitneach, tlachdmhor

please v toilich, riaraich; (intrans) còrd, taitinn **if you p.** mas e do thoil e, (pl & pol) mas e ur toil e

pleased a toilichte

pleasing a tlachdmhor, càilear

pleasure n tlachd f, toileachadh m

pleat n filleadh m, pleat f v figh, cuachaich, pleat

pleated a cuachach, pleatach

pledge n geall m, gealladh m, barantas m v geall, rach an geall, thoir barantas

plenary a làn-, iomlan **p. session** làn-sheisean m

plentiful a pailt, lìonmhor

plenty n pailteas m adv gu leòr

pleurisy n an grèim mòr m, pliùrais m

pliable a sùbailte, subailte, so-lùbte

pliers n greimire m

plight n cor m, càradh m

plod v saothraich, imich gu trom

plot n (of ground) goirtean m, pìos talmhainn m; (scheme) innleachd f, gùim m; (lit) plot(a) m v dèan innleachd/ gùim; (track) lorg/lean slighe

plough n crann m **the P.** an Crann v treabh

ploughman n treabhaiche m

plover n feadag f

ploy n plòidh f; (tactic) cleas m

pluck v spìon, buain

plucky a tapaidh

plug n plucan m, pluga m, cnag f; (in boat) tùc m **plughole** toll-sìolaidh m v dùin, plucaich; (of product) put

plum n pluma(i)s m

plumb v feuch doimhneachd

plumb a dìreach **p.-line** sreang-dhìreach f

plumber n plumair m

plummet v tuit gu grad

plump a reamhar, tiugh, sultmhor

plunder n creach f, cobhartach f m v spuinn, creach

plunge n tumadh m v tum; (thrust) sàth

plural a iomarra n, a iolra m

plus prep agus, le, a thuilleadh air

ply v saothraich; (supply) cùm ... ri; (shipping) ruith

pneumonia n am fiabhras-clèibhe m, teasach sgamhain f

poach v poidsig; (food) slaop

poacher n poidsear m

pocket n pòcaid f **p.-money** airgead-pòcaid m v cuir na p(h)òcaid etc, pòcaidich

pod n plaosg m

poem n dàn m, duan m

poet n bàrd m, filidh m

poetess n bana-bhàrd f

poetry n bàrdachd f

poignant a tiamhaidh

point n puing f; (headland) rubha m; (of pencil) gob m; (of view) barail f, sealladh m **what's the p.?** dè am feum a th' ann? v comharraich, seall

pointed a biorach; (*remark*) geur
poise n giùlan grinn m; (*balance*) co-chothrom m
poised a an co-chothrom, air mheidh
 p. to ... deiseil gu ...
poison n puinnsean m, nimh m v puinnseanaich
poisonous a puinnseanach, puinnseanta, nimheil
poke n (*bag*) poca m
poke v brod(an)aich; (*prod*) stob
 p. about rùraich
poker n brod-teine m, pòcair m
polar bear n mathan bàn m
polarize v pòlaraich, cuir calg-dhìreach an aghaidh a chèile
pole n pòla m, pòile m, cabar m **the North P.** am Pòla a Tuath **the South Pole** am Pòla a Deas
Pole n Pòlainneach m, (*female*) ban-Phòlainneach f
polecat n taghan m
police n poileas m **p. car** càr poilis m
 p. officer oifigear poilis m **p. station** stèisean poilis m
policeman n poileas m, poileasman m
policewoman n ban-phoileas f
policy n poileasaidh m
polish n lìomh f, lìomhadh m v lìomh, cuir lìomh air, lìomhaich
Polish a Pòlainneach
polished a lìomhte
polite a modhail
politic a glic, gleusta
political a poilitigeach **p. asylum** comraich phoilitigeach f **p. party** partaidh poilitigeach m
politically correct a ceart gu poilitigeach
politician n neach-poilitigs m

politics n poilitigs f
poll n cunntas cheann m; (*vote*) bhòtadh m; (*election*) taghadh m **p. tax** n cìs cheann f
pollen n poilean m
pollute v truaill, salaich
polluted a truaillte, air a t(h)ruailleadh *etc*
pollution n truailleadh m
polygon n ioma-cheàrnach f
pomp n greadhnachas m
pomposity n mòrchuis f
pompous a mòrchuiseach
pond n linne f, lòn m
ponder v beachd-smaoinich, cnuasaich, meòraich
ponderous a trom
pontificate v cuir às do chorp, dèan searmon de
pontoon n pontùn m
pony n pònaidh m
pool n linne f, glumag f, lòn m
poor a bochd, truagh
pop n (*sound*) brag m **p. music** ceòl pop m
Pope n am Pàp(a) m
poplar n pobhlar m
poppy n crom-lus m
popular a measail (aig daoine)
popularity n measalachd f
population n sluagh m; (*number*) àireamh-sluaigh f
porch n poirdse m
porcupine n gràineas m
pore n pòr m
pork n muicfheòil f, feòil muice f
pornography n drùiseantachd f
porous a pòrach, còsach
porpoise n pèileag f, cana m
porridge n lite f, brochan m

Insight: porridge

Porridge is a common breakfast dish in Scotland. It is made with oatmeal, water and salt and is taken with milk. There are two words for porridge in Gaelic – *brochan* and *lite*. They are dialectal variants, although *lite* can refer to a less thick type of porridge called gruel.

port *n* port *m*, caladh *m*, baile-puirt *m*; (*wine*) fìon-puirt *m*; (*naut*) clì *m*, an taobh clì *m*

portable *a* so-ghiùlan, a ghabhas giùlan

portent *n* comharra *m*, manadh *m*

porter *n* portair *m*, dorsair *m*; (*drink*) portair *m*

portion *n* earrann *f*, roinn *f*, cuid *f*

portrait *n* dealbh (neach) *f m*

portray *v* dèan cunntas/dealbh

Portuguese *n* Portagaileach *m*, (*female*) ban-Phortagaileach *f*; (*lang*) Portagaileis *f a* Portagaileach

pose *v* suidhich (thu *etc* fhèin), rach ann an cruth/riochd; (*question*) cuir ceist; (*problem*) adhbhraich; (*impersonate*) leig air/oirre a bhith na *etc*

posh *a* spaideil

position *n* suidheachadh *m*; (*in contest*) àite *m*; (*rank*) inbhe *f*, ìre *f*

positive *a* dòchasach, deimhinneach; (*certain*) dearbh-chinnteach; (*genuine*) dìreach, sònraichte **p. discrimination** leth-bhreith thaiceil *f*

possess *v* sealbhaich, gabh seilbh (de) **I don't even p. a watch** chan eil fiù 's uaireadair agam

possession *n* seilbh *f* **my possessions** mo chuid *f*

possessive *a* seilbheach

possibility *n* comas *m*, comasachd *f*, cothrom *m*

possible *a* comasach **it is not p. to do that** cha ghabh sin dèanamh, tha sin do-dhèanta

possibly *adv* is dòcha (gu), math dh'fhaodte (gu)

post *n* post *m*; (*position*) dreuchd *f* **postcode** còd puist *m* **p. office** oifis/oifig a' phuist *f v* post, cuir sa phost

postage *n* postachd *f*

postal *a* puist **p. vote** bhòt tron phost *f*

postcard *n* cairt-p(h)uist *f*

poster *n* postair *m*

postgraduate *n* iar-cheumnaiche *m a* iar-cheumnach

posthaste *adv* an làrach nam bonn

postman/postwoman *n* post(a) *m*

postpone *v* cuir dàil an, cuir dheth

postscript *n* fo-sgrìobhadh *m*

posture *n* giùlan *m*; (*polit*) seasamh *m*

pot *n* poit *f*, prais *f*

potassium *n* potasaidheam *m*

potato *n* buntàta *m*

potbellied *a* bronnach

potent *a* cumhachdach, làidir

potential *n* comas *m a* comasach air a bhith, a tha san t-sealladh

potion *n* deoch *f*

potter *n* crèadhadair *m*

pottery *n* crèadhadaireachd *f*; (*place*) ionad-crèadhaidh *m*

pouch *n* pòcaid *f* **tobacco p.** spliùchan *m*

poultice *n* fuar-lit *f*

poultry *n* cearcan *f pl*

pounce *v* leum air

pound *n* punnd *m*; (*money*) nota *m* **p. sterling** punnd Sasannach *m*

pound *v* pronn; (*impound*) punnd, cuir ann am punnd; (*strike*) buail

pour *v* (*trans*) dòirt **it poured with rain** bha dìle uisge ann

pout *v* cuir bus/gnoig air/oirre *etc*

poverty *n* bochdainn *f*

powder *n* fùdar *m*, pùdar *m v* cuir fùdar air; (*pulverize*) min-phronn

power *n* cumhachd *f m*; (*authority*) ùghdarras *m*

powerful *a* cumhachdach

powerless *a* gun chumhachd, lag

practical *a* practaigeach; (*skilled*) deas-làmhach

practice *n* cleachdadh *m*; (*performance*) cur an gnìomh *m*; (*instrument etc*) dol thairis air *m*

practise *v* bi ri …; (*perform*) cuir an gnìomh; (*instrument etc*) rach thairis air

pragmatic *a* pragmatach

pragmatism *n* pragmatachas *m*

prairie *n* prèiridh *m*

praise *n* moladh *m*, cliù *m v* mol

praiseworthy *a* ionmholta, ri m(h)oladh *etc*

pram *n* pram *m*

prance *v* leum, geàrr sùrdag

prank *n* cleas *m*

prattle v dèan cabadaich/gobaireachd
prawn n muasgan-caol m
pray v dèan ùrnaigh Also vn ag ùrnaigh
prayer n ùrnaigh f **p. meeting**
  coinneamh-ùrnaigh f
pre- pref ro-
preach v searmonaich, teagaisg
preacher n searmonaiche m
preamble n facal-toisich m
precarious a cugallach
precaution n earalas m
precede v rach/thig ro
precedent n ro-shampall m, eisimpleir f m
preceding a roimhe
precentor n neach togail fuinn m, neach
  cur a-mach na loidhne m
precept n àithne f, reachd m
precinct n crìoch(an) f pl, àrainn f;
  (district) ceàrn f **shopping p.** àrainn
  bhùthan
precious a prìseil, luachmhor **p. stone**
  seud m
precipice n bearradh m, stùc f
precipitate v (hasten) cabhagaich;
  (cause) adhbhraich
precipitate a bras, cabhagach
precipitous a cas
precise a pongail, mionaideach
precisely adv gu cruinn ceart
precision n pongalachd f, mionaideachd f
preclude v bac, dùin a-mach
precocious a ro-abaich, comasach
  ron àm
preconception n ro-bheachd m
predator n sealgair m
predatory a creachach, reubainneach
predecessor n neach a bh' ann
  roimhe m
predetermine v ro-rùnaich
predicament n càs m, teinn f
predict v ro-inn(i)s, dean fàisneachd air
predictable a ro-innseach, ris a bheil dùil
prediction n fàisneachd f
predominant a as bitheanta, buadhach
pre-empt v caisg ro-làimh
prefabricated a togte ro-làimh
preface n ro-ràdh m v can sa chiad dol
  a-mach

prefer v **prefers** 's fheàrr le …
preferable a nas fheàrr
preference n roghainn f m
preferential a am fàbhar (neach)
prefix n ro-leasachan m
pregnancy n leatrom m
pregnant a trom, torrach, air turas
prehistoric a ro-eachdraidheil
prejudge v ro-bhreithnich, thoir
  ro-bhreith air
prejudice n claon-bhàidh/bhreith
  f v claon-bharailich; (damage case etc)
  dochainn, mill
prejudiced a le claon-bharail
preliminary a tòiseachail
prelude n ro-thachartas m
premature a an-abaich, ron àm
premeditated a ro-bheachdaichte
premier n prìomhaire m a prìomh
  (+ len)
premiere n ciad shealladh m
premise n tùs-bheachd m
premises n aitreabh f, togalach m **on
  the p.** san àite (fhèin)
premium n (eg insurance) tàille f,
  tàilleabh m; (extra fee) sùim a chòrr **at a
  p.** is fèill mhòr air
premonition n ro-fhaireachdainn f,
  rabhadh m
prenatal a ro bhreith
preoccupation n cùram m
pre-ordain v ro-òrdaich
preparation n ullachadh m,
  deasachadh m
prepare v ullaich, deasaich
prepared a ullaichte, deasaichte
preposition n roimhear m
prepositional pronoun n ro-riochdair m
preposterous a gun sgot/chiall
prerequisite n riatanas m
Presbyterian n, a Clèireach m
presbytery n clèir f
prescribe v òrdaich, comharraich
prescribed a òrdaichte, comharraichte
prescription n òrdugh m, riaghailt f;
  (med) òrdugh-cungaidh m
prescriptive a òrdachail
presence n làthaireachd f

present n (*time*) an t-àm (a) tha (an) làthair m; (*gift*) tiodhlac m **at p.** an-ceartuair **the p. day** an là an-diugh m **the p. tense** an tràth làthaireach m a an làthair, làthaireach

present v nochd, taisbean; (*give*) thoir do, thoir seachad do, builich (air)

presentation n taisbeanadh m; (*gift*) tabhartas m

preservation n gleidheadh m

preserve v glèidh, cùm; (*food*) grèidh

presidency n uachdranachd f

president n ceann-suidhe m

press n (*printing*) clò m; (*newspapers*) na pàipearan m; (*journalists*) luchd-naidheachd m; (*cupboard*) preas m **p. conference** coinneamh naidheachd f **p. release** fios naidheachd m **p. statement** brath naidheachd m

press v fàisg, brùth, put; (*point*) leig cuideam air; (*urge*) cuir ìmpidh air, spàrr (air)

pressing a deatamach

pressure n bruthadh m, teannachadh m; (*stress*) èiginn f, eallach m; (*atmos*) tomhas-bruthaidh m **p. group** buidheann-tagraidh f m

pressurize v cuir/leig cuideam air

prestige n cliù m, ainm m, teist f

prestigious a cliùiteach, a sheallas inbhe

presumably adv 's fheudar (gu), a rèir c(h)oltais

presume v gabh air/oirre etc, rach dàn; (*assume*) bi dhen bheachd

presumptuous a ladarna, dalma

presuppose v bi dhen bheachd; (*infer*) gabh ris gu bheil

pretence n leisgeul m, leigeil air m

pretend v leig air/oirre etc, cuir an ìre

pretext n leisgeul m

pretty a brèagha, bòidheach adv an ìre mhath

prevail v buadhaich **p. upon** thoir air

prevailing a (*usual*) àbhaisteach **p. wind** gnàth-ghaoth f

prevalent a cumanta, bitheanta

prevaricate v dèan breug, bi ri mealltaireachd

prevent v bac, caisg

prevention n bacadh m, casg m

preview n ro-shealladh m

previous a eile

previously adv mu thràth, mar-thà, ro-làimh, roimhe

pre-war a ron chogadh

prey n creach f, cobhartach f m v spùinn, creach **p. upon** gabh brath air

price n prìs f **p. list** liosta phrìsean f v cuir prìs air

priceless a thar luach, prìseil thar tomhais

prick v bior, cuir bior an; (*met*) bior, brod, stuig

prickly a biorach; (*irritable*) calgach, crosta

pride n pròis f, uaill f, àrdan m; (*justified*) moit f

priest n sagart m

prim a ro ghrinn, ro fhìnealta

primarily adv sa chiad àite, gu h-àraid

primary a ciad, prìomh **p. school** bun-sgoil f

primate n àrd-easbaig m; (*biol*) prìomhaid m

prime a prìomh (+ len) **p. example** fìor dheagh eisimpleir f m **P. Minister** Prìomhaire m n làn-bhlàth m; (*phys*) trèine a neairt f

prime v cuir air ghleus

primitive a prìomhadail

primrose n sòbhrach f, sòbhrag f

prince n prionnsa m

princess n bana-phrionnsa f

principal n prionnsapal m, ceann(ard) m a prìomh (+ len)

principally adv gu sònraichte, gu h-àraid

principle n prionnsapal m

principled a prionnsapalta, le prionnsapail

print n clò m; (*footprint*) lorg f v clò-bhuail, cuir an clò

printer n clò-bhualadair m

prior a ro-làimh adv roimhe **p. to their arrival** mun do ràinig iad

prioritize v prìomhaich, dèan prìomhachas air

priority n prìomhachas m
prison n prìosan m
prisoner n prìosanach m
pristine a fìorghlan, gun mheang
privacy n uaigneas m
private a uaigneach, dìomhair, prìobhaideach **p. eye** lorgaire m **p. sector** roinn phrìobhaideach f n saighdear cumanta m **in p.** ann an dìomhaireachd
privately adv gu dìomhair, os ìosal, gu prìobhaideach
privilege n sochair f
privileged a fo shochair, math dheth; (information) dìomhair
prize n duais f v meas, cuir luach air
proactive a for-ghnìomhach
probable a coltach
probably adv is dòcha (gu/gun/gum/ nach)
probation n pròbhadh m; (period) àm dearbhaidh m
probationer n neach fo dhearbhadh m
probe n (implement) bior-tomhais m; (inquiry) rannsachadh m; (space) sireadh m v rannsaich, sir
problem n ceist f, duilgheadas m; (maths) cuistean m
problematic a na cheist/dhuilgheadas
procedure n modh f m, dòigh f, dòigh-obrach f
proceed v rach air adhart, gluais, lean (air/oirre etc)
proceedings n dol air adhart m, cùisean f pl; (leg) cùis-lagha f
proceeds n teachd a-steach m, toradh m
process n giullachd f, modh-obrachaidh f m, cùrsa m v làimhsich, dèilig ri
procession n caismeachd f, triall m
proclaim v aithris gu follaiseach
proclamation n aithris fhollaiseach f
procrastinate v dèan maill(e), màirnealaich, cuir dheth
procrastination n dàil f, maill(e) f, màirneal m
procreate v gin, sìolaich
procurator n procadair m **p. fiscal** neach-casaid a' Chrùin m, fiosgal m

procure v faigh, solaraich
prod v brod, stob; (encourage) brosnaich
prodigal a strùidheil, stròdhail **the P. Son** am Mac Stròdhail m
prodigious a anabarrach
produce n toradh m, cinneas m
produce v dèan; (show) nochd, taisbean, thoir am follais; (eg film) riochdaich
producer n (eg film) riochdaire m
product n toradh m; (result) buil f
production n dèanamh m; (artistic) riochdachadh m
productive a torrach, tarbhach
profane a mì-naomha
profess v cuir an cèill, aidich
profession n dreuchd f, obair f; (relig) aidmheil f
professional a dreuchdail, proifeiseanta
professor n ollamh m, proifeasair m
proficiency n comas m, alt m, liut m
proficient a comasach, ealanta
profile n leth-aghaidh f; (article) geàrr-iomradh m; (image) ìomhaigh f **she has a high p.** tha i gu mòr san fhollais
profit n prothaid f, buannachd f v prothaidich, dèan prothaid à, faigh buannachd à
profitable a prothaideach, buannachdail
profligate a ana-caithteach, mì-stuama
profound a domhainn
profuse a pailt
profusion n mòr-phailteas m, sgaoilteach f
prognosis n fàisneas m, ro-thuaiream f
programme n prògram m v prògram
progress n adhartas m **p. report** aithisg adhartais f v rach air adhart
progression n gluasad m; (continuity) leantainneachd f
progressive a adhartach
progressively adv mean air mhean
prohibit v toirmisg
prohibited a toirmisgte
prohibition n toirmeasg m, bacadh m
prohibitive a toirmeasgach; (price) ro dhaor
project n pròiseact f m

project v stob a-mach; (*on screen*) tilg; (*estimate*) dèan ro-mheasadh
projection n stob m; (*on screen*) tilgeil f; (*estimate*) ro-mheasadh m
projector n proiseactair m
proliferate v sìolaich, fàs lìonmhor
prolific a torrach; (*rich in*) beairteach
prolong v sìn a-mach, cuir dàil an
promenade n promanàd m; (*walk*) sràidireachd f
prominent a follaiseach, nochdte; (*to the fore*) inbheach
promiscuous a iol-fheiseach
promise n gealladh m, gealltanas m v geall, thoir gealladh
promising a gealltanach
promontory n rubha m, sròn f, àird f
promote v cuir air adhart/aghaidh; (*at work*) àrdaich, thoir àrdachadh do
promotion n cur air adhart m; (*at work*) àrdachadh (inbhe) m
prompt a clis, sgiobalta v spreig; (*remind*) cuir an cuimhne
prone a dual, buailteach do; (*lying*) air a b(h)eul fodha *etc*
pronoun n riochdair m **personal p.** rìochdair pearsanta
pronounce v fuaimnich; (*leg*) thoir a-mach binn
pronunciation n fuaimneachadh m
proof n dearbhadh m
prop n taic f, cùl-taic f v cùm suas, thoir taic do, cuir taic ri
propaganda n propaganda m
propel v iomain
propeller n proipeilear m
proper a iomchaidh, cubhaidh, dòigheil, ceart
properly adv gu cubhaidh, gu dòigheil, (gu) ceart
property n cuid f, seilbh f; (*attribute*) buadh f
prophecy n fàisneachd f, fàidheadaireachd f
prophesy v fàisnich, dèan fàidheadaireachd
prophet n fàidh m
propitious a fàbharach

proportion n cuid f, earrann f; (*symmetry*) cumadh m, cunbhalachd f, co-rèir m **in p. to** a rèir
proportional a co-rèireach, co-roinneil **p. representation** riochdachadh co-roinneil m
proposal n (*offer*) tairgse f; (*motion*) moladh m; (*of marriage*) tairgse-pòsaidh f
propose v tairg; (*motion*) mol
proposition n tairgse f; (*phil*) smaoineas m v (*sexual*) tairg feis
proprietor n sealbhadair m
propriety n freagarrachd f, iomchaidheachd f
propulsion n iomain f
prosaic a lom, tioram, neo-bheothail
proscribe v toirmisg, caisg
proscribed a toirmisgte
prose n rosg m
prosecute v tog casaid an aghaidh, cuir casaid às leth
prosecution n casaideachadh m; (*service*) luchd-casaid m
prospect n (*view*) sealladh m; (*met*) dùil f **in p.** san amharc
prospective a san amharc, ri teachd
prospectus n ro-shealladh m; (*institutional*) leabhran-iùil oilthigh/ colaiste/sgoile m
prosper v soirbhich
prosperity n soirbheachadh m
prosperous a soirbheachail
prostitute n siùrsach f, strìopach f
prostitution n siùrsachd f, strìopachas m; (*of talents*) mì-bhuileachadh m
prostrate a sleuchdte, sìnte
protect v dìon, teasraig
protection n dìon m
protective a dìona
protein n pròtain m
protest n gearan m, casaid f v gearain, tog casaid; (*against*) tog fianais an aghaidh (+ gen)
Protestant n, a Pròstanach m, (*female*) ban-Phròstanach f
protester n neach-togail-fianais m, casaidiche m

protocol n pròtacal m
protractor n protractair m
protrude v bi na stob a-mach, bi faicsinneach
proud a pròiseil, uailleil, àrdanach; (*justifiably*) moiteil
prove v dearbh; (*test*) feuch
proved, **proven** a dearbhte
proverb n seanfhacal m, gnàth-fhacal m
provide v solair, solaraich
providence n freastal m
province n roinn f
provincial a roinneil, a bhuineas dhan tuath; (*attitude*) beag-sheallach
provision n ullachadh m, solar m
  provisions lòn m
provisional a (*temporary*) sealach, car ùine; (*conditional*) air chùmhnant
proviso n cumha f, cùmhnant m
provocation n buaireadh m, stuigeadh m, cùis-fheirge f
provocative a buaireasach, buaireanta
provoke v cuir thuige, cuir conas air, stuig; (*engender*) adhbhraich
provost n pròbhaist m
prowess n comas m; (*in battle*) gaisge f
prowl v liùg
proximity n fagasachd f
proxy n neach-ionaid m, neach a ghabhas àite m
prude n neach nàrach m
prudence n crìonnachd f, faiceall f
prudent a crìonna, faiceallach, ciallach
prune n prùn m
prune v sgath, beàrr
psalm n salm f m
psalmody n salmadaireachd f **p. class** sgoil fhonn f
psalter n salmadair m
psyche n aigne f
psychiatrist n lighiche-inntinn m
psychiatry n leigheas-inntinn m
psychic a leis an dà shealladh; (*of psyche*) aignidheil
psychological a inntinn-eòlach
psychologist n eòlaiche-inntinn m
psychology n eòlas-inntinn m
ptarmigan n tàrmachan m

pub n taigh-seinnse m
puberty n inbhidheachd f
public n poball m, mòr-shluagh m
  a poblach **p. conveniences** goireasan poblach m pl **p. holiday** saor-latha poblach m, latha fèille m **p. house** taigh-seinnse m **p. inquiry** rannsachadh poblach m
publican n òstair m
publication n foillseachadh m
publicity n follaiseadh m
publicize v thoir am follais
publish v foillsich, cuir a-mach
publisher n foillsichear m
publishing n foillseachadh m
pudding n (*sweet*) mìlsean m **black/white p.** marag dhubh/gheal f
puddle n lòn m
puff n (*of wind*) osag f, oiteag f
puffin n buthaid f
pugnacious a buaireanta, cogail
puke v sgeith, cuir a-mach
pull n tarraing f, slaodadh m, draghadh m
  v tarraing, slaod, dragh
pullet n eireag f
pulley n ulag f
pulp n glaodhan m, taois f, pronnach f
pulpit n cùbaid f
pulse n (*med*) buille cuisle f
pulverize v mìn-phronn
pump n pump(a) m; (*dancing shoe*) bròg-dannsa f v tarraing, pump
pun n cainnt-chluich f m, geàrr-fhacal m
punch n dòrn m, buille f; (*tool*) tollair m; (*drink*) puinnse m
punctual a pongail, na uair, ris an uair
punctuation n puingeachadh m, pungadh m
puncture n toll m, tolladh m v toll
pungent a searbh, geur, guineach
punish v peanasaich, cronaich
punishment n peanas m, cronachadh m
punitive a peanasach
puny a crìon, beag
pup n cuilean m
pupil n sgoilear m; (*of eye*) clach na sùla f
puppet n pupaid f m, gille-mirein m
puppy n cuilean m

purchase v ceannaich
pure a fìorghlan
purgative n purgaid f
purge v glan, cairt, purgaidich
purification n glanadh m
purify v glan
purity n fìorghlaine f
purple a purpaidh, corcair
purport v leig ort, cùm a-mach
purpose n adhbhar m, rùn m
purposely adv a dh'aon ghnotha(i)ch
purr v dèan crònan
purse n sporan m
pursue v rach às dèidh/air tòir (+ gen); (met) lean
pursuit n tòir f, ruaig f; (pastime) cur-seachad m **in p. of** air tòir (+ gen)
pus n iongar m, brachadh m

push n putag f v put; (press) brùth
pushchair a carbad-leanaibh m
pushy a aghach
put v cuir **put aside** cuir mu seach, cuir an dàrna taobh **put off (the light)** cuir às/dheth (an solas) **put on clothes** cuir ort/umad etc aodach
putrid a grod, lobhte
putt v (golf) thoir gnogag do **putting the shot** putadh na cloiche m
putty n potaidh m, botaidh f
puzzle n tòimhseachan m, dubh-fhacal m v cuir fo imcheist; (intrans) bi an imcheist
pygmy n luchraban m, troich f m
pyjamas n deise-leapa f, aodach-oidhche m
pylon n crann-dealain m
pyramid n pioramaid f

Q

quadrangle n ceithir-cheàrnag f
quadruple v ceathraich
quadruplets n ceathrar (san aon bhreith) m
quagmire n bog(l)ach f, sùil-chritheach/chruthaich f
quaich n cuach f
quaint a neònach, seann-fhasanta
quake v rach air crith, criothnaich
qualification n (formal) teisteanas m; (attribute) feart m; (caveat) ceist f, teagamh m
qualified a (formally) le teisteanas; (equipped) uidheamaichte; (with caveat) le ceist/teagamh
qualify v thoir a-mach teisteanas; (be eligible) bi freagarrach (airson)
quality n buadh f, feart m, gnè f
quandary n imcheist f **in a q.** fo imcheist, eadar dhà bharail
quango n cuango m
quantify v àireamh(aich), tomhais meud
quantity n meud m, uiread m, uimhir f
quarrel n aimhreit f, còmhstri f, trod f m v rach far a chèile, troid, bi ag aimhreit
quarrelsome a aimhreiteach, connspaideach

quarry n cuaraidh f m; (prey) creach f
quarter n cairteal m, ceathramh m; (of year) ràith(e) f; (area) ceàrn f; (mercy) tròcair f **q. past one** cairteal/ceathramh an dèidh uair
quarterly n (magazine) ràitheachan m adv ràitheil, gach ràith(e), uair san ràith(e)
quarters n àite-fuirich m, cairtealan m pl
quartet(te) n (group) ceathrar m; (mus piece) ceòl-cheathrar m
quash v mùch, caisg, cuir an dara taobh
quatrain n ceathramh m, rann m
quaver n crith f; (mus) caman m
quay n cidhe m
queen n banrigh f
queer a neònach
quell v ceannsaich, mùch
quench v bàth, cuir às
quern n brà f
query n ceist f
quest n tòir f, iarraidh m, sireadh m
question n ceist f; (doubt) amharas m **q. mark** comharra-ceiste m v ceasnaich, faighnich, feòraich; (doubt) cuir teagamh an

Insight: queen

The word for queen, *banrigh*, literally means female king. Queen Elizabeth is known as *a' Bhanrigh Ealasaid* in Gaelic. *Ban* or *bana* is often used as a prefix to specify a female version. For instance, *caraid*, a friend, becomes *banacharaid*, a female friend, while *Ameireaganach* becomes *ban-Ameireaganach*, a female American.

questionable *a* teagmhach, a' togail ceist
questioning *n* ceasnachadh *m*
questionnaire *n* ceisteachan *m*
queue *n* ciudha *f*
quibble *n* gearan beag-seagh *m* *v* gearain mu nithean beag-seagh
quick *a* luath, ealamh, clis
quickly *adv* gu luath, gu h-ealamh, gu clis
quid *n* nota *f*
quiet *a* sàmhach, tostach **be q.!** bi sàmhach, (e)ist! *n* sàmhchair *f*, tost *m*
quieten *v* ciùinich; (*intrans*) fàs sàmhach
quietness *n* sàmhchair *f*, ciùineas *m*
quilt *n* cuibhrig(e) *f m*
quit *v* sguir, falbh, leig seachad; (*place*) fàg

quite *adv* (*fairly*) gu math, rudeigin, lethchar; (*completely*) gu tur, gu lèir, gu h-iomlan, buileach (*with neg*) **it wasn't q. ready** cha robh e buileach deiseil
quiver *v* crith, dèan ball-chrith
quiz *n* ceasnachadh *m*, farpais-cheist *f*
quorum *n* àireamh riaghailteach *f*, cuòram *m*
quota *n* cuid *f*, cuota *m*
quotation *n* (*extract*) pìos air a thogail à *m*, às-earrann *f*; (*estimate*) tuairmeas *m*; (*valuation*) luach *m* **q. marks** cromagan turrach *f pl*
quote *n* briathran (a labhradh) *m pl*; (*estimate*) tuairmeas *m v* (*extract*) tog à; (*cite*) tog mar ùghdarras; (*estimate*) thoir tuairmeas

R

rabbit *n* coineanach *m*, rabaid *f*
rabble *n* gràisg *f*
rabid *a* (*lit*) cuthachail; (*met*) dearg (+ *n/a* & *len*)
rabies *n* fibin *f*
race *n* rèis *f*; (*ethnic*) cinneadh *m*; (*genetic*) gineal *f* **racecourse** cùrsa-rèis *m* **racehorse** steud-each *m* **r. relations** dàimh cinnidh *m v* ruith
racial *a* cinneadail **r. discrimination** leth-bhreith chinneadail *f*
racing *n* rèiseadh *m* **r. car** càr-rèisidh *m*
racism *n* gràin-cinnidh *f*
racist *n* neach a tha ri gràin-cinnidh *f a* gràin-c(h)innidheach
rack *n* ealchainn *f*; (*for torture*) inneal pianaidh *m* **going to r. and ruin** a' dol a Thaigh Iain Ghròt(a)
racket *n* (*noise*) gleadhraich *f*; (*sport*) racaid *f*

radar *n* rèidear *m*
radiant *a* lainnireach, boillsgeach, deàlrach
radiate *v* deàlraich
radiation *n* rèididheachd *f*
radical *a* radaigeach, freumhail, bunasach
radio *n* rèidio *m*, radio *m*
radioactive *a* rèidio-beò
radiography *n* rèidiografaidh *m*
radiology *n* rèidio-eòlas *m*
radiotherapy *n* gath-leigheas *m*
radish *n* meacan-ruadh *m*
radium *n* rèidium *m*
radius *n* rèidius *m*, spòg *f*
raffle *n* crannchur-gill *m*
raft *n* ràth *m*
rafter *n* cabar *m*, taobhan *m*, tarsannan *m*
rag *n* luideag *f*, clobhd(a) *m*
rage *n* boile *f*, cuthach *m*

ragged *a* luideagach
raging *a* fon chuthach, air bhoil(e)
raid *n* ruaig *f*, ionnsaigh *f*, creach *f v* ruag, thoir ionnsaigh (air)
raider *n* creachadair *m*, neach-ionnsaigh *m*
rail *n* rèile *f*
railway *n* rathad-iarainn *m a* rèile
rain *n* uisge *m* **raincoat** còta-froise *m*
rainfall uisge *m* **rainforest** coille-uisge *f v* sil; (*heavily*) dòirt **it's raining** tha an t-uisge ann
rainbow *n* bogha-froise *m*
raise *v* tog, àrdaich **r. awareness** dùisg mothachadh, tog aire

rank *n* inbhe *f*: (*row*) rang *f m*, sreath *f m* **the r. and file** a' mhòr-chuid chumanta *f*, na mithean *m pl v* rangaich, cuir an òrdugh *a* (*intens*) tur, buileach; (*odour*) breun
rankle *v* fàg cais/ainmein air
ransack *v* rùraich; (*plunder*) creach
ransom *n* èirig *f v* saor/fuasgail (air èirig)
rant *v* bi ri blaomadaich **ranting and raving** ag èigheach 's ag uabhas
rap *n* buille *f*, sgailc *f*: (*on door*) gnogadh cruaidh *m* **take the rap** faigh/gabh a' choire
rape *n* èigneachadh *m v* èignich

Insight: rain

Rain, *uisge,* is not an unknown quantity in Scotland! To tell someone that it is raining, you say *tha an t-uisg' ann* (literally, the rain is in existence) or *tha i a' sileadh*. When it is raining heavily, you say *tha i a' dòrtadh*, it's pouring.

raisin *n* rèiseid *f*
rake *n* ràcan *m*; (*person*) raidhc *m*, ràcaire *m v* ràc
rally *n* (*gathering*) cruinneachadh *m v* misnich, thoir cruinn; (*intrans*) ath-chruinnich; (*from illness*) ath-bheothaich
ram *n* reithe *m*, rùda *m*
ramble *n* cuairt *f*, fàrsan *m v* bi a' cuairtearachd/rèabhaireachd; (*in talk*) bi ri blabhdaireachd
rambler *n* ramalair *m*, fàrsanach *m*, rèabhair(e) *m*
rambling *a* fàrsanach; (*talk*) sgaoilte; (*bot*) sreapach
ramification *n* ioma-bhuaidh *f*, buil *f*
ramp *n* ramp *m*
rampant *a* gun srian, gun cheannsachadh
ranch *n* rains(e) *f*
rancid *a* breun
rancour *n* gamhlas *m*
random *a* air thuaiream, tuaireamach
randy *a* macnasach
range *n* raon *m*; (*of mountains*) sreath bheanntan *f m*

rapid *a* bras, clis
rapids *n* bras-shruth *m*
rapport *n* co-bhàidh *f*
rapturous *a* mòr-aoibhneach
rare *a* tearc, ainneamh; (*in cooking*) gann-bhruich
rascal *n* blaigeard *m*, rasgal *m*
rash *n* broth *m a* bras, gun tùr
rasher *n* sliseag *f*
raspberry *n* subh-craoibh *m*
rat *n* radan *m*
rate *n* ìre *f*; (*speed*) astar *m* **r. of interest** ìre an rèidh *f* **the rates** na reataichean *m pl v* meas
rather *adv* rudeigin, car **r. than** seach, an àite (+ *gen*) **I'd r. go** b' fheàrr leam falbh
ratify *v* daingnich
ratio *n* co-mheas *m*
ration *n* cuibhreann *f m v* cùm ri cuibhreann
rational *a* ciallach, reusanta
rationale *n* feallsanachd *f*
rationalize *v* dèan leisgeul; (*operation etc*) cuir air stèidh ùr
rattle *n* gliogan *m*, glag *m*, glagadaich *f*: (*toy*) gliogan *m*

ravage v spùill, creach, cuir fàs
rave n hòro-gheallaidh f m v bi air
  bhoil(e) **r. about** dèan othail mu
  dheidhinn
raven n fitheach m
ravenous a cìocrach, gu fannachadh
ravine n mòr-ghil f
ravish v èignich
raw a amh **r. material** bun-stuth m
ray n gath m, leus m
raze v leag gu làr
razor n ealtainn f, ràsar m **r.-fish**
  muirsgian f
re- pref ath-
reach v ruig **r. for** sìn a dh'iarraidh
  (+ gen)
react v gluais, gabh ri, freagair **he**
  reacted badly to it chaidh e dona dha
reaction n gluasad m, gabhail ris m,
  freagairt f; (chem) iom-obrachadh m
reactor n reactar m
read v leugh
reader n leughadair m
readily adv gu toileach; (quickly) gu
  sgiobalta
reading n leughadh m
ready a deiseil, ullamh
reaffirm v daingnich
real a fìor
realistic a ciallach, practaigeach
reality n fìrinn f, fìorachd f **in r.** an dà-
  rìribh
realize v tuig; (fulfil) thoir gu buil; (sell)
  reic
really adv gu dearbh; (sceptically) seadh?
realm n rìoghachd f
reap v buain
reaper n buanaiche m; (mech) inneal-
  buana m
rear n deireadh m
rear v tog, àraich, altraim
reason n ciall f, reusan m; (cause)
  adhbhar m, fàth m v reusanaich
reasonable a reusanta, ciallach, coltach
reasoning n reusanachadh m
reassurance n fois-inntinn f
reassure v thoir fois-inntinn do
reassuring a fois-inntinneach

rebate n lasachadh m
rebel n reubaltach m v dèan ar-a-mach
  r. against rach an aghaidh (an t-sruth)
rebellion n ar-a-mach m
rebellious a ceannairceach
rebound v leum air ais **it will r. on him**
  thig e air ais air
rebuff n diùltadh m
rebuild v tog às ùr, ath-thog
rebuke v thoir achmhasan (do), cronaich
rebut v rach às àicheadh, cuir an
  aghaidh
recall v cuimhnich air, bi cuimhn' aig;
  (bring back) thoir air ais
recap n ath-shùil f
recede v rach air ais, sìolaidh
receipt n (written) cuidhteas m
receive v faigh; (react to) gabh ri;
  (welcome) fàiltich
recent a ùr, o chionn ghoirid
recently adv o chionn ghoirid
reception n gabhail ri m; (in hotel etc)
  fàilteachadh m; (event) cuirm f
receptionist n fàiltiche m
receptive a fosgailte (ri)
recess n cùil f; (vacation) fosadh m
recession n crìonadh m, seacadh m
recipe n reasabaidh m
recipient n neach-faighinn m, neach a
  gheibh m
reciprocal a air gach taobh
reciprocate v dèan dha rèir
recitation n aithris f
recite v aithris
reckless a neo-chùramach
reckon v cunnt; (consider) meas
reclaim v thoir air ais; (recover) faigh/
  iarr air ais
recline v sìn, laigh
recluse n aonaran m
reclusive a aon(a)ranach, lethoireach
recognize v aithnich; (admit) aidich
recoil v leum air ais **r. from** clisg (bh)o
recollect v cuimhnich
recollection n cuimhne f
recommend v mol
recommendation n moladh m
recommended a air a m(h)oladh etc

recompense n ath-dhìoladh m, èirig f
reconcile v (bring together) thoir gu chèile; (figures etc) rèitich **they were reconciled** thàinig iad gu rèite
reconciliation n (bringing together) toirt gu chèile f; (figures etc) rèite f
reconsider v ath-bheachdaich
reconstruction n ath-thogail f, ath-chruthachadh m
record n cunntas m, clàr m; (disc) clàr m v clàraich, cùm cunntas (air); (express) cuir an cèill; (mus) cuir air clàr
recorder n clàradair m; (mus) reacòrdair m
recording n clàr m, clàradh m
recount v aithris; (vote) ath-chunnt
recoup v faigh air ais
recover v (get back) faigh air ais; (improve) fàs nas fheàrr, rach am feabhas
recovery n faighinn/faotainn air ais f; (in health) fàs nas fheàrr m, dol am feabhas m
re-create v ath-chruthaich
recreation n cur-seachad m
recruit v tog
rectangle n ceart-cheàrnag f
rectangular a ceart-cheàrnach
rectify v ceartaich, cuir ceart
rector n (educ) ceannard m; (university) reachdair m; (relig) ministear m
recuperate v slànaich, rach am feabhas
recur v tachair a-rithist
recurrent a tillteach
recycle v ath-chleachd, ath-chuartaich
recycling n ath-chleachdadh m, ath-chuartachadh m
red a dearg; (hair) ruadh
redeem v (save) saor, fuasgail; (fin) ath-cheannaich
redirect v ath-sheòl
redistribute v ath-riaraich
redouble v (efforts) dèan spàirn is ath-spàirn
redraft v ath-dhreachd
redress n (fin) ath-dhìoladh m; (leg) furtachd f
reduce v lùghdaich, ìslich

reduced a lùghdaichte, air a lùghdachadh
reduction n lùghdachadh m, beagachadh m, ìsleachadh m
redundancy n pàigheadh dheth m; (superfluity) anbharr m **r. pay** airgead pàighidh dheth m
redundant a anbharra, gun fheum; (idle) gun obair **they were made r.** chaidh am pàigheadh dheth
reed n cuilc f; (mus) ribheid f
reef n bodha m, sgeir f; (a sail) riof f
reek v (smell) cuir fàileadh dheth/dhith etc; (smoke) cuir smùid/toit dheth/dhith etc
reel n r(u)idhle m; (of thread) piorna f m
re-elect v ath-thagh
re-examine v ath-sgrùd
refectory n biadhlann f
refer (to) v thoir iomradh/tarraing air; (pass to) cuir gu; (send back) till air ais
referee n rèitire m; (for job) teistiche m
reference n iomradh m, tarraing f; (testimonial) teisteanas f **with r. to** a thaobh (+ gen) **r. book** leabhar-fiosrachaidh m
referendum n reifreann m, referendum m
refine v glan; (met) grinnich
reflect v tilg air ais; (think) meòraich, cnuasaich
reflection n faileas m; (in mirror) dealbh-sgàthain f m; (thought) meòrachadh m, cnuasachadh m
reflective a meòrachail, breithneachail
reflex a neo-shaor-thoileach
reform n leasachadh m, ath-leasachadh m v leasaich, ath-leasaich
reformation n ath-leasachadh m **the R.** an t-Ath-Leasachadh
refrain v cùm (bh)o, sguir
refresh v ùraich
refreshment n (drink) deoch f; (renewal) ùrachadh m
refrigerator n inneal-fionnarachaidh m, frids m
refuel v ath-chonnaich, lìon le connadh a-rithist

refuge *n* tèarmann *m*, dìdean *m*
refugee *n* fògarrach *m*
refund *n* airgead air ais *m v* pàigh air ais, ath-dhìol
refuse *n* sgudal *m*, sprùilleach *m*
refuse *v* diùlt
refute *v* dearbh ceàrr
regain *v* ath-choisinn, ath-shealbhaich
regal *a* rìoghail
regard *n* meas *m*, sùim *f*, spèis *f* **with kind regards** leis gach deagh dhùrachd **as regards** a thaobh (+ *gen*) *v* (*consider*) meas; (*esteem*) thoir spèis do; (*pay heed to*) thoir aire do
regardless *adv* a dh'aindeoin (sin)
regatta *n* rèisean shoithichean *f pl*
regenerate *v* ath-nuadhaich
regeneration *n* ath-nuadhachadh *m*
regime *n* riaghladh *m*; (*system*) rèim *f*
regiment *n* rèisimeid *f*
region *n* roinn *f*, ceàrn *f*
regional *a* roinneil, roinne
register *n* clàr *m* **cash r.** clàradair-airgid *m v* clàraich; (*reveal*) leig ris; (*show up*) nochd
registrar *n* neach-clàraidh *m*
registration *n* clàradh *m*
registry *n* ionad-clàraidh *m*
regret *n* aithreachas *m*; (*sorrow*) duilichinn *f v* gabh aithreachas; (*be sorry*) bi duilich
regrettable *a* na adhbhar aithreachais; (*sad*) duilich
regular *a* cunbhalach, riaghailteach
regularity *n* cunbhalachd *f*
regulate *v* riaghlaich, rèitich
regulation *n* riaghailt *f*; (*act of*) riaghladh *m*
rehearsal *n* ruith thairis *f*
rehearse *v* ruith thairis air; (*go through*) ath-aithris
reign *n* rìoghachadh *m*
reimburse *v* pàigh air ais (airson)
rein *n* srian *f*
reindeer *n* rèin-fhiadh *m*
reinforce *v* daingnich, neartaich
reinstate *v* ath-shuidhich
reissue *v* cuir a-mach às ùr, ath-sgaoil

reiterate *v* ath-aithris
reject *v* diùlt
rejoice *v* dèan gàirdeachas/aoibhneas
rekindle *v* ath-bheothaich
relapse *n* tuiteam air ais *m*; (*med*) tilleadh tinneis *m*
relate *v* innis, aithris
related (to) *a* co-cheangailte ri; (*family*) càirdeach (do), an dàimh ri **r. by marriage** ann an cleamhnas
relation *n* co-cheangal *m*; (*relative*) neach-dàimh *m*, dàimh *f m* **in r. to** ann an dàimh ri
relationship *n* càirdeas *m*, dàimh *f m* **be in a r. with …** a bhith a' falbh le …
relative *n* neach-dàimh *m*, *pl* luchd-dàimh *m*, càirdean *m a* dàimheach **r. to** an coimeas ri
relaunch *v* cuir air bhog a-rithist
relax *v* gabh fois; (*rules etc*) lasaich, fuasgail
relaxation *n* fois *f*, tàmh *m*; (*pastime*) cur-seachad *m*
relaxed *a* socrach
relay *n* sreath (mu seach) *f m* **r. race** rèis phàirteach *f v* (*news etc*) sgaoil
release *v* fuasgail, leig às, cuir/leig mu sgaoil
relegate *v* cuir sìos
relent *v* taisich, gabh truas
relentless *a* gun sgur, gun abhsadh; (*implacable*) neo-thruacanta
relevance *n* buntainneas *m*
relevant *a* buntainneach, a' buntainn ri
reliable *a* earbsach
reliance *n* earbsa *f*, muinighin *f*
relief *n* fao(tha)chadh *m*, furtachd *f*; (*help*) cobhair *f*, cuideachadh *m*
relieve *v* furtaich, thoir fao(tha)chadh do; (*help*) cuidich **we were relieved** fhuair sinn fao(tha)chadh
religion *n* creideamh *m*
religious *a* cràbhach, diadhaidh
relinquish *v* leig/thoir seachad
relish *v* gabh fìor thlachd de/an
relocate *v* gluais (gu àite eile)
reluctant *a* ain-deònach **I was r. to do that** bha leisg(e) orm sin a dhèanamh

rely v cuir earbs(a) (an/ri)
remain v fuirich, fan
remainder n fuidheall m, còrr m
remains n fuidhleach m; (*corpse*) dust, duslach m
remark n iomradh m, facal m v thoir iomradh air; (*notice*) thoir fa-near
remarkable a sònraichte, suaicheanta, iongantach
remedial a leasachail
remedy n (*med*) leigheas m, ìocshlaint f; (*solution*) leasachadh m v leighis, slànaich; (*solve*) leasaich
remember v cuimhnich
remind v cuir an cuimhne, cuimhnich do
reminisce v cuimhnich (air)
remiss a dearmadach, neo-shuimeil
remit n raon-dleastanais/ùghdarrais m
remit v cuir air falbh; (*refer back*) till, cuir air ais; (*cancel*) math
remittance n pàigheadh m, sùim airgid f
remnant n fuidheall m, iarmad m
remorse n dubh-aithreachas m, agartas-cogais m
remorseful a làn aithreachais
remote a iomallach, cian, fad' às
removal n gluasad m; (*flitting*) imrich f
remove v thoir air falbh; (*move*) gluais
remunerate v ìoc do, pàigh
renaissance n ath-bheothachadh m **the R.** Linn an Ath-Bheothachaidh f m
rend v srac, reub
render v (*pay*) ìoc, liubhair; (*make*) dèan
rendezvous n àite-coinneachaidh m
renew v ath-nuadhaich, ùraich
renewal n ath-nuadhachadh m, ùrachadh m
rennet n binid f
renounce v leig bhuat, trèig, cuir cùl ri
renovate v ùraich, nuadhaich
renovation n nuadhachadh m, ùr-sgeadachadh m
renown n cliù m
renowned a cliùiteach, iomraiteach
rent n sracadh m, reubadh m; (*fin*) màl m v gabh air mhàl
rented a air mhàl
re-open v fosgail às ùr

reorganization n ath-eagrachadh m, ath-òrdachadh m
reorganize v ath-eagraich, cuir rian ùr air
repair v càirich **r. to** tog air/oirre *etc* gu
repay v pàigh air ais
repayment n pàigheadh air ais m
repeal v cuir à bith
repeat v can a-rithist, ath-aithris
repeatedly adv uair is uair
repel v till; (*be offensive to*) sgreamhaich, cuir sgàig air
repent v dèan/gabh aithreachas
repercussion n toradh m, buil f
repetition n ath-aithris f, ath-innse f
repetitive a a-rithist is a-rithist
replace v gabh àite (+ *gen*) **r. ... with ...** cuir ... an àite ...
re-plant v cuir a-rithist, ath-chuir
replay n ath-chluich f v ath-chluich
replenish v ath-lìon
replete a làn, buidheach
replica n mac-samhail m
reply n freagairt f v freagair
report n aithisg f, iomradh m v thoir cunntas/iomradh (air), dèan aithisg (air)
reporter n neach-naidheachd m
repossess v ath-shealbhaich, thoir air ais (bh)o
represent v riochdaich
representation n riochdachadh m
representative n riochdaire m a riochdachail, samhlach
repression n mùchadh m, ceannsachadh m
reprieve n allsachd f
reprimand n achmhasan m v cronaich, thoir achmasan do
reprint v ath-chlò-bhuail
reprisal n dìoghaltas m
reproach n cronachadh m; (*disgrace*) masladh m **beyond r.** gun choire sam bith
reproduce v gin; (*copy*) mac-samhlaich
reproduction n gintinn m; (*copy*) mac-samhlachadh m
reptile n pèist f, snàgair m
republic n poblachd f
republican n, a poblachdach m

repudiate v cuir cùl ri, diùlt gabhail ri
repulse v ruaig, cuir ruaig air
repulsive a gràineil, oillteil
reputable a le deagh chliù, measail
reputation n cliù m, ainm m
request n iarrtas m v iarr
require v feum; (ask) iarr
requirement n riatanas m, feumalachd f
requisite a riatanach, air a bheil feum
rescue n sàbhaladh m, teasairginn f
v sàbhail, teasairg
research n rannsachadh m, sgrùdadh m
v rannsaich, dèan sgrùdadh
researcher n neach-rannsachaidh m,
rannsaiche m
resemble v bi coltach ri
resent v fairich searbh mu, gabh san
t-sròin
resentful a searbh, tàmailteach
resentment n tàmailt f
reservation n (doubt) cumha m,
teagamh m; (booking) ro-chlàradh m
reserve v glèidh, taisg
reserved a fad' às, dùinte; (place, polit)
glèidhte
reservoir n tasgadh-uisge m; (met) stòr
m, stòras m
reside v fuirich, gabh còmhnaidh an
residence n àite/ionad-còmhnaidh m,
àros m
resident n neach-còmhnaidh m
residential a còmhnaidheach
residue n fuidheall m, còrr m
resign v leig dheth/dhith etc dreuchd,
thoir suas; (yield) gèill, bi leagte ri
resignation n leigeil dheth/dhith etc
dreuchd m; (yielding) gèilleadh m
resilient a fulangach
resin n ròiseid f, bìth f
resist v strì, cuir an aghaidh
resistance n strì f, cur an aghaidh m
resolute a seasmhach, gramail
resolution n (outcome) fuasgladh m;
(decision) rùn m; (resolve) seasmhachd f
resolve n rùn suidhichte m v cuir romhad,
rùnaich; (solve) fuasgail, rèitich
resonant a ath-fhuaimneach; (met) a'
dùsgadh …

resort n baile turasachd m; (recourse)
innleachd f, dòigh f
resource n goireas m, stòras m;
(ingenuity) innleachd f; (fin) ionmhas m
r. centre ionad ghoireasan m
resourceful a innleachdach
respect n spèis f, urram m **with r. to** a
thaobh (+ gen) v thoir spèis/urram do
respectable a measail, coltach
respectful a modhail, suimeil
respectively adv fa leth
respite n fao(tha)chadh m, anail f **r. care**
cùram fao(tha)chail m
respond v (answer) freagair; (act on)
dèilig ri
response n freagairt f
responsibility n dleastanas m, cùram m,
uallach m
responsible a cùramach; (accountable)
cunntachail; (behaviour) ciallach **r. for**
an urra ri
responsive a freagairteach, mothachail
rest n fois f, tàmh m; (mus) clos m **the r.**
(persons) càch; (things) an còrr v gabh
fois, leig anail
restaurant n taigh-bìdh m
restful a socair, foiseil
restless a an-fhoiseil, mì-stòlda,
luasganach, idrisgeach
restore v dèan suas às ùr; (give back)
thoir air ais; (of health) aisig gu slàinte
restrain v bac, caisg, ceannsaich
restrained a sriante, fo shrian
restraint n (curb) bacadh m, casg m;
(self-control) smachd m
restrict v cuingealaich, cuibhrich
restricted a cuingealaichte
restriction n cuingealachadh m,
cuibhreachadh m
result n buil f, toradh m **you'll see the r.!**
bidh a' bhuil ann!
resume v tòisich a-rithist; (recover) gabh
air ais
resurgence n ath-bheothachadh m,
dùsgadh m
resurrection n aiseirigh f
resuscitate v ath-bheothaich
retail a bùtha

retailer n ceannaiche m, marsanta m
retain v cùm, glèidh
retaliate v dìoghail, sabaidich air ais
retaliation n dìoghaltas m, sabaid air ais f
retard v bac, cùm air ais
retch v sgeith
retention n cumail f, gleidheadh m
retentive a glèidhteach
reticent a dùinte, diùid
retire v rach air chluainidh, leig dheth/ dhith dreuchd etc **I retired** leig mi dhìom mo dhreuchd
retired a air chluaineas/chluainidh
retirement n cluaineas m, leigeil dheth/ dhith etc dreuchd m
retort n freagairt gheur f v freagair gu geur/bras
retrace v rach air ais air
retract v tarraing air ais
retreat n ionad dìomhair m; (eccl) tèarmann m; (mil) ratreut m v teich, tarraing air ais
retrieve v faigh air ais; (met) leasaich
retrograde a ais-cheumach **a r. step** ceum air ais m
retrospect n coimhead/sealltainn air ais m **in r.** le sùil air ais
retrospective a ais-sheallach
return n tilleadh m; (fin) prothaid f **r. fare** faradh gach rathad m v till; (give back) cuir/thoir air ais
reunion n ath-choinneachadh m
reveal v nochd, taisbean, foillsich, leig ris
revealing a nochdte, follaiseach
revelation n taisbeanadh m; (eye-opener) sùileachan m **Book of Revelation** Leabhar an Taisbeanaidh m
revelry n fleadhachas m
revenge n dìoghaltas m **take r. on** v dèan dìoghaltas air
revenue n teachd a-steach m **Inland R.** Oifis nan Cìsean f
reverberate v ath-ghairm; (affect) thoir buaidh air
reverence n urram m, ùmhlachd f
reverend a urramach **the Rev** an t-Urramach (an t-Urr)

reverent a a' nochdadh spèis/urraim
reverse v rach air ais; (overturn) cuir car de
revert v till (gu)
review n breithneachadh m; (arts) lèirmheas m, sgrùdadh m v dèan breithneachadh air; (arts) dèan lèirmheas air, sgrùd
reviewer n lèirmheasaiche m
revise v ath-sgrùd, thoir sùil air ais air
revision n ath-sgrùdadh m, sùil air ais f
revitalise v ath-bheothaich
revival n ath-bheothachadh m; (relig) dùsgadh m
revive v ath-bheothaich, dùisg; (trans) ùraich
revoke v tarraing air ais
revolt n ar-a-mach m
revolting a gràineil, sgreamhail
revolution n car m, cuairt iomlan f; (polit) reabhlaid f, ar-a-mach m; (met) cruth-atharrachadh m, làn-thionndadh m
revolutionary n reabhlaideach m, neach ar-a-mach m a gu tur ùr; (polit) reabhlaideach
revolve v rach mun cuairt
revulsion n sgàig f
reward n duais f v thoir duais
rewrite v ath-sgrìobh
rhetoric n ùr-labhairt f, deas-chainnt f; (pej) glòireis f
rhetorical a ùr-labhrach, deas-chainnteach; (pej) glòireiseach
rheumatism n lòinidh f m
rhinoceros n sròn-adhairceach m
rhododendron n ròs-chraobh f
rhubarb n rùbarab m, ruadh-bhàrr m
rhyme n comhardadh m **internal r.** uaithne m v dèan comhardadh; (compose a verse) dèan rann
rhythm n ruitheam m, ruith f
rib n asna f m pl asnaichean, aisean f pl aisnean
ribbon n ribean m, ribinn f
rice n rus m
rich a beairteach, saidhbhir; (soil) torrach
riches n beairteas m, saidhbhreas m
rick n cruach f

rid v saor, fuasgail **get r. of** faigh cuidhteas (+ *nom*)
riddle n tòimhseachan m; (*agric*) ruideal m, criathar garbh m
ride v marcaich
rider n marcaiche m
ridge n druim m
ridicule n sgeig f, fanaid f v dèan fanaid air, dèan cùis-bhùirt de
ridiculous a gòrach, amaideach, luideach
riding n marcachd f
rife a pailt, lìonmhor
rifle n raidhfil f, isneach f
rift n sgoltadh m; (*between people*) sgaradh m
rig n rioga f; (*agric*) feannag f **oilrig** crann-ola m v (*equip*) uidheamaich, beairtich; (*manipulate*) claon
right n còir f, dlighe f; (*justice*) ceartas m a ceart; (*hand etc*) deas, ceart **r. away** sa bhad v cuir ceart
righteous a ionraic, fìreantach
rightful a dligheach
rights n còraichean f pl **civil r.** còraichean catharra
rigid a rag, do-lùbaidh
rigorous a cruaidh, mion
rigour n cruas m
rim n oir f m, bile f, iomall m
rind n rùsg m
ring n fàinne f m; (*area*) cearcall m, buaile f **r. finger** mac an aba m **r.-road** cuairt-rathad m v seirm **r. the bell** brùth an clag
rink n rinc m **ice r.** rinc deighe m
rinse v sgol, sruthail
riot n ùpraid f, iorghail f
riotous a ùpraideach, iorghaileach; (*prodigal*) stròdhail
rip v srac, reub
ripe a abaich
ripen v abaich
ripple n crith f, luasgan m, caitean m
rise v èirich
risk n cunnart m v feuch; (*put at risk*) cuir an cunnart
risky a cunnartach
ritual n deas-ghnàth m

rival n co-dheuchainniche m, co-fharpaiseach m
rivalry n còmhstri f, farpais f
river n abhainn f
riveting a aire-tharraingeach, drùidhteach
road n rathad m **r. sign** soidhne rathaid f
roam v rach air fàrsan
roar n beuc m, glaodh m, bùirean m v beuc, glaodh
roast n ròst f m a ròsta **r. beef** mairtfheòil ròsta f v ròist
rob v robaig, creach, goid air
robber n robair m, gadaiche m
robbery n goid f, robaireachd f, gadachd f
robe n fallaing f, trusgan m
robin redbreast n brù-dhearg m
robust a calma, làidir, foghainteach
rock n creag f, carraig f; (*substance*) clach f
rock v luaisg, tulg
rocket n rocaid f
rocking chair n sèithear-tulgaidh m
rocking horse n each-tulgach m
rock music n ceòl rog m
rocky a creagach
rod n slat f
rodent n criomach m
roe n earb f, ruadhag f; (*of fish*) iuchair f, glasag f **roebuck** boc-earba m
rogue n slaightear m, rògaire m
role n pàirt f m; (*in org*) dreuchd f; (*in society*) àite m **r.-play** gabhail riochd m
roll n roile f m v roilig, cuir car air char; (*fold*) paisg, fill
roller n roilear m **r.-coaster** roilear-còrsair m **r.-skate** bròg-roth f
Roman n, a Ròmanach m, (*female*) ban-Ròmanach f
Roman Catholic n, a Caitligeach m, (*female*) ban-Chaitligeach f
romance n romansachd f; (*story*) sgeul romansach m; (*love affair*) suirghe f
romantic a romansach
romp v bi a' ruideal
rone n guitear m, ròn f
roof n mullach m

rook n ròca(i)s f
room n rùm m, seòmar m; (*space*) àite m, rùm m
roomy a rùmail, farsaing
roost n spàrr m, spiris f
root n freumh m, bun m
rope n ròp(a) m, ball m
rosary n a' chonair(e) f, paidirean m
rose n ròs m
rot n grodadh m, lobhadh m v grod, lobh
rota n clàr-dleastanais m
rotate v cuir mun cuairt; (*intrans*) rach mun cuairt
rotten a grod, lobhte, breun
rotter n trustar m
rotund a cruinn
rough a garbh; (*hairy*) molach; (*temper*) garg
roughness n gairbhead m, gairge f
round n cuairt f, car m a cruinn adv mun cuairt, timcheall
roundabout n timcheallan m, cearcall-rathaid m
rouse v dùisg; (*stimulate*) brosnaich, piobraich
rousing a brosnachail, spreigearra
rout n ruaig f, sgiùrsadh m v rua(i)g, sgiùrs
route n rathad m, slighe f
routine n gnàth-chùrsa m a gnàthach
rove v bi a' ruagail, bi a' rèabhaireachd
row n (*line*) sreath f m
row n (*quarrel*) sabaid f, trod m v trod
row v (*boat*) iomair
rowan n caorann m
rowdy a gleadhrach
rowing n iomradh m **r. boat** bàta-ràmh m, geòla f
royal a rìoghail **the R. Family** an Teaghlach Rìoghail m
royalty n rìoghalachd f; (*fin*) dleasadh ùghdair m
rub v suath
rubber n rubair m
rubbish n sgudal m, treal(l)aich f **it's just r.** chan eil ann ach frachd **r. bin** biona-sgudail m **r. dump** lagais f, òtrach m
ruby n ruiteachan m, rùbaidh f
rucksack n màileid-droma f

rudder n stiùir f, falmadair m
ruddy a ruiteach, ruadh
rude a mì-mhodhail
rudeness n mì-mhodh m
rudimentary a bunaiteach, neo-leasaichte
rue v gabh aithreachas mu
rueful a dubhach, brònach, leamh
ruffian n brùid f m
ruffle v dèan ain-rèidh; (*met*) cuir colg air
rug n ruga m, brat-ùrlair m
rugby n rugbaidh m
rugged a garbh, corrach
ruin n sgrios m; (*site*) làrach f m, tobhta f v sgrios, mill
rule n riaghailt f; (*exercise of*) ceannas m **as a r.** mar as trice v riaghail, riaghlaich
ruler n riaghladair m **rulers** luchd-riaghlaidh m pl; (*measuring*) rùilear m
rum n ruma m
rumble v dèan torrann; (*stomach*) bi a' rùchdail
rumbling n torrann m, brùnsgal f; (*stomach*) rùchdail f
rummage v rùraich
rumour n fathann m
rump n dronn f, rumpall m
run n ruith f; (*transport*) slighe f v ruith; (*flee*) teich; (*melt*) leagh
runner n neach-ruith m
running n ruith f **r. costs** cosgais ruith f
runway n raon-laighe m
rupture v bris(t), sgàin, sgaoil
rural a dùthchail
ruse n innleachd f, clìc f
rush n dian-ruith f, sitheadh m, roid f v dèan cabhag/sitheadh **r. out** brùchd a-mach
rushes n luachair f
Russian n, a Ruiseanach m, (*female*) ban-Ruiseanach f; (*lang*) Ruisis f
rust n meirg f v meirg(ich)
rustic a dùthchail
rustling n siosarnaich f
rusty a meirgeach
rut n clais f; (*of deer*) dàmhair (nam fiadh) f **in a rut** san aon imire/eag
ruthless a cruaidh; (*pitiless*) gun iochd
rye n seagal m

S

Sabbath *n* an t-Sàbaid *f* **S. Day** Latha na Sàbaid *m*

sabotage *n* sabotàis *f*

sack *n* poca *m*, sac *m* **s.-race** rèis a' phoca *f*

sack *v* (*from work*) cuir à obair; (*destroy*) sgrios, creach

sacred *a* naomh, coisrigte

sacrifice *n* ìobairt *f v* ìobair

sacrilege *n* mì-naomhachadh *m*, aircealladh *m*

sad *a* brònach, dubhach, muladach; (*pitiful*) truagh

sadden *v* cuir bròn air, dèan dubhach

saddle *n* dìollaid *f*

sadness *n* bròn *m*, mulad *m*

safe *a* sàbhailte, tèarainte **s. and sound** slàn sàbhailte *n* ciste-tasgaidh *f*

safeguard *n* dìon *m v* dìon, geàrd

safety *n* sàbhailteachd *f*, tèarainteachd *f* **s.-belt** crios-sàbhalaidh *m* **s.-pin** prìne (banaltraim) *m*

sag *v* tuit

saga *n* sgeulachd *f*, mòr-sgeul *m*

sage *n* (*bot*) slàn-lus *m*; (*person*) saoi *m*

sail *n* seòl *m v* seòl, bi a' seòladh

sailor *n* seòladair *m*, maraiche *m*

saint *n* naomh *m*

saithe *n* saoithean *m*

sake *n* sgàth *m* **for the s. of** air sgàth (+ *gen*)

salad *n* sailead *m* **s. dressing** annlann saileid *m*

salary *n* tuarastal *m*

sale *n* reic *m*; (*reduced prices*) reic-saor *m* **s. of work** fèill-reic *f* **salesman** fear-reic *m* **salesperson** neach-reic *m*

saliva *n* seile *m*

salivate *v* seilich

sallow *a* lachdann

salmon *n* bradan *m*

salon *n* ionad *m* **beauty s.** ionad maise

salt *n* salann *m* **s. cellar** saillear *m* **s.-water** sàl *m a* saillte *v* saill

saltire *n* bratach na croise *f*

salty *a* saillte

salubrious *a* greadhnach

salutary *a* tairbheach **a s. warning** rabhadh feumail *m*

salute *n* (*mil*) nochdadh urraim *m v* nochd urram; (*acknowledge*) fàiltich, cuir fàilte air

salvage *v* dèan sàbhaladh air

salvation *n* teàrnadh *m*, saoradh *m*, slàinte *f* **Salvation Army** Arm an t-Saoraidh *m*

same *a* ionann, ceudna, ceart, aon

sameness *n* co-ionannachd *f*

sample *n* eisimpleir *f m*, sampall *m*; (*abstr*) taghadh *m v* feuch, blais

sanctify *v* naomhaich

sanctimonious *a* feall-chràbhach

sanction *n* (*approval*) aontachadh *m*, ùghdarras *m*; (*ban*) smachd-bhann *m*, òrdugh *m v* (*approve*) ceadaich, ùghdarraich; (*ratify*) daingnich

sanctuary *n* (*relig*) ionad coisrigte *m*; (*refuge*) comraich *f*, tèarmann *m*

sand *n* gainmheach *f* **s. dune** coilleag *f*, dùn gainmhich *m* **sandbank** oitir-ghainmhich *f*, banca-gainmhich *m* **sandpaper** pàipear-gainmhich *m* **sandstone** clach-ghainmhich *f*

sandal *n* cuaran *m*

sandpiper *n* fìdhlear *m*

sandwich *n* ceapaire *m*

sandy *a* gainmheil, gaineamhach

sane *a* ciallach

sanguine *a* dòchasach

sanitary *a* slàinteil, slàinte

sanitation *n* slàintealachd *f*

sanity *n* ciall *f*

Santa Claus *n* Bodach na Nollaig *m*

sap *n* snodhach *m*, sùgh *m v* sùgh, traogh

sapphire *n* gorm-leug *f*

sarcasm *n* searbhas *m*, searbh-chainnt *f*, leamhachas *m*

sarcastic *a* searbh, leamh, beumnach

sardine *n* sàrdain *m*

sardonic *a* sgaiteach

sash *n* crios *m*, bann *m*

Satan n an Sàtan m, an Donas m, an Droch Fhear m
satanic a diabhlaidh, deamhnaidh
satellite n saideal m
satin n sròl m a sròil
satire n aoir f
satirical a aoireil
satirize v aoir, dèan aoireadh
satisfaction n riarachadh m, sàsachadh m, toileachadh m
satisfactory a dòigheil, mar as còir
satisfied a riaraichte, sàsaichte, toilichte
satisfy v riaraich, sàsaich, toilich
satisfying a sàsachail
saturate v trom-fhliuch; (met) lèir-sgaoil
saturated a bog fliuch, trom-fhliuch; (met) loma-làn
Saturday n Disathairne m
sauce n sabhs m, leannra m
saucepan n sgeileid f
saucer n sàsar m, flat m
saucy a beadaidh
sauna n teaslann (smùide) f
saunter v spaidsirich
sausage n isbean m
savage a allaidh, borb
savagery n buirbe f
save v sàbhail, caomhain
saved a saorte, air a s(h)àbhaladh etc
saving(s) n sàbhaladh m, tasgadh m
  s. bond bann tasgaidh m
Saviour n an Slànaighear m
savour v feuch blas
savoury a blasta
saw n sàbh m **sawdust** min-sàibh f
  sawmill muileann-sàbhaidh f m
  v sàbh(aig)
saxifrage n lus nan cluas m
saxophone n sagsafòn m
say v can, abair
saying n ràdh m, facal m
scab n sgreab f, càrr f
scabies n am piocas m
scaffolding n sgafallachd f
scald v guail, sgald
scale n tomhas m; (size) meud m; (mus, geog) sgèile f; (on fish) lann f
scale v (climb) sreap

scallop n creachan(n) m
scalp n craiceann a' chinn m
scalpel n sgian lèigh f, lannsa f
scamper n ruith, thoir ruaig, teich
scampi n muasgain-chaola m pl
scan v sgrùd; (metr) bi a rèir meadrachd, meadaraich
scandal n sgainneal m, tuaileas m
scandalize v sgainnealaich
scandalous a maslach, tàmailteach, sgainnealach
Scandinavian n, a Lochlannach m
scanner n sganair m
scant(y) a gann, tearc
scapegoat n cùis-choireachaidh f
scar n làrach f m, leòn m
scarce a gann, tearc, ainneamh
scarcely adv air èiginn, is gann gu
scarcity n gainnead m, teirce f
scare n eagal m v cuir eagal air
scarecrow n bodach-ròcais/feannaig/ starraig m
scarf n sgarfa f, stoc m
scarlet n sgàrlaid f **s. fever** an teasach sgàrlaid f
scatter v sgap, sgaoil
scattered a sgapte
scene n (view, drama) sealladh m; (place) ionad m
scenery n sealladh m
scent n fàileadh m, boladh m, cùbhras m
scented a cùbhraidh
sceptic n, a eas-creidmheach m
sceptical a eas-creidmheach
scepticism n eas-creideamh m
schedule n clàr(-ama) m **ahead of s.** ron àm, tràth **on s.** ris an uair **behind s.** fadalach, air d(h)eireadh v cuir air clàr(-ama)
scheme n sgeama m, innleachd f, dòigh f v dèan sgeama/innleachd
schism n sgaradh m
scholar n sgoilear m
scholarship n sgoilearachd f, foghlam m
school n sgoil f **s.house** taigh-sgoile m **s.master** maighstir-sgoile m **s.mistress** ban-sgoilear, bana-mhaighstir-sgoile f
sciatica n siataig f

science n saidheans m
scientific a saidheansail
scientist n neach-saidheans m
scissors n siosar m
sclerosis n sglearòis f
scoff v mag, dèan fanaid (air)
scold v càin, cronaich
scone n sgona f m, bonnach m
scoop n liagh f, ladar m, taoman m
v cladhaich a-mach, tog a-mach
scope n comas m; (opportunity) cothrom
m; (extent) raon m, farsaingeachd f
score n (sport) sgòr m; (twenty) fichead
m; (cut) sgrìob f v (sport) cuir/faigh
tadhal; (cut) sgrìob
scorn n tàir f, dìmeas m v dèan tàir/
dìmeas air; (opportunity) leig seachad
scornful a tàireil
scorpion n sgairp f
Scot n Albannach m (female) ban-
Albannach f
Scots n (lang) Albais f, Beurla Ghallta f
Scottish a Albannach **S. Government**
Riaghaltas na h-Alba **S. Parliament**
Pàrlamaid na h-Alba
scoundrel n balgaire m
scour v sgùr
scourge v sgiùrs
scout n beachdair m
scowl v bi fo ghruaim, cuir drèin/mùig air/
oirre etc
scraggy a reangach
scramble v bi a' sporghail; (climb)
sreap
scrap n criomag f, mìr f; (fight) sabaid f,
tuasaid f
scrape v sgrìob **s. together** trus le èiginn
scratch n sgrìobadh m, sgrìob f, sgrìoch f
v sgròb, sgrìob; (itch) tachais
scrawl n sgròbaireachd f v dèan
sgròblaich
scream n sgiamh f m, sgreuch m v dèan
sgiamh/sgreuch
screech n sgread m, sgreuch m v dèan
sgread/sgreuch
screen n sgàilean m, sgrion m v (shelter)
dìon, sgàilich; (examine) cuir fo
sgrùdadh

screw n sgriubha m v sgriubh(aig)
screwdriver n sgriubhaire m
scribble n sgròbail m **a. quick s.** sgrìobag
ghoirid f v dean sgròbail
scribe n sgrìobhaiche m
script n sgrìobhadh m, clò m;
(handwriting) làmh-sgrìobha(i)dh f
scripture n sgriobtar m
scroll n rolla f v roilig
scrub v sgùr, nigh gu math
scruffy a piollagach, loireach
scruple n teagamh m, imcheist f
scrupulous a fìor chùramach,
mion-fhaiceallach
scrutinize v sgrùd
scrutiny n sgrùdadh m
scuffle n buaireas m
scullery n sguilearaidh f m, cùlaist f
sculptor n snaigheadair m
sculpture n snaigheadh m; (a piece of)
ìomhaigh shnaighte f
scum n rèim m, sgùm m; (slang) salchair
m pl
scurrilous a sgainnealach, tuaileasach
scythe n speal f v speal
sea n muir f m, cuan m, fairge f
seabed n grunnd na mara m, aigeann m
seagull n faoileag f
seal n ròn m; (document) seula m
v seulaich; (close) dùin
seam n (clothing) dùnadh m, fuaigheal m
seaman n maraiche m, seòladair m
search n lorg m, sireadh m **searchlight**
solas-siridh m v lorg, sir
seashore n cladach m, tràigh f
seasick a leis an tinneas-mhara, le cur
na mara
seasickness n an tinneas-mara m, cur na
mara m
season n ràith(e) f, seusan m; (time)
aimsir f, tràth m
season v (wood etc) seusanaich, grèidh;
(food) cuir blas ri
sea-spray n siaban m, marcan-sìne m
seat n suidheachan m, cathair f,
àite-suidhe m; (residence) àros m;
(in Parliament) seat f **s. belt** crios-
suidheachain m

sea trout *n* bànag *f*, gealag *f*
seaweed *n* feamainn *f*
secede *v* bris(t) air falbh, trèig
secluded *a* uaigneach, leathoireach
second *n* diog *m*
second *a* dara, dàrna
second *v* cuir taic ri; (*to post*)
 fo-fhastaich
secondary *a* dàrnacha, dhen dàrna ìre
 s. school àrd-sgoil *f*
seconder *n* neach-taice *m*
secondhand *a* ri/air ath-reic
secondly *adv* anns an dara h-àite, anns
 an dàrna h-àite
secrecy *n* dìomhaireachd *f*, cleith *f*
secret *n* rùn-dìomhair *m*, sgeul-rùin *m a*
 dìomhair, falaichte, falchaidh
secretariat *n* clèireachas *m*, rùnachas *m*
secretary *n* clèireach *m*, ban-chlèireach *f*;
 (*personal*) rùnaire *m* **S. of State** Rùnaire
 (na) Stàite *m*
secretive *a* falchaidh, ceilteach
secretly *adv* os ìosal, gun fhiosta (do
 dhaoine)
sect *n* dream *m*, treubh *f*
sectarian *a* dreamail, treubhail, fineil
section *n* roinn *f*, earrann *f*
sector *n* roinn *f*, raon *m*
secular *a* saoghalta
secure *a* tèarainte, seasgair *v* dèan
 cinnteach; (*lock*) gla(i)s; (*obtain*) faigh
security *n* (*abstr*) tèarainteachd *f*, dìon
 m; (*personnel*) luchd-dìon *m* **s. of tenure**
 còir-gabhaltais *f* **s. guard** geàrd-faire *m*
sedate *a* ciùin, stòlda
sedative *n* cungaidh stòlaidh *f*
sedge *n* seisg *f*
sediment *n* grùid *f*
seduce *v* thoir a thaobh, breug
seduction *n* toirt a thaobh *f*,
 breugadh *m*
see *v* faic **see you soon** chì mi (a)
 dh'aithghearr thu
seed *n* sìol *m*, fras *f*; (*offspring*) sliochd *m*,
 gineal *m*, iarmad *m v* sìolaich, cuir fras de
seek *v* iarr, sir, lorg
seem *v* bi mar … , leig air/oirre *etc* (a
 bhith)

seemly *a* iomchaidh, cubhaidh, coltach
seep *v* sìolaidh tro
seer *n* fiosaiche *m*, fàidh *m*
seethe *v* (*met*) bi fo chuthach
segment *n* gearradh-cuairteig *m*, roinn *f*
segregate *v* dealaich, sgar, tearb
segregation *n* dealachadh *m*, sgaradh
 m, tearbadh *m*
seize *v* glac, cuir làmh an, greimich air
seizure *n* glacadh *m*, grèim *m*
seldom *adv* ainneamh, gu tearc, gu
 h-ainmig
select *v* tagh, roghnaich
selection *n* taghadh *m*, roghainn *f m*
selective *a* roghnach
self *pron* fhèin, fèin
self-confidence *n* fèin-mhisneachd *f*
self-confident *a* fèin-mhisneachail
self-denial *n* fèin-àicheadh *m*
self-employed *a* ag obair air a c(h)eann
 fhèin *etc*, fèin-fhastaichte
self-explanatory *a* fèin-mhìneachail
self-government *n* fèin-riaghladh *m*
self-interest *n* fèin-bhuannachd *f*
selfish *a* fèineil, fèinchuiseach
selfishness *n* fèinealachd *f*
self-respect *n* fèin-mheas *m*
self-satisfied *a* fèin-riaraichte
self-service *n* fèin-fhrithealadh *m*
self-same *a* ceart, ionann
sell *v* reic
seller *n* reiceadair *m*, neach-reic *m*
semblance *n* samhla *m*, coltas *m*
semi- *pref* leth-
semi-circle *n* leth-chearcall *m*
semi-colon *n* leth-chòilean *m*, leth-
 stad *m*
semi-detached *a* leth-dhealaichte
seminal *a* mòr-bhuadhach; (*phys*)
 sìolach
seminar *n* co-chonaltradh *m*
senate *n* seanadh *m*
senator *n* seanadair *m*
send *v* cuir **s. word** cuir fios (gu) **s. for**
 cuir a dh'iarraidh
senile *a* seanntaidh
senior *a* as sine, nas sine, àrd- (+ *len*),
 prìomh (+ *len*)

sensation n mothachadh m,
faireachdainn f
sense n (wits) ciall f, toinisg f; (meaning)
brìgh f, seagh m; (faculty) ciadfath
f, mothachadh m **making no s.** gun
bhlèaram
senseless a gun chiall/sgot; (phys) gun
mhothachadh
sensibility n mothachas m
sensible a ciallach, tùrail
sensitive a mothachail; (contentious)
frionasach
sensory a mothachaidh
sensual a feòlmhor, collaidh
sensuous a ceudfathach
sentence n seantans f, rosgrann m; (leg)
binn f, breith f v thoir binn, dìt
sentiment n (thought) smaoin f;
(emotion) faireachdainn f
sentimental a maoth-inntinneach
separate a dealaichte, sgaraichte, air
leth, leis fhèin v dealaich, sgar, tearb,
roinn
separation n dealachadh m, sgaradh m
sept n fine f
September n an t-Sultain f
septic a lionnraichte, iongarach
sequel n na leanas **the s. to** a leanas
sequence n leanmhainn m, ruith f **in s.**
an sreath a chèile
serene a soineannta, ciùin, suaimhneach
serenity n soineanntachd f, ciùineas m,
suaimhneas m
sergeant n sàirdseant m
serial n leansgeul m
series n sreath f m
serious a cudromach, tromchuiseach;
(person) dùrachdach
seriously adv an da-rìribh
sermon n searmon m **preach s.**
searmonaich, dèan searmon
serpent n nathair f
serrated a eagach
servant n searbhanta f, seirbheiseach m,
sgalag f
serve v (food) fritheil, riaraich; (in office)
dèan seirbheis **s. one's time** thoir
a-mach ceàird

service n seirbheis f, frithealadh m;
(relig) seirbheis f; (dom) muinntireas m
s.-station stèisean-frithealaidh m
serviceable a feumail, iomchaidh
serviette n nèapaigin-bùird f m
servile a tràilleil
session n seisean m
set n seat(a) m a suidhichte, stèidh(ich)te;
(usual) gnàthach; (ready) deiseil
set v suidhich, socraich, stèidhich, cuir;
(sun) laigh, rach fodha **s. apart** cuir air
leth **s. fire to** cuir na theine, cuir teine
ri **s. off/out** tog air/oirre etc
s. out (outline) mìnich; (resolve) cuir
roimhe/roimhpe etc **s. up** cuir air
bhonn/chois **s. table** deasaich/seat
am bòrd
settee n seidhs(e) f
setter n cù-eunaich/luirg m
setting n suidheachadh m, seatadh m
s. of sun dol fodha na grèine m
settle v seatlaig, socraich; (intrans)
sìolaidh; (argument) rèitich; (inhabit)
tuinich, àitich
settled a stèidhichte, seatlaigte
settlement n socrachadh m; (resolution)
rèite f, rèiteachadh m; (habitation)
tuineachadh m
settler n tuiniche m, neach-
tuineachaidh m
seven n a seachd a seachd **s. people**
seachdnar m
seventeen a seachd-deug **s. cards**
seachd cairtean deug
seventh a seachdamh
seventy n trì fichead 's a deich m,
seachdad m
sever v sgar, dealaich
several a iomadh, iomadach
severe a cruaidh; (intense) dian; (of
person) gnù, gnuath, gruamach;
(criticism) feanntach
severity a cruas m, teinne f
sew v fuaigh, fuaigheil
sewage n giodar m, òtrachas m
sewer n sàibhear m
sewing n fuaigheal m **s. machine** beairt-
fuaigheil f

sex n gnè f, cineal m; (act) feis(e) f
 sex appeal tarraing chorporra f **sex
 discrimination** leth-bhreith (a thaobh)
 gnè f
sexist a gnè-thaobhach
sexual a gnèitheasach, gnèitheach
sexy a seagsaidh
shabby a robach; (treatment) suarach
shack n bothag f
shackle n geimheal m, ceangal m
 v geimhlich, cuingealaich
shade n sgàil f, dubhar m
shadow n faileas m, sgàil f, dubhar m
shadowy a faileasach, sgàileach
shady a dubharach; (met) a' togail
 amharais/teagaimh, mì-chneasta
shaft n cas f, samhach f; (mech) crann m;
 (of light) gath m; (lift, mine) toll m
shaggy a molach, ròmach
shake n crith f v crath, luaisg; (intrans)
 crith **s. hands with** beir/breith air làimh air
shaky a critheanach
shallow a ao-domhainn, tana; (met)
 staoin
sham n mealladh m
shambles n bùrach m
shame n nàire f, masladh m, tàmailt
 f **it's a s.** 's e call a th' ann v nàraich,
 maslaich
shameful a nàr, maslach
shameless a lugha-nàire, beag-nàrach
shampoo n siampù m, failcean m v failc
shamrock n seamrag f
shank n lurg(a) f, cas f
shape n cumadh m, cruth m v cum,
 dealbh, thoir cumadh air
shapeless a gun chumadh; (not shapely)
 neo-chuimir
shapely a cuimir, cumadail
share n roinn f, cuid f, cuibhreann f m,
 earrann f v roinn, pàirtich, riaraich **s. in**
 gabh pàirt an **s. and s. alike** dèan roinn
 a' mhic is an athar air **shareholder**
 neach-earrannan m pl luchd-
 earrannan
shark n siorc m **basking s.** cearban m
sharp a geur, biorach; (of person)
 geurchuiseach; (of practice) carach

sharpen v geuraich, faobharaich
shatter v bris(t) na mhìrean, bloighdich
shave n bearradh m, lomadh m **he had a
 close s.** (met) chaidh fìor shàbhaladh air
 v beàrr, lom(aich)
shawl n seàla f, guailleachan m
she pron i, (emph) ise
sheaf n sguab f m
shear v rùisg, lomair, beàrr
shearing n rùsgadh m, lomadh m,
 bearradh m
shears n deamhais f m
sheath n truaill f, duille f
shed n bothan m, sead(a) f m
shed v dòirt, sil; (staff) leig dheth
sheen n lainnir f
sheep n caora f **sheepdog** cù-chaorach
 m **sheepskin** craiceann-caorach m
sheepish a (met) similidh
sheer a fìor; (steep) cas
sheet n siota m; (bed) braith-lìn f; (of
 paper) duilleag f; (sail) sgòd-siùil m
 ice-s. clàr-deighe m
shelduck n cràdh-ghèadh m
shelf n sgeilp f; (of rock) sgeir f
shell n slige f, plaosg m
shellfish n maorach m
shelter n fasgadh m, dìon m **bus s.**
 ionad-fasgaidh bus m v (take) gabh
 fasgadh; (give) thoir fasgadh do
sheltered a fasgach
shepherd n cìobair m
sheriff n siorram m, siorraidh m **s. court**
 cùirt an t-siorraim f
sherry n searaidh m
shield n sgiath f v dìon, glèidh
shift v caraich, gluais
shifty a seòlta, carach
shilling n tastan m
shin n lurg f, lurgann f
shine n deàlradh m, gleans(a) m
 v deàlraich, soillsich, deàrrs
shingle n mol m, morghan m
shingles n deir f
shining a deàlrach, deàrrsach,
 boillsgeach
shinty n iomain f, camanachd f **s. stick**
 caman m

shiny *a* deàlrach, gleansach
ship *n* bàta *m*, soitheach *f m*, long *f*
v (*load*) cuir air bòrd; (*transport*) giùlain;
(*water*) leig a-steach uisge
shipbuilding *n* togail shoithichean *f*
shipyard *n* gàrradh-iarainn *m*
shire *n* siorr(am)achd *f*
shirk *v* seachain
shirt *n* lèine *f* **s.-sleeve** muilicheann lèine
m
shiver *n* crith *f*, gaoir *f v* crith, bi air chrith;
(*with cold*) bi ga lathadh *etc*
shivering *a* air chrith
shoal *n* tanalach *m*; (*of fish*) sgaoth *m*
shock *n* clisgeadh *m*, sgànradh *m*;
(*horror*) oillt *f*; (*of hair*) cnuaic *f*, cràic *f*
v (*startle*) cuir clisgeadh air, sgànraich;
(*horrify*) uabhasaich
shocking *a* sgriosail
shoddy *a* bochd, suarach, mu làimh
shoe *n* bròg *f*; (*horse*) crudha (eich) *m*
shoelace *n* barrall *m*
shoemaker *n* greusaiche *m*
shoot *n* faillean *m*, ògan *m*
shoot *v* (*gun*) loisg; (*in game*) srad, amais
air an lìon
shooting *n* losgadh *m*
shop *n* bùth *f*
shopkeeper *n* neach-bùtha *m*
shopping centre *n* ionad-bhùthan *m*
shore *n* cladach *m*, tràigh *f*
short *a* goirid, geàrr **s.-cut**
aithghearrachd *f* **s. leet** liosta thaghte *f*
shortlived diombuan **s.-sighted** geàrr-
sheallach **s. story** sgeulachd ghoirid *f*
s.-tempered cas, aithghearr (san nàdar)
s.-term *n* geàrr-ùine *f a* geàrr-ùineach
shortage dìth *f m*, gainne *f*
shortbread *n* aran-milis *m*
shortcoming *n* easbhaidh *f*
shorten *v* giorraich
shortly *adv a* dh'aithghearr
shorts *n* briogais ghoirid *f*
shot *n* (*of gun*) urchair *f*
shotgun *n* gunna-froise *m*
shoulder *n* gualainn *f*, slinnean *m*
shout *n* èigh *f*, glaodh *m v* èigh, glaodh

shove *n* putadh *m*, putag *f v* put
shovel *n* sluasaid *f v* obraich le sluasaid/
spaid
show *n* sealladh *m*, taisbeanadh *m*;
(*entertainment*) cuirm-chluich *f v* seall,
nochd, foillsich, taisbean
shower *n* fras *f*, meall *m*; (*appliance*)
frasair *m* **what a s.!** abair seat! *v* fras,
dòirt, sil
showery *a* frasach
showroom *n* seòmar-taisbeanaidh *m*
shred *n* mìr *m*, bìdeag *f*, criomag *f v* cuir
na stiallan
shrewd *a* glic, teòma, gleusta,
geurchuiseach
shriek *n* sgread *m*, sgreuch *m v* dèan
sgread/sgreuch
shrill *a* sgalanta, sgairteil
shrimp *n* carran *m*
shrine *n* ionad coisrigte *m*
shrink *v* seac; (*recoil*) bi fo gheilt, tarraing
air ais (bh)o
shrivel *v* crìon, searg
shrivelled *a* seargte
shroud *n* marbhphaisg *f*; (*naut*) cupaill *m pl*
shrub *n* preas *m*
shrubbery *n* preasarnach *f*
shrug *n* crathadh guailne *m v* crath
guailnean
shudder *n* ball-crith *f*, criothnachadh
m v criothnaich
shuffle *v* (*cards etc*) measgaich; (*gait*)
dragh do chasan
shun *v* seachain
shut *v* dùin *a* dùinte
shutter *n* còmhla (uinneige) *f*
shuttle *n* spàl *m* **shuttlecock** gleicean *m*
shy *a* diùid, socharach
sick *a* tinn, bochd, meadhanach
sicken *v* fàs tinn/bochd, gabh tinneas;
(*trans*) dèan tinn
sickle *n* corran *m*
sickness *n* tinneas *m*, bochdainn *f* **s.**
benefit sochair tinneis *f*
side *n* taobh *m*, cliathach *f* **s.-road** frith-
rathad *m* **s.-street** frith-shràid **sidewalk**
cabhsair *m f v* **s. with** gabh taobh
(*+ gen*) **sidetrack** thoir a thaobh

sideboard *n* preasa-tasgaidh *m*
sideline *n* iomall *m*; (*another activity*) frith-obair *f* *v* cuir gus an oir/an t-iomall
sidestep *v* (*met*) seachain; (*phys*) gabh ceum às an rathad
sideways *adv* air fiaradh, an comhair a t(h)ao(i)bh *etc*
sidle *v* siolp
siege *n* sèist *f* *m*
sieve *n* criathar *m*
sift *v* criathraich, rèitich
sigh *n* osna *f*, osann *f* *m* *v* leig osna/osann, osnaich
sight *n* sealladh *m*; (*faculty*) fradharc *m* **out of s.** às an t-sealladh **second s.** an dà shealladh
sightseeing *n* siubhal sheallaidhean *m*
sign *n* comharra *m*, soidhne *m* **signpost** post-seòlaidh *m*, post-soidhne *m* *v* soidhnig, cuir ainm ri; (*indicate*) dèan comharra
signal *n* comharra *m*, soidhne *m*
signature *n* ainm-sgrìobhte *m*
signet *n* fàinne seula *f*
significance *n* brìgh *f*; (*importance*) cudromachd *f*
significant *a* brìgheil; (*important*) cudromach
signify *v* comharraich, ciallaich
Sikh *n* Siog *m*, (*female*) ban-Siogach *f* *a* Siogach
silence *n* sàmhchair *f*, tost *m*
silent *a* sàmhach, na t(h)ost *etc*
silhouette *n* sgàil-riochd *m*
silicon *n* sileagon *m*
silk *n*, *a* sìoda *m*
silk(y)/silken *a* sìodach
sill *n* sòl *f*
silliness *n* gòraiche *f*, faoineas *m*
silly *a* gòrach, faoin
silt *n* eabar *m*
silver *n* airgead *m* *a* airgid, airgeadach
similar *a* coltach, ionann
similarity *n* coltas *m*, ionannachd *f*; (*resemblance*) suaip *f*
simile *n* samhla *m*
simmer *v* earr-bhruich
simple *a* sìmplidh; (*in mind*) slac, baoth

simplify *v* sìmplich
simplistic *a* ro shìmplidh
simply *adv* dìreach
simulate *v* leig ort
simultaneous *a* còmhla, mar-aon, aig an aon àm, co-amail
sin *n* peacadh *m* *v* peacaich
since *adv* (bh)o *conj* a chionn gu(n) *prep* (bh)o, o chionn (+ *gen*)
sincere *a* treibhdhireach, dùrachdach
sincerity *n* treibhdhireas *m*, dùrachd *f*
sinew *n* fèith *f*
sing *v* seinn, gabh òran
singe *v* dàth
singer *n* seinneadair *m*; (*female*) ban-s(h)einneadair *f*
single *a* singilte; (*not married*) gun phòsadh **s.-handed** leis/leatha (*etc*) fhèin, gun chuideachadh
singular *a* singilte; (*unusual*) sònraichte, àraid
sinister *a* (*threatening*) bagarrach; (*evil*) olc
sink *n* sinc(e) *f* *m*
sink *v* (*trans*) cuir fodha; (*intrans*) rach fodha
sinner *n* peacach *m*
sinuous *a* lùbach
sip *n* balgam *m*, drudhag *f* *v* gabh balgam/drudhag
siphon *n* pìob-èalaidh *f*
sir *n* an ridire *m*, sir *m*
siren *n* (*hooter*) dùdach *f* *m*, conacag *f*
sister *n* piuthar *f* **s.-in-law** piuthar-chèile *f*
sit *v* suidh, dèan suidhe
site *n* làrach *f* *m*, ionad *m* *v* suidhich
sitting-room *n* seòmar-suidhe *m*, rùm-suidhe *m*
situated *a* suidhichte, air a s(h)uidheachadh **well s.** air a dheagh shuidheachadh
situation *n* suidheachadh *m*
six *n*, *a* sia **s. people** sianar *m*
sixteen *n* a sia, *a* sia-deug *m* **s. letters** sia litrichean deug
sixth *a* siathamh
sixty *n*, *a* trì fichead *m*, seasgad *m*
sizeable *a* meadhanach mòr, meudmhor

size n meud m, meudachd f, tomhas m

skate n (*fish*) sgait f; (*ice*) spèil f, bròg-
spèilidh f v spèil

skating n spèileadh m

skeleton n cnàimhneach m

skelp n sgailc f

skerry n sgeir f

sketch n sgeidse f v dèan sgeidse

ski n sgì f pl sgithean v sgì

skid v sleamhnaich

skiff n coit f, sgoth m

skiing n sgitheadh m

skilful a sgileil, ealanta

skill n sgil f m

skilled a sgileil, ealanta

skim v (*eg milk*) thoir uachdar de;
(*intrans*) falbh air uachdar/bàrr (+ *gen*);
(*read*) dèan bloigh leughaidh (air)

skin n craiceann m; (*of animals*) bian
m, seiche f **by the s. of one's teeth**
dìreach air èiginn v feann, thoir an
craiceann de

skinny a caol, tana

skip n leum m, sùrdag f; (*rubbish*) tasgan
sgudail m v leum, dèan sùrdag

skipper n sgiobair m

skipping n sgiob(aige)adh m **s. rope**
ròp(a)-sgiobai(gi)dh m

skirt n sgiort(a) f

skulk v bi a' cùiltearachd

skull n claigeann m

sky n adhar m, speur m **skylight** fàirleus
m **skyline** fàire f

Skyeman n Sgitheanach m **Skyewoman**
ban-Sgitheanach f

skylark n uiseag f

slab n leac f

slack a slac, flagach; (*not busy*) sàmhach,
slac; (*lax*) lag

slacken v slac, lasaich

slam v slàraig, thoir slaic air; (*met*) càin,
thoir slaic air

slander n cùl-chàineadh m, tuaileas m
v cùl-chàin, sgainnealaich

slanderous a sgainnealach

slang n mith-chainnt f

slant n (*phys, met*) claonadh m,
fiaradh m

slanted a air a chlaonadh, le fiaradh ann;
(*biased*) claon, fiar

slap n sgailc f, pais f v thoir sgailc/pais do

slapdash a leibideach, gun diù

slash n gearradh m, sgath f v geàrr, sgath

slate n sglèat m v sglèat, cuir sglèat air

slater n sglèatair m

slaughter n marbhadh m, casgairt f
slaughterhouse taigh-spadaidh m
v spad, casgair, marbh

Slav/Slavonic n, a Slàbhach m, (*female*)
ban-Slàbhach f

slave n tràill f m

slavery n tràillealachd f, braighdeanas m

slay v marbh

sledge n càrn-slaoid m, slaodan m

sleek a slìom, mìn

sleep n cadal m **short s.** norrag f v caidil,
dèan cadal

sleeping bag n poca-cadail m

sleepless a gun chadal

sleepy a cadalach

sleet n flin(ne) m

sleeve n muilicheann f m, muinichill f m

slender a tana, seang

slice n slis f, sliseag f v slis, slisnich

sliced a sliseagach

slick a ealanta, le liut

slide n sleamhnag f v slaighd,
sleamhnaich

slight n dìmeas m, tàire f a beag, aotrom

slim a tana, seang, caol v fàs seang/caol,
caill cuideam

slime n làthach f, clàbar m

sling n (*med*) iris gàirdein f; (*weapon*)
crann-tabhaill m

slink v siap

slip n (*phys, met*) tuisleadh m; (*error*)
mearachd f v tuislich **s. up** dèan
mearachd

slipper n sliopair f m, slapag f

slippery a sleamhainn

slipshod a mu làimh

slipway n cidhe m; (*for launching*)
leathad cur air bhog m

slit n sgoltadh m v sgoilt, geàrr

slogan n sluagh-ghairm f

slope n leathad m, bruthach f m

sloping *a* ag aomadh
sloppy *a* bog; (*untidy*) mì-sgiobalta; (*shoddy*) leibideach, lapach
slot *n* beulag *f*
sloth *n* leisg(e) *f*
slothful *a* leisg
slovenly *a* robach, rapach
slow *a* slaodach, màirnealach
sludge *n* eabar *m*, làthach *f*
slug *n* seilcheag *f*
sluggish *a* slaodach, trom, gun sgoinn
slum *n* sluma *m*, bochd-cheàrn *f*
slump *v* tuit nad chnap; (*fin*) tuit gu mòr
slur *n* (*insult*) aithis *f*; (*of speech*) slugadh *m*, mabladh *m v* (*of speech*) sluig facail/faclan **cast a s.** aithisich
slush *n* sneachd(a) leaghte *m*
slut *n* luid *f*, sgliùrach *f*
sly *a* carach, slìogach
smack *n* deidhseag *f*
small *a* beag
smallpox *n* a' bhreac *f*
smart *a* grinn, spaideil; (*clever*) geur
smash *n* bris(t)eadh *m*; (*accident*) bualadh na chèile *m v* bris(t); (*tennis*) smoidsig
smashing *a* (*met*) sgoinneil
smear *v* smeur, liacair, smiùr
smell *n* fàileadh *m*, boladh *m v* (*trans*) feuch/tog fàileadh **it smells** tha fàileadh dheth
smelt *v* leagh
smile *n* fiamh-ghàire *m*, snodha-gàire *m*, faite-gàire *f v* dèan fiamh-ghàire, dèan snodha/faite-gàire
smirk *n* plìon(as) *m v* **he smirked** thàinig plìonas air
smith *n* gobha *m*
smock *n* lèine *f*
smoke *n* ceò *f m*, toit *f*, deatach *f v* (*tobacco*) gabh ceò/smoc, smoc(aig)
smoky *a* ceòthach
smooth *a* mìn, rèidh, còmhnard
smoothe *v* dèan rèidh
smother *v* mùch, tachd
smoulder *v* cnàmh-loisg

smudge *n* smal *m*, spuaic *f v* smalaich, cuir spuaic air
smug *a* riaraichte (leis/leatha fhèin *etc*)
smuggle *v* dèan cùl-mhùtaireachd
smuggler *n* cùl-mhùtaire *m*
smut *n* drabastachd *f*
smutty *a* drabasta
snack *n* blasad bìdh *m*, greimeag *f*
snag *n* duilgheadas *m*
snail *n* seilcheag *f*
snake *n* nathair *f*
snap *v* bris(t) le brag; (*bite*) dèan glamhadh
snapshot *n* mion-dhealbh *f m*; (*met*) dealbh aithghearr *f m*
snare *n* ribe *f m v* rib
snarl *v* dèan dranndan
snatch *v* glac, beir (air)
sneak *n* sniag *m*, lìogaire *m v* sniag, liùg, èalaidh
sneaky *a* sniagach, lìogach
sneer *v* dèan fanaid, cuir an neo-shùim
sneeze *n* sreothart *m v* dèan sreothart
sniff *n* boladh *m*, fàileadh *m v* gabh fàileadh/boladh **s. at** dèan tarcais air
snigger *n* siot-ghàire *f*
snip *v* geàrr le siosar
snipe *n* naosg *m*
snob *n* sodalan *m*, mòrchuisiche *m*
snobbery *n* sodalachd *f*, mòrchuiseachd *f*
snobbish *a* mòrchuiseach, sodalach
snooze *n* norrag *f*, snuachdan *m v* dèan norrag/snuachdan
snore *n* srann *f v* dèan srann
snort *n* srannartaich *f v* bi a' srannartaich
snotty *a* spliugach
snout *n* soc *m*, sròn *f*
snow *n* sneachd(a) *m* **snowball** ball-sneachd(a) *m* **snowdrift** cith(e) *m* **snowflake** pleòideag *f*, bleideag *f*, lòineag *f* **snowman** bodach-sneachd(a) *m* **snowstorm** stoirm s(h)neachd(a) *f m v* cuir sneachd(a)
snowdrop *n* gealag-làir *f*
snuff *n* snaoisean *m* **s.-box** bogsa/bucas snaoisein *m*
snug *a* seasgair, clùthmhor
snuggle *v* teann dlùth ri

Insight: snow

The Gaelic for snow is *sneachd(a)*. To comment that it is snowing, you say *tha i a' cur an t-sneachda* (literally, it is shedding the snow). You can also say *tha an sneachda ann* (literally there is snow). A snowman is *bodach-sneachda*. There are several words for a snowflake – *pleòideag, bleideag, lòineag.*

so *adv* cho; (*like this*) mar seo; (*therefore*) mar sin **so long as** cho fad 's a **so-and-so** a leithid seo a dhuine **s. much** uimhir *interj* seadh

soak *v* drùidh; (*eg clothes*) cuir am bogadh

soaking/soaked *a* bog fliuch

soap *n* siabann *m* **TV s.** siabann telebhisein

soar *v* itealaich gu h-àrd; (*fin*) àrdaich gu mòr

sob *n* glug caoinidh *m*

sober *a* sòbarra; (*moderate*) stuama, measarra *v* sòbraich, fuaraich, dèan/fàs sòbarra

soccer *n* ball-coise *m*

sociable *a* cuideachail, càirdeil

social *a* sòisealta, caidreabhach, comannach **S. Democrat** Deamocratach Sòisealta *m* **s. security** tèarainteachd shòisealta *f* **s. work** obair shòisealta *f*

socialism *n* sòisealachd *f*

socialist *n, a* sòisealach *m*

society *n* an comann-sòisealta *m*, sòisealtas *m*; (*body*) comann *m*

sociology *n* eòlas sòisealtais *m*

sock *n* stocainn *f*, socais *f*; (*blow*) sgleog *f*

socket *n* socaid *f* **electrical s.** bun-dealain *m*

sod *n* fòid *f*, sgrath *f*

soda *n* sòda *f m*

sodden *a* bog fliuch

sodium *n* sòidium *m*

sofa *n* sòfa *f*, langasaid *f*

soft *a* bog, maoth, socair **s.-hearted** tais-chridheach

soften *v* bogaich, maothaich

softness *n* buige *f*, maothachd *f*

software *n* bathar bog *m*

soggy *a* bog fliuch

soil *n* ùir *f*, talamh *m*

soil *v* salaich, truaill

soiled *a* loireach

solace *n* cofhurtachd *f*, furtachd *f*

solan goose *n* sùlaire *m* **young s.g.** guga *m*

solar *a* na grèine

sold *a* air a reic *etc*

solder *v* sobhdraich, solldraig

soldier *n* saighdear *m*

sole *n* bonn na coise *m*; (*fish*) lèabag/ leòbag-cheàrr *f*

sole *a* aon

solely *adv* a-mhàin

solemn *a* sòlaimte

solicit *v* (*request*) iarr

solicitor *n* neach-lagha *m*

solid *n* teann-stuth *m a* teann, cruaidh, daingeann; (*sound*) susbainteach

solidarity *n* dlùth-phàirteachas *m*, dìlseachd *f*

solidify *v* cruadhaich

solitary *a* aon(a)ranach, uaigneach

solitude *n* uaigneas *m*

solo *n* (*song*) òran aon-neach *m*, (*instrumental*) cluich aon-neach *f a* leis/ leatha *etc* fhèin

soloist *n* òranaiche *m*, neach-ciùil aona(i)r *m*

soluble *a* so-sgaoilte

solution *n* fuasgladh *m*; (*substance*) eadar-sgaoileadh *m*

solve *v* fuasgail

solvent *n* lionn-sgaoilidh *m*

solvent *a* comasach air pàigheadh

sombre *a* dubhach, gruamach; (*of dress*) dorch(a)

some *n* cuid *f*, roinn *f*, pàirt *f m*; (*people*) feadhainn *f*, cuid *f*

somebody *pron* cuideigin *f*, neacheigin *m*

somehow *adv* air dòigh air choreigin, air dòigheigin
someone *n* cuideigin *f*, neacheigin *m*
somersault *n* car a' mhuiltein *m* *v* dèan car a' mhuiltein
something *pron* rudeigin *m*, nìtheigin *m*
sometime *adv* uaireigin
sometimes *adv* uaireannan
somewhat *adv* rudeigin, beagan, car, lethchar
somewhere *adv* an àiteigin, am badeigin
son *n* mac *m*, gille *m* **son-in-law** cliamhainn *m*
song *n* òran *m*, amhran *m*
soon *adv* a dh'aithghearr, gu grad, an ùine ghoirid/gheàrr
soot *n* sùith *f m*
soothe *v* (*calm*) ciùinich; (*assuage*) thoir fao(tha)chadh do
soothing *a* sèimheachail
sophisticated *a* soifiostaigeach
sordid *a* suarach, salach
sore *a* goirt, cràiteach; (*resentful*) leamh *n* creuchd *f*, lot *m*
sorrow *n* bròn *m*, mulad *m*, tùrsa *f*
sorrowful *a* brònach, muladach, tùrsach
sorry *a* duilich
sort *n* seòrsa *m*, gnè *f* *v* cuir an òrdugh, seòrsaich; (*fix*) cuir air dòigh
so-so *a*, *adv* mu làimh, meadhanach
soul *n* anam *m* **we didn't see a s.** chan fhaca sinn duine beò
sound *n* fuaim *m*; (*topog*) caolas *m* *a* (*healthy*) slàn, fallain; (*reliable*) earbsach; (*advice*) glic **s. asleep** na s(h)uain *etc* chadail **s.-proof** fuaim-dhìonach *v* dèan fuaim; (*alarm*) gairm rabhadh; (*instrument*) sèid, seinn **s. out** faigh beachd (bh)o **that sounds fine/ reasonable** tha sin taghta/reusanta
soup *n* brot *m*, eanraich *f*
sour *a* goirt, geur, searbh
source *n* màthair-adhbhar *m*, bun *m*, freumh *m* **s. of river** bun aibhne *m*
south *n*, *a* deas *f* **the s.** an (àird a) deas *f* **the s.-east** an (àird an) ear-dheas *f* **the s.-west** an (àird an) iar-dheas *f*

southerly *a*, *adv* deas, à deas
southern *a* mu dheas, a deas
souvenir *n* cuimhneachan *m*
sovereign *n* rìgh *m* àrd-uachdaran *m*; (*coin*) sòbhran *m* *a* uachdarail, neo-eisimeileach
sovereignty *n* uachdaranachd *f*
sow *n* muc *f*, cràin *f*
sow *v* cuir (sìol)
space *n* rùm *m*, rèidhleach *m*, farsaingeachd *f*; (*atmos*) fànas *m*; (*gap*) beàrn *f* **spaceship** soitheach-fànais *f m* **s. shuttle** spàl-fànais *m*
spacious *a* farsaing, mòr, rùmail
spade *n* spaid *f*, caibe *m*
span *n* rèis *f*; (*lifetime*) rèis *f*, saoghal *m*; (*interval*) greis *f*
Spaniard *n* Spàinn(t)each *m*, (*female*) ban-Spàinn(t)each *f*
spaniel *n* cù-eunaich *m*
Spanish *n* (*lang*) Spàinn(t)is *f* *a* Spàinn(t)each
spanner *n* spanair *m*
spare *a* a chòrr, a bharrachd **s. part** pàirt-càraidh *f*
spare *v* caomhain, cumhain
spared *a* air a s(h)àbhaladh *etc* **if we are s.** ma bhios sinn air ar caomhnadh/cùmhnadh
spark *n* sradag *f*
sparkle *n* lainnir *f*, deàlradh *m* *v* lainnrich, deàlraich
sparkling *a* deàlrach, drìlseach
sparrow *n* gealbhonn *m*
sparrow-hawk *n* speireag *f*
sparse *a* gann
spasm *n* crupadh fèithe *m*
spasmodic *a* an-dràsta 's a-rithist
spastic *n*, *a* spastach *m*
spate *n* lighe *f*; (*met*) meall *m*
spawn *n* sìol *m*, cladh *m* *v* sìolaich, cladh
speak *v* abair, bruidhinn, labhair
speaker *n* neach-labhairt *m*, òraidiche *m*; (*mus etc*) labhradair *m* **the S.** an Labhraiche *m*
spear *n* sleagh *f*, gath *m*
special *a* àraidh, sònraichte
specialism *n* speisealachd *f*

specialist n speisealaiche m,
fìor-eòlaiche m a speisealta
specialize v speisealaich
specialized a speisealaichte
species n seòrsa m, gnè f
specific a sònraichte, àraid
specification n sònrachadh m, mion-
chomharrachadh m
specified a sònraichte, comharraichte
specify v sònraich, comharraich
specimen n sampall m, ball-sampaill m
specious a meallta
speck n smùirnean m, sal m, smal m
speckled a breac, ballach
spectacle n sealladh m
spectacles n speuclairean m pl, speuclair
m, glainneachan f pl
spectator n neach-amhairc/coimhid m
spectre n tannasg m
spectrum n speactram m
speculate v beachdaich, dèan tuairmeas
air; (fin) cuir airgead sa mhargadh
speculation n beachdachadh m,
tuairmeas m
speculative a beachdachail,
tuairmeasach
speech n cainnt f; (oration) òraid f
s. therapy leasachadh cainnt m
speechless a gun chainnt, balbh
speed n luaths m, astar m **s. limit** casg
astair m v rach luath, greas
spell n (of time) greis(eag) f; (charm)
seun m
spell v litrich
spelling n litreachadh m
spend v caith, cosg
spendthrift n caithtiche m a
caithteach
sperm n sìol(-ginidh) m
spew v cuir a-mach, sgeith
sphere n cruinne m; (met) raon m
spherical a cruinn
spice n spìosradh m v spìosraich, dèan
spìosrach
spicy a spìosrach
spider n damhan-allaidh m
spike n spìc f, bior m
spill v dòirt

spin v snìomh; (wheel) cuir caran **s.
around** grad-thionndaidh n (met)
snìomh m
spinach n bloinigean-gàrraidh m
spindle n dealgan m, fearsaid f
spindrift n cathadh-mara m, siaban m
spine n cnàimh-droma m
spinner n (person) snìomhadair m;
(mech) uidheam-snìomh f
spinning n snìomh m, calanas m
s.-wheel cuibheall-shnìomh f
spinster n maighdeann f, boireannach
gun phòsadh m
spiral n snìomhan m a snìomhanach
spire n stìopall m, binnean m
spirit n spiorad m, aigne f; (mettle)
meanmna m, misneachd f; (ghost)
tannasg m
spirited a aigeannach, misneachail,
meanmnach
spirits n (drink) deoch-làidir f
spiritual a spioradail
spit n smugaid f; (roasting) bior-ròstaidh
m v tilg smugaid
spite n gamhlas m, miosgainn f **in s. of**
a dh'aindeoin (+ gen)
spiteful a gamhlasach
spittle n seile m, ronn m
splash n steall f, splais f v steall, splaisig
splay-footed a spleadhach, pliutach
spleen n (anat) an dubh-chlèin f; (spite)
gamhlas m
splendid a gasta, taghta; (imposing)
greadhnach
splendour n greadhnachas m
splice v spla(o)idhs
splint n cleithean m
splinter n sgealb f, spealg f v spealg
split n sgoltadh m v sgoilt
splutter v (person) bi a' sgeamhadaich
spoil v mill, cuir a dholaidh
spoils n creach f, cobhartach f m
spoilt a air a m(h)illeadh etc, millte
spoke n spòg f, tarsannan m
spokesperson n neach-labhairt m,
labhraiche m **spokesman** fear-labhairt
m **spokeswoman** tè-labhairt f
sponge n spong m; (cake) spuinnse f

sponsor n neach-urrais m, goistidh m v rach mar neach-urrais, bi mar ghoistidh

sponsorship n urrasachd f, goistidheachd f

spontaneous a saor-thoileach, deònach

spoon n spàin f

sporadic a corra uair

spore n spòr m

sport n spòrs f

sporting a spòrsach

sports n lùth-chleasan m pl, geamachan m pl **s. centre** ionad-spòrs m

sportsman n neach-spòrs m

spot n spot f m; (place) àite m, bad m; (stain) smal m **on the s.** (time) an làrach nam bonn v (notice) mothaich do

spotless a gun smal

spotted a ballach, breac

spotty a guireanach

spouse n cèile f m, cèile-p(h)òsta f m

spout n srùb m, spùt m v spùt; (whale) sèid; (hold forth) cuir dheth/dhith etc

sprain n snìomh m, sgochadh m, siachadh m v cuir snìomh an, sgoch

sprawl v sìn a-mach; (of person) bi nad shlèibhtrich

spray n (sea) cathadh-mara m; (water) sradadh m; (aerosol) frasadair m; (bot) fleasg f v srad (air)

spread v sgaoil, sgap, sìn a-mach

spreadsheet n cliath-dhuilleag f

spree n (drinking) daorach f **shopping s.** splaoid ceannaich f

sprig n faillean m

sprightly a (of mood) beothail, suigeartach; (phys) frogail, spraiceil

spring n earrach m; (water) fuaran m; (leap) grad-leum m; (mech) sprionga m, cuairteag f **s.-tide** reothart m v grad-leum **s. from** thig/sruth (bh)o

springboard n (met) stèidh f

sprinkle v crath

sprinkling n craiteachan m

sprint n roid f, deann-ruith f; (race) dian-rèis f v dian-ruith, ruith le roid

sprout n buinneag f **Brussels sprouts** buinneagan Bruisealach f pl

spruce n giuthas Lochlannach m

spruce a deas, speiseanta

spur n spor m, brod m; (met) spreigeadh m v brod, stuig; (met) spursaig, spreig, piobraich

spurious a breugach

spurn v diùlt le tàir

spurt n briosgadh m, cabhag f; (of liquid) stealladh m

spy n beachdair m, neach-brathaidh m, brathadair m v bi ri beachdaireachd

squabble n connsachadh m, tuasaid f

squad n sguad m

squalid a robach, salach

squall n sgal/cnap-gaoithe m

squander v caith, dèan ana-caitheamh air, mì-bhuilich

square n ceàrnag f a ceithir-cheàrnach, ceàrnagach

squash v brùth, pronn

squat v crùb

squatter n sguatair m

squeak n bìog m v bi a' bìogail

squeal n sgiamh f m v dèan sgiamh

squeamish a òrraiseach

squeeze n fàsgadh m, bruthadh m v fàisg, brùth

squid n gibearnach f m

squint n claonadh m, fiaradh m a claon, fiar **s.-eyed** cam/fiar-shùileach **it is s.** tha e cam, tha fiaradh ann v seall claon

squirrel n feòrag f

squirt v steall, spùt

stab v sàth, stob

stabbing n sàthadh m, stobadh m

stabilize v bunailtich, cùm air bhunailt

stable a bunailteach, seasmhach

stable n stàball m

stack n stac(a) m, càrn m; (of hay, peat etc) cruach f v cruach, càrn; (shelves) cuir air sgeilp

stadium n lann-cluiche f

staff n luchd-obrach m; (stick) bata m **staffroom** seòmar luchd-obrach m

stag n damh (fèidh) m

stage n àrd-ùrlar m; (in process) ìre f

stagger v rach mu seach; (amaze) cuir fìor iongnadh air

staggering a (met) iongantach

stagnant *a* marbh, neo-ghluasadach
stagnate *v* bi/fàs marbhanta
staid *a* stòlda, suidhichte
stain *n* sal *m*, smal *m v* salaich, cuir/fàg smal air
stair *n* staidhre *f*
stake *n* post *m*; (*betting wager*) airgead-gill *m*
stalactite *n* aol-chluigean *m*
stalagmite *n* aol-charragh *f*
stale *a* sean, goirt
stalemate *n* closadh *m*, glasadh *m*
stalk *n* gas *f*
stalk *v* bi a' stalcaireachd **s. person** lean neach mun cuairt
stalker *n* stalcaire *m*; (*of person*) lorgair *m*
stall *n* stàile *f*
stall *v* cuir maill air
stallion *n* àigeach *m*
stalwart *a* sgairteil, calma, làidir
stamina *n* cùl *m*, smior *m*, cumail ris *m*
stammer *n* (s)gagachd *f*, stad *m* **she has a s.** tha stad na cainnt *v* bi (s)gagach
stamp *n* stamp(a) *f*; (*met*) comharra *m v* (*feet*) stamp; (*of letters*) cuir stampa air **s. out** cuir às do
stance *n* (*met*) seasamh *m*; (*phys*) dòigh-seasaimh *f*; (*site*) làrach *f m*
stand *n* seasamh *m*; (*stance*) ionad *m*; (*display*) taisbeanadh *m v* seas; (*endure*) fuiling, cuir suas ri; (*in election*) seas san taghadh
standard *n* inbhe *f*, ìre *f*, bun-tomhas *m*; (*flag*) meirghe *f* **s. of living** cor beòshlaint *m a* cumanta, cunbhalach, coitcheann **S. Grade** an Ìre Choitcheann *f*
standardize *v* cunbhalaich, dèan cunbhalach
standing *n* (*met*) seasamh *m*, inbhe *f a* na s(h)easamh *etc* **s. committee** gnàth-chomataidh *etc f* **s. orders** gnàth-riaghailtean *f pl* **s. stones** tursachan *m pl*
standstill *n* stad *m* **at a s.** na stad/t(h)àmh *etc*
stanza *n* rann *m*
staple *n* stìnleag *f*
staple *a* prìomh

star *n* rionnag *f*, reul *f v* comharraich le reul; (*in performance*) gabh prìomh phàirt
starboard *n* deas-bhòrd *m*
starch *n* stalc *m*, stuthaigeadh *m v* stalcaich, stuthaig
stare *v* geur-amhairc, spleuchd
starfish *n* crosgag *f*
stark *a* rag; (*absolute*) tur, fìor **s. naked** dearg-rùisgte
starling *n* druid *f*
starry *a* rionnagach, làn rionnagan
start *n* toiseach *m* **a sudden s.** clisgeadh *m v* tòisich; (*be startled*) clisg; (*sudden move*) leum
starter *n* neach-tòiseachaidh *m*; (*in engine*) inneal-spreigidh *m*
startle *v* clisg, cuir clisgeadh air
starvation *n* gort(a) *f*
starve *v* leig gort(a) air **s. to death** (*intrans*) bàsaich leis a' ghort **we were starving** bha an t-acras gar tolladh
state *n* staid *f*, cor *m*; (*country*) stàit *f*
state *v* can, cuir an cèill
stately *a* stàiteil
statement *n* aithris *f*, cunntas *m*
statesman *n* stàitire *m*
static *a* na stad, gun ghluasad
station *n* stèisean *m*; (*in life*) staid *f*, inbhe *f*
stationary *a* na stad, gun ghluasad
stationery *n* stuth-sgrìobhaidh *m*, pàipearachd *f*
statistical *a* staitistigeil, àireamhail
statistics *n* staitistearachd *f*
statue *n* ìomhaigh *f*
stature *n* àird *f*
status *n* inbhe *f*
statute *n* reachd *m*
statutory *a* reachdail, a rèir an lagha
staunch *a* daingeann, dìleas
staunch *v* caisg
stay *v* fuirich, fan
steadfast *a* daingeann, dìleas, diongmhalta
steady *a* seasmhach, daingeann, socraichte *v* socraich, daingnich
steak *n* staoig *f*

steal n goid f, mèirle f v goid, dèan mèirle
 s. away (intrans) liùg air falbh
stealing n goid f, mèirle f
steam n toit f, smùid f
steed n steud f, steud-each m
steel n cruaidh f, stàilinn f a dhen
 chruaidh, dhen stàilinn
steep a cas; (price) anabarrach daor
steep v bog, cuir am bogadh, tum
steeple n stìopall m
steer v stiùir, treòraich **s. clear of** cùm
 clìoras (+ nom)
steering n stiùireadh m **s. committee**
 comataidh stiùiridh f
stem n (bot) gas f
stench n boladh m, breuntas m
step n step m; (a pace) ceum m **s. by s.**
 ceum air cheum **take steps** (met) cuir
 mu dheidhinn
step a leth- **s.-brother** leth-bhràthair
 m **s.-sister** leth-phiuthar f **s.-daughter**
 nighean-cèile f **s.-son** dalta m **s.-father**
 oide m **s.-mother** muime f
stereotype n gnàth-iomhaigh f
sterile a seasg, aimrid; (ground) fàs;
 (med) sgaldach
sterilize v seasgaich; (ground) fàsaich;
 (med) sgald
sterling n airgead Bhreatainn m
 a pound s. not(a) Breatannach m
sterling a feartach, foghainteach
stern n deireadh m
stern a gruamach, dùr
stethoscope n steatasgop m
stew n stiubha f v stiubhaig
steward n stiùbhard m **stewardess**
 ban-stiùbhard f
stick n maide m, bioran m **walking s.**
 bata m
stick v (adhere to) steig; (become
 caught) rach an sàs; (endure)
 fuiling
sticker n steigear m
sticky a steigeach; (problem) righinn
stiff a rag
stiffen v ragaich
stiffness n raige f
stifle v mùch

stigma n adhbhar nàire m; (bot)
 stiogma m
stigmatize v dèan cùis-nàire de
still n poit-dhubh f, stail f
still a sàmhach, balbh; (weather) ciùin,
 fèathach
still adv an dèidh sin, a dh'aindeoin sin;
 (of time) fhathast
stimulant n stuth beothachaidh m
stimulate v brosnaich, spreig
stimulating a brosnachail, togarrach
stimulus n brosnachadh m, spreagadh m
sting n gath m, guin m v cuir gath ann,
 guin
stinginess n spìocaireachd f
stingy a spìocach
stink n tòchd m, samh m
stinking a breun, malcaidh
stipend n tuarastal m
stipulate v sònraich, cùmhnantaich
stir n othail f, ùinich f
stir v (food) cuir mun cuairt; (move)
 gluais; (stimulate) brosnaich **s. up** dùisg
stirk n gamhainn m
stirring a togarrach, brosnachail
stitch n (med, sewing) grèim m;
 (knitting) lùb f; (pain) grèim m; (of
 clothing) stiall f v fuaigh, fuaigheil
stoat n neas gheal f
stock n stoc m **s.-taking** cunntas stoc m
 v stocaich
stock exchange n margadh nan
 earrannan m
stockbroker n margaiche earrannan m
stocking n stocainn f
stocks n (fin) earrannan f pl
stodgy a trom
stoical a strìochdte
stoke v cùm connadh ri
stolen a air a g(h)oid etc
stomach n stamag f, goile f, maodal f
stone n clach f **S. Age** Linn na Cloiche m
 a cloiche
stonechat n clacharan m
stonemason n clachair m
stook n adag f, suidheachan m
stool n stòl m, furm m
stoop v crom, lùb, crùb

stooped *a* crom
stop *n* stad *m*; (*ban*) toirmeasg *m* **s.-cock**
goc *m* **s.-gap** neach/nì a lìonas beàrn *m*
v stad, cuir stad air; (*cease*) sguir, stad
stoppage *n* stad *m*, stopadh *m*,
grabadh *m*
stopper *n* àrc *f*, ceann *m*
storage *n* stòradh *m*, tasgadh *m*
store *n* stòr *m*; (*resources*) stòras *m*
v stòir, taisg
storey *n* lobhta *m*, làr *m*
stork *n* corra-bhàn *f*
storm *n* stoirm *f m*, doineann *f*, gailleann
f v thoir ionnsaigh air
stormy *a* stoirmeil, doineannach,
gailbheach
story *n* sgeul *m*, sgeulachd *f*, stòiridh *f m*
s.-teller sgeulaiche *m*, seanchaidh *m*
stout *n* leann dubh *m*
stout *a* garbh, tiugh; (*brave*) tapaidh
stove *n* stòbh(a) *f m*
straddle *v* rach gòbhlachan/casa-
gòbhlagain air
straggler *n* slaodaire *m*
straight *a* dìreach **s. away** *adv* sa
mhionaid, gun dàil
straighten *v* dìrich
strain *n* strèan *m*; (*phys*) teannachadh *m*,
snìomh *m*; (*mental*) uallach *m v* strèan;
(*phys*) teannaich, snìomh; (*filter*)
sìolaidh
strainer *n* sìol(t)achan *m*; (*for fence*)
strèanair *m*
straitjacket *n* cuing-cuirp *f*
strait(s) *n* caol *m*, caolas *m*; (*distress*)
cruaidh-theinn *f*
stramash *n* hù-bhitheil *f m*, ùpraid *f*
strand *n* dual *m*; (*shore*) tràigh *f*
strange *a* neònach, iongantach,
coimheach
stranger *n* coigreach *m*, srainnsear *m*
strangle *v* tachd, mùch
strap *n* strap *m*, iall *f v* strapaig, cuir
strap/bann air
strapping *a* tapaidh, mòr, calma
stratagem *n* cuilbheart *f*
strategic *a* ro-innleachdail
strategy *n* ro-innleachd *f*

strath *n* srath *m*
straw *n* connlach *f*, fodar *m*;
(*for drinking*) sràbh *m* **s. poll** beachd
air thuairmse *m*
strawberry *n* sùbh-làir *m*
stray *a* conadail, fuadain; (*wayward*) air
seachran *v* rach air seachran
streak *n* stiall *f*, srianag *f*
stream *n* sruth *m*
streamline *v* sìmplich
street *n* sràid *f*
strength *n* neart *m*, spionnadh *m*,
lùths *m*
strengthen *v* neartaich
strenuous *a* dian, saothrachail
stress *n* (*phys*) cuideam *m*; (*mental*)
uallach *m*, eallach *m v* cuir/leig
cuideam air
stretch *v* sìn, sgaoil, leudaich
strict *a* teann, cruaidh
stride *n* sìnteag *f*, searradh *m*
v sìnteagaich, dèan searradh
strife *n* strì *f*, còmhstri *f*
strike *n* (*ind*) stailc *f v* buail;
(*go on strike*) rach air stailc
striker *n* stailcear *m*; (*football*) neach-
ionnsaigh *m*
striking *a* comharraichte, sònraichte
string *n* sreang *f*; (*mus*) teud *m*
stringent *a* teann
strip *n* stiall *f v* thoir dheth/dhith *etc*
d' aodach
stripe *n* srianag *f*, sgrìob *f*
striped *a* srianach, sgrìobach
stripped *a* rùisgte, lomnochd
strive *v* dèan spàirn/strì
stroke *n* stràc *f m*, buille *f*; (*med*) stròc
m v slìob
stroll *v* gabh cuairt/ceum, spaidsir
strong *n* làidir, treun
structure *n* structair *m*, dèanamh *m*,
togail *f v* structair
struggle *n* gleac *m*, spàirn *f*, strì *f v* gleac,
dèan spàirn/strì
strut *v* falbh gu stràiceil
stub *n* bun *m*
stubble *n* asbhuain *f*; (*facial*) bun
feusaig *m*

stubborn *a* rag, rag-mhuinealach
stubbornness *n* raigeann *m*,
   rag-mhuinealas *m*
stubby *a* cutach, bunach
stuck *a* an sàs, steigte
stud *n* stud *f*; (*horses*) greigh *f*
student *n* oileanach *m*
studio *n* stiùidio *f*
studious *a* dèidheil air foghlam
study *n* ionnsachadh *m*; (*room*) seòmar-
   sgrùdaidh *m* *v* ionnsaich (mu); (*research*)
   sgrùd, cnuasaich; (*consider*) beachdaich
   (air)
stuff *n* stuth *m* *v* lìon, dinn
stumble *n* tuisleadh *m* *v* tuislich
stumbling-block *n* ceap-tuislidh *m*,
   cnap-starra *m*
stump *n* bun *m*, stoc *m*
stun *v* cuir an tuaineal, cuir
   tuainealaich air
stunt *n* cleas *m*
stupid *a* amaideach, gòrach
stupidity *n* amaideas *m*, gòraiche *f*
stupor *n* tuaineal *m*, neul *m*
sturdy *a* bunanta, gramail
stutter *v* bi manntach/gagach
stye *n* (s)leamhnagan *m*
style *n* stoidhle *f*, modh *f m*; (*fashion*)
   fasan *m*, stoidhle *f*; (*title*) tiotal *m* **with
   s.** le snas/loinn
stylish *a* fasanta, spaideil
sub- *pref* fo- (+ *len*)
sub-committee *n* fo-chomataidh *f*
subconscious *n* fo-mhothachadh *m*
sub-contract *v* fo-chunnraich
subdivide *v* fo-roinn
subdue *v* ceannsaich, cìosnaich
sub-heading *n* fo-thiotal *m*
subject *n* cuspair *m*; (*of talk etc*) ceann-
   labhairt/teagaisg *m*, cuspair *m*; (*citizen*)
   ìochdaran *m*
subject *v* ceannsaich, cuir fo smachd
   (+ *gen*) **s. to ...** cuir fo ...
subjective *a* pearsanta, suibseigeach
subject to *a* umhail do, fo smachd
   (+ *gen*), an urra ri
subjugate *v* ceannsaich
subjunctive *a* (*gram*) eisimeileach

sublime *a* òirdheirc
submarine *n* bàta-aigeil *m*
submerge *v* tum; (*trans*) cuir fodha;
   (*intrans*) rach fodha
submission *n* (*lodged*) tagradh *m*;
   (*yielding*) ùmhlachd *f*, gèill *f*
submissive *a* umha(i)l
submit *a* (*lodge, argue*) cuir a-steach,
   (t)agair; (*yield*) gèill, strìochd
subordinate *a* ìochdarach, fo- (+ *len*)
subscribe *v* fo-sgrìobh **s. to** gabh/thoir
   taic do
subscription *n* fo-sgrìobhadh *m*,
   sìnteas *m*
subsequent *a* a leanas, an dèidh
   làimhe
subsequently *adv* mar sin, na dhèidh
   sin, an dèidh làimhe
subside *v* sìolaidh, traogh, tràig
subsidence *n* dol sìos *m*, traoghadh *m*,
   ìsleachadh *m*, fo-thuiteam *m*
subsidiary *a* ìochdaireil, cuideachail,
   fo- (+ *len*)
subsidize *v* thoir subsadaidh/tabhartas
   do
subsidy *n* subsadaidh *m*, tabhartas *m*
subsistence *n* teachd-an-tìr *m*
substance *n* susbaint *f*, brìgh *f*;
   (*material*) stuth *m*
substantial *a* susbainteach, làidir,
   tàbhachdach
substantiate *v* dearbh, fìrinnich
substitute *n* stuth/nì-ionaid *m* (an)
   ionad *m*; (*person*) neach-ionaid *m*,
   riochdaire *m* *v* cuir an àite **s. for** gabh
   àite (+ *gen*)
sub-title *n* fo-thiotal *m*
subtle *a* seòlta
subtlety *n* seòltachd *f*
subtract *v* thoir (air falbh) (bh)o
suburb *n* iomall baile *m*
subversive *a* ceannairceach
subway *n* fo-shlighe *f*
succeed *v* soirbhich, rach le; (*follow*) lean
success *n* soirbheachadh *m*, buaidh *f*
successful *a* soirbheachail
successive *a* leantainneach, an dèidh a
   chèile

successor *n* neach-ionaid *m*, neach a
 thig an àite/às dèidh ... *m* (+ *gen*)
succinct *a* geàrr, cuimir
succulent *a* sùghmhor, blasta
succumb *v* gèill, strìochd
such *a*, *pron* (a) leithid, mar, dhen
 t-seòrsa **as s.** ann/innte fhèin
suck *v* deothail, deoc, sùigh
sudden *a* obann, grad, aithghearr
suddenly *adv* gu h-obann, gu grad, gu
 h-aithghearr
sue *v* thoir gu lagh
suet *n* geir *f*
suffer *v* fuiling; (*permit*) ceadaich
suffering *n* fulangas *m*
suffice *v* foghain
sufficient *a* leòr, cuibheasach
suffix *n* (iar-)leasachan *m*
suffocate *v* mùch
suffuse *v* sgaoil air feadh
sugar *n* siùcar *m*
suggest *v* mol, comhairlich, cuir an
 inntinn (+ *gen*)/air shùilibh do
suggestion *n* moladh *m*, cur an inntinn
 (+ *gen*)/air shùilibh *m*
suicide *n* fèin-mhurt *m* **commit s.** cuir às
 dhut fhèin
suit *n* deise *f*; (*law*) cùis(-lagha) *f*
suit *v* freagair
suitable *a* freagarrach, iomchaidh
suitcase *n* màileid *f*, baga *m*
suite *n* (*rooms*) sreath *f m*; (*furniture*)
 suidht *f*; (*mus*) sreath *f m*
suitor *n* suirghiche *m*
sullen *a* dùr, gnù
sully *v* salaich, truaill, cuir smal air
sulphur *n* sulfar *m*, pronnasg *m*
sulphuric *a* sulfarach, pronnasgach
sultry *a* bruthainneach
sum *n* àireamh *f*, sùim *f*
summarize *v* thoir geàrr-chunntas air,
 giorraich
summary *n* geàrr-chunntas *m*,
 giorrachadh *m*
summer *n* samhradh *m* **s. school** sgoil-
 shamhraidh *f*
summit *n* mullach *m*, bàrr *m* **s. meeting**
 àrd-choinneamh *f*

summon *v* gairm; (*leg*) sumain
summons *n* gairm *f*; (*leg*) bàirlinn *f*,
 sumanadh *m*
sumptuous *a* sòghail
sums *n* cunntadh *m*
sun *n* grian *f* **sundial** uaireadair-grèine *m*
 sunflower neòinean-grèine *m* **sunrise**
 èirigh na grèine *f* **sunset** dol fodha na
 grèine *m*, laighe na grèine *f* **sunshine**
 deàrrsadh na grèine *m* **sunbathe** *v*
 gabh a' ghrian, blian (thu/e/i *etc* fhèin)
 sunburnt *a* loisgte aig a' ghrèin
Sunday *n* Didòmhnaich *m*, Latha/Là na
 Sàbaid *m*
sundry *a* iomadaidh, measgaichte
sunk *a* air a dhol fodha
sunny *a* grianach
super *a* sgoinneil, barraichte *pref* os-,
 an(a)-
superannuation *n* peinnseanachadh *m*
superb *a* barraichte, sgoinneil
superficial *a* staoin, gun doimhneachd
superfluous *a* thar a' chòrr
superhuman *a* os-daonna
superintendent *n* stiùireadair *m*, àrd-
 neach-stiùiridh *m*
superior *n* uachdaran *m* *a* uachdarach,
 àrd
superiority *n* uachdarachd *f*, bàrr *m*,
 ceannas *m*
superlative *a* còrr, barraichte; (*gram*)
 feabhasach
supermarket *n* mòr-bhùth *f*
supernatural *a* os-nàdarra(ch)
supersede *v* gabh àite (+ *gen*), cuir às
 àite
superstition *n* saobh-chràbhadh *m*
superstitious *a* saobh-chràbhach
supervise *v* stiùir, cùm sùil air
supervision *n* stiùireadh *m*, cumail sùil
 air *f*
supervisor *n* neach-stiùiridh/coimhid *m*
supper *n* suipear *f*
supple *a* sùbailte, subailte
supplement *n* leasachadh *m*
supplementary *a* a bharrachd, leasachail
 s. benefit sochair-leasachaidh *f*
supplier *n* solaraiche *m*

supply *n* solarachadh *m*, solar *m*
  v solaraich, cùm ri **do s. work** obraich an
  àite cuideigin
support *n* taic *f*, tacsa *m*, cùl-taic *m*
  v thoir taic do, cuir/cùm taic ri, cuidich
supporter *n* neach-taic(e) *m*; (*sport*)
  neach-leantail/leantainn *m*
supportive *a* taiceil
suppose *v* saoil
suppress *v* cùm fodha, mùch
suppression *n* cumail fodha *f*,
  mùchadh *m*
supremacy *n* ceannasachd *f*, àrd-
  cheannas *m*
supreme *a* àrd-, sàr, barraichte
supremo *n* àrd-cheannard *m*
surcharge *n* for-chìs *f* *v* leag for-chìs air
sure *a* cinnteach, deimhinnte
surely *adv* is cinnteach, gu fìrinneach
surf *n* ròd *m*, rùid *m* *v* marcaich tuinn
  s. the net tràl an lìon
surface *n* uachdar *m*, leth a-muigh *m*
surfeit *n* sàth *m*, cus *m*
surge *n* onfhadh *m* *v* at, bòc
surgeon *n* lannsair *m*
surgery *n* obair-lannsa *f*; (*place*) ionad
  an dotair *m*; (*polit*) freastal-lann *f*
surly *a* gnù, greannach
surmise *v* saoil, bi dhen bharail
surmount *v* rach/faigh os cionn (+ *gen*)
surname *n* cinneadh *m*, sloinneadh *m*
surpass *v* thoir bàrr air
surplus *n* còrr *m*
surprise *n* iongnadh *m*, iongantas *m*
  v cuir iongnadh/iongantas air
  s. someone thig gun fhios air
surprising *a* iongantach, neònach
surrender *v* (*intrans*) strìochd, gèill;
  (*trans*) thoir suas
surround *v* cuartaich, iadh mu thimcheall
survey *n* tomhas *m*, sgrùdadh *m*
  v tomhais, sgrùd; (*look at*) gabh
  beachd air
surveyor *n* neach-tomhais/sgrùdaidh *m*
survive *v* mair beò, tàrr às **s. on** thig beò
  air
survivor *n* neach a tha beò/maireann *m*,
  neach a thàrr às *m*

susceptible *a* buailteach (do)
suspect *n* neach fo amharas *m* *v* bi/cuir
  an amharas **I s.** tha amharas agam (gu)
suspected *a* fo amharas
suspend *v* (*hang*) croch; (*defer*) cuir dàil
  an; (*from work*) cuir à dreuchd rè ùine
suspense *n* teagamh *m* **in s.** fo
  theagamh, a' feitheamh, air bhioran
suspension *n* crochadh *m*; (*from work*)
  cur à dreuchd rè ùine *m* **s. bridge**
  drochaid crochaidh *f*
suspicion *n* amharas *m*
suspicious *a* amharasach
sustain *v* cùm suas; (*suffer*) fuiling
sustainable *a* buan, seasmhach
sustenance *n* lòn *m*, beathachadh *m*
swallow *n* gòbhlan-gaoithe *m*
swallow *v* sluig
swamp *n* fèith *f*, bog(l)ach *f*
swan *n* eala *f*
swarm *n* sgaoth *m*
swarthy *a* doimhearra, ciar
sway *n* riaghladh *m*, seòladh *m* *v* luaisg;
  (*opinion*) gluais, buadhaich
swear *v* (*vow*) mionnaich, thoir mionnan,
  bòidich; (*curse*) bi ri guidheachan/
  mionnan
swearing *n* (*avowing*) mionnachadh *m*;
  (*cursing*) guidheachan *f* *m pl*
sweat *n* fallas *m* *v* cuir fallas (dheth/
  dhith *etc*)
sweatshirt *n* lèine spòrs *f*
sweaty *a* fallasach
Swede *n* Suaineach *m*, (*female*) ban-
  S(h)uaineach *f*
Swedish *a* Suaineach *n* (*lang*) Suainis *f*
sweep *v* sguab
sweeper *n* sguabadair *m*
sweet *n* mìlsean *m* *a* milis; (*scent*)
  cùbhraidh; (*sound*) binn
sweeten *v* mìlsich, dèan milis
sweetheart *n* leannan *m*, eudail *f*
sweets *n* suiteis *m pl*, siùcaran *m pl*
swell *v* at, sèid, bòc
swelling *n* at *m*, cnap *m*, bòcadh *m*
sweltering *a* brothallach, bruthainneach
swerve *v* claon, lùb, rach a thaobh
swift *n* gobhlan-gainmhich *m*

swift *a* luath, grad, siùbhlach, ealamh
swim *n* snàmh *m* *v* snàmh
swimmer *n* snàmhaiche *m*
swimming *n* snàmh *m* **s.-pool** amar-snà(i)mh *m*
swindle *v* thoir an car à, dèan foill (air)
swine *n* mucan *f pl*; (*slang*) trustar *m* **s. flu** flu na muice *m*
swing *n* (*action*) luasgadh *m*; (*for playing*) dreallag *f*; (*pendulum*) siùdan *m*; (*polit*) gluasad *m*; (*golf*) dòigh-bualaidh *f* **in full s.** fo làn-sheòl *v* luaisg; (*of pendulum*) dean siùdan; (*polit*) gluais
swingeing *a* cruaidh
swipe *n* sgailc *f*
Swiss *n, a* Eilbheiseach *m*, (*female*) ban-Eilbheiseach *f*
switch *n* suidse *f m*; (*wand*) slat *f*
switch *v* atharraich
swivel *n* udalan *m*, fulag *f*
swollen *a* air at/sèid
swoon *v* rach an neul, rach am paiseanadh
swoop *v* thig le roid/sitheadh **s. for** sguab leat, grad-ghlac
sword *n* claidheamh *m* **s.-dance** danns a' chlaidheimh *m*
swot *v* ionnsaich gu dian
syllable *n* lideadh *m*

syllabus *n* clàr-obrach *m*
symbol *n* samhla *m*
symbolical *a* samhlachail
symbolism *n* samhlachas *m*
symbolize *v* samhlaich, riochdaich
symmetrical *a* ceart-chumadail, cothromaichte
sympathetic *a* co-fhaireachail, truasail
sympathize *v* nochd co-fhaireachdainn
sympathy *n* co-fhaireachdainn *f*
symphony *n* (*mus piece*) siansadh *m*
symptom *n* comharra *m*
synchronize *v* co-thìmich
syndicate *n* comann iomairt *m*; (*media*) buidheann naidheachdais *f m*
synod *n* seanadh *m*
synonym *n* co-fhacal *m*
synopsis *n* geàrr-iomradh *m*, giorrachadh *m*
syntax *n* co-chàradh *m*
synthesis *n* co-chur *m*, co-thàthadh *m*
synthetic *a* co-thàthte; (*artificial*) fuadain
syphon *n* sùghachan *m*, lìonadair *m*
syringe *n* steallair *m*
syrup *n* siorap *f m*
system *n* siostam *m*, seòl *m*
systematic *a* rianail, òrdail, eagarach

T

table *n* bòrd *m*; (*figures*) clàr *m* **t.-tennis** teanas-bùird *m* **tablecloth** anart-bùird *m*, tubhailt(e) *f m*
tablet *n* pile *f*; (*block*) clàr *m*
tacit *a* gun ainmeachadh, gun a ràdh
tack *n* tacaid *f*; (*naut*) tac(a) *f*; (*lease*) tac *f*
tackle *n* acfhainn *f*, uidheam *f*; (*in sport*) dol an sàs *m* *v* rach an sàs ann
tactic *n* innleachd *f*, seòl *m*
tactical *a* innleachdail
tactile *n* beantainneach, beanailteach
tadpole *n* ceann-phollan *m*, ceann-simid *m*
tail *n* earball *m*, eàrr *f m*, feaman *m*
tailback ciudha charbadan *m*

tailor *n* tàillear *m*
tainted *a* trothach, air a t(h)ruailleadh *etc*, millte
take *v* gabh, thoir **it takes a long time** tha e a' toirt ùine mhòr **t. a photograph** tog dealbh
takeover *n* gabhail thairis *m*
takings *n* teachd-a-steach *m*
tale *n* sgeulachd *f*, sgeul *m*
talent *n* tàlant *m*, comas *m*, buadh *f*
talented *a* tàlantach, comasach
talk *n* bruidhinn *f*, cainnt *f*; (*chat*) còmhradh *m*; (*lecture*) òraid *f* *v* bruidhinn; (*chat*) dèan còmhradh
talkative *a* còmhraideach, bruidhneach, cabach

talking *n* bruidhinn *f*, labhairt *f*
tall *a* àrd
tallow *n* geir *f*, blona(i)g *f*, crèis *f*
tally *n* cunntas *m*, àireamh *f*
talon *n* spuir *m*, ionga *f*
tame *a* soitheamh, call(d)a, ceannsaichte
  v callaich, ceannsaich
tamper *v* buin/bean ri, mill
tan *n* dubhadh (-grèine) *m v* gabh
  a' ghrian; (*leather*) cairt
tang *n* blas geur *m*
tangent *n* beantan *m* **going off at a t.**
  a' dol bhàrr do sgeòil
tangible *a* so-bheantainn, susbainteach,
  a ghabhas làimhseachadh
tangle *n* troimh-a-chèile *f*; (*fishing line*)
  rocladh *m*; (*seaweed*) stamh *m v* rach an
  sàs/an lùib a chèile; (*fishing line*) rocail
tank *n* tanca *f m*
tanker *n* tancair *m*
tantalize *v* cùm air bhioran, leamhaich
tantamount *a* co-ionann, ionann
tantrum *n* prat *m*, dod *m*
tap *n* goc *m*, tap *f m*; (*sound*) gnogag
  f v (*sound*) thoir gnogag do; (*access*)
  tarraing air/à
tape *n* teip *f* **t.-measure** teip-tomhais *f*
  t.-recorder teip-chlàradair *m v* teip, cuir
  teip air; (*record*) cuir air teip, clàraich
taper *v* (*intrans*) fàs barra-chaol; (*trans*)
  dèan caol
tapestry *n* brat-grèise *m*
tar *n* teàrr *f*, bìth *f v* teàrr
tardy *a* athaiseach, màirnealach,
  slaodach
target *n* targaid *f* **t. audience** luchd-
  amais sònraichte *m v* cuimsich air
tariff *n* cìs *f*; (*prices*) clàr-phrìsean *m*
tarnish *v* smalaich, dubhaich
tarpaulin *n* cainb-thearra *f*
tart *n* pigheann *m*
tart *a* searbh, geur
tartan *n* tartan *m*, breacan *m*
task *n* obair *f*, gnìomh *m* **t.-force**
  buidheann-gnìomha *f m*
tassel *n* cluigean *m*, babag *f*
taste *n* blas *m*; (*judgement*)
  breithneachadh *m v* blais, feuch

tasteless *a* neo-bhlasta, gun bhlas; (*met*)
  neo-chubhaidh, mì-chiatach
tasty *a* blasta
tattle *n* goileam *m*
tattoo *n* tatù *m*
taunt *n* beum *m*, magadh *m*, tilgeil air *f*
  v beum, mag, tilg air
taut *a* teann
tawdry *a* suarach, gun snas/luach
tawny *a* lachdann, ciar
tawse *n* strap *m*, stràic *f*
tax *n* cìs *f*, càin *f* **income tax** cìs cosnaidh
  tax office oifis chìsean *f v* leag cìs, cuir
  cìs air
taxation *n* leagail cìse *m*, cìs *f*
taxi *n* tagsaidh *f m*
taxman *n* cìs-mhaor *m*
taxpayer *n* neach-pàighidh cìse *m*
tea *n* tì *f*, teatha *f* **teacup** cupa tì *m*,
  copan teatha *m* **teapot** poit-tì/teatha *f*
  teaspoon spàin-tì/teatha *f*
teach *v* teagaisg, ionnsaich
teacher *n* tidsear *f m*, neach-teagaisg *f*
teaching *n* teagasg *m*
teal *n* crann-lach *f*
team *n* sgioba *f m*
tear *n* deur *m*; (*rent*) sracadh *m v* srac,
  reub
tease *v* tarraing à, farranaich; (*comb
  out*) cìr
teat *n* sine *f*
technical *a* teicneòlach, teicnigeach
technician *n* teicneòlaiche *m*
technique *n* alt *m*, dòigh *f*
technological *a* teicneòlach
technology *n* teicneòlas *m*
tedious *a* sàrachail, sgìtheil, ràsanach
teeming *a* loma-làn, a' cur thairis
teenager *n* deugaire *m*
telecommunications *n* tele-
  chonaltradh *m*
telephone *n* fòn *f m*, teilefòn *m* **t.
  directory** leabhar a'/na fòn *m v* fòn(aig)
telephonist *n* neach-freagairt fòn *m*
telescope *n* prosbaig *f*, telesgop *f m*
teletext *n* tele-theacsa *m*
television *n* telebhisean *f m*
tell *v* innis, abair

telltale n cabaire m
temerity n ladarnas m
temper n nàdar m; (quick) sradag f
temperament n nàdar m, càil f
temperance n measarrachd f, stuamachd f
temperate a measarra, stuama; (atmos) eadar-mheadhanach
temperature n teòthachd f
temple n teampall m; (head) lethcheann m
tempo n luaths m
temporarily adv airson ùine ghoirid, rè tamaill
temporary a sealach, airson ùine ghoirid, rè seal
tempt v buair, tàlaidh
temptation n buaireadh m
ten n a deich a deich **ten people** deichnear f m
tenable a reusanta, a ghabhas seasamh
tenacious a leanailteach, righinn, greimeil
tenacity n leanailteachd f, rìghneas m
tenancy n gabhaltas m
tenant n neach-gabhail m
tend v fritheil, àraich; (incline) aom, bi buailteach
tendency n aomadh m, buailteachd f
tender n tairgse f v tairg, tabhann
tender a maoth, caoin
tenderness n maothalachd f, caomhalachd f
tenement n teanamaint m
tennis n teanas m
tenor n brìgh f, seagh m; (mus) teanor m
tense n tràth m **present/future/past t.** an tràth làthaireach/teachdail/caithte
tense a teann, rag
tension n teannachadh m, ragachadh m; (stress) strì f
tent n teant(a) f m
tentacle n greimiche m
tentative a teagmhach, mì-chinnteach
tenth n deicheamh m, an deicheamh cuid f a deicheamh
tenuous a (flimsy) lag; (fine) tana
tenure n còir-fearainn f, gabhaltas m

tepid a flodach; (met) meadh-bhlàth
term n (of time) teirm f; (end) crìoch f, ceann m; (condition) cùmhnant m, cumha m; (verbal) facal m, briathar m
terminal a (med) crìche
terminate v cuir crìoch air, crìochnaich
termination n crìochnachadh m; (med) casg-breith f
terminology n briathrachas m
tern n steàrnan m
terrible a eagalach, uabhasach, sgràthail
terrier n abhag f
terrific a sgoinneil, bàibheil
terrify v oilltich, cuir oillt/eagal air
terrifying a eagalach, oillteil
territory n tìr f, fonn m, fearann m
terror n eagal m, oillt f; (person) cùis-eagail f
terrorism n ceannairc f
terse a geàrr, cuimir
test n deuchainn f, ceasnachadh m
testament n tiomnadh m **the Old T.** an Seann Tiomnadh **the New T.** an Tiomnadh Nuadh
testicle n magairle f m, magairlean m, clach f
testify v thoir fianais
testimonial n teisteanas m
testimony n teisteas m, fianais f
tetchy a frionasach
tether n teadhair f, feist(e) f
text n teacsa m; (sermon) ceann-teagaisg m **textbook** teacs-leabhar m
textile n aodach fighte m
texture n dèanamh m, inneach m
than conj na **more t.** barrachd air **other t.** ach, a thuilleadh air
thank v thoir taing/buidheachas
thankful a taingeil, buidheach
thankless a gun taing; (ungrateful) mì-thaingeil, neo-ar-thaingeil
thanks n tapadh leat/leibh m **many t.** mòran taing
that dem a sin, siud dem pron sin, ud rel pron a **all t.** na conj gu, gum, gun adv cho **is it that late?** a bheil e/i cho anmoch sin?
thatch n tughadh m v tugh

Insight: thanks

There are several ways of expressing thanks in Gaelic. One of these is *tapadh leat* or *tapadh leibh*, thank you. *Tapadh leat* is used when speaking to someone you know well. *Tapadh leibh* is used in more formal situations or with older people. *Taing* is the word for thanks while *mòran taing* is the more effusive many thanks.

thaw *n* aiteamh *m* *v* bi ag aiteamh, leagh

the *def art* (*singular forms*) an, am (+ *b, f, m, p*), a' (+ *len*), an t- (+ *vowels*); (*plural*) na, na h- (+ *vowels*) (*See Forms of the article in Grammar*)

theatre *n* taigh-cluiche *m*

theft *n* mèirle *f*, goid *f*, braide *f*

their *poss pron* an, am, … aca

them *pers pron* iad, (*emph*) iadsan

theme *n* cuspair *m*; (*mus*) ùrlar *m*

themselves *emph pron* iad fhèin

then *adv* an sin, an uair sin; (*afterwards*) an dèidh sin; (*in that case*) mar sin, a-rèist(e)

thence *adv* às a sin, às an àite sin, (bh)o sin

theology *n* diadhachd *f*

theoretical *a* teòiridheach, beachdail

theory *n* teòiridh *f*, beachd *m*, beachd-smuain *m*

therapist *n* neach-slànachaidh *m*, leasaiche *m* **speech t.** leasaiche cainnt *m*

therapy *n* slànachadh *m*, leasachadh *m*

there *adv* an sin, an siud

thereabouts *adv* mu thimcheall sin

thereafter *adv* an dèidh sin, an uair sin

thereby *adv* le sin, leis a sin

therefore *adv* mar sin, air an adhbhar sin

thermal *a* tearmach

thermometer *n* teas-mheidh *f*

these *dem pron* iad seo

thesis *n* tràchdas *m*

they *pers pron* iad, (*emph*) iadsan

thick *a* tiugh, garbh

thicken *v* dèan nas tighe; (*intrans*) fàs nas tighe

thicket *n* doire d(h)ùmhail *f m*

thickness *n* tighead *m*

thief *n* mèirleach *m*, gadaiche *m*

thieve *v* goid, dèan mèirle

thigh *n* sliasaid *f*

thimble *n* meuran *m*

thin *a* tana, caol; (*scarce*) gann *v* tanaich

thing *n* nì *m*, rud *m* **how are things?** ciamar a tha cùisean?

think *v* smaoinich, saoil, meas

thinness *n* tainead *m*, caoilead *m*

third *n* trian *m*, treas cuid *f* *a* treas, tritheamh

thirdly *adv* san treas àite

thirst *n* pathadh *m*, tart *m*, iota(dh) *m*

thirsty *a* pàiteach, tartmhor, ìotmhor **are you t.?** a bheil am pathadh ort?

thirteen *n, a* trì-deug **t. minutes** trì mionaidean deug

thirteenth *a* treas … deug

thirty *n, a* deich air fhichead, trithead *m*

this *dem a* seo

thistle *n* cluaran *m*, fòghnan *m*

thole *v* fuiling

thong *n* iall *f*

thorn *n* dris *f*, droigheann *m*

thorny *a* driseach, droighneach; (*difficult*) connspaideach, ciogailteach

thorough *a* mionaideach, domhainn; (*complete*) fìor

those *dem pron* iad sin, iad siud

though *conj* ge, ged **as t.** mar gu/gun/gum

thought *n* smaoin *f*, smuain *f*

thoughtful *a* smaointeach; (*considerate*) tuigseach

thoughtless *a* beag diù, gun smaoin(eachadh)

thousand *n, a* mìle *f m*

thrash *v* slaic, sgiùrs; (*grain*) buail

thread *n* snàthainn *m*, snàithlean *m*

threadbare *a* lom

threat n bagairt f, maoidheadh m
threaten v bagair, maoidh
threatening a bagarrach
three n, a trì **t. people** triùir f m
  t.-legged trì-chasach **t.-quarters**
  trì-chairteil m pl
thresh v buail
threshold n stairs(n)each f, maide-
  buinn m
thrift n cùmhntachd f
thrifty a cùmhntach, glèidhteach
thrill n gaoir f v cuir gaoir an
thriller n gaoir-sgeul m
thrilling a fìor thogarrach, gad chur nad
  b(h)oil etc
thrive v soirbhich
throat n amha(i)ch f, sgòrnan m
throb v dèan plosgartaich
thrombosis n trombòis f, cleiteachd-
  fala f
throne n rìgh-chathair f
throng n sluagh mòr m, co-long f v
  dùmhlaich/lìon àite **t. to** còmh(dha)laich
throttle v tachd, mùch
through prep tro, tre, trìd **t. other**
  troimh-a-chèile
throughout adv o cheann gu ceann,
  feadh gach àite
throw n tilgeadh m, tilgeil m, sadail m,
  caitheamh m v tilg, sad, caith **t. up**
  dìobhair
thrush n smeòrach f; (med) craos-
  ghalar m
thrust n sàthadh m, sparradh m;
  (of argument) prìomh phuing f v sàth,
  spàrr
thud n turtar m
thug n ùmaidh m
thumb n òrdag f
thump n buille f, slaic f; (noise) trost m
  v buail, thoir slaic do
thunder n tàirneanach m **t. and
  lightning** tàirneanaich is dealanaich
thunderbolt n beithir f m
Thursday n Diardaoin m
thus adv mar seo, air an dòigh seo
thwart v cuir bacadh air
thyme n lus an rìgh m

tick n (sound) diog m, buille f; (moment)
  diog m; (mark) strìochag f; (insect)
  gartan m, mial-chaorach f
ticket n tiogaid f
tickle v diogail
tide n làn m, seòl-mara m, tìde-mhara f
  high t. muir-làn f m **low t.** muir-tràigh
  f m
tidy a sgiobalta v sgìoblaich
tie n bann m; (necktie) tàidh f v ceangail
tier n sreath f m, ìre f
tiger n tìgear m
tight a teann
tighten v teannaich
tights n stocainnean-teann f pl
tile n leacag f, taidhl f v leacaich, taidhl
till prep gu, gu ruig(e) conj gus
tiller n (f)ailm f, falmadair m; (of soil)
  treabhaiche m
tilt v aom
timber n fiodh m a fiodha
time n àm m, uair f; (period of) ùine
  f, tìde f; (abstr) tìm f **a long t. ago** o
  chionn f(h)ada **any t.** uair sam bith **for
  a long t.** airson ùine mhòir **from t. to
  t.** b(h)o àm gu àm **in a week's t.** an
  ceann seachdain **in t.** na uair **it's high
  t. you ...** tha làn-àm/thìde agad ... **on
  t.** ris an uair **plenty of t.** ùine/tìde gu
  leòr **what's the t.?** dè 'n uair a tha e? **at
  times** uaireannan v tomhais an ùine
timely adv an deagh àm
timetable n clàr-ama m v dèan clàr-ama
timid a gealtach, meata
timing n tomhas-ama m
timorous a eagalach, sgeunach,
  sgàthach
tin n staoin f; (can) tiona m, canastair m
  tin-opener fosglair chanastairean m
tinge n lì f, fiamh m v dath
tingle n biorgadaich f v (feel a tingling)
  fairich biorgadh
tinker n ceàrd m
tinkle v dèan/thoir gliong
tinsel n tionsail f
tint n fiamh-dhath m, bàn-dhath
  m, tuar m v dath
tiny a bìodach, meanbh, crìon

tip n bàrr m; (money) bonn-boise m
tipple v dèan pòit, gabh deoch
tipsy a air leth-mhisg, froganach
tiptoe n corra-biod(a) m **on t.** air chorra-biod(a)
tirade n sruth-cainnt m
tire v sgìthich, sàraich; (intrans) fàs sgìth, sgìthich
tired a sgìth
Tiree person n Tiristeach m, (female) ban-Thiristeach f
tiresome a sàrachail, leamh
tiring a sgìtheil
tissue n (cell) stuth (cealla) m; (muscle) maothran m **paper t.** nèapaigin pàipeir m
tit n (bird) gocan m, smutag f; (slang) cìoch f
tit-bit n grèim blasta m
title n tiotal m; (leg) còir f, dlighe f
to prep do (+ len), (to a) gu, (to the) chun (+ gen); (before verbs and place names) a (+ len); (after verbs) ri **are you going to the shop?** a bheil thu a' dol dhan bhùtha? **she went to a meeting** chaidh i gu coinneimh **are they going to the wedding?** a bheil iad a' dol chun na bainnse? **we are going to play football** tha sinn a' dol a chluich ball-coise **she spoke to him** bhruidhinn i ris adv **to and fro,** a-null 's a-nall
toad n muile-mhàg(ag) f
toast n tost m; (drink) deoch-slàinte f v tost(aig); (drink) òl deoch-slàinte
toaster n tostair m
tobacco n tombaca m
today adv an-diugh
toddler n pàiste m
toe n òrdag coise f
toffee n tofaidh m
together adv còmhla, le chèile
toil n saothair f, dubh-chosnadh m v saothraich
toilet n taigh-beag m **t. roll** roile toidhleit f m
token n comharra m; (memento) cuimhneachan m; (gift) àirleas m
tolerable a a ghabhas fhulang; (fairly good) meadhanach math

tolerance n fulangas m; (patience) foighidinn f
tolerant a fosgailte; (patient) foighidneach
tolerate v fuiling, ceadaich, bi fosgailte do
toll n cìs f
tomato n tomàto m
tomb n uaigh f, tuam m
tomcat n cat fireann m, cullach m
tome n leabhar mòr m
tomorrow adv a-màireach
ton n tunna m
tone n (sound) fuaim m; (mus) tòna f; (of voice) dòigh-labhairt f **t.-deaf** a ceòl-bhodhar
tongs n clobha m
tongue n teanga f; (lang) cainnt f, cànan f m
tonic n ìocshlaint f; (uplift) togail f
tonight adv a-nochd
tonsil n tonsail f
too adv ro (+ len); (also) cuideachd, mar an ceudna **too black** ro dhubh **too much** cus, tuilleadh 's a' chòir
tool n inneal m, ball-acfhainn m
tooth n fiacail f **back t.** fiacail-cùil **toothache** an dèideadh m **toothbrush** bruis-fhiaclan f **toothpaste** uachdar-fhiaclan m
top n mullach m, bàrr m, uachdar m **spinning t.** dòtaman m **on t. of** air muin (+ gen) **top-heavy** bàrr-throm v thoir bàrr air
topic n cuspair m, ceann(-còmhraidh) m
topical a àmail, sna naidheachdan
topsy-turvy a, adv bun-os-cionn, dromach-air-thearrach
torch n toirds f m, biùgan m
torment n àmhghar f m, dòrainn f v lèir
torpedo n spaileart m
torrent n tuil f, bras-shruth m, beum-slèibhe m
torrid a loisgeach; (met) fìor dhian
torso n colann f, com m
tortoise n sligeanach m
tortuous a snìomhach, toinnte, lùbach
torture n cràdh m, pianadh m v craidh, ceus

Tory n Tòraidh m **the T. Party** am Partaidh Tòraidheach m

toss v luaisg; (throw) tilg; (of a coin) cuir croinn

total a iomlan, uile n sùim (iomlan) f

totally adv gu lèir, gu h-iomlan, gu tur

touch v bean do, suath an, buin ri, làimhsich; (with emotion) drùidh air, maothaich

touching a (emotive) drùidhteach, maothach

touchy a frionasach

tough a cruaidh, righinn; (of meat etc) righinn

toughen v cruadhaich, rìghnich

tour n turas m, cuairt f

tourism n turasachd f

tourist n neach-turais m pl luchd-turais **t. information centre** ionad fiosrachaidh turasachd m **t. office** oifis turasachd f

tow v slaod, dragh

towards prep a dh'ionnsaigh (+ gen); gu, chun (+ gen); (purpose) a chum (+ gen)

towel n searbhadair m, tubhailt(e) f m

tower n tùr m

town n baile m, baile-mòr m **t. council** comhairle baile f **t. hall** talla baile m

township n baile m

toy n dèideag f v cluich

trace n lorg f v lorg

track n lorg f; (path) frith-rathad m, ceum m

tracksuit n deise-spòrs f

tract n leabhran m, tràchd f m; (of land) raonach m

tractor n tractar m

trade n malairt f; (craft) ceàird f **t. fair** fèill-mhalairt f **t. mark** comharra malairt m **t. union** aonadh-ciùird m v dèan malairt, malairtich

trader n neach-malairt m

tradition n dualchas; (oral) beul-aithris f

traditional a dualchasach, traidiseanta, beul-aithriseach

traffic n trafaig f **t. jam** stopadh trafaig m

traffic v dèan malairt

tragedy n cùis-mhulaid f; (liter) bròn-chluich f

tragic a muladach, cianail, dòrainneach

trail n lorg f, slighe f v bi air lorg (+ gen); (drag) slaod; (intrans) bi slaodach **t. after** triall às dèidh (+ gen)

trailer n trèilear m

train n trèan(a) f; (bride's) sguain f v trèan(aig), teagaisg, ionnsaich; (intrans) trèanaig, ionnsaich

trainee n foghlamach m, neach fo thrèanadh m

trainer n neach-trèanaidh m

trainers n brògan-trèanaidh f pl

training n trèanadh m, ionnsachadh m

trait n dual-nàdair m, stil f

traitor n neach-brathaidh m, brathadair m

tramp n (person) deòra(i)dh m; (walk) ruaig f v coisich le ceum trom

trample v saltair, stamp

trance n neul m

tranquil a ciùin, sìochail, sèimh

tranquillity n ciùineas m, sìth-thàmh m

tranquillizer n ciùineadair m, tàmhadair m

transaction n gnìomh-malairt m

transcend v rach thairis air, thoir bàrr air

transcribe v cuir an sgrìobhadh

transcript n riochd sgrìobhte m

transfer n gluasad f, aiseag m v gluais, aisig; (intrans) gluais gu

transfix v (met) beò-ghlac

transform v cruth-atharraich

transformation n cruth-atharrachadh m

transgress v bris(t) riaghailt/lagh, peacaich

transgression n bris(t)eadh riaghailt/ lagh(a) m, peacadh m

transient a diombuan, neo-mhaireann

transition n caochladh m, eadar-ghluasad f

transitional a trastach, san eadar-àm, eadar-amail

translate v eadar-theangaich; (move) gluais

translation n eadar-theangachadh m **simultaneous t.** eadar-theangachadh mar-aon

translator n eadar-theangair m
transmission n sgaoileadh m; (broadcast) craobh-sgaoileadh m, craoladh m
transmit v sgaoil; (broadcast) craobh-sgaoil, craol
transmitter n uidheam-sgaoilidh m; (mast) crann-sgaoilidh m
transparency n trìd-shoilleireachd f; (met) follaiseachd f
transparent a trìd-shoilleir; (met) follaiseach
transpire v thig am follais; (happen) tachair
transplant n ath-chur m **liver t.** ath-chur air grùthan v ath-chuir
transport n giùlan m, còmhdhail f **T. Dept** Roinn na Còmhdhail v giùlain, iomchair
transpose v atharraich òrdugh; (mus) cuir an gleus eile
transverse a tarsainn, trasta
trap n ribe f m v rib, glac
trash n sgudal m, smodal m
travel n siubhal m, taisteal m **t. agency** buidheann-siubhail f m **t. centre** ionad-siubhail m v siubhail
traveller n neach-siubhail m, taistealaiche m
travelling n siubhal m a siùbhlach **t.-people** luchd-siubhail m pl
traverse v triall, rach tarsainn
trawl n lìon-sguabaidh f v sgrìob, tràl(aig); (search) dèan sireadh farsaing
trawler n tràlair m, bàta-sgrìobaidh m
tray n treidhe f m, sgàl m
treacherous a cealgach, foilleil; (dangerous) cunnartach
treachery n cealg/ceilg f, foill f
treacle n trèicil m
tread v saltair
treason n brathadh m, feall f
treasure n ionmhas m, ulaidh f v cuir luach mòr air **he treasured her** bha meas a chridhe aige oirre
treasurer n ionmhasair m
treat n treat f, sòlas m; (event) cuirm f v thoir aoigheachd do; (deal with)

dèilig ri, làimhsich; (med) thoir aire do **t. someone to …** seas do làmh
treatment n làimhseachadh m, giullachd f
treaty n cùmhnant m, còrdadh m, cunnradh m
treble a trì-fillte; (of voice) àrd
tree n craobh f
trefoil n trì-bhileach m
tremble v criothnaich, bi air chrith
trembling a critheanach
tremendous a àibheiseach, sgoinneil **a t. loss** call cianail m **a t. help** cuideachadh mòr m
tremor n crith f
tremulous a critheanach; (anxious) iomagaineach
trench n clais f; (in war) trainnse f
trenchant a geur, cumhachdach
trend n claonadh m, gluasad m
trepidation n geilt f; (phys) crith-eagail f
trespass v rach thar chrìochan; (sin) peacaich
trial n deuchainn f, dearbhadh m; (leg) cùirt f
triangle n triantan m **equilateral t.** triantan ionann-thaobhach **isosceles t.** triantan co-chasach
triangular a triantanach
tribe n treubh f, sliochd m
tribulation n trioblaid f, àmhghar f m
tribunal n tribiùnal m
tribute n moladh m; (payment) càin f
trick n car m, cleas m v thoir an car à/ às, meall
trickle n beag-shileadh m, beag-shruth m v sil, sruth
tricycle n trì-rothach m, traidhsagal m
trifle n faoineas m, rud beag m; (sweet) mìlsean-measgaichte m, traidhfeal m
trifling a beag, suarach
trigger n iarann-leigidh m
trim a sgiobalta, cuimir, grinn v geàrr, lomaich; (decorate) snasaich
Trinity n Trianaid f **T. College** Colaiste na Trianaid f
trinket n faoin-sheud m
trio n triùir f m; (mus) ceòl-triùir m

trip n turas m, cuairt f, sgrìob f; (*stumble*) tuisleadh m v tuislich

triple a trì-fillte v trìoblaich

triplets n triùir f m

tripod n trì-chasach m

trite a beag-seagh

triumph n buaidh f; (*exultation*) buaidh-chaithream m v thoir buaidh, buadhaich

triumphant a (*victorious*) buadhmhor; (*exultant*) caithreamach

trivial a suarach, gun fhiù

trolley n troilidh f

trombone n trombòn m

troop n buidheann f m, cuideachd f, trùp m **t. of horses** greigh each f v triall

trophy n cuach buaidhe f

tropic n tropaig f **the Tropics** na Tropaigean f pl

tropical a tropaigeach

trot v dèan trotan, trot

trouble n dragh m, saothair f; (*dispute*) trioblaid f, buaireas m v cuir dragh air, buair

troublemaker n buaireadair m, neach-buairidh m

troublesome a draghail; (*causing trouble*) buaireasach

trough n amar m

trounce v liodraig

trousers n briogais f

trout n breac m **sea t.** bànag f

trowel n sgreadhail f

truancy n seachnadh-sgoile m

truant n seachnaiche(-sgoile) m

truce n fosadh (còmhraig) m

truck n truga f **have no t. with** na gabh gnothach ri

truculent a ceacharra

trudge v ceumnaich gu trom

true a fìor, fìrinneach; (*faithful*) dìleas; (*right*) ceart **a t. understanding** fìor thuigse

truly adv gu fìrinneach, gu dearbh, gu deimhinn(e) **yours t.** le dùrachd

trumpet n trombaid f

truncate v giorraich

truncheon n plocan m

trunk n stoc m, bun-craoibhe m; (*for storage*) ciste f; (*of animal*) sròn f, gnos m; (*anat*) com m **t. road** prìomh-rathad m

trust n earbsa f, creideas m; (*company*) urras m **the National T.** an t-Urras Nàiseanta v earb à, cuir muinighin an, thoir creideas do

trustee n urrasair m

trusting a earbsail

trustworthy a earbsach

truth n fìrinn f **in t.** gu fìrinneach **to tell the t.** a dh'innse na fìrinn

try v feuch

trying a deuchainneach

tryst n dàil f, coinneamh f; (*place*) àite-coinneachaidh m

tub n tuba f m, ballan m

tube n pìoban m, feadan m, tiùb f

tuberculosis n a' chaitheamh f

tuck v trus

Tuesday n Dimàirt m

tuft n dos m, toban m, topan m

tug n tarraing f, draghadh m; (*naut*) tuga f v tarraing, dragh, spìon

tuition n teagasg m, oideachadh m, ionnsachadh m

tulip n tiuilip f

tumble n tuiteam m **t. dryer** n car-thiormaichear m v tuit

tummy n brù f

tumour n at m, màm m, meall m

tumult n iorghail f, onghail f

tumultuous a iorghaileach, onghaileach

tune n fonn m, port m v gleus, cuir air ghleus

tuneful a ceòlmhor, fonnmhor

tuner n neach-gleusaidh m

tunnel n tunail f m

tup n reithe m, rùda m

turbine n roth-uidheam f

turbot n turbaid f

turbulence n buaireas m, luaisgeachd f

turbulent a buaireasach, luaisgeach

turf n (*ground*) bàrr-talmhainn m; (*a sod*) sgrath f, fò(i)d f

turgid a air at; (*style*) trom, iom-fhaclach

Turk n Turcach m, (*female*) ban-T(h)urcach f

turkey *n* eun-Frangach *m*, cearc Fhrangach *f*
Turkish *a* Turcach; (*lang*) Turcais *f*
turmoil *n* troimh-a-chèile *f*, ùpraid *f*
turn *n* tionndadh *m*, car *m*, lùb *f*; (*in sequence*) cuairt *f* **she took a t.** thàinig cuairt oirre *v* tionndaidh, cuir mun cuairt
turnip *n* tui(r)neap *m*, snèap *f*
turnout *n* na nochd
turnover *n* luach na malairt *m*; (*of staff etc*) atharrachadh *m*
turquoise *a* tuirc-ghorm
turret *n* turaid *f*
turtle *n* turtar *f*
tusk *n* starr-fhiacail *f*, tosg *m*
tussle *n* tuasaid *f*, strì *f*
tut! *interj* t(h)ud!
tutor *n* oide *m*
tutorial *n* tràth-oideachaidh *m*
twang *n* gliong *m*; (*lang*) blas *m*
tweak *v* cuir car de; (*met*) dèan atharrachadh beag air
tweed *n* clò (mòr) *m* **Harris T.** an Clò Mòr/Hearach *m*
tweezers *n* greimiche *m*
twelfth *a* dara … deug
twelve *n* a dhà-dheug *a* dà … dheug **t. disciples** dà dheisciobal dheug *m*
twentieth *a* ficheadamh
twenty *n*, *a* fichead *m*
twice *adv* dà uair, dà thuras
twig *n* faillean *m*, slat *f*
twilight *n* eadar-sholas *m*, camhanaich *f*, ciaradh *m*
twin *n* leth-aon *m pl* leth-aonan, càraid *f*
twine *v* toinn

twinge *n* biorgadh *m*
twinkle/twinkling *n* priobadh *m*; (*in eye*) drithleann *m* **in the t. of an eye** ann am priobadh na sùla *v* priob
twirl *n* roithleagan *m*; (*act*) ruidhleadh *m* *v* ruidhil mun cuairt
twist *n* toinneamh *m*, car *m*, snìomh *m* *v* toinn; (*story*) cuir car an; (*ankle*) cuir snìomh an
twisted *a* snìomhte, toinnte; (*nature*) coirbte
twit *n* amadan *m*, gloidhc *f*
twitch *n* spadhadh *m*, strangadh *m*
twitter *v* ceilearaich, dèan bìogail/bìdil; (*internet*) biodanaich
two *n* a dhà *a* dà **two people** dithis *f* **two-dimensional** dà-sheallach **two-faced** dà-aodannach, leam-leat **two-fold** dà-fhillte, dùbailte **two-ply** dà-dhualach
tycoon *n* toicear *m*, saidhbhriche *m*
type *n* seòrsa *m*; (*typ*) clò *m v* clò-sgrìobh, taidhp
typhoid *n* am fiabhras breac *m*
typhus *n* am fiabhras ballach *m*
typical *a* coltach, dualach **that's t. of him** tha sin cho coltach ris
typify *v* riochdaich, bi na (h-) *etc* eisimpleir de
typing *n* clò-sgrìobhadh *m*
typographical *a* clò-bhualaidh **t. error** mearachd clò-bhualaidh *f*
tyrannical *a* aintighearnail
tyrannize *v* dèan ainneart air
tyranny *n* aintighearnas *m*
tyrant *n* aintighearna *m*
tyre *n* taidhr *f*, taidhear *f*

U

ubiquitous *a* sa h-uile h-àite, uile-làthaireach
ugly *a* grànda
Uist person *n* Uibhisteach *m*, (*female*) ban-Uibhisteach *f*
ulcer *n* neasgaid *f*
ulterior *a* ìochdarach; (*met*) neo-fhollaiseach

ultimate *a* deireannach, mu dheireadh
ultimatum *n* rabhadh deireannach *m*
ultra *a* ro, sàr-, fìor, buileach
umbrage *n* oilbheum *m*
umbrella *n* sgàilean *m*
umpire *n* rèitire *m*, britheamh *m*
unable *a* eu-comasach **u. to** gun chomas

unacceptable *a* ... ris nach fhaodar gabhail

unaccompanied *a* na (h-)aonar *etc*; (*mus*) gun taic-ciùil

unaccustomed *a* neo-chleachdte (ri)

unadulterated *a* neo-thruaillte

unaided *a, adv* gun chuideachadh

unambiguous *a* (*lit*) aon-seaghach; (*met*) gun cheist

unanimous *a* aon-ghuthach, a dh'aon inntinn

unanimously *adv* gu h-aon-ghuthach

unappetizing *a* neo-bhlasta, mì-chàilear

unarmed *a* gun armachd, neo-armaichte

uncle *n* bràthair-athar/màthar *m*, uncail *m*

unclean *a* neòghlan

uncombed *a* gun chìreadh

uncomfortable *a* mì-chofhurtail

uncommon *a* neo-àbhaisteach, neo-chumanta

uncomplaining *a* neo-ghearaineach

unconcerned *a* gun chùram, gun dragh

unconditional *a* gun chùmhnantan/chumhachan

unconfirmed *a* gun daingneachadh

unconnected *a* gun cheangal, neo-cheangailte

Insight: unappetizing

Neo-bhlasta and *mì-chàilear* convey the meaning unappetizing. *Mi-* and *neo-* are negative prefixes which change the meaning of the adjective to the direct opposite of the original. Other common prefixes such as *ao-*, *do-* and *an-/ain-* perform the same function as the English prefix un- eg *aocoltach*, unlike, *an-iochdmhor*, unmerciful and *do-chreidsinn*, unbelievable.

---

unassuming *a* iriosal

unattainable *a* do-ruighinn, thar ruigse

unattended *a* gun neach na c(h)ois *etc*

unauthorized *a* gun ùghdarras, neo-cheadaichte

unavailing *a* gun tairbhe

unavoidable *a* do-sheachanta

unaware *a* gun fhios/mhothachadh

unbalanced *a* mì-chothromach

unbearable *a* do-fhulang

unbeatable *a* nach gabh beatadh

unbecoming *a* mì-chneasta

unbelief *n* eas-creideamh *m*

unbiased *a* gun chlaonadh

unborn *a* gun bhreith

unbreakable *a* nach gabh bris(t)eadh

unbroken *a* gun bhris(t)eadh

unbutton *v* fuasgail

unceasing *a* gun sgur/stad/abhsadh

uncertain *a* mì-chinnteach

uncertainty *n* mì-chinnt *f*

unchanging *a* neo-chaochlaideach

uncivil *a* gun mhodh

uncivilized *a* neo-shìobhalta, borbarra

unconscious *a* gun mhothachadh/fhaireachadh

unconstitutional *a* neo-reachdail

uncontested *a* gun fharpais

uncontrollable *a* thar smachd(achaidh)

uncooked *a* amh, gun chòcaireachd

uncouth *a* neo-ghrinn, amh

uncover *v* rùisg; (*met*) thoir gu follais

undecided *a* mì-chinnteach

undeniable *a* do-àicheadh

under *prep* fo *adv* fodha **it went u.** chaidh e/i fodha

undercurrent *n* fo-shruth *m*; (*met*) faireachdainn *f*

undercut *v* cuir air prìs nas ìsle

underestimate *v* meas fo luach

undergo *v* rach/theirig tro, fuiling

underground *a* fo thalamh **u. train** trèan(a) fo thalamh *f*

underhand *a* cealgach, clìceach

underline *v* (*lit*) cuir sgrìob/loidhne fo; (*met*) comharraich, dearbh

undermine *v* (*lit*) cladhaich fo; (*met*) lagaich

underneath prep fo adv shìos, gu h-ìosal/ìseal

underpass n fo-chaitoachas m, bealach fo thalamh m

underskirt n cota-bàn m

underspend n caiteachas fon t-sùim shuidhichte m v caith fon t-sùim shuidhichte

understand v tuig

understanding n tuigse f, breithneachadh m; (accord) còrdadh m

understanding a tuigseach

undertake v gabh os làimh

undertaker n neach-adhlacaidh m, adhlaicear m

undertaking n gnothach m, iomairt f

underway a fo sheòl, ga c(h)ur an gnìomh

underwear n fo-aodach m

undeserved a neo-thoillte

undisputed a gun chonnspaid, gun cheist, dearbhte

undo v fuasgail; (unpick) sgaoil; (abstr) mill

undoubtedly adv gun teagamh

undress v cuir/thoir aodach dheth, dhith etc **I undressed** chuir mi dhìom (m' aodach)

undue a neo-dhligheach; (excessive) cus

uneasy a mì-shaorsainneil

uneconomic a neo-eaconamach

uneducated a neo-fhoghlaim(ich)te, gun fhoghlam

unemployed a gun obair

unemployment n cion cosnaidh m, dìth obrach f m **u. benefit** sochair cion cosnaidh f

unequal a neo-ionann

uneven a mì-chothrom, mì-chòmhnard

unexpectedly adv gun dùil ris/rithe etc

unfair a mì-cheart, mì-chothromach

unfaithful a mì-dhìleas, neo-dhìleas

unfamiliar a coimheach **u. surroundings** àite far nach eil/robh mi etc eòlach

unfashionable a neo-fhasanta

unfasten v fuasgail

unfavourable a neo-fhàbharach

unfinished a neo-chrìochnaichte, gun chrìochnachadh

unfit a (phys) gun spionnadh; (unsuitable) mì-fhreagarrach, neo-iomchaidh; (unworthy) neo airidh

unforeseen a gun dùil ris/rithe etc

unfortunate a mì-fhortanach, mì-shealbhach

unfortunately adv gu mì-fhortanach, gu mì-shealbhach

unfriendly a neo-chàirdeil, fad' às

ungainly a liobasta, cliobach, spàgach

ungodly a ain-diadhaidh

ungrateful a mì-thaingeil

unhappy a mì-thoilichte, mì-shona

unhealthy a mì-fhallain

unholy a mì-naomh(a); (met) mì-chneasta

uniform n èideadh m, deise dreuchd f **firefighter's u.** èideadh smàladair m a aon-fhillte; (consistent) cunbhalach

unify v co-aonaich

unilateral a aon-taobhach

unimportant a neo-chudromach **that is u.** chan fhiach sin bruidhinn air

uninformed a aineolach, gun eòlas

uninspired a neo-thogarrach, marbhanta

unintentionally adv gun fhiosta, gun a bhith an rùn

uninterested a gun ùidh

uninvited a gun chuireadh/fhiathachadh

union n aonadh m **trade u.** aonadh luchd-ciùird

unique a gun choimeas, air leth **it was u.** cha robh a leithid ann

unison a aon-ghuthach

unit n aonad m

unite v aonaich

united a aonaichte **the U. Kingdom** an Rìoghachd Aonaichte f **the U. States** na Stàitean Aonaichte f pl **the U. Nations** na Dùthchannan Aonaichte f pl

unity n aonachd f

universal a uile-choitcheann, coitcheann

universe n cruinne m (f in gen), cruinne-cè m (f in gen), domhan m

university n oilthigh m

unjust a mì-cheart

unkind a mosach, gun choibhneas

unknown *a* neo-aithnichte
unlawful *a* mì-laghail
unleaded *a* gun luaidhe (ann/innte)
 u. petrol peatrail gun luaidhe *m*
unless *conj* mur(a), nas lugha na
unlicensed *a* gun cheadachd
unlike *a* ao-coltach (ri)
unlikely *a* mì-choltach
unlimited *a* gun chrìoch, neo-
 chrìochnach
unload *v* thoir an luchd de
unlock *v* fosgail (glas)
unlucky *a* mì-shealbhach
unmarried *a* gun phòsadh
unmistakable *a* do-àicheanta
unnatural *a* mì-nàdarra(ch)
unnecessary *a* neo-riatanach, gun
 fheum air
unobtainable *a* nach gabh faighinn,
 do-ruighinn
unobtrusive *a* neo-fhollaiseach/nochdte
unoccupied *a* falamh, bàn
unofficial *a* neo-oifigeil
unorthodox *a* neo-ghnàthach
unpack *v* falmhaich, thoir às
unpaid *a* gun phàigheadh/tuarastal
unpalatable *a* mì-bhlasta/-chàilear
unpardonable *a* nach fhaodar a
 mhathadh
unplayable *a* nach gabh cluich(e),
 do-chluiche
unpleasant *a* mì-thlachdmhor
unpopular *a* gun mheas air/oirre *etc*
unprecedented *a* gun choimeas, nach
 do thachair roimhe
unprepared *a* mì-dheiseil, neo-ullaichte
unproductive *a* gun tairbhe, neo-
 thorrach, neo-tharbhach
unprofessional *a* mì-phroifeiseanta
unprofitable *a* gun bhuannachd, neo-
 phrothaideach
unprotected *a* gun dìon
unqualified *a* gun teisteanas; (*total*)
 iomlan, fìor
unquestionably *adv* gun cheist
unravel *v* (*trans*) rèitich; (*intrans*) sgaoil
unreal *a* neo-fhìor
unrealistic *a* neo-phractaigeach

unreasonable *a* mì-reusanta
unrelated *a* gun bhuntainneas/
 cheangal
unreliable *a* neo-earbsach
unrest *n* an-fhois *f*; (*civil*) buaireadh *m*
unrestricted *a* gun bhacadh/chuing
unripe *a* an-abaich
unrivalled *a* gun choimeas, gun samhail
unruly *a* mì-rianail, tuasaideach;
 (*of children*) luathaireach
unsafe *a* mi-shàbhailte, cunnartach
unsatisfactory *a* neo-iomchaidh
 I found it u. cha robh mi riaraichte leis
unsavoury *a* (*taste*) mì-bhlasta; (*met*)
 mì-chneasta
unseemly *a* mì-chiatach
unselfish *a* neo-fhèineil
unsettled *a* neo-shuidhichte, mì-
 sheatlaigte
unsightly *a* grànda, mì-mhaiseach
unsophisticated *a* sìmplidh
unspecified *a* neo-ainmichte
unspoiled *a* gun mhilleadh
unstable *a* cugallach, neo-sheasmhach
unsteady *a* cugallach, mì-chothromach
unsuccessful *a* neo-shoirbheachail
unsuitable *a* mì-fhreagarrach
unsuspecting *a* gun amharas
unsympathetic *a* neo-fhaireachail, neo-
 thruasail, gun cho-fhaireachdainn
untested *a* gun dearbhadh/fheuchainn
unthinkable *a* nach gabh
 smaoineachadh (air)
untidy *a* mì-sgiobalta
untie *v* fuasgail
until *prep* gu *conj* gus **u. she returns** gus
 an till i
unto *prep* gu, do, chun (+ *gen*)
untrue *a* neo-fhìrinneach, fìor (*preceded
 by neg v*) **that's quite u.** chan eil sin
 idir fìor
untruth *n* breug *f*
untruthful *a* neo-fhìrinneach, neo-fhìor
unusual *a* neo-àbhaisteach, annasach
unused *a* gun chleachdadh, nach deach
 a chleachdadh
unveil *v* leig ris, taisbean
unwanted *a* gun iarraidh

unwarranted *a* gun adhbhar cothromach

unwell *a* tinn, bochd, meadhanach

unwieldy *a* doirbh a ghiùlain, lòdail, liobasta

unwilling *a* ain-deònach, mì-dheònach

unwind *v* thoir às an toinneamh, fuasgail; (*relax*) gabh fois

unwise *a* neo-ghlic, gòrach

unworthy *a* (*person*) neo-airidh; (*motive*) suarach

unwrap *v* thoir còmhdach de

up *prep* suas *adv* shuas **up the hill** suas an cnoc **were you up?** an robh thu shuas? **we were up until 2 o'clock** bha sinn an-àird(e) gu dà uair

upbringing *n* togail *f*, àrach *m*

update *n* cunntas às ùr *m v* ùraich, clàraich às ùr, thoir cunntas as ùr do

uphold *v* glèidh, thoir taic do, cùm suas

uplift *v* (*phys*) tog (suas); (*mental*) tog inntinn/meanmna

uplifting *a* brosnachail, a thogas meanmna

upon *prep* air, air muin (+ *gen*), air uachdar (+ *gen*)

upper *a* shuas, uachdrach

upright *a* dìreach; (*met*) dìreach, treibhdhireach, ceart

uproar *n* ùpraid *f*

uproot *v* spìon on fhreumh/bhun

upset *n* troimh-a-chèile *f*, bun-os-cionn *m a* troimh-a-chèile *v* cuir troimh-a-chèile/ bun-os-cionn

upshot *n* bun a bh' ann *m*, buil *f*

upside-down *adv* bun-os-cionn, a c(h)asan os a c(h)ionn *etc*

upstairs *a, adv* shuas an staidhre *adv* shuas an staidhre **going u.** a' dol suas an staidhre

up-to-date *a* an là an-diugh **u. fashions** fasain an là an-diugh

upwards *adv* suas

urban *a* baile

urbane *a* furm(h)ailteach

urge *n* miann *f m v* brosnaich, spàrr, cuir ìmpidh air

urgency *n* deatamachd *f*, èiginneachd/ èigeannachd *f*, cabhag *f*

urgent *a* èiginneach/èigeannach

urgently *adv* gu cabhagach, na (h-) èiginn *etc*

urine *n* mùn *m*

us *pron* sinn, *emph* sinne

usage *n* cleachdadh *m*, gnàths *m*

use *n* cleachdadh *m*, ùisneachadh *m*; (*usefulness*) feum *m* **what use is it?** dè am feum a th' ann? *v* cleachd, cuir gu feum, cuir an sàs, ùisnich

useful *a* feumail, gu feum

useless *a* gun fheum

user *n* neach-cleachdaidh *m*

usher *n* treòraiche *m v* treòraich a-steach

usual *a* àbhaisteach **as u.** mar as àbhaist, (*past tense*) mar a b' àbhaist

usually *adv* gu h-àbhaisteach, mar as/ (a) bu trice

usurp *v* gabh/glèidh gun chòir

utensil *n* soitheach *f m*, uidheam *f*, inneal *m*

uterus *n* machlag *f*

utility *n* goireas *m*, feum *m*

utilize *v* cleachd, cuir gu feum, cuir an sàs, ùisnich

utmost *a* as fhaide a-mach **I will do my u.** nì mi m' uile dhìcheall

utter *v* abair, can, labhair

utterly *adv* gu tur, uile-gu-lèir

U-turn *n* làn-char *m*, tur-atharrachadh *m*

V

vacancy *n* àite bàn/falamh *m*, beàrn *f m*

vacant *a* falamh, bàn, fàs

vacate *v* falmhaich, fàg

vacation *n* saor-làithean *m pl*, làithean-saora *m pl*

vaccination *n* banachdach *f*

vaccinate *v* thoir banachdach do

vacillate *v* bi eadar dhà bharail, bi sa bhonnalaich

vacuous *a* falamh, baoth

vacuum n falamhachd f
vacuum-cleaner n glanadair-sùghaidh m
vagina n faighean m
vagrant n siùbhlach m, faondrach m
vague a neo-shoilleir
vain a (futile) dìomhain, faoin; (proud) mòr às/aiste etc fhèin
valiant a calma, treubhach, foghainteach
valid a dligheach; (of time) a' seasamh
validate v dearbh
valley n gleann m; (wide, with river) srath m
valour n gaisge f
valuable a luachmhor, prìseil
valuation n meas m, luachadh m

vaseline n bhasailin m
vast a ro mhòr, àibheiseach
vault n (cellar) seilear m; (tomb) tuam m
vault v leum thairis air, geàrr sùrdag
veal n feòil-laoigh f
veer v gabh fiaradh, tionndaidh
vegetable(s) n glasraich f
vegetarian n glasraichear m, feòil-sheachnair m
vegetation n fàs-bheatha f
vehemence n dèineas m
vehement a dian, dealasach
vehicle n carbad m; (means) seòl m
veil n (on person) sgàile f, brat-gnùise m
   v còmhdaich, ceil, cuir fo sgàil

Insight: valley

There are two distinct words for a valley in Gaelic. *Gleann* is the term for a narrow valley or glen as in Glencoe, *Gleann Comhann*, while *srath* is a wide valley with a river running through it, as in Strathclyde, *Srath Chluaidh*.

value n luach m, fiach m v meas, cuir luach air, luach
valve n còmhla f, bhalbh f m
van n bhan(a) f; (front) toiseach m, tùs m
vandal n milltear m, sgriosadair m
vandalism n milleadh m, sgriosadh m
vanish v rach às an t-sealladh
vanity a dìomhanas m, faoineas m
vapour n deatach f, smùid f
variable a caochlaideach n caochladair m
variant n riochd eile m
variation n atharrachadh m, caochladh m; (mus) tionndadh m
varicose veins n fèithean borrach f pl
varied a eadar-dhealaichte
variety n (mixture) measgachadh m, caochladh m; (kind) seòrsa m, gnè f
various a iomadh, iomadach, eug-samhail
varnish n falaid m, bhàrnais f v cuir falaid/bhàrnais air, falaidich
vary v atharraich, caochail
vase n bhàs(a) f

vein n cuisle f, fèith-fala f **in that v.** air a' mhodh sin
velvet n meileabhaid f
veneer n snas-chraiceann m; (met) còmhdach uachdair m, sgeadachadh m
venerate v thoir mòr-spèis do
venereal a muineil **v. disease** a' bhreac Fhrangach f
vengeance n dìoghaltas m
venison n sitheann(-fèidh) f m
venom n nimh m, puinnsean m
venomous a nimheil
vent n fosgladh m, luidhear m v leig a-mach, leig ruith le
ventilate v fionnaraich, èadhraig
ventilation n fionnarachadh m, èadhraigeadh m
venture n iomairt f, oidhirp f v meantraig
venue n àite m, ionad m
Venus n Bheunas f
verb n gnìomhair m
verbatim adv facal air an fhacal
verbose a briathrach, ro bhriathrach, cabach
verdant a gorm, feurach

verdict n breith f

verge n oir f m; (of road) fàl m **on the v. of ...** an impis ... (+ vn)

verify v dearbh, fìrinnich, dèan cinnteach

veritable a fìor, cinnteach

vermin n (lice) mialan f pl; (rodents) criomairean m pl

versatile a iol-chomasach, làmhcharach

verse n rann m, earrann f; (poetry) bàrdachd f

version n (draft) dreach m; (of events) cunntas f m; (alternative) tionndadh m

versus prep an aghaidh (+ gen)

vertebrae n cnàmhan an droma m pl

vertebrate n druim-altach(an) m

vertical a dìreach

vertigo n tuaineal m, tuainealaich f

very a fìor (+ len), anabarrach; (same) ceart, dearbh (both + len) adv glè, fìor, ro (all + len)

vessel n soitheach f m **blood v.** balg fala m

vest n fo-lèine f; (waistcoat) siosacot m

vestibule n for-dhoras m

vestige n lorg f, comharra m

vet n lighiche-sprèidh m, bheat m

vet v sgrùd, breithnich

veteran n seann eòlach m; (soldier) seann saighdear m a seann, sean, eòlach

veto n crosadh m, bacadh m, bhèato m v cros, bac, dèan bhèato air

vex v leamhaich, buair, sàraich

vexation n leamhachas m, buaireadh m, sàrachadh m

via prep taobh (+ gen), tro

viability n comas obrachaidh m

viable a a ghabhas obrachadh

vial n searrag ghlainne f, meanbh-bhotal m

vibrate v crith, cuir air chrith, triob(h)uail

vibration n crith f, triob(h)ualadh m

vicar n piocair m, biocair m

vice n dubhailc f; (tool) bithis f, teanchair m

vice- pref iar-, leas- **vice-president** iar-cheann-suidhe m **vice-versa** adv agus a chaochladh

vicinity n àrainn f, nàbachas m

vicious a guineach, garg

victim n fulangaiche m, neach a dh'fhuiling(eas) m

victorious a buadhach, buadhmhor

victory n buaidh f

video n bhidio f m **videotape** teip bhidio f **v. conference** co-labhairt bhidio f

vie v strì (ri)

view n sealladh m; (opinion) beachd m v seall air, faic

viewer n neach-amhairc/coimhid m

viewpoint n àite-seallaidh/amhairc/coimhid m; (opinion) beachd m

vigil n faire f **keeping a v.** ri faire

vigilant a furachail

vigorous a sgairteil, calma

vigour n spionnadh m, sgairt f, treòir f

vile a gràineil, sgreataidh

vilify v màb, dubh-chàin

villa n taigh mòr m, taigh air leth m

village n baile beag m, clachan m

villain n slaightear m, eucorach m; (liter) droch fhear m

vindicate v dearbh; (justify) fìreanaich

vindictive a dìoghaltach

vine n fìonan f m, crann-fìona m vineyard fìon-lios m

vinegar n fìon geur m

violate v mill, bris(t)

violation n milleadh m, bris(t)eadh m; (of person) èigneachadh m

violence n fòirneart m, ainneart m

violent a fòirneartach, ainneartach **v. storm** gailleann f, doinneann f **he has a v. temper** tha leum eagalach na nàdar

violet n sail/dail-chuach f, bròg na cuthaig f

violin n fidheall f

violinist n fìdhlear m

viper n nathair-nimhe f

virgin n òigh f, maighdeann f

virginity n òigheachd f, maighdeannas m

virile n fearail, duineil

virtual a mas fhìor **v. reality** mas-fhìorachd f

virtually adv an impis (+ vn) **it's v. finished** cha mhòr nach eil e ullamh

virtue n subhailc f, deagh-bheus f, feart m

virtuous a subhailceach, beusach

virulent *a* nimhneach, geur
virus *n* bhìoras *m*
visa *n* bhìosa *f*
visage *n* aghaidh *f*, gnùis *f*
vis-à-vis *prep* a thaobh (+ *gen*); (*opposite*) aghaidh ri aghaidh
visibility *n* faicsinneachd *f*
visible *a* faicsinneach
vision *n* (*sight*) fradharc *m*, lèirsinn *f*; (*insight*) sealladh *m*, lèirsinn *f*; (*dream*) bruadar *m*, aisling *f*
visionary *n* neach le lèirsinn *m a* lèirsinneach
visit *n* tadhal *m*, cèilidh *f m v* tadhail, dèan cèilidh
visitor *n* neach-tadhail *m*, aoigh *m*, cèiliche *m*
visor *n* cidhis *f*
vista *n* sealladh *m*
visual *a* fradharcach, lèirsinne
visualize *v* dèan samhla sùla, dèan dealbh san inntinn
vital *a* beò, beathail; (*important*) ro chudromach
vitality *n* beathalachd *f*
vitamin *n* beothaman *m*
vitriol *n* (*acid*) searbhag loisgeach *f*; (*rancour*) nimhealachd *f*
vituperation *n* aithiseachadh *m*
vivacious *a* aigeannach, beothail
vivid *a* beò, boillsgeanta
vixen *n* sionnach boireann *m*
viz *adv* is e sin, 's e sin ri ràdh
vocabulary *n* (*of person*) stòr fhaclan *m*, (*glossary*) faclair *m*
vocal *a* guthach; (*outspoken*) àrd-ghuthach
vocation *n* (*work*) dreuchd *f*, ceàird *f*; (*calling*) gairm beatha *f*
vocative *a* gairmeach **v. case** an tuiseal gairmeach *m*
vociferous *a* sgairteach

vodka *n* bhodca *m*
vogue *n* fasan *m* **in v.** san fhasan
voice *n* guth *m v* cuir am briathran/an cèill
void *n* fàsalachd *f*; (*outer space*) fànas *m a* falamh, fàs
volatile *a* cugallach, caochlaideach, luaineach
volcano *n* beinn-theine *f*, b(h)olcàno *m*
volition *n* toil *f*
volley *n* (*of gun*) làdach *m*; (*sport*) bhòilidh *f*
volleyball *n* ball-làmhaich *m*
volt *n* bholt(a) *m*
voltage *n* bholtaids *f*, bholtachd *f*
voluble *a* sruth-chainnteach
volume *n* (*book*) leabhar *m*; (*capacity*) tomhas-lìonaidh *m*; (*size*) tomad *m*
voluntary *a* saor-thoileach **v. organization** buidheann s(h)aor-thoileach *f m*
volunteer *n* saor-thoileach *m v* tairg
voluptuous *a* (*shape*) làn-chumadail
vomit(ing) *n* cur a-mach *m*, sgeith *m*, dìobhairt *m v* cuir a-mach, sgeith, dìobhair
voracious *a* cìocrach, gionach, craosach
vote *n* bhòt(a) *f* **postal v.** bhòt(a) tron phost *v* bhòt
voter *n* neach-bhòtaidh *m*, bhòtair *m*
voting *n* bhòtadh *m* **v. system** siostam/modh bhòtaidh *m*
vouch *v* dearbh, thoir fianais
voucher *n* bileag fianais *f*, bileag-theist *f*
vow *n* bòid *f*, gealladh *m v* bòidich, mionnaich
vowel *n* fuaimreag *f*
voyage *n* turas-mara *m*, bhòidse *f*
vulgar *a* mì-chneasta, gràisgeil
vulnerable *a* (*to attack*) fosgailte (gu ionnsaigh); (*person*) so-leònte, dualach *a* g(h)oirteachadh *etc*
vulture *n* fang *f*

W

wade *v* grunnaich
wafer *n* abhlan *m*, slisneag *f*
waffle *n* (*met*) baoth-chòmhradh *m*, cainnt gun bhrìgh *f*

wag *n* àbhachdaiche *m*, sgeigire *m*
wage(s) *n* tuarastal *m*, duais *f*
wager *n* geall *m v* cuir geall, rach an urras

wagtail n breac-an-t-sìl m, breacan-buidhe m
wail(ing) n caoineadh m, gal m, burralaich f
waist n meadhan m
waistcoat n siosacot m, peitean m
wait n feitheamh m, stad m **they had a long w.** bha iad fada a' feitheamh v fuirich, feith, fan; (*serve*) fritheil
waiting-list n liosta-feitheimh f
waiting-room n seòmar-feitheimh m
waiter n fear-frithealaidh m
waitress n tè-fhrithealaidh f
waive v cuir an dàrna taobh
wake n faire f, taigh-fhaire m
wake(n) v dùisg
walk n cuairt f, ceum m v coisich, gabh ceum
walking-stick n bata m
wall n balla m; (*dyke*) gàrradh m
wallet n leabhar-pòcaid m
wallpaper n pàipear(-balla) m, bolt m v pàipearaich, boltaig
walnut n gall-chnò f
walrus n each-mara m, uàlras m
wand n slat f, slatag f
wander v rach air shiubhal; (*go astray*) rach air seachran; (*in mind*) rach iomrall
wanderer n siùbhlaiche m
wane v lùghdaich, crìon, searg
want n (*lack*) easbhaidh f, dìth f m; (*poverty*) bochdainn f v iarr; (*lack*) bi a dh'easbhaidh (+ *gen*)
wanton a drùiseil; (*reckless*) dalma
war n cogadh m **war memorial** cuimhneachan-cogaidh m v cog, cathaich
ward n (*hospital*) uàrd m; (*division*) roinn f **w. of court** neach fo chùram (cùrtach) m
warden n neach-gleidhidh m
warder n neach-faire m
wardrobe n preas-aodaich m
warehouse n taigh-bathair m
warfare n cogadh m
warm a blàth; (*personality*) coibhneil v blàthaich, gar
warmth n blàths m; (*personality*) tlàths m

warn v thoir rabhadh (do)
warning n rabhadh m
warp v claon, seac
warrant(y) n barantas m
warren n broclach f, toll m
warrior n laoch m, gaisgeach m, curaidh m
warship n long-chogaidh f
wart n foinne f m
wary a faiceallach, cùramach
was v bha (*See verb* **to be** *in Grammar*)
wash n nighe m, glanadh m, ionnlad m v nigh, ionnlaid
washer n (*mech*) cearclan m
washing n nigheadaireachd f
  w. machine inneal-nigheadaireachd m
  w.-powder fùdar nigheadaireachd m
  w.-up-liquid stuth-nighe shoithichean m
wasp n speach f, connspeach f
waste n (*misuse*) ana-caitheamh m; (*destruction*) sgrios m; (*rubbish*) sgudal m **w. of time** cosg tìde/ùine m **w.-paper basket** basgaid sgudail f a fàs v dèan mì-fheum de, dèan ana-caitheanaich; (*spoil*) mill
wasteful a caitheach, strùidheil
wasteland n talamh fàs m, àite fàsail m
waster n strùidhear m; (*slang*) duine gun fheum m
watch n faire f, caithris f; (*timepiece*) uaireadair m v cùm sùil air; (*TV etc*) coimhead; (*be careful*) thoir an aire **keep w.** v dèan/cùm faire, caithris
watchman n neach-faire m
water n uisge m, bùrn m **w. level** àird(e) an uisge f **w.-lily** duilleag-bhàthte f **w.-mill** muileann-uisge f m **w.-pipe** pìob-uisge f v uisgich, fliuch
watercress n biolaire f
waterfall n eas m
waterproof a uisge-dhìonach
watershed n (*geog*) druim-uisge m; (*met*) àm/adhbhar-tionndaidh m
watertight a dìonach
waulking n luadh m, luadhadh m **w. song** òran-luaidh m
wave n tonn m, stuagh f
wave v crath **w. (to)** smèid (ri)

waveband *n* bann *m* **Medium Wave** am Bann Meadhain

wavelength *n* bann *m* **on the same w.** air an aon ràmh

wavy *a* (*hair*) dualach

wax *n* cèir *f* *v* cèirich, cuir cèir air; (*grow*) fàs

way *n* (*route*) slighe *f*, rathad *m*; (*method*) dòigh *f* **w. of life** dòigh-beatha *f*

waylay *v* dèan feall-fhalach

wayward *a* claon, fiarach, frithearra

we *pron* sinn, (*emph*) sinne

weak *a* lag, fann, anfhann, lapach

weaken *v* lagaich; (*intrans*) fannaich

weakling *n* lagaich *m*, meathach *m*

weakness *n* laigse *f*, anfhannachd *f*

wealth *n* beairteas *m*, saidhbhreas *m*, ionmhas *m*

wealthy *a* beairteach, saidhbhir

wean *v* cuir bhàrr na cìche

weapon *n* ball-airm *m*, inneal-cogaidh *m*

wear *v* (*clothes*) caith, cuir umad/ort **w. out** cosg

weariness *n* sgìths *f m*, claoidh *f*

weary *a* sgìth, claoidhte *v* sgìthich, claoidh, sàraich **w. for** gabh fadachd ri

weasel *n* neas *f*

wed *v* pòs

wedder *n* molt *m*

wedding *n* banais *f*, pòsadh *m* **w. day** latha na bainnse *m*

wedge *n* geinn *m* *v* cuir geinn an

Wednesday *n* Diciadain *m*

wee *a* beag

weed *n* luibh *f m* *v* glan, priog

weedkiller *n* puinnsean luibhean *m*

week *n* seachdain *f* **this w. (coming)** an t-s. seo/sa (tighinn) **last w.** an t-s. seo/sa chaidh

weekend *n* deireadh seachdain *m*

weekly *a* gach seachdain, seachdaineach *adv* gach seachdain

weep *v* caoin, guil, dèan caoineadh/gal

weeping *n* caoineadh *m*, gal *m*, gul *m*

weigh *v* cothromaich, cuir air mheidh, tomhais **w. up** breithnich **w. anchor** tog acair

weight *n* cudthrom *m*, cuideam *m*, truimead *m* **lose w.** *v* caill cuideam

weird *a* air leth neònach

welcome *n* fàilte *f*, furan *m* *a* di-beathte; (*of development*) ris an dèanar toileachadh **you're w.** 's e do bheatha *v* (*person*) cuir fàilte air, fàiltich; (*development(s)*) dèan toileachadh ri

---

Insight: welcome

Fàilte is a well-known Gaelic word seen in signs in Highland towns like Oban where *Fàilte don Òban* means Welcome to Oban. You also find signs with *Ceud Mìle Fàilte* which are even more welcoming indicating 100,000 Welcomes! The word *Fàilte* is also known in Ireland, as in Bord Fáilte, the Irish Tourist Board.

---

weather *n* aimsir *f*, sìde *f* **w. forecast** tuairmse sìde *f* **under the w.** gun a bhith ann an sunnd *v* (*met*) seas ri, cùm ri; (*geol*) caith, caoinich

weave *v* figh

weaver *n* breabadair *m*, figheadair *m*

weaving *n* breabadaireachd *f*, figheadaireachd *f*

web *n* lìon *m*, eige *f* **the World-Wide Web** Lìon na Cruinne *m*

website *n* làrach-lìn *f m*

weld *v* tàth

welding *n* tàthadh *m*

welfare *n* sochair *f*, math *m* **w. state** stàit shochairean *f*

well *n* tobar *f m*, fuaran *m*

well *a* math, gasta; (*of health*) fallain *adv* gu math

well-behaved *a* modhail

well-dressed *a* spaideil, leòmach

well-informed *a* fiosrach

wellington *n* bòtann *f m*

well-known *a* ainmeil, iomraiteach
Welsh *a* Cuimreach *n* (*lang*) Cuimris *f*
Welshman *n* Cuimreach *m*
  Welshwoman ban-Chuimreach *f*
were *v* bha (*See verb* **to be** *in Grammar*)
west *n* an iar *f*, an àird an iar *f* **the w.**
  side an taobh siar *m a* siar *adv* an iar
westerly *a* on iar, às an àird an iar
western *a* siar **the W. Isles** na
  h-Eileanan Siar/an Iar
wet *a* fliuch *v* fliuch
whale *n* muc-mhara *f*
what *int* dè? *rel pron* an rud *a*; (*all that*)
  na *exclam* abair …! **w. a crowd!** abair
  sluagh!
whatever *pron* às bith, ge b'·e air bith,
  ge brith *a* sam bith
wheat *n* cruithneachd *f m*
wheel *n* cuibheall *f*, cuibhle *f*, roth *m* **w.-**
  house taigh-cuibhle *m*, taigh na cuibhle
  m v (*trans*) cuibhil, ruidhil; (*intrans*)
  tionndaidh mun cuairt **wheelbarrow**
  bara(-roth) *m* **wheelchair** sèithear-
  cuibhle *m*, cathair-chuibhle *f*
wheeze *n* pìochan, sèitean *m v* dèan
  pìochan, bi a' sèiteanaich
whelk *n* faochag *f*
when *int* cuin? *conj* nuair (a), an uair (a)
whence *adv* cò às, cò bhuaithe
whenever *adv* gach uair, ge b' e uair, àm
  sam bith
where *int* càite? *rel pron* far, san àite
  san
whereas *conj* ach; (*since*) a chionn
  ('s gu)
whereby *conj* leis, leis an do
wherever *adv* ge b' e càite, às bith càite,
  ge brith càite
whereupon *adv* le sin, leis a sin
whet *v* geuraich, faobharaich; (*appetite*)
  brod càil
whether *conj* co-dhiù, a/an/am (+ *v*)
which *int* cò, cò aca? *rel pron* a; (*neg*)
  nach
whichever *pron* ge b' e cò, às bith cò, ge
  brith cò
whiff *n* aithneachadh (fàil(e)idh) *m*; (*air*)
  oiteag *f*

while *n* treis *f*, greis *f*, tacan *m v* cuir
  seachad (an) ùine *adv* fhad 's, am feadh 's
whim *n* badhg *f*, badhgaid *f*, saobh-
  smaoin *f*
whimper *n* cnead *m*, sgiùgan *m*
whin *n* conasg *m*
whine *v* caoin, dèan caoidhearan;
  (*complain*) sìor ghearan
whinge *v* dèan cànran
whingeing *a* cànranach
whip *n* cuip *f v* cuip, sgiùrs
whiphand *n* làmh-an-uachda(i)r *f*
whirl *n* cuairt *f*, cuartag *f*
whirligig *n* gille-mirein *m*
whirlpool *n* ioma-shruth *m*, cuairt-shruth *m*
whirlwind *n* ioma-ghaoth *f*
whisk *v* sguab, sgiot, cuir mun cuairt
whisky *n* uisge-beatha *m*
whisper *n* cagar *m*, sanais *m v* cagair,
  cuir cagar
whispering *n* cagarsaich *f*,
  sainnsearachd *f*
whistle *n* fead *f*; (*mus*) feadag *f*, fìdeag *f*
  v dèan fead/feadaraich
white *a* geal; (*pale*) bàn **w.-board** bòrd-
  geal *m* **W. Paper** Pàipear Geal *m*
whitewash *n* aol-uisg(e) *m*, gealachadh
  m; (*met*) dreach eile/glan *m v* gealaich;
  (*met*) cuir dreach eile/glan air
whiting *n* cuidhteag *f*
who *int pron* cò? *rel pron* a; (*neg*) nach
whoever *pron* ge b' e cò, às bith cò, ge
  brith cò; neach sam bith *int pron* cò idir?
whole *a* slàn, iomlan, uile, gu lèir;
  (*healthy*) fallain
wholehearted *a* làn-(+ *a*), le *a* (h-)uile
  etc chridhe
wholesale *n* mòr-dhìol *m*, mòr-reic *m*
wholesome *a* slàn, fallain
wholly *adv* gu h-iomlan/buileach
whooping cough *n* an triuthach *f*
whose *int pron* cò leis?
why *int* carson? *adv* carson
wick *n* siobhag *f*, buaic *f*
wicked *a* olc, aingidh
wickedness *n* olc *m*, aingidheachd *f*
wide *a* farsaing, leathann **w.-ranging**
  farsaing

widely *adv* fad' is farsaing

widen *v* leudaich; (*intrans only*) fàs farsaing

widespread *a* (*common*) bitheanta, fad' is farsaing

widow(er) *n* banntrach *f* (*m*)

width *n* leud *m*

wield *v* làimhsich, obraich

wife *n* bean *f*, bean-phòsta *f*

wig *n* gruag *f*, pioraraig *f*

wild *a* fiadhaich, allaidh

wilderness *n* fàsach *m*

wildlife *n* fiadh-bheatha *f*

wile *n* cuilbheart *f*, car *m*

wilful *a* fada na c(h)eann *etc*, ceann-làidir

will *n* toil *f*, rùn *m*, deòin *f*; (*leg*) tiomnadh *m*

willing *a* deònach, toileach

willingly *a* gu deònach/toileach

willow *n* seileach *m*

willy-nilly *adv* a dheòin no (a) dh'aindeoin

wily *a* seòlta, carach

win *v* buannaich, coisinn, buinnig

wind *n* gaoth *f*; (*breath*) anail *f*
w. direction àird na gaoithe *f*

wind *v* (*around*) suain, toinn, fill; (*clock*) rothaig **w. up** thoir gu crìch; (*tease*) bi a' tarraing à

windfall *n* (*fin*) clabag *f*

winding *a* lùbach, cam, cama-lùbach

windmill *n* muileann-gaoithe *f m*

window *n* uinneag *f* **w.-pane** l(e)òsan (uinneige) *m* **w.-sill** sòl uinneige *m*

windpipe *n* pìob-sgòrnain *f*

windscreen *n* sgùl *m*, sgàile-gaoithe *m*

windsurfing *n* marcachd thonn *f*

windward *n* fuaradh *m*, taobh an fhuaraidh *m*

windy *a* gaothach, gailbheach, garbh

wine *n* fìon *m* **red w.** fìon dearg **white w.** fìon geal **w.-list** clàr-fìona *m*

wing *n* sgiath *f*

wink *n* priobadh *m*, caogadh *m*, sùil bheag *f v* priob, caog, dèan sùil bheag

winner *n* neach-buannachaidh *m*, buadhaiche *m*

winnow *v* fasgain

winter *n* an geamhradh *m v* geamhraich

wintry *a* geamhrachail

wipe *v* suath **w. off** glan dheth

wiper *n* suathair *m*

wire *n* uèir *f*, teud *m* **barbed w.** uèir-bhiorach/stobach *f*

wiry *a* seang

wisdom *n* gliocas *m*

wise *a* glic

wish *n* miann *f m*, toil *f*, togradh *m*, dùrachd *f v* miannaich, togair, luthaig, rùnaich

wisp *n* sop *m*

wistful *a* cianail, tiamhaidh

wit *n* eirmseachd *f*, geur-labhairt *f*; (*sense*) toinisg *f*

witch *n* bana-bhuidseach *f*

witchcraft *n* buidseachd *f*

with *prep* le, cuide ri, còmhla ri, leis (+ *art*)

withdraw *v* thoir air ais/falbh, tarraing a-mach/air ais

wither *v* searg, seac, crìon

withered *a* seargte, seacte, crìon

withhold *v* cùm air ais

within *adv* a-staigh *prep* taobh a-staigh (+ *gen*)

without *prep* gun, às aonais (+ *gen*)

withstand *v* seas ri

witness *a* (*abstr*) fianais *f v* thoir fianais

witty *a* eirmseach, geur

wizard *n* buidseach *m*, draoidh *m*

woeful *a* muladach, truagh

wolf *n* madadh-allaidh *m*

woman *n* bean *f*, boireannach *m*

womb *n* machlag *f*, bolg *m*, brù *f*

wonder *n* iongnadh *m*, iongantas *m v* gabh iongantas

wonderful *a* iongantach

woo *v* bi a' suirghe (air)

wood *n* fiodh *m*; (*forest*) coille *f*

wooden *a* fiodha

woodland *n* fearann coillteach *m*

woodpecker *n* snagan-daraich *m*

woodwork *n* saorsainneachd *f*

woodworm *n* (*insect*) raodan *m*; (*condition*) raodanas *m*

wool n clòimh f, olann f; (knitting) snàth m
woollen a clòimhe
woolly a clòimhe; (met) ceòthach, doilleir
word n facal m; (promise) gealladh m **w. for w.** facal air an fhacal **w. processing** rianachadh fhaclan m **w.-processor** rianadair fhaclan m
work n obair f, saothair f **workforce** luchd-obrach m **workshop** bùth-obrach f v obraich, saothraich
worker n obraiche m, neach-obrach m
working-party n buidheann-obrach f m
works n (place) ionad-obrach m **gasworks** ionad a' ghas m
world n saoghal m, cruinne m (f in gen)
worldly a saoghalta
worm n boiteag f, cnuimh f, durrag f
worn a caithte, breòite
worried a draghail, fo iomagain, fo chùram
worry n dragh m, iomagain f, cùram m v dèan dragh do, cuir dragh/iomnaidh air **I w. too much** bidh cus cùraim orm (mu rudan)
worse a nas miosa
worsen v fàs nas miosa
worship n adhradh m **family w.** adhradh teaghlaich, gabhail an Leabhair m v dèan adhradh Also vn ag adhradh
worst a as miosa
worth n fiach m, luach m a fiù, airidh air **it is not w. bothering about** chan fhiach/cha d' fhiach bodraigeadh mu dheidhinn
worthless a gun luach, gun fhiù
worthy a airidh, fiùghail, fiachail
wound n lot m, leòn m, creuchd f v leòn, lot

wounded a leònte
wounding a guineach
wrangle v connsaich, troid
wrap v paisg, fill **w. around** suain
wrapping paper n pàipear-còmhdaich m
wrath n corraich f, fearg f
wreath n blàth-fhleasg f
wreck n (naut) long-bhriste f; (of a person or article) ablach m v sgrios, mill
wren n dreathan-donn m
wrench v spìon
wrest v tarraing (bh)o
wrestle v bi a' carachd, gleac
wrestler n caraiche m, gleacadair m
wrestling n carachd f, gleac m
wretch n truaghan m
wretched a truagh, àmhgharach
wriggle v rach an lùban, toinneamhaich
wring v fàisg
wrinkle n preas m, roc f
wrinkled a preasach, liorcach, rocach
wrist n caol an dùirn m **wristband** bann dùirn m **wristwatch** uaireadair làimhe m
writ n sgrìobhainn-cùirte/cùrtach f
write v sgrìobh **w. up** dèan cunntas air **w. off** meas gun luach, dubh às
writer n sgrìobhadair m, sgrìobhaiche m
writhe v snìomh, bi gad aonagraich fhèin
writing n sgrìobhadh m **w.-paper** pàipear-sgrìobhaidh m
written a sgrìobhte
wrong n coire f, eucoir f, euceart m a ceàrr; (culpable) coireach, eucorach v dèan eucoir air
wry a cam, fiar, claon

X

xenophobia n gamhlas do choigrich m
Xmas n an Nollaig f

x-ray n x-ghath m a x-ghathach v x-ghathaich
xylophone n saidhleafòn m

Insight: xylophone
X is one of the letters of the English alphabet which does not feature in the Gaelic alphabet. Words with an X in the middle or at the end in English have a -gs- in Gaelic eg *bogsa*, a box. Words with an x at the beginning have s as in *saidhleafòn*, xylophone.

Y

yacht n sgoth-seòlaidh f, gheat f
yak n iac m
yank v spìon
yap v (dog) dèan comhart; (talk) bleadraig
yard n slat f; (enclosure) gàrradh m, lios f
  yardstick slat-t(h)omhais f
yarn n snàth m; (story) sgeulachd f,
  naidheachd f
yawn n mèaran m, mèanan m v bi a'/
  dèan mèaranaich/mèananaich Also vn
  a' mèaranaich, a' mèananaich
yawning n mèaranaich f, mèananaich f
year n bliadhna f this y. am-bliadhna
  next y. an-ath-bhliadhna last y. an-
  uiridh the y. before last a' bhòn-uiridh
  Happy New Y.! Bliadhna Mhath Ùr!
yearn v miannaich gu làidir, bi fo
  fhadachd airson
yearning n iarraidh f m, fadachd f
yeast n beirm f
yell n glaodh m, sgal m, sgairt f v glaodh
yellow n, a buidhe m
yelp n sgiamh f m; (of dog) tathann m v
  dèan sgiamh; (dog) dèan tathann
yes adv a Yes answer is represented by
  the positive form of the verb used in a
  question, eg a bheil thu sgìth? tha
  an e saor a th' ann? 's e am faca tu an
  gèam? chunnaic; (in agreement) seadh
yesterday adv an-dè the day before y.
  a' bhòn-dè

yet conj an dèidh sin, ach adv fhathast
  yet again aon uair eile
yew n iubhar m
yield n toradh m v thoir a-mach toradh;
  (submit) gèill, strìochd
yoga n iòga f
yoghurt n iogart f m
yoke n (phys, met) cuing f v (ready)
  beairtich; (oppress) cuingich
yolk (of egg) n buidheagan m
yon(der) adv thall, ud, an siud
you pron thu, (emph) thusa, (pl & pol)
  sibh, (emph) sibhse
young a òg **younger than** nas òige na
  youngest as òige n àl (òg) m; (people)
  òigridh f
youngster n òganach m
your poss pron do, d', t', (pl & pol)
  bhur, ur
yours poss pron leat, (emph) leatsa,
  (pl & pol) leibh, (emph) leibhse
yourself pron thu fhèin, (pl & pol) sibh
  fhèin, sib' fhèin
youth n (abstr) òige f; (person) òigear
  m, òganach m; (coll) òigridh f y. centre
  ionad-òigridh m y. club club òigridh m,
  buidheann-òigridh f m y. hostel ostail
  òigridh m
youthful a òg, ògail
Yuch/Yuck exclam (A) ghia!
Yule n Nollaig f

Insight: you

Gaelic, like French, employs two forms of the pronoun you. *Thu* is the form used when you know someone well while *sibh* is used in more formal situations and when being polite. Therefore, you would ask a friend how (s)he is with *ciamar a tha thu?* but say *ciamar a tha sibh?* to a stranger.

Z

zany a cleasach, àraid
zeal n eud m, dealas m
zealot n eudmhoraiche m

zealous a eudmhor, dealasach
zebra n seabra m z. crossing trast-rathad
  seabra m

zenith *n* bàrr *m*

zero *n* neoni *f* **z. tolerance** nach ceadaich an cron as lugha

zest *n* fonn *m*, sunnd *m*

zigzag *a* cam-fhiarach

zinc *n* sinc *m*

zip *n* siop *m*

zodiac *n* grian-chrios *m*, crios na grèine *m*

zone *n* raon *m*, ceàrn *f*, sòn *m*; (*geog*) bann *m*, crios *m* *v* suidhich raon/sòn

zoo *n* sù *m*, sutha *f*

zoologist *n* ainmh-eòlaiche *m*

zoology *n* ainmh-eòlas *m*

zoom *v* falbh le roid

Insight: zoo

Like x, z does not feature in the Gaelic alphabet. Words with an initial z such as zoo and zone are spelt with an s in Gaelic. Thus, *sù* or *sutha* is a zoo and *sòn* is a zone. You can guess what *seabra* and *sinc* are!

Personal names

Surnames **Sloinnidhean**

The forms of surnames for women and men differ from each other in Gaelic. Where a man's surname begins with **Mac**, a woman's begins with **Nic**. Thus, **Dòmhnall MacLeòid** (Donald MacLeod) but **Oighrig NicLeòid** (Effie MacLeod). With surnames other than those beginning with **Mac/Nic**, the female form of the noun is lenited. Thus, **Seumas Caimbeul** (James Campbell) but **Màiri Chaimbeul** (Mary Campbell).

As will be seen below, there is more than one Gaelic version of some names, one with **Mac/Nic** and one without, like **MacFhearghais/ Fearghasdan** (Ferguson). In addition, a form in **-ach** is often used when the person's surname and not his personal name is being used, eg **'Chunnaic mi an Granndach an-diugh'** ('I saw Grant today'). This practice is much less common with the surnames of women, but on the rare occasions on which it would be used, the female equivalent would be **'a' bhan(a)-Ghranndach'**. In the case of a few names, this form is as common or commoner in speech than the **Mac/Nic** form is, and so it has has been listed below in addition to the other form.

For convenience, the English names have all been spelt with a capital after Mac, but it is recognized that there are many variations on this, and also in other aspects (MacNeil/MacNeill etc). The same is true of Gaelic names, especially those which have the element **gille** (lad, servant) in them. Here we have rendered that element as **Ille** or **Ill**.

Beaton	*Peutan*	MacCorquodale	*MacCòrcadail,*
Black	*MacIlleDhuibh*		*MacThòrcadail*
Boyd	*Boidhd*	MacCrimmon	*MacCruimein*
Bruce	*Brus, Brusach*	MacDonald	*MacDhòmhnaill,*
Buchanan	*Bochanan*		*Dòmhnallach*
		MacDougall	*MacDhùghaill,*
Cameron	*Camshron*		*Dùghlach*
Campbell	*Caimbeul*	MacEachen	*MacEachainn*
Chisholm	*Siosal, Siosalach*	MacEachern,	*MacEacharna*
Cunningham	*Conaigean*	MacKechnie	
		MacFadyen	*MacPhàidein*
Douglas	*Dùghlas*	MacFarlane	*MacPhàrlain*
		MacGillivray	*MacIlleBhràth*
Ferguson	*Fearghasdan,*	MacGregor	*MacGriogair*
	MacFhearghais	MacInnes	*MacAonghais*
Finlayson	*Fionnlasdan,*	MacIntosh	*Mac an Tòisich*
	MacFhionnlaigh	MacIntyre	*Mac an t-Saoir*
Fraser	*Friseal*	MacIver	*MacÌomhair*
		MacKay	*MacAoidh*
Gillies	*MacIllÌosa*	MacKenzie	*MacCoinnich*
Graham	*Greum,*	MacKerlich	*MacTheàrlaich*
	Greumach	MacKinlay	*MacFhionnlaigh*
Grant	*Grannd*	MacKinnon	*MacFhionghain*
		MacLean	*MacIllEathain*
Henderson	*MacEanraig*	MacLellan	*MacIllFhaolain,*
			MacIllFhialain
Johnson	*MacIain*	MacLennan	*MacIllFhinnein*
		MacLeod	*MacLeòid*
Kennedy	*Ceanadach,*	MacMillan	*MacIlleMhaoil,*
	MacUalraig		*Mac a' Mhaoilein*
Kerr	*MacIlleChiar*	MacNab	*Mac an Aba*
		MacNeil	*MacNèill*
MacAllister	*MacAlasdair*	MacPhail	*MacPhàil*
MacArthur	*MacArtair*	MacPhee	*Mac-a-phì*
MacAskill	*MacAsgaill*	MacPherson	*Mac a' Phearsain*
MacAulay	*MacAmhlaigh*	MacQuarrie	*MacGuaire*
MacBain	*MacBheathain*	MacRae	*MacRath*
MacBeth	*MacBheatha*	MacRitchie	*MacRisnidh*

MacSween	*MacSuain*	Nicolson,	*MacNeacail*
MacTaggart	*Mac an t-Sagairt*	MacNicol	
MacVicar	*Mac a' Phiocair*		
MacVurich,	*MacMhuirich*	Robertson	*Robasdan,*
Currie			*MacDhonnchaidh*
Martin	*Màrtainn*	Ross	*Ros*
Matheson	*MacMhathain*		
	Matasanach	Smith	*Mac a' Ghobhainn*
Montgomery	*MacGumaraid*	Taylor	*Mac an Tàilleir*
Morrison	*Moireasdan,*	Thomson	*MacThòmais*
	MacIlleMhoire		
Munro	*Rothach, Mac an*	Urquhart	*Urchardan*
	Rothaich		
Murray	*Moireach*	Whyte	*MacIlleBhàin*

First names **Ciad ainmean**

Some of the names below are not etymologically related in the way that Alan and **Ailean** are but are used as equivalents, eg Claire/**Sorcha** and Kenneth/**Coinneach**.

Agnes	*Ùna*	Beth	*Beathag*
Alan	*Ailean*	Betty	*Beitidh*
Alasdair, Alexander	*Alasdair*		
Alec, Alex, Alick	*Ailig*	Cal(l)um, Malcolm	*Calum*
Alice	*Ailios, Ailis*	Catherine, Katherine	*Catrìona*
Andrew	*Anndra*	Cathleen, Kathleen	*Caitlin*
Angus	*Aonghas*	Charles	*Teàrlach*
Ann(e), Anna	*Anna, Annag*	Chrissie	*Crìosaidh,*
Archibald	*Gilleasbaig*		*Ciorstag*
Archie	*Eàirdsidh*	Christine, Christina	*Cairistìona,*
Arthur	*Artair*		*Ciorstag*
		Christoper	*Crìsdean*
Barbara	*Barabal*	Claire	*Sorcha*
Bessie	*Beasag*	Colin	*Cailean*

David	*Daibhidh*	Jack, Jock	*Seoc*
Deirdre	*Deirdre*	James	*Seumas*
Derek, Der(r)ick	*Ruairidh*	Jane	*Sìne*
Diarmid, Dermot	*Diarma(i)d*	Janet	*Seònaid*
Dolina, Dolly	*Doileag,*	Jessie	*Seasaidh*
	Doilìona,	Joan	*Seonag*
	Doilidh	John	*Iain, Seonaidh*
Donald	*Dòmhnall*	Johnny	*Seonaidh*
Donnie	*Donaidh*	Joseph	*Eòsaph, Iòsaph*
Douglas	*Dùghlas*	Julia	*Sìleas*
Duncan	*Donnchadh*		
		Kate	*Ceit, Ceiteag*
Edward	*Eideard, Ìomhar*	Katie	*Ceitidh,*
Effie, Euphemia	*Oighrig*		*Ceiteag*
Elizabeth	*Ealasaid*	Kenna	*Ceana*
Ewan, Ewen	*Eògha(i)nn*	Kenneth	*Coinneach*
		Kieran, Kieron	*Ciaran*
Farquhar	*Fearchar*	Kirsty	*Ciorstaidh*
Fergus	*Fearghas*		
Finlay	*Fionnlagh*	Lachlan	*Lachla(i)nn,*
Flora	*Flòraidh,*		*Lachann*
	Fionnghal		
		Maggie	*Magaidh*
George	*Seòras, Deòrsa*	Margaret	*Mai(gh)read*
Gilbert	*Gille-Brìghde*	Marion	*Mòr*
Gillespie	*Gilleasbaig*	Marjory	*Marsaili*
Gordon	*Gòrdan*	Mark	*Marc*
Graham	*Greum*	Martin	*Màrtainn*
		Mary	*Màiri*
Hector	*Eacha(i)nn*	May	*Màili*
Helen	*Eilidh*	Michael	*Mìcheal*
Henry	*Eanraig*	Morag	*Mòrag*
Hugh	*Ùisdean, Aodh,*	Murdo	*Murchadh*
	Eòghann	Myles	*Maoilios,*
			Maoileas
Ia(i)n	*Iain*		
Innes	*Aonghas*	Nancy	*Nansaidh*
Isobel, Ishbel	*Iseabail*	Neil, Niall	*Niall*
Ivor	*Ìomhar*	Norman	*Tormod*

Patrick	*Pàdraig*	Sheena	*Sìne*
Paul	*Pòl*	Sheila	*Sìle*
Peggy	*Peigi*	Stephen, Steven	*Steaphan*
Peter	*Peadar, Pàdraig*	Stewart	*Stiùbhart*
		Susan	*Siùsaidh*
Rachel	*Raonaid, Raghnaid*	Thomas	*Tòmas*
Ranald, Ronald	*Raghnall*	Torquil	*Torca(i)ll*
Robert	*Raibeart, Rob*		
Roderick	*Ruairidh*	Una	*Ùna*
Roy	*Ruadh*		
Ruth	*Rut*	William	*Uilleam*
Samuel, Sorley	*Somhairle*		
Sara(h)	*Sàra, Mòr*		

Place names

Aberdeen	*Obar Dheathain*	the Borders	*Na Crìochan*
Aberfeldy	*Obar Pheallaidh*	Bosnia	*Bosnia*
Aberfoyle	*Obar Phuill*	Bowmore	*Bogha Mòr*
Africa	*Afraga*	Braemar	*Bràigh Mhàrr*
Airdrie	*Àrd Ruighe*	Britain	*Breata(i)nn*
Albania	*Albàinia*	Brittany	*A' Bhreata(i)nn*
America	*Ameireaga(idh)*		*Bheag*
Argyll	*Earra-Ghàidheal*	Brussels	*A' Bhruiseal*
Arran	*Arainn*	Bulgaria	*Bulgàiria*
Asia	*(An) Àisia*	Bute	*Bòd*
the Atlantic	*An Cuan Siar*		
Ocean		the Cairngorms	*Am Monadh*
Athens	*Baile na h-Àithne*		*Ruadh*
Australia	*Astràilia*	Caithness	*Gallaibh*
Austria	*An Ostair*	Callander	*Calasraid*
Aviemore	*An Aghaidh Mhòr*	Campbeltown	*Ceann Loch (Chille*
Ayr	*Inbhir Àir*		*Chiarain)*
		Canada	*Canada*
Badenoch	*Bàideanach*	Canna	*Canaigh*
Ballachulish	*Bail' a' Chaolais*	Cape Breton	*Ceap Breatann*
Balmoral	*Baile Mhoireil*	Castlebay	*Bàgh a' Chaisteil*
Bannockburn	*Allt a' Bhonnaich*	Coll	*Col(l)a*
Barra	*Barraigh*	Colonsay	*Colbhasaigh*
Beauly	*A' Mhanachainn*	China	*Sìona*
Belfast	*Beul Feirste*	Cornwall	*A' Chòrn*
Belgium	*A' Bheilg*	Craignure	*Creag an Iubhair*
Benbecula	*Beinn na Fadhla/*	Crieff	*Craoibh*
	Beinn a' Bhadhla	Croatia	*Croatia*
Ben Nevis	*Beinn Nibheis*	Cromarty	*Cromba(i)dh*
Bernera(y)	*Beàrnaraigh*	the Cuillins	*An Cuilitheann*
Berwick	*Bearaig*	Culloden	*Cùil Lodair*
the Black Isle	*An t-Eilean Dubh*	Cumbernauld	*Comar nan Allt*
Blair Atholl	*Blàr (an) Athaill*	Czech Republic	*Poblachd na Seic*

Denmark	*An Danmhairg*	Gigha	*Giogha*
Dingwall	*Inbhir Pheofharain*	Glasgow	*Glaschu*
Dublin	*Baile Àtha Cliath*	Glencoe	*Gleann(a) Comhann*
Dumbarton	*Dùn Breatann*	Glenfinnan	*Gleann Fhionghain*
Dunfermline	*Dùn Phàrlain*	Golspie	*Goillspidh*
Dumfries	*Dùn Phris*	Greece	*A' Ghrèig*
Dunblane	*Dùn Blathain*	Greenock	*Grianaig*
Dundee	*Dùn Dèagh*		
Dunkeld	*Dùn Chailleann*	Harris	*Na Hearadh*
Dunoon	*Dùn Omhain*	the Hebrides	*Innse Gall*
Dunvegan	*Dùn Bheagain*	Helmsdale	*Bun Ilidh*
		the Highlands	*A' Ghàidhealtachd*
East Kilbride	*Cille Bhrìghde an*	Holland	*An Òlaind*
	Ear	Hungary	*An Ungair*
Edinburgh	*Dùn Èideann*	Huntly	*Hunndaidh*
Egypt	*An Èipheit*		
Eigg	*Eige*	Iceland	*Innis Tìle*
Elgin	*Eilginn*	India	*Na h-Innseachan*
England	*Sasa(i)nn*	Inveraray	*Inbhir Aora*
Eriskay	*Èirisgeigh*	Invergordon	*Inbhir Ghòrdain*
Estonia	*Estòinia*	Inverness	*Inbhir Nis*
Europe	*An Roinn Eòrpa*	Iona	*Ì (Chaluim*
			Chille)
Falkirk	*An Eaglais*	Iran	*Iran, Ioran*
	Bhreac	Iraq	*Iraq, Iorag*
Fife	*Fìobha*	Ireland	*Èirinn*
Finland	*Fionnlainn*	Islay	*Ìle*
Forres	*Farrais*	Isle of Man	*Eilean Mhanainn*
Fort Augustus	*Cille Chuimein*	Isle of Skye	*An t-Eilean*
Fort William	*An Gearastan,*		*Sgitheanach*
	An Gearasdan	Israel	*Israel, Iosarail*
France	*An Fhraing*	Italy	*An Eadailt*
Fraserburgh	*A' Bhrua(i)ch*		
		Japan	*Iapan*
Gairloch	*Geàrrloch*	Jerusalem	*Ierusalem*
Galloway	*Gall-Ghàidhealaibh*	Jordan	*Iòrdan*
Germany	*A' Ghearmailt*	Jura	*Diùra*

Kenya	Ceinia	Moidart	Mùideart
Killin	Cill Fhinn	Morvern	A' Mhorbhairne
Kilmarnock	Cille Mheàrnaig	Motherwell	Tobar na Màthar
Kingussie	Cinn a' Ghiùthsaich	Muck	Eilean nam Muc
		Mull	Muile
Kinlochleven	Ceann Loch Lìobhann		
		Nairn	Inbhir Narann
Kintyre	Cinn Tìre	Ness	Nis
Knoydart	Cnòideart	the Netherlands	An Tìr Ìosal
Kyle of Lochalsh	Caol Loch Aills(e)	Newtonmore	Bail' Ùr an t-Slèibh
Lanark	Lannraig	the North Sea	An Cuan a Tuath
Largs	Na Leargaidh Ghallta	North Uist	Uibhist a Tuath
		Norway	Nirribhidh
Latvia	Latbhia	Nova Scotia	Alba Nuadh
Leith	Lìte		
Lewis	Leòdhas	Oban	An t-Òban
Libya	Libia	Orkney	Arcaibh
Lismore	Lios Mòr		
Lithuania	Lituàinia	the Pacific Ocean	An Cuan Sèimh
Lochaber	Loch Abar	Paisley	Pàislig
Lochgilphead	Ceann Loch Gilb	Pakistan	Pagastan
Lochboisdale	Loch Baghasdail	Perth	Peairt
Lochinver	Loch an Inbhir	Peterhead	Ceann Phàdraig
Loch Lomond	Loch Laomainn	Pitlochry	Baile Chloichrigh
Lochmaddy	Loch nam Madadh	Plockton	Am Ploc
Loch Ness	Loch Nis	Poland	A' Phòlainn
London	Lunnainn	Port Ellen	Port Ilein
Lothian	Lodainn, Lobhdaidh	Portree	Port Rìgh, Port Ruighe
the Lowlands	A' Ghalltachd	Portugal	Portagail
Luing	(Eilean)Luinn		
Luxembourg	Lugsamburg	Raasay	Ratharsair, Ratharsaigh
Mallaig	Malaig	River Clyde	Abhainn Chluaidh
the Mediterranean	A' Mhuir Mheadhan-thìreach	River Forth	Abhainn Foirthe
		River Spey	Abhainn Spè, Uisge Spè
the Minch	An Cuan Sgìth	River Tay	Abhainn Tatha

River Tweed	*Abhainn Tuaidh*	Strathspey	*Srath Spè*
Romania	*Romàinia*	Sweden	*An t-Suain*
Rome	*An Ròimh*	Switzerland	*An Eilbheis*
Ross	*Ros*		
Rothesay	*Baile Bhòid*	Tain	*Baile Dhubhthaich*
Rum	*Rùm, Eilean Ruma*	Tarbert	*An Tairbeart*
Russia	*An Ruis, Ruisia*	Thurso	*Inbhir Theòrsa*
		Tiree	*Tiriodh, Tiridhe*
Scalpay	*Sgalpaigh*	Tobermory	*Tobar Mhoire*
Scandinavia	*Lochlann*	Tongue	*Tunga*
Scotland	*Alba*	Torridon	*Toirbheartan*
Serbia	*Serbia*	the Trossachs	*Na Tròiseachan*
Shetland	*Sealtainn*	Turkey	*An Tuirc*
Sleat	*Slèite*	Tyndrum	*Taigh an Droma*
Slovakia	*Slobhagia*		
Slovenia	*Slobhinia*	Uig	*Ùige, Ùig*
South Africa	*Afraga a Deas*	Uist	*Uibhist*
South Uist	*Uibhist a Deas*	Ullapool	*Ulapul*
Spain	*An Spàinn*	the United States	*Na Stàitean*
Staffin	*Stafainn, An Taobh Sear*		*Aonaichte*
St Andrews	*Cill Rìmhinn*	Vatersay	*Bhatarsaigh*
Stirling	*Sruighlea*		
Stornoway	*Steòrnabhagh*	Wales	*A' Chuimrigh*
Strathclyde	*Srath Chluaidh*	Wick	*Inbhir Ùige*

Grammar

Word order

In English, the subject precedes the verb. In Gaelic, the verb precedes the subject and is normally the first word in a sentence or question, eg

bha sinn anmoch	*we were late*
an glas mi an doras?	*shall I lock the door?*

In certain types of question, a question word precedes the verb:

cò bha siud?	*who was that?*

Another change in sequence between English and Gaelic arises with nouns and adjectives. Whereas in English the adjective precedes the noun, in Gaelic the noun generally precedes the adjective, eg

latha math	*(a) good day*

Adjectives are lenited if the noun they are qualifying is feminine in gender. Lenition is shown in the written form of a word by the insertion of an h after the first letter.

oidhche mhath	*good night*

There are a few exceptions to this convention. The adjectives *deagh* (good), *droch* (bad), *sàr* (excellent, supreme), *fìor* (true, absolute) and *seann* (old) are the main exceptions. These cause lenition, where applicable, of the following noun, eg

deagh bhiadh	*good food*
droch shìde	*bad weather*

sàr sheinneadair	*an excellent singer*
fìor charaid	*a true friend*
seann chù	*an old dog*

Adverbs

An adverb is formed by putting **gu** or **gu h-** before an adjective.
gu h- is used when the adjective begins with a vowel, eg

| **mòr** *(great)* | **gu mòr** *(greatly)* |
| **àrd** *(high)* | **gu h-àrd** *(above)* |

Forms of the article

There is no indefinite article in Gaelic – 'a window' is **uinneag**,
'a jacket' is **seacaid**. There are, however, several forms of the
definite article (equivalent to 'the' in English). The form of article
used varies according to the gender, number and case of the noun.
The various forms of the article are set out in the table below:

(a) Forms of the article with nouns in the nominative case

Gender & number	First letter of noun	Form of article	Example
Masculine singular	b, f, m, p a, e, i, o, u other letters	am an t- an	am bòrd an t-ubhal an leabhar
Feminine singular	b, c, g, m, p f	a' + (len) an + (len)	a' bhròg a' chaileag an fhreagairt an fhairge

Gender & number	First letter of noun	Form of article	Example
	sl, sn, sr, s + vowel	an t-	an t-sràid an t-seacaid
	other letters	an	an nighean an sgoil an uinneag
Masculine, feminine plural	consonant	na	na leabhraichean na sgoilearan
	vowel	na h-	na h-òrdagan na h-uinneagan

(b) Forms of the article with nouns in the genitive case

Gender & number	First letter of noun	Form of article	Example
Masculine singular	b, c, g, m, p	a' + (len)	am post → oifis a' phuist
	f	an + (len)	am fraoch → dath an fhraoich
	sl, sn, sr, s + vowel	an t-	an salann → blas an t-salainn
	other letters	an	an rathad → ceann an rathaid
Feminine singular	consonant	na	a' chailleach → còta na caillich
	vowel	na h-	an eaglais → doras na h-eaglaise
Masculine, feminine plural	b, f, m, p	nam	na bàird → obair nam bàrd
	other letters	nan	na leabhraichean → Comhairle nan Leabhraichean

(c) Forms of the article with nouns in the dative case

Gender & number	First letter of noun	Form of article	Example
Masculine singular	b, c, g, m, p	a' + (len)	am balach → leis a' bhalach
	f	an + (len)	am feur → anns an fheur
	sl, sn, sr, s + vowel	an t-	an salm → anns an t-salm
	other letters	an	an taigh → air an taigh
Feminine singular	b, c, g, m, p	a' + (len)	a' ghealach → air a' ghealaich
	f	an + (len)	an fheòrag → aig an fheòraig
	sl, sn, sr, s + vowel	an t-	an t-sràid → air an t-sràid
	other letters	an	an trèan → air an trèan an uinneag → air an uinneig
Masculine, feminine plural	consonant	na	na bùithean → anns na bùithean
	vowel	na h-	na h-òrain → ris na h-òrain

Regular verbs

Gaelic verbs have three forms:

- ▶ independent – normally the first word in a sentence
- ▶ dependent – used in subordinate clauses or after particles
- ▶ relative – used after relative pronouns

The root of the verb is the second person singular imperative, eg seall (look), literally, 'look you'.

The verb 'to be' apart, Gaelic verbs have no simple present tense. The present tense is formed by combining the verb 'to be' with the verbal noun of the verb being used.

eg *tha iad a' cluich* – they are playing

The verbal noun, as the name implies, can act both as verb or as noun. It is marked in English by the -ing ending.

eg *bha sinn a' snàmh* – we were swimming
   tha snàmh math dhut – swimming is good for you

Root	Verbal Noun	Infinitive	Subjunctive/ Conditional
bris	**a' briseadh**	**a bhriseadh**	**bhrisinn**
break	*breaking*	*to break*	*I would break*
cuir	**a' cur**	**a chur**	**chuirinn**
put	*putting*	*to put*	*I would put*
dùin	**a' dùnadh**	**a dhùnadh**	**dhùineadh e**
close/shut	*closing/shutting*	*to close/shut*	*he would close/ shut*
freagair	**a' freagairt**	**a fhreagairt**	**fhreagradh i**
answer	*answering*	*to answer*	*she would answer*
gabh	**a' gabhail**	**a ghabhail**	**ghabhadh tu**
take	*taking*	*to take*	*you would take*
las	**a' lasadh**	**a lasadh**	**lasainn**
light	*lighting*	*to light*	*I would light*
mill	**a' milleadh**	**a mhilleadh**	**mhilleadh tu**
spoil	*spoiling*	*to spoil*	*you would spoil*
nigh	**a' nighe**	**a nighe**	**nigheamaid**
wash/clean	*washing/ cleaning*	*to wash/clean*	*we would wash/ clean*
pòs	**a' pòsadh**	**a phòsadh**	**phòsadh iad**
marry	*marrying*	*to marry*	*they would marry*

(Contd)

Root	Verbal Noun	Infinitive	Subjunctive/ Conditional
ruith	**a' ruith**	**a ruith**	**ruitheadh sibh**
run	*running*	*to run*	*you (pl) would run*
suidh	**a' suidhe**	**a shuidhe**	**shuidheadh i**
sit	*sitting*	*to sit*	*she would sit*
tog	**a' togail**	**a thogail**	**thogadh iad**
lift	*lifting*	*to lift*	*they would lift*
aithnich	**ag aithn-eachadh**	**a dh'aithn-eachadh**	**dh'aithnicheadh sibh**
recognize	*recognizing*	*to recognize*	*you (pl) would recognize*
èirich	**ag èirigh**	**a dh'èirigh**	**dh'èireamaid**
rise	*rising*	*to rise*	*we would rise*
ith	**ag ithe**	**a dh'ithe**	**dh'itheadh e**
eat	*eating*	*to eat*	*he would eat*
òl	**ag òl**	**a dh'òl**	**dh'òlainn**
drink	*drinking*	*to drink*	*I would drink*
ullaich	**ag ullachadh**	**a dh'ullachadh**	**dh'ullaicheadh i**
prepare	*preparing*	*to prepare*	*she would prepare*
fuirich	**a' fuireach**	**a dh'fhuireach**	**dh'fhuiricheadh iad**
stay/wait	*staying/waiting*	*to stay/wait*	*they would stay/ wait*

NOTES

- ▶ there are different ways of forming verbal nouns
- ▶ verbal nouns beginning in consonants are preceded by *a'*
- ▶ verbal nouns beginning in vowels are preceded by *ag*
- ▶ the infinitive ('to') forms are related to the verbal noun forms
- ▶ there is no apostrophe after the *a* in the infinitive
- ▶ infinitive forms of verbs beginning in consonants are lenited where possible
- ▶ infinitive forms of verbs beginning in *f* followed by a vowel begin with *dh'* and are lenited. The *fh* combination is not pronounced and the verb is treated as if it began in a vowel

- subjunctive/conditional forms vary according to the person being referred to, or subject. The following is an example of the different forms of one verb:

chuirinn	*I would put*	**chuireamaid**	*we would put*
chuireadh tu	*you would put*	**chuireadh sibh**	*you (pl) would put*
chuireadh e	*he would put*	**chuireadh iad**	*they would put*
chuireadh i	*she would put*		

- the first person singular and plural have special forms which include the pronoun, while the pronoun is added separately in the second and third persons. However, in some areas *sinn* is retained in the first person plural, eg *chuireadh sinn*
- *thu* appears as *tu* in the subjunctive/conditional
- subjunctive/conditional forms of verbs beginning in consonants are lenited
- subjunctive/conditional forms of verbs beginning in vowels or *f* followed by a vowel begin with *dh'*

REGULAR VERBS: PAST TENSE

Root	Positive	Negative	Interrogative
bris	**bhris**	**cha do bhris**	**an do bhris?**
break	*broke*	*did not break*	*did ... break?*
cuir	**chuir**	**cha do chuir**	**an do chuir?**
put	*put*	*did not put*	*did ... put?*
dùin	**dhùin**	**cha do dhùin**	**an do dhùin?**
close/shut	*closed/shut*	*did not close/shut*	*did ... close/shut?*
freagair	**fhreagair**	**cha do fhreagair**	**an do fhreagair?**
answer	*answered*	*did not answer*	*did ... answer?*
gabh	**ghabh**	**cha do ghabh**	**an do ghabh?**
take	*took*	*did not take*	*did ... take?*
las	**las**	**cha do las**	**an do las?**
light	*lit*	*did not light*	*did ... light?*
mill	**mhill**	**cha do mhill**	**an do mhill?**
spoil	*spoilt*	*did not spoil*	*did ... spoil?*

(Contd)

Root	Positive	Negative	Interrogative
nigh	**nigh**	**cha do nigh**	**an do nigh?**
wash/clean	*washed/cleaned*	*did not wash/clean*	*did ... wash/clean?*
pòs	**phòs**	**cha do phòs**	**an do phòs?**
marry	*married*	*did not marry*	*did ... marry?*
ruith	**ruith**	**cha do ruith**	**an do ruith?**
run	*run*	*did not run*	*did ... run?*
suidh	**shuidh**	**cha do shuidh**	**an do shuidh?**
sit	*sat*	*did not sit*	*did ... sit?*
tog	**thog**	**cha do thog**	**an do thog?**
lift	*lifted*	*did not lift*	*did ... lift?*
aithnich	**dh'aithnich**	**cha do dh'aithnich**	**an do dh'aithnich?**
recognize	*recognized*	*did not recognize*	*did ... recognize?*
èirich	**dh'èirich**	**cha do dh'èirich**	**an do dh'èirich?**
rise	*rose*	*did not rise*	*did ... rise?*
ith	**dh'ith**	**cha do dh'ith**	**an do dh'ith?**
eat	*ate*	*did not eat*	*did ... eat?*
òl	**dh'òl**	**cha do dh'òl**	**an do dh'òl?**
drink	*drank*	*did not drink*	*did ... drink?*
ullaich	**dh'ullaich**	**cha do dh'ullaich**	**an do dh'ullaich?**
prepare	*prepared*	*did not prepare*	*did ... prepare?*
fuirich	**dh'fhuirich**	**cha do dh'fhuirich**	**an do dh'fhuirich?**
stay/wait	*stayed/waited*	*did not stay/wait*	*did ... stay/wait?*

NOTES

▶ positive forms of the past tense are derived by leniting the root form, where possible. Verbs beginning in *l*, *n*, *r* and *sg*, *sm*, *sp*, *st* retain the root form

▶ positive forms of verbs beginning in vowels begin with *dh'*

▶ negative forms of the past tense are marked by *cha do*

▶ interrogative (question) forms of the past tense are marked by *an do*

- the interrogative forms are answered, as appropriate, by the positive (yes) and negative (no) forms
  eg *an do dh'aithnich thu iad? dh'aithnich/cha do dh'aithnich*
  did you recognize them?   yes   no

REGULAR VERBS: FUTURE TENSE

Root	Positive	Negative	Interrogative
bris	**brisidh**	**cha bhris**	**am bris ...?**
break	*will break*	*will not break*	*will ... break?*
cuir	**cuiridh**	**cha chuir**	**an cuir ...?**
put	*will put*	*will not put*	*will ... put?*
dùin	**dùinidh**	**cha dhùin**	**an dùin ...?**
close/shut	*will close/shut*	*will not close/ shut*	*will ... close/shut?*
freagair	**freagraidh**	**cha fhreagair**	**am freagair ...?**
answer	*will answer*	*will not answer*	*will ... answer?*
gabh	**gabhaidh**	**cha ghabh**	**an gabh ...?**
take	*will take*	*will not take*	*will ... take?*
las	**lasaidh**	**cha las**	**an las ...?**
light	*will light*	*will not light*	*will ... light?*
mill	**millidh**	**cha mhill**	**am mill ...?**
spoil	*will spoil*	*will not spoil*	*will ... spoil?*
nigh	**nighidh**	**cha nigh**	**an nigh ...?**
wash/clean	*will wash/clean*	*will not wash/ clean*	*will ... wash/ clean?*
pòs	**pòsaidh**	**cha phòs**	**am pòs ...?**
marry	*will marry*	*will not marry*	*will ... marry?*
ruith	**ruithidh**	**cha ruith**	**an ruith ...?**
run	*will run*	*will not run*	*will ... run?*
suidh	**suidhidh**	**cha shuidh**	**an suidh ...?**
sit	*will sit*	*will not sit*	*will ... sit?*
tog	**togaidh**	**cha thog**	**an tog ...?**
lift	*will lift*	*will not lift*	*will ... lift?*
aithnich	**aithnichidh**	**chan aithnich**	**an aithnich ...?**
recognize	*will recognize*	*will not recognize*	*will ... recognize?*

(Contd)

Root	Positive	Negative	Interrogative
èirich	**èiridh**	**chan èirich**	**an èirich ...?**
rise	*will rise*	*will not rise*	*will ... rise?*
ith	**ithidh**	**chan ith**	**an ith ...?**
eat	*will eat*	*will not eat*	*will ... eat?*
òl	**òlaidh**	**chan òl**	**an òl ...?**
drink	*will drink*	*will not drink*	*will ... drink?*
ullaich	**ullaichidh**	**chan ullaich**	**an ullaich ...?**
prepare	*will prepare*	*will not prepare*	*will ... prepare?*
fuirich	**fuirichidh**	**chan fhuirich**	**am fuirich ...?**
stay/wait	*will stay/wait*	*will not stay/wait*	*will ... stay/wait?*

NOTES

▶ positive forms of the future are generally derived by adding -*idh* or -*aidh* to the root form. The former is added when the last vowel in the root is *i* or *e*, and -*aidh* is added when the last vowel is *a, o* or *u*

▶ a few verbs, eg *freagair*, drop part of the second syllable before adding the -*(a)idh* element

▶ negative forms are marked by *cha* or *chan*. Chan is used before vowels and before *f* followed by a vowel

▶ interrogative (question) forms are marked by *an* or *am*. Am is used before verbs beginning in *b, f, m, p*

▶ the interrogative forms are answered, as appropriate, by the positive (Yes) and negative (No) forms
eg *an gabh thu cofaidh?*   *gabhaidh/cha ghabh, tapadh leat*
 will you have a coffee?   yes/no, thank you

▶ some alternative forms not involving lenition of *d, s* and *t* are not listed above eg *cha dùin, cha suidh, cha tog*

IRREGULAR VERBS

Root	Verbal Noun	Infinitive	Subjunctive/ Conditional
abair	**ag ràdh**	**a ràdh**	**theirinn**
say	*saying*	*to say*	*I would say*

Root	Verbal Noun	Infinitive	Subjunctive/ Conditional
beir	**a' breith/ a' beireachdainn**	**a bhreith/ a bheireachdainn**	**bheireadh i**
catch	*catching*	*to catch*	*she would catch*
cluinn	**a' cluinntinn**	**a chluinntinn**	**chluinneamaid**
hear	*hearing*	*to hear*	*we would hear*
dèan	**a' dèanamh**	**a dhèanamh**	**dhèanainn**
do, make	*doing, making*	*to do, make*	*I would do, make*
faic	**a' faicinn**	**a dh'fhaicinn**	**chitheadh tu**
see	*seeing*	*to see*	*you would see*
faigh	**a' faighinn**	**a dh'fhaighinn**	**gheibheadh iad**
get	*getting*	*to get*	*they would get*
rach	**a' dol**	**a dhol**	**rachainn**
go	*going*	*to go*	*I would go*
ruig	**a' ruighinn/ a' ruigsinn**	**a ruighinn/ a ruigsinn**	**ruigeadh sibh**
arrive, reach	*arriving, reaching*	*to arrive, reach*	*you would arrive, reach*
thoir/tabhair	**a' toirt/ a' tabhairt**	**a thoirt/ a thabhairt**	**thoireamaid**
give, take, bring	*giving, taking, bringing*	*to give, take, bring*	*we would give, take, bring*
thig	**a' tighinn**	**a thighinn**	**thigeadh e**
come	*coming*	*to come*	*he would come*

IRREGULAR VERBS: PAST TENSE

Root	Positive	Negative	Interrogative
abair	**thuirt/ thubhairt**	**cha tuirt/ tubhairt**	**an tuirt/ tubhairt ...?**
say	*said*	*did not say*	*did ... say?*
beir	**rug**	**cha do rug**	**an do rug ...?**
catch	*caught*	*did not catch*	*did ... catch?*
cluinn	**chuala**	**cha chuala**	**an cuala ...?**
hear	*heard*	*did not hear*	*did ... hear?*
dèan	**rinn**	**cha do rinn**	**an do rinn ...?**
do, make	*did, made*	*did not do, make*	*did ... do, make?*

(Contd)

Root	Positive	Negative	Interrogative
faic	**chunnaic**	**chan fhaca**	**am faca ...?**
see	*saw*	*did not see*	*did ... see?*
faigh	**fhuair**	**cha d' fhuair**	**an d' fhuair ...?**
get	*got*	*did not get*	*did ... get?*
rach	**chaidh**	**cha deach**	**an deach ...?**
go	*went*	*did not go*	*did ... go?*
ruig	**ràinig**	**cha do ràinig**	**an do ràinig ...?**
arrive, reach	*arrived, reached*	*did not arrive, reach*	*did ... arrive, reach?*
thoir/tabhair	**thug**	**cha tug**	**an tug ...?**
give, take, bring	*gave, took, brought*	*did not give, take, bring*	*did .... give, take, bring*
thig	**thàinig**	**cha tàinig**	**an tàinig ...?**
come	*came*	*did not come*	*did ... come?*

IRREGULAR VERBS: FUTURE TENSE

abair	**their**	**chan abair**	**an abair ...?**
say	*will say*	*will not say*	*will ... say?*
beir	**beiridh**	**cha bheir**	**am beir ...?**
catch	*will catch*	*will not catch*	*will ... catch?*
cluinn	**cluinnidh**	**cha chluinn**	**an cluinn ...?**
hear	*will hear*	*will not hear*	*will ... hear?*
dèan	**nì**	**cha dèan**	**an dèan ...?**
do, make	*will do, make*	*will not do, make*	*will ... do, make*
faic	**chì**	**chan fhaic**	**am faic ...?**
see	*will see*	*will not see*	*will ... see?*
faigh	**gheibh**	**chan fhaigh**	**am faigh ...?**
get	*will get*	*will not get*	*will ... get?*
rach	**thèid**	**cha tèid**	**an tèid ...?**
go	*will go*	*will not go*	*will ... go?*
ruig	**ruigidh**	**cha ruig**	**an ruig ...?**
arrive, reach	*will arrive, reach*	*will not arrive, reach*	*will ... arrive, reach?*

thoir/tabhair	bheir	cha toir/ tabhair	an toir/ tabhair ...?
give, take, bring	will give, take, bring	will not give, take, bring	will ... give, take, bring?
thig	thig	cha tig	an tig ...?
come	will come	will not come	will ... come?

The verb 'to be'

There are two separate strands of the verb 'to be' in Gaelic. One is based on **bi** and the other, known as the assertive form, is based on **is**.

These strands are set out separately below:

BI FORMS

Root	Present positive	Present negative	Present interrogative
bi	**tha**	**chan eil**	**a bheil?**
	am, is, are	am not, is not, are not	am?, is?, are?
	Past positive **bha**	**Past negative** **cha robh**	**Past interrogative** **an robh?**
	was, were	was not, were not	was ... not?, were ... not?
	Future positive **bidh/bithidh**	**Future negative** **cha bhi**	**Future interrogative** **am bi?**
	will be	will not be	will ... be?
	Present relative	**Present dependent** **positive**	**Present dependent** **negative**
	a tha	**gu bheil**	**nach eil**
	who/which/ that is	that ... is	that ... is not
	Past relative	**Past dependent** **positive**	**Past dependent** **negative**
	a bha	**gun robh**	**nach robh**
	who/which/that was/were	that ... was/were	that ... was/were not

(Contd)

	Future relative	Future dependent positive	Future dependent negative
	a bhitheas/ a bhios	**gum bi**	**nach bi**
	who/which/that will be	*that … will be*	*that … will not be*
2ⁿᵈ pl. imp.	**Infinitive**	**Subjunctive/ conditional dependent**	**Subjunctive/ conditional**
bithibh	**a bhith**	**bhithinn**	**gum bithinn**
be (pl)	*to be*	*I would be*	*that I would be*
		bhiodh/ bhitheadh …	**gum biodh/ bitheadh**
		you/he/she/it/ they would be	*that he/she/it/ they would be*
		bhitheamaid, bhitheadh sinn	**gum bitheamaid, gum bitheadh sinn**
		we would be	*that we would be*

ASSERTIVE FORMS

Present Positive	Present Negative	Present Interrogative
is/'s	**cha(n)**	**an, am**
am, is, are	*am not, is not, are not*	*am?, is?, are?*
Past Positive & Conditional positive	**Past Negative & Conditional negative**	**Past Interrogative & Conditional interrogative**
bu/b'	**cha bu, cha b'**	**am bu? am b'?**
was, were, would be	*was not, were not, would not be*	*was?, were?, would … be?*
Present relative	**Present Dependent positive**	**Present Dependent negative**
as	**gur**	**nach**
that am, that is, that are	*that am, that is, that are*	*that am not, that is not, that are not*

Past Relative & Conditional relative	Past Dependent positive & Conditional dependent positive	Past Dependent negative & Conditional dependent negative
(a) bu, b'	gum bu, gum b'	nach bu, nach b'
that was,	*that was,*	*that was not,*
that were,	*that were,*	*that were not,*
that would be	*that would be*	*that would not be*

Is is often reduced to **'S** in pronunciation and in writing, while **Bu** becomes **B'** before a word beginning in a vowel.

The Assertive forms are used to highlight, identify and define a particular point, eg

's e àite snog a th' ann	*it's a nice place*
's ann à Ile a tha iad	*they are from Islay*
cha b' ise a bh' ann idir	*it wasn't her at all*
b' ann a-raoir a thachair e	*it was last night it happened*

'S and **B'** are followed by pronouns when the point being highlighted or identified is a person or thing. They are accompanied by *ann* when reference is being made to a place or time.

The various forms of **Is** and **Bu** feature in a number of phrases in combination with a noun or adjective and a prepositional pronoun. These phrases convey the meanings carried by certain verbs in English, eg

's toil/toigh leam	*I like*
's caomh leis	*he likes*
's fheàrr leatha	*she prefers*
's beag orm	*I dislike*
's lugha air	*he hates*
chan àbhaist dhomh	*I don't usually*
an urrainn dhut?	*can you?*
bu chòir dhi	*she should/ought to*
an aithne dhuibh?	*do you (pl) know?*

The prepositional pronouns

Preposition		Singular		
	1st	2nd	3rd Masc	3rd Fem
aig *at*	agam *at me*	agad *at you*	aige *at him/it*	aice *at her/it*
air *on*	orm *on me*	ort *on you*	air *on him/it*	oirre on *her/it*
ann *in*	annam *in me*	annad *in you*	ann *in him/it*	innte *in her/it*
às *out of*	asam *out of me*	asad *out of you*	às *out of him/it*	aiste *out of her/it*
bho *from*	bhuam	bhuat	bhuaithe	bhuaipe
o	uam	uat	uaithe	uaipe
	from me	*from you*	*from her/it*	*from her/it*
de *of, off*	dhìom *of me*	dhìot *of you*	dheth *of him/it*	dhith *of her/it*
do *to*	dhomh *to me*	dhut *to you*	dha *to him/it*	dhi *to her/it*
eadar *between*	-	-	-	-
fo *under*	fodham	fodhad	fodha	fòidhpe
	under me	*under you*	*under him/it*	*under her/it*
gu/chun *to*	thugam *to me*	thugad *to you*	thuige *to him/it*	thuice *to her/it*
le *with, by*	leam *with me*	leat *with you*	leis *with him/it*	leatha *with her/it*
mu *about*	umam	umad	uime	uimpe
	about me	*about you*	*about him/it*	*about her/it*
ri *to*	rium *to me*	riut *to you*	ris *to him/it*	rithe *to her/it*
ro/roimh	romham	romhad	roimhe	roimhpe
before	*before me*	*before you*	*before him/it*	*before her/it*
tro/troimh	tromham	tromhad	troimhe	troimhpe
through	*through me*	*through you*	*through him/it*	*through her/it*
thar *over*	tharam	tharad	thairis (air)	thairte
	over me	*over you*	*over him/it*	*over her/it*

| | Plural | | |
	1st	2nd	3rd
aig *at*	againn *at us*	agaibh *at you*	aca *at them*
air *on*	oirnn *on us*	oirbh *on you*	orra *on them*
ann *in*	annainn *in us*	annaibh *in you*	annta *in them*
às *out of*	asainn *out of us*	asaibh *out of you*	asta *out of them*
bho *from*	bhuainn *from us*	bhuaibh *from you*	bhuapa *from them*
o	uainn	uaibh	uapa
de *of, off*	dhinn *of us*	dhibh *of you*	dhiubh *of them*
do *to*	dhuinn *to us*	dhuibh *to you*	dhaibh *to them*
eadar *between*	eadarainn *between us*	eadaraibh *between you*	eatarra *between them*
fo *under*	fodhainn *under us*	fodhaibh *under you*	fòdhpa *under them*
gu/chun *to*	thugainn *to us*	thugaibh *to you*	thuca *to them*
le *with, by*	leinn *with us*	leibh *with you*	leotha *with them*
mu *about*	umainn *about us*	umaibh *about you*	umpa *about them*
ri *to*	rinn *to us*	ribh *to you*	riutha *to them*
ro/roimh *before*	romhainn *before us*	romhaibh *before you*	romhpa *before them*
tro/troimh *through*	tromhainn *through us*	tromhaibh *through you*	tromhpa *through them*
thar *over*	tharainn *over us*	tharaibh *over you*	tharta *over them*